English
Novel
Explication

Supplement III, 1980-1985

Compiled by
Christian J. W. Kloesel

THE SHOE STRING PRESS, INC.   1986

© 1986 The Shoe String Press, Inc.
Hamden, Connecticut 06514

Printed in the United States of America

The paper in this book meets the guidelines for permanence and durability
of the Committee on Production Guidelines for Book Longevity of the
Council on Library Resources. ∞

Library of Congress Cataloging-in-Publication Data
(Revised for vol. 3)

English novel explication. Supplement.

Supplements: English novel explication /
compiled by Helen H. Palmer & Anne Jane Dyson.
Supplement I / compiled by Peter L. Abernethy,
Christian J. W. Kloesel, Jeffrey R. Smitten;
supplement II / compiled by Christian J. W.
Kloesel, Jeffrey R. Smitten; supplement III /
compiled by Christian J. W. Kloesel.
1. English fiction—Explication—Bibliography.
I. Abernethy, Peter L. II. Kloesel, Christian
J. W. III. Smitten, Jeffrey R. IV. English novel
explication.
Z2014.F5P26   Suppl. [PR821]   016.823′009   84-137107
ISBN 0-208-01464-0 (v. 1)
ISBN 0-208-02092-6 (v. 3)

CONTENTS

PREFACE

This third supplement extends the *English Novel Explication* series from 1980 through 1985. Accordingly, it has been my primary obligation to gather materials published in these years, although I have added some earlier items not included in the second supplement, as well as a few from 1986. Readers should be reminded, however, that it has not been possible to include all items published between 1980 and 1985, especially those appearing toward the end of the five-year period. Because *English Novel Explication* is a continuing series, it must have a fixed date of publication. That date cannot be affected by printing and library binding schedules or by the inevitable delays in acquisitions and interlibrary loans. Consequently, readers not finding an item they expect to be here must, I regret, consult the next supplement.

The scope of the present supplement is the same as that of the two previous ones. The very broad definition of the term "novel" is again based on Ernest A. Baker's *History of the English Novel*, and that is why such works as *Le Morte Darthur, The Pilgrim's Progress, Gulliver's Travels, Rasselas*, and *Down and Out in Paris and London* are included. An "English novelist" is a writer born in England, Scotland, Ireland, Wales, or the Commonwealth who has lived in Great Britain during some significant portion of his/her creative years. This definition excludes writers like Henry James and Brian Moore, and it includes others like Doris Lessing, Malcolm Lowry, and V.S. Naipaul. By "explication" is meant the interpretation of the *meaning* of a novel. Consequently, discussions of structure, diction, theme, imagery, or symbolism are included here, whereas those wholly devoted to sources and influence, critical reception, biography, or bibliography are excluded.

The format of the present supplement is similar to that of the two earlier ones, although a few additional modifications have been introduced. To conserve space, I have abbreviated book titles more drastically than before. Full titles, together with complete bibliographical information, may be found in the LIST OF BOOKS INDEXED. In addition, I have used the generally accepted abbreviations of the journals of the American and Australian Modern Language Associations (*PMLA* and *AUMLA*), and have abbreviated several frequently repeated words in journal and serial titles. These words include Academy (Acad), American (Am), Assocation (Assoc), British (Brit), Bulletin (Bull), Chronicle (Chron), College (Coll), Comparative (Compar), Contemporary (Contemp), Critical (Crit), Department (Dept), English (Engl), History (Hist), Humanities (Hum), Institute (Inst), International (Intl), Journal (J), Language (Lang), Library (Lib), Literary (Liter), Literature (Lit), Magazine (Mag), Modern (Mod), Newsletter (Newsl), Philological (Philol), Philosophy (Philos), Proceedings (Proc), Psychology (Psych), Publications (Publs), Quarterly (Q), Research (Res), Review (R), Society (Soc), Studies (Stud), Supplement (Suppl), and University (Univ). A few abbreviations, like *ELH* or *PTL*, are themselves journal titles. Finally, I have used

shortened periodical citations with the author entries. The first citation of a
periodical article for a given author appears in full. Subsequent citations of
that article *within the author entry* are reduced to a short form consisting of
the critic's name and a shortened version of the article's title. If the same
article also includes discussion of a novel by another author, it is given again
in full under the appropriate author entry.

Readers should remember that, as in the two previous supplements, page
numbers in a citation correspond to the passage of explication for a given
novel and not necessarily to the entire article or book. When an entire book
is devoted to explication of the novel under which it appears, it is generally
listed without page numbers.

Thanks to the staff of the Interlibrary Loan Department of the library at
Indiana University-Purdue University at Indianapolis and to Cathy Clark and
Barbara Shields—and to English novelists and their critics.

Indianapolis, Indiana   C. J. W. K.
May 1986

RICHARD ADAMS

Watership Down, 1972

Anderson, Celia Catlett. "Troy, Carthage, and *Watership Down*." *Children's Lit Assoc Q* 8:1 (1983), 12–13.

Chapman, Edgar L. "The Shaman as Hero and Spiritual Leader: Richard Adams' Mythmaking in *Watership Down* and *Shardik*." *Mythlore* 5:2 (1978), 7–11.

Finger, Hans. "*Watership Down*," in Hermann Weiand, ed., *Insight V*, 26–32.

Pawling, Christopher. "*Watership Down*: Rolling Back the 1960s," in Pawling, ed., *Popular Fiction*, 212–233.

Rodriguez, Francisco Collado. "*Watership Down*: Tale and Myth." *Intl Fiction R* 12 (1985), 39–42.

Rose, Jacqueline. *The Case of Peter Pan*, 129–130.

Sell, Roger D. "*Watership Down* and the Rehabilitation of Pleasure." *Neuphilologische Mitteilungen* 82 (1981), 28–35.

Sutherland, John. *Bestsellers*, 112–115.

Swinfen, Ann. *In Defence*, 37–43, 218–229.

GRACE AGUILAR

The Vale of Cedars, 1872

Zatlin, Linda Gertner. *The Nineteenth-Century Anglo-Jewish Novel*, 33–40.

WILLIAM HARRISON AINSWORTH

Jack Sheppard, 1839

Hill, Jonathan E. "Cruikshank, Ainsworth, and Tableau Illustration." *Victorian Stud* 23 (1980), 430–459.

Watt, George. *The Fallen Woman*, 11–15.

RICHARD ALDINGTON

The Colonel's Daughter, 1931

Crawford, Fred D. *Mixing Memory*, 13–15.

Death of a Hero, 1929

Crawford, Fred D. *Mixing Memory*, 10–13.

Gates, Norman T. "*Images of War* and *Death of a Hero*: Aldington's Twice-Used Images." *Mod Brit Lit* 4 (1979), 120–127.

BRIAN ALDISS

An Age, 1967

Griffin, Brian, and David Wingrove. *Apertures*, 111–122.

Barefoot in the Head, 1969

Greenland, Colin. *The Entropy Exhibition*, 87–91.
Griffin, Brian, and David Wingrove. *Apertures*, 122–135.

The Canopy of Time, 1959

Wagar, W. Warren. "Round Trips to Doomsday," in Eric S. Rabkin et al., eds., *The End of the World*, 94–95.

The Dark Light-Years, 1964

Greenland, Colin. *The Entropy Exhibition*, 75–77.
Griffin, Brian, and David Wingrove. *Apertures*, 72–77.

Earthworks, 1965

Griffin, Brian, and David Wingrove. *Apertures*, 77–81.

The Eighty-Minute Hour, 1975

Griffin, Brian, and David Wingrove. *Apertures*, 173–175.

Enemies of the System, 1978

Griffin, Brian, and David Wingrove. *Apertures*, 215–222.

Frankenstein Unbound, 1973

Griffin, Brian, and David Wingrove. *Apertures*, 162–169.
McLeod, Patrick G. "Frankenstein: Unbound and Otherwise." *Extrapolation* 21 (1980), 158–166.
McNelly, Willis E. "Brian W. Aldiss," in E. F. Bleiler, ed., *Science Fiction Writers*, 253–254.

Greybeard, 1964

Griffin, Brian, and David Wingrove. *Apertures*, 86–94.

Hothouse, 1962

Griffin, Brian, and David Wingrove. *Apertures*, 41–55.
Wagar, W. Warren. "The Rebellion of Nature," in Eric S. Rabkin et al., eds., *The End of the World*, 153–154.
Wendland, Albert. *Science, Myth*, 122–126.

The Interpreter, 1960

Griffin, Brian, and David Wingrove. *Apertures*, 58–62.

Life in the West, 1980

Griffin, Brian, and David Wingrove. *Apertures*, 222–228.

The Malacia Tapestry, 1976

Griffin, Brian, and David Wingrove. *Apertures*, 203–211.
Parrinder, Patrick. *Science Fiction . . . Teaching*, 24–27.

The Male Response, 1961

    Griffin, Brian, and David Wingrove. *Apertures*, 63–65.

Moreau's Other Island, 1980

    Griffin, Brian, and David Wingrove. *Apertures*, 170–173.

Non-Stop, 1958

    Griffin, Brian, and David Wingrove. *Apertures*, 8–18.

The Primal Urge, 1961

    Griffin, Brian, and David Wingrove. *Apertures*, 63–67.

Report on Probability A, 1968

    Greenland, Colin. *The Entropy Exhibition*, 85–87.
    Griffin, Brian, and David Wingrove. *Apertures*, 135–146.

A Rude Awakening, 1978

    Griffin, Brian, and David Wingrove. *Apertures*, 156–158.

A Soldier Erect, 1971

    Griffin, Brian, and David Wingrove. *Apertures*, 155–157.

KINGSLEY AMIS

The Alteration, 1976

    Füger, Wilhelm. "Streifzüge durch Allotopia: Zur Topographie des fiktionalen Gestaltungsraums." *Anglia* 102 (1984), 367–376.
    Gardner, Philip. *Kingsley Amis*, 83–91.
    Sutherland, John. *Bestsellers*, 242–244.

The Anti-Death League, 1966

    Gardner, Philip. *Kingsley Amis*, 63–71.
    Green, Martin. *The English Novel*, 150–155.

Ending Up, 1974

    Gardner, Philip. *Kingsley Amis*, 99–105.
    Green, Martin. *The English Novel*, 162–166.
    McCort, Dennis. "The Dreadful Weight of Days: The Hilarious Heroism of Old Age in Kingsley Amis's *Ending Up*." *Sphinx* 4:2 (1982), 101–108.

Girl, 20, 1971

    Claas, Dietmar. "Kingsley Amis, *Girl, 20*," in Rainer Lengeler, ed., *Englische Literatur*, 256–267.
    Gardner, Philip. *Kingsley Amis*, 92–99.
    McEwan, Neil. *The Survival of the Novel*, 93–96.

The Green Man, 1969

    Gardner, Philip. *Kingsley Amis*, 71–76.
    McEwan, Neil. *The Survival of the Novel*, 87–93.

I Like It Here, 1958

> Gardner, Philip. *Kingsley Amis*, 50–53.
> Macleod, Norman. "A Trip to Greeneland: The Plagiarizing Narrator of Kingsley Amis's *I Like It Here*." *Stud in the Novel* 17 (1985), 203–216.

I Want It Now, 1969

> Gardner, Philip. *Kingsley Amis*, 58–62.

Jake's Thing, 1978

> Gardner, Philip. *Kingsley Amis*, 105–112.
> McDermott, John. "Kingsley and the Women." *Crit Q* 27:3 (1985), 65–71.
> Wilson, Keith. "Jim, Jake and the Years Between: The Will to Stasis in the Contemporary British Novel." *Ariel* 13:1 (1982), 66–69.

Lucky Jim, 1954

> Bell, Robert H. " 'True Comic Edge' in *Lucky Jim*." *Am Humor* 8:2 (1981), 1–7.
> Gardner, Philip. *Kingsley Amis*, 22–36.
> Green, Martin. *The English Novel*, 138–144.
> Kenyon, J. P. "*Lucky Jim* and After: The Business of University Novels." *Encounter*, June 1980, 81–84.
> Leech, Geoffrey N., and Michael H. Short. *Style in Fiction*, 165–166.
> Swinden, Patrick. *The English Novel*, 197–201.
> Wilson, Keith. "Jim, Jake and the Years Between," 55–62.

One Fat Englishman, 1963

> Gardner, Philip. *Kingsley Amis*, 53–57.

The Riverside Villas Murder, 1973

> Gardner, Philip. *Kingsley Amis*, 78–82.

Russian Hide-and-Seek, 1980

> Füger, Wilhelm. "Streifzüge durch Allotopia," 382–390.

Take A Girl Like You, 1960

> Gardner, Philip. *Kingsley Amis*, 42–48.
> McEwan, Neil. *The Survival of the Novel*, 83–86.
> Swinden, Patrick. *The English Novel*, 196–198.

That Uncertain Feeling, 1955

> Gardner, Philip. *Kingsley Amis*, 37–42.

PENELOPE AUBIN

The Life of Madam de Beaumont, 1721

> Suhr, Heidrun. *Englische Romanautorinnen*, 36–39.

JANE AUSTEN

Emma, 1816

Adams, Timothy Dow. "To Know the Dancer from the Dance: Dance as a Metaphor of Marriage in Four Novels of Jane Austen." *Stud in the Novel* 14 (1982), 60–63.

Auerbach, Nina. *Romantic Imprisonment*, 45–49.

Barfoot, C. C. *The Thread*, 62–84, 115–116.

Barker, Gerard A. *Grandison's Heirs*, 167–169.

Bodenheimer, Rosemarie. "Looking at the Landscape in Jane Austen." *Stud in Engl Lit, 1500–1900* 21 (1981), 611–613.

Boles, Carolyn G. "Jane Austen and the Reader: Rhetorical Techniques in *Northanger Abbey, Pride and Prejudice*, and *Emma*." *Emporia State Res Stud* 30 (1981), 152–167.

Booth, Wayne C. "Emma, *Emma*, and the Question of Feminism." *Persuasions* 5 (1983), 29–40.

Boyd, Zelda. "Jane Austen's 'Must': The Will and the World." *Nineteenth-Century Fiction* 39 (1984), 134–136.

Brownstein, Rachel M. *Becoming a Heroine*, 84–86, 90–99.

Cantrell, D. Dean. "Porcine Tittle-Tattle." *Persuasions* 4 (1982), 14–15.

Creese, Richard. "Austen's *Emma*." *Explicator* 44:2 (1986), 21–23.

Dash, Irene G. "Emma Crosses the Channel." *Names* 31 (1983), 191–196.

De Rose, Peter L. *Jane Austen*, 65–90.

De Rose, Peter L. "Marriage and Self-Knowledge in *Emma* and *Pride and Prejudice*." *Renascence* 30 (1978), 199–216.

Drew, Philip. "Jane Austen and Bishop Butler." *Nineteenth-Century Fiction* 35 (1980), 135–136, 144–146.

Ebine, Hiroshi. "*Emma* no Plot." *Eigo Seinen* (Tokyo) 126 (1981), 554–558.

Edwards, Lee R. *Psyche as Hero*, 65–72.

Fergus, Jan. *Jane Austen*, 133–142.

Fergus, Jan S. "Sex and Social Life in Jane Austen's Novels," in David Monaghan, ed., *Jane Austen*, 82–84.

Figes, Eva. *Sex and Subterfuge*, 107–110.

Fleishman, Avrom. "Two Faces of Emma." *Women & Lit* 3 (1983), 248–256.

Fried, Cathy. "Some Notes on 'parish business' in *Emma*." *Persuasions* 1 (1979), 17, 24.

Fry, Paul H. "Georgic Comedy: The Fictive Territory of Jane Austen's *Emma*." *Stud in the Novel* 11 (1979), 129–142.

Gilbert, Sandra M., and Susan Gubar. *The Madwoman*, 157–160.

Groves, David. "The Two Picnics in *Emma*." *Persuasions* 5 (1983), 6–7.

Halperin, John. *The Life*, 267–278.

Hanaway, Ann C. L. "On Reading *Emma* for the First Time at Age Seventeen." *Persuasions* 5 (1983), 15–16.

Hardy, John. *Jane Austen's Heroines*, 82–108.

Hilliard, Raymond F. "*Emma*: Dancing Without Space to Turn In," in Paula R. Backscheider, ed., *Probability*, 275–295.

Hough, Graham. "Narrative and Dialogue in Jane Austen," in his *Selected Essays*, 47–82.

Hunt, Linda C. "A Woman's Portion: Jane Austen and the Female Character," in Mary Anne Schofield and Cecilia Macheski, eds., *Fetter'd or Free?*, 20–22.

Irwin, Michael. *Picturing*, 145–148.

James, Selma. *The Ladies*, 26–28, 50–52.

Jefferson, Douglas. *Jane Austen's "Emma,"* 15–87.

Johnson, Claudia L. "The 'Operations of Time, and the Changes of the Human Mind': Jane Austen and Dr. Johnson Again." *Mod Lang Q* 44 (1983), 34–35.

Kirkham, Margaret. *Jane Austen*, 121–143.

Kurrik, Maire Jaanus. *Literature and Negation*, 82–96.

Lauritzen, Monica. *Jane Austen's "Emma,"* 43–152.

Leech, Geoffrey N., and Michael H. Short. *Style in Fiction*, 274–275.

Leimberg, Inge. " 'Humble Independence': Das Thema und seine dichterische Verwirklichung in Jane Austens *Emma*." *Germanisch-Romanische Monatsschrift* 30 (1980), 395–416.

Lemos, Brunilda Reichmann. "Language and Character in Jane Austen's *Emma*." *Revista Letras* 28 (1979), 95–105.

Lenta, Margaret. "Jane Fairfax and Jane Eyre: Educating Women." *Ariel* 12:4 (1981), 27–34.

Litvak, Joseph. "Reading Characters: Self, Society, and Text in *Emma*." *PMLA* 100 (1985), 763–771.

Macey, Samuel L. *Money and the Novel*, 155–158.

McMaster, Juliet. *Jane Austen*, 19–27, 40–42, 55–59, 66–67, 74–75.

Marie, Beatrice. "*Emma* and the Democracy of Desire." *Stud in the Novel* 17 (1985), 1–11.

Merrett, Robert James. "The Concept of Mind in *Emma*." *Engl Stud in Canada* 6 (1980), 39–54.

Monaghan, David. *Jane Austen*, 115–142.

Monaghan, David. "Jane Austen and the Position of Women," in Monaghan, ed., *Jane Austen*, 115–117.

Morgan, Susan. *In the Meantime*, 23–50.

Myer, Valerie Grosvenor. *Jane Austen*, 50–53, 59–63.

Nardin, Jane. "Children and Their Families in Jane Austen's Novels." *Women & Lit* 3 (1983), 78–81, 84–85.

Nardin, Jane. "Jane Austen and the Problem of Leisure," in David Monaghan, ed., *Jane Austen*, 135–137.

Odmark, John. *An Understanding*, 24–34, 74–78, 107–114, 150–155, 172–174.

Paris, Bernard J. " 'Creations inside a Creation': The Case of Emma Woodhouse." *Psychocultural R* 2 (1978), 119–138.

Parke, Catherine. "Vision and Revision: A Model for Reading the Eighteenth-Century Novel of Education." *Eighteenth-Century Stud* 16 (1982–83), 169–173.

Pickrel, Paul. "*Emma* as Sequel." *Nineteenth-Century Fiction* 40 (1985), 135–153.

Pickrel, Paul. "Lionel Trilling and *Emma*: A Reconsideration." *Nineteenth-Century Fiction* 40 (1985), 297–311.

Piggott, Patrick. *The Innocent Diversion*, 77–110.

Polhemus, Robert M. *Comic Faith*, 24–59.

Poovey, Mary. " 'The True English Style'." *Persuasions* 5 (1983), 48–51.

Preston, John. "The Silence of the Novel." *Mod Lang R* 74 (1979), 265–267.

Reeves, Charles Eric. "A Voice of Unrest: Conrad's Rhetoric of the Unspeakable." *Texas Stud in Lit and Lang* 27 (1985), 284–286.

Roberts, Warren. *Jane Austen*, 36–42, 149–154, 192–195.

Rosmarin, Adena. " 'Misreading' *Emma*: The Powers and Perfidies of Interpretive History." *ELH* 51 (1984), 315–339.

Rumrich, John Peter. "The Importance of Being Frank." *Essays in Lit* (Macomb) 8 (1981), 97–104.

Sciullo, Luciana. "Miss Bates, personaggio chiave di *Emma*." *Quaderni di Lingue e Letterature* 2 (1977), 91–98.

Smith, Mack. "The Document of Falsimilitude: Frank's Epistles and Misinterpretation in *Emma*." *Massachusetts Stud in Engl* 9:4 (1984), 52–69.

Stewart, Ralph. "Fairfax, Churchill, and Jane Austen's *Emma*." *Univ of Hartford Stud in Lit* 14:3 (1982), 96–100.

Stout, Janis P. "Jane Austen's Proposal Scenes and the Limitations of Language." *Stud in the Novel* 14 (1982), 318–319.

Tamm, Merike. "Performing Heroinism in Austen's *Sense and Sensibility* and *Emma*." *Papers on Lang & Lit* 15 (1979), 401–406.

Teyssandier, Hubert. *Les formes de le création*, 156–193.

Todd, Janet. *Women's Friendship*, 274–301.

Vargish, Thomas. *The Providential Aesthetic*, 48–50.

Voss-Clesly, Patricia. *Tendencies of Character*, 196–198, 264–271, 340–354, 521–527, 659–693.

Weinsheimer, Joel. "*Emma* and Its Critics: The Value of Tact." *Women & Lit* 3 (1983), 257–271.

Weinsheimer, Joel. "Theory of Character: *Emma*." *Poetics Today* 1:1–2 (1979), 185–211.

Wilt, Judith. *Ghosts of the Gothic*, 153–172.

Wilt, Judith. "Jane Austen's Men: Inside/Outside 'the Mystery'." *Women & Lit* 2 (1981), 71–73.

Wilt, Judith. "The Powers of the Instrument: or Jane, Frank, and the Pianoforte." *Persuasions* 5 (1983), 41–47.

Lady Susan, 1871

> Epstein, Julia L. "Jane Austen's Juvenilia and the Female Epistolary Tradition." *Papers on Lang & Lit* 21 (1985), 409–411.
> Piggott, Patrick. *The Innocent Diversion*, 35–36.

Love and Friendship, 1922

> Epstein, Julia L. "Jane Austen's Juvenilia," 405–409.
> Figes, Eva. *Sex and Subterfuge*, 79–81.
> Gilbert, Sandra M., and Susan Gubar. *The Madwoman*, 113–119.
> Voss-Clesly, Patricia. *Tendencies of Character*, 158–162.

Mansfield Park, 1814

> Adams, Timothy Dow. "To Know the Dancer," 63–64.
> Auerbach, Nina. "Jane Austen's Dangerous Charm: Feeling as One Ought about Fanny Price." *Persuasions* 2 (1980), 9–11. [Also in *Women & Lit* 3 (1983), 208–221.]
> Auerbach, Nina. *Romantic Imprisonment*, 22–37.
> Banfield, Ann. "The Influence of Place: Jane Austen and the Novel of Social Consciousness," in David Monaghan, ed., *Jane Austen*, 33–44.
> Barfoot, C. C. *The Thread*, 39–61, 115.
> Bodenheimer, Rosemarie. "Looking at the Landscape," 613–618.
> Boyd, Zelda. "Jane Austen's 'Must'," 138–142.
> Burlin, Katrin R. " 'At the Crossroads': Sister Authors and the Sister Arts," in Mary Anne Schofield and Cecilia Macheski, eds., *Fetter'd or Free?*, 72–79.
> Cohn, Maggie Hunt. "Suppressed Desires in *Mansfield Park*." *Persuasions* 2 (1980), 27–28.
> Cowart, David. "Wise and Foolish Virgins (and Matrons) in *Mansfield Park*." *South Atlantic Bull* 44:2 (1979), 76–82.
> Daleski, H. M. *Unities*, 129–150.
> De Rose, Peter L. *Jane Austen*, 37–60.
> Drew, Philip. "Jane Austen and Bishop Butler," 136–142.
> Fergus, Jan. *Jane Austen*, 125–133.
> Fergus, Jan. "Sex and Social Life," 77–82.
> Figes, Eva. *Sex and Subterfuge*, 101–109.
> Flahiff, F. T. "Place and Replacement in *Mansfield Park*." *Univ of Toronto Q* 54 (1985), 221–232.
> Fleishman, Avrom. "How Many Beliefs Had Lady Jane?" *Persuasions* 2 (1980), 19.
> Gilbert, Sandra M., and Susan Gubar. *The Madwoman*, 163–168.
> Gillis, Christina Marsden. "Garden, Sermon, and Novel in *Mansfield Park*: Exercises in Legibility." *Novel* 18 (1985), 117–125.
> Giuffre, Giulia. "Sex, Self and Society in *Mansfield Park*." *Sydney Stud in Engl* 9 (1983–84), 76–93.
> Grove, Robin. "Jane Austen's Free Enquiry: *Mansfield Park*." *Crit R* (Canberra) 25 (1983), 132–150.

Halperin, John. *The Life*, 234–250.

Halperin, John. "The Novelist as Heroine in *Mansfield Park*: A Study in Autobiography." *Mod Lang Q* 44 (1983), 136–156.

Hardy, John. *Jane Austen's Heroines*, 58–81.

Harris, Jocelyn. " 'As if they had been living friends': *Sir Charles Grandison* into *Mansfield Park*." *Bull of Res in the Hum* 83 (1980), 360–403.

Hart, John. "Jane Austen's Sailors: Gentlemen in the Military Capacity." *Persuasions* 4 (1982), 18–20.

Hassler, Donald M. *Comic Tones*, 60–63.

Hunt, Linda C. "A Woman's Portion," 16–20, 23–24.

Irwin, Michael. *Picturing*, 127–132.

Johnson, Claudia L. "The 'Operations of Time'," 32–34.

Jones, Myrddin. "Feelings of Youth and Nature in *Mansfield Park*." *English* 29 (1980), 221–231.

Keener, Frederick M. *The Chain of Becoming*, 276–287, 297–299.

Kelly, Gary. "Reading Aloud in *Mansfield Park*." *Nineteenth-Century Fiction* 37 (1982), 29–49.

Kilroy, G. J. F. "*Mansfield Park* in Two Volumes." *English* 34 (1985), 115–128.

Kirkham, Margaret. "Feminist Irony and the Priceless Heroine of *Mansfield Park*." *Women & Lit* 3 (1983), 231–246.

Kirkham, Margaret. *Jane Austen*, 101–120.

Koppel, Gene. "The Role of Contingency in *Mansfield Park*: The Necessity of an Ambiguous Conclusion." *Southern R* (Adelaide) 15 (1982), 306–312.

Koppel, Gene. "The Theme of Contingency in *Mansfield Park*." *Persuasions* 2 (1980), 20.

Leech, Geoffrey N., and Michael H. Short. *Style in Fiction*, 167–168.

Lenta, Margaret. "Androgyny and Authority in *Mansfield Park*." *Stud in the Novel* 15 (1983), 169–181.

Lovell, Terry. "Jane Austen and the Gentry: A Study in Literature and Ideology," in Diana Laurenson, ed., *The Sociology*, 15–16, 22–32.

McDonnell, Jane. " 'A Little Spirit of Independence': Sexual Politics and the Bildungsroman in *Mansfield Park*." *Novel* 17 (1984), 197–214.

Macey, Samuel L. *Money and the Novel*, 150–151, 154–155, 161–164.

McKenzie, Alan T. "The Derivation and Distribution of 'Consequence' in *Mansfield Park*." *Nineteenth-Century Fiction* 40 (1985), 281–296.

McMaster, Juliet. *Jane Austen*, 32–36, 52–55, 70–72.

Meyersohn, Marylea. "What Fanny Knew: A Quiet Auditor of the Whole." *Women & Lit* 3 (1983), 224–230.

Millard, Mary. "The Outs and Not Outs." *Persuasions* 2 (1980), 24–25.

Moler, Kenneth L. "Miss Price All Alone: Metaphors of Distance in *Mansfield Park*." *Stud in the Novel* 17 (1985), 189–192.

Moler, Kenneth L. " 'Only Connect': Emotional Strength and Health in *Mansfield Park*." *Engl Stud* 64 (1983), 144–152.

Monaghan, David. *Jane Austen*, 93–114.

Moore, Susan. "The Heroine of *Mansfield Park*." *Engl Stud* 63 (1982), 139–144.

Morgan, Susan. *In the Meantime*, 132–165.

Myer, Valerie Grosvenor. *Jane Austen*, 28–32, 94–96, 101–104, 118–120, 138–146.

Nardin, Jane. "Children," 82–84.

Nardin, Jane. "Jane Austen," 132–135.

Odmark, John. *An Understanding*, 12–24, 69–74, 102–107, 144–148, 184–186.

Piggott, Patrick. *The Innocent Diversion*, 64–76.

Polhemus, Robert M. *Comic Faith*, 25–27.

Preston, John. "The Silence of the Novel," 257–262, 264–265.

Ram, Atma. "Frail and Weak: A Portrait of Fanny Price." *Panjab Univ Res Bull* 8:1–2 (1977), 27–34.

Roberts, Warren. *Jane Austen*, 33–37, 50–55, 97–100, 133–151, 206–208.

Ruoff, Gene W. "The Sense of a Beginning: *Mansfield Park* and Romantic Narrative." *Wordsworth Circle* 10 (1979), 174–185.

Schwerin, Erna. "*Mansfield Park*: A Note on the Elopement of Henry and Maria." *Persuasions* 2 (1980), 22–23, 25.

Smith, Leroy W. "*Mansfield Park*: The Revolt of the 'Feminine' Woman," in David Monaghan, ed., *Jane Austen*, 143–157.

Spacks, Patricia Meyer. "Muted Discord: Generational Conflict in Jane Austen," in David Monaghan, ed., *Jane Austen*, 173–176.

Spring, David. "The Social Context of *Mansfield Park*." *Persuasions* 2 (1980), 14.

Steele, Pamela. "In Sickness and in Health: Jane Austen's Metaphor." *Stud in the Novel* 14 (1982), 156–159.

Stout, Janis P. "Jane Austen's Proposal Scenes," 318.

Tamm, Merike. "Performing Heroinism," 400–401.

Teyssandier, Hubert. *Les formes de la création*, 125–156.

Todd, Janet. *Women's Friendship*, 246–274.

Voss-Clesly, Patricia. *Tendencies of Character*, 191–196, 250–264, 502–511, 555–562, 723–725, 790–839.

Walton, James. "*Mansfield Park*: The Circle Squared," in *Studies in Nineteenth Century Literature* (2), 44–108.

Webb, Igor. *From Custom to Capital*, 58–72, 88–90, 101–123, 158–160, 189–191, 193–195.

Wilt, Judith. *Ghosts of the Gothic*, 142–144, 151–153.

Wilt, Judith. "Jane Austen's Men," 70–71.

Northanger Abbey, 1818

Adams, Timothy Dow. "To Know the Dancer," 57–59.

Anderson, Walter E. "From Northanger to Woodston: Catherine's Education to Common Life." *Philol Q* 63 (1984), 493–507.

Baguley, David. "Parody and the Realist Novel." *Univ of Toronto Q* 55 (1985), 98–100.

Barfoot, C. C. *The Thread*, 10–17, 113–114.

Bodenheimer, Rosemarie. "Looking at the Landscape," 607.

Boles, Carolyn G. "Jane Austen and the Reader," 152–167.

Boyd, Zelda. "Jane Austen's 'Must'," 127–134.

Brownstein, Rachel M. *Becoming a Heroine*, 92–94.

Butler, Marilyn. "Disregarded Designs: Jane Austen's Sense of the Volume," in David Monaghan, ed., *Jane Austen*, 56–58.

Butler, Marilyn. "The Woman at the Window: Ann Radcliffe in the Novels of Mary Wollstonecraft and Jane Austen." *Women & Lit* 1 (1980), 135–140.

De Rose, Peter L. *Jane Austen*, 15–33.

Fergus, Jan. *Jane Austen*, 11–38.

Figes, Eva. *Sex and Subterfuge*, 82–85.

Fowler, Marian. " 'Substance and Shadow': Conventions of the Marriage Market in *Northanger Abbey*." *Engl Stud in Canada* 6 (1980), 277–289.

Gilbert, Sandra M., and Susan Gubar. *The Madwoman*, 128–145.

Gordon, Jan B. "Narrative Enclosure as Textual Ruin: An Archaeology of Gothic Consciousness." *Dickens Stud Annual* 11 (1983), 231–233.

Halperin, John. *The Life*, 101–115.

Hardy, John. *Jane Austen's Heroines*, 1–18.

Hennessy, Brendan. *The Gothic Novel*, 30–32.

Hopkins, Robert. "General Tilney and Affairs of State: The Political Gothic of *Northanger Abbey*." *Philol Q* 57 (1978), 213–224.

Howells, Coral Ann. *Love, Mystery*, 114–130.

James, Selma. *The Ladies*, 46–49.

Keener, Frederick M. *The Chain of Becoming*, 249–276.

Kent, Christopher. " 'Real Solemn History' and Social History," in David Monaghan, ed., *Jane Austen*, 97–99.

Kirkham, Margaret. *Jane Austen*, 88–90.

Lewis, Paul. "Mysterious Laughter: Humor and Fear in Gothic Fiction." *Genre* 14 (1981), 316–318.

MacDonald, Susan Peck. "Jane Austen and the Tradition of the Absent Mother," in Cathy N. Davidson and E. M. Broner, eds., *The Lost Tradition*, 61–64.

Macey, Samuel L. *Money and the Novel*, 146–148.

McMaster, Juliet. *Jane Austen*, 46–48, 64–65.

Marais, Trudi. "*Northanger Abbey* in the '80s." *CRUX* 14:3 (1980), 42–43.

May, Leland Chandler. *Parodies of the Gothic Novel*, 12–44.

Moler, Kenneth L. "Some Verbal Tactics of General Tilney." *Persuasions* 6 (1984), 10–12.

Monaghan, David. "Jane Austen," 117–118.

Monaghan, David. *Jane Austen*, 16–41.

Morgan, Susan. *In the Meantime*, 51–76.

Morrow, Patrick D. "Sublime or Sensible: *The Mysteries of Udolpho* and *Northanger Abbey*," in his *Tradition*, 106–117.

Myer, Valerie Grosvenor. *Jane Austen*, 86–91, 124–126.

Nardin, Jane. "Children," 74–75.

Nardin, Jane. "Jane Austen," 125–128.

Odmark, John. *An Understanding*, 4–6, 45–50, 118–121.

Paulson, Ronald. "Gothic Fiction and the French Revolution." *ELH* 48 (1981), 532–534.

Piggott, Patrick. *The Innocent Diversion*, 39–41.

Roberts, Warren. *Jane Austen*, 22–31, 109–111, 178–180.

Spacks, Patricia Meyer. "Muted Discord," 170–172.

Stout, Janis P. "Jane Austen's Proposal Scenes," 317–318.

Voss-Clesly, Patricia. *Tendencies of Character*, 165–176, 494–497, 553–555, 614–639, 708–716, 765–771.

Weiss, Fredric. *The Antic Spectre*, 198–206.

Williams, Merryn. *Women in the English Novel*, 44–46.

Wilt, Judith. *Ghosts of the Gothic*, 124–151, 161–164.

Persuasion, 1818

Auerbach, Nina. *Romantic Imprisonment*, 38–54.

Barfoot, C. C. *The Thread*, 85–111, 116–118.

Bernikow, Louise. *Among Women*, 220–223.

Bodenheimer, Rosemarie. "Looking at the Landscape," 618–623.

Burrows, J. F. "*Persuasion* and Its 'Sets of People'." *Sydney Stud in Engl* 2 (1976–77), 3–23.

Butler, Marilyn. "Disregarded Designs," 61–64.

Cerny, Lothar. "Das gute Ende des Romans: Jane Austens *Persuasion*." *Anglia* 102 (1984), 80–100.

Collins, K. K. "Prejudice, *Persuasion*, and the Puzzle of Mrs. Smith." *Persuasions* 6 (1984), 40–43.

Davison, Trevor. "Jane Austen and the 'Process' of *Persuasion*." *Durham Univ J* 77 (1984–85), 43–47.

De Rose, Peter L. *Jane Austen*, 93–111.

Drew, Philip. "Jane Austen and Bishop Butler," 132–134.

Fergus, Jan. *Jane Austen*, 143–148.

Fergus, Jan. "Sex and Social Life," 75–77.

Figes, Eva. *Sex and Subterfuge*, 110–112.

Gay, Penny. "The Romanticism of *Persuasion*." *Sydney Stud in Engl* 5 (1979–80), 15–30.

Gilbert, Sandra M., and Susan Gubar. *The Madwoman*, 174–183.

Grant, John E. "Shows of Mourning in the Text of Jane Austen's *Persuasion*." *Mod Philology* 80 (1983), 283–286.

Groves, David. "Knowing One's Species Better: Social Satire in *Persuasion*." *Persuasions* 6 (1984), 13–15.

Grylls, David. *Guardians and Angels*, 115–117.

Halperin, John. *The Life*, 300–311.

Hardy, John. *Jane Austen's Heroines*, 109–127.

Harris, Jocelyn. "Anne Eliot, the Wife of Bath, and Other Friends." *Women & Lit* 3 (1983), 273–292.

Hart, John. "Jane Austen's Sailors," 18–20.

Hufstader, Alice. "Family Patterns in *Persuasion*." *Persuasions* 6 (1984), 21–23.

Hunt, Linda C. "A Woman's Portion," 22–26.

Ireland, K. R. "Future Recollections of Immortality: Temporal Articulation in Jane Austen's *Persuasion*." *Novel* 13 (1980), 204–220.

James, Selma. *The Ladies*, 16–20.

Johnson, Claudia L. "The 'Operations of Time'," 35–38.

Johnson, Judy Van Sickle. "The Bodily Frame: Learning Romance in *Persuasion*." *Nineteenth-Century Fiction* 38 (1983), 43–61.

Keener, Frederick M. *The Chain of Becoming*, 286–307.

Kern, Jean B. "The Old Maid, or 'to grow old, and be poor, and laughed at'," in Mary Anne Schofield and Cecilia Macheski, eds., *Fetter'd or Free?*, 210–211.

Kirkham, Margaret. *Jane Austen*, 144–160.

Koppel, Gene. "The Mystery of the Self in *Persuasion*." *Persuasions* 6 (1984), 48–53.

Leech, Geoffrey N., and Michael H. Short. *Style in Fiction*, 226–227.

MacDonald, Susan Peck. "Jane Austen," 65–67.

Macey, Samuel L. *Money and the Novel*, 149–150, 153–154, 162–163.

McMaster, Juliet. *Jane Austen*, 18–27, 36–40, 59–61, 72–74.

Marshall, P. Scott. "Techniques of Persuasion in *Persuasion*: A Lawyer's Viewpoint." *Persuasions* 6 (1984), 44–47.

Molan, Ann. "Persuasion in *Persuasion*." *Crit R* 24 (1982), 16–29.

Monaghan, David. "Jane Austen," 118–121.

Monaghan, David. *Jane Austen*, 143–162.

Morgan, Susan. *In the Meantime*, 166–198.

Myer, Valerie Grosvenor. *Jane Austen*, 48–50.

Nardin, Jane. "Children," 85–86.

Nardin, Jane. "Jane Austen," 137–141.

Odmark, John. *An Understanding*, 33–40, 82–89, 114–118, 159–161.

Piggott, Patrick. *The Innocent Diversion*, 111–130.

Poovey, Mary. "*Persuasion* and the Promises of Love," in Carolyn G. Heilbrun and Margaret R. Higonnet, eds., *The Representation of Women*, 156–177.

Roberts, Warren. *Jane Austen*, 56–59, 100–149, 151–154, 195–202.

Ruoff, Gene W. "The Triumph of *Persuasion*: Jane Austen and the Creation of Woman." *Persuasions* 6 (1984), 54–61.

Sieferman, Sylvia. "*Persuasion*: The Motive for Metaphor." *Stud in the Novel* 11 (1979), 283–300.

Smith, Grahame. *The Novel & Society*, 116–145.

Soulsby, Sarah E. "Some Notes on Jane Austen's *Persuasion*." *J of Engl* (Sana'a Univ) 4 (1977), 43–50.

14

AUSTEN

Spence, Jon. "The Abiding Possibilities of Nature in *Persuasion*." *Stud in Engl Lit, 1500–1900* 21 (1981), 625–636.

Stout, Janis P. "Jane Austen's Proposal Scenes," 319–321.

Swanson, Janice Bowman. "Toward a Rhetoric of Self: The Art of *Persuasion*." *Nineteenth-Century Fiction* 36 (1981), 1–21.

Tanner, Tony. "In Between: Anne Elliot Marries a Sailor and Charlotte Heywood Goes to the Seaside," in David Monaghan, ed., *Jane Austen*, 180–187.

Voss-Clesly, Patricia. *Tendencies of Character*, 191–196, 250–264, 814–839.

Wilt, Judith. "Jane Austen's Men," 73–75.

Pride and Prejudice, 1813

Adams, Timothy Dow. "To Know the Dancer," 59–60.

Allen, Dennis W. "No Love for Lydia: The Fate of Desire in *Pride and Prejudice*." *Texas Stud in Lit and Lang* 27 (1985), 425–440.

Armstrong, Nancy. "Inside Greimas's Square: Literary Characters and Cultural Constraints," in Wendy Steiner, ed., *The Sign*, 52–66.

Armstrong, Nancy. "The Rise of Feminine Authority in the Novel." *Novel* 15 (1982), 139–142.

Barfoot, C. C. "Choice against Fate in *Sense and Sensibility* and *Pride and Prejudice*." *Dutch Q R of Anglo-American Letters* 10 (1980), 176–198.

Barfoot, C. C. *The Thread*, 30–38, 114–115.

Barker, Gerard A. *Grandison's Heirs*, 150–167.

Bodenheimer, Rosemarie. "Looking at the Landscape," 610–611.

Boles, Carolyn G. "Jane Austen and the Reader," 152–167.

Boyd, Zelda. "Jane Austen's 'Must'," 136–138, 142–143.

Brown, Carole O. "Dwindling into a Wife: A Jane Austen Heroine Grows Up." *Intl J of Women's Stud* 5 (1982), 460–469.

Brownstein, Rachel M. *Becoming a Heroine*, 118–134.

Bruns, Gerald L. *Inventions*, 111–124.

Burlin, Katrin R. " 'Pictures of Perfection' at Pemberley: Art in *Pride and Prejudice*." *Women & Lit* 3 (1983), 155–167.

Burrows, J. F. "A Measure of Excellence: Modes of Comparison in *Pride and Prejudice*." *Sydney Stud in Engl* 5 (1979–80), 38–59.

Caywood, Cynthia L. "*Pride and Prejudice* and the Belief in Choice: Jane Austen's Fantastical Vision," in Anne C. Hargrove and Maurine Magliocco, eds., *Portraits of Marriage*, 31–37.

De Rose, Peter L. *Jane Austen*, 65–90.

De Rose, Peter L. "Marriage and Self-Knowledge," 199–216.

Epstein, Julia L. "Jane Austen's Juvenilia," 412–414.

Fergus, Jan. *Jane Austen*, 87–120.

Figes, Eva. *Sex and Subterfuge*, 97–101.

Flavin, Louise. "From Classic to Modern: The Marriage Theme in *Pride and Prejudice*," in *Literature*, 101–105.

Giuffre, Giulia. "The Ethical Mode of *Pride and Prejudice*." *Sydney Stud in Engl* 6 (1980–81), 17–29.

Halperin, John. *The Life*, 65–78.

Hardy, John. *Jane Austen's Heroines*, 36–57.

Hennelly, Mark M., Jr. "*Pride and Prejudice*: The Eyes Have It." *Women & Lit* 3 (1983), 187–205.

Higbie, Robert. *Character & Structure*, 101–119.

Higgins, Elizabeth Jean. *Reading the Novel*, 5–12.

Howells, Coral Ann. *Love, Mystery*, 96–99.

Irwin, Michael. *Picturing*, 37–40, 113–115.

James, Selma. *The Ladies*, 28–37.

Johnson, Claudia L. "The 'Operations of Time'," 28–31.

Kelly, Gary. "The Art of Reading in *Pride and Prejudice*." *Engl Stud in Canada* 10 (1984), 156–169.

Kent, Christopher. " 'Real Solemn History'," 99–101.

Kirkham, Margaret. *Jane Austen*, 91–92.

Konigsberg, Ira. *Narrative Technique*, 213–256.

Leech, Geoffrey N., and Michael H. Short. *Style in Fiction*, 291–294, 315–316.

Lellis, George, and H. Philip Bolton. "Pride but No Prejudice," in Michael Klein and Gillian Parker, eds., *The English Novel*, 44–51.

Litz, A. Walton. "The Picturesque in *Pride and Prejudice*." *Persuasions* 1 (1979), 13, 15, 20–24.

Lovell, Terry. "Jane Austen and the Gentry," 24–29.

MacDonald, Susan Peck. "Jane Austen," 64–65.

Macey, Samuel L. *Money and the Novel*, 148–153, 158–161.

McKeon, Zahava Karl. *Novels and Arguments*, 36–38, 46–52.

McMaster, Juliet. *Jane Austen*, 17–27, 48–52, 63–64, 75–76, 79–80.

McMaster, Juliet and Rowland. *The Novel from Sterne to James*, 19–35.

Mason, Philip. *The English Gentleman*, 71–74.

Milligan, Ian. *The Novel in English*, 74–89.

Monaghan, David. "Jane Austen," 107–108.

Monaghan, David. *Jane Austen*, 64–92.

Morgan, Susan. *In the Meantime*, 77–106.

Myer, Valerie Grosvenor. *Jane Austen*, 72–78.

Nardin, Jane. "Children," 75–77.

Nardin, Jane. "Jane Austen," 125–128.

Newman, Karen. "Can This Marriage Be Saved: Jane Austen Makes Sense of an Ending." *ELH* 50 (1983), 696–708.

Newton, Judith Lowder. "*Pride and Prejudice*: Power, Fantasy, and Subversion in Jane Austen." *Feminist Stud* 4 (1978), 27–42.

Newton, Judith Lowder. *Women, Power, and Subversion*, 55–85.

Odmark, John. *An Understanding*, 10–13, 61–69, 100–102, 106–108, 148–150.

Petit, J.-P. "Jane Austen: *Pride and Prejudice*," in Pierre Coustillas et al., eds., *Le roman anglais*, 127–138.

Piggott, Patrick. *The Innocent Diversion*, 50–63.

Roberts, Warren. *Jane Austen*, 47–53, 105–107, 173–176, 180–182.

Satz, Martha. "An Epistemological Understanding of *Pride and Prejudice*: Humility and Objectivity." *Women & Lit* 3 (1983), 171–183.

Sherry, James. "*Pride and Prejudice*: The Limits of Society." *Stud in Engl Lit, 1500–1900* 19 (1979), 609–622.

Stout, Janis P. "Jane Austen's Proposal Scenes," 316–317, 321–325.

Voss-Clesly, Patricia. *Tendencies of Character*, 185–191, 514–521, 537–545, 639–659, 721–723, 776–790.

Webb, Igor. *From Custom to Capital*, 49–58, 158–160, 172–176, 194–196.

Weinsheimer, Joel. "Impedance as Value: *Roderick Random* and *Pride and Prejudice*." *PTL* 3 (1978), 139–166.

Wiesenfarth, Joseph. "The Case of *Pride and Prejudice*." *Stud in the Novel* 16 (1984), 261–271.

Williams, Merryn. *Women in the English Novel*, 45–47.

Woolf, David. *An Aspect of Fiction*.

Sanditon, 1925

Fergus, Jan. *Jane Austen*, 148–149.

Ganner-Rauth, Heidi. "To Be Continued? Sequels and Continuations of Nineteenth-Century Novels and Novel Fragments." *Engl Stud* 64 (1983), 133–135.

Halperin, John. "Jane Austen's Anti-Romantic Fragment: Some Notes on *Sanditon*." *Tulsa Stud in Women's Lit* 2 (1983), 183–190.

Halperin, John. *The Life*, 326–335.

Kirkham, Margaret. *Jane Austen*, 144–160.

Piggott, Patrick. *The Innocent Diversion*, 37–39.

Roberts, Warren. *Jane Austen*, 59–67.

Tanner, Tony. "In Between," 187–193.

Tayler, Irene. "Jane Austen Looks Ahead," in Mary Anne Schofield and Cecilia Macheski, eds., *Fetter'd or Free?*, 428–433.

Sense and Sensibility, 1811

Auerbach, Nina. *Romantic Imprisonment*, 13–15, 41–43.

Barfoot, C. C. "Choice against Fate," 176–198.

Barfoot, C. C. *The Thread*, 17–29, 114.

Bodenheimer, Rosemarie. "Looking at the Landscape," 607–610.

Boyd, Zelda. "The Language of Supposing: Modal Auxiliaries in *Sense and Sensibility*." *Women & Lit* 3 (1983), 142–152.

Brownstein, Rachel M. *Becoming a Heroine*, 112–114.

Butler, Marilyn. "Disregarded Designs," 58–60.

Craddock, Patricia. "The Almanac of *Sense and Sensibility*." *Notes and Queries* 26 (1979), 222–226.

De Rose, Peter L. *Jane Austen*, 93–111.

Drew, Philip. "Jane Austen and Bishop Butler," 134–135.

Fergus, Jan. *Jane Austen*, 39–60.

Figes, Eva. *Sex and Subterfuge*, 89–97.

Frazer, June M. "The Apprenticeship of Elinor Dashwood." *Persuasions* 3 (1981), 6.

Hagstrum, Jean H. *Sex and Sensibility*, 268–274.

Halperin, John. *The Life*, 83–95.

Hardy, John. *Jane Austen's Heroines*, 19–35.

Jefferson, Ann. *The Nouveau Roman*, 89–91.

Johnson, Claudia L. "The 'Operations of Time'," 26–28.

Johnson, Claudia L. "The 'Twilight of Probability': Uncertainty and Hope in *Sense and Sensibility*." *Philol Q* 62 (1983), 171–185.

Kaplan, Deborah. "Achieving Authority: Jane Austen's First Published Novel." *Nineteenth-Century Fiction* 37 (1983), 535–551.

Kirkham, Margaret. *Jane Austen*, 86–87.

Klieneberger, H. R. *The Novel*, 30–34.

Leech, Geoffrey N., and Michael H. Short. *Style in Fiction*, 272–274.

Leighton, Angela. "Sense and Silences: Reading Jane Austen Again." *Women & Lit* 3 (1983), 128–140.

Macey, Samuel L. *Money and the Novel*, 150–152, 158–164.

McMaster, Juliet. *Jane Austen*, 16–27, 65–66, 68–69.

Millard, Mary. "The Extraordinary Fate of Marianne Dashwood." *Persuasions* 3 (1981), 5.

Monaghan, David. *Jane Austen*, 42–63.

Morgan, Susan. *In the Meantime*, 109–131.

Myer, Valerie Grosvenor. *Jane Austen*, 43–46, 64–66, 127–130.

Nardin, Jane. "Children," 77–78.

Nardin, Jane. "Jane Austen," 128–129.

Nollen, Elizabeth. "Ann Radcliffe's *A Sicilian Romance*: A New Source for Jane Austen's *Sense and Sensibility*." *Engl Lang Notes* 22:2 (1984), 30–37.

Odmark, John. *An Understanding*, 6–10, 51–60, 92–102, 155–157.

Piggott, Patrick. *The Innocent Diversion*, 42–49.

Ram, Atma. "Heroines in *Sense and Sensibility*." *Panjab Univ Res Bull* 7:2 (1976), 19–23.

Reinstein, P. Gila. "Moral Priorities in *Sense and Sensibility*." *Renascence* 35 (1983), 269–283.

Roberts, Warren. *Jane Austen*, 44–47, 174–177.

Séjourné, Philippe. "Les Intentions de Jane Austen dans *Sense and Sensibility*: Héritage et innovation," in *Hommage à Emile Gasquet*, 149–158.

Shoben, Edward Joseph, Jr. "Impulse and Virtue in Jane Austen: Sense and Sensibility in Two Centuries." *Hudson R* 35 (1982), 529–539.

Spacks, Patricia Meyer. "The Difference It Makes." *Soundings* 64 (1981), 343–360.

Spacks, Patricia Meyer. "Sisters," in Mary Anne Schofield and Cecilia Macheski, eds., *Fetter'd or Free?*, 146–150.

Steele, Pamela. "In Sickness and in Health," 152–157.

Tamm, Merike. "Performing Heroism," 396–400.
Usaily, M. A. al-. "Jane Austen's *Sense and Sensibility*." *J of Engl* (Sana'a Univ) 4 (1977), 73–87.
Voss-Clesly, Patricia. *Tendencies of Character*, 176–185, 497–502, 545–553, 716–721, 771–776.
Watt, Ian. "Jane Austen and the Traditions of Comic Aggression: *Sense and Sensibility*." *Persuasions* 3 (1981), 14–15, 24–28.
Zeman, Anthea. *Presumptuous Girls*, 154–156.

The Watsons, 1871

Ganner-Rauth, Heidi. "To Be Continued?," 130–133.
Kern, Jean B. "The Old Maid,," 211–212.

ELIZABETH AYRTON

Two Years in My Afternoon, 1972

Zeman, Anthea. *Presumptuous Girls*, 138–140.

MICHAEL AYRTON

The Maze Maker, 1967

Oettli, Simone. "The Maze Maker." *Kenyon R* 5 (1983), 67–84.

ROBERT BAGE

Hermsprong, or Man as He Is Not, 1796

Punter, David. "Fictional Representation of the Law in the Eighteenth Century." *Eighteenth-Century Stud* 16 (1982–83), 66–67.
Scheuermann, Mona. "Redefining the Filial Tie: Eighteenth-Century English Novelists from Brooke to Bage." *Etudes Anglaises* 37 (1984), 395–398.
Scheuermann, Mona. *Social Protest*, 203–229.
Sheriff, John K. *The Good-Natured Man*, 64–70.

ENID BAGNOLD

The Squire, 1938

Beauman, Nicola. *A Very Great Profession*, 117–119.

BERYL BAINBRIDGE

The Bottle Factory Outing, 1974

Crosland, Margaret. *Beyond the Lighthouse*, 200–201.

The Dressmaker, 1973

Crosland, Margaret. *Beyond the Lighthouse*, 199–200.

Sweet William, 1975

    Crosland, Margaret. *Beyond the Lighthouse*, 201–203.

ROBERT MICHAEL BALLANTYNE

The Coral Island, 1858

    McEwan, Neil. *The Survival of the Novel*, 147–161.

    Mannsaker, Frances M. "The Dog that didn't Bark: The Subject Races in Imperial Fiction at the Turn of the Century," in David Dabydeen, ed., *The Black Presence*, 114–117.

    Rose, Jacqueline. *The Case of Peter Pan*, 78–79.

J. G. BALLARD

The Atrocity Exhibition, 1969

    Brigg, Peter. *J. G. Ballard*, 56–66.

    Greenland, Colin. *The Entropy Exhibition*, 114–117.

    Platzner, Robert L. "The Metamorphic Vision of J. G. Ballard." *Essays in Lit* (Macomb) 10 (1983), 214–216.

Concrete Island, 1974

    Brigg, Peter. *J. G. Ballard*, 67–74.

    Dowling, Terry. "Alternative Reality and Deviant Logic in J. G. Ballard's Second 'Disaster' Trilogy." *Science Fiction* 1:1 (1977), 6–18.

Crash, 1972

    Brigg, Peter. *J. G. Ballard*, 67–74.

    Dowling, Terry. "Alternative Reality," 6–18.

The Crystal World, 1966

    Brigg, Peter. *J. G. Ballard*, 51–55.

    Firsching, Lorenz J. "J. G. Ballard's Ambiguous Apocalypse." *Science-Fiction Stud* 12 (1985), 305–308.

    Platzner, Robert L. "The Metamorphic Vision," 211–212.

    Stableford, Brian M. "J. G. Ballard," in E. F. Bleiler, ed., *Science Fiction Writers*, 279–280.

    Wendland, Albert. *Science, Myth*, 150–155.

The Drought, 1964

    Brigg, Peter. *J. G. Ballard*, 48–51.

    Firsching, Lorenz J. "J. G. Ballard's Ambiguous Apocalypse," 303–305.

The Drowned World, 1962

    Brigg, Peter. *J. G. Ballard*, 46–49.

    Firsching, Lorenz J. "J. G. Ballard's Ambiguous Apocalypse," 302–303.

    Platzner, Robert L. "The Metamorphic Vision," 212–214.

    Wendland, Albert. *Science, Myth*, 147–151.

Empire of the Sun, 1984
  Brigg, Peter. *J. G. Ballard*, 106–108.
Hello America, 1981
  Brigg, Peter. *J. G. Ballard*, 99–105.
High-Rise, 1975
  Brigg, Peter. *J. G. Ballard*, 70–76.
  Dowling, Terry. "Alternative Reality," 6–18.
The Unlimited Dream Company, 1979
  Brigg, Peter. *J. G. Ballard*, 96–99.
The Wind from Nowhere, 1962
  Brigg, Peter. *J. G. Ballard*, 46–49.
  Firsching, Lorenz J. "J. G. Ballard's Ambiguous Apocalypse," 301.

JOHN BANIM

The Boyne Water, 1826
  Cahalan, James M. *Great Hatred*, 49–55.
The Conformists, 1830
  Cahalan, James M. *Great Hatred*, 60–62.
The Last Baron of Crana, 1830
  Cahalan, James M. *Great Hatred*, 55–60.
The Nowlans, 1826
  Cronin, John. *The Anglo-Irish Novel*, 45–57.

MICHAEL BANIM

The Croppy, 1826
  Cahalan, James M. *Great Hatred*, 62–65.

JOHN BANVILLE

Birchwood, 1973
  Imhoff, Rüdiger. "John Banville's Supreme Fiction." *Irish Univ R* 11
    (1981), 63–69.
Doctor Copernicus, 1976
  Imhoff, Rüdiger. "John Banville's Supreme Fiction," 69–73.
Kepler, 1981
  Imhoff, Rüdiger. "John Banville's Supreme Fiction," 73–86.
Nightspawn, 1971
  Imhoff, Rüdiger. "John Banville's Supreme Fiction," 59–63.

H. R. BARBOR

Against the Red Sky, 1922

Klaus, H. Gustav. "Silhouettes of Revolution: Some Neglected Novels of the Early 1920s," in Klaus, ed., *The Socialist Novel*, 97–100.

SABINE BARING-GOULD

Mehalah, 1880

Sutton, Max Keith. "Baring-Gould's *Mehalah* and *Red Spider*: Sources for Hardy's *Tess*?" *Engl Lit in Transition* 24 (1981), 94–96.

Red Spider, 1887

Sutton, Max Keith. "Baring-Gould's *Mehalah* and *Red Spider*," 91–94.

JAMES BARKE

Major Operation, 1936

Klaus, H. Gustav. *The Literature*, 121–123.

JANE BARKER

Exilius, 1715

Beasley, Jerry C. "Politics and Moral Idealism: The Achievement of Some Early Women Novelists," in Mary Anne Schofield and Cecilia Macheski, eds., *Fetter'd or Free?*, 227–229.

Love's Intrigues, 1713

Kern, Jean B. "The Old Maid, or 'to grow old, and be poor, and laughed at'," in Mary Anne Schofield and Cecilia Macheski, eds., *Fetter'd or Free?*, 204–205.
Suhr, Heidrun. *Englische Romanautorinnen*, 43–45.

A Patch-Work Screen for the Ladies, 1723

Kern, Jean B. "The Old Maid," 205–206.
Suhr, Heidrun. *Englische Romanautorinnen*, 45–47.

EATON STANNARD BARRETT

The Heroine, 1813

Lewis, Paul. "Gothic and Mock Gothic: The Repudiation of Fantasy in Barrett's *Heroine*." *Engl Lang Notes* 21:2 (1983), 44–52.
May, Leland Chandler. *Parodies of the Gothic Novel*, 73–92.
Weiss, Fredric. *The Antic Spectre*, 206–212.

JAMES MATTHEW BARRIE

The Little White Bird, 1902

Hunter, Lynette. "J. M. Barrie: The Rejection of Fantasy." *Scottish Liter J* 5:1 (1978), 46–51.

Rose, Jacqueline. *The Case of Peter Pan*, 20–34.

Peter and Wendy, 1911

Rose, Jacqueline. *The Case of Peter Pan*, 66–78, 83–86, 127–130.

Peter Pan in Kensington Gardens, 1906

Griffith, John. "Making Wishes Innocent: *Peter Pan*." *The Lion and the Unicorn* 3:1 (1979), 28–37.

STAN BARSTOW

A Kind of Loving, 1960

Paul, Ronald. *"Fire in Our Hearts,"* 67–69.

H. E. BATES

Catherine Foster, 1929

Vannatta, Dennis. *H. E. Bates*, 27–30.

Charlotte's Row, 1931

Vannatta, Dennis. *H. E. Bates*, 30–31.

Dear Life, 1949

Vannatta, Dennis. *H. E. Bates*, 72–75.

The Distant Horns of Summer, 1967

Vannatta, Dennis. *H. E. Bates*, 105–107.

Fair Stood the Wind for France, 1944

Vannatta, Dennis. *H. E. Bates*, 58–61.

The Fallow Land, 1932

Vannatta, Dennis. *H. E. Bates*, 43–45.

The Feast of July, 1954

Vannatta, Dennis. *H. E. Bates*, 95–97.

A House of Women, 1936

Vannatta, Dennis. *H. E. Bates*, 46–47.

The Jacaranda Tree, 1949

Vannatta, Dennis. *H. E. Bates*, 68–71.

Love for Lydia, 1952

Vannatta, Dennis. *H. E. Bates*, 93–95.

A Moment in Time, 1964

> Vannatta, Dennis. *H. E. Bates*, 104–105.

The Poacher, 1935

> Vannatta, Dennis. *H. E. Bates*, 45–46.

The Purple Plain, 1947

> Vannatta, Dennis. *H. E. Bates*, 66–68.

The Sleepless Moon, 1956

> Vannatta, Dennis. *H. E. Bates*, 97–98.

Spella Ho, 1938

> Vannatta, Dennis. *H. E. Bates*, 47–49.

The Two Sisters, 1926

> Vannatta, Dennis. *H. E. Bates*, 9–13.

RALPH BATES

The Olive Field, 1936

> Klaus, H. Gustav. *The Literature*, 111–114.

SAMUEL BECKETT

Company, 1980

> Bair, Deirdre. " 'Back the Way He Came . . . or in Some Quite Different Direction': *Company* in the Canon of Samuel Beckett's Writing." *Pennsylvania Engl* 9:1 (1982), 12–19.
>
> Baldwin, Helene L. "Memories, Echoes, and Trinities in Beckett's *Company*." *Christianity & Lit* 32:2 (1983), 37–42.
>
> Burgin, Richard. "*Company*." *Parabola* 6:4 (1981), 116–118.
>
> Butler, Lance St. John. *Samuel Beckett*, 192–194.
>
> Dobrez, L. A. C. "Samuel Beckett and the Impossibility of Lit. Crit." *Southern R* (Adelaide) 16 (1983), 74–76, 78–85.
>
> Levy, Eric P. "*Company*: The Mirror of Beckettian Mimesis." *J of Beckett Stud* 8 (1982), 95–104.
>
> Moorjani, Angela B. *Abysmal Games*, 133–147.
>
> Pilling, John. "*Company* by Samuel Beckett." *J of Beckett Stud* 7 (1982), 127–131.
>
> Read, David. "Beckett's Search for Unseeable and Unmakeable: *Company* and *Ill Seen Ill Said*." *Mod Fiction Stud* 29 (1983), 111–125.
>
> Smith, Frederik N. "Beckett's Verbal Slapstick." *Mod Fiction Stud* 29 (1983), 53–55.
>
> Zurbrugg, Nicholas. "From 'Gleam' to 'Gloom': The Volte Face between the Criticism and Fiction of Samuel Beckett." *AUMLA* 55 (1981), 32–34.

How It Is, 1964

Binns, Ronald. "Beckett, Lowry and the Anti-Novel," in Malcolm Bradbury and David Palmer, eds., *The Contemporary English Novel*, 99–100.

Butler, Lance St. John. *Samuel Beckett*, 163–165.

Cohn, Ruby. *"Comment c'est* par le bout," in Harold Bloom, ed., *Samuel Beckett*, 83–101.

Elovaara, Raili. *The Problem of Identity*, 267–275.

Esslin, Martin. *Mediations*, 108–109.

Gidal, Peter. *Understanding Beckett*, 46–47.

Gluck, Barbara Reich. *Beckett and Joyce*, 119–120.

Hutchings, William. " 'Shat into Grace' Or, A Tale of a Turd: Why It Is How It Is in Samuel Beckett's *How It Is*." *Papers on Lang & Lit* 21 (1985), 64–87.

Knowlson, James, and John Pilling. *Frescoes of the Skull*, 61–78.

Moorjani, Angela B. *Abysmal Games*, 53, 61–65.

Simon, Alfred. *Beckett*, 244–247.

Smith, Frederik N. "Beckett's Verbal Slapstick," 50–52.

Ill Seen Ill Said, 1982

Butler, Lance St. John. *Samuel Beckett*, 192–194.

Moorjani, Angela B. *Abysmal Games*, 147–151.

Read, David. "Beckett's Search," 113–125.

The Lost Ones, 1971

Brater, Enoch. "Mis-takes, Mathematical and Otherwise, in *The Lost Ones*." *Mod Fiction Stud* 29 (1983), 93–109.

Butler, Lance St. John. *Samuel Beckett*, 171–173.

Knowlson, James, and John Pilling. *Frescoes of the Skull*, 156–167.

Moorjani, Angela B. *Abysmal Games*, 95–96.

Murphy, Peter. "The Nature of Allegory in *The Lost Ones*, or the Quincunx Realistically Considered." *J of Beckett Stud* 7 (1982), 71–88.

Smith, Frederik N. "Beckett's Verbal Slapstick," 52–53.

Malone Dies, 1956

Binns, Ronald. "Beckett, Lowry," 98.

Christensen, Inger. *The Meaning of Metafiction*, 121–135.

Elovaara, Raili. *The Problem of Identity*, 166–185.

Esslin, Martin. *Mediations*, 102–103.

Gluck, Barbara Reich. *Beckett and Joyce*, 112–115, 126–140.

Henkle, Roger B. "Beckett and the Comedy of Bourgeois Experience." *Thalia* 3:1 (1980), 37–38.

Hildebrandt, Hans-Hagen. *Becketts Proust-Bilder*, 52–70.

Kawin, Bruce F. *The Mind of the Novel*, 275–278.

Keil, Flod Van. "Over Becketts trilogie: *Molloy, Malone meurt, L'Inno-mable*." *Nieuw Vlaams Tijdschrift* 34 (1981), 826–839.

Kellman, Steven G. *The Self-Begetting Novel*, 130–143.

Moorjani, Angela B. *Abysmal Games*, 51–52, 54–56, 120–127.

Renner, Charlotte. "The Self-Multiplying Narrators of *Molloy, Malone Dies*, and *The Unnamable*." *J of Narrative Technique* 11 (1981), 12–29.

Schröder, Wolfgang. *Reflektierter Roman*, 78–82.

Shahane, Vasant A. "Samuel Beckett's Trilogy: A Study in Complex Form," in I. K. Masih, ed., *An Indian Response*, 31–32.

Simon, Alfred. *Beckett*, 221–222.

Smith, Roch C. "Naming the M/inotaur: Beckett's Trilogy and the Failure of Narrative." *Mod Fiction Stud* 29 (1983), 73–80.

Stewart, Garrett. "Signing Off: Dickens and Thackeray, Woolf and Beckett," in William E. Cain, ed., *Philosophical Approaches*, 130–138.

Tagliaferri, Aldo. *Beckett*, 59–63, 94–101, 161–170.

Woodward, Kathleen. "Transitional Objects and the Isolate: Samuel Beckett's *Malone Dies*." *Contemp Lit* 26 (1985), 140–154.

Mercier et Camier, 1970

Castillo, Debra A. "Beckett's Metaphorical Towns." *Mod Fiction Stud* 28 (1982), 191–200.

Culik, Hugh. "Entropic Order: Beckett's *Mercier et Camier*." *Eire-Ireland* 17:1 (1982), 91–106.

Elovaara, Raili. *The Problem of Identity*, 76–79.

Gluck, Barbara Reich. *Beckett and Joyce*, 100–104.

Kenner, Hugh. "Life in the Box," in Harold Bloom, ed., *Samuel Beckett*, 36–39.

Moorjani, Angela B. *Abysmal Games*, 43–45, 96.

Schröder, Wolfgang. *Reflektierter Roman*, 58–59.

Simon, Alfred. *Beckett*, 214–216.

Molloy, 1955

Acheson, James. "The Art of Failure: Samuel Beckett's *Molloy*." *Southern Hum R* 17 (1983), 1–16.

Benson, Michael. "Moving Bodies in Hardy and Beckett." *Essays in Criticism* 34 (1984), 237–238.

Binns, Ronald. "Beckett, Lowry," 97–98.

Bové, Paul A. "The Image of the Creator in Beckett's Postmodern Writing." *Philos and Lit* 4 (1980), 54–64.

Castillo, Debra A. "Beckett's Metaphorical Towns," 194–200.

Christensen, Inger. *The Meaning of Metafiction*, 99–120.

Cousineau, Thomas J. "*Molloy* and the Paternal Metaphor." *Mod Fiction Stud* 29 (1983), 81–91.

Culik, Hugh. "Samuel Beckett's *Molloy*: Transformation and Loss." *Am Imago* 39 (1982), 21–29.

Cushman, Keith. "*Molloy*: Beckett's 'Nourishing and Economical Irish Stew'." *Univ of Dayton R* 15:3 (1982), 75–82.

Elovaara, Raili. *The Problem of Identity*, 80–165.

Esslin, Martin. *Mediations*, 100–102.

Frye, Northrop. "The Nightmare Life in Death," in Harold Bloom, ed., *Samuel Beckett*, 21–23.

Gluck, Barbara Reich. *Beckett and Joyce*, 113–115, 126–140.

Groves, David. "Beckett's *Molloy*." *Explicator* 41:3 (1983), 53–54.

Henkle, Roger B. "Beckett and the Comedy," 35–37.

Hildebrandt, Hans-Hagen. *Becketts Proust-Bilder*, 95–98.

Kawin, Bruce F. *The Mind of the Novel*, 272–275.

Keil, Flod Van. "Over Becketts trilogie," 826–839.

Kellman, Steven G. *The Self-Begetting Novel*, 130–143.

Kern, Edith. "Moran-Molloy: The Hero as Author," in Harold Bloom, ed., *Samuel Beckett*, 7–16.

Kroll, Jeri L. " 'I Create, Therefore I Am': The Artist's Mind in Samuel Beckett's Fiction." *AUMLA* 55 (1981), 46–52.

Moorjani, Angela B. *Abysmal Games*, 39–51, 96–120.

O'Hara, J. D. "Jung and the Narratives of *Molloy*." *J of Beckett Stud* 7 (1982), 19–47.

Pearce, Richard. "From Joyce to Beckett: The Tale That Wags the Telling," in Bernard Benstock, ed., *The Seventh of Joyce*, 47–49.

Phillips, K. J. "Beckett's *Molloy* and *The Odyssey*." *Intl Fiction R* 11 (1984), 19–24.

Rabinovitz, Rubin. "*Molloy* and the Archetypal Traveller." *J of Beckett Stud* 5 (1979), 25–44.

Renner, Charlotte. "The Self-Multiplying Narrators," 12–29.

Rolin-Janziti, Jeanne. "Le Système générateur dans *Molloy* de Samuel Beckett." *Lingua e Stile* 16 (1981), 255–270.

Schröder, Wolfgang. *Reflektierter Roman*, 38–45, 101–102.

Shahane, Vasant A. "Samuel Beckett's Trilogy," 28–31.

Simon, Alfred. *Beckett*, 218–220.

Smith, Frederik N. "Beckett's Verbal Slapstick," 48–49.

Smith, Roch C. "Naming the M/inotaur," 73–80.

Tagliaferri, Aldo. *Beckett*, 37–59, 71–75, 91–101, 161–170.

Murphy, 1938

Acheson, James. "Murphy's Metaphysics." *J of Beckett Stud* 5 (1979), 9–23.

Ackerley, C. J. " 'In the Beginning Was the Pun': Samuel Beckett's *Murphy*." *AUMLA* 55 (1981), 15–22.

Arthur, Kateryna. "Murphy, Gerontion and Dante." *AUMLA* 55 (1981), 54–67.

Brugière, Bernard. "*Murphy* de Samuel Beckett: ironie et parodie dans un récit de quête." *Etudes Anglaises* 35 (1982), 39–56.

Butler, Lance St. John. *Samuel Beckett*, 23–25, 197–198.

Castillo, Debra A. "Beckett's Metaphorical Towns," 192–200.

Cousineau, Thomas J. "Descartes, Lacan, and Murphy." *Coll Lit* 11 (1984), 223–232.

Culik, Hugh. "Mindful of the Body: Medical Allusions in Beckett's *Murphy*." *Eire-Ireland* 14:1 (1979), 84–101.

Eade, J. C. "The Seventh Scarf: A Note on *Murphy*." *J of Beckett Stud* 7 (1982), 115–117.

Elovaara, Raili. *The Problem of Identity*, 29–48.

Esslin, Martin. *Mediations*, 96–97.

Fiérobe, Claude. "Murphy, Celia et les autres," in *L'Autre dans la sensibilité*, 107–116.

Fletcher, John. "Reading Beckett with Iris Murdoch's Eyes." *AUMLA* 55 (1981), 7–14.

Freese, Wolfgang, and Angela B. Moorjani. "The Esoteric and the Trivia: Chess and Go in the Novels of Beckett and Kawabata." *Perspectives on Contemp Lit* 6 (1980), 37–48.

Frye, Northrop. "The Nightmare Life," 18–19.

Gluck, Barbara Reich. *Beckett and Joyce*, 71–86.

Hildebrandt, Hans-Hagen. *Becketts Proust-Bilder*, 90–91.

Jones, Anthony. "The French Murphy: From 'Rare Bird' to 'Cancre'." *J of Beckett Stud* 6 (1980), 37–50.

Mooney, Michael E. "Presocratic Scepticism: Samuel Beckett's *Murphy* Reconsidered." *ELH* 49 (1982), 214–232.

Moorjani, Angela B. *Abysmal Games*, 18–22, 24–25, 70–83.

Rabinovitz, Rubin. *The Development*, 71–96, 104–118, 185–221.

Rafroidi, Patrick. "Pas de shamrocks pour Sam Beckett? La dimension irlandaise de *Murphy*." *Etudes Irlandaises* 7 (1982), 71–80.

Schröder, Wolfgang. *Reflektierter Roman*, 59–66.

Simon, Alfred. *Beckett*, 207–209.

Smith, Frederik N. "Beckett's Verbal Slapstick," 45–46.

Stuart, Malcolm. "Notes on Place and Place Names in *Murphy*." *Recherches Anglaises et Américaines* 14 (1981), 227–235.

Susini, Christian. "Murphomania: Murphy et sa catharsis."*Recherches Anglaises et Américaines* 14 (1981), 213–225.

Waters, Maureen. *The Comic Irishman*, 110–122.

The Unnamable, 1958

Binns, Ronald. "Beckett, Lowry," 98–99.

Butler, Lance St. John. *Samuel Beckett*, 35–37, 123–127, 133–136.

Christensen, Inger. *The Meaning of Metafiction*, 135–150.

Elovaara, Raili. *The Problem of Identity*, 186–256.

Esslin, Martin. *Mediations*, 104–107.

Foster, Dennis A. "All Here Is Sin: The Obligation in *The Unnamable*." *Boundary 2* 12:1 (1983), 81–99.

Frye, Northrop. "The Nightmare Life," 23–25.

Gluck, Barbara Reich. *Beckett and Joyce*, 126–140.

Hildebrandt, Hans-Hagen. *Becketts Proust-Bilder*, 71–89.

Hill, Leslie. "The Name, the Body, 'The Unnameable'." *Oxford Liter R* 6:1 (1983), 52–67.

Hutchings, William. " 'The Unintelligible Terms of an Incomprehensible Damnation': Samuel Beckett's *The Unnamable*, Sheol, and *St. Erkenwald.*" *Twentieth Century Lit* 27 (1981), 98–111.

Kawin, Bruce F. *The Mind of the Novel*, 277–286.

Keil, Flod Van. "Over Becketts trilogie," 826–839.

Kellman, Steven G. *The Self-Begetting Novel*, 130–143.

Kurrik, Maire Jaanus. *Literature and Negation*, 224–230.

Moorjani, Angela B. *Abysmal Games*, 52–53, 56–61, 127–132.

Renner, Charlotte. "The Self-Multiplying Narrators," 12–29.

Schröder, Wolfgang. *Reflektierter Roman*, 46–57, 83–88, 92–100, 103–110.

Shahane, Vasant A. "Samuel Beckett's Trilogy," 32–33.

Simon, Alfred. *Beckett*, 230–232.

Smith, Frederik N. "Beckett's Verbal Slapstick," 49–50.

Smith, Roch C. "Naming the M/inotaur," 73–80.

Tagliaferri, Aldo. *Beckett*, 63–68, 76–83, 92–152, 161–170.

Thiher, Allen. *Words in Reflection*, 128–132.

Watt, 1953

Benson, Michael. "Moving Bodies," 236–237.

Brater, Enoch. "Privilege, Perspective, and Point of View in *Watt.*" *Coll Lit* 8 (1981), 209–226.

Butler, Lance St. John. *Samuel Beckett*, 20–22, 47–49, 198–200.

Büttner, Gottfried. *Samuel Beckett's Novel "Watt,"* 5–164.

Büttner, Marie Renate. "*Watt* von Samuel Beckett." *Christengemeinschaft* 50 (1978), 63–65.

Cousineau, Thomas J. "*Watt*: Language as Interdiction and Consolation." *J of Beckett Stud* 4 (1979), 1–13.

Culik, Hugh. "The Place of *Watt* in Beckett's Development." *Mod Fiction Stud* 29 (1983), 57–71.

Di Pietro, John C. *Structures in Beckett's "Watt,"* 1–105.

Dobrez, L. A. C. "Samuel Beckett and the Impossibility," 79–80.

Elovaara, Raili. *The Problem of Identity*, 48–73.

Esslin, Martin. *Mediations*, 98–100.

Gluck, Barbara Reich. *Beckett and Joyce*, 86–100.

Harrington, John P. "The Irish Landscape in Samuel Beckett's *Watt.*" *J of Narrative Technique* 11 (1981), 1–9.

Kawin, Bruce F. *The Mind of the Novel*, 64–70.

Leech, Geoffrey N., and Michael H. Short. *Style in Fiction*, 252–254.

Moorjani, Angela B. *Abysmal Games*, 26–39, 83–93.

Pearce, Richard. "From Joyce to Beckett," 46–47.

Posnock, Ross. "Beckett, Valéry and *Watt.*" *J of Beckett Stud* 6 (1980), 51–62.

Rabinovitz, Rubin. *The Development*, 124–142, 151–169.

Robinson, Fred Miller. "Samuel Beckett: *Watt,*" in Harold Bloom, ed., *Samuel Beckett*, 147–192.

Schröder, Wolfgang. *Reflektierter Roman*, 26–38.

Simon, Alfred. *Beckett*, 209–213.
Smith, Frederik N. "Beckett's Verbal Slapstick," 46–48.
Thiher, Allen. *Words in Reflection*, 102–105.
Winston, Mathew. "*Watt*'s First Footnote." *J of Mod Lit* 6 (1977), 69–82.

WILLIAM BECKFORD

Azemia, 1797

Fothergill, Brian. *Beckford*, 245–247.
Reddin, Chitra Pershad. *Forms of Evil*, 63–65.

Vathek, 1786

Craig, Randall. "Beckford's Inversion of Romance in *Vathek*." *Orbis Litterarum* 39 (1984), 95–105.
Dédéyan, Charles. *Dante dans le romantisme*, 61–66.
Fothergill, Brian. *Beckford*, 128–134.
Garber, Frederick. "Beckford, Delacroix and Byronic Orientalism." *Compar Lit Stud* 18 (1981), 321–325.
Hennessy, Brendan. *The Gothic Novel*, 14–18.
Hyland, Peter. "*Vathek*, Heaven and Hell." *Res Stud* 50 (1982), 99–105.
Lange, Bernd-Peter. "Orientierungsarbeit: Radikale Fantasie in William Beckfords *Vathek*." *Zeitschrift für Anglistik und Amerikanistik* 33 (1985), 33–42.
Le Tellier, Robert Ignatius. *An Intensifying Vision*, 19–21, 69–70, 78–79, 90–94, 121–122, 154–155.
Le Tellier, Robert Ignatius. *Kindred Spirits*, 166–168, 222–223.
Lin, Alan. "Toward a Theory of Common Sense: Beckford's *Vathek* and Johnson's *Rasselas*." *Texas Stud in Lit and Lang* 26 (1984), 183–211.
MacAndrew, Elizabeth. *The Gothic Tradition*, 71–73.
Mochi, Giovanna. "L'inferno rassicurante di *Vathek*." *Paragone* 350 (1979), 64–102.
Reddin, Chitra Pershad. *Forms of Evil*, 60–63, 117–120, 217–218, 238–239, 249–251.
Vigil, Julioan Josue. "A Nightmare in Literary Criticism." *New Mexico Highlands Univ J* 1 (1979), 48–50.
Weiss, Fredric. *The Antic Spectre*, 84–122.

MAX BEERBOHM

Zuleika Dobson, 1911

Grushow, Ira. *The Imaginary Reminiscences*, 20–21, 37–41.
Viscusi, Robert. "A Dandy's Diary: The Manuscripts of Max Beerbohm's *Zuleika Dobson*." *Princeton Univ Lib Chron* 40 (1979), 234–256.
Viscusi, Robert. *Max Beerbohm*, 133–228.

BRENDAN BEHAN

Borstal Boy, 1959

Brown, Richard. *"Borstal Boy*: Structure and Meaning." *Colby Lib Q* 21 (1985), 188–197.
Paul, Ronald. *"Fire in Our Hearts,"* 106–121.
Phelps, Corey. "Borstal Revisited," in E. H. Mikhail, ed., *The Art of Brendan Behan*, 91–108.
Thomsen, Christian W. "Brendan Behan: Literat zwischen Revolution und Showbusiness," in J. Kornelius et al., eds., *Einführung*, 95–98.
Waters, Maureen. *The Comic Irishman*, 166–170.

APHRA BEHN

The Fair Jilt, 1688

Kelly, Gary. " 'Intrigue' and 'Gallantry': The XVIIth Century French Nouvelle and the 'Novels' of Aphra Behn." *Revue de Littérature Comparée* 218 (1981), 188–190.

The History of Agnes de Castro, 1688

Kelly, Gary. " 'Intrigue' and 'Gallantry'," 187–188.

Love Letters Between a Nobleman and His Sister, 1683–87

Perry, Ruth. *Women*, 24–26, 157–159.

Oroonoko, 1688

Beasley, Jerry C. "Politics and Moral Idealism: The Achievement of Some Early Women Novelists," in Mary Anne Schofield and Cecilia Macheski, eds., *Fetter'd or Free?*, 221.
Hagstrum, Jean H. *Sex and Sensibility*, 78–80.
Hayden, Lucy K. "The Black Presence in Eighteenth-Century British Novels." *Coll Lang Assoc J* 24 (1981), 404–407.
Helman, Albert. "Mrs. Behn en haar *Oroonoko*." *Maatstaf* 30 (1982), 1–44.
Houston, Beverle. "Usurpation and Dismemberment: Oedipal Tyranny in *Oroonoko*." *Lit and Psych* 32:1 (1986), 30–35.
Kelly, Gary. " 'Intrigue' and 'Gallantry'," 185–187, 193–194.
Pache, Walter. *Profit and Delight*, 67–73.
Spengemann, William C. "The Earliest American Novel: Aphra Behn's *Oroonoko*." *Nineteenth-Century Fiction* 38 (1984), 384–414.

HILAIRE BELLOC

Belinda, 1928

Markel, Michael H. *Hilaire Belloc*, 91–93.

A Change in the Cabinet, 1909

McCarthy, John P. *Hilaire Belloc*, 188–190.

Emmanuel Burden, 1904

  Markel, Michael H. *Hilaire Belloc*, 81–84.
  Wilson, A. N. *Hilaire Belloc*, 125–129.

The Girondin, 1911

  Markel, Michael H. *Hilaire Belloc*, 89–90.

The Haunted House, 1927

  Markel, Michael H. *Hilaire Belloc*, 97–98.

Mr. Clutterbuck's Election, 1908

  Markel, Michael H. *Hilaire Belloc*, 84–86.

Pongo and the Bull, 1910

  Wilson, A. N. *Hilaire Belloc*, 167–169.

The Postmaster-General, 1932

  Markel, Michael H. *Hilaire Belloc*, 86–88.

ANNA MARIA BENNETT

Anna, or Memoirs of a Welch Heiress, 1785

  Suhr, Heidrun. *Englische Romanautorinnen*, 219–223.

ARNOLD BENNETT

Anna of the Five Towns, 1902

  Batchelor, John. *The Edwardian Novelists*, 162–166.
  Broomfield, Olga R. R. *Arnold Bennett*, 32–41.
  Hunter, Jefferson. *Edwardian Fiction*, 210–213.
  Marroni, Francesco. "*Anna of the Five Towns* ovvero il margine della libertà." *Lettore di Provincia* 43 (1980), 26–35.
  Norton, David. "Lawrence, Wells and Bennett: Influence and Tradition." *AUMLA* 54 (1980), 177–181.
  Scheick, William J. "Compassion and Fictional Structure: The Example of Gissing and Bennett." *Stud in the Novel* 15 (1983), 305–310.
  Stubbs, Patricia. *Women and Fiction*, 198–199.
  Voss, James. "Arnold Bennett's Realism: Social Process and the Individual in *Anna of the Five Towns*." *Orbis Litterarum* 38 (1983), 168–183.

Buried Alive, 1908

  Broomfield, Olga R. R. *Arnold Bennett*, 58–59.

The Card, 1911

  Broomfield, Olga R. R. *Arnold Bennett*, 87–89.

Clayhanger, 1910

> Batchelor, John. *The Edwardian Novelists*, 152–161.
> Broomfield, Olga R. R. *Arnold Bennett*, 76–85.
> Hunter, Jefferson. *Edwardian Fiction*, 210–214.
> Leech, Geoffrey N., and Michael H. Short. *Style in Fiction*, 175–176.
> Lincoln, Andrew. "The Sociology of Bennett's *Clayhanger*." *Engl Lit in Transition* 27 (1984), 188–198.

The Glimpse, 1909

> Broomfield, Olga R. R. *Arnold Bennett*, 74–76.

Grand Babylon Hotel, 1902

> Broomfield, Olga R. R. *Arnold Bennett*, 30–32.

Hilda Lessways, 1911

> Broomfield, Olga R. R. *Arnold Bennett*, 85–87.

Imperial Palace, 1930

> Broomfield, Olga R. R. *Arnold Bennett*, 117–122.

Leonora, 1903

> Broomfield, Olga R. R. *Arnold Bennett*, 43–46.

The Lion's Share, 1916

> Broomfield, Olga R. R. *Arnold Bennett*, 96–98.

Lord Raingo, 1926

> Broomfield, Olga R. R. *Arnold Bennett*, 111–115.

A Man from the North, 1898

> Batchelor, John. *The Edwardian Novelists*, 157–159, 161–163.
> Broomfield, Olga R. R. *Arnold Bennett*, 23–28.

The Old Wives' Tale, 1908

> Batchelor, John. *The Edwardian Novelists*, 170–177.
> Broomfield, Olga R. R. *Arnold Bennett*, 60–73.
> Denjean, Albert. "Euphorie et dysphorie dans *The Old Wives' Tale* d'A. Bennett." *Cahiers Victoriens et Edouardiens* 15 (1982), 79–86.
> Fromm, Gloria G. "Remythologizing Arnold Bennett." *Novel* 16 (1982), 23–31.
> Hunter, Jefferson. *Edwardian Fiction*, 210–214.
> Meckier, Jerome. "Aldous Huxley and the Congenital Novelists: New Ideas about the Novel of Ideas." *Southern R* (Adelaide) 13 (1980), 213–214.
> Stubbs, Patricia. *Women and Fiction*, 199–201.

The Pretty Lady, 1918

> Broomfield, Olga R. R. *Arnold Bennett*, 99–102.

Riceyman Steps, 1923

> Broomfield, Olga R. R. *Arnold Bennett*, 103–109.

The Roll-Call, 1918

 Broomfield, Olga R. R. *Arnold Bennett*, 98–99.

Sacred and Profane Love, 1905

 Broomfield, Olga R. R. *Arnold Bennett*, 48–50.
 Stubbs, Patricia. *Women and Fiction*, 206–208.

These Twain, 1915

 Broomfield, Olga R. R. *Arnold Bennett*, 48–50.

Whom God Hath Joined, 1906

 Broomfield, Olga R. R. *Arnold Bennett*, 51–55.

STELLA BENSON

Goodbye, Stranger, 1926

 Bedell, R. Meredith. *Stella Benson*, 85–97.

I Pose, 1915

 Bedell, R. Meredith. *Stella Benson*, 24–39.

Living Alone, 1919

 Bedell, R. Meredith. *Stella Benson*, 53–61.

Pipers and a Dancer, 1924

 Bedell, R. Meredith. *Stella Benson*, 72–84.

The Poor Man, 1922

 Bedell, R. Meredith. *Stella Benson*, 62–72.

This is the End, 1917

 Bedell, R. Meredith. *Stella Benson*, 40–53.

Tobit Transplanted, 1931

 Bedell, R. Meredith. *Stella Benson*, 97–110.

JOHN BERGER

Corker's Freedom, 1964

 Craig, Randall. "Fiction and Freedom: The Novels of John Berger."
 Dalhousie R 63 (1983–84), 671–676.
 McMahon, Joseph H. "Marxist Fictions: The Novels of John Berger."
 Contemp Lit 23 (1982), 213–216.

The Foot of Clive, 1962

 McMahon, Joseph H. "Marxist Fictions," 209–213.

G., 1972

 Bergonzi, Bernard. "Fictions of History," in Malcolm Bradbury and
 David Palmer, eds., *The Contemporary English Novel*, 50–51.

Craig, Randall. "Fiction and Freedom," 676–683.
James, David E. "Cubism as Revolutionary Realism: John Berger and
    G." *Minnesota R* 21 (1983), 92–107.
McMahon, Joseph H. "Marxist Fictions," 216–224.

A Painter of Our Time, 1959

Craig, Randall. "Fiction and Freedom," 668–671.
McMahon, Joseph H. "Marxist Fictions," 205–209.

WALTER BESANT

The Inner House, 1888

Abrash, Merritt. "Is There Life After Immortality?," in Carl B. Yoke
    and Donald M. Hassler, eds., *Death and the Serpent*, 22–25.

RICHARD D. BLACKMORE

Lorna Doone, 1869

Smith, J. B. "Possible Sources for the Legend of Wizard's Slough in
    R. D. Blackmore's *Lorna Doone.*" *Lore and Lang* 3:2 (1980), 36–41.
Sutton, Max Keith. "*The Prelude* and *Lorna Doone.*" *Wordsworth
    Circle* 13 (1982), 193–197.

ALGERNON BLACKWOOD

The Centaur, 1911

Reaver, J. Russell. "From Seed to Fruit: The Doubling of Psychic
    Landscapes in Algernon Blackwood's *The Centaur.*" *Romantist* 4–5
    (1980–81), 55–58.

GEORGE BLAKE

The Shipbuilders, 1935

Bold, Alan. *Modern Scottish Literature*, 231–233.

SIMON BLUMENFIELD

Jew Boy, 1935

Worpole, Ken. *Dockers and Detectives*, 97–99.

They Won't Let You Live, 1939

Worpole, Ken. *Dockers and Detectives*, 100–101.

GEORGE BORROW

Lavengro, 1851

Collie, Michael. *George Borrow*, 184–228.
Collie, Michael. "George Borrow's Joseph Sell." *Nineteenth-Century Fiction* 37 (1982), 133–145.

The Romany Rye, 1857

Collie, Michael. *George Borrow*, 211–228.

LUCIE M. BOSTON

The Children of Green Knowe, 1954

Swinfen, Ann. *In Defence*, 49–52.

ELIZABETH BOWEN

The Death of the Heart, 1938

Blodgett, Harriet. *Patterns of Reality*, 114–153.
Chessman, Harriet S. "Women and Language in the Fiction of Elizabeth Bowen." *Twentieth Century Lit* 29 (1983), 78–81.
Coates, John. "In Praise of Civility: Conservative Values in Elizabeth Bowen's *The Death of the Heart*." *Renascence* 37 (1985), 248–265.
Lee, Hermione. *Elizabeth Bowen*, 104–128.

Eva Trout, 1969

Blodgett, Harriet. *Patterns of Reality*, 74–83.
Chessman, Harriet S. "Women and Language," 81–84.
Lee, Hermione. *Elizabeth Bowen*, 206–211.

Friends and Relations, 1931

Blodgett, Harriet. *Patterns of Reality*, 52–55.
Lee, Hermione. *Elizabeth Bowen*, 62–66.

The Heat of the Day, 1949

Blodgett, Harriet. *Patterns of Reality*, 154–189.
Brothers, Barbara. "Pattern and Void: Bowen's Irish Landscapes and *The Heat of the Day*." *Mosaic* 12:3 (1979), 129–138.
Chessman, Harriet S. "Women and Language," 71–78.
Crosland, Margaret. *Beyond the Lighthouse*, 65–67.
Lee, Hermione. *Elizabeth Bowen*, 164–188.
Watson, Barbara Bellow. "Variations on an Enigma: Elizabeth Bowen's War Novel." *Southern Hum R* 15 (1981), 131–150.

The Hotel, 1927

Blodgett, Harriet. *Patterns of Reality*, 26–38.
Lee, Hermione. *Elizabeth Bowen*, 58–61.

The House in Paris, 1935

Adams, Timothy Dow. " 'Bend Sinister': Duration in Elizabeth Bowen's *The House in Paris.*" *Intl Fiction R* 7 (1980), 49–52.
Blodgett, Harriet. *Patterns of Reality*, 84–113.
Lee, Hermione. *Elizabeth Bowen*, 80–103.

The Last September, 1929

Blodgett, Harriet. *Patterns of Reality*, 38–45.
Lee, Hermione. *Elizabeth Bowen*, 15–18, 43–53.
Quinn, Antoinette. "Elizabeth Bowen's Irish Stories: 1939 to 1945," in Heinz Kosok, ed., *Studies*, 314–315.
Scanlan, Margaret. "Rumors of War: Elizabeth Bowen's *Last September* and J. G. Farrell's *Troubles.*" *Eire-Ireland* 20:2 (1985), 70–79.
Tuohy, Frank. "Five Fierce Ladies," in Masaru Sekine, ed., *Irish Writers*, 203–204.

The Little Girls, 1964

Blodgett, Harriet. *Patterns of Reality*, 68–74.
Lee, Hermione. *Elizabeth Bowen*, 199–206.

To the North, 1932

Blodgett, Harriet. *Patterns of Reality*, 55–68.
Lee, Hermione. *Elizabeth Bowen*, 66–79.

A World of Love, 1955

Blodgett, Harriet. *Patterns of Reality*, 45–52.
Lee, Hermione. *Elizabeth Bowen*, 189–198.
McGowan, Martha. "The Enclosed Garden in Elizabeth Bowen's *A World of Love.*" *Eire-Ireland* 16:1 (1981), 55–70.

MALCOLM BRADBURY

The History Man, 1975

Todd, Richard. "Malcolm Bradbury's *The History Man*: The Novelist as Reluctant Impresario." *Dutch Q R of Anglo-American Letters* 11 (1981), 162–182.

G. F. BRADBY

The Lanchester Tradition, 1913

Quigly, Isabel. *The Heirs of Tom Brown*, 189–196.

MARY ELIZABETH BRADDON

Aurora Floyd, 1863

Hughes, Winifred. *The Maniac*, 128–131, 187–189.
Trodd, Anthea. "The Policeman and the Lady: Significant Encounters in Mid-Victorian Fiction." *Victorian Stud* 27 (1984), 446.

Charlotte's Inheritance, 1868

Peterson, Audrey. *Victorian Masters*, 167–169.

Henry Dunbar, 1864

Peterson, Audrey. *Victorian Masters*, 164–167.

John Marchmont's Legacy, 1863

Hughes, Winifred. *The Maniac*, 131–133.

Lady Audley's Secret, 1862

Auerbach, Nina. *Woman and the Demon*, 78–81, 107–108.
Hughes, Winifred. *The Maniac*, 120–122, 124–128.
Peterson, Audrey. *Victorian Masters*, 161–164.
Showalter, Elaine. "Family Secrets and Domestic Subversion: Rebellion in the Novels of the 1860s," in Anthony S. Wohl, ed., *The Victorian Family*, 111–113.
Showalter, Elaine. *A Literature*, 163–168.
Welsh, Alexander. *George Eliot*, 20–24.

Strangers and Pilgrims, 1873

Putzell, Sara Moore. "Attracting the Majority: M. E. Braddon and George Eliot." *George Eliot Fellowship R* 11 (1980), 14–19.

JOHN BRAINE

Room at the Top, 1957

Laing, Stuart. "*Room at the Top*: The Morality of Affluence," in Christopher Pawling, ed., *Popular Fiction*, 157–182.
Paul, Ronald. *"Fire in Our Hearts,"* 57–59.

JOHN BRODERICK

The Fugitives, 1962

O'Rourke, Brian. *The Conscience of the Race*, 27–28, 37–39.

ANNE BRONTË

Agnes Grey, 1847

Easson, Angus. "Anne Brontë and the Glow-Worms." *Notes and Queries* 26 (1979), 299–300.
Pollard, Arthur. "The Brontës and Their Father's Faith." *Essays & Stud 1984*, 52–53.
Rataboul, Louis J. *Le pasteur anglican*, 172–174, 234–235.
Scott, P. J. M. *Anne Brontë*, 9–43.

The Tenant of Wildfell Hall, 1848

Chitham, Edward, and Tom Winnifrith. *Brontë Facts*, 99–109.
Figes, Eva. *Sex and Subterfuge*, 163–165.

Gilbert, Sandra M., and Susan Gubar. *The Madwoman*, 80–83.

Gordon, Jan B. "Gossip, Diary, Letter, Text: Anne Brontë's Narrative *Tenant* and the Problematic of the Gothic Sequel." *ELH* 51 (1984), 719–742.

Jackson, Arlene M. "The Question of Credibility in Anne Brontë's *The Tenant of Wildfell Hall*." *Engl Stud* 63 (1982), 198–206.

McMaster, Juliet. " 'Imbecile Laughter' and 'Desperate Earnest' in *The Tenant of Wildfell Hall*." *Mod Lang Q* 43 (1982), 352–368.

Mitchell, Sally. *The Fallen Angel*, 64–65.

Pollard, Arthur. "The Brontës," 53–54.

Scott, P. J. M. *Anne Brontë*, 73–124.

Williams, Merryn. *Women in the English Novel*, 101–105.

CHARLOTTE BRONTË

Jane Eyre, 1847

Adams, Harriet Farwell. "Domesticating the Brutal Passion in Nineteenth-Century Fiction." *Victorian Newsl* 67 (1985), 8.

Adams, Maurianne. "Family Disintegration and Creative Reintegration: The Case of Charlotte Brontë and *Jane Eyre*," in Anthony S. Wohl, ed., *The Victorian Family*, 148–176.

Armstrong, Nancy. "The Rise of Feminine Authority in the Novel." *Novel* 15 (1982), 136–138.

Auerbach, Nina. *Romantic Imprisonment*, 67–70, 196–204.

Beaty, Jerome. "Jane Eyre at Gateshead: Mixed Signals in the Text and Context," in James R. Kincaid and Albert J. Kuhn, eds., *Victorian Literature*, 168–194.

Berg, Temma F. "From Pamela to Jane Grey; or, How Not to Become the Heroine of Your Own Text." *Stud in the Novel* 17 (1985), 123–130.

Berman, Ronald. "The Innocent Observer." *Children's Lit* 9 (1981), 40–50.

Bodenheimer, Rosemarie. "Jane Eyre in Search of Her Story." *Papers on Lang & Lit* 16 (1980), 387–402.

Butery, Karen Ann. "Jane Eyre's Flights from Decision." *Liter R* 24 (1981), 222–251.

Bystrom, Valerie Ann. "The Abyss of Sympathy: The Conventions of Pathos in Eighteenth and Nineteenth Century British Novels." *Criticism* 23 (1981), 228–229.

Castillo, Debra A. *The Translated World*, 266–270, 275–277.

Chase, Karen. *Eros & Psyche*, 47–91.

Chitham, Edward. *The Brontës' Irish Background*, 14–16, 109–111, 142–144.

Chitham, Edward, and Tom Winnifrith. *Brontë Facts*, 9–13.

Costa de Beauregard, Raphaëlle. "La femme dans *Jane Eyre* (1847)." *Caliban* 17 (1980), 57–67.

Cowart, David. "Oedipal Dynamics in *Jane Eyre*." *Lit and Psych* 31:1 (1981), 33–37.

Dale, Peter Allan. "Heretical Narration: Charlotte Brontë's Search for Endlessness." *Religion & Lit* 16:3 (1984), 1–6.

Daleski, H. M. *The Divided Heroine*, 5–6.

Davies, Stevie. "*Jane Eyre*: Exile and Grace." *Durham Univ J* 77 (1984–85), 223–227.

Dunn, Richard J. "The Natural Heart: Jane Eyre's Romanticism." *Wordsworth Circle* 10 (1979), 197–204.

Edwards, Lee R. *Psyche as Hero*, 72–91.

El-Ayouty, Amin. "A Structural Study of *Jane Eyre*." *J of Engl* (Sana'a Univ) 8 (1980), 109–125.

Ellis, Kate, and E. Ann Kaplan. "Feminism in Brontë's Novel and Its Film Versions," in Michael Klein and Gillian Parker, eds., *The English Novel*, 83–94.

Figes, Eva. *Sex and Subterfuge*, 125–138.

Fitzgerald, Joan. "Charlotte Brontë, Mary Taylor and the Working Woman," in Agostino Lombardo, ed., *Studi inglesi*, 93–124.

Foster, Shirley. *Victorian Women's Fiction*, 84–92.

Freeman, Janet H. "Speech and Silence in *Jane Eyre*." *Stud in Engl Lit, 1500–1900* 24 (1984), 683–700.

Fulton, E. Margaret. "Jane Eyre: The Development of a Female Consciousness." *Engl Stud in Canada* 5 (1979), 432–446.

Gezari, Janet K. "Marriage or Career: Goals for Women in Charlotte Brontë's Novels." *Bucknell R* 24:1 (1978), 83–86.

Gilbert, Sandra M., and Susan Gubar. *The Madwoman*, 336–371.

Griffin, Gail B. "The Humanization of Edward Rochester." *Women & Lit* 2 (1981), 118–129.

Hardy, Barbara. *Forms of Feeling*, 109–117.

Hennelly, Mark M., Jr. "*Jane Eyre*'s Reading Lesson." *ELH* 51 (1984), 693–713.

Horne, Margot. "From the Window-Seat to the Red Room: Innocence to Experience in *Jane Eyre*." *Dutch Q R of Anglo-American Letters* 10 (1980), 199–213.

Howells, Coral Ann. *Love, Mystery*, 159–187.

Jack, Ian. "Novels and 'Those Necessary Evils': Annotating the Brontës." *Essays in Criticism* 32 (1982), 321–327.

Kestner, Joseph. "Charlotte Brontë and Charlotte Elizabeth Tonna: A Possible Source for *Jane Eyre*." *Papers on Lang & Lit* 20 (1984), 96–98.

Kucich, John. "Passionate Reserve and Reserved Passion in the Works of Charlotte Brontë." *ELH* 52 (1985), 916–936.

Landow, George P. *Victorian Types*, 97–99.

Lee, Hermione. "Emblems and Enigmas in *Jane Eyre*." *English* 30 (1981), 233–253.

Lenta, Margaret. "Jane Fairfax and Jane Eyre: Educating Women." *Ariel* 12:4 (1981), 34–41.

Longford, Elizabeth. *Eminent Victorian Women*, 30–31, 51–53.

Margalioth, Daniel. "Passion and Duty: A Study of Charlotte Brontë's *Jane Eyre*." *Hebrew Univ Stud in Lit* 7 (1979), 182–213.

Merrett, Robert James. "The Conduct of Spiritual Autobiography in *Jane Eyre*." *Renascence* 37 (1984), 2–15.

Miller, Margaret. "Happily Ever After: Marriage in Charlotte Brontë's Novels." *Massachusetts Stud in Engl* 8:2 (1982), 24–25.

Nestor, Pauline. *Female Friendships*, 104–112.

Petit, Jean-Pierre. "Charlotte Brontë: *Jane Eyre*," in Pierre Coustillas et al., eds., *Le roman anglais*, 150–162.

Platzner, Robert Leonard. *The Metaphysical Novel*, 70–100.

Politi, Jina. "*Jane Eyre* Class-ified." *Lit and Hist* 8 (1982), 56–66.

Pollard, Arthur. "The Brontës and Their Father's Faith." *Essays & Stud 1984*, 58–61.

Qualls, Barry V. *The Secular Pilgrims*, 44–46, 51–69.

Rapaport, Herman. "*Jane Eyre* and the *Mot Tabou*." *Mod Lang Notes* 94 (1979), 1093–1104.

Rataboul, Louis J. *Le pasteur anglican*, 195–202.

Roberts, Doreen. "*Jane Eyre* and 'The Warped System of Things'," in Ian Gregor, ed., *Reading the Victorian Novel*, 131–147.

Rodolff, Rebecca. "From the Ending of *The Professor* to the Conception of *Jane Eyre*." *Philol Q* 61 (1982), 71–87.

Rowe, Margaret Moan. "Beyond Equality: Ideas and Images in *Jane Eyre*." *Ball State Univ Forum* 21:4 (1980), 5–9.

Rule, Philip C. "The Function of Allusion in *Jane Eyre*." *Mod Lang Stud* 15:4 (1985), 165–169.

Sadoff, Dianne F. *Monsters of Affection*, 130–135, 143–148, 156–162.

Schmidt, Helen von. "The Dark Abyss, the Broad Expanse: Versions of the Self in *Jane Eyre* and *Great Expectations*." *Dickens Q* 2 (1985), 84–91.

Senf, Carol. "*Jane Eyre*: The Prison-House of Victorian Marriage." *J of Women's Stud in Lit* 1 (1979), 353–359.

Showalter, Elaine. *A Literature*, 114–125.

Stone, Donald D. *The Romantic Impulse*, 113–120.

Taylor, Anne Robinson. *Male Novelists*, 103–112.

Tromly, Annette. *The Cover of the Mask*, 42–61.

Twitchell, James B. *The Living Dead*, 66–73.

Vargish, Thomas. *The Providential Aesthetic*, 58–67.

Webb, Igor. *From Custom to Capital*, 70–86, 158–160.

Weiss, Barbara. "The Dilemma of Happily Ever After: Marriage and the Victorian Novel," in Anne C. Hargrove and Maurine Magliocco, eds., *Portraits of Marriage*, 78.

Westwater, Martha. "Rochester and Greg and Jane and Julia: A Study in Art and Reality." *Brontë Soc Transactions* 18:4 (1984), 286–290.

Wheeler, Michael. *English Fiction*, 55–63.

Williams, Merryn. *Women in the English Novel*, 90–92.

Wyatt, Jean. "A Patriarch of One's Own: *Jane Eyre* and Romantic Love." *Tulsa Stud in Women's Lit* 4 (1985), 199–214.

Zeman, Anthea. *Presumptuous Girls*, 49–51.

The Professor, 1857

Figes, Eva. *Sex and Subterfuge*, 120–126.
Foster, Shirley. *Victorian Women's Fiction*, 79–84.
Gilbert, Sandra M., and Susan Gubar. *The Madwoman*, 315–335.
Hardy, Barbara. *Forms of Feeling*, 104–109.
Hirota, Minoru. "*The Professor*: Charlotte Brontë's Narrative Technique and Its Limitations." *Stud in Engl Lang and Lit* (Fukuoka) 31 (1981), 39–64. [In Japanese.]
Kucich, John. "Passionate Reserve," 915–936.
Miller, Margaret. "Happily Ever After," 22–24.
Nestor, Pauline. *Female Friendships*, 125–133.
Rodolff, Rebecca. "From the Ending of *The Professor*," 71–87.
Stone, Donald D. *The Romantic Impulse*, 110–113.
Tromly, Annette. *The Cover of the Mask*, 20–41.

Shirley, 1849

Belkin, Roslyn. "Rejects of the Marketplace: Old Maids in Charlotte Brontë's *Shirley*." *Intl J of Women's Stud* 4:1 (1981), 50–66.
Bergmann, Helena. *Between Obedience and Freedom*, 82–85, 98–102, 117–119, 142–148.
Chase, Karen. *Eros & Psyche*, 79–81.
Chitham, Edward. *The Brontës' Irish Background*, 146–148.
Eagleton, Mary, and David Pierce. *Attitudes to Class*, 47–52.
Figes, Eva. *Sex and Subterfuge*, 158–162.
Fitzgerald, Joan. "Charlotte Brontë, Mary Taylor," 93–124.
Foster, Shirley. *Victorian Women's Fiction*, 92–101.
Gezari, Janet K. "Marriage or Career," 86–92.
Gilbert, Sandra M., and Susan Gubar. *The Madwoman*, 372–398.
Godwin-Jones, Robert. "George Sand, Charlotte Brontë, and the Industrial Novel," in Natalie Datlof et al., eds., *George Sand Papers*, 161–170.
Hunt, Linda C. "Substance and Balm: The Question of Female Friendship in *Shirley* and *Villette*." *Tulsa Stud in Women's Lit* 1 (1982), 55–66.
Kestner, Joseph. *Protest and Reform*, 125–135.
Kucich, John. "Passionate Reserve," 918–936.
Miller, Margaret. "Happily Ever After," 25–28.
Nestor, Pauline. *Female Friendships*, 112–124.
Qualls, Barry V. *The Secular Pilgrims*, 46–49, 70–73.
Rataboul, Louis J. *Le pasteur anglican*, 166–172.
Rogal, Samuel J. "The Methodist Connection in Charlotte Brontë's *Shirley*." *Victorians Inst J* 10 (1981–82), 1–13.
Sadoff, Dianne F. *Monsters of Affection*, 131–135, 149–151, 154–156.
Stone, Donald D. *The Romantic Impulse*, 120–126.
Vargish, Thomas. *The Providential Aesthetic*, 67–70.
Webb, Igor. *From Custom to Capital*, 121–161.
Weiss, Barbara. "The Dilemma of Happily Ever After," 78–80.
Williams, Merryn. *Women in the English Novel*, 92–94.

Villette, 1853

Auerbach, Nina. *Romantic Imprisonment*, 204–211.

Bennett, James R. "Plot Repetition: Theme and Variation of Narrative Macro-Episodes." *Papers on Lang & Lit* 17 (1981), 411–412.

Bernikow, Louise. *Among Women*, 207–212.

Blair, David. "Wilkie Collins and the Crisis of Suspense," in Ian Gregor, ed., *Reading the Victorian Novel*, 45–48.

Bledsoe, Robert. "Snow Beneath Snow: A Reconsideration of the Virgin in *Villette*." *Women & Lit* 1 (1980), 214–220.

Brownstein, Rachel M. *Becoming a Heroine*, 154–181.

Carlisle, Janice. "The Face in the Mirror: *Villette* and the Conventions of Autobiography." *ELH* 46 (1979), 262–287.

Carlisle, Janice. "A Prelude to *Villette*: Charlotte Brontë's Reading, 1850–52." *Bull of Res in the Hum* 82 (1979), 403–423.

Chase, Karen. *Eros & Psyche*, 66–70, 81–84.

Crosby, Christina. "Charlotte Brontë's Haunted Text." *Stud in Engl Lit, 1500–1900* 24 (1984), 701–715.

Dale, Peter Allan. "Heretical Narration," 6–22.

Foster, Shirley. " 'A Suggestive Book': A Source for *Villette*." *Etudes Anglaises* 35 (1982), 177–184.

Foster, Shirley. *Victorian Women's Fiction*, 101–107.

Gendron, Charisse. "Harriet Martineau and Virginia Woolf Reading *Villette*." *Victorians Inst J* 11 (1982–83), 13–21.

Gilbert, Sandra M., and Susan Gubar. *The Madwoman*, 399–440.

Hardy, Barbara. *Forms of Feeling*, 117–128.

Heilman, Robert B. "Tulip-Hood, Streaks, and Other Strange Bedfellows: Style in *Villette*." *Stud in the Novel* 14 (1982), 223–245.

Hunt, Linda. "*Villette*: The Inward and the Outward Life." *Victorians Inst J* 11 (1982–83), 23–31.

Hunt, Linda C. "Substance and Balm," 55–66.

Jacobus, Mary. "The Buried Letter: Feminism and Romanticism in *Villette*," in Jacobus, ed., *Women Writing*, 42–59.

Kinkead-Weekes, Mark. "The Voicing of Fictions," in Ian Gregor, ed., *Reading the Victorian Novel*, 176–183.

Kucich, John. "Passionate Reserve," 917–936.

Lenta, Margaret. "The Tone of Protest: An Interpretation of Charlotte Brontë's *Villette*." *Engl Stud* 64 (1983), 422–432.

Miller, Margaret. "Happily Ever After," 28–33.

Nestor, Pauline. *Female Friendships*, 124–140.

Newton, Judith Lowder. *Women, Power, and Subversion*, 86–124.

Ping, Tang Soo. "C. Brontë's *Villette*." *Explicator* 42:1 (1983), 25–26.

Plotz, Judith. " 'Potatoes in a Cellar': Charlotte Brontë's *Villette* and the Feminist Imagination." *J of Women's Stud in Lit* 1 (1979), 74–87.

Qualls, Barry V. *The Secular Pilgrims*, 49–50, 73–84.

Rabinowitz, Nancy Soirkin. " 'Faithful Narrator' or 'Partial Eulogist': First-Person Narration in Brontë's *Villette*." *J of Narrative Technique* 15 (1985), 244–253.

Sadoff, Dianne F. *Monsters of Affection*, 151–156, 161–169.
Stokes, John. "Rachel's 'Terrible Beauty': An Actress among the Novelists." *ELH* 51 (1984), 779–782.
Stone, Donald D. *The Romantic Impulse*, 126–132.
Tromly, Annette. *The Cover of the Mask*, 62–88.
Vargish, Thomas. *The Providential Aesthetic*, 70–88.
Weiss, Barbara. "The Dilemma of Happily Ever After," 80.
Wheeler, Michael. *English Fiction*, 57–59.
Williams, Merryn. *Women in the English Novel*, 94–97.
Wright, Terence. "Rhythm in the Novel." *Mod Lang R* 80 (1985), 12–15.

EMILY BRONTË

Wuthering Heights, 1847

Andreani, Patrizia. "L'altra morte: *Cime tempestose* di Emily Brontë." *Lettere di Provincia* 43 (1980), 36–44.
Armstrong, Nancy. "Emily Brontë In and Out of Her Time." *Genre* 15 (1982), 243–262.
Bal, Mieke. "Notes on Narrative Embedding." *Poetics Today* 2:2 (1981), 41–59.
Benvenuto, Richard. *Emily Brontë*, 85–118.
Bolton, Françoise. "*Les Hauts de Hurlevent*: Superposition de genres," in *Le genre du roman*, 105–111.
Burgan, Mary. " 'Some Fit Parentage': Identity and the Cycle of Generations in *Wuthering Heights*." *Philol Q* 61 (1982), 395–411.
Chitham, Edward. *The Brontës' Irish Background*, 123–133.
Chitham, Edward, and Tom Winnifrith. *Brontë Facts*, 84–90, 99–109.
Clarke, Graham. " 'Bound in Moss and Cloth': Reading a Long Victorian Novel," in Ian Gregor, ed., *Reading the Victorian Novel*, 64–68.
Daleski, H. M. *The Divided Heroine*, 25–46.
Davies, Stevie. *Emily Brontë*, 95–170.
Federico, Annette R. "The Waif at the Window: Emily Brontë's Feminine *Bildungsroman*." *Victorian Newsl* 68 (1985), 26–28.
Figes, Eva. *Sex and Subterfuge*, 139–150.
Frankenberg, Ronald. "Styles of Marxism; Styles of Criticism—*Wuthering Heights*: A Case Study," in Diana Laurenson, ed., *The Sociology*, 109–141.
Garrett, Peter K. *The Victorian Multiplot Novel*, 18–22.
Gilbert, Sandra M., and Susan Gubar. *The Madwoman*, 248–308.
Gilmour, Robin. "Scott and the Victorian Novel: The Case of *Wuthering Heights*," in J. H. Alexander and David Hewitt, eds., *Scott and His Influence*, 366–371.
Goetz, William R. "Genealogy and Incest in *Wuthering Heights*." *Stud in the Novel* 14 (1982), 359–374.
Goff, Barbara Munson. "Between Natural Theology and Natural Selection: Breeding the Human Animal in *Wuthering Heights*." *Victorian Stud* 27 (1984), 477–508.

Gordon, Jan B. "Narrative Enclosure as Textual Ruin: An Archaeology of Gothic Consciousness." *Dickens Stud Annual* 11 (1983), 215–218.

Gregor, Ian. "Reading a Story: Sequence, Pace, and Recollection," in Gregor, ed., *Reading the Victorian Novel*, 92–98.

Hardy, Barbara. *Forms of Feeling*, 97–103.

Harrington, John. "Wyler as *Auteur*," in Michael Klein and Gillian Parker, eds., *The English Novel*, 67–82.

Harris, Anne Leslie. "Psychological Time in *Wuthering Heights*." *Intl Fiction R* 7 (1980), 112–117.

Higgins, Elizabeth Jean. *Reading the Novel*, 125–132.

Hirota, Minoru. "The Elements of American Romance in *Wuthering Heights*: Concurrent Origin and Themes Found in *Wuthering Heights* and 'The Fall of the House of Usher'." *Stud in Engl Lang and Lit* (Fukuoka) 30 (1980), 57–75.

Hutson, Nancy W. "The Androgynous Soul." *Publs of the Arkansas Philol Assoc* 9:2 (1983), 43–56.

Jack, Ian. "Novels and 'Those Necessary Evils': Annotating the Brontës." *Essays in Criticism* 32 (1982), 321–327.

Jackson, Rosemary. *Fantasy*, 128–129.

Jefferson, Douglas. "Irresistible Narrative: The Art of *Wuthering Heights*." *Brontë Soc Transactions* 17:5 (1980), 337–347.

Kavanagh, James H. *Emily Brontë*, 15–98.

Kestner, Joseph. "John Gibson Lockhart's *Matthew Wald* and Emily Brontë's *Wuthering Heights*." *Wordsworth Circle* 13 (1982), 94–96.

Law, Pamela. "Reading *Wuthering Heights*." *Sydney Stud in Engl* 7 (1981–82), 49–54.

Leech, Geoffrey N., and Michael H. Short. *Style in Fiction*, 262–263.

Longford, Elizabeth. *Eminent Victorian Women*, 53–54.

MacAndrew, Elizabeth. *The Gothic Tradition*, 183–186, 203–206.

McCarthy, Terence. "The Incompetent Narrator of *Wuthering Heights*." *Mod Lang Q* 42 (1981), 48–64.

McInerney, Peter. "Satanic Conceits in *Frankenstein* and *Wuthering Heights*." *Milton and the Romantics* 4 (1980), 1–15.

McKinsty, Susan J. "Desire's Dreams: Power and Passion in *Wuthering Heights*." *Coll Lit* 12 (1985), 141–146.

McLemore, Joy Ellis. "Edgar Linton: Master of Thrushcross Grange." *RE: Artes Liberales* 8:1 (1981), 13–26.

Madden, David. *A Primer*, 229–235.

Mafud Haye, Hilda. "La empatia y lo demoniaco en *Wuthering Heights*." *Nueva Revista del Pacifico* 19–20 (1981), 14–21.

Matthews, John T. "Framing in *Wuthering Heights*." *Texas Stud in Lit and Lang* 27 (1985), 25–58.

Miller, J. Hillis. *Fiction and Repetition*, 42–72.

Miller, J. Hillis. "*Wuthering Heights* and the Ellipses of Interpretation." *Notre Dame Engl J* 12 (1980), 85–100.

Milligan, Ian. *The Novel in English*, 36–38.

Napier, Elizabeth R. "The Problem of Boundaries in *Wuthering Heights.*" *Philol Q* 63 (1984), 95–106.

Oates, Joyce Carol. "The Magnanimity of *Wuthering Heights.*" *Crit Inquiry* 9 (1982), 435–449.

Paris, Bernard J. " 'Hush, hush! He's a human being': A Psychological Approach to Heathcliff." *Women & Lit* 2 (1981), 101–116.

Petit, Jean-Pierre. "Emily Brontë: *Wuthering Heights,*" in Pierre Coustillas et al., eds., *Le roman anglais*, 163–178.

Petit, Jean-Pierre. *L'oeuvre*, 15–227.

Platzner, Robert Leonard. *The Metaphysical Novel*, 100–139.

Reed, Michael D. "The Power of Wuthering Heights: A Psychoanalytic Examination." *Psychocultural R* 1 (1977), 21–42.

Rohrberger, Mary. "The Merging of Antinomies: Surreality in *Wuthering Heights,*" in Mary Lynn Johnson and Seraphia D. Leyda, eds., *Reconciliations*, 177–193.

Rousseau, Kathleen G. "The Lyric Visualisation in *Wuthering Heights*: Selected Passages." *Brontë Soc Transactions* 18:1 (1981), 30–34.

Scheick, William J. "Fictional Structure and Ethics in the Edwardian, Modern and Contemporary Novel." *Philol Q* 63 (1984), 294–295.

Senf, Carol A. "Emily Brontë's Version of Feminist History: *Wuthering Heights.*" *Essays in Lit* (Macomb) 12 (1985), 201–212.

Smith, Grahame. *The Novel & Society*, 34–36.

Stevenson, W. H. "*Wuthering Heights*: The Facts." *Essays in Criticism* 35 (1985), 149–165.

Stone, Donald D. *The Romantic Impulse*, 42–44.

Tobin, Patricia Drechsel. *Time and the Novel*, 38–42.

Twitchell, James B. *The Living Dead*, 116–122.

Usuda, Akira. "*Wuthering Heights* e no shikaku." *Eigo Seinen* (Tokyo) 125 (1979), 109, 160, 223, 273, 312, 367, 408, 456, 512, 560.

Weiss, Barbara. "The Dilemma of Happily Ever After: Marriage and the Victorian Novel," in Anne C. Hargrove and Maurine Magliocco, eds., *Portraits of Marriage*, 80–81.

Wheeler, Michael. *English Fiction*, 63–67.

Wilcockson, Colin. " 'Fair(y) Annie's Wedding': A Note on *Wuthering Heights.*" *Essays in Criticism* 33 (1983), 259–260.

Williams, Anne. "Natural Supernaturalism in *Wuthering Heights.*" *Stud in Philology* 82 (1985), 104–127.

Williams, Merryn. *Women in the English Novel*, 97–101.

Zeman, Anthea. *Presumptuous Girls*, 97–99.

FRANCES BROOKE

The History of Emily Montague, 1769

Edwards, Mary Jane. "Frances Brooke's *The History of Emily Montague*: A Biographical Context." *Engl Stud in Canada* 7 (1981), 171–181.

Edwards, Mary Jane. "Frances Brooke's Politics and *The History of Emily Montague*," in John Moss, ed., *Beginnings*, 19–27.

Shohet, Linda. "An Essay on *The History of Emily Montague*," in John Moss, ed., *Beginnings*, 28–34.

Lady Julia Mandeville, 1763

McMullen, Lorraine. "Frances Brooke's Early Fiction." *Canadian Lit* 86 (1980), 31–40.

HENRY BROOKE

The Fool of Quality, 1764–1770

Scheuermann, Mona. "Redefining the Filial Tie: Eighteenth-Century English Novelists from Brooke to Bage." *Etudes Anglaises* 37 (1984), 386–389.

Scheuermann, Mona. *Social Protest*, 41–68.

Shroff, Homai J. *The Eighteenth Century Novel*, 77–81.

CHRISTINE BROOKE-ROSE

Thru, 1975

Kafalenos, Emma. "Textasy: Christine Brooke-Rose's *Thru*." *Intl Fiction R* 7 (1980), 43–46.

Rimmon-Kenan, Shlomith. "Ambiguity and Narrative Levels: Christine Brooke-Rose's *Thru*." *Poetics Today* 3:1 (1982), 21–31.

RHODA BROUGHTON

Cometh Up as a Flower, 1867

Showalter, Elaine. *A Literature*, 173–175.

Terry, R. C. *Victorian Popular Fiction*, 114–116.

Good-bye, Sweetheart!, 1872

Terry, R. C. *Victorian Popular Fiction*, 118–122.

Joan, 1876

Terry, R. C. *Victorian Popular Fiction*, 122–127.

Not Wisely, but Too Well, 1867

Terry, R. C. *Victorian Popular Fiction*, 111–114.

Red as a Rose is She, 1870

Terry, R. C. *Victorian Popular Fiction*, 116–118.

Second Thoughts, 1880

Terry, R. C. *Victorian Popular Fiction*, 127–129.

GEORGE DOUGLAS BROWN

The House with the Green Shutters, 1901

Bold, Alan. *Modern Scottish Literature*, 108–116.
Campbell, Ian. "George Douglas Brown: A Study in Objectivity," in Campbell, ed., *Nineteenth-Century Scottish Fiction*, 148–162.
Campbell, Ian. "*The House with the Green Shutters*: Some Second Thoughts." *Bibliotheck* 10:4 (1981), 99–106.
Manson, John. "Young Gourlay." *Scottish Liter J* 7:2 (1980), 44–54.
Sommers, Jeffrey. [*"The House with the Green Shutters."*] *Stud in Scottish Lit* 19 (1984), 252–258.

GEORGE MACKAY BROWN

Greenvoe, 1972

Bold, Alan. *Modern Scottish Literature*, 242–246.

Magnus, 1974

Bold, Alan. *Modern Scottish Literature*, 246–248.
Huberman, Elizabeth. "George Mackay Brown's *Magnus*." *Stud in Scottish Lit* 16 (1981), 122–133.

JOHN BRUNNER

Stand on Zanzibar, 1968

Pfeiffer, John R. "John Brunner," in E. F. Bleiler, ed., *Science Fiction Writers*, 299–300.

MARY BRUNTON

Discipline, 1814

Smith, Sarah W.R. "Men, Women, and Money: The Case of Mary Brunton," in Mary Anne Schofield and Cecilia Macheski, eds., *Fetter'd or Free?*, 44–56.

Self-Control, 1811

Burlin, Katrin R. " 'At the Crossroads': Sister Authors and the Sister Arts," in Mary Anne Schofield and Cecilia Macheski, eds., *Fetter'd or Free?*, 65–68.
Smith, Sarah W.R. "Men, Women, and Money," 44–56.

JOHN BUCHAN

The Courts of the Morning, 1929

Bedell, Jeanne F. "Romance and Moral Certainty: The Espionage Fiction of John Buchan." *Midwest Q* 22 (1981), 240–241.

A Lodge in the Wilderness, 1906

Hunter, Jefferson. *Edwardian Fiction*, 109–111.

Mr. Standfast, 1918

Bedell, Jeanne F. "Romance and Moral Certainty," 236–238.

The Power-House, 1913

Ray, Philip E. "The Villain in the Spy Novels of John Buchan." *Engl Lit in Transition* 24 (1981), 86–88.

Prester John, 1910

Bedell, Jeanne F. "Romance and Moral Certainty," 232–234.
Couzens, T. J. " 'The Old Africa of a Boy's Dream': Towards Interpreting Buchan's *Prester John*." *African Perspective* (Johannesburg) 13 (1980), 34–57. [Also in *Engl Stud in Africa* 24 (1981), 1–23.]
Daniell, David. "Buchan and 'The Black General'," in David Dabydeen, ed., *The Black Presence*, 136–152.
Hunter, Jefferson. *Edwardian Fiction*, 122–123.

The Thirty-Nine Steps, 1915

Bedell, Jeanne F. "Romance and Moral Certainty," 234–235.
Calendrillo, Linda T. "Role Playing and 'Atmosphere' in Four Modern British Spy Novels." *Clues* 3:1 (1982), 111–119.
Ray, Philip E. "The Villain," 85–88.

The Three Hostages, 1924

Ray, Philip E. "The Villain," 81–82.

WILLIAM BUCKLEY

Croppies Lie Down, 1903

Cahalan, James M. *Great Hatred*, 103–108.

EDWARD BULWER-LYTTON

Alice, 1838

Engel, Elliot, and Margaret F. King. *The Victorian Novel*, 57–58.
King, Margaret F., and Elliot Engel. "The Emerging Carlylean Hero in Bulwer's Novels of the 1830s." *Nineteenth-Century Fiction* 36 (1981), 293–294.

The Caxtons, 1849

Lamarca Margalef, Jordi. *Ciencia y literatura*, 109–110.

The Coming Race, 1871

Lamarca Margalef, Jordi. *Ciencia y literatura*, 61–62, 92, 160.
Knepper, B. G. "*The Coming Race*: Hell? or Paradise Foretasted?," in Eric S. Rabkin et al., eds., *No Place Else*, 11–30.

Suvin, Darko. "The Extraordinary Voyage, the Future War, and Bulwer's *The Coming Race*: Three Sub-Genres in British Science Fiction, 1871–1885." *Lit and Hist* 10 (1984), 242–246.

Ernest Maltravers, 1837

Engel, Elliot, and Margaret F. King. *The Victorian Novel*, 53–58.
King, Margaret F., and Elliot Engel. "The Emerging Carlylean Hero," 290–293.
Mitchell, Sally. *The Fallen Angel*, 46–49.

Eugene Aram, 1832

Engel, Elliot, and Margaret F. King. *The Victorian Novel*, 44–46, 48–49.
King, Margaret F., and Elliot Engel. "The Emerging Carlylean Hero," 282–284.

Godolphin, 1833

Engel, Elliot, and Margaret F. King. *The Victorian Novel*, 46–48, 54–55.
Graham, Peter W. "Bulwer the *Moraliste*." *Dickens Stud Annual* 9 (1981), 152–156.
King, Margaret F., and Elliot Engel. "The Emerging Carlylean Hero," 284–286.

Kenelm Chillingly, 1873

Rataboul, Louis J. *Le pasteur anglican*, 359–360.

The Last Days of Pompeii, 1834

Durand, Michel. "*Les Martyrs, Les Derniers Jours de Pompei* et *Fabiola*, ou les romans des premiers siècles chrétiens en France et en Angleterre de 1809 à 1854." *Confluents* 1 (1975), 73–89.
Engel, Elliot, and Margaret F. King. *The Victorian Novel*, 49–51.
King, Margaret F., and Elliot Engel. "The Emerging Carlylean Hero," 287–288.

My Novel, 1853

Rataboul, Louis J. *Le pasteur anglican*, 153–158.

Paul Clifford, 1830

Engel, Elliot, and Margaret F. King. *The Victorian Novel*, 42–44.
King, Margaret F., and Elliot Engel. "The Emerging Carlylean Hero," 280–282.

Pelham, 1828

Gilmour, Robin. *The Idea of the Gentleman*, 48–51, 53–55.
Graham, Peter W. "Bulwer the *Moraliste*," 144–149.
Graham, Peter W. "Pelham as Paragon: Bulwer's Ideal Aristocrat." *Victorians Inst J* 9 (1980–81), 71–81.
Hart, Francis Russell. "The Regency Novel of Fashion," in Samuel I. Mintz et al., eds., *From Smollett to James*, 129–133.

Rienzi, 1835

Brown, Andrew. "Metaphysics and Melodrama: Bulwer's *Rienzi*." *Nineteenth-Century Fiction* 36 (1981), 261–276.

Engel, Elliot, and Margaret F. King. *The Victorian Novel*, 50–53.

King, Margaret F., and Elliot Engel. "The Emerging Carlylean Hero," 288–290.

Witemeyer, Hugh. "George Eliot's *Romola* and Bulwer Lytton's *Rienzi*." *Stud in the Novel* 15 (1983), 62–71.

Zanoni, 1842

Coates, John. "*Zanoni* by Bulwer-Lytton: A Discussion of Its 'Philosophy' and Its Possible Influences." *Durham Univ J* 76 (1983–84), 223–233.

Punter, David. *The Literature of Terror*, 171–174.

JOHN BUNYAN

The Life and Death of Mr. Badman, 1680

Knott, John R., Jr. "Bunyan and the Holy Community." *Stud in Philology* 80 (1983), 205–206.

The Pilgrim's Progress, 1678

Bacon, Ernest W. *Pilgrim and Dreamer*, 135–142.

Beatty, Bernard. "Rival Fables: *The Pilgrim's Progress* and Dryden's *The Hind and the Panther*," in Vincent Newey, ed., *"The Pilgrim's Progress,"* 263–281.

Campbell, Gordon. "The Theology of *The Pilgrim's Progress*," in Vincent Newey, ed., *"The Pilgrim's Progress,"* 251–262.

Daly, Peter M. *Literature*, 172–174.

Davis, Nick. "The Problem of Misfortune in *The Pilgrim's Progress*," in Vincent Newey, ed., *"The Pilgrim's Progress,"* 182–204.

Edwards, Philip. "The Journey in *The Pilgrim's Progress*," in Vincent Newey, ed., *"The Pilgrim's Progress,"* 111–117.

Forrest, James F. "Vision, Form, and the Imagination in the Second Part of *The Pilgrim's Progress* (1684)." *J of Narrative Technique* 13 (1983), 109–115.

Hammond, Brean S. "*The Pilgrim's Progress*: Satire and Social Comment," in Vincent Newey, ed., *"The Pilgrim's Progress,"* 118–131.

Hardy, Barbara. *Forms of Feeling*, 20–22.

Haskin, Dayton. "The Burden of Interpretation in *The Pilgrim's Progress*." *Stud in Philology* 79 (1982), 256–278.

Keeble, N. H. "Christiana's Key: The Unity of *The Pilgrim's Progress*," in Vincent Newey, ed., *"The Pilgrim's Progress,"* 1–20.

Knott, John R., Jr. "Bunyan and the Holy Community," 200–225.

Manlove, C. N. "The Image of the Journey in *Pilgrim's Progress*: Narrative versus Allegory." *J of Narrative Technique* 10 (1980), 16–35.

Metscher, Thomas. "Subversive, Radical and Revolutionary Traditions in European Literature between 1300 and the Age of Bunyan." *Zeitschrift für Anglistik und Amerikanistik* 29 (1981), 12–20.

Milligan, Ian. *The Novel in English*, 23–25.

Mills, David. "The Dreams of Bunyan and Langland," in Vincent Newey, ed., *"The Pilgrim's Progress,"* 154–181.

Nellist, Brian. *"The Pilgrim's Progress* and Allegory," in Vincent Newey, ed., *"The Pilgrim's Progress,"* 132–153.

Newey, Vincent. "Bunyan and the Confines of the Mind," in Newey, ed., *"The Pilgrim's Progress,"* 21–48.

Newman, S. J. "Bunyan's Solidness," in Vincent Newey, ed., *"The Pilgrim's Progress,"* 225–250.

Nuttall, Geoffrey F. "The Heart of *The Pilgrim's Progress,"* in Peter Newman Brooks, ed., *Reformation Principle*, 227–239.

Seed, David. "Dialogue and Debate in *The Pilgrim's Progress,"* in Vincent Newey, ed., *"The Pilgrim's Progress,"* 69–90.

Sharrock, Roger. "Life and Story in *The Pilgrim's Progress,"* in Vincent Newey, ed., *"The Pilgrim's Progress,"* 49–68.

Shrimpton, Nick. "Bunyan's Military Metaphor," in Vincent Newey, ed., *"The Pilgrim's Progress,"* 205–224.

Stranahan, Brainerd P. "Bunyan and the Epistle to the Hebrews: His Source for the Idea of Pilgrimage in *The Pilgrim's Progress." Stud in Philology* 79 (1982), 279–296.

Titlestad, P. J. H. "Bunyan and the Puritan Contribution to the Growth of the English Novel." *Communique* (Pietersburg) 5:2 (1980), 24–35.

Turner, James. "Bunyan's Sense of Place," in Vincent Newey, ed., *"The Pilgrim's Progress,"* 91–110.

Williams, Ioan. *The Idea of the Novel*, 150–152.

ANTHONY BURGESS

Abba Abba, 1977

Coale, Samuel. *Anthony Burgess*, 149–153.

Beard's Roman Women, 1976

Coale, Samuel. *Anthony Burgess*, 110–116.

Lucas, Timothy R. "The Old Shelley Game: Prometheus & Predestination in Burgess' Works." *Mod Fiction Stud* 27 (1981), 477–478.

Beds in the East, 1959

Coale, Samuel. *Anthony Burgess*, 29–32, 36–38.

Crawford, Fred D. *Mixing Memory*, 142–144.

A Clockwork Orange, 1962

Bowie, Robert. "Freedom and Art in *A Clockwork Orange*: Anthony Burgess and the Christian Premises of Dostoevsky." *Thought* 56 (1981), 402–416.

Boyum, Joy Gould. *Double Exposure*, 162–168.

Coale, Samuel. *Anthony Burgess*, 84–98.

Coleman, Julian. "Burgess' *A Clockwork Orange*." *Explicator* 42:1 (1983), 62–63.

Escuret-Bertrand, A. "*A Clockwork Orange*: Anthony Burgess," in *Autour de l'idée*, 169–191.

Fowler, Roger. "Anti-Language in Fiction." *Style* 13 (1979), 268–270.

Guetti, James. *Word-Music*, 54–76.

Leech, Geoffrey N., and Michael H. Short. *Style in Fiction*, 265–266.

Mentzer, Thomas L. "The Ethics of Behavior Modification: *A Clockwork Orange* Revisited." *Essays in Arts and Sciences* 9 (1980), 93–105.

Rabinovitz, Rubin. "Ethical Values in Anthony Burgess's *Clockwork Orange*." *Stud in the Novel* 11 (1979), 43–49.

Ray, Philip E. "Alex before and after: A New Approach to Burgess' *A Clockwork Orange*." *Mod Fiction Stud* 27 (1981), 479–487.

Sheldon, Leslie E. "Newspeak and Nadsat: The Disintegration of Language in *1984* and *A Clockwork Orange*." *Stud in Contemp Satire* 6 (1979), 7–13.

Sobchack, Vivian C. "Decor as Theme: *A Clockwork Orange*." *Lit/Film Q* 9 (1981), 92–102.

Winkler, Willi. "Den Menschen aufs Spiel gesetzt: Der Schriftsteller Anthony Burgess." *Merkur* 37:419 (1983), 572–576.

The Clockwork Testament, 1974

Coale, Samuel. *Anthony Burgess*, 175–178.

Coale, Samuel. "The Ludic Loves of Anthony Burgess." *Mod Fiction Stud* 27 (1981), 462–463.

Mérigot, Bernard. "Le Signifiant Balzac: Lecture de *The Clockwork Testament* d'Anthony Burgess," in Claude Duchet et al., eds., *Sociocritique*, 122–136.

Devil of a State, 1961

Coale, Samuel. *Anthony Burgess*, 40–47.

Crawford, Fred D. *Mixing Memory*, 145–149.

McNeil, David. "Anthony Burgess: Composer of Comic Fiction." *Intl Fiction R* 10 (1983), 95–97.

The Doctor Is Sick, 1960

Coale, Samuel. *Anthony Burgess*, 105–110.

Earthly Powers, 1980

Aggeler, Geoffrey. "Faust in the Labyrinth: Burgess' *Earthly Powers*." *Mod Fiction Stud* 27 (1981), 517–531.

Baranger, Colette. "Quelques aspects des modes d'écriture comparés dans *Earthly Powers* d'Anthony Burgess et dans *Darkness Visible* de William Golding." *Etudes Anglaises* 36 (1983), 154–158.

Coale, Samuel. *Anthony Burgess*, 183–194.

Enderby, 1968

Coale, Samuel. *Anthony Burgess*, 162–166.

Enderby Outside, 1968

 Coale, Samuel. *Anthony Burgess*, 171–174.

The Enemy in the Blanket, 1958

 Crawford, Fred D. *Mixing Memory*, 140–142.

The Eve of St. Venus, 1964

 Coale, Samuel. *Anthony Burgess*, 145–149.

Honey for the Bears, 1963

 Coale, Samuel. *Anthony Burgess*, 58–67.

Inside Mr. Enderby, 1963

 Coale, Samuel. *Anthony Burgess*, 166–170.
 Coale, Samuel. "The Ludic Loves," 461–462.

The Long Day Wanes, 1965

 Coale, Samuel. *Anthony Burgess*, 28–40.
 McNeil, David. "Anthony Burgess," 92–94.

Man of Nazareth, 1979

 Coale, Samuel. *Anthony Burgess*, 180–183.

MF, 1971

 Coale, Samuel. *Anthony Burgess*, 116–124.
 Coale, Samuel. "The Ludic Loves," 455–457.
 Lucas, Timothy R. "The Old Shelley Game," 467–477.
 Reeve, N. H. "Reflections on 'Fictionality'," in Malcolm Bradbury and David Palmer, eds., *The Contemporary English Novel*, 127–130.

Napoleon Symphony, 1974

 Beyer, Manfred. "Anthony Burgess, *Napoleon Symphony*," in Rainer Lengeler, ed., *Englische Literatur*, 312–327.
 Coale, Samuel. *Anthony Burgess*, 125–134.
 Coale, Samuel. "The Ludic Loves," 457–459.

1985, 1978

 Coale, Samuel. *Anthony Burgess*, 75–77.
 Schulte-Middelich, Bernd. " '1984 is not going to be like that at all': Anthony Burgess' Alternative in *1985*." *Literatur in Wissenschaft und Unterricht* 17 (1984), 211–231.
 Stinson, John J. "Better to Be Hot or Cold: *1985* and the Dynamic of the Manichaean Duoverse." *Mod Fiction Stud* 27 (1981), 505–516.
 Whellens, Arthur. "Anthony Burgess's *1985*." *Studi dell'Istituto Linguistico* 5 (1982), 223–244.
 Wilson, Keith. "Jim, Jake and the Years Between: The Will to Stasis in the Contemporary British Novel." *Ariel* 13:1 (1982), 66–67.

Nothing Like the Sun, 1964

 Coale, Samuel. *Anthony Burgess*, 153–162.

One Hand Clapping, 1961

    Coale, Samuel. *Anthony Burgess*, 139–145.

The Right to an Answer, 1960

    Coale, Samuel. *Anthony Burgess*, 48–54.

Time for a Tiger, 1956

    Coale, Samuel. *Anthony Burgess*, 33–35.

Tremor of Intent, 1966

    Bly, James I. "Sonata Form in *Tremor of Intent.*" *Mod Fiction Stud* 27 (1981), 489–504.
    Coale, Samuel. *Anthony Burgess*, 67–75.
    Coale, Samuel. "The Ludic Loves," 459–461.
    Duffy, Charles F. "From Espionage to Eschatology: Anthony Burgess's *Tremor of Intent.*" *Renascence* 32 (1980), 79–87.
    Palumbo, Ronald J. "Names and Games in *Tremor of Intent.*" *Engl Lang Notes* 18 (1980), 48–51.

A Vision of Battlements, 1965

    Coale, Samuel. *Anthony Burgess*, 19–28.

The Wanting Seed, 1962

    Coale, Samuel. *Anthony Burgess*, 77–84.
    Crawford, Fred D. *Mixing Memory*, 149–152.
    Dorenkamp, John H. "Anthony Burgess and the Future of Man: *The Wanting Seed.*" *Univ of Dayton R* 15 (1981), 107–111.
    Juillard, M. "Compétence linguistique et performance stylistique d'Anthony Burgess dans *The Wanting Seed*," in *Etudes anglo-américaines*, 69–82.

FANNY BURNEY

Camilla, 1796

    Bloom, Lilian D. "Fanny Burney's *Camilla*: The Author as Editor." *Bull of Res in the Hum* 82 (1979), 367–393.
    Brown, Martha G. "Fanny Burney's 'Feminism': Gender or Genre?," in Mary Anne Schofield and Cecilia Macheski, eds., *Fetter'd or Free?*, 30–38.
    Doody, Margaret Anne. "George Eliot and the Eighteenth-Century Novel." *Nineteenth-Century Fiction* 35 (1980), 286–287.
    Figes, Eva. *Sex and Subterfuge*, 45–53.
    Hart, Francis Russell. "The Regency Novel of Fashion," in Samuel I. Mintz et al., eds., *From Smollett to James*, 102–106.
    Voss-Clesly, Patricia. *Tendencies of Character*, 138–143, 477–480, 579–586.

Cecilia, 1782

Brown, Martha G. "Fanny Burney's 'Feminism'," 30–38.
Doody, Margaret Anne. "George Eliot," 284–286.
Fergus, Jan. *Jane Austen*, 62–72.
Figes, Eva. *Sex and Subterfuge*, 41–45.
Hart, Francis Russell. "The Regency Novel," 100–102.
Konigsberg, Ira. *Narrative Technique*, 216–218.
Shroff, Homai J. *The Eighteenth Century Novel*, 14–15, 46–47, 235–240, 248–253.
Todd, Janet. *Women's Friendship*, 312–314.
Voss-Clesly, Patricia. *Tendencies of Character*, 132–138, 572–578.

Evelina, 1778

Anderson, Earl R. "Footnotes More Pedestrian Than Sublime: A Historical Background for the Foot-Races in *Evelina* and *Humphry Clinker*." *Eighteenth-Century Stud* 14 (1980), 56–68.
Barker, Gerard A. *Grandison's Heirs*, 70–83.
Brown, Martha G. "Fanny Burney's 'Feminism'," 30–38.
Dobbin, Marjorie W. "The Novel, Women's Awarenness, and Fanny Burney." *Engl Lang Notes* 22:3 (1985), 46–52.
Figes, Eva. *Sex and Subterfuge*, 33–42.
Hart, Francis Russell. "The Regency Novel," 95–100.
Hollahan, Eugene. "The Orpheus Allusion in *Evelina* (1778) and *La Peste*." *Compar Lit Stud* 16 (1979), 111–113, 116–119.
Jeffery, David M. "Manners, Morals, Magic, and *Evelina*." *Enlightenment Essays* 9 (1978), 35–47.
MacDonald, Susan Peck. "Jane Austen and the Tradition of the Absent Mother," in Cathy N. Davidson and E. M. Broner, eds., *The Lost Tradition*, 59–61.
Newton, Judith Lowder. *Women, Power, and Subversion*, 23–54.
Olshin, Toby A. " 'To Whom I Most Belong': The Role of Family in *Evelina*." *Eighteenth-Century Life* 6:1 (1980), 29–40.
Parke, Catherine. "Vision and Revision: A Model for Reading the Eighteenth-Century Novel of Education." *Eighteenth-Century Stud* 16 (1982–83), 166–169.
Poovey, Mary. "Fathers and Daughters: The Trauma of Growing Up Female." *Women & Lit* 2 (1981), 52–57.
Scheuermann, Mona. "Redefining the Filial Tie: Eighteenth-Century English Novelists from Brooke to Bage." *Etudes Anglaises* 37 (1984), 390–392.
Scheuermann, Mona. *Social Protest*, 69–88.
Sherbo, Arthur. "Addenda to 'Footnotes More Pedestrian than Sublime'." *Eighteenth-Century Stud* 14 (1981), 313–316.
Shroff, Homai J. *The Eighteenth Century Novel*, 43–45, 237–253.
Suhr, Heidrun. *Englische Romanautorinnen*, 186–194.
Voss-Clesly, Patricia. *Tendencies of Character*, 123–131, 462–465, 737–741.
Zeman, Anthea. *Presumptuous Girls*, 12–14.

The Wanderer, 1814

Brown, Martha G. "Fanny Burney's 'Feminism'," 30–38.
Figes, Eva. *Sex and Subterfuge*, 53–55.
Suhr, Heidrun. *Englische Romanautorinnen*, 196–199.
Teyssandier, Hubert. *Les formes de la création*, 53–66.
Todd, Janet. *Women's Friendship*, 314–318.

ALAN BURNS

The Angry Brigade, 1973

Reeve, N. H. "Reflections on 'Fictionality'," in Malcolm Bradbury and David Palmer, eds., *The Contemporary English Novel*, 121–123.

Babel, 1969

Reeve, N. H. "Reflections on 'Fictionality'," 117–118.

Celebrations, 1967

Reeve, N. H. "Reflections on 'Fictionality'," 116–117.

Dreamerika!, 1972

Reeve, N. H. "Reflections on 'Fictionality'," 118–121.

SAMUEL BUTLER

Erewhon, 1872

Coates, Paul. *The Realist Fantasy*, 96–98.
Dollerup, Cay. "Religious Satire in the Frame of Samuel Butler's *Erewhon*," in Graham D. Caie et al., eds., *Occasional Papers*, 155–173.
Fuerst, John A. "Concepts of Physiology Reproduction, and Evolution of Machines in Samuel Butler's *Erewhon* and George Eliot's *Impressions of Theophrastus Such*." *Samuel Butler Newsl* 4:2 (1981), 31–53.
Gounelas, Ruth. "Samuel Butler's Cambridge Background, and *Erewhon*." *Engl Lit in Transition* 24 (1981), 17–33.
Norrman, Ralf. *Samuel Butler*, 171–193.
Remington, Thomas J. " 'The Mirror up to Nature': Reflections of Victorianism in Samuel Butler's *Erewhon*," in Eric S. Rabkin et al., eds., *No Place Else*, 33–52.
Sharma, Govind Narain. "Butler's *Erewhon*: The Machine as Object and Symbol." *Samuel Butler Newsl* 3:1 (1980), 3–12.
Suvin, Darko. "Victorian Science Fiction, 1871–85: The Rise of the Alternative History Sub-Genre." *Science-Fiction Stud* 10 (1983), 151–153.

The Way of All Flesh, 1903

Grylls, David. *Guardians and Angels*, 153–172.
Jeffers, Thomas L. *Samuel Butler*, 38–46, 59–62, 87–103, 106–126.

Jolicoeur, C. "Christian Mythology and Narrative Structure in Butler's *The Way of All Flesh.*" *Cahiers Victoriens et Edouardiens* 16 (1982), 125–137.

Leech, Geoffrey N., and Michael H. Short. *Style in Fiction*, 134–135, 278–279.

Morton, Peter. *The Vital Science*, 174–194.

Nadel, Ira Bruce. "From Fathers and Sons to Sons and Lovers." *Dalhousie R* 59 (1979), 227–229.

Norrman, Ralf. *Samuel Butler*, 110–135, 194–238.

Rataboul, Louis J. *Le pasteur anglican*, 192–195, 405–406.

Rosenman, John B. "Evangelicalism in *The Way of All Flesh.*" *Coll Lang Assoc J* 26 (1982), 76–97.

Tobin, Patricia Drechsel. *Time and the Novel*, 46–51.

Wheeler, Michael. *English Fiction*, 168–169.

Wisenthal, J. L. "Samuel Butler's Epistle to the Victorians: *The Way of All Flesh* and Unlovely Paul." *Mosaic* 13:1 (1979), 17–29.

Yeasted, Rita. "The Handelian Quality of Butler's *The Way of All Flesh.*" *Mod Lang Stud* 9:2 (1979), 23–32.

A. S. BYATT

The Virgin in the Garden, 1978

Dusinberre, Juliet. "Forms of Reality in A. S. Byatt's *The Virgin in the Garden.*" *Critique* (Atlanta) 24 (1982), 55–61.

WILLIAM CARLETON

The Black Prophet, 1847

Cronin, John. *The Anglo-Irish Novel*, 88–97.

Reynolds, Lorna. "Irish Women in Legend, Literature and Life," in S. F. Gallagher, ed., *Woman in Irish Legend*, 16–17.

Redmond Count O'Hanlon, 1862

Cahalan, James M. *Great Hatred*, 81–84.

ETHEL CARNIE

This Slavery, 1925

Klaus, H. Gustav. "Silhouettes of Revolution: Some Neglected Novels of the Early 1920s," in Klaus, ed., *The Socialist Novel*, 94–97.

LEWIS CARROLL

Alice's Adventures in Wonderland, 1865

Auerbach, Nina. *Romantic Imprisonment*, 130–168.

Balais, Marcel. "La Systématisation binaire en sémantique." *Confluents* 7 (1981), 135–144.

Brockway, Robert W. "The *Descensus ad Inferos* of Lewis Carroll." *Dalhousie R* 62 (1982), 36–42.

Demurova, Nina. "Toward a Definition of *Alice*'s Genre: The Folktale and Fairy-Tale Connections," in Edward Guiliano, ed., *Lewis Carroll*, 75–88.

Dreyer, Laurence. "The Mathematical References to the Adoption of the Gregorian Calendar in Lewis Carroll's *Alice's Adventures in Wonderland.*" *Victorian Newsl* 60 (1981), 24–26.

Gabriele, Mark. "*Alice in Wonderland*: Problem of Identity—Aggressive Content and Form Control." *Am Imago* 39 (1982), 369–389.

Hancher, Michael. "Humpty Dumpty and Verbal Meaning." *J of Aesthetics and Art Criticism* 40 (1981), 49–58.

Hancher, Michael. "The Placement of Tenniel's *Alice* Illustrations." *Harvard Lib Bull* 30 (1982), 237–252.

Hancher, Michael. "Pragmatics in Wonderland." *Bucknell R* 28:2 (1983), 165–182.

Hancher, Michael. "*Punch* and *Alice*: Through Tenniel's Looking-Glass," in Edward Guiliano, ed., *Lewis Carroll*, 26–49.

Henkle, Roger B. "Carroll's Narratives Underground: 'Modernism' and Form," in Edward Guiliano, ed., *Lewis Carroll*, 89–100.

Higbie, Robert. "Lewis Carroll and the Victorian Reaction against Doubt." *Thalia* 3:1 (1980), 21–26.

Kelly, Richard. " 'If You Don't Know What a Gryphon Is': Text and Illustration in *Alice's Adventures in Wonderland*," in Edward Guiliano, ed., *Lewis Carroll*, 62–74.

Kurrik, Maire Jaanus. *Literature and Negation*, 197–205.

Little, Edmund. *The Fantasts*, 39–53.

Madden, William A. "Framing the *Alices*." *PMLA* 101 (1986), 362–371.

Mango, Susan. "Alice in Two Wonderlands: Lewis Carroll in German." *SubStance* 16 (1977), 63–84.

Mellor, Anne K. *English Romantic Irony*, 168–173.

Morton, Lionel. "Memory in the Alice Books." *Nineteenth-Century Fiction* 33 (1978), 285–308.

Natov, Roni. "The Persistence of Alice." *The Lion and the Unicorn* 3:1 (1979), 38–61.

Oates, Joyce Carol. "Wonderlands." *Georgia R* 38 (1984), 495–498.

Otten, Terry. "After Innocence: Alice in the Garden," in Edward Guiliano, ed., *Lewis Carroll*, 50–61.

Paterson, Gary H. "Stephen and Alice: Not So Strange Bedfellows." *Interpretations* 15:1 (1983), 60–69.

Pattison, Robert. *The Child Figure*, 151–159.

Petersen, Robert C. "To Sleep, Perchance to Dream: Alice Takes a Little Nap." *Jabberwocky* 8 (1979), 27–37.

Pycior, Helena M. "At the Intersection of Mathematics and Humor: Lewis Carroll's *Alices* and Symbolical Algebra." *Victorian Stud* 28 (1984), 149–170.

Rackin, Donald. "Love and Death in Carroll's *Alices*." *Engl Lang Notes* 20:2 (1982), 26–45.

Reichertz, Ronald. "Carroll's *Alice in Wonderland*." *Explicator* 43:2 (1985), 21–22.

Suchan, James. "Alice's Journey from Alien to Artist." *Children's Lit* 7 (1978), 78–92.

Takahashi, Yasunari. *Alice no kuni no kotobatachi*.

Takayama, Hiroshi. *Alice Gari*.

Taylor, Steven M. "Wanderers in Wonderland: Fantasy in the Works of Carroll and Arrabal," in William Coyle, ed., *Aspects of Fantasy*, 164–172.

Thoiron, Philippe. "La Méthode stylostatistique: Brève présentation et application à une comparaison des passages narratifs et des passages dialogués de *Alice's Adventures in Wonderland*." *Confluents* 4 (1978), 141–176.

Thoiron, Philippe. "Richesse lexicale et structure d'ordre." *Confluents* 7 (1981), 23–46.

Tiedemann, Rüdiger von. "Alice bei den Surrealisten: Zur Rezeption Lewis Carrolls." *Arcadia* 17 (1982), 61–80.

Valencia, Gabriela C. de. "Notas para un estudio linguistico de la *Alicia* de Carroll." *Lenguaje* 11 (1980), 93–103.

Warren, Austin. "Carroll and His Alice Books." *Sewanee R* 88 (1980), 341–353.

Sylvie and Bruno, 1889

Deleuze, Gilles. "The Schizophrenic and Language: Surface and Depth in Lewis Carroll and Antonin Artaud," in Josué V. Harari, ed., *Textual Strategies*, 280–282.

Higbie, Robert. "Lewis Carroll," 26–27.

Prickett, Stephen. *Victorian Fantasy*, 137–140.

Through the Looking-Glass, 1871

Auerbach, Nina. *Romantic Imprisonment*, 130–168.

Brockway, Robert W. "The *Descensus ad Inferos*," 36–42.

Clark, Beverly Lyon. "Carroll's Well-Versed Narrative: *Through the Looking-Glass*." *Engl Lang Notes* 20:2 (1982), 65–76.

Hancher, Michael. "John Tenniel, Horace Mayhew, and the White Knight." *Jabberwocky* 8 (1979), 98–107.

Henkle, Roger B. "Carroll's Narratives," 89–100.

Higbie, Robert. "Lewis Carroll," 21–26.

Imholtz, August A., Jr. "Jam Sempiterne: A Note on Time in *Through the Looking-Glass*." *Jabberwocky* 8 (1978–79), 13–15.

Knoepflmacher, U. C. "The Balancing of Child and Adult: An Approach to Victorian Fantasies for Children." *Nineteenth-Century Fiction* 37 (1983), 511–518.

Little, Edmund. *The Fantasts*, 39–53.

Madden, William A. "Framing the *Alices*," 362–371.

Martinich, A. P. "A Theory of Communication and the Depth of Humor." *J of Liter Semantics* 10 (1981), 20–31.

Mellor, Anne K. *English Romantic Irony*, 174–178.

Morton, Lionel. "Memory in the Alice Books," 285–308.

Oates, Joyce Carol. "Wonderlands," 495–498.

Polhemus, Robert M. *Comic Faith*, 245–293.

Prickett, Stephen. *Victorian Fantasy*, 135–137, 140–142, 144–145.

Pycior, Helena M. "At the Intersection of Mathematics," 149–170.

Rackin, Donald. "Love and Death," 26–45.

Warren, Austin. "Carroll and His Alice Books," 341–353.

JOYCE CARY

The African Witch, 1936

Fisher, Barbara. *Joyce Cary*, 168–174.

Hall, Dennis. *Joyce Cary*, 32–44.

Klooß, Wolfgang. *Die englische Kolonialpolitik*, 148–149, 150–153, 156–296.

Majumdar, Bimalendu. *Joyce Cary*, 32–42.

Aissa Saved, 1932

Downes, Brian. " 'Almost a Fabulous Treatment': A Reading of Joyce Cary's *Aissa Saved*." *Work in Progress* 3 (1980), 52–62.

Fisher, Barbara. *Joyce Cary*, 150–158.

Hall, Dennis. *Joyce Cary*, 14–21.

Klooß, Wolfgang. *Die englische Kolonialpolitik*, 146–147, 156–296.

Majumdar, Bimalendu. *Joyce Cary*, 16–22.

An American Visitor, 1933

Fisher, Barbara. *Joyce Cary*, 158–167.

Hall, Dennis. *Joyce Cary*, 22–32.

Klooß, Wolfgang. *Die englische Kolonialpolitik*, 144–148, 156–296.

Majumdar, Bimalendu. *Joyce Cary*, 22–32.

The Captive and the Free, 1959

Christian, Edwin Ernest. "*The Captive and the Free*: Joyce Cary's Christianity." *Christianity & Lit* 33:3 (1984), 12–21.

Fisher, Barbara. *Joyce Cary*, 304–329.

Hall, Dennis. *Joyce Cary*, 131–145.

Majumdar, Bimalendu. *Joyce Cary*, 185–200.

Roby, Kinley E. *Joyce Cary*, 98–104.

Castle Corner, 1938

Cook, Cornelia. *Joyce Cary*, 40–45, 49–56.

Echeruo, Michael J. C. *Joyce Cary*, 26–28.

Fisher, Barbara. *Joyce Cary*, 175–186.

Fisher, Barbara. "Joyce Cary as an Anglo-Irish Writer," in Heinz Kosok, ed., *Studies*, 299–302.

Majumdar, Bimalendu. *Joyce Cary*, 55–66.

Charley Is My Darling, 1940

   Cook, Cornelia. *Joyce Cary*, 70–79.
   Echeruo, Michael J. C. *Joyce Cary*, 30–42.
   Fisher, Barbara. *Joyce Cary*, 199–201.
   Hall, Dennis. *Joyce Cary*, 53–56.
   Majumdar, Bimalendu. *Joyce Cary*, 90–99.

Except the Lord, 1953

   Cook, Cornelia. *Joyce Cary*, 206–217.
   Echeruo, Michael J. C. *Joyce Cary*, 107–126, 138–140.
   Fisher, Barbara. *Joyce Cary*, 281–294.
   Hall, Dennis. *Joyce Cary*, 115–121.
   Majumdar, Bimalendu. *Joyce Cary*, 157–169.
   Roby, Kinley E. *Joyce Cary*, 89–94.

A Fearful Joy, 1949

   Cook, Cornelia. *Joyce Cary*, 153–157, 168–173.
   Fisher, Barbara. *Joyce Cary*, 251–265.
   Hall, Dennis. *Joyce Cary*, 93–98.
   Majumdar, Bimalendu. *Joyce Cary*, 76–87.
   Roby, Kinley E. *Joyce Cary*, 53–58.

Herself Surprised, 1941

   Cook, Cornelia. *Joyce Cary*, 99–107.
   Echeruo, Michael J. C. *Joyce Cary*, 61–70.
   Fisher, Barbara. *Joyce Cary*, 211–217.
   Hall, Dennis. *Joyce Cary*, 66–68, 72–73.
   McCrea, Brian. "The Murder of Sara Monday: Art and Morality in
      Joyce Cary's *First Trilogy*." *Essays in Lit* (Macomb) 7 (1980), 45–53.
   Majumdar, Bimalendu. *Joyce Cary*, 112–121.
   Roby, Kinley E. *Joyce Cary*, 60–67.

The Horse's Mouth, 1944

   Auerbach, Nina. *Romantic Imprisonment*, 80–82.
   Clews, Hetty. *The Only Teller*, 114–120.
   Cook, Cornelia. *Joyce Cary*, 131–149.
   Echeruo, Michael J. C. *Joyce Cary*, 71–91.
   Fisher, Barbara. *Joyce Cary*, 223–238.
   Hall, Dennis. *Joyce Cary*, 84–90.
   McCrea, Brian. "The Murder of Sara Monday," 45–53.
   Majumdar, Bimalendu. *Joyce Cary*, 132–143.
   Roby, Kinley E. *Joyce Cary*, 76–82.
   Yeager, D. M. "Love and Mirth in *The Horse's Mouth*." *Renascence* 33
      (1981), 131–141.

A House of Children, 1941

   Cook, Cornelia. *Joyce Cary*, 81–93.
   Fisher, Barbara. *Joyce Cary*, 28–31, 201–210.

Fisher, Barbara. "Joyce Cary as an Anglo-Irish Writer," 302–304.
Hall, Dennis. *Joyce Cary*, 56–61.
Majumdar, Bimalendu. *Joyce Cary*, 99–110.

Mister Johnson, 1939

Cook, Cornelia. *Joyce Cary*, 59–70, 72–79.
Fisher, Barbara. *Joyce Cary*, 197–199.
Hall, Dennis. *Joyce Cary*, 44–53.
Klooß, Wolfgang. *Die englische Kolonialpolitik*, 135–137, 149–150, 153–154, 156–296.
Majumdar, Bimalendu. *Joyce Cary*, 42–51.
Milbury-Steen, Sarah L. *European and African Stereotypes*, 78–88.
Okonkwo, Juliet I. "Joyce Cary, *Mister Johnson*." *Okike* 13 (1979), 111–123.

The Moonlight, 1946

Cook, Cornelia. *Joyce Cary*, 153–168.
Fisher, Barbara. *Joyce Cary*, 239–251.
Hall, Dennis. *Joyce Cary*, 90–93.
Majumdar, Bimalendu. *Joyce Cary*, 67–76.
Roby, Kinley E. *Joyce Cary*, 49–53.

Not Honour More, 1955

Cook, Cornelia. *Joyce Cary*, 217–227.
Echeruo, Michael J. C. *Joyce Cary*, 126–137.
Fisher, Barbara. *Joyce Cary*, 294–303.
Hall, Dennis. *Joyce Cary*, 121–124.
Majumdar, Bimalendu. *Joyce Cary*, 169–181.
Roby, Kinley E. *Joyce Cary*, 94–97.

Prisoner of Grace, 1952

Cook, Cornelia. *Joyce Cary*, 183–206.
Echeruo, Michael J. C. *Joyce Cary*, 97–109.
Fisher, Barbara. *Joyce Cary*, 266–281.
Hall, Dennis. *Joyce Cary*, 103–115.
Majumdar, Bimalendu. *Joyce Cary*, 147–157.
Roby, Kinley E. *Joyce Cary*, 85–89.

To Be a Pilgrim, 1942

Cook, Cornelia. *Joyce Cary*, 107–131.
Echeruo, Michael J. C. *Joyce Cary*, 48–60.
Fisher, Barbara. *Joyce Cary*, 119–121, 217–223.
Hall, Dennis. *Joyce Cary*, 73–84.
McCrea, Brian. "The Murder of Sara Monday," 45–53.
Majumdar, Bimalendu. *Joyce Cary*, 121–132.
Roby, Kinley E. *Joyce Cary*, 67–75.

DAVID CAUTE

The Occupation, 1971

Bergonzi, Bernard. "Fictions of History," in Malcolm Bradbury and David Palmer, eds., *The Contemporary English Novel,* 46–49.

JOY CHANT

The Grey Mane of Morning, 1977

Elgin, Don D. *The Comedy,* 163–176.

Red Moon and Black Mountain, 1970

Elgin, Don D. *The Comedy,* 154–162.

Elgin, Don D. "The Comedy of Fantasy: An Ecological Perspective in Joy Chant's *Red Moon and Black Mountain,*" in William Coyle, ed., *Aspects of Fantasy,* 221–230.

SID CHAPLIN

The Day of the Sardine, 1961

Paul, Ronald. *"Fire in Our Hearts,"* 64–67.

G. K. CHESTERTON

The Ball and the Cross, 1910

Blissett, William. *"The Ball and the Cross* (1910)." *Chesterton R* 8:1 (1982), 30–34.

Hunter, Jefferson. *Edwardian Fiction,* 56–57.

The Club of Queer Trades, 1905

Quinn, Joseph. *"The Club of Queer Trades." Chesterton R* 5 (1978–79), 79–86.

The Flying Inn, 1914

Coates, John D. *Chesterton,* 85–97, 111–114.

The Man Who Was Thursday, 1908

Beckman, Peter. "God and the Keystone Cops: Some Observations Concerning G. K. Chesterton's *The Man Who Was Thursday,*" in Ann Boaden, ed., *The Masks,* 71–82.

Coates, John D. *Chesterton,* 214–222.

Conners, Joseph B. "The Starry Pinnacle of the Commonplace." *Chesterton R* 5 (1978–79), 48–61.

Denis, Yves. *G. K. Chesterton,* 382–388.

Leigh, David J. "Politics and Perspective in *The Man Who Was Thursday." Chesterton R* 7 (1981), 329–336.

Manalive, 1912

>   Coates, John D. *Chesterton*, 222–228.
>   Denis, Yves. *G. K. Chesterton*, 169–171, 184–185.

The Napoleon of Notting Hill, 1904

>   Coates, John D. *Chesterton*, 102–106, 135–143.
>   d'Haussy, Christiane. *La vision du monde*, 99–102, 124–125.
>   Kerridge, Roy. "The Prophets of Notting Hill." *Chesterton R* 6 (1979–80), 116–130.

The Return of Don Quixote, 1927

>   Coates, John D. *Chesterton*, 115–123.

JOHN CHRISTOPHER

The Winchester Trilogy, 1970–72

>   Swinfen, Ann. *In Defence*, 202–218.

ARTHUR C. CLARKE

Against the Fall of Night, 1948

>   Hollow, John. *Against the Night*, 37–45.
>   Rabkin, Eric S. "Fairy Tales and Science Fiction," in George E. Slusser et al., eds., *Bridges*, 88–89.

Childhood's End, 1953

>   Goldman, Stephen H. "Immortal Man and Mortal Overlord: The Case for Intertextuality," in Carl B. Yoke and Donald M. Hassler, eds., *Death and the Serpent*, 193–207.
>   Hollow, John. *Against the Night*, 66–87.
>   Hull, Elizabeth Anne. "Fire and Ice: The Ironic Imagery of Arthur C. Clarke's *Childhood's End*." *Extrapolation* 24 (1983), 13–30.
>   Rabkin, Eric S. *Arthur C. Clarke*, 22–29.

The City and the Stars, 1956

>   Dunn, Thomas P., and Richard D. Erlich. "Environmental Concerns in Arthur C. Clarke's *The City and the Stars*," in William Coyle, ed., *Aspects of Fantasy*, 203–209.
>   Hollow, John. *Against the Night*, 117–127.
>   Rabkin, Eric S. *Arthur C. Clarke*, 30–35.
>   Rabkin, Eric S. "Fairy Tales," 88–89.
>   Rabkin, Eric S. "The Unconscious City," in George E. Slusser and Eric S. Rabkin, eds., *Hard Science Fiction*, 31–34.
>   Wolfe, Gary K. *The Known and the Unknown*, 110–116.

The Deep Range, 1968

>   Hollow, John. *Against the Night*, 104–110.

Dolphin Island, 1963

> Hollow, John. *Against the Night*, 113–117.

A Fall of Moondust, 1961

> Hollow, John. *Against the Night*, 110–113.

The Fountains of Paradise, 1978

> Hollow, John. *Against the Night*, 174–178.
> Hume, Kathryn. "The Edifice Complex: Motive and Accomplishment in *The Fountains of Paradise*." *Extrapolation* 24 (1983), 380–387.

Imperial Earth, 1975

> Hollow, John. *Against the Night*, 165–174.

Islands in the Sky, 1952

> Hollow, John. *Against the Night*, 47–52.

Prelude to Space, 1947

> Hollow, John. *Against the Night*, 58–65.

Rendezvous with Rama, 1973

> Hanzo, Thomas A. "The Past of Science Fiction," in George E. Slusser et al., eds., *Bridges*, 145–146.
> Hollow, John. *Against the Night*, 159–165.
> Parrinder, Patrick. *Science Fiction . . . Teaching*, 108–110.
> Rabkin, Eric S. *Arthur C. Clarke*, 45–52.
> Ruddick, Nicholas. "The World Turned Inside Out: Decoding Clarke's *Rendezvous with Rama*." *Science-Fiction Stud* 12 (1985), 42–48.
> Wendland, Albert. *Science, Myth*, 100–105.

The Sands of Mars, 1952

> Hollow, John. *Against the Night*, 52–58.

2001: A Space Odyssey, 1968

> Boylan, Jay H. "Hal in *2001: A Space Odyssey*: The Lover Sings His Song." *J of Popular Culture* 18:4 (1985), 53–56.
> Hollow, John. *Against the Night*, 128–154.
> Otten, Terry. "The Fallen and Evolving Worlds of *2001*." *Mosaic* 13:3–4 (1980), 41–50.
> Pielke, Robert G. "*Star Wars* vs. *2001*: A Question of Identity." *Extrapolation* 24 (1983), 144–154.
> Rabkin, Eric S. *Arthur C. Clarke*, 36–44.
> Spector, Judith A. "Science Fiction and the Sex War: A Womb of One's Own." *Lit and Psych* 31:1 (1981), 22–29.
> Stover, Leon. "Social Science Fiction," in Jack Williamson, ed., *Teaching Science Fiction*, 138–140.

2010: Odyssey Two, 1982

> Hollow, John. *Against the Night*, 178–187.

PAULINE CLARKE

The Twelve and the Genii, 1962

Swinfen, Ann. *In Defence*, 124–128.

JOHN CLELAND

Fanny Hill, 1748

Brooks-Davies, Douglas. "The Mythology of Love: Venerean (and Related) Iconography in Pope, Fielding, Cleland and Sterne," in Paul-Gabriel Boucé, ed., *Sexuality*, 184–186.

Markley, Robert. "Language, Power, and Sexuality in Cleland's *Fanny Hill*." *Philol Q* 63 (1984), 343–354.

Miller, Nancy K. *The Heroine's Text*, 51–66.

Miller, Nancy K. " 'I's' in Drag: The Sex of Recollection." *Eighteenth Century* 22 (1981), 47–57.

Roussel, Roy. *The Conversation*, 37–66.

Taylor, Anne Robinson. *Male Novelists*, 92–95.

Todd, Janet. *Women's Friendship*, 69–100.

JOHN COLLIER

Defy the Foul Fiend, 1934

Richardson, Betty. *John Collier*, 60–71.

His Monkey Wife, 1930

Richardson, Betty. *John Collier*, 33–46.

Tom's A-Cold, 1933

Richardson, Betty. *John Collier*, 47–59.

WILKIE COLLINS

Antonina, 1850

Sayers, Dorothy L. *Wilkie Collins*, 61–72.

Armadale, 1866

Blair, David. "Wilkie Collins and the Crisis of Suspense," in Ian Gregor, ed., *Reading the Victorian Novel*, 39–45.

Gates, Barbara T. "Wilkie Collins's Suicides: 'Truth As It Is in Nature'." *Dickens Stud Annual* 12 (1983), 308–309.

Hughes, Winifred. *The Maniac*, 155–161.

Peterson, Audrey. *Victorian Masters*, 54–57.

Williams, Merryn. *Women in the English Novel*, 135–137.

Basil, 1852

Bedell, Jeanne F. "Wilkie Collins," in Earl F. Bargainnier, ed., *Twelve Englishmen*, 19–21, 24–28.
Sayers, Dorothy L. *Wilkie Collins*, 78–92.

The Fallen Leaves, 1879

Gates, Barbara T. "Wilkie Collins's Suicides," 309–311.
Mitchell, Sally. *The Fallen Angel*, 132–133.
Watt, George. *The Fallen Woman*, 98–104.

Heart and Science, 1883

Gates, Barbara T. "Wilkie Collins's Suicides," 314–316.

Hide and Seek, 1854

Sayers, Dorothy L. *Wilkie Collins*, 102–110.

The Law and the Lady, 1875

Gates, Barbara T. "Wilkie Collins's Suicides," 311–314.

Man and Wife, 1870

Bedell, Jeanne F. "Wilkie Collins," 22–24.
Mitchell, Sally. *The Fallen Angel*, 129–130.
Newby, Richard L. "Wilkie Collins's *Man and Wife*: Kingsley's Athlete Scouted." *McNeese R* 26 (1979–80), 47–54.
Watt, George. *The Fallen Woman*, 105–107.

The Memoirs of a Picture, 1805

Sayers, Dorothy L. *Wilkie Collins*, 29–34.

The Moonstone, 1868

Bedell, Jeanne F. "Wilkie Collins," 28–29.
Böker, Uwe. "Entwicklung des Unbewussten in der viktorianischen Kriminalliteratur: Andrew Forresters' 'A Child Found Dead' und Wilkie Collins' *The Moonstone*." *Deutsche Vierteljahrsschrift für Literaturwissenschaft und Geistesgeschichte* 55 (1981), 665–683.
Frick, Patricia Miller. "Wilkie Collins's 'Little Jewel': The Meaning of *The Moonstone*." *Philol Q* 63 (1984), 313–319.
Hennelly, Mark M., Jr. "Detecting Collins' Diamond: From Serpentstone to Moonstone." *Nineteenth-Century Fiction* 39 (1984), 25–47.
Hughes, Winifred. *The Maniac*, 161–165.
Lonoff, Sue. "Multiple Narratives & Relative Truths: A Study of *The Ring and the Book*, *The Woman in White*, and *The Moonstone*." *Browning Inst Stud* 10 (1982), 143–159.
Malcolm, David. "Victorian Modernism: Wilkie Collins." *Stud in Engl Lit* (Japan) 61 (1984), 44–48.
Miller, D. A. "From *roman policier* to *roman-police*: Wilkie Collins's *The Moonstone*." *Novel* 13 (1980), 153–170.
Miller, David. "Romanzo poliziesco, romanzo-polizia: *The Moonstone* di Wilkie Collins." *Calibano* 3 (1979), 100–120.

Muller, Charles. "*The Moonstone*: Victorian Detective Novel." *Communique* (Pietersburg) 5:1 (1980), 1–24.

Murfin, Ross C. "The Art of Representation: Collins' *The Moonstone* and Dickens' Example." *ELH* 49 (1982), 653–671.

Nadel, Ira Bruce. "Science and *The Moonstone*." *Dickens Stud Annual* 11 (1983), 239–257.

Peterson, Audrey. *Victorian Masters*, 57–66.

Trodd, Anthea. "The Policeman and the Lady: Significant Encounters in Mid-Victorian Fiction." *Victorian Stud* 27 (1984), 446–449.

The New Magdalen, 1873

Mitchell, Sally. *The Fallen Angel*, 130–132.

Watt, George. *The Fallen Woman*, 107–117.

No Name, 1862

Baker, William. "Wilkie Collins, Dickens and *No Name*." *Dickens Stud Newsl* 11 (1980), 49–52.

Bedell, Jeanne F. "Wilkie Collins," 16–18.

Gates, Barbara T. "Wilkie Collins's Suicides," 306–308.

Hughes, Winifred. *The Maniac*, 145–155.

Peterson, Audrey. *Victorian Masters*, 50–54.

The Woman in White, 1860

Auerbach, Nina. *Woman and the Demon*, 135–143.

Bedell, Jeanne F. "Wilkie Collins," 15–16.

Blair, David. "Wilkie Collins," 36–39.

Coates, J. D. "Techniques of Terror in *The Woman in White*." *Durham Univ J* 73 (1980–81), 177–189.

Hennelly, Mark M., Jr. "Reading Detection in *The Woman in White*." *Texas Stud in Lit and Lang* 22 (1980), 449–465.

Hughes, Winifred. *The Maniac*, 138–144.

Kurata, Marilyn J. "Italians with White Mice Again: *Middlemarch* and *The Woman in White*." *Engl Lang Notes* 22:4 (1985), 46–47.

Leavy, Barbara Fass. "Wilkie Collins' Cinderella: The History of Psychology and *The Woman in White*." *Dickens Stud Annual* 10 (1982), 91–135.

Lonoff, Sue. "Multiple Narratives & Relative Truths," 143–159.

Malcolm, David. "Victorian Modernism," 44–48.

Meckier, Jerome. "Wilkie Collins's *The Woman in White*: Providence Against the Evils of Propriety." *J of Brit Stud* 22:1 (1982), 104–126.

Milligan, Ian. *The Novel in English*, 151–153.

Peterson, Audrey. *Victorian Masters*, 39–50.

Punter, David. *The Literature of Terror*, 223–228.

MARY COLLYER

Letters from Felicia to Charlotte, 1744

Suhr, Heidrun. *Englische Romanautorinnen*, 172–174.

JACK COMMON

The Ampersand, 1954

Paul, Ronald. *"Fire in Our Hearts,"* 89–99.

Kiddar's Luck, 1951

Paul, Ronald. *"Fire in Our Hearts,"* 80–89.

IVY COMPTON-BURNETT

Brothers and Sisters, 1929

Rowsell, Mary Dalton. *"Brothers and Sisters*: A Most Complex Relation." *Twentieth Century Lit* 25 (1979), 207–222.

A Family and a Fortune, 1939

Potter, Lois. "Show and Dumb Show in *A Family and a Fortune.*" *Twentieth Century Lit* 25 (1979), 194–206.

A House and Its Head, 1935

McFarlane, Brian. "Ivy Compton-Burnett's *A House and Its Head*: Truth and Wit." *Southern R* (Adelaide) 11 (1978), 154–164.

Manservant and Maidservant, 1947

Lewis, Constance. *"Manservant and Maidservant*: A Pivotal Novel." *Twentieth Century Lit* 25 (1979), 224–234.

JOSEPH CONRAD

Almayer's Folly, 1895

Batchelor, John. *The Edwardian Novelists*, 28–30.

Bonney, William W. *Thorns & Arabesques*, 89–96.

Brodie, Susan Lundvall. "Conrad's Feminine Perspective." *Conradiana* 16 (1984), 146–147.

Bruffee, Kenneth A. *Elegiac Romance*, 74–76, 86–88.

Gillon, Adam. *Joseph Conrad*, 18–20.

Hawkins, Hunt. "Conrad and the Psychology of Colonialism," in Ross C. Murfin, ed., *Conrad Revisited*, 73–77.

Hunter, Allan. *Joseph Conrad*, 59–64.

Inamdar, F. A. *Image and Symbol*, 1–9, 11–15.

Land, Stephen K. *Paradox and Polarity*, 13–27.

McClure, John. "Problematic Presence: The Colonial Other in Kipling and Conrad," in David Dabydeen, ed., *The Black Presence*, 155–157.

McClure, John A. *Kipling & Conrad*, 99–107.

McLauchlan, Juliet. "Almayer and Willems: 'How Not To Be'." *Conradiana* 11 (1979), 113–122.

Maisonnat, Claude. *"Almayer's Folly*; ou, la question de la voix." *Recherches Anglaises et Américaines* 15 (1982), 21–38.

Page, Norman. *A Conrad Companion*, 68–72.

Schwarz, Daniel R. *Conrad*, 3–20.

Slights, William W. E. "Anagram, Myth, and the Structure of *Almayer's Folly*." *Ariel* 11:3 (1980), 23–36.

Tennant, Roger. *Joseph Conrad*, 48–56, 97–100.

Watt, Ian. *Conrad*, 34–67.

Watts, Cedric. "The Covert Plot of *Almayer's Folly*: A Structural Discovery." *Conradiana* 15 (1983), 227–229.

The Arrow of Gold, 1919

Geddes, Gary. *Conrad's Later Novels*, 115–143.

Hunter, Allan. *Joseph Conrad*, 109–110.

Inamdar, F. A. *Image and Symbol*, 187–189.

La Bossière, Camille R. *Joseph Conrad*, 61–63.

Land, Stephen K. *Paradox and Polarity*, 232–249.

Mursia, Ugo. *Scritti Conradiani*, 118–123.

Page, Norman. *A Conrad Companion*, 122–126.

Schwarz, Daniel R. *Conrad: The Later Fiction*, 125–140.

Tennant, Roger. *Joseph Conrad*, 229–231.

Chance, 1913

Batchelor, John. *The Edwardian Novelists*, 81–85.

Geddes, Gary. *Conrad's Later Novels*, 11–40.

Gillon, Adam. *Joseph Conrad*, 140–144.

Inamdar, F. A. *Image and Symbol*, 174–178.

Johnson, Julie M. "The Damsel and Her Knights: The Goddess and the Grail in Conrad's *Chance*." *Conradiana* 13 (1981), 221–226.

La Bossière, Camille R. *Joseph Conrad*, 56–59.

Land, Stephen K. *Paradox and Polarity*, 179–191.

Mursia, Ugo. *Scritti Conradiani*, 107–112.

Page, Norman. *A Conrad Companion*, 110–113.

Purdy, Dwight H. *Joseph Conrad's Bible*, 85–88.

Rude, Donald. "Joseph Conrad's *Chance*." *Book Collector* 27 (1978), 343–347.

Schwarz, Daniel R. *Conrad: The Later Fiction*, 40–59.

Schwarz, Daniel R. "The Continuity of Conrad's Later Novels," in Ross C. Murfin, ed., *Conrad Revisited*, 162–164.

Siegle, Robert. "The Two Texts of *Chance*." *Conradiana* 16 (1984), 83–101.

Lord Jim, 1900

Aithal, S. Krishnamoorthy. "Conrad's *Lord Jim*." *Explicator* 38:1 (1979), 3–4.

Armstrong, Paul B. "The Hermeneutics of Literary Impressionism: Interpretation and Reality in James, Conrad, and Ford." *Centennial R* 27 (1983), 250–254.

Barza, Steven. "Bonds of Empathy: The Widening Audience in *Lord Jim*." *Midwest Q* 25 (1984), 220–232.

Batchelor, John. *The Edwardian Novelists*, 45–57.

Bender, T. K. "Authorial Privilege in Joseph Conrad," in Serge Lusignan and John S. North, eds., *Computing*, 51–58.

Bevan, Ernest, Jr. "Marlow and Jim: The Reconstructed Past." *Conradiana* 15 (1983), 191–200.

Bonney, William W. *Thorns & Arabesques*, 27–30.

Bruffee, Kenneth A. *Elegiac Romance*, 90–92, 96–98, 103–132, 192–196.

Caserio, Robert L. "Joseph Conrad, Dickensian Novelist of the Nineteenth Century: A Dissent from Ian Watt." *Nineteenth-Century Fiction* 36 (1981), 341–347.

Conroy, Mark. *Modernism*, 99–117.

Cottom, Daniel. "*Lord Jim*: Destruction Through Time." *Centennial R* 27 (1983), 10–29.

Craig, Randall. "Swapping Yarns: The Oral Mode of *Lord Jim*." *Conradiana* 13 (1981), 181–191.

Darras, Jacques. *Joseph Conrad*, 23–33.

Das, R. J. *Joseph Conrad*, 68–70.

Davidson, Arnold E. "The Abdication of Lord Jim." *Conradiana* 13 (1981), 19–31.

Doody, Terrence. *Confession and Community*, 133–161.

El-Ayouty, Amin. "Romantic Realism in Conrad's *Lord Jim*." *J of Engl* (Sana'a Univ) 6 (1979), 54–78.

Galen, Nina. "Stephen Crane as a Source for Conrad's Jim." *Nineteenth-Century Fiction* 38 (1983), 78–96.

Gillon, Adam. *Joseph Conrad*, 84–98.

Hawkins, Hunt. "Conrad and the Psychology," 77–80.

Hervouet, Yves. "Aspects of Flaubertian Influence on Conrad's Fiction." *Revue de Littérature Comparée* 226 (1983), 185–197.

Hunter, Allan. *Joseph Conrad*, 29–31, 41–57, 91–101, 113–116.

Hunter, Jefferson. *Edwardian Fiction*, 128–133.

Inamdar, F. A. *Image and Symbol*, 71–99.

Johnson, Bruce. "Conrad's Impressionism and Watt's 'Delayed Decoding'," in Ross C. Murfin, ed., *Conrad Revisited*, 63–64.

Jones, Michael P. *Conrad's Heroism*, 81–100.

La Bossière, Camille R. *Joseph Conrad*, 37–44.

Land, Stephen K. *Paradox and Polarity*, 79–92.

McClure, John. "Problematic Presence," 158–159.

McClure, John A. *Kipling & Conrad*, 121–130.

Madden, David. *A Primer*, 306–308.

Martin, Joseph. "Conrad and the Aesthetic Movement." *Conradiana* 17 (1985), 200–206.

Mason, Philip. *The English Gentleman*, 189–195.

Miller, J. Hillis. *Fiction and Repetition*, 22–41.

Morf, Gustav. *The Polish Shades*, 143–158.

O'Hanlon, Redmond. *Joseph Conrad*, 28–34, 58–90, 92–100, 110–129, 134–142.

72 CONRAD

Page, Norman. *A Conrad Companion*, 86–93.
Platzner, Robert Leonard. *The Metaphysical Novel*, 216–284.
Purdy, Dwight H. *Joseph Conrad's Bible*, 106–110.
Raimond, Jean. "Jim et Axel Heyst ou les mirages de l'ailleurs: Deux avatars conradiens de Don Quichotte et de Robinson," in *Images de l'ailleurs*, 77–95.
Raimond, Jean. "Joseph Conrad: *Lord Jim*," in Pierre Coustillas et al., eds., *Le roman anglais*, 271–283.
Raval, Suresh. "Narrative and Authority in *Lord Jim*: Conrad's Art of Failure." *ELH* 48 (1981), 387–408.
Reeves, Charles Eric. "A Voice of Unrest: Conrad's Rhetoric of the Unspeakable." *Texas Stud in Lit and Lang* 27 (1985), 292–293.
Ricks, Christopher. "The Pink Toads in *Lord Jim*." *Essays in Criticism* 31 (1981), 142–144.
Scheick, William J. "Fictional Structure and Ethics in the Edwardian, Modern and Contemporary Novel." *Philol Q* 63 (1984), 302–307.
Schug, Charles. *The Romantic Genesis*, 160–188.
Schwarz, Daniel R. *Conrad*, 76–94.
Schwarz, Daniel R. *Conrad: The Later Fiction*, 34–36, 41–44.
Seidel, Michael. "Isolation and Narrative Power: A Meditation on Conrad at the Boundaries." *Criticism* 27 (1985), 73–84, 90–92.
Shires, Linda M. "The 'Privileged' Reader and Narrative Methodology in *Lord Jim*." *Conradiana* 17 (1985), 19–28.
Shukla, Narain Prasad. "The Light Imagery in *Lord Jim*." *Osmania J of Engl Stud* 15 (1979), 43–48.
Simpson, David. *Fetishism and Imagination*, 102–105, 107–111.
Tennant, Roger. *Joseph Conrad*, 48–56, 136–150.
Thornton, Lawrence. "Conrad, Flaubert, and Marlow: Possession and Exorcism." *Compar Lit* 34 (1982), 146–156.
Thornton, Lawrence. *Unbodied Hope*, 81–97.
Turner, Rosa Shand. "The Redemptive Act of Narrating: Reclaiming the Trace of *Lord Jim*." *Ball State Univ Forum* 21:4 (1980), 53–57.
Vidan, Ivo. "Time Sequence in Spatial Fiction," in Jeffrey R. Smitten and Ann Daghistany, eds., *Spatial Form*, 135–143.
Watt, Ian. *Conrad*, 254–356.
Watt, Ian P. "The Ending of *Lord Jim*." *Conradiana* 11 (1979), 3–19.
Weiand, Hermann J. "*Lord Jim*," in Weiand, ed., *Insight V*, 53–66.
Weinstein, Philip M. *The Semantics of Desire*, 148–166.
White, Allon. *The Uses of Obscurity*, 73–74.
Yoshida, Tetsuo. "Joseph Conrad and His 'Teutonic' Character Schomberg." *Stud in Engl Lit* (Japan), Engl Number 1980, 6–8.

The Nigger of the "Narcissus," 1897

Batchelor, John. *The Edwardian Novelists*, 31–36.
Bonney, William W. "Joseph Conrad and the Betrayal of Language." *Nineteenth-Century Fiction* 34 (1979), 140–142, 145–153.
Bonney, William W. *Thorns & Arabesques*, 162–175, 204–206, 215–222.

Fogel, Aaron. *Coercion to Speak*, 39–44, 47–53, 86–89.

Foulke, R. D. "Creed and Conduct in *The Nigger of the 'Narcissus'*." *Conradiana* 12 (1980), 105–125.

Gillon, Adam. *Joseph Conrad*, 37–49.

Hervouet, Yves. "Aspects of Flaubertian Influence on Conrad's Fiction." *Revue de Littérature Comparée* 225 (1983), 13–19.

Humphries, Reynold. "How to Change the Subject: Narrative, Reader and Ideology in *The Nigger of the 'Narcissus'*." *Recherches Anglaises et Américaines* 15 (1982), 39–50.

Hunter, Jefferson. *Edwardian Fiction*, 216–218.

Inamdar, F. A. *Image and Symbol*, 19–42.

Jones, Michael P. *Conrad's Heroism*, 45–63.

Kay, Arthur. "Joseph Conrad's Use of Key Names in *The Nigger of the 'Narcissus'*." *Names* 29 (1981), 178–180.

Land, Stephen K. *Paradox and Polarity*, 49–63.

Lester, John. "Conrad's Narrators in *The Nigger of the 'Narcissus'*." *Conradiana* 12 (1980), 163–172.

Levenson, Michael. "The Modernist Narrator on the Victorian Sailing Ship." *Browning Inst Stud* 11 (1983), 101–112.

Lothe, Jakob. "Variations of Narrative in *The Nigger of the 'Narcissus'*." *Conradiana* 16 (1984), 215–223.

Page, Norman. *A Conrad Companion*, 76–85.

Purdy, Dwight H. *Joseph Conrad's Bible*, 23–31.

Reeves, Charles Eric. "A Voice of Unrest," 294–298.

Schwarz, Daniel R. *Conrad*, 35–51.

Watt, Ian. *Conrad*, 68–125.

Willy, Todd G. "The Conquest of the Commodore: Conrad's Rigging of 'The Nigger' for the Henley Regatta." *Conradiana* 17 (1985), 171–180.

Nostromo, 1904

Armstrong, Paul B. "Conrad's Contradictory Politics: The Ontology of Society in *Nostromo*." *Twentieth Century Lit* 31 (1985), 1–19.

Batchelor, John. *The Edwardian Novelists*, 57–66.

Bonney, William W. "Joseph Conrad and the Betrayal," 131–133, 142–144.

Bonney, William W. *Thorns & Arabesques*, 109–124, 128–131, 157–160.

Brodie, Susan Lundvall. "Conrad's Feminine Perspective," 144–146.

Christmas, Peter. "Conrad's *Nostromo*: A Tale of Europe." *Lit and Hist* 6 (1980), 59–80.

Coates, Paul. *The Realist Fantasy*, 125–127.

Conroy, Mark. "Lost in Azuera: The Fate of Sulaco and Conrad's *Nostromo*." *Glyph* 8 (1981), 148–169.

Conroy, Mark. *Modernism*, 118–140.

Curreli, Mario. "Aspetti della tecnica narrativa nel *Nostromo* di Conrad." *Studi dell'Istituto Linguistico* 2 (1979), 153–185.

Curreli, Mario. "Fictional Suicide and Personal Rescue: The Case-History of *Nostromo*." *Studi dell'Istituto Linguistico* 4 (1981), 97–121.

Curreli, Mario. "Gli schiavi dell'argento del *Nostromo* di Conrad." *Studi dell'Istituto Linguistico* 3 (1980), 61–86.

Darras, Jacques. *Joseph Conrad*, 109–119.

Das, R. J. *Joseph Conrad*, 33–35, 72–74.

Dobrinsky, Joseph. "Conrad, *Nostromo* and the Silver: A Psychobiographical Reading." *Cahiers Victoriens et Edouardiens* 11 (1980), 93–116.

Fogel, Aaron. *Coercion to Speak*, 25–30, 94–145.

Gillon, Adam. *Joseph Conrad*, 98–111.

Hervouet, Yves. "Aspects of Flaubertian Influence," 203–204.

Hunter, Allan. *Joseph Conrad*, 124–151.

Hunter, Jefferson. *Edwardian Fiction*, 142–152.

Inamdar, F. A. *Image and Symbol*, 100–124.

Jones, Michael P. *Conrad's Heroism*, 122–124.

La Bossière, Camille R. *Joseph Conrad*, 74–79.

Land, Stephen K. *Paradox and Polarity*, 108–111, 131–141.

Langland, Elizabeth. "Society as Formal Protagonist: The Examples of *Nostromo* and *Barchester Towers*." *Crit Inquiry* 9 (1982), 359–378.

Leech, Geoffrey N., and Michael H. Short. *Style in Fiction*, 258–259, 269–270.

Levine, George. "The Hero as Dilettante: *Middlemarch* and *Nostromo*," in Anne Smith, ed., *George Eliot*, 152–177.

Lindsay, Clarence B. "The Loss of Youth in *Nostromo*." *Stud in the Novel* 12 (1980), 114–129.

McAlindon, T. "*Nostromo*: Conrad's Organicist Philosophy of History." *Mosaic* 15:3 (1982), 27–41.

McClure, John A. *Kipling & Conrad*, 155–167.

Mnthali, Felix. "Continuity and Change in Conrad and Ngugi." *Kunapipi* 3:1 (1981), 103–106.

Morf, Gustav. *The Polish Shades*, 160–177.

Mursia, Ugo. *Scritti Conradiani*, 72–100.

Page, Norman. *A Conrad Companion*, 94–99.

Purdy, Dwight H. *Joseph Conrad's Bible*, 15–19, 42–44, 70–72.

Schwarz, Daniel R. *Conrad*, 135–156.

Simpson, David. *Fetishism and Imagination*, 113–116.

Smith, Peter. *Public and Private Value*, 183–214.

Thornton, Lawrence. *Unbodied Hope*, 82–84.

Toker, Leona. "A Nabokovian Character in Conrad's *Nostromo*." *Revue de Littérature Comparée* 233 (1985), 15–29.

Vidan, Ivo. "Time Sequence," 146–148.

Weinstein, Philip M. *The Semantics of Desire*, 166–184.

The Rescue, 1920

Bonney, William W. *Thorns & Arabesques*, 125–148.
Brodie, Susan Lundvall. "Conrad's Feminine Perspective," 149–151.
Caserio, Robert. "*The Rescue* and the Ring of Meaning," in Ross C. Murfin, ed., *Conrad Revisited*, 125–149.
Geddes, Gary. *Conrad's Later Novels*, 145–171.
Gillon, Adam. *Joseph Conrad*, 168–169.
Inamdar, F. A. *Image and Symbol*, 189–194.
La Bossière, Camille R. *Joseph Conrad*, 63–66.
Land, Stephen K. *Paradox and Polarity*, 250–269.
McClure, John A. *Kipling & Conrad*, 115–120.
Page, Norman. *A Conrad Companion*, 127–128.
Purdy, Dwight H. *Joseph Conrad's Bible*, 2–4, 77–82, 146–149.
Schwarz, Daniel R. *Conrad: The Later Fiction*, 105–124.

The Rover, 1923

Geddes, Gary. *Conrad's Later Novels*, 173–195.
Inamdar, F. A. *Image and Symbol*, 195–198.
La Bossière, Camille R. *Joseph Conrad*, 66–68.
Land, Stephen K. *Paradox and Polarity*, 270–281.
Page, Norman. *A Conrad Companion*, 129–131.
Schwarz, Daniel R. *Conrad: The Later Fiction*, 139–154.
Schwarz, Daniel R. "The Continuity," 164–168.

The Secret Agent, 1907

Arac, Jonathan. "Romanticism, the Self, and the City: *The Secret Agent* in Literary History." *Boundary 2* 9:1 (1980), 75–88.
Batchelor, John. *The Edwardian Novelists*, 66–73.
Biles, Jack I. "Winnie Verloc: Agent of Death." *Conradiana* 13 (1981), 101–106.
Calendrillo, Linda T. "Role Playing and 'Atmosphere' in Four Modern British Spy Novels." *Clues* 3:1 (1982), 111–119.
Conroy, Mark. *Modernism*, 139–155.
Conroy, Mark. "The Panoptical City: The Structure of Suspicion in *The Secret Agent*." *Conradiana* 15 (1983), 203–217.
Darras, Jacques. *Joseph Conrad*, 99–107.
Das, R. J. *Joseph Conrad*, 33–36.
Davidson, Arnold E. "The Sign of Conrad's Secret Agent." *Coll Lit* 8:1 (1981), 33–41.
D'Elia, Gaetano. "L'anarchismo e l'acrobata in *The Secret Agent*," in Agostino Lombardo, ed., *Studi inglesi*, 211–243.
Dolan, Paul. "The Plot in *The Secret Agent*." *Conradiana* 16 (1984), 225–233.
Eagleton, Terry. "Form, Ideology and *The Secret Agent*," in Diana Laurenson, ed., *The Sociology*, 55–63.
Fleishman, Avrom. "The Landscape of Hysteria in *The Secret Agent*," in Ross C. Murfin, ed., *Conrad Revisited*, 89–105.

Fogel, Aaron. *Coercion to Speak*, 30–33, 146–179.

Fogel, Daniel Mark. " 'The Last Cab' in James's 'The Papers' and in *The Secret Agent*: Conrad's Cues from the Master." *Mod Fiction Stud* 29 (1983), 227–233.

Gillon, Adam. *Joseph Conrad*, 112–122.

Goodwin, James. "Conrad and Hitchcock: Secret Sharers," in Michael Klein and Gillian Parker, eds., *The English Novel*, 218–227.

Held, George. "Conrad's Oxymoronic Imagination in *The Secret Agent*." *Conradiana* 17 (1985), 93–107.

Hollahan, Eugene. "The Globe and the Bomb: Apollonian and Dionysian Symbology in Conrad's *The Secret Agent*." *Intl J of Symbology* 8 (1977), 65–72.

Holubetz, Margarete. " 'Bad World for Poor People': Social Criticism in *The Secret Agent*." *Arbeiten aus Anglistik und Amerikanistik* 7 (1982), 13–22.

Houze, William C. "*The Secret Agent* from Novel to Play: The Implications of Conrad's Handling of Structure." *Conradiana* 13 (1981), 109–119.

Hubbard, Francis A. *Theories of Action*, 23–52.

Hunter, Allan. *Joseph Conrad*, 153–216.

Hunter, Jefferson. *Edwardian Fiction*, 230–234.

Inamdar, F. A. *Image and Symbol*, 125–137.

Johnson, Bruce. "Conrad's Impressionism," 58–62.

Jones, Michael P. *Conrad's Heroism*, 118–122.

Kennedy, Chris. "Systemic Grammar and Its Use in Literary Analysis," in Ronald Carter, ed., *Language and Literature*, 83–99.

Krahé, Peter. "Zur Psychologie des Erzählers in Joseph Conrads *The Secret Agent*." *Germanisch-Romanische Monatsschrift* 31 (1981), 156–169.

La Bossière, Camille R. *Joseph Conrad*, 79–82.

Land, Stephen K. *Paradox and Polarity*, 143–156.

Leech, Geoffrey N., and Michael H. Short. *Style in Fiction*, 219–220, 236–238, 330–331, 335–336.

Lesser, Wendy. "From Dickens to Conrad: A Sentimental Journey." *ELH* 52 (1985), 201–207.

Lewitter, L. R. "Conrad, Dostoyevsky, and the Russo-Polish Antagonism." *Mod Lang R* 79 (1984), 657–658.

McConnell, Frank. *Storytelling*, 175–180.

Merivale, P. "*Catch–22* and *The Secret Agent*: Mechanical Man, the Hole in the Centre, and the 'Principle of Inbuilt Chaos'." *Engl Stud in Canada* 7 (1981), 426–436.

Morf, Gustav. *The Polish Shades*, 178–184.

Mursia, Ugo. *Scritti Conradiani*, 101–104.

Page, Norman. *A Conrad Companion*, 100–105.

Price, Martin. "Conrad: Satire and Fiction." *Yearbook of Engl Stud* 14 (1984), 233–242.

Purdy, Dwight H. *Joseph Conrad's Bible*, 55–57, 96–101.

Ray, Martin. "Conrad, Nordau, and Other Degenerates: The Psychology of *The Secret Agent.*" *Conradiana* 16 (1984), 125–139.

Redwine, Bruce. "Deception and Intention in *The Secret Agent.*" *Conradiana* 11 (1979), 253–265.

Schultz, Robert. "*The Secret Agent*: Conrad's 'Perfect Detonator'." *Midwest Q* 22 (1981), 218–229.

Schwarz, Daniel R. *Conrad*, 157–176.

Sizemore, Christine W. " 'The Small Cardboard Box': A Symbol of the City and of Winnie Verloc in Conrad's *The Secret Agent.*" *Mod Fiction Stud* 24 (1978), 23–39.

Spensley, R. M. "Zola and Conrad: The Influence of *Pot-Bouille* on *The Secret Agent.*" *Conradiana* 11 (1979), 185–188.

Stine, Peter. "Conrad's Secrets in *The Secret Agent.*" *Conradiana* 13 (1981), 123–137.

Zaal, J. "The Modulation of Terror: The Oblique Elements in *The Secret Agent.*" *Univ of Cape Town Stud in Engl* 11 (1981), 29–42.

Under Western Eyes, 1911

Batchelor, John. *The Edwardian Novelists*, 74–81.

Brodie, Susan Lundvall. "Conrad's Feminine Perspective," 143–144.

Cobley, Evelyn. "Political Ambiguities in *Under Western Eyes* and *Doktor Faustus.*" *Canadian R of Compar Lit* 10 (1983), 377–388.

Cousineau, Thomas J. "The Ambiguity of Razumov's Confession in *Under Western Eyes.*" *Conradiana* 18 (1986), 27–40.

Darras, Jacques. *Joseph Conrad*, 121–137.

Fogel, Aaron. *Coercion to Speak*, 180–218.

Gillon, Adam. *Joseph Conrad*, 122–131.

Hervouet, Yves. "Conrad's Debt to French Authors in *Under Western Eyes.*" *Conradiana* 14 (1982), 113–123.

Hunter, Allan. *Joseph Conrad*, 220–239.

Inamdar, F. A. *Image and Symbol*, 160–174.

Jones, Michael P. *Conrad's Heroism*, 126–130.

Kermode, Frank. *The Art of Telling*, 139–153.

Kermode, Frank. "Secrets and Narrative Sequence." *Crit Inquiry* 7 (1980), 89–101.

La Bossière, Camille R. *Joseph Conrad*, 83–86.

La Bossière, Camille R. " 'A Matter of Feeling': A Note on Conrad's Comedy of Errors in *Under Western Eyes.*" *Thalia* 2:1–2 (1979), 35–37.

Land, Stephen K. *Paradox and Polarity*, 158–167.

Lewitter, L. R. "Conrad, Dostoyevsky," 659–663.

Moore, Gene M. "Chronotypes and Voices in *Under Western Eyes.*" *Conradiana* 18 (1986), 9–23.

Morf, Gustav. *The Polish Shades*, 184–193.

Moser, Thomas C. "Ford Madox Hueffer and *Under Western Eyes.*" *Conradiana* 15 (1983), 169–177.

Mursia, Ugo. *Scritti Conradiani*, 105–107.

Page, Norman. *A Conrad Companion*, 106–109.

Purdy, Dwight H. *Joseph Conrad's Bible*, 72–77, 111–118.

Purdy, Dwight H. " 'Peace that Passeth Understanding': The Professor's English Bible in *Under Western Eyes*." *Conradiana* 13 (1981), 83–92.

Schwarz, Daniel R. *Conrad*, 195–211.

Szittya, Penn R. "Metafiction: The Double Narration of *Under Western Eyes*." *ELH* 48 (1981), 817–838.

Tennant, Roger. *Joseph Conrad*, 178–180, 189–190.

Thornton, Lawrence. *Unbodied Hope*, 81–84.

Tsukui, Yoshimitsu. "Rinri no Fuzai: *Under Western Eyes*." *Oberon* (Tokyo) 18:1 (1979), 84–94.

White, Allon. *The Uses of Obscurity*, 109–110.

Victory, 1915

Batchelor, John. *The Edwardian Novelists*, 85–88.

Bonney, William W. *Thorns & Arabesques*, 175–194.

Brodie, Susan Lundvall. "Conrad's Feminine Perspective," 147–149.

Coates, Paul. *The Realist Fantasy*, 128–130.

Daleski, H. M. *Unities*, 99–110.

Daleski, H. M. "*Victory* and Patterns of Self-Division," in Ross C. Murfin, ed., *Conrad Revisited*, 107–123.

Geddes, Gary. *Conrad's Later Novels*, 41–80.

Gillon, Adam. "Conrad's *Victory* and Nabokov's *Lolita*: Imitations of Imitations." *Conradiana* 12 (1980), 51–70.

Gillon, Adam. *Joseph Conrad*, 144–152.

Haugaard, Janet Butler. "Conrad's *Victory*: Another Look at Axel Heyst." *Lit and Psych* 31:3 (1981), 33–46.

Inamdar, F. A. *Image and Symbol*, 138–159.

Jones, Michael P. *Conrad's Heroism*, 130–132.

Karl, Frederick R. "*Victory*: Its Origin and Development." *Conradiana* 15 (1983), 23–45.

La Bossière, Camille R. *Joseph Conrad*, 86–90.

Land, Stephen K. *Paradox and Polarity*, 192–207.

Madden, David. *A Primer*, 293–300.

Martin, Joseph. "Conrad and the Aesthetic Movement," 206–212.

Meyers, Jeffrey. "Lord Nelson and Conrad's *Victory*." *Papers on Lang and Lit* 19 (1983), 419–426.

Meyers, Jeffrey. "The Ranee of Sarawak and Conrad's *Victory*." *Conradiana* 18 (1986), 41–44.

Mursia, Ugo. *Scritti Conradiani*, 113–117.

Orlich, Rose. "The Psychology of Love in Conrad's *Victory*." *Conradiana* 13 (1981), 65–71.

Page, Norman. *A Conrad Companion*, 114–118.

Purdy, Dwight H. *Joseph Conrad's Bible*, 38–40, 44–46, 120–144.

Purdy, Dwight H. "Paul and the Pardoner in Conrad's *Victory*." *Texas Stud in Lit and Lang* 23 (1981), 197–211.

Raimond, Jean. "Jim et Axel Heyst," 77–95.

Raval, Suresh. "Conrad's *Victory*: Skepticism and Experience." *Nineteenth-Century Fiction* 34 (1980), 414–433.

Schwarz, Daniel R. *Conrad: The Later Fiction*, 60–80.

Shukla, Narain Prasad. "The Theme of Escape in Conrad's *Victory*." *J of the Dept of Engl* (Calcutta Univ) 17:1 (1981–82), 99–106.

Stammler, H. A. "Joseph Conrad's Novel *Victory* and Nikolaj Leskov's Chronicle *Soboriane*: Affinities and Resemblances." *Wiener Slavistisches Jahrbuch* 25 (1979), 125–139.

Tennant, Roger. *Joseph Conrad*, 206–208.

Viola, André. "La symbolique du Mandala dans *Victory* de Joseph Conrad." *Cahiers Victoriens et Edouardiens* 16 (1982), 105–124.

Watts, Cedric. "Reflections on *Victory*." *Conradiana* 15 (1983), 73–79.

Yoshida, Tetsuo. "Joseph Conrad and His 'Teutonic' Character," 8–21.

JOSEPH CONRAD AND FORD MADOX FORD

The Inheritors, 1901

Green Robert. *Ford Madox Ford*, 12–26.

Romance, 1903

Brebach, Raymond. *Joseph Conrad, Ford Madox Ford*, 1–112.

Moser, Thomas C. *The Life in the Fiction*, 47–51.

Snitow, Ann Barr. *Ford Madox Ford*, 48–58.

EDMUND COOPER

All Fools' Day, 1966

Wagar, W. Warren. "The Rebellion of Nature," in Eric S. Rabkin et al., eds., *The End of the World*, 157–158.

SUSAN COOPER

The Dark Is Rising, 1965–77

Swinfen, Ann. *In Defence*, 141–146.

MARIE CORELLI

Aurora Floyd, 1862

Stubbs, Patricia. *Women and Fiction*, 46–48.

Thelma, 1887

Christensen, Inger. "Ground Untrodden: Images of Norway in Nineteenth-Century English Fiction." *Edda*, 1985, 355–356.

The Treasure of Heaven, 1906

> Roberts, Helen. "Propaganda and Ideology in Women's Fiction," in Diana Laurenson, ed., *The Sociology*, 165–166.

DANIEL CORKERY

The Threshold of Quiet, 1917

> Gonzalez, Alexander G. "A Re-Evaluation of Daniel Corkery's Fiction." *Irish Univ R* 14 (1984), 198–201.

HELEN CRESSWELL

The Outlanders, 1970

> Swinfen, Ann. *In Defence*, 71–74.

GEORGE CROLY

Salathiel, 1827

> Tracy, Ann Blaisdell. *Patterns of Fear*, 276–280.

A. J. CRONIN

Beyond This Place, 1953

> Salwak, Dale. *A. J. Cronin*, 106–111.

The Citadel, 1937

> Salwak, Dale. *A. J. Cronin*, 60–71.

Grand Canary, 1933

> Salwak, Dale. *A. J. Cronin*, 38–49.

The Green Years, 1944

> Salwak, Dale. *A. J. Cronin*, 86–95.

Hatter's Castle, 1931

> Salwak, Dale. *A. J. Cronin*, 20–32.

The Judas Tree, 1961

> Salwak, Dale. *A. J. Cronin*, 121–125.

The Keys of the Kingdom, 1941

> Salwak, Dale. *A. J. Cronin*, 72–85.

The Northern Light, 1958

> Salwak, Dale. *A. J. Cronin*, 117–120.

A Pocketful of Rye, 1969

> Salwak, Dale. *A. J. Cronin*, 127–128.

Shannon's Way, 1948
  Salwak, Dale. *A. J. Cronin*, 95–101.
A Song of Sixpence, 1964
  Salwak, Dale. *A. J. Cronin*, 125–127.
The Spanish Gardener, 1950
  Salwak, Dale. *A. J. Cronin*, 102–106.
The Stars Look Down, 1935
  Salwak, Dale. *A. J. Cronin*, 50–59.
A Thing of Beauty, 1956
  Salwak, Dale. *A. J. Cronin*, 112–117.
Three Loves, 1932
  Salwak, Dale. *A. J. Cronin*, 32–37.

CHARLOTTE DACRE

The Libertine, 1807
  Tracy, Ann Blaisdell. *Patterns of Fear*, 181–184.
The Passions, 1811
  Tracy, Ann Blaisdell. *Patterns of Fear*, 120–121, 138–140, 173–175.
Zofloya, 1806
  Magnier, Mireille. "Zofloya et le moine," in *Autour de l'idée*, 227–231.
  Tracy, Ann Blaisdell. *Patterns of Fear*, 86–88, 109–110, 121–122, 166–
    168.

THOMAS DAY

The History of Sandford and Merton, 1783–89
  Scheuermann, Mona. *Social Protest*, 41–68.

DANIEL DEFOE

Captain Singleton, 1720
  Alkon, Paul K. *Defoe*, 33–36, 171–182.
  Alkon, Paul K. "The Odds Against Friday: Defoe, Bayes, and Inverse
    Probability," in Paula R. Backscheider, ed., *Probability*, 41–43.
  Birdsall, Virginia Ogden. *Defoe's Perpetual Seekers*, 50–72.
  Boardman, Michael M. *Defoe*, 100–108.
  Kenny, Virginia C. *The Country-House Ethos*, 84–88.
  Macey, Samuel L. "Mercenary Motivation in Defoe's Errant Protago-
    nists." *Dalhousie R* 64 (1984), 101–111.
  Macey, Samuel L. *Money and the Novel*, 36–38, 50–53.

Rogers, Pat. "Speaking with Compass: The Ground Covered in Two Works by Defoe." *Stud in the Liter Imagination* 15:2 (1982), 103–113.

Colonel Jacque, 1722

Alkon, Paul K. *Defoe*, 59–76, 94–102, 133–135.
Bell, Ian A. *Defoe's Fiction*, 80–82, 124–126.
Birdsall, Virginia Ogden. *Defoe's Perpetual Seekers*, 121–142.
Boardman, Michael M. *Defoe*, 135–138.
Dupas, Jean-Claude. "La Passion de l'or chez Defoe," in *La Passion dans le monde*, 61–71.
Hartveit, Lars. "A Chequer-Work of Formulae: A Reading of Defoe's *Colonel Jack*." *Engl Stud* 63 (1982), 122–133.
Kenny, Virginia C. *The Country-House Ethos*, 96–101.
Leinster-Mackay, D. P. *The Educational World*, 77–78.
Macey, Samuel L. "Mercenary Motivation," 101–111.
Macey, Samuel L. *Money and the Novel*, 42–43, 53–54, 58–61, 68–69.
Mohr, Hans-Ulrich. "Texte als funktionale Äquivalente: Mandevilles *Fable of the Bees* und Defoes *Col. Jack*," in Johann N. Schmidt, ed., *Of Private Vices*, 63–102.
Novak, Maximillian E. *Eighteenth-Century English Literature*, 61–62.
Pache, Walter. *Profit and Delight*, 182–201.
Williams, Ioan. *The Idea of the Novel*, 151–153.

Journal of the Plague Year, 1722

Alkon, Paul K. *Defoe*, 207–224, 248–250.
Bell, Ian A. *Defoe's Fiction*, 85–88.
Birdsall, Virginia Ogden. *Defoe's Perpetual Seekers*, 101–120.
Boardman, Michael M. *Defoe*, 82–96.
Burke, John J., Jr. "Observing the Observer in Historical Fictions by Defoe." *Philol Q* 61 (1982), 20–27.
McNeil, David. "*A Journal of the Plague Year*: Defoe and Claustrophobia." *Southern R* (Adelaide) 16 (1983), 374–384.
Novak, Maximillian E. *Eighteenth-Century English Literature*, 58–59.
Novak, Maximillian E. *Realism*, 64–68.
Novak, Maximillian E. "The Unmentionable and the Ineffable in Defoe's Fiction." *Stud in the Liter Imagination* 15:2 (1982), 99–102.
Pache, Walter. *Profit and Delight*, 162–181.
Rogers, Pat. *Eighteenth Century Encounters*, 151–166.
Stephanson, Raymond. " 'T's a speaking Sight': Imagery as Narrative Technique in Defoe's *A Journal of the Plague Year*." *Dalhousie R* 62 (1982–83), 680–691.

The Memoirs of a Cavalier, 1720

Backscheider, Paula R. "Defoe's Prodigal Sons." *Stud in the Liter Imagination* 15:2 (1982), 10–11, 16–18.
Boardman, Michael M. *Defoe*, 71–80.
Burke, John J., Jr. "Observing the Observer," 14–20.

Haywood, Ian. "Dreams in Pregnancy: The Opening of Defoe's *Memoirs of a Cavalier* and Smollett's *Roderick Random*." *Am Notes and Queries* 20 (1982), 71–73.
Merrett, Robert James. *Daniel Defoe's . . . Ideas*, 102–105.
Novak, Maximillian E. *Realism*, 48–65, 68–70.
Sokolyansky, Mark G. "The Diary and Its Role in the Genesis of the English Novel." *Zeitschrift für Anglistik und Amerikanistik* 28 (1980), 344–348.

Moll Flanders, 1722

Alkon, Paul K. *Defoe*, 50–52, 76–80, 110–132, 141–143.
Auerbach, Nina. *Romantic Imprisonment*, 59–66.
Bartmann, Susanna. "Defoe's Daydream: Becoming Moll Flanders." *Visible Lang* 14 (1980), 283–305.
Bell, Ian A. *Defoe's Fiction*, 115–153, 155–157, 164–167, 169–173, 176–179, 182–184.
Bell, Ian A. "Narrators and Narrative in Defoe." *Novel* 18 (1985), 158–165.
Birdsall, Virginia Ogden. *Defoe's Perpetual Seekers*, 73–100.
Blewett, David. "Changing Attitudes toward Marriage in the Time of Defoe: The Case of Moll Flanders." *Huntington Lib Q* 44 (1981), 85–88.
Boardman, Michael M. *Defoe*, 110–135.
Borck, Jim Springer. "One Woman's Prospects: Defoe's *Moll Flanders* and the Ironies in Restoration Self-Image." *Forum* (Houston) 17:1 (1979), 10–16.
Chaber, Lois A. "Matriarchal Mirror: Women and Capital in *Moll Flanders*." *PMLA* 97 (1982), 212–223.
Clews, Hetty. *The Only Teller*, 102–105.
Curtis, Laura A. *The Elusive Daniel Defoe*, 138–160.
Doody, Terrence. *Confession and Community*, 43–55.
Erickson, Robert A. "Moll's Fate: 'Mother Midnight' and *Moll Flanders*." *Stud in Philology* 76 (1979), 75–100.
Gaskin, Bob. "Moll Flanders: Consistency in a Psychopath." *Lamar J of the Hum* 6:1 (1980), 5–18.
Goetsch, Paul. "Defoes *Moll Flanders* und der Leser." *Germanisch-Romanische Monatsschrift* 30 (1980), 271–286.
Grossi, Marina. "*Moll Flanders* e il viaggio della conoscenza tra libertà e necessità." *Acme* 33 (1980), 407–425.
Hammond, Brean S. "Repentance: Solution to the Clash of Moralities in *Moll Flanders*." *Engl Stud* 61 (1980), 329–337.
Kenny, Virginia C. *The Country-House Ethos*, 90–96.
Konigsberg, Ira. *Narrative Technique*, 18–49.
Macey, Samuel L. "Mercenary Motivation," 101–111.
Macey, Samuel L. *Money and the Novel*, 32–35, 43–44, 55–56, 59–61, 69–71.
Maddox, James. "On Defoe's *Roxana*." *ELH* 51 (1984), 683–688.

Merrett, Robert James. *Daniel Defoe's . . . Ideas*, 83–85.

Miller, Nancy K. *The Heroine's Text*, 3–20.

Novak, Maximillian E. *Eighteenth-Century English Literature*, 60–61.

Novak, Maximillian E. *Realism*, 71–98.

Novak, Maximillian E. "The Unmentionable and the Ineffable," 95–97.

O'Neill, John H. "The Experience of Error: Ironic Entrapment in Augustan Narrative Satire." *Papers on Lang & Lit* 18 (1982), 278–284.

Pache, Walter. *Profit and Delight*, 142–161, 204–210.

Price, John Valdimir. "Patterns of Sexual Behaviour in Some Eighteenth-Century Novels," in Paul-Gabriel Boucé, ed., *Sexuality*, 164–165, 173.

Reed, Walter L. *An Exemplary History*, 95–116.

Reishman, John. "Joy in the Wasteland: Moll Flanders' Discovery of the Modern Landscape." *Tennessee Philol Bull* 19 (1982), 15.

Richetti, John. "The Family, Sex, and Marriage in Defoe's *Moll Flanders* and *Roxana*." *Stud in the Liter Imagination* 15:2 (1982), 23–35.

Riggan, William. *Picaros*, 61–64.

Rogers, Henry N., III. "The Two Faces of Moll." *J of Narrative Technique* 9 (1979), 117–124.

Rogers, Pat. "Classics and Chapbooks," in Isabel Rivers, ed., *Books and Their Readers*, 39–41.

Smith, Grahame. *The Novel & Society*, 49–66.

Soniller, Didier. "Utilisation et transformation par Defoe dans *Moll Flanders* du *Mariage trompeur* de Cervantès." *Revue de Littérature Comparée* 217 (1981), 30–38.

du Sorbier, Françoise. "Héroines de la marginalité: Moll Flanders et Roxana," in *La Marginalité*, 67–71, 76–77.

Spadaccini, Nicholas. "Daniel Defoe and the Spanish Picaresque Tradition: The Case of *Moll Flanders*." *Ideologies and Lit* 2:6 (1978), 10–26.

Taylor, Anne Robinson. *Male Novelists*, 29–37.

Vaid, Sudesh. *The Divided Mind*, 92–116, 137–139.

Weisgerber, Jean. *L'espace romanesque*, 73–91.

Wilson, Bruce L. " 'Sex and the Single Girl' in the Eighteenth Century: An Essay on Marriage and the Puritan Myth." *J of Women's Stud in Lit* 1 (1979), 195–219.

Robinson Crusoe, 1719

Alkon, Paul K. *Defoe*, 143–167, 187–199.

Alkon, Paul K. "The Odds Against Friday," 29–59.

Backscheider, Paula R. "Defoe's Prodigal Sons," 8–10, 11–16.

Baer, Joel H. " 'The Complicated Plot of Piracy': Aspects of English Criminal Law and the Image of the Pirate in Defoe." *Eighteenth Century* 23 (1982), 5–26.

Bell, Ian A. *Defoe's Fiction*, 3–8, 47–53, 73–115, 169–173, 176–179, 184–186.

Bell, Ian A. "Narrators and Narrative," 154–157.

Bignami, Marialuisa. "Defoe e Salgari," in Agostino Lombardo, ed., *Studi inglesi*, 373–383.

Birdsall, Virginia Ogden. *Defoe's Perpetual Seekers*, 24–49.

Birkner, Gerd. "Das Utopische in *Robinson Crusoe*." *Literatur in Wissenschaft und Unterricht* 14 (1981), 73–87.

Blackburn, Timothy C. "Friday's Religion: Its Nature and Importance in *Robinson Crusoe*." *Eighteenth-Century Stud* 18 (1985), 360–382.

Blewett, David. "The Retirement Myth in *Robinson Crusoe*: A Reconsideration." *Stud in the Liter Imagination* 15:2 (1982), 37–50.

Boardman, Michael M. *Defoe*, 10–15, 25–62.

Butler, Mary E. "The Effect of the Narrator's Rhetorical Uncertainty on the Fiction of *Robinson Crusoe*." *Stud in the Novel* 15 (1983), 77–88.

Cottom, Daniel. "*Robinson Crusoe*: The Empire's New Clothes." *Eighteenth Century* 22 (1981), 271–286.

Curtis, Laura A. *The Elusive Daniel Defoe*, 62–88.

Daly, Peter M. *Literature*, 174–176.

Ducroq, Jean. "Relations de voyages et récits symboliques: *Robinson* et *Gulliver*." *Stud on Voltaire and the Eighteenth Century* 215 (1982), 1–8.

Dupas, Jean-Claude. "La Passion de l'or," 61–71.

Erickson, Robert A. "Starting Over with *Robinson Crusoe*." *Stud in the Liter Imagination* 15:2 (1982), 51–73.

Gillespie, Gerald. "Erring and Wayfaring in Baroque Fiction: The World as Labyrinth and Garden." *Revue de Littérature Comparée* 231 (1984), 297–299.

Hardy, Barbara. *Forms of Feeling*, 22–24.

Hayden, Lucy K. "The Black Presence in Eighteenth-Century British Novels." *Coll Lang Assoc J* 24 (1981), 407–410.

Heims, Neil. "*Robinson Crusoe* and the Fear of Being Eaten." *Colby Lib Q* 19 (1983), 190–193.

Hunter, J. Paul. "Fielding and the Disappearance of Heroes," in Robert Folkenflik, ed., *The English Hero*, 130–131.

Kalb, Gertrud. "Travel Literature Reinterpreted: *Robinson Crusoe* und die religiöse Thematik der Reiseliteratur." *Anglia* 101 (1983), 407–420.

Kenny, Virginia C. *The Country-House Ethos*, 101–105.

Landow, George P. *Images of Crisis*, 103–108.

Leinster-Mackay, D. P. *The Educational World*, 9–11.

Macey, Samuel L. "Mercenary Motivation," 101–111.

Macey, Samuel L. *Money and the Novel*, 47–51.

Mackiewicz, Wolfgang. *Providenz und Adaption in Defoes "Robinson Crusoe."*

Maddox, James H., Jr. "Interpreter Crusoe." *ELH* 51 (1984), 33–50.

Merrett, Robert James. *Daniel Defoe's . . . Ideas*, 85–87.

Midgley, Mary. "The Vulnerable World and Its Claims on Us." *Georgia R* 39 (1985), 739–740, 753–754.

Moore, Catherine E. "Robinson and Xury and Inkle and Yarico." *Engl Lang Notes* 19 (1981), 24–29.

Moore, Catherine E. "Robinson Crusoe's Two Servants: The Measure of His Conversion," in Jack M. Durant and M. Thomas Hester, eds., *A Fair Day*, 111–118.

Neumeister, Sebastian. "Saint-John Perse et le mythe de Robinson." *Cahiers Saint-John Perse* 2 (1979), 61–76.

Novak, Maximillian E. *Eighteenth-Century English Literature*, 54–57.

Novak, Maximillian E. *Realism*, 23–46.

Novak, Maximillian E. "Sincerity, Delusion, and Character in the Fiction of Defoe and the 'Sincerity Crisis' of His Time," in Douglas Lane Patey and Timothy Keegan, eds., *Augustan Studies*, 116–121.

Novak, Maximillian E. "The Unmentionable and the Ineffable," 91–94.

O'Hanlon, Redmond. *Joseph Conrad*, 90–93.

Pache, Walter. *Profit and Delight*, 99–109, 117–141.

Parker, Gillian. "Crusoe Through the Looking-Glass," in Michael Klein and Gillian Parker, eds., *The English Novel*, 14–27.

Rogers, Pat. "Classics and Chapbooks," 28–39.

Rogers, Pat. *"Robinson Crusoe,"* 51–125.

Sankey, Margaret. "Meaning through Intertextuality: Isomorphism of Defoe's *Robinson Crusoe* and Tournier's *Vendredi ou les limbes du Pacifique*." *Australian J of French Stud* 18 (1981), 77–88.

Seidel, Michael. "Crusoe in Exile." *PMLA* 96 (1981), 363–374.

Sill, Geoffrey M. "Defoe's Two Versions of the Outlaw." *Engl Stud* 64 (1983), 125–126.

Smith, Grahame. *The Novel & Society*, 47–66.

Speck, W. A. *Society and Literature*, 62–64.

Thomsen, Christian W. *Menschenfresser*, 98–101.

White, Michael. "Reading and Rewriting: The Production of an Economic *Robinson Crusoe*." *Southern R* (Adelaide) 15 (1982), 115–139.

Zabus, Jeanne de Chantal. *"The Tempest* and *Robinson Crusoe*: A Structuralist 'Attention'." *Engl Stud in Canada* 9 (1983), 151–161.

Zeitz, Lisa Margaret. " 'A Checker-Work of Providence': The Shaping of *Robinson Crusoe*." *Engl Stud in Canada* 9 (1983), 255–269.

Zelnick, Stephen. "Ideology as Narrative: Critical Approaches to *Robinson Crusoe*." *Bucknell R* 27:1 (1982), 79–100.

Roxana, 1724

Alkon, Paul K. *Defoe*, 52–58, 136–142, 185–187.

Backscheider, Paula R. " 'I Died for Love': Esteem in Eighteenth-Century Novels by Women," in Mary Anne Schofield and Cecilia Macheski, eds., *Fetter'd or Free?*, 164–165.

Bell, Ian A. *Defoe's Fiction*, 153–189.

Bell, Ian A. "Narrators and Narrative," 165–172.

Bennett, James R. "Plot Repetition: Theme and Variation of Narrative Macro-Episodes." *Papers on Lang & Lit* 17 (1981), 411.

Birdsall, Virginia Ogden. *Defoe's Perpetual Seekers*, 143–170.

Boardman, Michael M. *Defoe*, 140–155.

Castle, Terry J. " 'Amy, who knew my Disease': A Psychosexual Pattern in Defoe's *Roxana*." *ELH* 46 (1979), 81–95.

Curtis, Laura A. *The Elusive Daniel Defoe*, 169–174.

Durant, David. "Roxana's Fictions." *Stud in the Novel* 13 (1981), 225–236.

Gasquet, Emile. "*Roxana* de Defoe: Tensions et ruptures," in *Hommage à Emile Gasquet*, 221–228.

Macey, Samuel L. "Mercenary Motivation," 101–111.

Macey, Samuel L. *Money and the Novel*, 32–36, 43–45, 47–48, 64–65, 79–80.

Maddox, James. "On Defoe's *Roxana*," 669–688.

Novak, Maximillian E. *Eighteenth-Century English Literature*, 62–63.

Novak, Maximillian E. *Realism*, 99–120.

Novak, Maximillian E. "The Unmentionable and the Ineffable," 85–91, 97–99.

Pache, Walter. *Profit and Delight*, 202–220.

Richetti, John. "The Family, Sex, and Marriage," 23–35.

Sloman, Judith. "The Time Scheme of Defoe's *Roxana*." *Engl Stud in Canada* 5 (1979), 406–418.

du Sorbier, Françoise. "Héroines de la marginalité, 71–77.

Stephanson, Raymond. "Defoe's 'Malade Imaginaire': The Historical Foundation of Mental Illness in *Roxana*." *Huntington Lib Q* 45 (1982), 99–115.

Stephanson, Raymond. "Defoe's *Roxana*: The Unresolved Experiment in Characterization." *Stud in the Novel* 12 (1980), 279–288.

Taylor, Anne Robinson. *Male Novelists*, 29–40, 44–47, 50–52.

Vaid, Sudesh. *The Divided Mind*, 116–139.

E. M. DELAFIELD

The Chip and the Block, 1925

McCullen, Maurice L. *E. M. Delafield*, 32–33.

Consequences, 1919

Beauman, Nicola. *A Very Great Profession*, 46–49.

McCullen, Maurice L. *E. M. Delafield*, 21–23.

Faster! Faster!, 1936

McCullen, Maurice L. *E. M. Delafield*, 86–87.

Gay Life, 1933

McCullen, Maurice L. *E. M. Delafield*, 84–86.

Jill, 1926

McCullen, Maurice L. *E. M. Delafield*, 33–35.

Late and Soon, 1943

McCullen, Maurice L. *E. M. Delafield*, 107–114.

No One Now Will Know, 1941

McCullen, Maurice L. *E. M. Delafield*, 100–106.

Nothing Is Safe, 1937

McCullen, Maurice L. *E. M. Delafield*, 87–88.

Thank Heaven Fasting, 1932

McCullen, Maurice L. *E. M. Delafield*, 79–84.

The Way Things Are, 1927

McCullen, Maurice L. *E. M. Delafield*, 35–40.

WALTER DE LA MARE

The Return, 1910

Bonnerot, Luce. "Walter de la Mare ou la transgression fantastique: Etude de deux textes." *Caliban* 16 (1979), 19–22.

ETHEL M. DELL

The Way of an Eagle, 1912

Beauman, Nicola. *A Very Great Profession*, 178–183.

THOMAS DELONEY

The Gentle Craft, c. 1598

Wright, Eugene P. *Thomas Deloney*, 86–117.

Jack of Newbury, 1597

Jordan, Constance. "The 'Art of Clothing': Role-Playing in Deloney's Fiction." *Engl Liter Renaissance* 11 (1981), 183–193.
Loretelli, Rosamaria. "Thomas Deloney e il *Novel*: Una morfogenesi mancata," in Agostino Lombardo, ed., *Studi inglesi*, 53–75.
Wright, Eugene P. *Thomas Deloney*, 59–74.

Thomas of Reading, 1597

Domnarski, William. "A Different Thomas Deloney: *Thomas of Reading* Reconsidered." *Renaissance and Reformation* 6 (1982), 197–202.
Jordan, Constance. "The 'Art of Clothing'," 183–193.
Wright, Eugene P. *Thomas Deloney*, 74–86.

NIGEL DENNIS

Cards of Identity, 1955

Saltzman, Arthur. "*Cards of Identity* and the Case of the Sundered Self." *Stud in Contemp Satire* 9 (1982), 9–16.

THOMAS DE QUINCEY

Klosterheim, 1832

Gordon, Jan B. "De Quincey as Gothic Parasite: The Dynamic of Supplementarity," in Robert Lance Snyder, ed., *Thomas De Quincey*, 256–260.

Lindop, Grevel. "Innocence and Revenge: The Problem of De Quincey's Fiction," in Robert Lance Snyder, ed., *Thomas De Quincey*, 228–231.

Snyder, Robert Lance. "*Klosterheim*: De Quincey's Gothic Masque." *Res Stud* 49 (1981), 129–142.

CHARLES DICKENS

Barnaby Rudge, 1841

Adrian, Arthur A. *Dickens*, 96–99.

Craig, David. "The Crowd in Dickens," in Robert Giddings, ed., *The Changing World*, 75–77.

Friedberg, Joan B. "Alienation and Integration in *Barnaby Rudge*." *Dickens Stud Newsl* 11 (1980), 11–15.

Gilmour, Robin. *The Idea of the Gentleman*, 20–21.

Grylls, David. *Guardians and Angels*, 137–139.

Hardy, Barbara. *Charles Dickens*, 48–50.

Hollington, Michael. *Dickens and the Grotesque*, 100–110.

Leech, Geoffrey N., and Michael H. Short. *Style in Fiction*, 226–227.

McGowan, John P. "Mystery and History in *Barnaby Rudge*." *Dickens Stud Annual* 9 (1981), 33–48.

McMaster, Juliet. " 'Better to be Silly': From Vision to Reality in *Barnaby Rudge*." *Dickens Stud Annual* 13 (1984), 1–16.

Magnet, Myron. *Dickens and the Social Order*, 51–171.

Middlebro', Tom. "Burke, Dickens and the Gordon Riots." *Hum Assoc R* 31 (1980), 87–95.

Perkins, Donald. *Charles Dickens*, 74–82.

Rice, Thomas J. "The Politics of *Barnaby Rudge*," in Robert Giddings, ed., *The Changing World*, 51–68.

Rosenberg, Brian. "Physical Opposition in *Barnaby Rudge*." *Victorian Newsl* 67 (1985), 21–22.

Sadoff, Dianne F. "The Dead Father: *Barnaby Rudge*, *David Copperfield*, and *Great Expectations*." *Papers on Lang & Lit* 18 (1982), 43–48.

Sadoff, Dianne F. *Monsters of Affection*, 27–30.

Schwarzbach, F. S. *Dickens*, 77–79.

Sroka, Kenneth M. "Echoes of *Old Mortality* in Dickens and Katherine Anne Porter," in J. H. Alexander and David Hewitt, eds., *Scott and His Influence*, 351–358.

Walder, Dennis. *Dickens and Religion*, 91–106.

Weiss, Barbara. "The Dilemma of Happily Ever After: Marriage and the Victorian Novel," in Anne C. Hargrove and Maurine Magliocco, eds., *Portraits of Marriage*, 68–69.

Zelicovici, Dvora. "Grip the Raven: A Rehabilitation." *Dickensian* 77 (1981), 151–153.

Bleak House, 1853

Adrian, Arthur A. *Dickens*, 123–125.

Altick, Richard D. "*Bleak House*: The Reach of Chapter One." *Dickens Stud Annual* 8 (1980), 73–99.

Bassus, Jean-Marie. "Dickens' Spacemanship in *Bleak House*." *Cahiers Victoriens et Edouardiens* 20 (1984), 5–16.

Beckwith, Marc. "Catabasis in *Bleak House*: Bucket as Sibyl." *Dickens Q* 1 (1984), 2–6.

Beer, Gillian. "Origins and Oblivion in Victorian Narrative," in Ruth Bernard Yeazell, ed., *Sex*, 77–79.

Belmont, Anthony M., Jr. "Qualitative Progression and the Dual Narrative in Dickens' *Bleak House*." *Publs of the Arkansas Philol Assoc* 7:2 (1981), 1–8.

Blain, Virginia. "Double Vision and the Double Standard in *Bleak House*: A Feminist Perspective." *Lit and Hist* 11 (1985), 31–43.

Bolton, H. Philip. "*Bleak House* and the Playhouse." *Dickens Stud Annual* 12 (1983), 81–90.

Briad, Edith. "Hortense, Rigaud/Lagnier/Blandois and Co.: Dickens's French Characters," in Sylvère Monod, ed., *Charles Dickens*, 25–34.

Brooks, Chris. *Signs for the Times*, 53–63.

Brown, James M. *Dickens*, 57–84.

Bystrom, Valerie Ann. "The Abyss of Sympathy: The Conventions of Pathos in Eighteenth and Nineteenth Century British Novels." *Criticism* 23 (1981), 220–222, 226–228.

Chase, Karen. *Eros & Psyche*, 92–135.

Chaudhuri, Brahma. "The Interpolated Chapter in *Bleak House*." *Dickensian* 81 (1985), 103–104.

Chaudhuri, Brahma. "Speculation about the Plot of *Bleak House*." *Dickens Q* 1 (1984), 57.

Chevalier, Jean-Louis. "Le Mariage d'Esther." *Cahiers Victoriens et Edouardiens* 20 (1984), 29–38.

Conlon, Raymond. "*Bleak House*'s Miss Barbary: A Psychological Miniature." *Dickens Stud Newsl* 14 (1983), 90–92.

Connor, Steven. *Charles Dickens*, 59–88.

Conrow, Margaret. "Wife-Abuse in Dickens's Fiction." *Dickens Stud Newsl* 14 (1983), 45–47.

Cox, Don Richard. "The Birds of *Bleak House*." *Dickens Stud Newsl* 11 (1980), 6–11.

Creevy, Patrick J. "In Time and Out: The Tempo of Life in *Bleak House*." *Dickens Stud Annual* 12 (1983), 63–79.

Daleski, H. M. "Dickens and the Proleptic Uncanny." *Dickens Stud Annual* 13 (1984), 202–204.

Dusseau, John L. "The Bleak House in Charles Dickens." *Sewanee R* 92 (1984), 592–594.

Eggert, Paul. "The Real Esther Summerson." *Dickens Stud Newsl* 11 (1980), 74–81.

Eldredge, Patricia R. "The Lost Self of Esther Summerson: A Horneyan Interpretation of *Bleak House*." *Liter R* 24 (1981), 252–278.

Erickson, Donald H. "*Bleak House* and Victorian Art and Illustration: Charles Dickens's Visual Narrative Style." *J of Narrative Technique* 13 (1983), 31–43.

Fenstermaker, John J. "Language Abuse in *Bleak House*: The First Monthly Installment," in James R. Kincaid and Albert J. Kuhn, eds., *Victorian Literature*, 240–256.

Fiérobe, Claude. "Les Inventaires de *Bleak House*." *Cahiers Victoriens et Edouardiens* 20 (1984), 19–27.

Foley, Brian. "Dickens Revised: 'Bartleby' and *Bleak House*." *Essays in Lit* (Macomb) 12 (1985), 241–248.

Ford, George H. "Light in Darkness: Gas, Oil, and Tallow in Dickens's *Bleak House*," in Samuel I. Mintz et al., eds., *From Smollett to James*, 183–210.

Forsyth, Neil. "Wonderful Chains: Dickens and Coincidence." *Mod Philology* 83 (1985), 158–161.

Frazee, John P. "The Character of Esther and the Narrative Structure of *Bleak House*." *Stud in the Novel* 17 (1985), 227–238.

Garrett, Peter K. *The Victorian Multiplot Novel*, 59–71.

Georgas, Marilyn. "Dickens, Defoe, the Devil and the Dedlocks: The Faust Motif in *Bleak House*." *Dickens Stud Annual* 10 (1982), 23–42.

Gold, Joel J. "Mrs Jellyby: Dickens's Inside Joke." *Dickensian* 79 (1983), 35–38.

Goldfarb, Russell M. "John Jarndyce of *Bleak House*." *Stud in the Novel* 12 (1980), 144–151.

Grant, Allan. *A Preface*, 115–118, 128–130.

Hanzo, Thomas A. "Paternity and the Subject in *Bleak House*," in Robert Con Davis, ed., *The Fictional Father*, 27–47.

Hardy, Barbara. *Charles Dickens*, 70–74.

Hardy, Barbara. *Forms of Feeling*, 54–56, 73–76.

Herbert, Christopher. "The Occult in *Bleak House*." *Novel* 17 (1984), 101–115.

Hollington, Michael. *Dickens and the Grotesque*, 199–205.

Hornback, Bert G. *'The Hero'*, 100–102.

Hornback, Bert G. "The Other Portion of *Bleak House*," in Robert Giddings, ed., *The Changing World*, 180–195.

Horton, Susan R. *The Reader*, 33–34, 93–95.

Ikeler, A. Abott. "The Philanthropic Sham: Dickens' Corrective Method in *Bleak House*." *Coll Lang Assoc J* 24 (1981), 497–512.

Irwin, Michael. *Picturing*, 71–73, 97–99.

Irwin, Michael. "Readings of Melodrama," in Ian Gregor, ed., *Reading the Victorian Novel*, 16–19.

Jacobs, Naomi. "Of Grace and Grease: Two Oily Clergymen." *Dickens Stud Newsl* 12 (1981), 47–48.

Kearns, Michael S. " 'But I Cried Very Much': Esther Summerson as Narrator." *Dickens Q* 1 (1984), 121–128.

Kennedy, Valerie. "*Bleak House*: More Trouble with Esther?" *J of Women's Stud in Lit* 1 (1979), 330–347.

Kucich, John. *Excess and Restraint*, 75–87, 94–99, 129–131, 145–152.

Larson, Janet. "Biblical Reading in the Later Dickens: The Book of Job According to *Bleak House*." *Dickens Stud Annual* 13 (1984), 35–72.

Larson, Janet L. "The Battle of Biblical Books in Esther's Narrative." *Nineteenth-Century Fiction* 38 (1983), 131–160.

Lecker, Barbara. "The Split Characters of Charles Dickens." *Stud in Engl Lit, 1500–1900* 19 (1979), 692–693. [Also in *Engl Stud* 62 (1981), 429–441.]

Leech, Geoffrey N., and Michael H. Short. *Style in Fiction*, 63–64, 169–170, 327–329.

Lesser, Wendy. "From Dickens to Conrad: A Sentimental Journey." *ELH* 52 (1985), 199–200.

Levy, Diane Wolfe. "Dickens' *Bleak House*." *Explicator* 38:3 (1980), 40–42.

McCusker, Jane A. "The Games Esther Plays: Chapter Three of *Bleak House*." *Dickensian* 81 (1985), 163–174.

McMaster, Juliet and Rowland. *The Novel*, 42–44, 60–63.

Mason, Philip. *The English Gentleman*, 123–125.

Meckier, Jerome. "Hidden Rivalries in Victorian Fiction: The Case of the Two Esthers," in Robert Giddings, ed., *The Changing World*, 219–237.

Mendez, Charlotte Walker. "Scriveners Forlorn: Dickens's Nemo and Melville's Bartleby." *Dickens Stud Newsl* 11 (1980), 33–37.

Metz, Nancy Aycock. "Narrative Gesturing in *Bleak House*." *Dickensian* 77 (1981), 13–22.

Milligan, Ian. *The Novel in English*, 102–104.

Murfin, Ross C. "The Art of Representation: Collins' *The Moonstone* and Dickens' Example." *ELH* 49 (1982), 668–671.

Neary, John M. "*Bleak House*: From Phenomena to Story." *Massachusetts Stud in Engl* 9:4 (1984), 13–30.

Nelson, Harland S. *Charles Dickens*, 145–189.

Newsom, Robert. *Dickens*, 11–151.

Perkins, Donald. *Charles Dickens*, 18–19, 26–28, 48–53, 87–88, 94–95, 97–99.

Peterson, Audrey. *Victorian Masters*, 88–98.

Ragussis, Michael. "The Ghostly Signs of *Bleak House*." *Nineteenth-Century Fiction* 34 (1979), 253–280.

Reed, John R. "Freedom, Fate, and the Future in *Bleak House*." *CLIO* 8 (1979), 175–191.

Riffaterre, Michael. "Intertextual Representation: On Mimesis as Interpretive Discourse." *Crit Inquiry* 11 (1984), 154–159.

Rives, Françoise. "*Bleak House* roman picaresque?" *Caliban* 20 (1983), 51–60.

Rosner, Mary. "Drizzle, Darkness, and Dinosaurs: Defining the World of *Bleak House*." *Dickens Stud Newsl* 13 (1982), 99–108.

Qualls, Barry V. *The Secular Pilgrims*, 112–121.

Reynolds, Margaret. " 'In Chancery' Again: Dickens and Prize-Fighting." *Dickens Stud Newsl* 14 (1983), 48–50.

Sadoff, Dianne F. *Monsters of Affection*, 14–17.

Schwarzbach, F. S. *Dickens*, 116–142.

Schwarzbach, F. S. "The Fever of *Bleak House*." *Engl Lang Notes* 20:3–4 (1983), 21–27.

Scott, P. J. M. *Reality and Comic Confidence*, 61–121.

Shand, G. B. "Middleton's *Phoenix* and the Opening of *Bleak House*." *Dickensian* 78 (1982), 93–95.

Senf, Carol A. "*Bleak House*: Dickens, Esther, and the Androgynous Mind." *Victorian Newsl* 64 (1983), 21–27.

Senf, Carol A. "*Bleak House*: The Need for Social Exorcism." *Dickens Stud Newsl* 11 (1980), 70–73.

Simpson, David. *Fetishism and Imagination*, 56–59.

Smithers, David Waldron. *Dickens's Doctors*, 58–65.

Stewart, Garrett. "The New Mortality of *Bleak House*." *ELH* 45 (1978), 443–485.

Stewart, Garrett. "The Secret Life of Death in Dickens." *Dickens Stud Annual* 11 (1983), 197–199.

Stokes, Edward. *Hawthorne's Influence*, 28–59.

Stone, Donald D. *The Romantic Impulse*, 266–271.

Tarantelli, Carole Beebe. "Nella città industriale: il personaggio è l'abbandono alla morte." *Calibano* 3 (1979), 38–67.

Taylor, Anne Robinson. *Male Novelists*, 129–151.

Tsomondo, Thorell. " 'A Habitable Doll's House': *Beginning* in *Bleak House*." *Victorian Newsl* 62 (1982), 3–7.

Vargish, Thomas. *The Providential Aesthetic*, 95–97, 113–115, 130–132.

Walder, Dennis. *Dickens and Religion*, 153–170.

Ward, John C. " 'The Virtues of the Mothers': Powerful Women in *Bleak House*." *Dickens Stud Newsl* 14 (1983), 37–42.

Waters, Catherine. "The Dilettante and the Artist in Dickens' *Bleak House*." *Southern R* (Adelaide) 17 (1984), 232–248.

Welsh, Alexander. "Blackmail Studies in *Martin Chuzzlewit* and *Bleak House*." *Dickens Stud Annual* 11 (1983), 29–34.

Wilson, Philip James. "Notice on the Megalosaurus or Great Fossil Lizard of Stonefield: Observations on the Beginning of *Bleak House*." *Dickensian* 78 (1982), 97–103.

Woods, Irene E. "On the Significance of Jarndyce and Jarndyce." *Dickens Q* 1 (1984), 81–86.

Young, Saundra K. "Uneasy Relations: Possibilities for Eloquence in *Bleak House*." *Dickens Stud Annual* 9 (1981), 67–83.

The Chimes, 1844

Hollington, Michael. *Dickens and the Grotesque*, 158–160.

Kurata, Marilyn J. "*The Chimes*: Dickens's Re-Casting of 'Young Goodman Brown'." *Am Notes and Queries* 22:1–2 (1983), 10–12.

Kurata, Marilyn J. "Fantasy and Realism: A Defense of *The Chimes*." *Dickens Stud Annual* 13 (1984), 19–32.

Perkins, Donald. *Charles Dickens*, 25–26.

Prickett, Stephen. *Victorian Fantasy*, 62–64.

Shelden, Michael. "Dickens, *The Chimes*, and the Anti-Corn Law League." *Victorian Stud* 25 (1982), 329–353.

A Christmas Carol, 1843

Anastaplo, George. "Notes from Charles Dickens's *Christmas Carol*." *Interpretation: J of Political Philos* 7:1 (1978), 52–73.

Carlisle, Janice. *The Sense of an Audience*, 46–49.

Daleski, H. M. "Dickens and the Proleptic Uncanny," 197–198.

Hardy, Barbara. *Charles Dickens*, 55–58.

Hollington, Michael. *Dickens and the Grotesque*, 156–158.

Keyser, Lester J. "A Scrooge for All Seasons," in Michael Klein and Gillian Parker, eds., *The English Novel*, 121–131.

Perkins, Donald. *Charles Dickens*, 106–122.

Prickett, Stephen. *Victorian Fantasy*, 54–64.

Walder, Dennis. *Dickens and Religion*, 120–124.

David Copperfield, 1850

Adrian, Arthur A. *Dickens*, 81–86, 109–114.

Auerbach, Nina. *Woman and the Demon*, 84–88.

Baumgarten, Murray. "Writing and *David Copperfield*." *Dickens Stud Annual* 14 (1985), 39–57.

Berman, Ronald. "The Innocent Observer." *Children's Lit* 9 (1981), 40–50.

Bodenheimer, Rosemarie. "Dickens and the Art of Pastoral." *Centennial R* 23 (1979), 458–461.

Brooks, Chris. *Signs for the Times*, 40–52.

Buckley, Jerome H. "The Identity of David Copperfield," in James R. Kincaid and Albert J. Kuhn, eds., *Victorian Literature*, 225–237.

Cameron, J. M. "Dickens and the Angels." *Univ of Toronto Q* 50 (1980/81), 170–171.

Carabine, Keith. "Reading *David Copperfield*," in Ian Gregor, ed., *Reading the Victorian Novel*, 150–165.

Carr, Jean Ferguson. "David Copperfield's 'Written Memory'," in Richard J. Dunn, ed., *Approaches*, 88–94.

Clark, Beverly Lyon. "*David Copperfield* in a Children's Literature Course," in Richard J. Dunn, ed., *Approaches*, 49–53.

Crick, Brian. " 'Mr. Peggoty's Dream Comes True': Fathers and Husbands; Wives and Daughters." *Univ of Toronto Q* 54 (1984), 38–55.

Dawson, Carl. *Victorian Noon*, 123–143.

DeGraaff, Robert M. "Self-Articulating Characters in *David Copperfield*." *J of Narrative Technique* 14 (1984), 214–221.

Dobrinsky, Joseph. "Tommy Traddles as a Dickensian Hero?" *Cahiers Victoriens et Edouardiens* 20 (1984), 55–63.

Dusseau, John L. "The Bleak House in Charles Dickens," 588–592.

Dutt, Dattatreya. "Father, Mother, and Son: The Archetypal Structure of *David Copperfield*." *CIEFL Bull* 16:1 (1980), 41–49.

Dutton, A. R. "Jonson and David Copperfield: Dickens and Bartholomew Fair." *Engl Lang Notes* 16 (1979), 227–232.

Eigner, Edwin M. "*David Copperfield* and the Benevolent Spirit." *Dickens Stud Annual* 14 (1985), 1–13.

Eigner, Edwin M. "The Lunatic at the Window: Magic Casements of *David Copperfield*." *Dickens Q* 2 (1985), 18–21.

Forsyth, Neil. "Wonderful Chains," 156–158.

Friedman, Stanley. "*David Copperfield*: An Introduction to a Dickens Course," in Richard J. Dunn, ed., *Approaches*, 81–87.

Garson, Marjoric. "Inclusion and Exclusion: The Morif of the Copyist in *David Copperfield*." *Etudes Anglaises* 36 (1983), 401–413.

Gilmour, Robin. *The Idea of the Gentleman*, 112–118.

Grant, Allan. *A Preface*, 109–114.

Grill, Neil. "Home and Homeless in *David Copperfield*." *Dickens Stud Newsl* 11 (1980), 108–111.

Hanna, Susan J. "*Copperfield* on Trial: Meeting the Opposition," in Richard J. Dunn, ed., *Approaches*, 33–39.

Hardy, Barbara. *Charles Dickens*, 63–69.

Hennelly, Mark M., Jr. "*David Copperfield*: 'The Theme of This Incomprehensible Conundrum Was the Moon'." *Stud in the Novel* 10 (1978), 375–396.

Higbie, Robert. *Character & Structure*, 129–162.

Hirsch, Gordon D. "A Psychoanalytic Rereading of *David Copperfield*." *Victorian Newsl* 58 (1980), 1–5. [Also in Wendell Stacy Johnson, ed., *Charles Dickens*, 83–93.]

Holland, J. Gill. "*David Copperfield*: Parallel Reading for Undergraduates," in Richard J. Dunn, ed., *Approaches*, 102–106.

Hollington, Michael. *Dickens and the Grotesque*, 179–187.

Hornback, Bert G. *'The Hero'*, 1–85, 101–104.

Horton, Susan R. "Making Sense of *David Copperfield*," in Richard J. Dunn, ed., *Approaches*, 131–140.

Irwin, Michael. *Picturing*, 64–66, 76–81, 102–106, 118–122.

Irwin, Michael. "Readings of Melodrama," 21–24.

Jackson, Arlene M. "Agnes Wickfield and the Church Leitmotif in *David Copperfield*." *Dickens Stud Annual* 9 (1981), 53–65.

Jacobson, Wendy S. "Brothers and Sisters in *David Copperfield*." *Engl Stud in Africa* 25 (1982), 11–27.

Jefferson, Ann. *The Nouveau Roman*, 169–172.

Jordan, John O. "The Social Sub-text of *David Copperfield*." *Dickens Stud Annual* 14 (1985), 61–90.

Joseph, Gerhard. "Fathers and Sons: *David Copperfield* in a Course on Victorian Autobiographical Prose," in Richard J. Dunn, ed., *Approaches*, 71–80.

Keyte, J. M., and M. L. Robinson. "Mr Dick the Schizophrenic." *Dickensian* 76 (1980), 37–39.

Kinkead-Weekes, Mark. "The Voicing of Fictions," in Ian Gregor, ed., *Reading the Victorian Novel*, 169–176.

Kishtainy, Khalid. *The Prostitute*, 129–130.

Konick, Willis. "The Chords of Memory: Teaching *David Copperfield* in the Context of World Literature," in Richard J. Dunn, ed., *Approaches*, 61–70.

Kort, Melissa Sue. " 'I have taken with fear and trembling to authorship': *David Copperfield* in the Composition Classroom," in Richard J. Dunn, ed., *Approaches*, 95–101.

Lankford, William T. " 'The Deep of Time': Narrative Order in *David Copperfield*." *ELH* 46 (1979), 452–466.

Leech, Geoffrey N., and Michael H. Short. *Style in Fiction*, 338–339.

Leitch, Thomas M. "Dickens' Problem Child," in Richard J. Dunn, ed., *Approaches*, 40–48.

Luhr, William. "Dickens's Narrative, Hollywood's Vignette," in Michael Klein and Gillian Parker, eds., *The English Novel*, 132–142.

Lund, Michael. "Testing by Installments the 'Undisciplined Heart' of *David Copperfield*'s Reader," in Richard J. Dunn, ed., *Approaches*, 114–121.

Lutman, Stephen. "Reading Illustrations: Pictures in *David Copperfield*," in Ian Gregor, ed., *Reading the Victorian Novel*, 196–223.

McGowan, John P. "*David Copperfield*: The Trial of Realism." *Nineteenth-Century Fiction* 34 (1979), 1–19.

MacKay, Carol Hanbery. "Surrealization and the Redoubled Self: Fantasy in *David Copperfield* and *Pendennis*." *Dickens Stud Annual* 14 (1985), 241–261.

MacPike, Loralee. *Dostoevsky's Dickens*, 121–194.

Mafud Haye, Consuelo. "David Copperfield, el nino favorito de Charles Dickens." *Nueva Revista del Pacifico* 13–14 (1979), 42–51.

Manning, Sylvia. "David Copperfield and Scheherazada: The Necessity of Narrative." *Stud in the Novel* 14 (1982), 327–335.

Miller, D. A. "Secret Subjects, Open Secrets." *Dickens Stud Annual* 14 (1985), 17–37.

Miller, Michael G. "Murdstone, Heep, and the Structure of *David Copperfield*." *Dickens Stud Newsl* 11 (1980), 65–70.

Patten, Robert L. "Autobiography into Autobiography: The Evolution of *David Copperfield*," in George P. Landow, ed., *Approaches*, 269–291.

Pattison, Robert. *The Child Figure*, 122–127.

Perkins, Donald. *Charles Dickens*, 31–32, 38–39, 60–62.

Reibetanz, J. M. "Villain, Victim and Hero: Structure and Theme in *David Copperfield*." *Dalhousie R* 59 (1979), 321–335.

Rodolff, Rebecca. "What David Copperfield Remembers of Dora's Death." *Dickensian* 77 (1981), 32–39.

Sadoff, Dianne F. "The Dead Father," 48–50.

Sadoff, Dianne F. "*Locus Suspectus*: Narrative, Castration, and the Uncanny." *Dickens Stud Annual* 13 (1984), 211–212, 214–215.

Sadoff, Dianne F. *Monsters of Affection*, 38–46.

Sadoff, Dianne F. "Teaching *David Copperfield*: Language, Psychoanalysis, and Feminism," in Richard J. Dunn, ed., *Approaches*, 122–130.

Scanlan, Margaret. "An Introduction to Fiction: *David Copperfield* in the Genre Course," in Richard J. Dunn, ed., *Approaches*, 54–60.

Seehase, Georg. "Eine 'englische' Geschichte des jungen Menschen: Zur literaturgeschichtlichen Stellung des Romans *David Copperfield* (1849) von Charles Dickens." *Zeitschrift für Anglistik und Amerikanistik* 32 (1984), 220–229.

Sell, Roger D. "Projection Characters in *David Copperfield*." *Studia Neophilologica* 55 (1983), 19–29.

Shelston, Alan. "Past and Present in *David Copperfield*." *Crit Q* 27:3 (1985), 17–32.

Sheridan, Daniel. "*David Copperfield*: Different Readers, Different Approaches," in Richard J. Dunn, ed., *Approaches*, 23–32.

Smithers, David Waldron. *Dickens's Doctors*, 52–57.

Steig, Michael. "*David Copperfield* and Shared Reader Response," in Richard J. Dunn, ed., *Approaches*, 141–148.

Stewart, Garrett. "The Secret Life of Death," 192–195, 199–206.

Stone, Donald D. *The Romantic Impulse*, 261–266.

Stone, Harry. "What's in a Name: Fantasy and Calculation in Dickens." *Dickens Stud Annual* 14 (1985), 194–197.

Sullivan, Patricia Rosalind. "A Student Response to the Genuine Fear and Pain in *Mort à crédit* and *David Copperfield*." *Recovering Lit* 7:2–3 (1979), 42–52.

Talbot, Norman. "The Naming and the Namers of the Hero: A Study in *David Copperfield*." *Southern R* (Adelaide) 11 (1978), 267–282.

Taylor, Anne Robinson. *Male Novelists*, 126–128, 138–140.

Thomas, Deborah A. "Dickens and Indigestion: The Deadly Dinners of the Rich." *Dickens Stud Newsl* 14 (1983), 7–11.

Thurin, Susan Schoenbauer. "The Relationship between Dora and Agnes." *Dickens Stud Newsl* 12 (1981), 103–108.

Tschumi, Raymond. "Dickens and Switzerland." *Engl Stud* 60 (1979), 444–445.

Vargish, Thomas. *The Providential Aesthetic*, 127–130.

Walder, Dennis. *Dickens and Religion*, 144–153.

Weinstein, Philip M. *The Semantics of Desire*, 22–47.

Welsh, Alexander. "Writing and Copying in the Age of Steam," in James R. Kincaid and Albert J. Kuhn, eds., *Victorian Literature*, 43–45.

Wheeler, Michael. *English Fiction*, 75–78.

Wijesinha, Rajiva. *The Androgynous Trollope*, 150–152.

Williams, Merryn. *Women in the English Novel*, 81–84.

Worth, George J. "*Multum in Parvo*: The Ninth Chapter of *David Copperfield*," in Richard J. Dunn, ed., *Approaches*, 107–113.

Dombey and Son, 1848

Adrian, Arthur A. *Dickens*, 99–105, 120–122.

Auerbach, Nina. *Romantic Imprisonment*, 67–129.

Box, Terry J. "Young Paul Dombey: A Case of Progeria." *RE: Artes Liberales* 9:2 (1983), 17–21.

Brooks, Chris. *Signs for the Times*, 36–40.

Carlisle, Janice. *The Sense of an Audience*, 16–18, 64–95.

Clark, Robert. "Riddling the Family Firm: The Sexual Economy in *Dombey and Son*." *ELH* 51 (1984), 69–82.

Collins, Philip. "Dickens and Industrialism." *Stud in Engl Lit, 1500–1900* 20 (1980), 667–669.

Connor, Steven. *Charles Dickens*, 22–55.

Eagleton, Mary, and David Pierce. *Attitudes to Class*, 41–42, 73–75.

Fiérobe, Claude. "Le Train, image de l'ailleurs, dans quelques oeuvres de Dickens," in *Images de l'ailleurs*, 65–75.

Grant, Allan. *A Preface*, 103–109.

Hardy, Barbara. *Charles Dickens*, 58–63.

Hardy, Barbara. *Forms of Feeling*, 51–54, 68–73.

Higbie, Robert. *Character & Structure*, 129–161.

Hill, Nancy K. *A Reformer's Art*, 62–79, 91–95.

Hollington, Michael. *Dickens and the Grotesque*, 170–179.

Horton, Susan R. *Interpreting, Interpreting*.

Horton, Susan R. *The Reader*, 16–23.

Humpherys, Anne. "*Dombey and Son*: Carker the Manager." *Nineteenth-Century Fiction* 34 (1980), 397–413.

Ingham, Patricia. "Speech and Non-Communication in *Dombey and Son*." *R of Engl Stud* 30 (1979), 144–153.

Irwin, Michael. *Picturing*, 27–30.

Jackson, Rosemary. "The Silenced Text: Shades of Gothic in Victorian Fiction." *Minnesota R* 13 (1979), 102–105.

Kishtainy, Khalid. *The Prostitute*, 29–30, 126–128.

Kucich, John. *Excess and Restraint*, 27–31.

Lecker, Barbara. "The Split Characters," 689–690.

Leech, Geoffrey N., and Michael H. Short. *Style in Fiction*, 57–63, 310–315.

McMaster, Juliet and Rowland. *The Novel*, 56–58.

Nelson, Harland S. *Charles Dickens*, 107–109.

Pattison, Robert. *The Child Figure*, 87–92.

Perkins, Donald. *Charles Dickens*, 58–59.

Qualls, Barry V. *The Secular Pilgrims*, 93–98.

Sadoff, Dianne F. *Monsters of Affection*, 60–64.

Schwarzbach, F. S. *Dickens*, 101–113.

Simpson, David. *Fetishism and Imagination*, 48–50, 52–54, 58–61.

Smithers, David Waldron. *Dickens's Doctors*, 48–51.

Stewart, Garrett. "The Secret Life of Death," 182–184.

Vargish, Thomas. *The Providential Aesthetic*, 138–145.

Walder, Dennis. *Dickens and Religion*, 124–140.

Weiss, Barbara. "The Dilemma of Happily Ever After," 70–72.

Wijesinha, Rajiva. *The Androgynous Trollope*, 23–28.

Williams, Merryn. *Women in the English Novel*, 78–81.

Yelin, Louise. "Strategies for Survival: Florence and Edith in *Dombey and Son*." *Victorian Stud* 22 (1979), 297–319.

Zelicovici, Dvora. "Tema con Variazioni in *Dombey and Son*." *Mod Lang Stud* 15:4 (1985), 270–279.

Zwinger, Lynda. "The Fear of the Father: Dombey and Daughter." *Nineteenth-Century Fiction* 39 (1985), 420–440.

Great Expectations, 1861

Adrian, Arthur A. *Dickens*, 86–91.

Auerbach, Nina. *Romantic Imprisonment*, 74–78.

Auerbach, Nina. *Woman and the Demon*, 142–144.

Baumgarten, Murray. "Calligraphy and Code: Writing in *Great Expectations*." *Dickens Stud Annual* 11 (1983), 61–72.

Bodenheimer, Rosemarie. "Dickens and the Art of Pastoral," 461–467.

Brooks, Peter. "Repetition, Repression, and Return: *Great Expectations* and the Study of Plot." *New Liter Hist* 11 (1980), 503–526.

Brown, James M. *Dickens*, 127–142.

Cameron, J. M. "Dickens and the Angels," 169–170.

Chaney, Lois E. "Pip and the Fairchild Family." *Dickensian* 79 (1983), 162–163.

Coniff, Gerald. " 'The Prison of This Lower World'," in Wendell Stacy Johnson, ed., *Charles Dickens*, 119–120.

Connor, Steven. *Charles Dickens*, 114–144.

Conrow, Margaret. "Wife-Abuse," 43–44.

Craig, David M. "Origins, Ends, and Pip's Two Selves." *Res Stud* 47 (1979), 17–26.

Crawford, John W. "The Garden Imagery in *Great Expectations*," in his *Discourse*, 109–114.

Daleski, H. M. "Dickens and the Proleptic Uncanny," 198–202.

Daleski, H. M. *The Divided Heroine*, 23–24.

Drew, Philip. *The Meaning of Freedom*, 302–307.

Eigner, Edwin M. "The Absent Clown in *Great Expectations.*" *Dickens Stud Annual* 11 (1983), 115–129.

Finney, Gail. "Garden Paradigms in 19th-Century Fiction." *Compar Lit* 36 (1984), 30–33.

Foll, Scott. "*Great Expectations* and the 'Uncommercial' Sketch Book." *Dickensian* 81 (1985), 109–115.

Forsyth, Neil. "Wonderful Chains," 163–165.

French, A. L. "Old Pip: The Ending of *Great Expectations.*" *Essays in Criticism* 29 (1979), 357–360.

Garrett, Peter K. *The Victorian Multiplot Novel*, 85–89.

Gervais, David. "The Prose and Poetry of *Great Expectations.*" *Dickens Stud Annual* 13 (1984), 85–111.

Gilbert, Elliot L. " 'In Primal Sympathy': *Great Expectations* and the Secret Life." *Dickens Stud Annual* 11 (1983), 89–111.

Gilmour, Robin. *The Idea of the Gentleman*, 105–146.

Ginsburg, Michael Peled. "Dickens and the Uncanny: Repression and Displacement in *Great Expectations.*" *Dickens Stud Annual* 13 (1984), 115–123.

Grant, Allan. *A Preface*, 125–155.

Gribble, Jennifer. "Pip and Estella: Expectations of Love." *Sydney Stud in Engl* 2 (1976–77), 126–138.

Hara, Eiichi. "Name and No Name: The Identity of Dickensian Heroes." *Stud in Engl Lit* (Japan), Engl Number 1982, 29–35.

Hardy, Barbara. *Charles Dickens*, 83–86.

Hardy, Barbara. *Forms of Feeling*, 58–63.

Hartog, Curt. "The Rape of Miss Havisham." *Stud in the Novel* 14 (1982), 248–263.

Hill, Nancy K. *A Reformer's Art*, 124–134.

Hollington, Michael. *Dickens and the Grotesque*, 216–228.

Irwin, Michael. *Picturing*, 59–61, 120–122.

Jackson, David. *Encounters*, 163–183.

Johnson, Wendell Stacy. *Sons and Fathers*, 97–98, 101–105.

Jordan, John O. "The Medium of *Great Expectations.*" *Dickens Stud Annual* 11 (1983), 73–87.

Kelly, Mary Ann. "The Function of Wemmick of Little Britain and Wemmick of Walworth." *Dickens Stud Newsl* 14 (1983), 145–148.

Kennedy, George E. "The Weakened Will Redeemed." *Dickensian* 79 (1983), 77–82.

Kestner, Joseph A. *The Spatiality*, 117–121.

Kotzin, Michael C. "Herbert Pocket as Pip's Double." *Dickensian* 79 (1983), 95–102.

Kucich, John. *Excess and Restraint*, 66–85, 91–94, 100–102, 110–114.

Kurrik, Maire Jaanus. *Literature and Negation*, 168–183.

Lecker, Barbara. "The Split Characters," 696–703.

Levit, Donald J. "The Unity of *Great Expectations*." *Letras de Deusto* 9:18 (1979), 131–143.

McEwan, Neil. *The Survival of the Novel*, 28–30.

MacKay, Carol Hanbery. "A Novel's Journey into Film: The Case of *Great Expectations*." *Lit/Film Q* 13 (1985), 127–132.

McMaster, Juliet and Rowland. *The Novel*, 51–52, 71–86.

Manlove, Colin N. "Neither Here Nor There: Uneasiness in *Great Expectations*." *Dickens Stud Annual* 8 (1980), 61–70.

Martin, Graham. *"Great Expectations,"* 1–89.

Maxwell, Richard. "Dickens's Omniscience." *ELH* 46 (1979), 304–309.

Milligan, Ian. *The Novel in English*, 39–43.

Moynahan, Julian. "Seeing the Book, Reading the Movie," in Michael Klein and Gillian Parker, eds., *The English Novel*, 143–154.

Newsom, Robert. "The Hero's Shame." *Dickens Stud Annual* 11 (1983), 18–19.

Perkins, Donald. *Charles Dickens*, 21–22, 46–47.

Raimond, J. "Charles Dickens: *Great Expectations*," in Pierre Coustillas et al., eds., *Le roman anglais*, 210–223.

Rawlins, Jack P. "Great Expiations: Dickens and the Betrayal of the Child." *Stud in Engl Lit, 1500–1900* 23 (1983), 667–683.

Rosenberg, Edgar. "Last Words on *Great Expectations*: A Textual Brief on the Six Endings." *Dickens Stud Annual* 9 (1981), 87–107.

Sadoff, Dianne F. "The Dead Father," 50–57.

Sadoff, Dianne F. *"Locus Suspectus,"* 211–212, 215–219.

Sadoff, Dianne F. *Monsters of Affection*, 29–39.

Schmidt, Helen von. "The Dark Abyss, the Broad Expanse: Versions of the Self in *Jane Eyre* and *Great Expectations*." *Dickens Q* 2 (1985), 84–91.

Schwartz, Roberta C. "The Moral Fable of *Great Expectations*." *North Dakota Q* 47:1 (1979), 55–66.

Schwarzbach, F. S. *Dickens*, 171–174, 184–193.

Simpson, David. *Fetishism and Imagination*, 51–54.

Spenko, James Leo. "The Return of the Repressed in *Great Expectations*." *Lit and Psych* 30 (1980), 133–145.

Stewart, Garrett. "The Secret Life of Death," 190–192, 195–197.

Stokes, Edward. *Hawthorne's Influence*, 74–77.

Taylor, Anne Robinson. *Male Novelists*, 129–131.

Taylor, Anya. "Devoured Hearts in *Great Expectations*." *Dickens Stud Newsl* 13 (1982), 65–71.

Thomson, David T., Jr. "Pip: The Divided Self." *Psychocultural R* 1 (1977), 49–67.

Thomson, Douglass H. "The Passing of Another's Shadow: A Third Ending to *Great Expectations*." *Dickens Q* 1 (1984), 94–96.

Thurin, Susan Schoenbauer. "To Be Brought Up 'By Hand'." *Victorian Newsl* 64 (1983), 27–29.

Tracy, Robert. "Reading Dickens' Writing." *Dickens Stud Annual* 11 (1983), 46–57.

Tsuneoka, Ashie. "The Language of *Great Expectations.*" *Hiroshima Stud in Engl Lang and Lit* 27 (1982), 76–77.

Vargish, Thomas. *The Providential Aesthetic*, 150–156.

Walder, Dennis. *Dickens and Religion*, 199–204.

Weiser, Irwin. "Dickens' *Great Expectations.*" *Explicator* 39:4 (1981), 14–15.

Weiser, Irwin. "Reformed, But Unrewarded: Pip's Progress." *Dickens Stud Newsl* 14 (1983), 143–145.

Weiss, Barbara. "The Dilemma of Happily Ever After," 73.

Weissman, Judith. "Dickens' *Great Expectations*: Pip's Arrested Development." *Am Imago* 38 (1981), 105–126.

Wheeler, Michael. *English Fiction*, 101–103.

Wijesinha, Rajiva. *The Androgynous Trollope*, 32–36.

Wilson, William A. "The Magic Circle of Genius: Dickens' Translation of Shakespearean Drama in *Great Expectations.*" *Nineteenth-Century Fiction* 40 (1985), 154–174.

Witt, Richard. "The Death of Miss Havisham." *Dickensian* 80 (1984), 151–156.

Wright, Terence. "The Imperfect Ideal of the Novel." *Mod Lang R* 73 (1978), 8–9.

Hard Times, 1854

Adrian, Arthur A. *Dickens*, 114–117.

Arneson, Richard J. "Benthamite Utilitarianism and *Hard Times.*" *Philos and Lit* 2 (1978), 60–74.

Belcher, Diane Dewhurst. "Dickens's Mrs. Sparsit and the Politics of Service." *Dickens Q* 2 (1985), 92–97.

Belcher, Margaret S. "Bulwer's Mr Bluff: A Suggestion for *Hard Times.*" *Dickensian* 78 (1982), 105–109.

Bergmann, Helena. *Between Obedience and Freedom*, 40–44, 80–82, 109–111, 115–117, 129–134.

Brooks, Chris. *Signs for the Times*, 63–69.

Campbell, Jane. " 'Competing Towers of Babel': Some Patterns of Language in *Hard Times.*" *Engl Stud in Canada* 10 (1984), 416–434.

Collins, Philip. "Dickens and Industrialism," 662–665.

Connor, Steven. *Charles Dickens*, 89–106.

Eagleton, Mary, and David Pierce. *Attitudes to Class*, 42–47.

Fowler, Roger. "Polyphony and Problematic in *Hard Times*," in Robert Giddings, ed., *The Changing World*, 91–107.

Gallagher, Catherine. "*Hard Times* and *North and South*: The Family and Society in Two Industrial Novels." *Arizona Q* 36 (1980), 71–84.

Gallagher, Catherine. *The Industrial Reformation*, 147–166.

Hardy, Barbara. *Charles Dickens*, 75–77.

Hill, Nancy K. *A Reformer's Art*, 110–123.

Hirshfield, Claire. "*Hard Times* and the Teacher of History: An Interdisciplinary Approach." *Dickens Stud Newsl* 13 (1982), 33–37.

Hollington, Michael. *Dickens and the Grotesque*, 205–211.

Jefferson, D. W. "Mr Gradgrind's Facts." *Essays in Criticism* 35 (1985), 197–211.

Johnson, Wendell Stacy. *Sons and Fathers*, 89–90, 92–96.

McGillis, Roderick F. "Plum Pies and Factories: Cross Connections in *Hard Times*." *Dickens Stud Newsl* 11 (1980), 102–107.

Matsuoka, Mitsuharu. "On Dickens's Changed View of Society: Fancy and Affection in *Hard Times*." *Hiroshima Stud in Engl Lang and Lit* 27 (1982), 79–81.

Meier, Stefanie. *Animation*, 137–148.

Naslund, Sena Jeter. "Mr. Sleary's Lisp: A Note on *Hard Times*." *Dickens Stud Newsl* 12 (1981), 42–46.

Nelson, Harland S. *Charles Dickens*, 197–199.

Organ, Dennis. "Compression and Explosion: Pattern in *Hard Times*." *RE: Artes Liberales* 8:1 (1981), 29–37.

Ousby, Ian. "Figurative Language in *Hard Times*." *Durham Univ J* 74 (1981–82), 103–109.

Perkins, Donald. *Charles Dickens*, 56–58.

Schwarzbach, F. S. *Dickens*, 143–150.

Spector, Stephen J. "Masters of Metonymy: *Hard Times* and Knowing the Working Class." *ELH* 51 (1984), 365–381.

Stokes, Edward. *Hawthorne's Influence*, 59–69.

Stone, Donald D. *The Romantic Impulse*, 276–278.

Tarantelli, Carole Beebe. *Ritratto di ignoto*, 137–169.

Wallis, Bruce L. "Dickens' *Hard Times*." *Explicator* 44:2 (1986), 26–27.

Webb, Igor. *From Custom to Capital*, 86–100, 189–192.

Weiss, Barbara. "The Dilemma of Happily Ever After," 72–73.

Wheeler, Michael. *English Fiction*, 79–81.

Wijesinha, Rajiva. *The Androgynous Trollope*, 29–32.

Winkgens, Meinhard. "Das Problem der 'historischen Wahrheit' in dem Roman *Hard Times* von Charles Dickens." *Poetica* 12 (1980), 24–58.

The Haunted Man, 1847

Herron, Jerry. "*The Haunted Man* and the Two Scrooges." *Stud in Short Fiction* 19 (1982), 45–50.

Spence, Gordon. "The Haunted Man and Barbox Brothers." *Dickensian* 76 (1980), 150–157.

Little Dorrit, 1857

Adrian, Arthur A. *Dickens*, 125–128.

Briad, Edith. "Hortense, Rigaud," 25–34.

Brooks, Chris. *Signs for the Times*, 70–83.

Brown, James M. *Dickens*, 85–114.

Carlisle, Janice. *The Sense of an Audience*, 96–118.

Collins, Philip. "Dickens and Industrialism," 665–666.

Collins, Philip. "*Little Dorrit*: The Prison and the Critics." *Times Liter Suppl*, 18 April 1980, 445–446.

Coniff, Gerald. " 'The Prison of This Lower World'," 116–118.

Conrow, Margaret. "Wife-Abuse," 44–45.

Daleski, H. M. "Dickens and the Proleptic Uncanny," 196.

Drew, Philip. *The Meaning of Freedom*, 296–301.

Forsyth, Neil. "Wonderful Chains," 161–162.

Frow, John. "Voice and Register in *Little Dorrit*." *Compar Lit* 33 (1981), 258–270.

Garrett, Peter K. *The Victorian Multiplot Novel*, 71–85.

Hardy, Barbara. *Charles Dickens*, 77–82.

Hardy, Barbara. *Forms of Feeling*, 56–58.

Hartog, Dirk Den. "*Little Dorrit*: Dickens's Dialogue with Wordsworth." *Crit R* (Canberra) 23 (1981), 3–19.

Heaman, Robert J. "Love and Communication in *Little Dorrit*." *Dickens Stud Newsl* 12 (1981), 39–42.

Higbie, Robert. *Character & Structure*, 127–146.

Hill, Nancy K. "Picturesque Satire in *Little Dorrit*." *Hartford Univ Stud in Lit* 11 (1979), 212–222.

Hill, Nancy K. *A Reformer's Art*, 30–43.

Hollington, Michael. *Dickens and the Grotesque*, 145–150.

Horton, Susan R. *The Reader*, 26–28, 114–117.

Kelly, Mary Ann. "Imagination, Fantasy, and Memory in *Little Dorrit*." *Dickens Stud Newsl* 13 (1982), 48–50.

Landow, George P. *Images of Crisis*, 198–199.

Larson, Janet. "Apocalyptic Style in *Little Dorrit*." *Dickens Q* 1 (1984), 41–48.

Larson, Janet. "The Arts in These Latter Days: Carlylean Prophecy in *Little Dorrit*." *Dickens Stud Annual* 8 (1980), 139–181.

Lecker, Barbara. "The Split Characters," 696–698.

Lund, Roger D. "Genteel Fictions: Caricature and Satirical Design in *Little Dorrit*." *Dickens Stud Annual* 10 (1982), 45–64.

McMaster, Juliet and Rowland. *The Novel*, 63–69.

MacPike, Loralee. "Dickens and Dostoyevsky: The Technique of Reverse Influence," in Robert Giddings, ed., *The Changing World*, 199–213.

McSweeney, Kerry. *Four Contemporary Novelists*, 16–18.

Man, Glenn K. S. "Affirmation in Dickens' *Little Dorrit*." *Essays in Lit* (Macomb) 6 (1979), 43–54.

Mason, Mary. "Deixis: A Point of Entry to *Little Dorrit*," in Ronald Carter, ed., *Language*, 29–38.

Maxwell, Richard. "Dickens's Omniscience," 299–304.

Metz, Nancy Aycock. "Physician as Cliché and as Character." *Dickens Stud Newsl* 13 (1982), 38–42.

Mott, Graham. "Was there a Stain upon Little Dorrit?" *Dickensian* 76 (1980), 31–35.

Naef-Hinderling, Annabeth. *The Search*, 96–128.

Nelson, Harland S. *Charles Dickens*, 114–118.

Perkins, Donald. *Charles Dickens*, 85–87.

Petch, Simon. "*Little Dorrit*: Some Visions of Pastoral." *Sydney Stud in Engl* 7 (1981–82), 102–114.

Qualls, Barry V. *The Secular Pilgrims*, 102–105.

Ray, Kalyan B. "Nomenclature and Satire in *Little Dorrit*." *Dickens Q* 1 (1984), 10–11.

Roberts, Bette B. "Travel versus Imprisonment: The 'Fellow Travellers' in *Little Dorrit*." *Dickens Stud Newsl* 13 (1982), 109–112.

Rogers, Henry N., III. "Shadows of Irony: The Comic Structure of *Little Dorrit*." *Publs of the Arkansas Philol Assoc* 5:2–3 (1979), 58–63.

Rosenberg, Brian. "*Resurrection* and *Little Dorrit*: Tolstoy and Dickens Reconsidered." *Stud in the Novel* 17 (1985), 27–36.

Sadoff, Dianne F. *Monsters of Affection*, 56–60.

Sadoff, Dianne F. "Storytelling and the Figure of the Father in *Little Dorrit*." *PMLA* 95 (1980), 234–244.

Schwarzbach, F. S. *Dickens*, 150–171.

Scott, P. J. M. *Reality and Comic Confidence*, 122–204.

Showalter, Elaine. "Guilt, Authority, and the Shadows of *Little Dorrit*." *Nineteenth-Century Fiction* 34 (1979), 20–40.

Simpson, David. *Fetishism and Imagination*, 47–51.

Smith, Peter. *Public and Private Value*, 15–48.

Smithers, David Waldron. *Dickens's Doctors*, 66–72.

Springer, Marlene. "Teaching Dickens: A Note on *Little Dorrit*." *J of Engl Teaching Techniques* 10:1 (1980), 53–58.

Stein, Robert A. "Arthur Clennam and the Trouble with *Little Dorrit*." *Papers on Lang & Lit* 17 (1981), 181–197.

Stokes, Edward. *Hawthorne's Influence*, 70–72.

Stone, Harry. "What's in a Name," 197–198.

Thomas, Deborah A. "Dickens and Indigestion," 7–11.

Tschumi, Raymond. "Dickens and Switzerland," 445.

Vargish, Thomas. *The Providential Aesthetic*, 145–150.

Walder, Dennis. *Dickens and Religion*, 170–195.

Weinstein, Philip M. *The Semantics of Desire*, 48–72.

Weiss, Barbara. "The Dilemma of Happily Ever After," 73–74.

Weiss, Barbara. "Secret Pockets and Secret Breasts: *Little Dorrit* and the Commercial Scandals of the Fifties." *Dickens Stud Annual* 10 (1982), 67–75.

Wheeler, Michael. *English Fiction*, 82–88.

Wijesinha, Rajiva. *The Androgynous Trollope*, 75–77, 129–131.

Wright, Terence. "The Imperfect Ideal," 10–11.

Zelicovici, Dvora. "Circularity and Linearity in *Little Dorrit*." *Dickens Q* 1 (1984), 50–53.

Zelicovici, Dvora. "The First Chapter of *Little Dorrit*: Overture to the Novel." *Ariel* 13:2 (1982), 47–63.

Martin Chuzzlewit, 1844

Adrian, Arthur A. *Dickens*, 108–109.

Barickman, Richard. "The Subversive Methods of Dickens' Early Fiction: *Martin Chuzzlewit*," in Wendell Stacy Johnson, ed., *Charles Dickens*, 37–50.

Berthold, Michael Coulson. "Ontological Insecurity in *Martin Chuzzlewit*." *Dickens Stud Newsl* 14 (1983), 135–142.

Blaisdell, Lowell L. "The Origins of the Satire in the Watertoast Episode of *Martin Chuzzlewit*." *Dickensian* 77 (1981), 92–100.

Conrow, Margaret. "Wife-Abuse," 43–44.

Garrett, Peter K. *The Victorian Multiplot Novel*, 39–41.

Grant, Allan. *A Preface*, 82–84.

Hardy, Barbara. *Charles Dickens*, 50–55.

Higgins, Elizabeth Jean. *Reading the Novel*, 34–40.

Hollington, Michael. *Dickens and the Grotesque*, 123–135.

Irwin, Michael. *Picturing*, 73–76.

Lecker, Barbara. "The Split Characters," 693–696.

McCarthy, Patrick J. "The Language of *Martin Chuzzlewit*." *Stud in Engl Lit, 1500–1900* 20 (1980), 637–649.

Magnet, Myron. *Dickens and the Social Order*, 203–237.

Meckier, Jerome. "Dickens Discovers America, Dickens Discovers Dickens: The First Visit Reconsidered." *Mod Lang R* 79 (1984), 266–277.

Monod, Sylvère. *Martin Chuzzlewit*, 1–197.

Nelson, Harland S. *Charles Dickens*, 98–100.

Olofson, Harold. "The Birds and the Barber: An Anthropological Analysis of a Joke in Charles Dickens' *Martin Chuzzlewit*," in Michael A. Salter, ed., *Play*, 104–112.

Peterson, Audrey. *Victorian Masters*, 82–85.

Polhemus, Robert M. *Comic Faith*, 88–123.

Schwarzbach, F. S. *Dickens*, 80–100.

Smithers, David Waldron. *Dickens's Doctors*, 41–45.

Sulfridge, Cynthia. "*Martin Chuzzlewit*: Dickens's Prodigal and the Myth of the Wandering Son." *Stud in the Novel* 11 (1979), 318–324.

Vargish, Thomas. *The Providential Aesthetic*, 125–127.

Walder, Dennis. *Dickens and Religion*, 113–121.

Welsh, Alexander. "Blackmail Studies," 28–34.

The Mystery of Edwin Drood, 1870

Beer, John. "*Edwin Drood* and the Mystery of Apartness." *Dickens Stud Annual* 13 (1984), 143–184.

Bleiler, Everett F. "The Names in *Drood*." *Dickens Q* 1 (1984), 88–93, 137–141.

Carr, John Dickson. "John Dickson Carr's Solution to *The Mystery of Edwin Drood*." *Armchair Detective* 14 (1981), 291–294.

Cordery, Gareth. "The Cathedral as Setting and Symbol in *The Mystery of Edwin Drood*." *Dickens Stud Newsl* 10 (1979), 97–103.

Cox, Arthur J. "Dickens's Last Book: More Mysteries Than One." *Armchair Detective* 14 (1981), 31–36.

Fisher, Ben. "Edwin's Mystery and Its History: Or, Another Look at Datchery." *Mystery FANcier* 4 (1980), 6–8.

Fleissner, Robert F. "A Drood Awakening." *Dickens Stud Newsl* 11 (1980), 17–18.

Fleissner, Robert F. "*Drood* the Obscure: The Evidence of the Names." *Armchair Detective* 13 (1980), 12–16.

Flynn, Judith Prescott. " 'Fugitive and Cloistered Virtue': Innocence and Evil in *Edwin Drood*." *Engl Stud in Canada* 9 (1983), 312–323.

Forsyte, Charles. *The Decoding of Edwin Drood*.

Forsyte, Charles. "Drood and the Bean-stalk." *Dickensian* 80 (1984), 74–87.

Garrett, Peter K. *The Victorian Multiplot Novel*, 23–25.

Hardy, Barbara. *Charles Dickens*, 91–92.

Hill, Nancy K. *A Reformer's Art*, 135–148.

Hollington, Michael. *Dickens and the Grotesque*, 238–244.

Hornback, Bert G. *'The Hero'*, 119–155.

Lane, Lauriat, Jr. "*The Mystery of Edwin Drood* De/Re/Encoded." *Intl Fiction R* 9 (1982), 120–124.

O'Mealy, Joseph H. " 'Some stray sort of ambition . . .': John Jasper's Great Expectations." *Dickens Q* 2 (1985), 129–136.

Perkins, Donald. *Charles Dickens*, 22–23, 104–105.

Peterson, Audrey. *Victorian Masters*, 99–119.

Rataboul, Louis J. *Le pasteur anglican*, 137–139.

Robson, W. W. "*The Mystery of Edwin Drood*: The Solution." *Times Liter Suppl*, 11 Nov. 1983, 1246.

Schroeder, Natalie. "Echoes of *Paradise Lost* in *The Mystery of Edwin Drood*." *Dickens Stud Newsl* 13 (1982), 42–47.

Schwarzbach, F. S. *Dickens*, 216–219.

Stone, Harry. "What's in a Name," 199–203.

Thomas, Marilyn. "*Edwin Drood*: A Bone Yard Awaiting Resurrection." *Dickens Q* 2 (1985), 12–18.

Wales, Kathleen. "Dickens and Interior Monologue: The Opening of *Edwin Drood* Reconsidered." *Lang and Style* 17 (1984), 234–246.

Wheeler, Michael. *English Fiction*, 106–108.

Nicholas Nickleby, 1839

Day, Gary H. "The Relevance of the Nickleby Stories." *Dickensian* 81 (1985), 52–55.

Edgar, David. "Adapting *Nickleby*," in Robert Giddings, ed., *The Changing World*, 135–147.

Garrett, Peter K. *The Victorian Multiplot Novel*, 53–55.

Glancy, Ruth F. "Dickens and Christmas: His Framed-Tale Themes." *Nineteenth-Century Fiction* 35 (1980), 55–56.

Hardy, Barbara. *Charles Dickens*, 39–45.

Hardy, Barbara. *Forms of Feeling*, 50–51, 63–73.

Hollington, Michael. *Dickens and the Grotesque*, 65–73.

Magnet, Myron. *Dickens and the Social Order*, 11–48.

Marks, Patricia. "Time in *Nicholas Nickleby*." *Victorian Newsl* 55 (1979), 23–26.

Russell, N. "*Nicholas Nickleby* and the Commercial Crisis of 1825." *Dickensian* 77 (1981), 144–149.

Schwarzbach, F. S. *Dickens*, 43–68.

Smith, Grahame. *The Novel & Society*, 183–190.

Smithers, David Waldron. *Dickens's Doctors*, 36–40.

Zelicovici, Dvora. "Grip the Raven: A Rehabilitation." *Dickensian* 77 (1981), 151–153.

The Old Curiosity Shop, 1841

Auerbach, Nina. *Woman and the Demon*, 82–88.

Brooks, Chris. *Signs for the Times*, 23–35.

Dvorak, Wilfred P. "On the Knocking at the Gate in *The Old Curiosity Shop*." *Stud in the Novel* 16 (1984), 304–311.

Ermarth, Elizabeth. "Fictional Consensus and Female Casualties," in Carolyn G. Heilbrun and Margaret R. Higonnet, eds., *The Representation of Women*, 6–7.

Fleissner, Robert F. " 'Fancy's (K)Nell' Retolled." *Dickens Stud Newsl* 13 (1982), 76–79.

Grant, Allan. *A Preface*, 100–103.

Hardy, Barbara. *Charles Dickens*, 45–48.

Hardy, Barbara. *Forms of Feeling*, 66–68.

Hill, Nancy K. *A Reformer's Art*, 98–111.

Hollington, Michael. *Dickens and the Grotesque*, 79–91.

Horton, Susan R. *The Reader*, 110–121.

James, W. L. G. "The Portrayal of Death and 'Substance of Life': Aspects of the Modern Reader's Response to 'Victorianism'," in Ian Gregor, ed., *Reading the Victorian Novel*, 226–233.

Kucich, John. *Excess and Restraint*, 21–24, 62–90, 102–104, 121–125, 180–190.

MacPike, Loralee. *Dostoevsky's Dickens*, 19–117.

MacPike, Loralee. " 'The Old Cupiosity Shape': Changing Views of Little Nell." *Dickens Stud Newsl* 12 (1981), 33–38, 70–76.

Maxwell, Richard. "Crowds and Creativity in *The Old Curiosity Shop*." *J of Engl and Germanic Philology* 78 (1979), 49–71.

Mayer, Hans. *Outsiders*, 338–341.

Meier, Stefanie. *Animation*, 133–137.

Naef-Hinderling, Annabeth. *The Search*, 61–95.

Nelson, Harland S. *Charles Dickens*, 100–103.

Pattison, Robert. *The Child Figure*, 76–80, 82–84.

Qualls, Barry V. *The Secular Pilgrims*, 90–92, 98–100.

Sadoff, Dianne F. *Monsters of Affection*, 19–21.

Schlicke, Paul. "A 'Discipline of Feeling': Macready's *Lear* and *The Old Curiosity Shop*." *Dickensian* 76 (1980), 78–89.

Stewart, Garrett. "The Secret Life of Death," 180–182.

Stewart, Thomas H. "Bliss and Dickens: A Note on Little Nell and 'Little Willie'." *Univ of Mississippi Stud in Engl* 1 (1980), 125–126.

Stone, Donald D. *The Romantic Impulse*, 272–276.

Vargish, Thomas. *The Providential Aesthetic*, 99–101.

Walder, Dennis. *Dickens and Religion*, 66–92.

Wheeler, Michael. *English Fiction*, 27–29.

White, Isabella. "The Uses of Death in *The Old Curiosity Shop*." *Kentucky Philol Assoc Bull*, 1982, 29–40.

Winslow, Joan D. "*The Old Curiosity Shop*: The Meaning of Nell's Fate." *Dickensian* 77 (1981), 162–167.

Oliver Twist, 1838

Adrian, Arthur A. *Dickens*, 72–80.

Beaty, Jerome. "Jane Eyre at Gateshead: Mixed Signals in the Text and Context," in James R. Kincaid and Albert J. Kuhn, eds., *Victorian Literature*, 178–182.

Bodenheimer, Rosemarie. "Dickens and the Art of Pastoral," 453–458.

Brody, Benjamin. "Brainwashing and *Oliver Twist*." *Univ of Hartford Stud in Lit* 14:2 (1982), 61–66.

Brueck, Katherine T. "Poverty and Villainy in *Oliver Twist*: Unraveling the Paradox." *Dickens Stud Newsl* 12 (1981), 66–69.

Cameron, J. M. "Dickens and the Angels," 163–166.

Crawford, Iain. "Time and Structure in *Oliver Twist*." *Dickensian* 77 (1981), 23–31.

Daleski, H. M. "Dickens and the Proleptic Uncanny," 195–196, 204–206.

Daleski, H. M. *The Divided Heroine*, 12–14.

Edgerton, Larry.. "Dickens' *Oliver Twist*." *Explicator* 40:1 (1981), 28–30.

Fleissner, Robert F. "Dickens' *Oliver Twist*." *Explicator* 41:3 (1983), 30–31.

Forsyth, Neil. "Wonderful Chains," 152–156.

Garrett, Peter K. *The Victorian Multiplot Novel*, 28–30.

Gilmour, Robin. *The Idea of the Gentleman*, 113–115.

Grant, Allan. *A Preface*, 96–99, 122–125.

Hara, Eiichi. "Name and No Name," 23–29.

Hardy, Barbara. *Charles Dickens*, 29–39.

Hardy, Barbara. *Forms of Feeling*, 46–50.

Hill, Nancy K. *A Reformer's Art*, 55–62.

Hollington, Michael. *Dickens and the Grotesque*, 58–65.

Hornback, Bert G. '*The Hero*', 49–51.

Ingham, Patricia. "The Name of the Hero in *Oliver Twist*." *R of Engl Stud* 33 (1982), 188–189.

James, Louis. "The View from Brick Lane: Contrasting Perspectives in Working-Class and Middle-Class Fiction of the Early Victorian Period." *Yearbook of Engl Stud* 11 (1981), 88–94.

Johnson, Wendell Stacy. *Sons and Fathers*, 90–91, 96–97.

Kucich, John. *Excess and Restraint*, 205–207.

McMaster, Juliet. "Diabolic Trinity in Oliver Twist." *Dalhousie R* 61 (1981), 263–276.

Naman, Anne Aresty. *The Jew*, 58–79.

Newsom, Robert. "The Hero's Shame," 13–17.

Perkins, Donald. *Charles Dickens*, 16–17, 28–29, 37–38, 66–71, 88–92.

Punter, David. *The Literature of Terror*, 217–222.

Sadoff, Dianne F. *"Locus Suspectus,"* 212–214, 221–223.

Schwarzbach, F. S. *Dickens*, 43–68.

Smithers, David Waldron. *Dickens's Doctors*, 31–35.

Tharaud, Barry. "Two Film Versions of *Oliver Twist*: Moral Vision in Film and Literature." *Dickens Stud Newsl* 11 (1980), 41–46.

Tick, Stanley. "*Oliver Twist*: 'A stronger hand than chance'." *Renascence* 33 (1981), 225–239.

Vargish, Thomas. *The Providential Aesthetic*, 135–138.

Walder, Dennis. *Dickens and Religion*, 42–66.

Watt, George. *The Fallen Woman*, 11–17.

Wheeler, Burton M. "The Text and Plan of *Oliver Twist*." *Dickens Stud Annual* 12 (1983), 41–58.

Zatlin, Linda Gertner. *The Nineteenth-Century Anglo-Jewish Novel*, 123–127.

Our Mutual Friend, 1865

Adrian, Arthur A. *Dickens*, 128–130.

Barbour, Judith. "Euphemism and Paternalism in *Our Mutual Friend*." *Sydney Stud in Engl* 7 (1981–82), 55–68.

Beiderwell, Bruce. "The Coherence of *Our Mutual Friend*." *J of Narrative Technique* 15 (1985), 234–242.

Bennett, Kenneth C. "Surrogate Religion in *Our Mutual Friend* and *The Mill on the Floss*." *Victorians Inst J* 10 (1981–82), 15–25.

Brattin, Joel. "Dickens' Creation of Bradley Headstone." *Dickens Stud Annual* 14 (1985), 147–164.

Brown, James M. *Dickens*, 143–165.

Clarke, Ian. "Two Names in *Our Mutual Friend*." *Dickens Stud Newsl* 14 (1983), 12–14.

Coates, Paul. *The Realist Fantasy*, 66–70.

Collins, Angus P. "Dickens and *Our Mutual Friend*: Fancy as Self-Preservation." *Etudes Anglaises* 38 (1985), 257–265.

Collins, Angus P. "A Rhetorical Use of the 'Fancy' in *Our Mutual Friend*." *Dickens Stud Newsl* 12 (1981), 108–110.

Connor, Steven. *Charles Dickens*, 144–158.

Cotsell, Michael. "The Book of Insolvent Fates: Financial Speculation in *Our Mutual Friend*." *Dickens Stud Annual* 13 (1984), 125–140.

Cotsell, Michael. " 'Do I never read in the newspapers': Dickens's Last Attack on the Poor Law." *Dickens Stud Newsl* 14 (1983), 81–90.

Cotsell, Michael. "Mr Venus Rises from the Counter: Dickens's Taxidermist and his Contribution to *Our Mutual Friend*." *Dickensian* 80 (1984), 105–113.

Cotsell, Michael. "Secretary or Sad Clerk? The Problem with John Harmon." *Dickens Q* 1 (1984), 130–136.

David, Deirdre. *Fictions of Resolution*, 53–128.

Dvorak, Wilfred P. "Charles Dickens' *Our Mutual Friend* and Frederick Somner Merryweather's *Lives and Anecdotes of Misers*." *Dickens Stud Annual* 9 (1981), 117–139.

Garrett, Peter K. *The Victorian Multiplot Novel*, 89–94.

Gibbon, Frank. "R. H. Horne and *Our Mutual Friend*." *Dickensian* 81 (1985), 140–143.

Gitter, Elisabeth G. "The Power of Women's Hair in the Victorian Imagination." *PMLA* 99 (1984), 943–946.

Hara, Eiichi. "Name and No Name," 35–39.

Hardy, Barbara. *Charles Dickens*, 88–91.

Hirsch, Gordon D. "Psychological Patterns in the Double Plot of *Our Mutual Friend*." *Hartford Univ Stud in Lit* 12 (1980), 195–219.

Hollington, Michael. *Dickens and the Grotesque*, 231–238.

Horne, Lewis. "*Our Mutual Friend* and the Test of Worthiness." *Dalhousie R* 62 (1982), 292–301.

Hutter, Albert D. "Dismemberment and Articulation in *Our Mutual Friend*." *Dickens Stud Annual* 11 (1983), 135–163.

Kiely, Robert. "Plotting and Scheming: The Design of Design in *Our Mutual Friend*." *Dickens Stud Annual* 12 (1983), 267–282.

Knowles, Owen. "Veneering and the Age of Veneer: A Source and Background for *Our Mutual Friend*." *Dickensian* 81 (1985), 88–96.

Kucich, John. "Dickens' Fantastic Rhetoric: The Semantics of Reality and Unreality in *Our Mutual Friend*." *Dickens Stud Annual* 14 (1985), 167–187.

Kucich, John. "Repression and Representation: Dickens's General Economy." *Nineteenth-Century Fiction* 38 (1983), 70–77.

Kurrik, Maire Jaanus. *Literature and Negation*, 194–197.

Lesser, Wendy. "From Dickens to Conrad," 197–199.

McMaster, Juliet and Rowland. *The Novel*, 48–49.

Mason, Philip. *The English Gentleman*, 126–130.

Meckier, Jerome. "Boffin and Podsnap in Utopia." *Dickensian* 77 (1981), 154–161.

Metz, Nancy Aycock. "The Artistic Reclamation of Waste in *Our Mutual Friend*." *Nineteenth-Century Fiction* 34 (1979), 59–72.

Milligan, Ian. *The Novel in English*, 153–155.

Mundhenk, Rosemary. "The Education of the Reader in *Our Mutual Friend*." *Nineteenth-Century Fiction* 34 (1979), 41–58.

Naman, Anne Aresty. *The Jew*, 79–88.

Nelson, Harland S. *Charles Dickens*, 105–107.

Newsom, Robert. " 'To Scatter Dust': Fancy and Authenticity in *Our Mutual Friend*." *Dickens Stud Annual* 8 (1980), 39–58.

Perkins, Donald. *Charles Dickens*, 92–94, 103–104.

Qualls, Barry V. *The Secular Pilgrims*, 106–108, 121–135.

Rataboul, Louis J. *Le pasteur anglican*, 136–137.

Robson, John M. "*Our Mutual Friend*: A Rhetorical Approach to the First Number," in Wendell Stacy Johnson, ed., *Charles Dickens*, 159–183.

Schwarzbach, F. S. *Dickens*, 194–212.

Scott, P. J. M. *Reality and Comic Confidence*, 11–60.

Stewart, Garrett. "Signing Off: Dickens and Thackeray, Woolf and Beckett," in William E. Cain, ed., *Philosophical Approaches*, 118–120.

Stewart, Thomas H. "Bliss and Dickens: A Note on Little Nell and 'Little Willie'." *Univ of Mississippi Stud in Engl* 1 (1980), 125–126.

Stokes, Edward. *Hawthorne's Influence*, 77–83.

Stone, Donald D. *The Romantic Impulse*, 278–281.

Stone, Harry. "What's in a Name," 198–199.

Thomas, Deborah A. "Dickens and Indigestion," 7–11.

Trodd, Anthea. "The Policeman and the Lady: Significant Encounters in Mid-Victorian Fiction." *Victorian Stud* 27 (1984), 451–452.

Vargish, Thomas. *The Providential Aesthetic*, 156–162.

Walder, Dennis. *Dickens and Religion*, 204–208.

Weiss, Barbara. "The Dilemma of Happily Ever After," 74–75.

Wheeler, Michael. *English Fiction*, 103–106.

Wijesinha, Rajiva. *The Androgynous Trollope*, 73–75.

Yeazell, Ruth Bernard. "Podsnappery, Sexuality, and the English Novel." *Crit Inquiry* 9 (1982), 339–357.

The Pickwick Papers, 1837

Chase, Karen. *Eros & Psyche*, 25–46.

Connor, Steven. *Charles Dickens*, 8–19.

Dusseau, John L. "The Bleak House in Charles Dickens," 586–588.

Engel, Elliot. "The Maturing of a Comic Artist: Dickens' Leap from *Sketches by Boz* to *Pickwick Papers*." *Victorians Inst J* 9 (1980–81), 39–47.

Engel, Elliot, and Margaret F. King. *The Victorian Novel*, 130–134.

Feltes, N. N. "The Moment of *Pickwick*, or the Production of a Commodity Text." *Lit and Hist* 10 (1984), 203–213.

Filmer, Paul. "Dickens, Pickwick and Realism: On the Importance of Language to Socio-Literary Relations," in Diana Laurenson, ed., *The Sociology*, 75–87.

Grylls, David. *Guardians and Angels*, 132–134.

Hardy, Barbara. *Charles Dickens*, 25–29.

Hill, Nancy K. *A Reformer's Art*, 15–26.

Hirsch, Gordon D. "Mr. Pickwick's Impotence." *Sphinx* 9 (1979), 28–35.

Hollington, Michael. *Dickens and the Grotesque*, 44–49.

Hornback, Bert G. *'The Hero'*, 37–39.

Jackson, Rosemary. "The Silenced Text," 101–102.

Lamarca Margalef, Jordi. *Ciencia y literatura*, 106–108.

McMaster, Juliet. "Visual Design in *Pickwick Papers*." *Stud in Engl Lit, 1500–1900* 23 (1983), 595–614.

Marlow, James E. "Pickwick's Writing: Propriety and Language." *ELH* 52 (1985), 939–962.

Marlow, James E. "Popular Culture, Pugilism, and Pickwick." *J of Popular Culture* 15:4 (1982), 16–30.

Mason, Philip. *The English Gentleman*, 120–122.

Mouchard, Claude. "L'ange de l'intime." *Quinzaine Littéraire* 316 (1980), 13–14.

Perkins, Donald. *Charles Dickens*, 14–16, 35–37, 64–66.

Prange, Roy L., Jr. "The Case against Mrs. Cluppins." *Dickens Stud Newsl* 11 (1980), 112–114.

Reed, Walter L. *An Exemplary History*, 168–182.

Schwarzbach, F. S. *Dickens*, 43–68.

Simpson, Jacqueline. "Urban Legends in *The Pickwick Papers*." *J of Am Folklore* 96:382 (1983), 462–470.

Smith, Grahame. *The Novel & Society*, 174–182.

Smithers, David Waldron. *Dickens's Doctors*, 27–30.

Stewart, Garrett. "Signing Off," 118–120.

Strange, Glyn A. "Paired Episodes in *Pickwick*." *Dickens Stud Newsl* 12 (1981), 6–8.

Tanaka, Takanobu. "Benevolence and Laughter as the Predominant Qualities of *The Pickwick Papers*." *Hiroshima Stud in Engl Lang and Lit* 27 (1982), 77–79.

Vega Ritter, Max. "De quelques mécanismes de l'humour dans les *Pickwick Papers*." *Cahiers Victoriens et Edouardiens* 20 (1984), 39–53.

Walder, Dennis. *Dickens and Religion*, 17–43.

Welsh, Alexander. *Reflections*, 9–15, 25–36, 108–112, 119–123.

Wheeler, Michael. *English Fiction*, 23–26.

A Tale of Two Cities, 1859

Baumgarten, Murray. "Writing the Revolution." *Dickens Stud Annual* 12 (1983), 161–175.

Bossche, Chris R. Vanden. "Prophetic Closure and Disclosing Narrative: *The French Revolution* and *A Tale of Two Cities*." *Dickens Stud Annual* 12 (1983), 209–218.

Britwum, Atta. "Dickens's War against the Militancy of the Oppressed." *Victorian Newsl* 65 (1984), 16–18.

Brooks, Chris. *Signs for the Times*, 84–95.

Brown, James M. *Dickens*, 115–126.

Collins, Philip. "Dickens and French Wickedness," in Sylvère Monod, ed., *Charles Dickens*, 35–46.

Court, Franklin E. "Boots, Barbarism, and the New Order in Dickens' *Tale of Two Cities*." *Victorians Inst J* 9 (1980–81), 29–37.

Craig, David. "The Crowd," 77–81.

Dunn, Richard J. "A Tale for Two Dramatists." *Dickens Stud Annual* 12 (1983), 117–123.

Eigner, Edwin M. "Charles Darnay and Revolutionary Identity." *Dickens Stud Annual* 12 (1983), 147–157.

Fleming, Margaret B. "Archetypes in *A Tale of Two Cities*," in *Literature*, 14–21.

Frank, Lawrence. "Dickens' *A Tale of Two Cities*: The Poetics of Impasse." *Am Imago* 36 (1979), 125–144.

Gallagher, Catherine. "The Duplicity of Doubling in *A Tale of Two Cities*." *Dickens Stud Annual* 12 (1983), 125–144.

Gilbert, Elliot L. " 'To Awake from History': Carlyle, Thackeray, and *A Tale of Two Cities*." *Dickens Stud Annual* 12 (1983), 252–264.

Gitter, Elisabeth G. "The Power of Women's Hair," 943–946.

Hardy, Barbara. *Charles Dickens*, 82–83.

Hollington, Michael. *Dickens and the Grotesque*, 110–118.

Irwin, Michael. *Picturing*, 67–71.

Kucich, John. *Excess and Restraint*, 87–91, 114–121, 168–177.

Kucich, John. "The Purity of Violence: *A Tale of Two Cities*." *Dickens Stud Annual* 8 (1980), 119–134.

Lecker, Barbara. "The Split Characters," 698–699.

Lindley, Dwight N. "Clio and Three Historical Novels." *Dickens Stud Annual* 10 (1982), 80–85.

MacKay, Carol Hanbery. "The Rhetoric of Soliloquy in *The French Revolution* and *A Tale of Two Cities*." *Dickens Stud Annual* 12 (1983), 197–204.

McMaster, Juliet and Rowland. *The Novel*, 39–42.

Mengel, Ewald. "The Poisoned Fountain: Dickens's Use of a Traditional Symbol in *A Tale of Two Cities*." *Dickensian* 80 (1984), 26–32.

Nelson, Harland S. *Charles Dickens*, 117–118.

O'Mealy, Joseph H. "Dickens' *A Tale of Two Cities*." *Explicator* 42:2 (1984), 10–12.

Perkins, Donald. *Charles Dickens*, 20–21.

Rignall, J. M. "Dickens and the Catastrophic Continuum of History in *A Tale of Two Cities*." *ELH* 51 (1984), 575–586.

Sadoff, Dianne F. *Monsters of Affection*, 52–57.

Sadrin, Anny. "*A Tale of Two Cities*: Théatre-Roman." *Cahiers Victoriens et Edouardiens* 20 (1984), 65–83.

Sanders, Andrew. "Dickens's French Historical Novel," in Sylvère Monod, ed., *Charles Dickens*, 61–68.

Sanders, Andrew. "Monsieur heretofore the Marquis: Dickens's St. Evrémonde." *Dickensian* 81 (1985), 148–155.

Schwarzbach, F. S. *Dickens*, 174–178.

Smithers, David Waldron. *Dickens's Doctors*, 83–85.

Stewart, Garrett. "The Secret Life of Death," 184–190.

Stokes, Edward. *Hawthorne's Influence*, 72–74.

Tetzeli von Rosador, Kurt. "Geschichtsrhetorik und Geschichtsauffassung in Charles Dickens' *A Tale of Two Cities*." *Germanisch-Romanische Monatsschrift* 35 (1985), 301–313.

Tick, Stanley. "Cruncher on Resurrection: A Tale of Charles Dickens." *Renascence* 33 (1981), 86–98.

Timko, Michael. "Splendid Impressions and Picturesque Means: Dickens, Carlyle, and *The French Revolution*." *Dickens Stud Annual* 12 (1983), 177–194.

Tucker, David G. "The Reception of *A Tale of Two Cities*." *Dickens Stud Newsl* 10 (1979), 8–13, 51–56.

Vargish, Thomas. *The Providential Aesthetic*, 132–134.

Vernier, Jean-Pierre. "Lecture de *A Tale of Two Cities*," in Sylvère Monod, ed., *Charles Dickens*, 69–76.

Walder, Dennis. *Dickens and Religion*, 197–200.

EILIS DILLON

Across the Bitter Sea, 1973

Cahalan, James M. *Great Hatred*, 192–195.

Blood Relations, 1973

Cahalan, James M. *Great Hatred*, 192–195.

BENJAMIN DISRAELI

Alroy, 1832

Braun, Thom. *Disraeli the Novelist*, 57–61.

Engel, Elliot, and Margaret F. King. *The Victorian Novel*, 76–81.

Schwarz, Daniel R. *Disraeli's Fiction*, 41–52.

Coningsby, 1844

Braun, Thom. *Disraeli the Novelist*, 73–89.

Matthews, John. "Literature and Politics: A Disraelian View." *Engl Stud in Canada* 10 (1984), 184–186.

O'Kell, Robert. "Disraeli's *Coningsby*: Political Manifesto or Psychological Romance?" *Victorian Stud* 23 (1979), 57–78.

Schwarz, Daniel R. *Disraeli's Fiction*, 81–104.

Contarini Fleming, 1832

Beaty, Jerome. "Jane Eyre at Gateshead: Mixed Signals in the Text and Context," in James R. Kincaid and Albert J. Kuhn, eds., *Victorian Literature*, 172–178.

Braun, Thom. *Disraeli the Novelist*, 50–54.

Clausson, Nils. "English Catholics and Roman Catholicism in Disraeli's Novels." *Nineteenth-Century Fiction* 33 (1979), 459–460.

Engel, Elliot, and Margaret F. King. *The Victorian Novel*, 71–77.

Matthews, John. "Literature and Politics," 180–181.

Schwarz, Daniel R. *Disraeli's Fiction*, 31–42, 51–54.
Stone, Donald D. *The Romantic Impulse*, 82–84.

Henrietta Temple, 1837

Braun, Thom. *Disraeli the Novelist*, 67–70.
Engel, Elliot, and Margaret F. King. *The Victorian Novel*, 80–84.
Schwarz, Daniel R. *Disraeli's Fiction*, 55–70.

Lothair, 1870

Braun, Thom. *Disraeli the Novelist*, 1–8, 132–137.
Buschkühl, Matthias. *Die irische . . . Frage*, 1–205.
Clausson, Nils. "English Catholics," 466–474.
Schwarz, Daniel R. *Disraeli's Fiction*, 125–138.

Sybil, 1845

Bergmann, Helena. *Between Obedience and Freedom*, 44–47, 58–62, 96–98, 148–152.
Braun, Thom. *Disraeli the Novelist*, 73–83, 85–89, 91–110.
Clausson, Nils. "English Catholics," 460–466.
Clausson, Nils. "*Lady Chatterley's Lover* and the Condition-of-England Novel." *Engl Stud in Canada* 8 (1982), 297–300.
De Stasio, Clotilde. *Lo Scrittore*, 51–65.
Gallagher, Catherine. *The Industrial Reformation*, 200–218.
Kestner, Joseph. *Protest and Reform*, 109–113.
Rataboul, Louis J. *Le pasteur anglican*, 249–252.
Schwarz, Daniel R. *Disraeli's Fiction*, 105–124.
Tarantelli, Carole Beebe. *Ritratto di ignoto*, 96–117.
Yeazell, Ruth Bernard. "Podsnappery, Sexuality, and the English Novel." *Crit Inquiry* 9 (1982), 353–354.
Yeazell, Ruth Bernard. "Why Political Novels Have Heroines: *Sybil*, *Mary Barton*, and *Felix Holt*." *Novel* 18 (1985), 128–132.

Tancred, 1847

Braun, Thom. *Disraeli the Novelist*, 113–118.
Schwarz, Daniel R. *Disraeli's Fiction*, 81–104.
Stokes, John. "Rachel's 'Terrible Beauty': An Actress among the Novelists." *ELH* 51 (1984), 777–779.
Stone, Donald D. *The Romantic Impulse*, 90–93.

Venetia, 1837

Engel, Elliot, and Margaret F. King. *The Victorian Novel*, 83–86.
Schwarz, Daniel R. *Disraeli's Fiction*, 56–65, 70–77.
Stone, Donald D. *The Romantic Impulse*, 86–88.

Vivian Grey, 1826–1827

Braun, Thom. *Disraeli the Novelist*, 28–35.
Clausson, Nils. "English Catholics," 456–457.
Engel, Elliot, and Margaret F. King. *The Victorian Novel*, 61–65.

Hart, Francis Russell. "The Regency Novel of Fashion," in Samuel I.
Mintz et al., eds., *From Smollett to James*, 129–133.
Matthews, John. "Literature and Politics," 174–178.
Schwarz, Daniel R. *Disraeli's Fiction*, 8–21, 51–54.

The Young Duke, 1831

Braun, Thom. *Disraeli the Novelist*, 43–48.
Clausson, Nils. "English Catholics," 458–459.
Davis, Jana. "Disraeli's *The Young Duke*: The Rhetoric of Heroism."
Disraeli Newsl 5:2 (1980), 26–42.
Engel, Elliot, and Margaret F. King. *The Victorian Novel*, 65–71.
Schwarz, Daniel R. *Disraeli's Fiction*, 20–31, 51–54.

NORMAN DOUGLAS

South Wind, 1917

Bold, Alan. *Modern Scottish Literature*, 190–193.
Dasenbrock, Reed Way. "Norman Douglas and the Denizens of Siren
Land." *Deus Loci* 5:4 (1982), 1–9.
Woodcock, George. "Norman Douglas: The Willing Exile." *Ariel* 13:4
(1982), 99–101.

ARTHUR CONAN DOYLE

The Hound of the Baskervilles, 1902

Brody, Howard. "The Location of Baskerville Hall." *Baker Street J* 29
(1979), 229–234, 247.
Christensen, Peter. "The Nature of Evil in *The Hound of the Basker-
villes*." *Baker Street J* 29 (1979), 209–211, 213.
Clausen, Christopher. "Sherlock Holmes, Order, and the Late-Victo-
rian Mind." *Georgia R* 38 (1984), 116–121.
Cox, Don Richard. *Arthur Conan Doyle*, 84–93.
Ferguson, Paul F. "Narrative Vision in *The Hound of the Baskervilles*."
Clues 1:2 (1980), 24–30.
Green, C. Maureen. "A Study of the Legend of the Hound of the
Baskervilles." *Baker Street J* 31 (1981), 40–43.
Sheridan, Daniel. "Later Victorian Ghost Stories: The Literature of
Belief." *Gothic* 2 (1980), 33–36.

The Land of Mist, 1926

Cox, Don Richard. *Arthur Conan Doyle*, 191–194.

The Maracot Deep, 1929

Cox, Don Richard. *Arthur Conan Doyle*, 196–200.

The Sign of the Four, 1890

Clausen, Christopher. "Sherlock Holmes," 109–110.
Cox, Don Richard. *Arthur Conan Doyle*, 43–48.

Farrell, Kirby. "Heroism, Culture, and Dread in *The Sign of Four*." *Stud in the Novel* 16 (1984), 32–48.

Guffey, George R. "Noise, Information, and Statistics in Stanislaw Lem's *The Investigation*," in George E. Slusser and Eric S. Rabkin, eds., *Hard Science Fiction*, 164–167.

Linsenmeyer, John. "Further Thoughts on *The Sign of the Four*." *Baker Street J* 25 (1975), 133–139.

A Study in Scarlet, 1887

Bonfantini, Massimo A., and Giampaolo Proni. "To Guess or Not To Guess," in Umberto Eco and Thomas A. Sebeok, eds., *The Sign of Three*, 119–123.

Clausen, Christopher. "Sherlock Holmes," 106–109.

Cox, Don Richard. *Arthur Conan Doyle*, 36–42.

Melander, Wayne. "Sierra Blanco—Found (?)." *Baker Street J* 31 (1981), 83–89.

Peterson, Audrey. *Victorian Masters*, 204–207.

Roberts, Randy. "Dr. Watson's Warning." *Baker Street J* 31 (1981), 80–82.

Roberts, Randy. "Oscar Wilde and Sherlock Holmes: A Literary Mystery." *Clues* 1:1 (1980), 41–45.

Williams, Molly Gabriel. "What Watson Did Not Know." *Baker Street J* 29 (1979), 150–151.

The Valley of Fear, 1915

Cox, Don Richard. *Arthur Conan Doyle*, 126–132.

MARGARET DRABBLE

The Garrick Year, 1964

Creighton, Joanne V. *Margaret Drabble*, 45–50.

Cunningham, Gail. "Women and Children First: The Novels of Margaret Drabble," in Thomas F. Staley, ed., *Twentieth-Century Women Novelists*, 131–132, 136–137.

Moran, Mary Hurley. *Margaret Drabble*, 46–47, 65–66, 74–75, 85–86.

Pruessner, Dee. "Patterns in *The Garrick Year*," in Dorey Schmidt and Jan Seale, eds., *Margaret Drabble*, 117–126.

Rose, Ellen Cronan. *The Novels*, 7–14.

Ruderman, Judith. "An Invitation to a Dinner Party: Margaret Drabble on Women and Food," in Dorey Schmidt and Jan Seale, eds., *Margaret Drabble*, 104–107.

Sadler, Lynn Veach. *Margaret Drabble*, 73–83.

Whittier, Gayle. "Mistresses and Madonnas in the Novels of Margaret Drabble." *Women & Lit* 1 (1980), 199–204.

The Ice Age, 1977

Creighton, Joanne V. *Margaret Drabble*, 94–101.

Cunningham, Gail. "Women and Children First," 130–132, 138–139.

Gindin, James. "Three Recent British Novels and an American Response." *Michigan Q R* 17 (1978), 223–246.

Gullette, Margaret Morganroth. "Ugly Ducklings and Swans: Margaret Drabble's Fable of Progress in the Middle Years." *Mod Lang Q* 44 (1983), 296–299.

Hansen, Elaine Tuttle. "The Uses of Imagination: Margaret Drabble's *The Ice Age*," in Ellen Cronan Rose, ed., *Critical Essays*, 151–168.

Irvine, Lorna. "No Sense of an Ending: Drabble's Continuous Fictions," in Ellen Cronan Rose, ed., *Critical Essays*, 80–82.

Joseph, Gerhard. "The *Antigone* as Cultural Touchstone: Matthew Arnold, Hegel, George Eliot, Virginia Woolf, and Margaret Drabble." *PMLA* 96 (1981), 29–30.

Korenman, Joan S. "The 'Liberation' of Margaret Drabble." *Critique* (Atlanta) 21:3 (1980), 69–71.

Lay, Mary M. "Temporal Ordering in the Fiction of Margaret Drabble." *Critique* (Atlanta) 21:3 (1980), 81–83.

Levitt, Morton P. "The New Victorians: Margaret Drabble as Trollope," in Dorey Schmidt and Jan Seale, eds., *Margaret Drabble*, 174–175.

Moran, Mary H. "Spots of Joy in the Midst of Darkness: The Universe of Margaret Drabble," in Dorey Schmidt and Jan Seale, eds., *Margaret Drabble*, 39–40.

Moran, Mary Hurley. *Margaret Drabble*, 55–56, 71–72, 76–77, 83–84, 102–104.

Pickering, Jean. "Margaret Drabble's Sense of the Middle Problem." *Twentieth Century Lit* 30 (1984), 478–479.

Rose, Ellen Cronan. *The Novels*, 112–129.

Sadler, Lynn Veach. *Margaret Drabble*, 101–114.

Stovel, Nora Foster. "The Aerial View of Modern Britain: The Airplane as a Vehicle for Idealism and Satire." *Ariel* 15:3 (1984), 29–30.

Wilson, Keith. "Jim, Jake and the Years Between: The Will to Stasis in the Contemporary British Novel." *Ariel* 13:1 (1982), 62–66.

Jerusalem the Golden, 1967

Creighton, Joanne V. *Margaret Drabble*, 67–73.

Edwards, Lee R. "*Jerusalem the Golden*: A Fable for Our Times." *Women's Stud* 6 (1979), 321–334.

Gullette, Margaret Morganroth. "Ugly Ducklings," 288–293.

Harper, Michael F. "Margaret Drabble and the Resurrection of the English Novel." *Contemp Lit* 23 (1982), 158–161. [Also in Ellen Cronan Rose, ed., *Critical Essays*, 62–63.]

Hatvary, Laurel T. "Carrie Meeber and Clara Maugham: Sisters under the Skin." *Notes on Mod Am Lit* 5:4 (1981), #26.

Lambert, Ellen Z. "Margaret Drabble and the Sense of Possibility." *Univ of Toronto Q* 49 (1980), 237–241. [Also in Ellen Cronan Rose, ed., *Critical Essays*, 40–43.]

Mayer, Suzanne H. "Margaret Drabble's Short Stories: Worksheets for Her Novels," in Dorey Schmidt and Jan Seale, eds., *Margaret Drabble*, 78–81.

Moran, Mary Hurley. *Margaret Drabble*, 50–52, 93–94, 111–112.

Rose, Ellen Cronan. *The Novels*, 28–48.

Sadler, Lynn Veach. *Margaret Drabble*, 16–23.

Stovel, Nora F. "Margaret Drabble's Golden Vision," in Dorey Schmidt and Jan Seale, eds., *Margaret Drabble*, 6–9.

The Middle Ground, 1980

Bromberg, Pamela S. "Narrative in Drabble's *The Middle Ground*: Relativity versus Teleology." *Contemp Lit* 24 (1983), 463–479.

Campbell, Jane. "Reaching Outwards: Versions of Reality in *The Middle Ground*." *J of Narrative Technique* 14 (1984), 17–30.

Creighton, Joanne V. *Margaret Drabble*, 101–112.

Efrig, Gail. "*The Middle Ground*," in Dorey Schmidt and Jan Seale, eds., *Margaret Drabble*, 178–184.

Elkins, Mary Jane. "Alenoushka's Return: Motifs and Movement in Margaret Drabble's *The Middle Ground*," in Ellen Cronan Rose, ed., *Critical Essays*, 169–180.

Gullette, Margaret Morganroth. "Ugly Ducklings," 285–287, 302–304.

Irvine, Lorna. "No Sense of an Ending," 82–84.

Moran, Mary Hurley. *Margaret Drabble*, 27–28, 33–36, 45–46, 56–58, 70–71, 77–78, 104–105, 112–115.

Pickering, Jean. "Margaret Drabble's Sense," 479–483.

Rose, Ellen Cronan. "Drabble's *The Middle Ground*: 'Mid-Life' Narrative Strategies." *Critique* (Atlanta) 23:3 (1982), 69–81.

Rubenstein, Roberta. "From Detritus to Discovery: Margaret Drabble's *The Middle Ground*." *J of Narrative Technique* 14 (1984), 1–15.

Ruderman, Judith. "An Invitation to a Dinner Party," 112–115.

Sadler, Lynn Veach. *Margaret Drabble*, 114–129.

Sadler, Lynn Veach. " 'The Society We Have': The Search for Meaning in Drabble's *The Middle Ground*." *Critique* (Atlanta) 23:3 (1982), 83–92.

Vosluisant, Marie-Jeanne. " 'The Survival of the Fittest': Résistance du moi et manipulation d'autrui dans *The Realms of Gold* et *The Middle Ground* de Margaret Drabble," in *L'Autre dans la sensibilité*, 151–163.

The Millstone, 1965

Creighton, Joanne V. *Margaret Drabble*, 50–55.

Cunningham, Gail. "Women and Children First," 131–136, 139–145.

Harper, Michael F. "Margaret Drabble," 157–160 [60–62].

Moran, Mary Hurley. *Margaret Drabble*, 44–45, 82–83, 109–110.

Rose, Ellen Cronan. *The Novels*, 15–23.

Sadler, Lynn Veach. *Margaret Drabble*, 25–35.

Sörbö, Linda Ricketts. "The Way Contemporary Women Write: An Analysis of Margaret Drabble's *The Millstone*." *Edda*, 1981, 93–101.

Whittier, Gayle. "Mistresses and Madonnas," 197–199, 202–204.

The Needle's Eye, 1972

Creighton, Joanne V. *Margaret Drabble*, 74–81.

Davidson, Arnold E. "Parables of Grace in *The Needle's Eye*," in Dorey Schmidt and Jan Seale, eds., *Margaret Drabble*, 66–74.

Dixson, Barbara. "Patterned Figurative Language in *The Needle's Eye*," in Dorey Schmidt and Jan Seale, eds., *Margaret Drabble*, 128–137.

Gullette, Margaret Morganroth. "Ugly Ducklings," 293–295.

Hasler, Jörg. "Margaret Drabble, *The Needle's Eye*," in Rainer Lengeler, ed., *Englische Literatur*, 278–288.

Irvine, Lorna. "No Sense of an Ending," 78–79.

Korenman, Joan S. "The 'Liberation'," 64–65.

Lay, Mary M. "Margaret Drabble's *The Needle's Eye*: Jamesian Perception of Self." *Coll Lang Assoc J* 28 (1984), 33–45.

Lay, Mary M. "Temporal Ordering," 76–79.

Moran, Mary Hurley. *Margaret Drabble*, 6–7, 38–39, 41–42, 47–48, 53–54, 69–70, 75–76.

Pickering, Jean. "Margaret Drabble's Sense," 477.

Rose, Ellen Cronan. *The Novels*, 71–93.

Ruderman, Judith. "An Invitation to a Dinner Party," 107–109.

Sadler, Lynn Veach. *Margaret Drabble*, 53–63.

Sage, Lorna. "Female Fictions: The Women Novelists," in Malcolm Bradbury and David Palmer, eds., *The Contemporary English Novel*, 74–76.

Showalter, Elaine. *A Literature*, 306–307.

Realms of Gold, 1975

Bromberg, Pamela S. "Romantic Revisionism in Margaret Drabble's *The Realms of Gold*," in Dorey Schmidt and Jan Seale, eds., *Margaret Drabble*, 48–63.

Creighton, Joanne V. *Margaret Drabble*, 81–90.

Cunningham, Gail. "Women and Children First," 145–151.

Davis, Cynthia A. "Unfolding Form: Narrative Approach and Theme in *The Realms of Gold*." *Mod Lang Q* 40 (1979), 390–402. [Also in Ellen Cronan Rose, ed., *Critical Essays*, 141–151.]

Gullette, Margaret Morganroth. "Ugly Ducklings," 299–302.

Harper, Michael F. "Margaret Drabble," 164–168 [66–70].

Irvine, Lorna. "No Sense of an Ending," 79.

Kaplan, Carey. "A Vision of Power in Margaret Drabble's *The Realms of Gold*." *J of Women's Stud in Lit* 1 (1979), 233–242. [Also in Ellen Cronan Rose, ed., *Critical Essays*, 133–140.]

Korenman, Joan S. "The 'Liberation'," 65–69.

Lambert, Ellen Z. "Margaret Drabble," 241–249 [44–51].

Lay, Mary M. "Temporal Ordering," 79–81.

Levitt, Morton P. "The New Victorians," 172–173.

Little, Judy. *Comedy and the Woman Writer*, 184–189.

Little, Judy. "Margaret Drabble and the Romantic Imagination: *The Realms of Gold*." *Prairie Schooner* 55 (1981), 241–252.

Moran, Mary H. "Spots of Joy," 40–43.

Moran, Mary Hurley. *Margaret Drabble*, 32–33, 54–55, 64–65, 67–68, 100–102.

Pickering, Jean. "Margaret Drabble's Sense," 477–478.

Pratt, Annis. *Archetypal Patterns*, 91–92.

Rose, Ellen Cronan. *The Novels*, 94–111.

Rowe, Margaret M. "The Uses of the Past in Margaret Drabble's *The Realms of Gold*," in Dorey Schmidt and Jan Seale, eds., *Margaret Drabble*, 158–166.

Ruderman, Judith. "An Invitation to a Dinner Party," 109–112.

Sadler, Lynn Veach. *Margaret Drabble*, 85–101.

Sage, Lorna. "Female Fictions," 76–77.

Stovel, Nora F. "Margaret Drabble's Golden Vision," 9–11.

Vosluisant, Marie-Jeanne. " 'The Survival of the Fittest'," 151–163.

Whittier, Gayle. "Mistresses and Madonnas," 209–213.

A Summer Bird-Cage, 1963

Creighton, Joanne V. *Margaret Drabble*, 39–45.

Davidson, Arnold E. "Pride and Prejudice in Margaret Drabble's *A Summer Bird-Cage*." *Arizona Q* 38 (1982), 303–310.

Harper, Michael F. "Margaret Drabble," 155–157 [58–60].

Lambert, Ellen Z. "Margaret Drabble," 229–237 [32–39].

Moran, Mary Hurley. *Margaret Drabble*, 43–44, 72–73, 84–85, 110–111.

Rose, Ellen Cronan. *The Novels*, 1–7.

Sadler, Lynn Veach. *Margaret Drabble*, 9–16.

Zeman, Anthea. *Presumptuous Girls*, 34–37, 39–41.

The Waterfall, 1969

Berg, Temma F. "From Pamela to Jane Grey; or, How Not to Become the Heroine of Your Own Text." *Stud in the Novel* 17 (1985), 130–134.

Creighton, Joanne V. *Margaret Drabble*, 55–64.

Creighton, Joanne V. "Reading Margaret Drabble's *The Waterfall*," in Ellen Cronan Rose, ed., *Critical Essays*, 106–118.

Fuoroli, Caryn. "Sophistry or Simple Truth? Narrative Technique in Margaret Drabble's *The Waterfall*." *J of Narrative Technique* 11 (1981), 110–123.

Harper, Michael F. "Margaret Drabble," 161–164 [63–66].

Irvine, Lorna. "No Sense of an Ending," 77–78.

Korenman, Joan S. "The 'Liberation'," 62–64.

Levitt, Morton P. "The New Victorians," 170–172.

Mayer, Suzanne H. "Margaret Drabble's Short Stories," 81–82.

Moran, Mary Hurley. *Margaret Drabble*, 28–29, 40–41, 52–53, 86–89.

Pratt, Annis. *Archetypal Patterns*, 90–91.
Rose, Ellen Cronan. "Feminine Endings—and Beginnings: Margaret Drabble's *The Waterfall*." *Contemp Lit* 21 (1980), 81–99.
Rose, Ellen Cronan. *The Novels*, 49–70.
Rubenstein, Roberta. "*The Waterfall*: The Myth of Psyche, Romantic Tradition, and the Female Quest," in Dorey Schmidt and Jan Seale, eds., *Margaret Drabble*, 139–156.
Sadler, Lynn Veach. *Margaret Drabble*, 41–49.
Skoller, Eleanor Honig. "The Progress of a Letter: Truth, Feminism, and *The Waterfall*," in Ellen Cronan Rose, ed., *Critical Essays*, 119–131.
Walker, Nancy. "Women Drifting: Drabble's *The Waterfall* and Chopin's *The Awakening*." *Denver Q* 17:4 (1983), 88–96.
Whittier, Gayle. "Mistresses and Madonnas," 204–208.

DAPHNE DU MAURIER

Rebecca, 1938

Bromley, Roger. "The Gentry, Bourgeois Hegemony and Popular Fiction." *Lit and Hist* 7 (1981), 166–176.

GEORGE DU MAURIER

The Martian, 1897

Kelly, Richard. *George Du Maurier*, 125–153.

Peter Ibbetson, 1891

Allen, Richard J. "Documentary Realism and Artistic Licence: A Note on an Emblematic Prison Gate in *The Nether World* and *Peter Ibbetson*." *Gissing Newsl* 17:2 (1981), 22–23.
Kelly, Richard. *George Du Maurier*, 57–84.

Trilby, 1894

Auerbach, Nina. "Magi and Maidens: The Romance of the Victorian Freud." *Crit Inquiry* 8 (1981), 284–289.
Auerbach, Nina. *Woman and the Demon*, 17–21.
Kelly, Richard. *George Du Maurier*, 87–123.
Lamarca Margalef, Jordi. *Ciencia y literatura*, 63–64.
Zatlin, Linda Gertner. *The Nineteenth-Century Anglo-Jewish Novel*, 127–131.

JANE DUNCAN

My Friend Sashie, 1972

Bold, Alan. *Modern Scottish Literature*, 218–220.

LAWRENCE DURRELL

The Alexandria Quartet, 1961

Ashworth, Ann. "Durrell's Hermetic Puer and Senex in *The Alexandria Quartet*." *Critique* (Atlanta) 26 (1985), 67–78.

Brewer, Jennifer L. "Character and Psychological Place: The Justine/ Sophia Relation." *Deus Loci* 5 (1981), 236–239.

Cornu, Marie-Renée. *La dynamique du "Quatuor d'Alexandrie."*

Creed, Walter G. *The Muse of Science.*

Franklin, Steve. "Space-Time and Creativity in Lawrence Durrell's *Alexandria Quartet*." *Perspectives on Contemp Lit* 5 (1979), 55–61.

Ghinste, Josée van de. *Lawrence Durrell*, 11–179.

Kellman, Steven G. *The Self-Begetting Novel*, 93–97.

Lemon, Lee T. *Portraits of the Artist*, 11–42.

Lewis, Nancy W. "Two Thematic Applications of Einsteinian Field Structure in *The Alexandria Quartet*." *Deus Loci* 6:1 (1982), 1–10.

Morrison, Ray. " 'A Mirror Reference to Reality': Justine as a Schopenhauerian Woman in *The Alexandria Quartet*." *Deus Loci* 5 (1981), 42–50.

Musumarra, Adriana. "Mito e metafora nell'Alessandria di Durrell," in Agostino Lombardo, ed., *Studi inglesi*, 321–352.

Nichols, J. R. "The Paradise of Bitter Fruit: Lawrence Durrell's *Alexandria Quartet*." *Deus Loci* 5 (1981), 224–234.

Nichols, James R. "Lawrence Durrell's *Alexandria Quartet*: The Paradisc of Bitter Fruit." *Deus Loci* 3:2 (1979), 9–16.

Peirce, Carol Marshall. " 'Wrinkled Deep in Time': *The Alexandria Quartet* as Many-Layered Palimpsest." *Deus Loci* 2:4 (1979), 11–28.

Pinchin, Jane Lagoudis. "Durrell's Fatal Cleopatra." *Deus Loci* 5 (1981), 24–39. [Also in *Mod Fiction Stud* 28 (1982), 229–236.]

Riggan, William. *Picaros*, 11–13.

Robillard, Douglas, Jr. "In the Capital of Memory: The Alexandria of Durrell and Cavafy." *Deus Loci* 5 (1981), 78–87.

Schwerdt, Lisa. "Coming of Age in Alexandria: The Narrator." *Deus Loci* 5 (1981), 210–221.

Stromberg, Robert L. "The Contribution of Relativity to the Inconsistency of Form in *The Alexandria Quartet*." *Deus Loci* 5 (1981), 246–256.

Thornton, Lawrence. *Unbodied Hope*, 129–148.

Volkoff, Vladimir. *Lawrence le Magnifique*, 15–140.

The Black Book, 1938

Richtofen, Patrick von. "Lawrence Durrell, Prince of Denmark." *Deus Loci* 4:2 (1980), 3–11.

Livia, 1978

MacNiven, Ian S. "Steps to *Livia*: The State of Durrell's Fiction." *Deus Loci* 5 (1981), 330–347.

Monsieur: or, The Prince of Darkness, 1974

Carley, James P. "An Interview with Lawrence Durrell on the Background to *Monsieur* and Its Sequels." *Malahat R* 51 (1979), 42–46.

Carley, James P. "Lawrence Durrell's Avignon Quincunx and Gnostic Heresy." *Deus Loci* 5 (1981), 284–304.

MacNiven, Ian S. "Steps to *Livia*," 330–347.

Nunquam, 1970

Dickson, Gregory. "Spengler's Theory of Architecture in Durrell's *Tunc* and *Nunquam*." *Deus Loci* 5 (1981), 272–280.

Kersnowski, Frank. "Paradox and Resolution in Durrell's *Tunc* and *Nunquam*." *Deus Loci* 7:1 (1983), 1–13.

Mablekos, Carole. "Lawrence Durrell's *Tunc* and *Nunquam*: Rebirth Now or Never." *Sphinx* 4:1 (1981), 48–54.

Tunc, 1968

Dickson, Gregory. "Spengler's Theory," 272–280.

Kersnowski, Frank. "Paradox and Resolution," 1–13.

Mablekos, Carole. "Lawrence Durrell's *Tunc* and *Nunquam*," 48–54.

ERIC RUCKER EDDISON

A Fish Dinner in Memison, 1941

Pesch, Helmut W. "The Sign of the Worm: Images of Death and Immortality in the Fiction of E. R. Eddison," in Carl B. Yoke and Donald M. Hassler, eds., *Death and the Serpent*, 95–100.

The Mezentian Gate, 1958

Pesch, Helmut W. "The Sign of the Worm," 95–100.

Mistress of Mistresses, 1935

Pesch, Helmut W. "The Sign of the Worm," 95–100.

The Worm Ouroboros, 1922

Pesch, Helmut W. "The Sign of the Worm," 91–95.

MARIA EDGEWORTH

The Absentee, 1812

Colgan, Maurice. "After Rackrent: Ascendancy Nationalism in Maria Edgeworth's Later Irish Novels," in Heinz Kosok, ed., *Studies*, 37–39.

Harden, Elizabeth. *Maria Edgeworth*, 107–112.

Hart, Francis Russell. "The Regency Novel of Fashion," in Samuel I. Mintz et al., eds., *From Smollett to James*, 110–112.

Tracy, Robert. "Maria Edgeworth and Lady Morgan: Legality versus Legitimacy." *Nineteenth-Century Fiction* 40 (1985), 10–16.

Warner, Alan. *A Guide*, 47–48.
Williams, Merryn. *Women in the English Novel*, 65–67.

Belinda, 1801

Atkinson, Colin B., and Jo Atkinson. "Maria Edgeworth, *Belinda*, and Women's Rights." *Eire-Ireland* 19:4 (1984), 94–118.

Burlin, Katrin R. " 'At the Crossroads': Sister Authors and the Sister Arts," in Mary Anne Schofield and Cecilia Macheski, eds., *Fetter'd or Free?*, 69–71.

Figes, Eva. *Sex and Subterfuge*, 87–89.

Harden, Elizabeth. *Maria Edgeworth*, 50–56.

Hart, Francis Russell. "The Regency Novel," 106–109.

Topliss, Iain. "Mary Wollstonecraft and Maria Edgeworth's Modern Ladies." *Etudes Irlandaises* 6 (1981), 23–28.

Voss-Clesly, Patricia. *Tendencies of Character*, 143–149, 465–469, 481–485, 587–595, 737–741, 752–754, 757–761.

Williams, Merryn. *Women in the English Novel*, 62–64.

Zeman, Anthea. *Presumptuous Girls*, 14–16.

Castle Rackrent, 1800

Connelly, Joseph F. "Transparent Poses: *Castle Rackrent* and *The Memoirs of Barry Lyndon*." *Eire-Ireland* 14:2 (1979), 37–43.

Cronin, John. *The Anglo-Irish Novel*, 25–39.

Figes, Eva. *Sex and Subterfuge*, 25–27, 85–87.

Harden, Elizabeth. *Maria Edgeworth*, 94–103.

Jeffares, A. Norman. "Anglo-Irish Literature: Treatment for Radio," in Masaru Sekine, ed., *Irish Writers*, 88–89.

Kestner, Joseph. *Protest and Reform*, 26–28.

Mortimer, Anthony. "*Castle Rackrent* and Its Historical Contexts." *Etudes Irlandaises* 9 (1984), 107–121.

Omasreiter, Ria. *Travels*, 213–224.

Sheeran, P. F. "Colonists and Colonized: Some Aspects of Anglo-Irish Literature from Swift to Joyce." *Yearbook of Engl Stud* 13 (1983), 104–106.

Tracy, Robert. "Maria Edgeworth and Lady Morgan," 1–4.

Warner, Alan. *A Guide*, 43–47.

Ennui, 1809

Colgan, Maurice. "After Rackrent," 37.

Harden, Elizabeth. *Maria Edgeworth*, 103–107.

Tracy, Robert. "Maria Edgeworth and Lady Morgan," 4–7.

Harrington, 1817

Harden, Elizabeth. *Maria Edgeworth*, 87–93.

Papay, Twila Yates. "A Near-Miss on the Psychological Novel: Maria Edgeworth's *Harrington*," in Mary Anne Schofield and Cecilia Macheski, eds., *Fetter'd or Free?*, 360–368.

Helen, 1834

Harden, Elizabeth. *Maria Edgeworth*, 66–74.
Voss-Clesly, Patricia. *Tendencies of Character*, 152–153, 469–476, 485–489, 603–611.

Lenora, 1806

Harden, Elizabeth. *Maria Edgeworth*, 56–61.
Topliss, Iain. "Mary Wollstonecraft," 25–28.

The Modern Griselda, 1805

Harden, Elizabeth. *Maria Edgeworth*, 47–50.
Topliss, Iain. "Mary Wollstonecraft," 24.

Ormond, 1817

Colgan, Maurice. "After Rackrent," 39–42.
Howard, William. "Regional Perspective in Early Nineteenth-Century Fiction: The Case of *Ormond*." *Wordsworth Circle* 10 (1979), 331–338.
Reilly, Pamela. "The Influence of *Waverley* on Maria Edgeworth's *Ormond*," in J. H. Alexander and David Hewitt, eds., *Scott and His Influence*, 290–297.
Tracy, Robert. "Maria Edgeworth and Lady Morgan," 16–19.
Warner, Alan. *A Guide*, 48–49.

Patronage, 1814

Harden, Elizabeth. *Maria Edgeworth*, 81–87.
Teyssandier, Hubert. *Les formes de la création*, 72–94.

Vivian, 1812

Harden, Elizabeth. *Maria Edgeworth*, 76–81.
Voss-Clesly, Patricia. *Tendencies of Character*, 149–152, 469–476, 489–490, 595–603, 750–752, 790–814.

GEORGE ELIOT

Adam Bede, 1859

Ashton, Rosemary. *George Eliot*, 27–35.
Atkins, Dorothy. *George Eliot*, 91–157.
Auerbach, Nina. "The Rise of the Fallen Woman." *Nineteenth-Century Fiction* 35 (1980), 44–50.
Auerbach, Nina. *Romantic Imprisonment*, 260–265.
Auerbach, Nina. *Woman and the Demon*, 174–178.
Bell, Loren C. "A Kind of Madness: Hetty Sorrel's Infanticide." *Platte Valley R* 11:1 (1983), 82–87.
Burch, Beth. "Eliot's *Adam Bede*." *Explicator* 40:1 (1981), 27–28.
Cameron, J. M. "Dickens and the Angels." *Univ of Toronto Q* 50 (1980/81), 166–167.
Carlisle, Janice. *The Sense of an Audience*, 187–213.

Clayton, Jay. "Visionary Power and Narrative Form: Wordsworth and *Adam Bede*." *ELH* 46 (1979), 645–671.

Dalal, D. S. *George Eliot*, 95–98, 127–135, 207–212.

Doyle, Mary Ellen. *The Sympathetic Response*, 23–55.

Eagleton, Mary, and David Pierce. *Attitudes to Class*, 56–59.

Ermarth, Elizabeth Deeds. *George Eliot*, 68–77.

Ferris, Ina. "The Reader in the Rhetoric of Realism: Scott, Thackeray and Eliot," in J. H. Alexander and David Hewitt, eds., *Scott and His Influence*, 389–391.

Fisher, Philip. *Making Up Society*, 39–65.

Foster, Shirley. *Victorian Women's Fiction*, 201–203, 207–208.

Harris, Mason. "Infanticide and Respectability: Hetty Sorrel as Abandoned Child in *Adam Bede*." *Engl Stud in Canada* 9 (1983), 177–194.

Hunter, Shelagh. *Victorian Idyllic Fiction*, 120–166.

Jones, Lawrence. "George Eliot and Pastoral Tragicomedy in Hardy's *Far from the Madding Crowd*." *Stud in Philology* 77 (1980), 415–425.

Kestner, Joseph A. *The Spatiality*, 37–40.

Longford, Elizabeth. *Eminent Victorian Women*, 77–78.

Malcolm, David. "*Adam Bede* and the Unions: 'A . . . Proletarian Novel'." *Zeitschrift für Anglistik und Amerikanistik* 31 (1983), 5–15.

Mann, Karen B. *The Language*, 10–12, 70–72, 100–102, 139–142, 153–155, 157–159, 189–191.

Mitchell, Sally. *The Fallen Angel*, 66–69.

Myers, William. *The Teaching*, 25–37, 110–112, 145–150.

Nestor, Pauline. *Female Friendships*, 173–175.

Newton, K. M. *George Eliot*, 38–39, 55–56, 86–90.

Palliser, Charles. "*Adam Bede* and 'the Story of the Past'," in Anne Smith, ed., *George Eliot*, 55–76.

Pinion, F. B. *A George Eliot Companion*, 92–107.

Putzell, Sara Moore. "George Eliot's Location of Value in History." *Renascence* 32 (1980), 174–175.

Putzell-Korab, Sara M. *The Evolving Consciousness*, 26–30.

Qualls, Barry V. *The Secular Pilgrims*, 143–146.

Rataboul, Louis J. *Le pasteur anglican*, 129–131, 202–203.

Sadoff, Dianne F. *Monsters of Affection*, 107–112.

Schug, Charles. *The Romantic Genesis*, 49–59.

Shuttleworth, Sally. *George Eliot*, 24–50.

Stokes, Edward. *Hawthorne's Influence*, 122–146.

Stone, Donald D. *The Romantic Impulse*, 205–210.

Vargish, Thomas. *The Providential Aesthetic*, 165–181.

Watt, George. *The Fallen Woman*, 68–71.

Welsh, Alexander. *George Eliot*, 137–141, 149–153.

Wiesenfarth, Joseph. *George Eliot's Mythmaking*, 77–95.

Williams, Merryn. *Women in the English Novel*, 140–143.

Witemeyer, Hugh. *George Eliot*, 48–54, 108–120.

Wright, T. R. "From Bumps to Morals: The Phrenological Background to George Eliot's Moral Framework." *R of Engl Stud* 33 (1982), 39–40.

Daniel Deronda, 1876

Alley, Henry. "Literature and the Miscast Marriages of *Middlemarch* and *Daniel Deronda*." *Cithara* 19:1 (1979), 21–25.

Alley, Henry. "New Year's at the Abbey: Point of View in the Pivotal Chapters of *Daniel Deronda*." *J of Narrative Technique* 9 (1979), 147–155.

Argyle, Gisela. *German Elements*, 62–85.

Ashton, Rosemary. *George Eliot*, 83–93.

Auerbach, Emily. "The Domesticated *Maestro*: George Eliot's Klesmer." *Papers on Lang & Lit* 19 (1983), 280–292.

Baker, William. "George Eliot and Zionism," in Alice Shalvi, ed., *"Daniel Deronda,"* 47–63.

Beer, Gillian. "Beyond Determinism: George Eliot and Virginia Woolf," in Mary Jacobus, ed., *Women Writing*, 90–94.

Belkin, Roslyn. "What George Eliot Knew: Women and Power in *Daniel Deronda*." *Intl J of Women's Stud* 4 (1981), 472–483.

Belsey, Catherine. "Re-Reading the Great Tradition," in Peter Widdowson, ed., *Re-Reading*, 121–135.

Brownstein, Rachel M. *Becoming a Heroine*, 203–238.

Calimani, Dario. *"Daniel Deronda* tra *Novel* e *Romance,"* in Agostino Lombardo, ed., *Studi inglesi*, 125–164.

Caraes, Colette. "La peur dans *Daniel Deronda* de G. Eliot." *Cahiers Victoriens et Edouardiens* 15 (1982), 63–70.

Carlisle, Janice. *The Sense of an Audience*, 216–219.

Caron, James. "The Rhetoric of Magic in *Daniel Deronda*." *Stud in the Novel* 15 (1983), 1–9.

Carpenter, Mary Wilson. "The Apocalypse of the Old Testament: *Daniel Deronda* and the Interpretation of Interpretation." *PMLA* 99 (1984), 56–67.

Collister, Peter. "Portraits of 'Audacious Youth': George Eliot and Mrs Humphry Ward." *Engl Stud* 64 (1983), 299–317.

Dalal, D. S. *George Eliot*, 82–88, 114–122, 167–170, 237–241.

Dale, Peter. "Symbolic Representation and the Means of Revolution in *Daniel Deronda*." *Victorian Newsl* 59 (1981), 25–30.

Daleski, H. M. "Owning and Disowning: The Unity of *Daniel Deronda,"* in Alice Shalvi, ed., *"Daniel Deronda,"* 67–85.

Daleski, H. M. *Unities*, 27–38.

Daniels, Elizabeth A. "A Meredithian Glance at Gwendolen Harleth," in Gordon S. Haight and Rosemary T. VanArsdel, eds., *George Eliot*, 28–37.

David, Deirdre. *Fictions of Resolution*, 136–204.

Doyle, Mary Ellen. *The Sympathetic Response*, 159–170.

Edwards, P. D. "*Daniel Deronda*: New Elements and Long Familiar Types." *Sydney Stud in Engl* 6 (1980–81), 49–61.

Ermarth, Elizabeth Deeds. *George Eliot*, 121–131.

Fischer, Sandra K. "Eliot's *Daniel Deronda*." *Explicator* 37:3 (1979), 21–22.

Fisher, Philip. *Making Up Society*, 203–227.

Foltinek, Herbert. "George Eliot und der unwissende Erzähler." *Germanisch-Romanische Monatsschrift* 33 (1983), 172–178.

Foster, Shirley. *Victorian Women's Fiction*, 210–214.

Gallagher, Catherine. "George Eliot and *Daniel Deronda*: The Prostitute and the Jewish Question," in Ruth Bernard Yeazell, ed., *Sex*, 39–60.

Garrett, Peter K. *The Victorian Multiplot Novel*, 167–179.

Goldberg, S. L. "Morality and Literature; with Some Reflections on *Daniel Deronda*." *Crit R* 22 (1980), 3–20.

Goode, John. " 'The Affections Clad with Knowledge': Woman's Duty and the Public Life." *Lit and Hist* 9 (1983), 38–41.

Hardy, Barbara. *Forms of Feeling*, 139–142.

Hochman, Baruch. "*Daniel Deronda*: The Zionist Plot and the Problematic of George Eliot's Art," in Alice Shalvi, ed., *"Daniel Deronda,"* 113–133.

Howe, Irving. "George Eliot and the Jews." *Partisan R* 46 (1979), 359–375.

Howells, Coral Ann. "Dreams and Visions in George Eliot's Fiction." *AUMLA* 56 (1981), 178–181.

Huzzard, John A. "The Emergence of Women in Society as Revealed in George Eliot's *Romola* and *Daniel Deronda*." *George Eliot Fellowship R* 12 (1981), 10–12.

Irwin, Michael. *Picturing*, 61–64.

Jumeau, Alain. "Héritiers et héritages dans *Daniel Deronda*." *Etudes Anglaises* 38 (1985), 24–35.

Kubitschek, Missy Dehn. "Eliot as Activist: Marriage and Politics in *Daniel Deronda*." *Coll Lang Assoc J* 28 (1984), 176–189.

Leech, Geoffrey N., and Michael H. Short. *Style in Fiction*, 282–286.

Lerner, Laurence. "George Eliot's Struggle with Realism," in Alice Shalvi, ed., *"Daniel Deronda,"* 89–109.

Levine, George. "George Eliot's Hypothesis of Reality." *Nineteenth-Century Fiction* 35 (1980), 17–28.

Levine, Herbert J. "The Marriage of Allegory and Realism in *Daniel Deronda*." *Genre* 15 (1982), 421–443.

McCarron, Robert. "Evil and Eliot's Religion of Humanity: Grandcourt in *Daniel Deronda*." *Ariel* 11:1 (1980), 71–87.

McCobb, E. A. "*Daniel Deronda* as Will and Representation: George Eliot and Schopenhauer." *Mod Lang R* 80 (1985), 533–549.

McCobb, E. A. "The Morality of Musical Genius: Schopenhauerian Views in *Daniel Deronda*." *Forum for Mod Lang Stud* 19 (1983), 321–330.

McVeagh, John. *Tradefull Merchants*, 146–147.

Mann, Karen B. "George Eliot's Language of Nature: Production and Consumption." *ELH* 48 (1981), 212–215.

Mann, Karen B. *The Language*, 32–39, 45–47, 54–59, 70–78, 93–96, 100–105, 109–112, 127–131, 134–139, 147–150, 154–157, 163–165.

Mann, Karen B. "Self, Shell and World: George Eliot's Language of Space." *Genre* 15 (1982), 450–457, 471–474.

Martin, Carol A. "No Angel in the House: Victorian Mothers and Daughters in George Eliot and Elizabeth Gaskell." *Midwest Q* 24 (1983), 306–312.

Mayer, Hans. *Outsiders*, 342–345.

Milner, Ian. "*Daniel Deronda* and Contemporary English Society," in Magdi Wahba, ed., *Centenary Essays*, 69–86.

Mintz, Alan. "*Daniel Deronda* and the Messianic Vocation," in Alice Shalvi, ed., *"Daniel Deronda,"* 137–156.

Moldstad, David. "The Dantean Purgatorial Metaphor in *Daniel Deronda*." *Papers on Lang & Lit* 19 (1983), 183–198.

Myers, William. *The Teaching*, 176–182, 210–228.

Nadel, Ira Bruce. "From Fathers and Sons to Sons and Lovers." *Dalhousie R* 59 (1979), 232–233.

Naman, Anne Aresty. *The Jew*, 162–203.

Nestor, Pauline. *Female Friendships*, 193–195, 199–201.

Newton, K. M. "*Daniel Deronda* and Circumcision." *Essays in Criticism* 31 (1981), 313–325.

Newton, K. M. *George Eliot*, 168–200.

Panitz, Esther L. *The Alien*, 117–119.

Pell, Nancy. "The Fathers' Daughters in *Daniel Deronda*." *Nineteenth-Century Fiction* 36 (1982), 424–451.

Pinion, F. B. *A George Eliot Companion*, 201–218.

Poole, Adrian. " 'Hidden Affinities' in *Daniel Deronda*." *Essays in Criticism* 33 (1983), 294–310.

Putzell, Sara Moore. "Attracting the Majority: M. E. Braddon and George Eliot." *George Eliot Fellowship R* 11 (1980), 14–19.

Putzell, Sara Moore. "George Eliot's Location of Value," 168–169, 175.

Putzell-Korab, Sara M. *The Evolving Consciousness*, 111–134.

Putzell-Korab, Sara M. "The Role of the Prophet: The Rationality of Daniel Deronda's Idealist Mission." *Nineteenth-Century Fiction* 37 (1982), 170–187.

Pykett, Lyn. "Typology and the End(s) of History in *Daniel Deronda*." *Lit and Hist* 9 (1983), 62–72.

Qualls, Barry V. *The Secular Pilgrims*, 168–187.

Raider, Ruth. " 'The Flash of Fervour': *Daniel Deronda*," in Ian Gregor, ed., *Reading the Victorian Novel*, 253–271.

Reed, John R., and Jerry Herron. "George Eliot's Illegitimate Children." *Nineteenth-Century Fiction* 40 (1985), 179–181.

Robertson, Linda K. "Education and *Daniel Deronda*: Three of Eliot's Concepts." *George Eliot Fellowship R* 14 (1983), 56–60.

Scribner, Margo. "*Daniel Deronda* and *Ivanhoe*: The Dark Lady and the Knight." *Graduate Engl Papers* 9:1 (1979), 3–8.

Shuttleworth, Sally. *George Eliot*, 175–200.

Shuttleworth, Sally. "The Language of Science and Psychology in George Eliot's *Daniel Deronda*," in James Paradis and Thomas Postlewait, eds., *Victorian Science*, 269–298.

Smith, Grahame. *The Novel & Society*, 193–211.

Stange, G. Robert. "The Voices of the Essayist." *Nineteenth-Century Fiction* 35 (1980), 328–330.

Still, Judith. "Rousseau in *Daniel Deronda*." *Revue de Littérature Comparée* 221 (1982), 62–77.

Stokes, Edward. *Hawthorne's Influence*, 207–209.

Stokes, John. "Rachel's 'Terrible Beauty': An Actress among the Novelists." *ELH* 51 (1984), 784–789.

Stone, Donald D. *The Romantic Impulse*, 240–248.

Stott, G. St. John. "*Daniel Deronda*: George Eliot's 'Negro Nove'." *George Eliot Fellowship R* 16 (1985), 44–48.

Vargish, Thomas. *The Providential Aesthetic*, 228–243.

Weinstein, Philip M. *The Semantics of Desire*, 89–103.

Weiss, Barbara. "The Dilemma of Happily Ever After: Marriage and the Victorian Novel," in Anne C. Hargrove and Maurine Magliocco, eds., *Portraits of Marriage*, 84.

Welsh, Alexander. *George Eliot*, 259–273, 276–334, 341–344.

Werses, Shmuel. "The Jewish Reception of *Daniel Deronda*," in Alice Shalvi, ed., *"Daniel Deronda,"* 11–43.

Wiesenfarth, Joseph. "*Antique Gems* from *Romola* to *Daniel Deronda*," in Gordon S. Haight and Rosemary T. VanArsdel, eds., *George Eliot*, 60–62.

Wiesenfarth, Joseph. *George Eliot's Mythmaking*, 210–212, 215–230.

Wijesinha, Rajiva. *The Androgynous Trollope*, 265–268.

Williams, Merryn. *Women in the English Novel*, 149–154.

Wilt, Judith. *Ghosts of the Gothic*, 209–230.

Witemeyer, Hugh. *George Eliot*, 64–66, 92–104, 120–124, 140–142.

Wright, T. R. "From Bumps to Morals," 41–43.

Wright, T. R. "George Eliot and Positivism: A Reassessment." *Mod Lang R* 76 (1981), 270–272.

Zimmerman, Bonnie. "Gwendolen Harleth and 'The Girl of the Period'," in Anne Smith, ed., *George Eliot*, 196–215.

Zimmerman, Bonnie. " 'The Mother's History' in George Eliot's Life, Literature and Political Ideology," in Cathy N. Davidson and E. M. Broner, eds., *The Lost Tradition*, 91–93.

Felix Holt, 1866

Ashton, Rosemary. *George Eliot*, 57–62.

Atkins, Dorothy. *George Eliot*, 166–169.

Bergmann, Helena. "Politics through Love: Felix Holt and the Industrial Novel." *Moderna Språk* 74 (1980), 219–226.

Butwin, Joseph. "The Pacification of the Crowd: From 'Janet's Repentance' to *Felix Holt*." *Nineteenth-Century Fiction* 35 (1980), 366–371.

Cohen, Susan R. "Avoiding the High Prophetic Strain: DeQuincey's Mail-Coach and *Felix Holt*." *Victorian Newsl* 64 (1983), 19–20.

Dalal, D. S. *George Eliot*, 71–77, 150–157.

Doyle, Mary Ellen. *The Sympathetic Response*, 93–115.

Ermarth, Elizabeth Deeds. *George Eliot*, 102–107.

Ermarth, Elizabeth Deeds. "George Eliot's Conception of Sympathy." *Nineteenth-Century Fiction* 40 (1985), 36–42.

Fisher, Philip. *Making Up Society*, 144–162.

Gallagher, Catherine. "The Failure of Realism: *Felix Holt*." *Nineteenth- Century Fiction* 35 (1980), 378–384.

Gallagher, Catherine. *The Industrial Reformation*, 237–252.

Kestner, Joseph. *Protest and Reform*, 193–195, 200–208.

Longford, Elizabeth. *Eminent Victorian Women*, 79.

McCormack, Kathleen. "The Sybil and the Hyena: George Eliot's Wollstonecraftian Feminism." *Dalhousie R* 63 (1983–84), 611–612.

McVeagh, John. *Tradefull Merchants*, 145–146.

Mann, Karen B. "George Eliot's Language," 209–211.

Mann, Karen B. *The Language*, 48–50, 70–72, 83–85, 93–95, 99–104, 121–124, 157–160.

Meckier, Jerome. "Hidden Rivalries in Victorian Fiction: The Case of the Two Esthers," in Robert Giddings, ed., *The Changing World*, 219–237.

Myers, William. *The Teaching*, 71–85, 113–115, 168–175.

Nestor, Pauline. *Female Friendships*, 188–191.

Newton, K. M. *George Eliot*, 40–50, 76–78.

Pinion, F. B. "Coincidence and Consequence Relative to a Scene in *Felix Holt*." *George Eliot Fellowship R* 10 (1979), 7–9.

Pinion, F. B. *A George Eliot Companion*, 153–164.

Putzell-Korab, Sara M. *The Evolving Consciousness*, 87–89.

Qualls, Barry V. *The Secular Pilgrims*, 159–162.

Sadoff, Dianne F. *Monsters of Affection*, 71–73, 78–81, 106–107.

Sandler, Florence. "The Unity of *Felix Holt*," in Gordon S. Haight and Rosemary T. VanArsdel, eds., *George Eliot*, 137–151.

Sheets, Robin. "*Felix Holt*: Language, the Bible, and the Problematic of Meaning." *Nineteenth-Century Fiction* 37 (1982), 146–169.

Shuttleworth, Sally. *George Eliot*, 115–141.

Stokes, Edward. *Hawthorne's Influence*, 189–197.

Stone, Donald D. *The Romantic Impulse*, 225–230.

Vance, Norman. "Law, Religion and the Unity of *Felix Holt*," in Anne Smith, ed., *George Eliot*, 103–121.

Vargish, Thomas. *The Providential Aesthetic*, 211–216.

Welsh, Alexander. *George Eliot*, 195–208, 210–220.

Wiesenfarth, Joseph. *George Eliot's Mythmaking*, 170–185.

Wijesinha, Rajiva. *The Androgynous Trollope*, 263–265.

Yeazell, Ruth Bernard. "Why Political Novels Have Heroines: *Sybil*, *Mary Barton*, and *Felix Holt*." *Novel* 18 (1985), 137–144.

Zimmerman, Bonnie. "*Felix Holt* and the True Power of Womanhood." *ELH* 46 (1979), 432–449.

Middlemarch, 1872

Adams, Harriet Farwell. "Domesticating the Brutal Passion in Nineteenth-Century Fiction." *Victorian Newsl* 67 (1985), 9.

Adams, Harriet Farwell. "Dorothea and 'Miss Brooke' in *Middlemarch*." *Nineteenth-Century Fiction* 39 (1984), 69–90.

Adams, Harriet Farwell. "Prelude and Finale to *Middlemarch*." *Victorian Newsl* 68 (1985), 9–11.

Alley, Henry. "Literature and the Miscast Marriages," 21–25.

Alley, Henry. "The Subterranean Intellectual of *Middlemarch*." *Midwest Q* 20 (1979), 347–361.

Alley, Henry M. "*Middlemarch*: Three Italian Journeys." *George Eliot Fellowship R* 16 (1985), 74–79.

Altick, Richard D. "Anachronisms in *Middlemarch*: A Note." *Nineteenth-Century Fiction* 33 (1978), 366–372.

apRoberts, Ruth. "*Middlemarch* and the New Humanity," in Gordon S. Haight and Rosemary T. VanArsdel, eds., *George Eliot*, 38–46.

Argyle, Gisela. *German Elements*, 39–60.

Ashton, Rosemary. *George Eliot*, 68–82.

Ashton, Rosemary D. "The Intellectual 'Medium' of *Middlemarch*." *R of Engl Stud* 30 (1979), 154–168.

Atkins, Dorothy. "The Philosophical Basis for George Eliot's Feminist Stance in *Middlemarch*." *Publs of the Arkansas Philol Assoc* 5:2–3 (1979), 23–29.

Auerbach, Nina. *Romantic Imprisonment*, 85–90, 263–267.

Bellringer, Alan W. "The Study of Provincial Life in *Middlemarch*." *English* 28 (1979), 219–244.

Bennett, James R. "Scenic Structure of Judgement in *Middlemarch*." *Essays & Stud 1984*, 62–74.

Bonaparte, Felicia. "*Middlemarch*: The Genesis of Myth in the English Novel—The Relationship Between Literary Form and the Modern Predicament." *Notre Dame Engl J* 13 (1981), 107–148.

Brody, Selma. "Origins of George Eliot's 'Pier-Glass' Image." *Engl Lang Notes* 22:2 (1984), 55–58.

Brown, Julia Prewitt. *A Reader's Guide*, 42–44, 78–79.

Carroll, David. "George Eliot: The Sibyl of Mercia." *Stud in the Novel* 15 (1983), 18–21.

Castillo, Debra A. *The Translated World*, 265–266, 270–275, 277–281.

Chase, Karen. *Eros & Psyche*, 136–187.

Clark-Beattie, Rosemary. "*Middlemarch*'s Dialogic Style." *J of Narrative Technique* 15 (1985), 199–216.

Cosslett, Tess. *The 'Scientific Movement'*, 75–97.

Court, Franklin E. "The Image of St. Theresa in *Middlemarch* and Positive Ethics." *Victorian Newsl* 63 (1983), 21–25.

Dalal, D. S. *George Eliot*, 77–82, 111–114, 157–166, 233–237.

Doody, Margaret Anne. "George Eliot and the Eighteenth-Century Novel." *Nineteenth-Century Fiction* 35 (1980), 261–264, 279–280, 290–291.

Doyle, Mary Ellen. *The Sympathetic Response*, 117–156.

Eagleton, Mary, and David Pierce. *Attitudes to Class*, 63–68, 108–110.

Edwards, Lee R. *Psyche as Hero*, 91–103.

Ermarth, Elizabeth Deeds. *George Eliot*, 110–121.

Fisher, Philip. *Making Up Society*, 163–202.

Foltinek, Herbert. "George Eliot und der unwissende Erzähler," 167–172.

Forster, Jean-Paul. "George Eliot: The Language and Drama of Reticence." *Engl Stud* 64 (1983), 433–446.

Foster, Shirley. *Victorian Women's Fiction*, 218–222.

Garrett, Peter K. *The Victorian Multiplot Novel*, 135–167.

Gilbert, Sandra M., and Susan Gubar. *The Madwoman*, 499–532.

Ginsburg, Michal Peled. "Pseudonym, Epigraphs, and Narrative Voice: *Middlemarch* and the Problem of Authorship." *ELH* 47 (1980), 542–556.

Goldsberry, Dennis. "Goethe and George Eliot's *Middlemarch*." *USF Lang Q* 16:3–4 (1978), 9–44.

Gordon, Jan. "Origins, *Middlemarch*, Endings: George Eliot's Crisis of the Antecedent," in Anne Smith, ed., *George Eliot*, 124–149.

Graver, Suzanne. "Mill, *Middlemarch*, and Marriage," in Anne C. Hargrove and Maurine Magliocco, eds., *Portraits of Marriage*, 55–63.

Greene, Mildred Sarah. "G. Eliot's *Middlemarch*." *Explicator* 42:3 (1984), 26–28.

Greenstein, Susan M. "The Question of Vocation: From *Romola* to *Middlemarch*." *Nineteenth-Century Fiction* 35 (1981), 487–505.

Hardy, Barbara. *Forms of Feeling*, 132–139, 148–156.

Hardy, Barbara. "*Middlemarch*, Chapter 85." *Nineteenth-Century Fiction* 35 (1980), 435–441.

Heilman, Robert B. " 'Stealthy Convergence' in *Middlemarch*," in Gordon S. Haight and Rosemary T. VanArsdel, eds., *George Eliot*, 47–54.

Hertz, Neil. "Recognizing Casaubon." *Glyph* 6 (1979), 24–41.

Higgins, Elizabeth Jean. *Reading the Novel*, 206–213.

Hooton, Joy W. "*Middlemarch* and Time." *Southern R* (Adelaide) 13 (1980), 188–201.

Hulcoop, John F. " 'This Petty Medium': In the Middle of *Middlemarch*," in Gordon S. Haight and Rosemary T, VanArsdel, eds., *George Eliot*, 153–164.

Irwin, Michael. *Picturing*, 112–117, 139–141.

Jacobus, Mary. "The Difference of View," in Jacobus, ed., *Women Writing*, 17–19.

Joseph, Gerhard. "The *Antigone* as Cultural Touchstone: Matthew Arnold, Hegel, George Eliot, Virginia Woolf, and Margaret Drabble." *PMLA* 96 (1981), 25–27.

Kurata, Marilyn J. "Italians with White Mice Again: *Middlemarch* and *The Woman in White*." *Engl Lang Notes* 22:4 (1985), 45–47.

Kurrik, Maire Jaanus. *Literature and Negation*, 108–119.

Levine, George. "George Eliot's Hypothesis," 12–17.

Levine, George. "The Hero as Dilettante: *Middlemarch* and *Nostromo*," in Anne Smith, ed., *George Eliot*, 152–177.

Longford, Elizabeth. *Eminent Victorian Women*, 80–81.

McCabe, Colin. *James Joyce*, 16–19.

McCobb, E. A. "Of Women and Doctors: *Middlemarch* and Wilhelmine von Hillern's *Ein Arzt der Seele*." *Neophilologus* 68 (1984), 571–585.

McCormack, Kathleen. "The Sybil and the Hyena," 602–607, 610–611.

McGowan, John P. "The Turn of George Eliot's Realism." *Nineteenth-Century Fiction* 35 (1980), 183–192.

Mann, Karen B. "George Eliot's Language," 206–209.

Mann, Karen B. *The Language*, 26–28, 34–36, 71–74, 93–95, 100–104, 125–127, 145–147, 150–157, 160–163, 194–196.

Mann, Karen B. "Self, Shell and World," 458–461.

Marotta, Kenny. "*Middlemarch*: The 'Home Epic'." *Genre* 15 (1982), 403–418.

Martin, Carol A. "No Angel in the House," 303–304.

Mason, Philip. *The English Gentleman*, 15–20.

Meikle, Susan. "Fruit and Seed: The Finale to *Middlemarch*," in Anne Smith, ed., *George Eliot*, 181–194.

Miller, J. Hillis. "*Middlemarch*, Chapter 85." *Nineteenth-Century Fiction* 35 (1980), 441–448.

Myers, William. *The Teaching*, 115–118, 187–206.

Newton, K. M. *George Eliot*, 123–167.

Peskin, S. G. "Music in *Middlemarch*." *Engl Stud in Africa* 23 (1980), 75–81.

Petit, J.-P. "George Eliot: *Middlemarch*," in Pierre Coustillas et al., eds., *Le roman anglais*, 224–233.

Pinion, F. B. *A George Eliot Companion*, 179–200.

Poirier, Richard. "*Middlemarch*, Chapter 85." *Nineteenth-Century Fiction* 35 (1980), 448–453.

Postlethwaite, Diana. *Making It Whole*, 234–261.

Putzell, Sara Moore. "George Eliot's Location of Value," 169–171.

Putzell-Korab, Sara M. *The Evolving Consciousness*, 31–43, 89–110.

Putzell-Korab, Sara M., and Martine Watson Brownley. "Dorothea and Her Husbands: Some Autobiographical Sources for Speculation." *Victorian Newsl* 68 (1985), 15–19.

Rataboul, Louis J. *Le pasteur anglican*, 122–125, 203.

Reed, John R., and Jerry Herron. "George Eliot's Illegitimate Children," 182–184.

Ringler, Ellin. "*Middlemarch*: A Feminist Perspective." *Stud in the Novel* 15 (1983), 55–60.

Robson, John M. "Narrative Transitions in *Middlemarch*." *Hum Assoc R* 31 (1980), 97–120.

Rosowski, Susan J. "The Novel of Awakening." *Genre* 12 (1979), 328–332.

Sadoff, Dianne F. *Monsters of Affection*, 74–78, 98–99, 117–118.

Shuttleworth, Sally. *George Eliot*, 142–174.

Spence, Martin. "C. Brontë's *Jane Eyre* and G. Eliot's *Middlemarch*." *Explicator* 43:3 (1985), 10–11.

Spivey, Ted R. *The Journey beyond Tragedy*, 20–24, 28–32.

Stokes, Edward. *Hawthorne's Influence*, 198–207.

Stone, Donald D. *The Romantic Impulse*, 234–240.

Stoneman, Patsy. "G. Eliot: *Middlemarch* (1871–2)," in D. A. Williams, ed., *The Monster*, 102–130.

Taiot, Mary E. "Target Structures in *Middlemarch*," in Robert S. Haller, ed., *Papers*, 403–413.

Taylor, Anne Robinson. *Male Novelists*, 115–118.

Vargish, Thomas. *The Providential Aesthetic*, 216–228.

Weiss, Barbara. "The Dilemma of Happily Ever After," 83–84.

Welsh, Alexander. *George Eliot*, 195–200, 211–214, 216–258.

Wheeler, Michael. *English Fiction*, 131–137.

Wiesenfarth, Joseph. "*Antique Gems*," 59–60.

Wiesenfarth, Joseph. *George Eliot's Mythmaking*, 186–209.

Wiesenfarth, Joseph. "The Greeks, the Germans, and George Eliot." *Browning Inst Stud* 10 (1982), 93–103.

Wiesenfarth, Joseph. "*Middlemarch*: The Language of Art." *PMLA* 97 (1982), 363–377.

Wijesinha, Rajiva. *The Androgynous Trollope*, 255–262, 282–291.

Wilhelm, Cherry. "Conservative Reform in *Middlemarch*." *Theoria* (Natal) 53 (1979), 47–57.

Williams, Merryn. *Women in the English Novel*, 146–149.

Wilt, Judith. *Ghosts of the Gothic*, 173–179, 203–206.

Witemeyer, Hugh. *George Eliot*, 41–43, 79–87, 110–112, 150–155.

Wright, T. R. "From Bumps to Morals," 45–46.

Zeman, Anthea. *Presumptuous Girls*, 32–33, 58–60.

The Mill on the Floss, 1860

Adam, Ian. "The Ambivalence of *The Mill on the Floss*," in Gordon S. Haight and Rosemary T. VanArsdel, eds., *George Eliot*, 122–135.

Adams, Harriet Farwell. "Domesticating the Brutal Passion," 9.

Alley, Henry. "The Complete and Incomplete Educations of *The Mill on the Floss*." *Rocky Mountain R of Lang and Lit* 33 (1979), 184–201.

Arac, Jonathan. "Rhetoric and Realism in Nineteenth-Century Fiction: Hyperbole in *The Mill on the Floss*." *ELH* 46 (1979), 673–690.

Ashton, Rosemary. *George Eliot*, 36–46.

Auerbach, Nina. *Romantic Imprisonment*, 230–249.

Beer, Gillian. "Beyond Determinism," 87–89.

Bennett, Kenneth C. "Surrogate Religion in *Our Mutual Friend* and *The Mill on the Floss*." *Victorians Inst J* 10 (1981–82), 15–25.

Buckley, Jerome H. "George Eliot's Double Life: *The Mill on the Floss* as a Bildungsroman," in Samuel I. Mintz et al., eds., *From Smollett to James*, 211–236.

Bushnell, John P. "Maggie Tulliver's 'Stored-up Force': A Re-reading of *The Mill on the Floss*." *Stud in the Novel* 16 (1984), 378–393.

Campbell, Thomas J. "From Country to Town: The Growth of Abstract Consciousness in *The Mill on the Floss*." *Res Stud* 49 (1981), 107–115.

Carroll, David. "George Eliot: The Sibyl of Mercia," 21–22.

Dalal, D. S. *George Eliot*, 60–63, 99–101, 136–140, 160–163, 212–218.

Daleski, H. M. *The Divided Heroine*, 47–68.

Daleski, H. M. "Lawrence and George Eliot: The Genesis of *The White Peacock*," in Jeffrey Meyers, ed., *D. H. Lawrence*, 54–62.

Doody, Margaret Anne. "George Eliot," 265–267.

Doyle, Mary Ellen. *The Sympathetic Response*, 57–89.

Drew, Philip. *The Meaning of Freedom*, 284–293.

Eagleton, Mary, and David Pierce. *Attitudes to Class*, 59–63.

El-Ayouty, Amin. "Romantic Realism in *The Mill on the Floss*." *Cairo Stud in Engl* 32 (1978), 41–58.

Ermarth, Elizabeth Deeds. *George Eliot*, 77–89.

Fisher, Philip. *Making Up Society*, 66–98.

Foster, Shirley. *Victorian Women's Fiction*, 205–207.

Gemmette, Elizabeth Villiers. "G. Eliot's *Mill on the Floss* and Hardy's *Jude the Obscure*." *Explicator* 42:3 (1984), 28–30.

Goldberg, S. L. " 'Poetry' as Moral Thinking: *The Mill on the Floss*." *Crit R* 24 (1982), 55–79.

Goode, John. " 'The Affections Clad with Knowledge'," 41–44.

Gregor, Ian. "Reading a Story: Sequence, Pace, and Recollection," in Gregor, ed., *Reading the Victorian Novel*, 105–109.

Guth, Barbara. "Philip: The Tragedy of *The Mill on the Floss*." *Stud in the Novel* 15 (1983), 356–362.

Harris, Margaret. "The Narrator of *The Mill on the Floss*." *Sydney Stud in Engl* 3 (1977–78), 32–46.

Howells, Coral Ann. "Dreams and Visions," 172–175.

Huzzard, John A. "George Eliot and Education." *George Eliot Fellowship R* 11 (1980), 11–14.

Irwin, Michael. *Picturing*, 139–141.

Jacobus, Mary. "The Question of Language: Men of Maxims and *The Mill on the Floss*." *Crit Inquiry* 8 (1981), 212–222.

Jeffers, Thomas L. "Myth and Morals in *The Mill on the Floss*." *Midwest Q* 20 (1979), 332–346.

Kelly, Mary Ann. "The Narrative Emphasis on the Power of the Imagination in *The Mill on the Floss.*" *George Eliot Fellowship R* 14 (1983), 86–93.

Knoepflmacher, U. C. "Genre and the Integration of Gender: From Wordsworth to George Eliot to Virginia Woolf," in James R. Kincaid and Albert J. Kuhn, eds., *Victorian Literature*, 102–107.

Kucich, John. "George Eliot and Objects: Meaning and Matter in *The Mill on the Floss.*" *Dickens Stud Annual* 12 (1983), 319–336.

Lee, A. Robert. "*The Mill on the Floss*: 'Memory' and the Reading Experience," in Ian Gregor, ed., *Reading the Victorian Novel*, 72–90.

Levay, John. "Maggie as Muse: The Philip-Maggie Relationship in *The Mill on the Floss.*" *Engl Stud in Canada* 9 (1983), 69–78.

Longford, Elizabeth. *Eminent Victorian Women*, 78.

McCobb, E. A. "Keller's Influence on *The Mill on the Floss*: A Reassessment." *German Life and Letters* 33 (1980), 199–208.

McCormack, Kathleen. "The Sybil and the Hyena," 607–610.

McDonnell, Jane. " 'Perfect Goodness' or 'The Wider Life': *The Mill on the Floss* as Bildungsroman." *Genre* 15 (1982), 379–400.

McGowan, John P. "The Turn of George Eliot's Realism," 176–183.

McMaster, Juliet. "George Eliot's Language of the Sense," in Gordon S. Haight and Rosemary T. VanArsdel, eds., *George Eliot*, 22–25.

McSweeney, Kerry. "The Ending of *The Mill on the Floss.*" *Engl Stud in Canada* 12 (1986), 55–66.

McVeagh, John. *Tradefull Merchants*, 144–145.

Mann, Karen B. "George Eliot's Language," 196–198.

Mann, Karen B. *The Language*, 13–15, 86–89, 100–104, 142–144, 147–150.

Mann, Karen B. "Self, Shell and World," 461–463.

Martin, Carol A. "No Angel in the House," 304–306.

Martin, Carol A. "Pastoral and Romance in George Eliot's *The Mill on the Floss.*" *Coll Lang Assoc J* 28 (1984), 78–101.

Martin, Graham. "*The Mill on the Floss* and the Unreliable Narrator," in Anne Smith, ed., *George Eliot*, 36–54.

Mason, Kenneth M., Jr. "George Eliot's *Mill on the Floss*: Tragic Harvest and Pastoral Deceit." *J of Narrative Technique* 15 (1985), 169–180.

Miller, Nancy K. "Emphasis Added: Plots and Plausibilities in Women's Fiction." *PMLA* 96 (1981), 44–47.

Mundhenk, Rosemary. "Patterns of Irresolution in Eliot's *The Mill on the Floss.*" *J of Narrative Technique* 13 (1983), 20–28.

Myers, William. *The Teaching*, 45–55, 64–69, 160–163.

New, Peter. *Fiction and Purpose*, 154–230.

Newton, Judith Lowder. *Women, Power, and Subversion*, 125–157.

Newton, K. M. *George Eliot*, 101–122.

Pattison, Robert. *The Child Figure*, 101–107.

Peterson, Carla L. "The Heroine as Reader in the Nineteenth-Century Novel: Emma Bovary and Maggie Tulliver." *Compar Lit Stud* 17 (1980), 169–182.

Pinion, F. B. *A George Eliot Companion*, 107–121.

Putzell, Sara Moore. "George Eliot's Location of Value," 171–173.

Putzell-Korab, Sara M. *The Evolving Consciousness*, 44–63, 79–81.

Qualls, Barry V. *The Secular Pilgrims*, 146–149, 156–159.

Rataboul, Louis J. *Le pasteur anglican*, 128–129.

Reed, John R., and Jerry Herron. "George Eliot's Illegitimate Children," 181–182.

Sadoff, Dianne F. *Monsters of Affection*, 70–71, 78–88.

Schultze, Bruno. "Textbrüchigkeit und ästhetisches Urteil: Zur Interpretationsproblematik von George Eliots *The Mill on the Floss*," in Hans-Heinrich Freitag and Peter Hühn, eds., *Literarische Ansichten*, 209–230.

Showalter, Elaine. *A Literature*, 125–132.

Shuttleworth, Sally. *George Eliot*, 51–77.

Stokes, Edward. *Hawthorne's Influence*, 146–159.

Stone, Donald D. *The Romantic Impulse*, 212–218.

Tanner, Tony. *Adultery in the Novel*, 66–72.

Vargish, Thomas. *The Providential Aesthetic*, 181–196.

Wasserman, Renata R. Mautner. "Narrative Logic and the Form of Tradition in *The Mill on the Floss*." *Stud in the Novel* 14 (1982), 266–278.

Weinstein, Philip M. *The Semantics of Desire*, 74–89.

Welsh, Alexander. *George Eliot*, 118–121, 141–153, 170–172.

Wiesenfarth, Joseph. *George Eliot's Mythmaking*, 96–123.

Wilt, Judith. "Steamboat Surfacing: Scott and the English Novelists." *Nineteenth-Century Fiction* 35 (1981), 472–475.

Woodward, Wendy. "The Solitariness of Selfhood: Maggie Tulliver and the Female Community at St Ogg's." *Engl Stud in Africa* 28 (1985), 47–54.

Wright, T. R. "From Bumps to Morals," 40–41.

Romola, 1863

Ashton, Rosemary. *George Eliot*, 50–56.

Bamlett, Steve. " 'A Way-Worn Ancestry Returning': The Function of the Representation of Peasants in the Novel," in Kathleen Parkinson and Martin Priestman, eds., *Peasants and Countrymen*, 158–172.

Bullough, Geoffrey. "The Making of *Romola*," in Magdi Wahba, ed., *Centenary Essays*, 15–35.

Butwin, Joseph. "The Pacification," 359–366.

Chase, Karen. "The Modern Family and the Ancient Image in *Romola*." *Dickens Stud Annual* 14 (1985), 303–325.

Dalal, D. S. *George Eliot*, 66–71, 104–108, 145–150, 223–229.

De Jong, Mary Gosselink. "*Romola*: A *Bildungsroman* for Feminists?" *South Atlantic R* 49:4 (1984), 75–86.

De Jong, Mary. "Tito: A Portrait of Fear." *George Eliot Fellowship R* 14 (1983), 18–22.

Ermarth, Elizabeth Deeds. *George Eliot*, 93–97.

Ermarth, Elizabeth Deeds. "George Eliot's . . . Sympathy," 27–31.

Fisher, Philip. *Making Up Society*, 111–143.

Foster, Shirley. *Victorian Women's Fiction*, 216–218.

Gezari, Janet K. "*Romola* and the Myth of Apocalypse," in Anne Smith, ed., *George Eliot*, 77–101.

Goode, John. " 'The Affections Clad with Knowledge'," 44–49.

Greenstein, Susan M. "The Question of Vocation," 487–505.

Howells, Coral Ann. "Dreams and Visions," 175–178.

Huzzard, John A. "The Emergence of Women," 10–12.

Lindley, Dwight N. "Clio and Three Historical Novels." *Dickens Stud Annual* 10 (1982), 85–88.

Longford, Elizabeth. *Eminent Victorian Women*, 78–79.

McCobb, Anthony. "Kleist's *Der Findling*: The 'Backbone' of George Eliot's *Romola*." *Forum for Mod Lang Stud* 16 (1980), 172–173.

Mann, Karen B. *The Language*, 77–83, 100–104, 157–159.

Myers, William. *The Teaching*, 39–42, 58–64, 93–100, 165–167, 236–238.

Nestor, Pauline. *Female Friendships*, 195–197.

Neufeldt, Victor A. "The Madonna and the Gypsy." *Stud in the Novel* 15 (1983), 44–53.

Newton, K. M. *George Eliot*, 13–27, 66–75.

Paxton, Nancy L. "George Eliot and the City: The Imprisonment of Culture," in Susan Merrill Squier, ed., *Women Writers*, 71–94.

Pinion, F. B. *A George Eliot Companion*, 141–152.

Putzell-Korab, Sara M. *The Evolving Consciousness*, 68–79.

Sadoff, Dianne F. *Monsters of Affection*, 88–104.

Shaw, Harry E. "Scott and George Eliot: The Lure of the Symbolic," in J. H. Alexander and David Hewitt, eds., *Scott and His Influence*, 397–399.

Shuttleworth, Sally. *George Eliot*, 96–114.

Stokes, Edward. *Hawthorne's Influence*, 173–189.

Stone, Donald D. *The Romantic Impulse*, 221–225.

Thurin, Susan Schoenbauer. "The Madonna and the Child Wife in *Romola*." *Tulsa Stud in Women's Lit* 4 (1985), 217–231.

Vargish, Thomas. *The Providential Aesthetic*, 205–211.

Welsh, Alexander. *George Eliot*, 169–200.

Wiesenfarth, Joseph. "*Antique Gems*," 55–59.

Wiesenfarth, Joseph. *George Eliot's Mythmaking*, 146–169.

Wijesinha, Rajiva. *The Androgynous Trollope*, 277–282.

Wilt, Judith. *Ghosts of the Gothic*, 187–205.

Witemeyer, Hugh. *George Eliot*, 56–61, 157–170.

Witemeyer, Hugh. "George Eliot's *Romola* and Bulwer Lytton's *Rienzi*." *Stud in the Novel* 15 (1983), 62–71.

Wright, T. R. "From Bumps to Morals," 42–45.

Scenes of Clerical Life, 1858

Ashton, Rosemary. *George Eliot*, 22–27.
Atkins, Dorothy. *George Eliot*, 164–166.
Butwin, Joseph. "The Pacification," 355–358.
Carlisle, Janice. *The Sense of an Audience*, 166–186.
Carroll, David. " 'Janet's Repentance' and the Myth of the Organic."
    Nineteenth-Century Fiction 35 (1980), 336–348.
Ermarth, Elizabeth Deeds. *George Eliot*, 60–68.
Gilbert, Sandra M., and Susan Gubar. *The Madwoman*, 484–491.
Hardy, Barbara. *Forms of Feeling*, 145–148.
Jumeau, Alain. "*Scenes of Clerical Life*: George Eliot sur les chemins
    de la 'conversion'." *Etudes Anglaises* 33 (1980), 268–281.
Knoepflmacher, U. C. "Unveiling Men: Power and Masculinity in
    George Eliot's Fiction." *Women & Lit* 2 (1981), 136–141.
Landow, George P. *Victorian Types*, 99–103.
Mann, Karen B. "George Eliot's Language," 191–192, 198–205.
Mann, Karen B. "Self, Shell and World," 464–470.
Pinion, F. B. *A George Eliot Companion*, 77–92.
Shaw, Harry E. "Scott and George Eliot," 393–397.
Stokes, Edward. *Hawthorne's Influence*, 114–122.
Stone, Donald D. *The Romantic Impulse*, 202–205.
Wiesenfarth, Joseph. *George Eliot's Mythmaking*, 57–76.
Wijesinha, Rajiva. *The Androgynous Trollope*, 269–277.

Silas Marner, 1861

Ashton, Rosemary. *George Eliot*, 47–50.
Cohen, Susan R. " 'A History and a Metamorphosis': Continuity and
    Discontinuity in *Silas Marner*." *Texas Stud in Lit and Lang* 25 (1983),
    410–425.
Dalal, D. S. *George Eliot*, 63–66, 101–104, 140–145, 218–223.
Dessner, Lawrence Jay. "The Autobiographical Matrix of *Silas
    Marner*." *Stud in the Novel* 11 (1979), 251–278.
Ermarth, Elizabeth Deeds. *George Eliot*, 97–102.
Ermarth, Elizabeth Deeds. "George Eliot's . . . Sympathy," 31–36.
Fisher, Philip. *Making Up Society*, 99–110.
Gilbert, Sandra M. "Life's Empty Pack: Notes toward a Literary
    Daughteronomy." *Crit Inquiry* 11 (1985), 358–365.
Hawes, Donald. "Chance in *Silas Marner*." *English* 31 (1982), 213–218.
Knoepflmacher, U. C. "Genre and the Integration of Gender," 108–110.
McLaverty, James. "Comtean Fetishism in *Silas Marner*." *Nineteenth-
    Century Fiction* 36 (1981), 318–336.
McMaster, Juliet. "George Eliot's Language," 15–16.
Mann, Karen B. *The Language*, 49–51, 100–104, 119–121.
Myers, William. *The Teaching*, 20–23, 42–45, 163–165.
Newton, K. M. *George Eliot*, 84–86, 97–99.
Pattison, Robert. *The Child Figure*, 96–101.
Pinion, F. B. *A George Eliot Companion*, 130–141.

Preston, John. "The Community of the Novel: *Silas Marner*." *Compar Criticism* 2 (1980), 109–130.
Preston, John. "*Silas Marner*: The Community of the Novel." *George Eliot Fellowship R* 11 (1980), 8–10.
Putzell-Korab, Sara M. *The Evolving Consciousness*, 65–67.
Qualls, Barry V. *The Secular Pilgrims*, 149–155.
Reed, John R., and Jerry Herron. "George Eliot's Illegitimate Children," 178–179.
Rochelson, Meri-Jane. "The Weaver of Raveloe: Metaphor as Narrative Persuasion in *Silas Marner*." *Stud in the Novel* 15 (1983), 35–42.
Sadoff, Dianne F. *Monsters of Affection*, 71–73, 108–110.
Shuttleworth, Sally. *George Eliot*, 78–95.
Stokes, Edward. *Hawthorne's Influence*, 159–173.
Stone, Donald D. *The Romantic Impulse*, 218–220.
Vargish, Thomas. *The Providential Aesthetic*, 196–205.
Welsh, Alexander. *George Eliot*, 163–170.
Wheeler, Michael. *English Fiction*, 126–131.
Wiesenfarth, Joseph. *George Eliot's Mythmaking*, 124–145.
Woolf, David. *An Aspect of Fiction*.

BENJAMIN FARJEON

Aaron the Jew, 1894

Zatlin, Linda Gertner. *The Nineteenth-Century Anglo-Jewish Novel*, 77–79.

Pride of Race, 1900

Zatlin, Linda Gertner. *The Nineteenth-Century Anglo-Jewish Novel*, 79–81, 85–86.

PENELOPE FARMER

A Castle of Bone, 1972

Swinfen, Ann. *In Defence*, 67–71.

Charlotte Sometimes, 1969

Swinfen, Ann. *In Defence*, 55–58.

J. G. FARRELL

The Siege of Krishnapur, 1973

Bergonzi, Bernard. "Fictions of History," in Malcolm Bradbury and David Palmer, eds., *The Contemporary English Novel*, 61–64.
Singh, Frances B. "Progress and History in J. G. Farrell's *The Siege of Krishnapur*." *Chandrabhaga* 2 (1979), 23–39.

The Singapore Grip, 1978

>   Bergonzi, Bernard. "Fictions of History," 64–65.

Troubles, 1970

>   Bergonzi, Bernard. "Fictions of History," 57–61.
>   Hartveit, Lars. "Affinity or Influence? Sir Walter Scott and J. G. Farrell as Historical Novelists," in J. H. Alexander and David Hewitt, eds., *Scott and His Influence*, 414–420.
>   Kim, Suzanne. "Histoire et roman." *Etudes Anglaises* 36 (1983), 174–177.
>   Scanlan, Margaret. "Rumors of War: Elizabeth Bowen's *Last September* and J. G. Farrell's *Troubles*." *Eire-Ireland* 20:2 (1985), 79–89.

MICHAEL FARRELL

Thy Tears Might Cease, 1963

>   O'Rourke, Brian. *The Conscience of the Race*, 24–25.

ELAINE FEINSTEIN

The Circle, 1970

>   Zeman, Anthea. *Presumptuous Girls*, 69–71.

SUSAN FERRIER

Destiny, 1831

>   Cullinan, Mary. *Susan Ferrier*, 91–105.

The Inheritance, 1824

>   Cullinan, Mary. *Susan Ferrier*, 66–90.
>   Hart, Francis Russell. "The Regency Novel of Fashion," in Samuel I. Mintz et al., eds., *From Smollett to James*, 115–117.

Marriage, 1818

>   Cullinan, Mary. *Susan Ferrier*, 40–65.
>   Hart, Francis Russell. "The Regency Novel," 113–115.
>   Teyssandier, Hubert. *Les formes de la création*, 94–118.

HENRY FIELDING

Amelia, 1752

>   Battestin, Martin C. "Fielding, *Amelia*, and the 'Constitution' of England," in Jan Fergus, ed., *Literature and Society*, 1–11.
>   Cleary, Thomas R. *Henry Fielding*, 286–291.
>   Dircks, Richard J. *Henry Fielding*, 107–120.

Fraser, Donald. "Lying and Concealment in *Amelia*," in K. G. Simpson, ed., *Henry Fielding*, 174–196.

Golden, Morris. "Fielding's Politics," in K. G. Simpson, ed., *Henry Fielding*, 51–53.

Hagstrum, Jean H. *Sex and Sensibility*, 180–185.

Kalpakgian, Mitchell. *The Marvellous*, 105–143.

Keener, Frederick M. *The Chain of Becoming*, 48–54.

Knight, Charles A. "The Narrative Structure of Fielding's *Amelia*." *Ariel* 11:1 (1980), 31–44.

Lenta, Margaret. "Comedy, Tragedy and Feminism: The Novels of Richardson and Fielding." *Engl Stud in Africa* 26 (1983), 14–25.

Low, Donald. "Mr. Fielding of Bow Street," in K. G. Simpson, ed., *Henry Fielding*, 28–31.

McCrea, Brian. "Politics and Narrative Technique in Fielding's *Amelia*." *J of Narrative Technique* 13 (1983), 131–138.

Macey, Samuel L. *Money and the Novel*, 140–145.

Mulford, Carla. "Booth's Progress and the Resolution of *Amelia*." *Stud in the Novel* 16 (1984), 20–28.

Nathan, Sabine. "Humes Auffassung von Moral und Fieldings *Amelia*." *Zeitschrift für Anglistik und Amerikanistik* 28 (1980), 219–224.

Osland, Dianne. "Fielding's *Amelia*: Problem Child or Problem Reader?" *J of Narrative Technique* 10 (1980), 56–66.

Peereboom, John James. *Fielding Practice*, 26–33, 77–79.

Rogers, Pat. *Henry Fielding*, 193–197.

Sabor, Peter. "*Amelia* and *Sir Charles Grandison*: The Convergence of Fielding and Richardson." *Wascana R* 17:2 (1982), 3–18.

Scheuermann, Mona. "Man Not Providence: Fielding's *Amelia* as a Novel of Social Criticism." *Forum for Mod Lang Stud* 20 (1984), 106–121.

Scheuermann, Mona. *Social Protest*, 13–40.

Sell, Roger D. *The Reluctant Naturalism of "Amelia."*

Shroff, Homai J. *The Eighteenth Century Novel*, 128–136, 144–146, 150–155, 158–160.

Todd, Janet. *Women's Friendship*, 332–336.

Voogd, Peter Jan de. *Henry Fielding*, 166–176.

Williams, Ioan. *The Idea of the Novel*, 194–200.

Wynne, Edith J. "Latitudinarian Philosophy in Fielding's *Amelia*." *Publs of the Missouri Philol Assoc* 4 (1979), 33–38.

Jonathan Wild, 1743

Cleary, Thomas R. *Henry Fielding*, 190–197.

Dircks, Richard J. *Henry Fielding*, 69–80.

Felsenstein, Frank. " 'Newgate with the mask on': A View of *Jonathan Wild*." *Zeitschrift für Anglistik und Amerikanistik* 28 (1980), 211–218.

Kalpakgian, Mitchell. *The Marvellous*, 182–193.

McKenzie, Alan T. "The Physiology of Deceit in Fielding's Works." *Dalhousie R* 62 (1982), 141–144.

Merrett, Robert James. *Daniel Defoe's . . . Ideas*, 94–96.
Peereboom, John James. *Fielding Practice*, 20–21.
Reilly, Patrick. "Fielding's Magisterial Art," in K. G. Simpson, ed., *Henry Fielding*, 83–86.
Rinehart, Hollis. "Fielding's Chapter 'Of Proverbs': (*Jonathan Wild* [1743], Book 2, Chapter 12): Sources, Allusions, and Interpretation." *Mod Philology* 77 (1980), 291–296.
Rinehart, Hollis. "The Role of Walpole in Fielding's *Jonathan Wild*." *Engl Stud in Canada* 5 (1979), 420–430.
Rogers, Pat. *Henry Fielding*, 136–138.

Joseph Andrews, 1742

Baguley, David. "Parody and the Realist Novel." *Univ of Toronto Q* 55 (1985), 95–98.
Baker, Sheridan. "Fielding's Comic Epic-in-Prose Romances Again." *Philol Q* 58 (1979), 63–78.
Brooks-Davies, Douglas. "The Mythology of Love: Venerean (and Related) Iconography in Pope, Fielding, Cleland and Sterne," in Paul-Gabriel Boucé, ed., *Sexuality*, 181–184.
Burns, Bryan. "The Story-telling in *Joseph Andrews*," in K. G. Simpson, ed., *Henry Fielding*, 119–135.
Caminero, Juventino. "Joseph Andrews y Don Quijote de la Mancha: Dos castos varones." *Letras de Deusto* 9:18 (1979), 95–129.
Christensen, Bryce J. "The Man-of-the-Hill and Mr. Wilson: Mirth and Misanthropy in Fielding's *Tom Jones* and *Joseph Andrews*." *Ball State Univ Forum* 23:3 (1983), 18–23.
Church, Margaret. *Structure and Theme*, 13–36.
Cleary, Thomas R. *Henry Fielding*, 168–173.
Dircks, Richard J. *Henry Fielding*, 45–66.
Evans, James E. "Fielding, *The Whole Duty of Man*, *Shamela*, and *Joseph Andrews*." *Philol Q* 61 (1982), 217–218.
Evans, James E. "The World According to Paul: Comedy and Theology in *Joseph Andrews*." *Ariel* 15:1 (1984), 45–54.
Hunter, J. Paul. "Fielding and the Disappearance of Heroes," in Robert Folkenflik, ed., *The English Hero*, 134–137.
Kalpakgian, Mitchell. *The Marvellous*, 20–50.
Keener, Frederick M. *The Chain of Becoming*, 43–47.
Laban, Lawrence F. "Visualizing Fielding's Point of View," in Michael Klein and Gillian Parker, eds., *The English Novel*, 28–35.
Lenta, M. "From *Pamela* to *Joseph Andrews*: An Investigation of the Relationship between Two Originals." *Engl Stud in Africa* 23 (1980), 63–74.
McCrea, Brian. "Rewriting Pamela: Social Change and Religious Faith in *Joseph Andrews*." *Stud in the Novel* 16 (1984), 137–147.
Macey, Samuel L. *Money and the Novel*, 125–132, 169–171.
McKenzie, Alan T. "The Physiology of Deceit," 144–146.

Merrett, Robert. "The Principles of Fielding's Legal Satire and Social Reform." *Dalhousie R* 62 (1982), 238–240.

Novak, Maximillian E. *Eighteenth-Century English Literature*, 127–128.

Osland, Dianne. "Tied Back to Back: The Discourse Between the Poet and Player and the Exhortations of Parson Adams in *Joseph Andrews*." *J of Narrative Technique* 12 (1982), 191–198.

Peereboom, John James. *Fielding Practice*, 11–16, 21–23, 39–40, 43–44, 48–49, 83–84.

Perl, Jeffrey M. "Anagogic Surfaces: How to Read *Joseph Andrews*." *Eighteenth Century* 22 (1981), 249–270.

Price, John Valdimir. "Patterns of Sexual Behaviour in Some Eighteenth-Century Novels," in Paul-Gabriel Boucé, ed., *Sexuality*, 167–169.

Punter, David. "Fictional Representation of the Law in the Eighteenth Century." *Eighteenth-Century Stud* 16 (1982–83), 51–52.

Reed, Walter L. *An Exemplary History*, 117–136.

Rhodes, Neil. "The Innocence of *Joseph Andrews*," in K. G. Simpson, ed., *Henry Fielding*, 101–117.

Rogers, Pat. *Henry Fielding*, 121–126.

Seehase, Georg. "Henry Fielding und der realistische Roman: Der sich wandelnde Erzählerstandpunkt." *Zeitschrift für Anglistik und Amerikanistik* 28 (1980), 202–204.

Sheriff, John K. *The Good-Natured Man*, 35–37.

Shroff, Homai J. *The Eighteenth Century Novel*, 85–86, 154–157.

Simon, Richard Keller. *The Labyrinth*, 27–52.

Stephanson, Raymond. "The Education of the Reader in Fielding's *Joseph Andrews*." *Philol Q* 61 (1982), 243–257.

Tandrup, Birthe. "The Technique of Qualification in Fielding's *Joseph Andrews* and *Tom Jones*." *Orbis Litterarum* 37 (1982), 227–240.

Tichy, Ales. "The Inorganic Plot of *Joseph Andrews*." *Brno Stud in Engl* 14 (1981), 149–157.

Voogd, Peter Jan de. *Henry Fielding*, 115–123.

Welsh, Alexander. *Reflections*, 20–25, 40–43, 106–108.

Williams, Ioan. *The Idea of the Novel*, 189–192.

Shamela, 1741

Cleary, Thomas R. *Henry Fielding*, 150–152.

Evans, James E. "Fielding, *The Whole Duty of Man*," 212–217.

Macey, Samuel L. *Money and the Novel*, 123–126.

Rogers, Pat. *Henry Fielding*, 113–116.

Tom Jones, 1749

Amory, Hugh. "The History of 'The Adventures of a Foundling': Revising *Tom Jones*." *Harvard Lib Bull* 27 (1979), 277–303.

Amory, Hugh. "*Tom Jones* among the Compositors: An Examination." *Harvard Lib Bull* 26 (1978), 172–192.

Baker, Sheridan. "Fielding's Comic Epic-in-Prose Romances," 63–78.

Barfoot, C. C. *The Thread*, 155–157.

Behrens, Laurence. "The Argument of *Tom Jones*." *Lit/Film Q* 8 (1980), 22–33.

Benstock, Shari. "At the Margin of Discourse: Footnotes in the Fictional Text." *PMLA* 98 (1983), 205–207.

Breuer, Horst. "Dramatische Gestaltungsmittel in Henry Fieldings *Tom Jones*." *Anglia* 99 (1981), 332–354.

Butler, Lance St. John. "Fielding and Shaftesbury Reconsidered: The Case of *Tom Jones*," in K. G. Simpson, ed., *Henry Fielding*, 56–73.

Christensen, Bryce J. "The Man-of-the-Hill and Mr. Wilson," 18–23.

Cleary, Thomas R. *Henry Fielding*, 263–274.

Dircks, Richard J. *Henry Fielding*, 81–106.

Donaldson, Ian. "Fielding, Richardson, and the Ends of the Novel." *Essays in Criticism* 32 (1982), 40–45.

Ek, Grete. "Glory, Jest, and Riddle: The Masque of Tom Jones in London." *Engl Stud* 60 (1979), 148–158.

Figes, Eva. *Sex and Subterfuge*, 13–15.

Golden, Morris. "Fielding's Politics," 50–53.

Golden, Morris. "Public Context and Imagining Self in *Tom Jones*." *Papers on Lang & Lit* 20 (1984), 273–292.

Hafner, Dieter. *"Tom Jones,"* 27–249.

Hahn, H. George. "Main Lines of Criticism of Fielding's *Tom Jones*, 1900–1978." *Brit Stud Monitor* 10 (1980), 8–35.

Hall, Michael L. "Incest and Morality in *Tom Jones*." *South Central Bull* 41:4 (1981), 101–104.

Hardy, Barbara. *Forms of Feeling*, 31–36.

Hassall, Anthony J. *Henry Fielding's "Tom Jones,"* 1–111.

Higbie, Robert. *Character & Structure*, 29–34.

Hodges, Laura F. "Aristotle's *Nicomachean Ethics* and *Tom Jones*." *Philol Q* 63 (1984), 223–235.

Hunter, J. Paul. "Fielding," 136–142.

Insdorf, Annette, and Sharon Goodman. "A Whisper and a Wink," in Michael Klein and Gillian Parker, eds., *The English Novel*, 36–43.

Kalpakgian, Mitchell. *The Marvellous*, 55–98.

Keener, Frederick M. *The Chain of Becoming*, 47–48, 50–52, 61–62.

Kinkead-Weekes, Mark. "Out of the Thicket in *Tom Jones*," in K. G. Simpson, ed., *Henry Fielding*, 137–156.

Knight, Charles A. *"Tom Jones*: The Meaning of the 'Main Design'." *Genre* 12 (1979), 379–399.

Konigsberg, Ira. *Narrative Technique*, 100–156.

Koppel, Gene S. "Sexual Education and Sexual Values in *Tom Jones*: Confusion at the Core?" *Stud in the Novel* 12 (1980), 1–8.

Kraft, Quentin G. "Narrative Transformation in *Tom Jones*: An Episode in the Emergence of the English Novel." *Eighteenth Century* 26 (1985), 23–45.

Lenta, Margaret. "Comedy, Tragedy and Feminism," 14–25.

Lindboe, Berit R. " 'O, *Shakespear*, Had I Thy Pen!': Fielding's Use of Shakespeare in *Tom Jones*." *Stud in the Novel* 14 (1982), 303–315.

Löffler, Arno. "Sophie Western und das Welttheater: Zum Verhältnis von idealer Norm und satirischer Kritik in *Tom Jones*." *Germanisch-Romanische Monatsschrift* 35 (1985), 27–39.

Lynch, James J. "Moral Sense and the Narrator of *Tom Jones*." *Stud in Engl Lit, 1500–1900* 25 (1985), 599–614.

McCrea, Brian. "Romances, Newspapers, and the Style of Fielding's True History." *Stud in Engl Lit, 1500–1900* 21 (1981), 471–480.

Macey, Samuel L. *Money and the Novel*, 56–57, 106–107, 132–141.

McKenzie, Alan T. "The Physiology of Deceit," 146–150.

McVeagh, John. *Tradefull Merchants*, 77–79.

Mafud Haye, Hilda. "Satira e ironia comica en *Tom Jones*." *Nueva Revista del Pacifico* 6 (1977), 11–23.

Merrett, Robert. "The Principles of Fielding's Legal Satire," 241–246.

Merrett, Robert James. "Empiricism and Judgment in Fielding's *Tom Jones*." *Ariel* 11:3 (1980), 3–20.

Miller, Henry Knight. *Henry Fielding's "Tom Jones,"* 22–101.

Milligan, Ian. *The Novel in English*, 66–68.

Novak, Maximillian E. *Eighteenth-Century English Literature*, 129–132.

Oakleaf, David. "Sliding Down Together: Fielding, Addison, and the Pleasures of the Imagination in *Tom Jones*." *Engl Stud in Canada* 9 (1983), 402–415.

O'Brien, Timothy D. "The Hungry Author and Narrative Performance in *Tom Jones*." *Stud in Engl Lit, 1500–1900* 25 (1985), 615–632.

Pache, Walter. *Profit and Delight*, 221–243.

Peereboom, John James. *Fielding Practice*, 16–19, 23–25, 40–43, 67–72, 75–76.

Preston, John. "The Silence of the Novel." *Mod Lang R* 74 (1979), 262–263.

Ribble, Frederick G. "Aristotle and the 'Prudence' Theme of *Tom Jones*." *Eighteenth-Century Stud* 15 (1981), 26–47.

Rogers, Pat. *Henry Fielding*, 158–164.

Rostrig, Maren-Sofie. "New Perspectives on Fielding's Narrative Art," in Stig Johansson and Bjorn Tysdahl, eds., *Papers*, 183–197.

Sander, Hans-Jochen. " 'Menschliche Natur' und Individualität in Fieldings *Tom Jones* und im spätbürgerlichen englischen Roman." *Zeitschrift für Anglistik und Amerikanistik* 28 (1980), 237–239.

Schonhorn, Manuel. "Fielding's Ecphrastic Moment: Tom Jones and his Egyptian Majesty." *Stud in Philology* 78 (1981), 305–323.

Seamon, Roger G. "Narrative Practice and the Theoretical Distinction between History and Fiction." *Genre* 16 (1983), 209–210.

Seehase, Georg. "Henry Fielding und der realistische Roman," 204–206.

Sells, L. F. "*Tom Jones* and *The Secrets of the Invisible World.*" *Notes and Queries* 28 (1981), 231–233.

Shroff, Homai J. *The Eighteenth Century Novel*, 24–26, 123–132, 134–150, 157–159.

Simon, Richard Keller. *The Labyrinth*, 53–77.

Simpson, K. G. "Technique as Judgement in *Tom Jones*," in Simpson, ed., *Henry Fielding*, 158–172.

Smith, Grahame. *The Novel & Society*, 92–114.

Snow, Malinda. "The Judgment of Evidence in *Tom Jones*." *South Atlantic R* 48:2 (1983), 37–49.

Speck, W. A. *Society and Literature*, 152–154.

Tandrup, Birthe. "The Technique," 227–240.

Torrance, Robert M. *The Comic Hero*, 187–196.

Trickett, Rachel. " 'Curious Eye': Some Aspects of Visual Description in Eighteenth-Century Literature," in Douglas Lane Patey and Timothy Keegan, eds., *Augustan Studies*, 247–249.

Voogd, Peter Jan de. *Henry Fielding*, 110–118, 121–127, 157–159.

Weisgerber, Jean. *L'espace romanesque*, 117–139.

Weissman, Judith. "The Man of the Hill and the Gypsies in *Tom Jones*: Satire, Utopia, and the Novel." *Ball State Univ Forum* 22:1 (1981), 60–68.

Williams, Ioan. *The Idea of the Novel*, 192–198.

SARAH FIELDING

The Countess of Dellwyn, 1759

Downs-Miers, Deborah. "Springing the Trap: Subtexts and Subversions," in Mary Anne Schofield and Cecilia Macheski, eds., *Fetter'd or Free?*, 313–316.

The Cry, 1754

Downs-Miers, Deborah. "Springing the Trap," 312–313, 316–317, 320–323.

David Simple, 1744–1753

Barker, Gerard A. "*David Simple*: The Novel of Sensibility in Embryo." *Mod Lang Stud* 12:2 (1982), 69–80.

Downs-Miers, Deborah. "Springing the Trap," 311–312.

Suhr, Heidrun. *Englische Romanautorinnen*, 164–166.

The Governess, 1749

Downs-Miers, Deborah. "Springing the Trap," 314–316.

The History of Ophelia, 1760

Downs-Miers, Deborah. "Springing the Trap," 318–320.

Suhr, Heidrun. *Englische Romanautorinnen*, 167–171.

RONALD FIRBANK

Caprice, 1917

    Severi, Rita. "Comunicazione e metacomunicazione in *Caprice* di Ronald Firbank." *Paragone* 336 (1978), 57–71.

FORD MADOX FORD

A Call, 1910

    Green Robert. *Ford Madox Ford*, 56–62.

The *Fifth Queen* Trilogy, 1962

    Batchelor, John. *The Edwardian Novelists*, 105–109.

    Gass, William. "The Neglect of *The Fifth Queen*," in Sondra J. Stang, ed., *The Presence*, 25–43.

    Moser, Thomas C. *The Life in the Fiction*, 61–64.

    Newman, Judie. "Ford Madox Ford's *Fifth Queen* Trilogy: Mythical Fiction and Political Letters." *Etudes Anglaises* 38 (1985), 397–410.

The Good Soldier, 1915

    Armstrong, Paul B. "The Epistemology of *The Good Soldier*: A Phenomenological Reconsideration." *Criticism* 22 (1980), 230–251.

    Armstrong, Paul B. "The Hermeneutics of Literary Impressionism: Interpretation and Reality in James, Conrad, and Ford." *Centennial R* 27 (1983), 255–257.

    Bailin, Miriam. " 'An Extraordinarily Safe Castle': Aesthetics as Refuge in *The Good Soldier*." *Mod Fiction Stud* 30 (1984), 621–636.

    Batchelor, John. *The Edwardian Novelists*, 109–113.

    Bonds, Diane Stockmar. "The Seeing Eye and the Slothful Heart: The Narrator of Ford's *The Good Soldier*." *Engl Lit in Transition* 25 (1982), 21–26.

    Bruffee, Kenneth A. *Elegiac Romance*, 141–150.

    Cheng, Vincent J. "Religious Differences in *The Good Soldier*: The 'Protest' Scene." *Renascence* 37 (1985), 238–247.

    Clews, Hetty. *The Only Teller*, 141–152.

    Crawford, Fred D. *Mixing Memory*, 26–28.

    Creed, Walter G. "*The Good Soldier*: Knowing and Judging." *Engl Lit in Transition* 23 (1980), 215–228.

    Donoghue, Denis. "Listening to the Saddest Story." *Sewanee R* 88 (1980), 557–571. [Also in Sondra J. Stang, ed., *The Presence*, 44–54.]

    Eggenschwiler, David. "Very Like a Whale: The Comical-Tragical Illusions of *The Good Soldier*." *Genre* 12 (1979), 401–414.

    Fleishman, Avrom. "The Genre of *The Good Soldier*: Ford's Comic Mastery." *Stud in the Liter Imagination* 13:1 (1980), 31–41.

    Gardiner, Judith Kegan. "Rhys Recalls Ford: *Quartet* and *The Good Soldier*." *Tulsa Stud in Women's Lit* 1:1 (1982), 67–81.

    Green, Robert. *Ford Madox Ford*, 33–36, 49–78, 80–109.

Green, Robert. "*The Good Soldier*: Ford's Cubist Novel." *Modernist Stud* 3 (1979), 49–59.

Hartford, Gordon. "Ford and *The Good Soldier*: A Bid for Tragedy." *Engl Stud in Africa* 23 (1980), 93–102.

Hessler, John G. "Dowell and *The Good Soldier*: The Narrator Re-Examined." *J of Narrative Technique* 9 (1979), 53–60.

Levenson, Michael. "Character in *The Good Soldier*." *Twentieth Century Lit* 30 (1984), 373–386.

Lynn, David H. "Watching the Orchards Robbed: Dowell and *The Good Soldier*." *Stud in the Novel* 16 (1984), 410–423.

McDougal, Stuart Y. " 'Where Even the Saddest Stories Are Gay': Provence and *The Good Soldier*." *J of Mod Lit* 7 (1979), 552–554.

Micklus, Robert. "Dowell's Passion in *The Good Soldier*." *Engl Lit in Transition* 22 (1979), 281–290.

Moser, Thomas C. *The Life in the Fiction*, 154–180.

Reichert, John. "Poor Florence Indeed! or: *The Good Soldier* Retold." *Stud in the Novel* 14 (1982), 161–178.

Rentz, Kathryn C. "The Question of James's Influence on Ford's *The Good Soldier*." *Engl Lit in Transition* 25 (1982), 104–111.

Sale, Roger. "Ford's Coming of Age: *The Good Soldier* and *Parade's End*," in Sondra J. Stang, ed., *The Presence*, 55–62.

Snitow, Ann Barr. *Ford Madox Ford*, 159–190.

Thornton, Lawrence. *Unbodied Hope*, 98–114.

Ladies Whose Bright Eyes, 1911

Moser, Thomas C. *The Life in the Fiction*, 82–86.

Last Post, 1928

Green Robert. *Ford Madox Ford*, 162–167.

A Man Could Stand Up —, 1926

Green Robert. *Ford Madox Ford*, 133–134, 136–137, 140–141, 146–147, 159–164.
Moser, Thomas C. *The Life in the Fiction*, 248–253.

The Marsden Case, 1923

Green Robert. *Ford Madox Ford*, 125–128.
Moser, Thomas C. *The Life in the Fiction*, 209–213.
Snitow, Ann Barr. *Ford Madox Ford*, 201–204.

Mr. Apollo, 1908

Moser, Thomas C. *The Life in the Fiction*, 72–76.
Snitow, Ann Barr. *Ford Madox Ford*, 115–120.

No More Parades, 1925

Green Robert. *Ford Madox Ford*, 154–157.
Moser, Thomas C. *The Life in the Fiction*, 228–241.

Parade's End, 1950

Brightman, Christopher. "Ford Madox Ford: Art Criticism and *Parade's End*." *Theoria* (Natal) 59 (1982), 63–74.

Colbert, Robert Edward. "*Parade's End*: Ford Madox Ford's Fabricated World." *Res Stud* 48 (1980), 63–70.

Crawford, Fred D. *Mixing Memory*, 28–30.

Green Robert. *Ford Madox Ford*, 121–167.

Lytle, Andrew. "A Partial Reading of *Parade's End*, or The Hero as an Old Furniture Dealer," in Sondra J. Stang, ed., *The Presence*, 77–95.

Moore, Gene M. "The Tory in a Time of Change: Social Aspects of Ford Madox Ford's *Parade's End*." *Twentieth Century Lit* 28 (1982), 49–67.

Moser, Thomas C. *The Life in the Fiction*, 215–254.

Page, Norman. "Living as Ritual in *Parade's End*." *Stud in the Liter Imagination* 13:1 (1980), 43–50.

Sale, Roger. "Ford's Coming of Age," 63–76.

Snitow, Ann Barr. *Ford Madox Ford*, 207–233.

The Simple Life, 1911

Batchelor, John. *The Edwardian Novelists*, 115–117.

Some Do Not, 1924

Green Robert. *Ford Madox Ford*, 114–117, 150–160.

Moser, Thomas C. *The Life in the Fiction*, 213–248.

EMANUEL FORDE

Ornatus and Artesia, 1595?

Falke, Anne. " 'The Work Well Done that Pleaseth All': Emanuel Forde and the Seventeenth-Century Popular Chivalric Romance." *Stud in Philology* 78 (1981), 241–254.

E. M. FORSTER

Howards End, 1910

Amur, G. S. "Hellenic Heroines and Sexless Angels: Images of Woman in Forster's Novels," in Vasant A. Shahane, ed., *Approaches*, 27–29.

Ansari, A. A. "*Howards End*: The Pattern of Antinomies." *Aligarh J of Engl Stud* 5 (1980), 66–82.

Aronson, Alex. *Music and the Novel*, 77–79.

Barrett, Elizabeth. "The Advance Beyond Daintiness: Voice and Myth in *Howards End*," in Judith Scherer Herz and Robert K. Martin, eds., *E. M. Forster*, 155–166.

Batchelor, John. *The Edwardian Novelists*, 225–232.

Bellman Nerozzi, Patrizia. "Il gattopardo di E. M. Forster," in Agostino Lombardo, ed., *Studi inglesi*, 353–371.

Buhariwala, Shernavaz. *Arcades to a Dome*, 98–130.

Chakrabarty, Surabhi. "Bi-Tonality in Fiction: Leonard Bast in E. M. Forster's *Howards End*." *J of the Dept of Engl* (Calcutta Univ) 17:2 (1981–82), 1–25.

Chakrabarty, Surabhi. "Forster's *Howards End*: Character of Margaret." *J of the Dept of Engl* (Calcutta Univ) 17:1 (1981–82), 54–74.

Daleski, H. M. *Unities*, 111–125.

Dowling, David. *Bloomsbury Aesthetics*, 60–67.

Eagleton, Mary, and David Pierce. *Attitudes to Class*, 95–101.

Ebbatson, Roger. *Lawrence and the Nature Tradition*, 223–227.

Elert, Kerstin. *Portraits of Women*, 94–103.

Firchow, Peter. "E. M. Forster's *Howards End*: From Pleasant Land to Waste Land." *Cahiers Victoriens et Edouardiens* 11 (1980), 119–134.

Firchow, Peter E. "Germany and Germanic Mythology in *Howards End*." *Compar Lit* 33 (1981), 50–68.

Gardner, Philip. "E. M. Forster and 'the possession of England'." *Mod Lang Q* 42 (1981), 176–179.

Gillie, Christopher. *A Preface*, 117–126.

Golden, Kenneth L. "Jung, Modern Dissociation, and Forster's *Howards End*." *Coll Lang Assoc J* 29 (1985), 221–231.

Gordon, Jan B. "The Third Cheer: 'Voice' in Forster." *Twentieth Century Lit* 31 (1985), 321–324.

Green, Martin. *The English Novel*, 55–57.

Hamlet, Betsy L. "A Comparative Study of Two Motifs in *Howards End*, *Dubliners*, and *The Waste Land*." *Notes on Contemp Lit* 13:3 (1983), 2–4.

Hanquart, Evelyne. "Divertissements et divertissement: la musique et E. M. Forster." *Cahiers Victoriens et Edouardiens* 19 (1984), 59–61.

Hanquart, Evelyne. "The Evolution of the Mother-Figure in E. M. Forster's Fictional Work," in Vasant A. Shahane, ed., *Approaches*, 65–67.

Heims, Neil. "Forster's *Howards End*." *Explicator* 42:1 (1983), 39–41.

Hoy, Pat C., II. "The Narrow, Rich Staircase in Forster's *Howards End*." *Twentieth Century Lit* 31 (1985), 221–234.

Hunter, Jefferson. *Edwardian Fiction*, 241–245, 251–253.

Levenson, Michael. "Liberalism and Symbolism in *Howards End*." *Papers on Lang & Lit* 21 (1985), 295–316.

McDowell, Frederick P. W. *E. M. Forster*, 65–84.

Parkinson, R. N. "The Inheritors; or A Single Ticket for Howards End," in G. K. Das and John Beer, eds., *E. M. Forster*, 55–68.

Pinkerton, Mary. "Ambiguous Connections: Leonard Bast's Role in *Howards End*." *Twentieth Century Lit* 31 (1985), 236–245.

Rivenberg, Paul R. "The Role of the Essayist-Commentator in *Howards End*," in Judith Scherer Herz and Robert K. Martin, eds., *E. M. Forster*, 167–175.

Roman, A. M. "Fêtes religieuses et noces païennes dans les romans de E. M. Forster." *Cahiers Victoriens et Edouardiens* 19 (1984), 71–72.

Rosecrance, Barbara. *Forster's Narrative Vision*, 111–149.

Schwarz, Daniel R. "The Originality of E. M. Forster." *Mod Fiction Stud* 29 (1983), 633–635.

Scott, P. J. M. *E. M. Forster*, 110–130.

Stape, J. H. "Leonard's 'Fatal Forgotten Umbrella': Sex and the Manuscript Revision to *Howards End*." *J of Mod Lit* 9 (1981–82), 123–132.

Summers, Claude J. *E. M. Forster*, 105–139.

Thomson, Douglass H. "From Words to Things: Margaret's Progress in *Howards End*." *Stud in the Novel* 15 (1983), 122–132.

Walch, Günter. "Humanistische Abbildfunktion als Voraussetzung des realistischen Romanschaffens E. M. Forsters." *Zeitschrift für Anglistik und Amerikanistik* 29 (1981), 296–304.

Weatherhead, Andrea K. "*Howards End*: Beethoven's *Fifth*." *Twentieth Century Lit* 31 (1985), 247–263.

The Longest Journey, 1907

Amur, G. S. "Hellenic Heroines," 25–26, 32.

Batchelor, John. *The Edwardian Novelists*, 217–221.

Brown, Tony. "Edward Carpenter and the Discussion of the Cow in *The Longest Journey*." *R of Engl Stud* 33 (1982), 58–62.

Buhariwala, Shernavaz. *Arcades to a Dome*, 43–72.

Dowling, David. *Bloomsbury Aesthetics*, 54–60.

Ebbatson, Roger. *Lawrence and the Nature Tradition*, 217–222.

Elert, Kerstin. *Portraits of Women*, 86–89, 122–125.

Faber, M. D. "E. M. Forster's *The Longest Journey*: Doubled Offspring and Ambivalent Mothers." *Univ of Hartford Stud in Lit* 17:1 (1985), 19–34.

Furbank, P. N. "The Philosophy of E. M. Forster," in Judith Scherer Herz and Robert K. Martin, eds., *E. M. Forster*, 44–49.

Gardner, Philip. "E. M. Forster," 173–175.

Gillie, Christopher. *A Preface*, 113–116.

Hanquart, Evelyne. "The Evolution of the Mother-Figure," 61–63.

Levine, June Perry. "The Tame in Pursuit of the Savage: The Posthumous Fiction of E. M. Forster." *PMLA* 99 (1984), 82–84.

McDowell, Frederick P. W. *E. M. Forster*, 46–64.

Martin, Robert K. "The Paterian Mode in Forster's Fiction: *The Longest Journey* to *Pharos and Pharillon*," in Judith Scherer Herz and Robert K. Martin, eds., *E. M. Forster*, 106–109.

Roman, A. M. "Fêtes religieuses et noces païennes," 67–69.

Rosenbaum, S. P. "*The Longest Journey*: E. M. Forster's Refutation of Idealism," in G. K. Das and John Beer, eds., *E. M. Forster*, 32–54.

Schultz, Robert A. "Analogues of Argument in Fictional Narrative." *Poetics* 8 (1979), 231–244.

Schwarz, Daniel R. "The Originality," 630–633.

Scott, P. J. M. *E. M. Forster*, 83–101.

Simon, Richard Keller. "E. M. Forster's Critique of Laughter and the
Comic: The First Three Novels as Dialectic." *Twentieth Century Lit*
31 (1985), 207–211, 214–220.
Stubbs, Patricia. *Women and Fiction*, 213–214.
Summers, Claude J. *E. M. Forster*, 49–76.

Maurice, 1971

Adams, Stephen. *The Homosexual*, 106–119.
Batchelor, John. *The Edwardian Novelists*, 208–213.
Brake, Mike. "The Image of the Homosexual in Contemporary English
and American Fiction," in Diana Laurenson, ed., *The Sociology*,
182–183.
Buhariwala, Shernavaz. *Arcades to a Dome*, 133–155.
Dowling, David. *Bloomsbury Aesthetics*, 67–70.
Ebbatson, Roger. *The Evolutionary Self*, 57–75.
Ebbatson, Roger. *Lawrence and the Nature Tradition*, 227–234.
Friend, Robert. "*Maurice*: E. M. Forster's Sexual *Bildungsroman*."
Hebrew Univ Stud in Lit 7 (1979), 271–297.
Gardner, Philip. "E. M. Forster," 179–181.
Gardner, Philip. "The Evolution of E. M. Forster's *Maurice*," in Judith
Scherer Herz and Robert K. Martin, eds., *E. M. Forster*, 204–221.
Gillie, Christopher. *A Preface*, 126–128.
Grant, Kathleen. "*Maurice* as Fantasy," in Judith Scherer Herz and
Robert K. Martin, eds., *E. M. Forster*, 191–202.
Hanquart, Evelyne. "Romans et nouvelles inachevés d'E. M. Forster."
Etudes Anglaises 35 (1982), 165–172.
King, Dixie. "The Influence of Forster's *Maurice* on *Lady Chatterley's
Lover*." *Contemp Lit* 23 (1982), 76–82.
Levine, June Perry. "The Tame in Pursuit," 74–81.
McDowell, Frederick P. W. *E. M. Forster*, 85–95.
Nadel, Ira Bruce. "Moments in the Greenwood: *Maurice* in Context,"
in Judith Scherer Herz and Robert K. Martin, eds., *E. M. Forster*,
177–189.
Page, Norman. *E. M. Forster's Posthumous Fiction*, 67–102.
Rosecrance, Barbara. *Forster's Narrative Vision*, 150–174.
Scott, P. J. M. *E. M. Forster*, 135–137.
Summers, Claude J. *E. M. Forster*, 141–180.
Theogood, Jack. "Worlds Apart: Apropos E. M. Forster's *Maurice*."
Recovering Lit 12 (1984), 41–50.

A Passage to India, 1924

Ali, Ahmed. "E. M. Forster and India," in Judith Scherer Herz and
Robert K. Martin, eds., *E. M. Forster*, 278–282.
Amur, G. S. "Hellenic Heroines," 29–30.
Aronson, Alex. *Music and the Novel*, 145–149.
Barrett, Elizabeth. "Comedy, Courtesy, and *A Passage to India*." *Engl
Stud in Canada* 10 (1984), 77–92.

Beer, Gillian. " 'But Nothing in India is Identifiable': Negation and Identification in *A Passage to India*," in Vasant A. Shahane, ed., *Approaches*, 9–23.

Beer, Gillian. "Negation in *A Passage to India*." *Essays in Criticism* 30 (1980), 151–166.

Beer, John. "Echoes, Reflections, Correspondences: Some Central Romantic Themes and *A Passage to India*," in Vasant A. Shahane, ed., *Approaches*, 70–95.

Beer, John. "*A Passage to India*, the French New Novel and English Romanticism," in Judith Scherer Herz and Robert K. Martin, eds., *E. M. Forster*, 124–150.

Bhardwaj, R. S. "Forster on Love and Liberty," in Vasant A. Shahane, ed., *Approaches*, 102–105.

Bodenheimer, Rosemarie. "The Romantic Impasse in *A Passage to India*." *Criticism* 22 (1980), 40–56.

Buhariwala, Shernavaz. *Arcades to a Dome*, 158–194.

Butter, Peter H. "*A Passage to India*," in Hermann J. Weiand, ed., *Insight V*, 69–79.

Colmer, John. "Promise and Withdrawal in *A Passage to India*," in G. K. Das and John Beer, eds., *E. M. Forster*, 117–128.

Conradi, Peter. "The Metaphysical Hostess: The Cult of Personal Relations in the Modern English Novel." *ELH* 48 (1981), 439–443.

Crawford, Fred D. *Mixing Memory*, 23–26.

Daleski, H. M. *Unities*, 59–79.

Das, G. K. "E. M. Forster and Hindu Mythology," in Judith Scherer Herz and Robert K. Martin, eds., *E. M. Forster*, 251–255.

Dowling, David. *Bloomsbury Aesthetics*, 71–84.

Dowling, David. "*A Passage to India* through 'The Spaces between the Words'." *J of Narrative Technique* 15 (1985), 256–265.

Drew, John. "A Passage via Alexandria?," in G. K. Das and John Beer, eds., *E. M. Forster*, 89–101.

Gillie, Christopher. *A Preface*, 130–157.

Green, Martin. *The English Novel*, 57–59.

Hanquart, Evelyne. "Divertissements et divertissement," 61–65.

Hanquart, Evelyne. "The Evolution of the Mother-Figure," 67–68.

Hawkins, Hunt. "Forster's Critique of Imperialism in *A Passage to India*." *South Atlantic R* 48:1 (1983), 54–64.

Higgins, Elizabeth Jean. *Reading the Novel*, 377–382.

Irwin, Archibald E. "*Déjà lu*: Forster's Self-Echoes in *A Passage to India*." *J of Mod Lit* 7 (1979), 456–470.

Leech, Geoffrey N., and Michael H. Short. *Style in Fiction*, 245–249.

Lewis, Robin Jared. "E. M. Forster: The Indian Diary," in Vasant A. Shahane, ed., *Approaches*, 127–136.

McDowell, Frederick P. W. *E. M. Forster*, 102–130.

Noble, R. W. "*A Passage to India*: The Genesis of E. M. Forster's Novel." *Encounter*, Feb. 1980, 51–61.

Orange, Michael. "Language and Silence in *A Passage to India*," in G. K. Das and John Beer, eds., *E. M. Forster*, 142–160.

Parry, Benita. "*A Passage to India*: Epitaph or Manifesto?," in G. K. Das and John Beer, eds., *E. M. Forster*, 129–141.

Peat, Derek. "Pattern and Meaning: *A Passage to India*." *Southern R* (Adelaide) 11 (1978), 183–187.

Petry, Alice Hall. "Fantasy, Prophecy, and *A Passage to India*." *Dutch Q R of Anglo-American Letters* 12 (1982), 99–112.

Pradhan, S. V. "*A Passage to India*: Realism Versus Symbolism, A Marxist Analysis." *Dalhousie R* 60 (1980), 300–314.

Rahman, Shaista. "Onomastic Devices in Forster's *A Passage to India*." *Liter Onomastic Stud* 10 (1983), 55–74.

Raizada, Harish. "The Double Vision of Love-Hate Relations in *A Passage to India*." *Aligarh J of Engl Stud* 5 (1980), 83–101.

Ram, Atma. "E. M. Forster: A Friend of India." *Commonwealth Q* 4:15 (1980), 110–113.

Rao, E. Nageswara. "The Dialogue is the Thing: A Contrastive Analysis of Fictional Speech in Forster and Anand," in Vasant A. Shahane, ed., *Approaches*, 139–146.

Rath, Sura Prasad. "Language of 'Expansion': Forster's 'Connecting' Metaphor in *A Passage to India*." *South Asian R* 4 (1980), 70–78.

Roman, A. M. "Fêtes religieuses et noces païennes," 69–71.

Rosecrance, Barbara. *Forster's Narrative Vision*, 184–236.

Rosecrance, Barbara. "*A Passage to India*: The Dominant Voice," in Judith Scherer Herz and Robert K. Martin, eds., *E. M. Forster*, 234–243.

Sahni, Chaman L. "E. M. Forster's *A Passage to India*: The Islamic Dimension." *Cahiers Victoriens et Edouardiens* 17 (1983), 73–86.

Sahni, Chaman L. *Forster's "A Passage to India,"* 11–159.

Schwarz, Daniel R. "The Originality," 635–640.

Scott, P. J. M. *E. M. Forster*, 150–184.

Selig, Robert L. " 'God is Love': On an Unpublished Forster Letter and the Ironic Use of Myth in *A Passage to India*." *J of Mod Lit* 7 (1979), 471–487.

Shahane, V. A. "Life's Walking Shadows in *A Passage to India*," in G. K. Das and John Beer, eds., *E. M. Forster*, 109–116.

Shahane, Vasant A. "Echoes of Plotinus in Forster's *A Passage to India*," in Shahane, ed., *Approaches*, 162–177.

Shahane, Vasant A. "Forster's Inner Passage to India," in Judith Scherer Herz and Robert K. Martin, eds., *E. M. Forster*, 267–276.

Shahane, Vasant A. "Mrs. Moore's Experience in The Marabar Caves: A Zen Buddhist Reading." *Twentieth Century Lit* 31 (1985), 279–285.

Shamsul Islam. *Chronicles of the Raj*, 18–28, 34–43.

Singh, Brijraj. "Mrs. Moore, Prof. Godbole and the Supernatural: Some Comments on *A Passage to India*." *Liter Criterion* 15:2 (1980), 44–53.

Singh, Frances B. "*A Passage to India*, the National Movement, and Independence." *Twentieth Century Lit* 31 (1985), 265–276.

Sivaramkrishna, M. "Epiphany and History: The Dialectic of Transcendence and *A Passage to India*," in Vasant A. Shahane, ed., *Approaches*, 148–161.

Summers, Claude J. *E. M. Forster*, 181–236.

Thumboo, Edwin. "E. M. Forster's Inner Passage to India: Dewas, Alexandria and the Road to Mau," in Vasant A. Shahane, ed., *Approaches*, 40–57.

Tinsley, Molly B. "Muddle et Cetera: Syntax in *A Passage to India*." *J of Narrative Technique* 9 (1979), 191–198. [Also in Judith Scherer Herz and Robert K. Martin, eds., *E. M. Forster*, 257–266.]

A Room with a View, 1908

Amur, G. S. "Hellenic Heroines," 25, 31–32.

Batchelor, John. *The Edwardian Novelists*, 221–225.

Buhariwala, Shernavaz. *Arcades to a Dome*, 75–96.

Dowling, David. *Bloomsbury Aesthetics*, 49–54.

Elert, Kerstin. *Portraits of Women*, 89–94, 125–130.

Gillie, Christopher. *A Preface*, 68–71.

Gordon, Jan B. "The Third Cheer," 318–321.

Hunter, Jefferson. *Edwardian Fiction*, 173–176.

McDowell, Frederick P. W. *E. M. Forster*, 18–29.

Rosecrance, Barbara. *Forster's Narrative Vision*, 83–110.

Ross, Michael L. "Forster's Arnoldian Comedy: Hebraism, Hellenism, and *A Room with a View*." *Engl Lit in Transition* 23 (1980), 155–165.

Scott, P. J. M. *E. M. Forster*, 63–81.

Simon, Richard Keller. "E. M. Forster's Critique," 211–220.

Summers, Claude J. *E. M. Forster*, 77–104.

Thumboo, Edwin. "E. M. Forster's Inner Passage," 38–39.

Where Angels Fear to Tread, 1905

Amur, G. S. "Hellenic Heroines," 27, 30–32.

Batchelor, John. *The Edwardian Novelists*, 213–217.

Bhardwaj, R. S. "Forster on Love and Liberty," 102–105.

Buhariwala, Shernavaz. *Arcades to a Dome*, 16–40.

Dowling, David. *Bloomsbury Aesthetics*, 44–49.

Elert, Kerstin. *Portraits of Women*, 80–86, 118–122.

Gillie, Christopher. *A Preface*, 96–111.

Gordon, Jan B. "The Third Cheer," 316–318.

Hanquart, Evelyne. "The Evolution of the Mother-Figure," 61.

Levine, June Perry. "The Tame in Pursuit," 81–82.

McDowell, Frederick P. W. *E. M. Forster*, 29–38.

Rosecrance, Barbara. *Forster's Narrative Vision*, 19–51.

Rosenbaum, S. P. "Towards a Literary History of *Monteriano*." *Twentieth Century Lit* 31 (1985), 180–196.

Schwarz, Daniel R. "The Originality," 629–630.

Scott, P. J. M. *E. M. Forster*, 38–55.

Simon, Richard Keller. "E. M. Forster's Critique," 204–207, 214–220.

Summers, Claude J. *E. M. Forster*, 25–48.
Thumboo, Edwin. "E. M. Forster's Inner Passage," 38–40.
Walch, Günter. "Humanistische Abbildfunktion," 295–296.

JOHN FOWLES

The Collector, 1963

Bagchee, Syhamal. "*The Collector*: The Paradoxical Imagination of John Fowles." *J of Mod Lit* 8 (1980–81), 219–234.

Beatty, Patricia V. "John Fowles' Clegg: Captive Landlord of Eden." *Ariel* 13:3 (1982), 73–80.

Davidson, Arnold E. "Caliban and the Captive Maiden: John Fowles' *The Collector* and Irving Wallace's *The Fan Club*." *Stud in the Hum* 8:2 (1981), 28–33.

Fawkner, H. W. *The Timescapes*, 73–75.

Huffaker, Robert. *John Fowles*, 73–90.

Lemon, Lee T. *Portraits of the Artist*, 131–133.

Loveday, Simon. *The Romances*, 11–28.

McSweeney, Kerry. *Four Contemporary Novelists*, 129–135.

Riggan, William. *Picaros*, 3–10.

Thorpe, Michael. *John Fowles*, 13–17.

Wolfe, Peter. *John Fowles*, 45–47, 51–80.

Woodcock, Bruce. *Male Mythologies*, 27–43.

Daniel Martin, 1977

Alter, Robert. "*Daniel Martin* and the Mimetic Task." *Genre* 14 (1981), 65–78. [Also in Jackson I. Cope and Geoffrey Green, eds., *Novel vs. Fiction*, 65–78.]

Andrews, Maureen Gillespie. "Nature in John Fowles's *Daniel Martin* and *The Tree*." *Mod Fiction Stud* 31 (1985), 150–155.

Arlett, Robert. "*Daniel Martin* and the Contemporary Epic Novel." *Mod Fiction Stud* 31 (1985), 173–185.

Barnum, Carol. "John Fowles's *Daniel Martin*: A Vision of Whole Sight." *Liter R* 25 (1981), 64–79.

Bernstein, John. "John Fowles' Use of Ibsen in *Daniel Martin*." *Notes on Contemp Lit* 9:4 (1979), 10.

Boomsma, Patricia J. " 'Whole Sight': Fowles, Lukacs and *Daniel Martin*." *J of Mod Lit* 8 (1980–81), 325–336.

Chittick, Kathryn. "The Laboratory of Narrative and John Fowles's *Daniel Martin*." *Engl Stud in Canada* 11 (1985), 70–80.

Fawkner, H. W. *The Timescapes*, 43–49, 59–66, 91–105.

Ferris, Ina. "Realist Intention and Mythic Impulse in *Daniel Martin*." *J of Narrative Technique* 12 (1982), 146–152.

Gindin, James. "Three Recent British Novels and an American Response." *Michigan Q R* 17 (1978), 223–246.

Huffaker, Robert. *John Fowles*, 32–43.

Lemon, Lee T. *Portraits of the Artist*, 119–136.

Lewis, Janet E., and Barry N. Olshen. "John Fowles and the Medieval Romance Tradition." *Mod Fiction Stud* 31 (1985), 27–28.

Loveday, Simon. *The Romances*, 103–128.

Loveday, Simon. "The Style of John Fowles: Tense and Person in the First Chapter of *Daniel Martin*." *J of Narrative Technique* 10 (1980), 198–204.

McSweeney, Kerry. *Four Contemporary Novelists*, 143–149.

Park, Sue. "John Fowles, Daniel Martin, and Simon Wolfe." *Mod Fiction Stud* 31 (1985), 165–171.

Park, Sue. "Time and Ruins in John Fowles's *Daniel Martin*." *Mod Fiction Stud* 31 (1985), 157–163.

Swann, C. S. B. "*Daniel Martin*." *Delta* 59 (1979), 1–6.

Thorpe, Michael. *John Fowles*, 35–43.

Wolfe, Peter. *John Fowles*, 170–196.

Woodcock, Bruce. *Male Mythologies*, 115–145.

Wymard, Eleanor B. " 'A New Version of the Midas Touch': *Daniel Martin* and *The World According to Garp*." *Mod Fiction Stud* 27 (1981), 284–286.

The French Lieutenant's Woman, 1969

Barber, Susanna, and Richard Messer. "*The French Lieutenant's Woman* and Individualization." *Lit/Film Q* 12 (1984), 225–229.

Bergonzi, Bernard. "Fictions of History," in Malcolm Bradbury and David Palmer, eds., *The Contemporary English Novel*, 54–56.

Boyum, Joy Gould. *Double Exposure*, 104–110.

Brown, Ruth Christiani. "*The French Lieutenant's Woman* and *Pierre*: Echo and Answer." *Mod Fiction Stud* 31 (1985), 115–131.

Burden, Robert. "The Novel Interrogates Itself: Parody as Self-Consciousness in Contemporary English Fiction," in Malcolm Bradbury and David Palmer, eds., *The Contemporary English Novel*, 147–153.

Byatt, A. S. "People in Paper Houses: Attitudes to 'Realism' and 'Experiment' in English Postwar Fiction," in Malcolm Bradbury and David Palmer, eds., *The Contemporary English Novel*, 27–29.

Castangt, Jean-Claude, and René Gallet. "Quelques aspects des relations entre personnages," in *Etudes sur . . . Fowles*, 25–31.

Castangt, Jean-Claude, and René Gallet. "La symbolique spatiale," in *Etudes sur . . . Fowles*, 43–49.

Catherine, Dominique, and Ginette Emprin. "Aspects de la technique narrative: les relations narrateur/lecteur/personnages," in *Etudes sur . . . Fowles*, 15–22.

Coates, Paul. *The Realist Fantasy*, 183–187.

Conradi, Peter J. "*The French Lieutenant's Woman*: Novel, Screenplay, Film." *Crit Q* 24 (1982), 41–57.

DeVitis, A. A., and Lisa M. Schwerdt. "*The French Lieutenant's Woman* and 'Las Meninas': Correspondences of Art." *Intl Fiction R* 12 (1985), 102–104.

Fawkner, H. W. *The Timescapes*, 100–101, 105–106, 113–121, 124–130, 153–155.

Guth, Deborah. "Archetypal Worlds Reappraised: *The French Lieutenant's Woman* and *Le Grand Meaulnes*." *Compar Lit Stud* 22 (1985), 244–251.

D'Haen, Theo. *Text to Reader*, 25–42.

Hagopian, John V. "Bad Faith in *The French Lieutenant's Woman*." *Contemp Lit* 23 (1982), 191–201.

Hagopian, John V. "*The French Lieutenant's Woman*," in Hermann J. Weiand, ed., *Insight V*, 81–87.

Hellegouarc'h, Elisabeth, and Sylviane Troadec. "L'image du victorianisme," in *Etudes sur . . . Fowles*, 35–41.

Higdon, David Leon. "Endgames in John Fowles's *The French Lieutenant's Woman*." *Engl Stud* 65 (1984), 350–361.

Hogan, Ken. "Fowles' Narrative Style in *The French Lieutenant's Woman*." *CCTE Proc* 48 (1983), 54–63.

Holmes, Frederick M. "The Novel, Illusion, and Reality: The Paradox of Omniscience in *The French Lieutenant's Woman*." *J of Narrative Technique* 11 (1981), 184–196.

Huffaker, Robert. *John Fowles*, 91–115.

Johnson, A. J. B. "Realism in *The French Lieutenant's Woman*." *J of Mod Lit* 8 (1980–81), 287–302.

Kim, Suzanne. "Histoire et roman." *Etudes Anglaises* 36 (1983), 177–180.

Le Bouille, Lucien. "L'oeuvre de John Fowles: Esquisse de quelques grandes lignes," in *Etudes sur . . . Fowles*, 9–13.

Lemon, Lee T. *Portraits of the Artist*, 112–117, 122–127, 141–144.

Lewis, Janet E., and Barry N. Olshen. "John Fowles," 26–27.

Loveday, Simon. *The Romances*, 48–81.

McDaniel, Ellen. "Games and Godgames in *The Magus* and *The French Lieutenant's Woman*." *Mod Fiction Stud* 31 (1985), 36–42.

McEwan, Neil. *The Survival*, 20–37.

McKeon, Zahava Karl. *Novels and Arguments*, 123–129.

McSweeney, Kerry. *Four Contemporary Novelists*, 135–142.

Mansfield, Elizabeth. "A Sequence of Endings: The Manuscripts of *The French Lieutenant's Woman*." *J of Mod Lit* 8 (1980–81), 275–286.

Mazis, Glen A. "The 'Riteful' Play of Time in *The French Lieutenant's Woman*." *Soundings* 16 (1983), 296–316.

Nelles, William. "Problems for Narrative Theory: *The French Lieutenant's Woman*." *Style* 18 (1984), 207–215.

Scruggs, Charles. "The Two Endings of *The French Lieutenant's Woman*." *Mod Fiction Stud* 31 (1985), 95–112.

Siegle, Robert. "The Concept of the Author in Barthes, Foucault, and Fowles." *Coll Lit* 10 (1983), 129–137.

Smith, Frederik N. "Revision and the Style of Revision in *The French Lieutenant's Woman*." *Mod Fiction Stud* 31 (1985), 85–94.

Spitz, Ellen Handler. "On Interpretation of Film as Dream: *The French Lieutenant's Woman*." *Post Script* 2:1 (1982), 13–29.

Sweet-Hurd, Evelyn. "Victorian Echoes in John Fowles's *The French Lieutenant's Woman*." *Notes on Contemp Lit* 13:2 (1983), 2–5.

Thorpe, Michael. *John Fowles*, 25–31.

Whall, Tony. "Karel Reisz's *The French Lieutenant's Woman*: Only the Name Remains the Same." *Lit/Film Q* 10 (1982), 75–81.

Wolfe, Peter. *John Fowles*, 122–169.

Woodcock, Bruce. *Male Mythologies*, 81–113.

The Magus, 1966

Billy, Ted. "*Homo Solitarius*: Isolation and Estrangement in *The Magus*." *Res Stud* 48 (1980), 129–141.

Boccia, Michael. " 'Visions and Revisions': John Fowles's New Version of *The Magus*." *J of Mod Lit* 8 (1980–81), 235–246.

Fawkner, H. W. *The Timescapes*, 53–62, 89–91, 102–113, 125–130.

Glaserfeld, Ernst von. "Reflections on John Fowles's *The Magus* and the Construction of Reality." *Georgia R* 33 (1979), 444–448.

Harris, Richard L. "*The Magus* and 'The Miller's Tale': John Fowles on the Courtly Mode." *Ariel* 14:2 (1983), 3–16.

Holmes, Frederick M. "Art, Truth, and John Fowles's *The Magus*." *Mod Fiction Stud* 31 (1985), 45–55.

Holmes, Frederick M. "Fictions, Reality, and the Authority of the Novelist: Barth's *The Sot-Weed Factor* and Fowles's *The Magus*." *Engl Stud in Canada* 11 (1985), 346–359.

Huffaker, Robert. *John Fowles*, 44–72.

Hussey, Barbara L. "John Fowles's *The Magus*: The Book and the World." *Intl Fiction R* 10 (1983), 19–26.

Leech, Geoffrey N., and Michael H. Short. *Style in Fiction*, 289–290.

Lewis, Janet E., and Barry N. Olshen. "John Fowles," 19–22, 24–26.

Lindroth, James R. "The Architecture of Revision: Fowles and the Agora." *Mod Fiction Stud* 31 (1985), 57–68.

Loveday, Simon. "Magus or Midas?" *Oxford Liter R* 2:3 (1977), 34–35.

Loveday, Simon. *The Romances*, 29–47.

McDaniel, Ellen. "Games and Godgames," 33–42.

McDaniel, Ellen. "*The Magus*: Fowles's Tarot Quest." *J of Mod Lit* 8 (1980–81), 247–260.

McSweeney, Kerry. *Four Contemporary Novelists*, 121–129.

Nadeau, Robert L. "Fowles and Physics: A Study of *The Magus: A Revised Version*." *J of Mod Lit* 8 (1980–81), 261–274.

Newman, Robert D. " 'An Anagram Made Flesh': The Transformation of Nicholas Urfe in Fowles' *The Magus*." *Notes on Contemp Lit* 12:4 (1982), 9.

Novak, Frank G., Jr. "The Dialectics of Debasement in *The Magus*." *Mod Fiction Stud* 31 (1985), 71–82.

Palmer, William J. "Fowles' *The Magus*: The Vortex as Myth, Metaphor, and Masque," in Victor Carrabino, ed., *The Power of Myth*, 66–74.

Poirier, Suzanne. "*L'Astrée* Revisited: A 17th Century Model for *The Magus*." *Compar Lit Stud* 17 (1980), 269–285.

Pollock, John J. "Conchis as Allegorical Figure in *The Magus*." *Notes on Contemp Lit* 10:1 (1980), 10.

Thorpe, Michael. *John Fowles*, 17–25.

Wade, Cory. " 'Mystery Enough at Noon': John Fowles's Revision of *The Magus*." *Southern R* 15 (1979), 717–723.

Wainwright, J. A. "The Illusion of 'Things as they are': *The Magus* versus *The Magus A Revised Version*." *Dalhousie R* 63 (1983), 107–118.

Wolfe, Peter. *John Fowles*, 81–121.

Woodcock, Bruce. *Male Mythologies*, 45–79.

Mantissa, 1982

Fawkner, H. W. "The Neurocognitive Significance of John Fowles's *Mantissa*." *Studia Neophilologica* 56 (1984), 51–57.

Fawkner, H. W. *The Timescapes*, 131–144.

Gotts, Ian. "Fowles' *Mantissa*: Funfair in Another Village." *Critique* (Atlanta) 26 (1985), 81–94.

Woodcock, Bruce. *Male Mythologies*, 147–164.

JULIA FRANKAU

Dr. Phillips, 1887

Zatlin, Linda Gertner. *The Nineteenth-Century Anglo-Jewish Novel*, 98–105.

JAMES ANTHONY FROUDE

The Nemesis of Faith, 1849

Gracie, William J., Jr. "Faith of Our Fathers: The Autobiographical Novels of James Anthony Froude." *Victorians Inst J* 10 (1981–82), 27–43.

Rataboul, Louis J. *Le pasteur anglican*, 391–397.

Shadows of the Clouds, 1847

Gracie, William J., Jr. "Faith of Our Fathers," 27–43.

JOHN GALSWORTHY

Beyond, 1917

Fréchet, Alec. *John Galsworthy*, 82–84.

The Burning Spear, 1919

Fréchet, Alec. *John Galsworthy*, 84–86.

The Country House, 1907

Batchelor, John. *The Edwardian Novelists*, 195–198.
Fréchet, Alec. *John Galsworthy*, 69–71, 136–139, 148–150, 166–170.
Hunter, Jefferson. *Edwardian Fiction*, 200–202.

The Dark Flower, 1913

Fréchet, Alec. *John Galsworthy*, 72–76, 79–81, 141–146.

End of the Chapter, 1934

Fréchet, Alec. *John Galsworthy*, 102–107.

The Forsyte Saga, 1922

Dubasinskij, I. A. *"Saga o Forsaitax."*
Fréchet, Alec. *John Galsworthy*, 89–97, 164–168.
Hojoh, Fumio. "The *Femme Fatale* in Irene Forsyte: A Reading of Galsworthy's *The Forsyte Saga*." *Stud in Engl Lit* (Japan), Engl Number 1980, 23–37.
McQuitty, Peter. "The Forsyte Chronicles: A Nineteenth-Century Liberal View of English History." *Engl Lit in Transition* 23 (1980), 99–114.

Fraternity, 1909

Batchelor, John. *The Edwardian Novelists*, 198–202.
Fréchet, Alec. *John Galsworthy*, 71–73, 110–112, 146–150.
Hunter, Jefferson. *Edwardian Fiction*, 224–226.

In Chancery, 1920

Fréchet, Alec. *John Galsworthy*, 89–91, 94–96.

The Island Pharisees, 1904

Fréchet, Alec. *John Galsworthy*, 64–66, 140–141.
Hunter, Jefferson. *Edwardian Fiction*, 232–240.

Jocelyn, 1898

Fréchet, Alec. *John Galsworthy*, 58–61.

Maid in Waiting, 1931

Fréchet, Alec. *John Galsworthy*, 102–104.

The Man of Property, 1906

Batchelor, John. *The Edwardian Novelists*, 188–195.
Buttigieg, Joseph A. "Individual Freedom in a Structured Universe: Spencer, Galsworthy, and *The Man of Property*." *Res Stud* 48 (1980), 198–209.
Coudriow, Jacques. "La femme dans l'oeuvre de John Galsworthy." *Caliban* 17 (1980), 82–90.
Fréchet, Alec. *John Galsworthy*, 66–68, 89–95, 157–159.
Hunter, Jefferson. *Edwardian Fiction*, 202–204.
McDorman, Kathryne S. "Tarnished Brass: The Imperial Heroes of John Galsworthy and H. G. Wells." *North Dakota Q* 50:1 (1982), 37–45.

A Modern Comedy, 1929

    Fréchet, Alec. *John Galsworthy*, 97–102.

Over the River, 1933

    Fréchet, Alec. *John Galsworthy*, 105–107.

The Patrician, 1911

    Batchelor, John. *The Edwardian Novelists*, 204–207.
    Fréchet, Alec. *John Galsworthy*, 77–79, 146–152.

Saint's Progress, 1919

    Fréchet, Alec. *John Galsworthy*, 75–77, 86–88.

Swan Song, 1927

    Fréchet, Alec. *John Galsworthy*, 100–102.

The White Monkey, 1924

    Fréchet, Alec. *John Galsworthy*, 97–99.

JOHN GALT

Annals of the Parish, 1821

    Buchan, David. "Galt's *Annals*: Treatise and Fable," in Ian Campbell,
      ed., *Nineteenth-Century Scottish Fiction*, 18–35.
    Gibault, Henri. *John Galt*, 92–106.
    McClure, J. Derrick. "Scots and English in *Annals of the Parish* and
      The Provost," in Christopher A. Whatley, ed., *John Galt*, 195–210.
    Scott, P. H. *John Galt*, 25–37.
    Simpson, Kenneth G. "Ironic Self-Revelation in *Annals of the Parish*,"
      in Christopher A. Whatley, ed., *John Galt*, 64–88.
    Whatley, Christopher A. "*Annals of the Parish* and History," in What-
      ley, ed., *John Galt*, 51–62.

The Ayrshire Legatees, 1820–1821

    Campbell, Ian. "Town and Country: *The Ayrshire Legatees*," in Chris-
      topher A. Whatley, ed., *John Galt*, 92–105.
    Gibault, Henri. *John Galt*, 119–127.
    Scott, P. H. *John Galt*, 39–48.

Bogle Corbet, 1831

    Gibault, Henri. *John Galt*, 140–143.
    Scott, P. H. *John Galt*, 99–104.

The Earthquake, 1820

    Gibault, Henri. *John Galt*, 55–56.

Eben Erskine, 1833

    Gibault, Henri. *John Galt*, 59–60.

The Entail, 1822

> Costain, Keith M. "Mind-Forg'd Manacles: John Galt's *The Entail* as Romantic Tragicomedy," in Christopher A. Whatley, ed., *John Galt,* 164–192.
> Gibault, Henri. *John Galt,* 145–171.
> McClure, J. D. "The Language of *The Entail.*" *Scottish Liter J* 8:1 (1981), 30–50.
> Scott, P. H. *John Galt,* 63–69.

The Gathering of the West, 1823

> Gibault, Henri. *John Galt,* 129–130.

Glenfell, 1820

> Gibault, Henri. *John Galt,* 46–47.

The Last of the Lairds, 1826

> Gibault, Henri. *John Galt,* 173–177.
> Gordon, Ian A. "Plastic Surgery on a Nineteenth-Century Novel: John Galt, William Blackwood, Dr. D. M. Moir and *The Last of the Lairds.*" *Library* 32 (1977), 246–255.
> Scott, P. H. *John Galt,* 71–77.

Lawrie Todd, 1830

> Gibault, Henri. *John Galt,* 136–140.
> Scott, P. H. *John Galt,* 93–99.

The Majolo, 1816–1820

> Gibault, Henri. *John Galt,* 45–46.

The Member, 1832

> Scott, P. H. *John Galt,* 104–107.
> Ward, John T. "*The Member* and Parliamentary Reform," in Christopher A. Whatley, ed., *John Galt,* 151–161.

The Omen, 1826

> Gibault, Henri. *John Galt,* 47–48.

The Provost, 1822

> Carnie, R. H. "Names in John Galt's *The Provost,*" in J. H. Alexander and David Hewitt, eds., *Scott and His Influence,* 298–306.
> Gibault, Henri. *John Galt,* 106–115.
> McClure, J. Derrick. "Scots and English," 195–210.
> Scott, P. H. *John Galt,* 50–59.

The Radical, 1832

> Scott, P. H. *John Galt,* 107–108.

Ringan Gilhaize, 1823

> de Groot, H. B. "Scott and Galt: *Old Mortality* and *Ringan Gilhaize,*" in J. H. Alexander and David Hewitt, eds., *Scott and His Influence,* 321–329.

Gibault, Henri. *John Galt*, 179–192.
Mack, Douglas S. " 'The Rage of Fanaticism in Former Days': James Hogg's *Confessions of a Justified Sinner* and the Controversy over *Old Mortality*," in Ian Campbell, ed., *Nineteenth-Century Scottish Fiction*, 39–42.
MacQueen, John. "*Ringan Gilhaize* and Particular Providence," in Christopher A. Whatley, ed., *John Galt*, 107–119.
Scott, P. H. *John Galt*, 78–92.
Wilson, Patricia J. "John Galt at Work: Comments on the MS. of *Ringan Gilhaize*." *Stud in Scottish Lit* 20 (1985), 160–176.
Wilson, Patricia J. "*Ringan Gilhaize*: A Neglected Masterpiece?," in Christopher A. Whatley, ed., *John Galt*, 120–148.
Wilson, Patricia J. "*Ringan Gilhaize*: The Product of an Informing Vision." *Scottish Liter J* 8:1 (1981), 52–67.

Rothelan, 1824

Gibault, Henri. *John Galt*, 68–70.

Sir Andrew Wylie, 1822

Gibault, Henri. *John Galt*, 130–135.
Scott, P. H. *John Galt*, 60–63.

Southennan, 1830

Gibault, Henri. *John Galt*, 70–74.

The Spaewife, 1823

Gibault, Henri. *John Galt*, 66–68.

Stanley Buxton, 1832

Gibault, Henri. *John Galt*, 56–59.

The Steam-Boat, 1822

Gibault, Henri. *John Galt*, 127–129.

The Stolen Child, 1833

Gibault, Henri. *John Galt*, 60–61.

LEON GARFIELD

The Ghost Downstairs, 1972

Swinfen, Ann. *In Defence*, 159–168.

GEORGE GASCOIGNE

The Adventures of Master F. J., 1573

Hedley, Jane. "Allegoria: Gascoigne's Master Trope." *Engl Liter Renaissance* 11 (1981), 148–164.
Rowe, George E. "Interpretation, Sixteenth-Century Readers, and George Gascoigne's 'The Adventures of Master F. J.' " *ELH* 489 (1981), 271–286.

Schöwerling, Rainer. "George Gascoignes *The Adventures of Master F. J.*: Der erste psychologische Roman der englischen Literatur?" *Germanisch-Romanische Monatsschrift* 31 (1981), 129–138.

ELIZABETH GASKELL

Cousin Phillis, 1865

Duthie, Enid L. *The Themes*, 174–176.
Foster, Shirley. *Victorian Women's Fiction*, 172–175.
Hunter, Shelagh. *Victorian Idyllic Fiction*, 80–83, 93–103.
Nestor, Pauline. *Female Friendships*, 62–65.

Cranford, 1853

Duthie, Enid L. *The Themes*, 37–44, 124–126.
Foster, Shirley. *Victorian Women's Fiction*, 166–172.
Fowler, Rowena. "*Cranford*: Cow in Grey Flannel or Lion *Couchant*?" *Stud in Engl Lit, 1500–1900* 24 (1984), 717–729.
Griffith, George V. "What Kind of Book is *Cranford*?" *Ariel* 14:2 (1983), 53–64.
Hunter, Shelagh. *Victorian Idyllic Fiction*, 80–93.
Lansbury, Coral. *Elizabeth Gaskell*, 71–77.
Nestor, Pauline. *Female Friendships*, 49–57.
Stone, Donald D. *The Romantic Impulse*, 153–155.

Mary Barton, 1848

Abalain, H. "Le refus de la marginalité: le combat d'Elizabeth Gaskell pour la réinsertion et la réhabilitation de la *femme déchue* dans la société," in *La Marginalité*, 107–109.
Bergmann, Helena. *Between Obedience and Freedom*, 29–36, 91–92, 107–109, 125–129.
Bodenheimer, Rosemarie. "Private Grief and Public Acts in *Mary Barton*." *Dickens Stud Annual* 9 (1981), 195–214.
Crick, Brian. "The Implications of the Title Changes and Textual Revisions in Mrs. Gaskell's *Mary Barton: A Tale of Manchester Life*." *Notes and Queries* 27 (1980), 514–519.
Culross, Jack L. "*Mary Barton*: A Revaluation." *Bull of the John Rylands Univ Lib of Manchester* 61 (1978), 42–59.
De Stasio, Clotilde. *Lo Scrittore*, 31–50.
Diedrich, Maria. " 'A life of pain': Die Darstellung des Landlebens in den Industrieromanen Elizabeth Gaskells." *Archiv für das Studium der neueren Sprachen und Literaturen* 222 (1985), 49–53.
Duthie, Enid L. *The Themes*, 75–80, 158–163, 181–183.
Eagleton, Mary, and David Pierce. *Attitudes to Class*, 34–38.
Figes, Eva. *Sex and Subterfuge*, 154–159.
Foster, Shirley. *Victorian Women's Fiction*, 143–147.
Fryckstedt, Monica Correa. "The Early Industrial Novel: *Mary Barton* and Its Predecessors." *Bull of the John Rylands Univ Lib of Manchester* 63 (1980), 11–30.

Fryckstedt, Monica Correa. *Elizabeth Gaskell's "Mary Barton,"* 87–119, 170–180.

Fryckstedt, Monica Correa. *"Mary Barton* and the *Reports of the Ministry of the Poor."* *Studia Neophilologica* 52 (1980), 333–336.

Gallagher, Catherine. *The Industrial Reformation*, 62–87.

Hunter, Shelagh. *Victorian Idyllic Fiction*, 104–110.

Ingenito, Michele. *"Mary Barton,"* 5–142.

James, W. L. G. "The Portrayal of Death and 'Substance of Life': Aspects of the Modern Reader's Response to 'Victorianism'," in Ian Gregor, ed., *Reading the Victorian Novel*, 237–240.

Jordan, Elaine. "Spectres and Scorpions: Allusion and Confusion in *Mary Barton."* *Lit and Hist* 7 (1981), 48–61.

Kestner, Joseph. "Men in Female Condition of England Novels." *Women & Lit* 2 (1981), 92–95.

Kestner, Joseph. *Protest and Reform*, 14–20.

Lansbury, Coral. *Elizabeth Gaskell*, 10–22.

Nakazato, Shigeyasu. "On Elizabeth Gaskell's *Mary Barton*: A Study of the Novelist's Realism and Idealism." *Bull of Seisen Women's Coll* (Japan) 28 (1980), 20–31.

Stone, Donald D. *The Romantic Impulse*, 146–149.

Webb, Igor. *From Custom to Capital*, 191–192, 194–197.

Welsh, Alexander. *Reflections*, 132–136.

Williams, Merryn. *Women in the English Novel*, 106–108.

Yeazell, Ruth Bernard. "Why Political Novels Have Heroines: *Sybil, Mary Barton,* and *Felix Holt."* *Novel* 18 (1985), 132–137.

My Lady Ludlow, 1859

Rataboul, Louis J. *Le pasteur anglican*, 263–264.

North and South, 1855

Bergmann, Helena. *Between Obedience and Freedom*, 36–38, 70–76, 92–96, 135–142.

Bodenheimer, Rosemarie. *"North and South*: A Permanent State of Change." *Nineteenth-Century Fiction* 34 (1979), 281–301.

Campbell, Ian. "Mrs. Gaskell's *North and South* and the Art of the Possible." *Dickens Stud Annual* 8 (1980), 231–249.

Coustillas, P. "Mrs. Gaskell: *North and South,"* in Coustillas et al., eds., *Le roman anglais*, 187–198.

David, Deirdre. *Fictions of Resolution*, 1–49.

Diedrich, Maria. " 'A life of pain'," 53–60.

Duthie, Enid L. *The Themes*, 75–79, 84–86, 94–97.

Eagleton, Mary, and David Pierce. *Attitudes to Class*, 33–41, 43–44.

Easson, Angus. "Mr. Hale's Doubts in *North and South."* *R of Engl Stud* 31 (1980), 30–40.

Foster, Shirley. *Victorian Women's Fiction*, 147–153.

Gallagher, Catherine. *"Hard Times* and *North and South*: The Family and Society in Two Industrial Novels." *Arizona Q* 36 (1980), 84–96.

Gallagher, Catherine. *The Industrial Reformation*, 166–184.

Hunter, Shelagh. *Victorian Idyllic Fiction*, 110–119.

Kestner, Joseph. "Men in Female Condition," 95–99.

Kestner, Joseph. *Protest and Reform*, 163–170.

Lansbury, Coral. *Elizabeth Gaskell*, 35–47.

Martin, Carol A. "Gaskell, Darwin, and *North and South*." *Stud in the Novel* 15 (1983), 91–105.

Nestor, Pauline. *Female Friendships*, 68–70.

Newton, Judith Lowder. *Women, Power, and Subversion*, 162–169.

Rataboul, Louis J. *Le pasteur anglican*, 387–388.

Stone, Donald D. *The Romantic Impulse*, 156–160.

Trodd, Anthea. "The Policeman and the Lady: Significant Encounters in Mid-Victorian Fiction." *Victorian Stud* 27 (1984), 453–455.

Weiss, Barbara. "The Dilemma of Happily Ever After: Marriage and the Victorian Novel," in Anne C. Hargrove and Maurine Magliocco, eds., *Portraits of Marriage*, 81–82.

Wheeler, Michael. *English Fiction*, 69–72.

Ruth, 1853

Abalain, H. "Le refus de la marginalité," 111–121.

Auerbach, Nina. *Woman and the Demon*, 169–171.

Duthie, Enid L. *The Themes*, 73–75, 154–156.

Foster, Shirley. *Victorian Women's Fiction*, 153–155.

Fryckstedt, Monica Correa. *Elizabeth Gaskell's . . . "Ruth,"* 120–166, 180–195.

Kestner, Joseph. *Protest and Reform*, 160–163.

Lansbury, Coral. *Elizabeth Gaskell*, 23–34.

Mitchell, Sally. *The Fallen Angel*, 32–42.

Stone, Donald D. *The Romantic Impulse*, 149–153.

Watt, George. *The Fallen Woman*, 19–40.

Williams, Merryn. *Women in the English Novel*, 111–114.

Sylvia's Lovers, 1863

Duthie, Enid L. *The Themes*, 29–31, 172–174.

Foster, Shirley. *Victorian Women's Fiction*, 157–162.

Kestner, Joseph. *Protest and Reform*, 193–201.

Lansbury, Coral. *Elizabeth Gaskell*, 93–103.

Rignall, J. M. "The Historical Double: *Waverley*, *Sylvia's Lovers*, *The Trumpet-Major*." *Essays in Criticism* 34 (1984), 22–27.

Stone, Donald D. *The Romantic Impulse*, 161–165.

Williams, Merryn. *Women in the English Novel*, 115–117.

Wives and Daughters, 1866

Berke, Jacqueline, and Laura Berke. "Mothers and Daughters in *Wives and Daughters*: A Study of Elizabeth Gaskell's Last Novel," in Cathy N. Davidson and E. M. Broner, eds., *The Lost Tradition*, 95–108.

Duthie, Enid L. *The Themes*, 52–55, 96–98.

Foster, Shirley. *Victorian Women's Fiction*, 175–181.

Irwin, Michael. *Picturing*, 50–53.
Lansbury, Coral. *Elizabeth Gaskell*, 104–116.
Martin, Carol A. "No Angel in the House: Victorian Mothers and Daughters in George Eliot and Elizabeth Gaskell." *Midwest Q* 24 (1983), 301–303.
Stone, Donald D. *The Romantic Impulse*, 167–172.
Wheeler, Michael. *English Fiction*, 72–74.

PHILIP GIBBS

Young Anarchy, 1926

Laing, Stuart. "Philip Gibbs and the Newsreel Novel." *Lit and Hist* 7 (1981), 187–201.

GEORGE GISSING

Born in Exile, 1892

Alden, Patricia. "Gissing's Mimic Men." *Gissing Newsl* 17:3 (1981), 3–11.
Allen, M. D. "A New Source for *Born in Exile*?" *Gissing Newsl* 16:3 (1980), 25–30.
Browne, W. Francis. "Gissing's *Born in Exile*: Spiritual Distance between Author and Character." *Gissing Newsl* 15:2 (1979), 5–27.
Coustillas, P. "George Gissing: *Born in Exile*," in Coustillas et al., eds., *Le roman anglais*, 247–257.
De Stasio, Clotilde. *Lo Scrittore*, 126–128.
Korg, Jacob. "The Paradox of Success and Failure in the Novels of George Gissing." *Gissing Newsl* 19:3 (1983), 18–19.
Lamarca Margalef, Jordi. *Ciencia y literatura*, 170–172.
Leavis, L. R. "The Late Nineteenth Century Novel and the Change towards the Sexual: Gissing, Hardy and Lawrence." *Engl Stud* 66 (1985), 40.
Selig, Robert L. *George Gissing*, 63–71.
Swann, Charles. "Sincerity and Authenticity: The Problem of Identity in *Born in Exile*." *Lit and Hist* 10 (1984), 165–186.

The Crown of Life, 1899

Argyle, Gisela. *German Elements*, 142–146.
Grylls, David. "Determinism and Determination in Gissing." *Mod Lang Q* 45 (1984), 79–80.
Selig, Robert L. *George Gissing*, 103–105.

Demos, 1886

Argyle, Gisela. *German Elements*, 113–121.
De Stasio, Clotilde. *Lo Scrittore*, 108–110.
Grylls, David. "Determinism and Determination," 78–79.

Rataboul, Louis J. *Le pasteur anglican*, 274–278.
Selig, Robert L. *George Gissing*, 31–34.

Denzil Quarrier, 1892

Brook, Clifford. "References to Wakefield in *Denzil Quarrier*." *Gissing Newsl* 17:3 (1981), 11–19.
Halperin, John. "Gissing, Marriage, and Women's Rights: The Case of *Denzil Quarrier*." *Gissing Newsl* 15:1 Supplement (1979), 1–10.
Selig, Robert L. *George Gissing*, 88–91.
Tintner, Adeline R. "*Denzil Quarrier*: Gissing's Ibsen Novel." *Engl Stud* 64 (1983), 225–232.
Walker, Brian Robert. "Gissing out of Context: *Denzil Quarrier*." *Gissing Newsl* 19:3 (1983), 1–14.

The Emancipated, 1890

Collie, Michael. "George Gissing, Cosmopolitan." *Engl Stud in Canada* 7 (1981), 167–169.
Grylls, David. "Determinism and Determination," 71–76.
Harrison, John R. "*The Emancipated*: Gissing's Treatment of Women and Religious Emancipation." *Gissing Newsl* 17:2 (1981), 1–8.
Selig, Robert L. *George Gissing*, 48–52.

Eve's Ransom, 1895

Bowlby, Rachel. *Just Looking*, 35–51.
Coustillas, Pierre. "George Gissing, *Eve's Ransom*." *Gissing Newsl* 17:3 (1981), 28–30.
Selig, Robert L. *George Gissing*, 91–95.

In the Year of Jubilee, 1894

Browne, W. Francis. "Gissing: The Reluctant Prophet." *Gissing Newsl* 16:2 (1980), 1–13.
Selig, Robert L. *George Gissing*, 78–82.

Isabel Clarendon, 1886

Argyle, Gisela. *German Elements*, 111–121.
Selig, Robert L. *George Gissing*, 41–45.

A Life's Morning, 1888

Morse, G. O. "An Appreciation of *A Life's Morning*." *Gissing Newsl* 18:4 (1982), 1–21.
Selig, Robert L. *George Gissing*, 45–48.

The Nether World, 1889

Allen, Richard J. "Documentary Realism and Artistic Licence: A Note on an Emblematic Prison Gate in *The Nether World* and *Peter Ibbetson*." *Gissing Newsl* 17:2 (1981), 20–23.
De Stasio, Clotilde. *Lo Scrittore*, 110–123.
Hoyas Solis, José Antonio. "Speech and Character: Dialect in the Novels of George Gissing." *Gissing Newsl* 22:1 (1986), 18–24.

Ingle, Stephen. *Socialist Thought*, 20–22.

McVeagh, John. *Tradefull Merchants*, 155–156.

Selig, Robert L. *George Gissing*, 37–40.

Theman, Diana L. "Continuing the Debate." *Gissing Newsl* 22:1 (1986), 31–39.

Wright, T. R. "George Gissing: Positivist in the Dawn." *Gissing Newsl* 20:2 (1984), 16–17.

New Grub Street, 1891

Bowlby, Rachel. *Just Looking*, 98–117.

Coustillas, Pierre. "Pessimism in Gissing's *New Grub Street*: Its Nature and Manifestations." *Cahiers Victoriens et Edouardiens* 11 (1980), 45–64.

Cross, Nigel. *The Common Writer*, 223–239.

De Stasio, Clotilde. *Lo Scrittore*, 124–126.

Eakin, David B. "The Unmaking of the Artist: Woman and Economics in Gissing's *New Grub Street*." *Cahiers Victoriens et Edouardiens* 13 (1981), 43–51.

Guillaume, André. "The Jamesian Pattern in George Gissing's *New Grub Street*." *Gissing Newsl* 20:1 (1984), 28–33.

Irwin, Michael. *Picturing*, 93–96.

Jolicoeur, Claude. "L'écrivain, grand-prêtre de la littérature ou *New Grub Street*, allégorie de l'âme de l'artiste." *Cahiers Victoriens et Edouardiens* 15 (1982), 71–76.

Korg, Jacob. "The Paradox of Success and Failure," 19–22.

Leavis, L. R. "The Late Nineteenth Century Novel," 38–39.

Makinen, M. A. "The Three Points of View in *New Grub Street*." *Gissing Newsl* 17:1 (1981), 8–13.

Selig, Robert L. *George Gissing*, 53–62.

Tintner, Adeline R. "*New Grub Street* and Juvenal's *Satire* III: 'Free Play Among Classic Ghosts'." *Gissing Newsl* 18:3 (1982), 1–21.

Wright, T. R. "George Gissing," 14–15.

The Odd Women, 1893

Chase, Karen. "The Literal Heroine: A Study of Gissing's *The Odd Women*." *Criticism* 26 (1984), 231–243.

Cotes, Alison. "Gissing, Grant Allen and 'Free Union'." *Gissing Newsl* 19:4 (1983), 1–16.

Eakin, David B. "Gissing and Women: A Response." *Gissing Newsl* 15:3 (1979), 15–19.

Edwards, Lee R. *Psyche as Hero*, 152–156, 168–174.

Kennedy, George E. "Gissing's Narrative of Change: *The Odd Women*." *Gissing Newsl* 18:2 (1982), 12–26.

Kropholler, P. F. "Notes on *The Odd Women*." *Gissing Newsl* 15:3 (1979), 19–23.

Leavis, L. R. "The Late Nineteenth Century Novel," 40–41.

Lesser, Wendy. "Even-Handed Oddness: George Gissing's *The Odd Women.*" *Hudson R* 37 (1984), 209–220.

Linehan, Katherine Bailey. "*The Odd Women*: Gissing's Imaginative Approach to Feminism." *Mod Lang Q* 40 (1979), 358–375.

Selig, Robert L. *George Gissing*, 72–78.

Selig, Robert L. "The Gospel of Work in *The Odd Women*: Gissing's Double Standard." *Gissing Newsl* 15:1 Supplement (1979), 17–25.

Stetz, Margaret Diane. 'Objectified Autobiography' in the Plots of George Gissing's Novels." *Gissing Newsl* 18:2 (1982), 4–6.

Wright, T. R. "George Gissing," 15–16.

Our Friend the Charlatan, 1901

Selig, Robert L. *George Gissing*, 105–107.

The Paying Guest, 1895

Selig, Robert L. *George Gissing*, 97–99.

The Private Papers of Henry Ryecroft, 1903

De Stasio, Clotilde. *Lo Scrittore*, 129–141.

Frye, Lowell T. " 'An Author at Grass': Ironic Intent in Gissing's *The Private Papers of Henry Ryecroft.*" *Engl Lit in Transition* 24 (1981), 41–50.

Poston, Lawrence. "Three Versions of Victorian Pastoral." *Genre* 13 (1980), 320–328.

Selig, Robert L. *George Gissing*, 132–135.

Wright, T. R. "George Gissing," 17–18.

Sleeping Fires, 1895

Selig, Robert L. *George Gissing*, 95–97.

Thyrza, 1887

Selig, Robert L. *George Gissing*, 34–37.

The Town Traveller, 1898

Brigley, Judith. "*The Town Traveller*: A Comic Novel." *Gissing Newsl* 16:3 (1980), 15–25.

Hoyas Solis, José Antonio. "Speech and Character," 24–29.

Selig, Robert L. *George Gissing*, 100–102.

The Unclassed, 1884

Bemelmans, J. W. M. " 'A Permanent Interest of a Minor Kind': Charlotte Brontë and George Gissing's *The Unclassed.*" *Brontë Soc Transactions* 18:5 (1985), 383–390.

De Stasio, Clotilde. *Lo Scrittore*, 106–108.

Halperin, John. "On *The Unclassed* as Autobiography." *Gissing Newsl* 15:4 (1979), 3–11.

Markow, Alice B. "George Gissing's *The Unclassed*: A Problematic Variation of the Dissociative Pattern." *Lit and Psych* 30 (1980), 182–190.

Powell, Robert S. "Gissing and 'the impertinent Ego': A Comparison of Editions of *The Unclassed.*" *Gissing Newsl* 16:1 (1980), 18–34.

Scheick, William J. "Compassion and Fictional Structure: The Example of Gissing and Bennett." *Stud in the Novel* 15 (1983), 294–305.

Selig, Robert L. *George Gissing,* 27–31.

Watt, George. *The Fallen Woman,* 119–145.

Veranilda, 1904

Dowling, David. "*Veranilda*: A Revaluation." *Gissing Newsl* 18:2 (1982), 27–31.

Harrison, John R. "The Rejected *Veranilda* Preface: Wells's View of Gissing as a Novelist." *Gissing Newsl* 18:4 (1982), 24–30.

Selig, Robert L. *George Gissing,* 110–111.

The Whirlpool, 1897

Argyle, Gisela. *German Elements,* 134–142.

Argyle, Gisela. "Gissing's *The Whirlpool* and Schopenhauer." *Gissing Newsl* 17:4 (1981), 3–19.

Buckley, William K. "George Gissing's *The Whirlpool*: The Plight of Urban Men and Women." *Recovering Lit* 7:1 (1979), 5–39.

Collinson, C. S. "*The Whirlpool* and *The House of Mirth.*" *Gissing Newsl* 16:4 (1980), 12–16.

Reed, John R. "A Friend to Mammon: Speculation in Victorian Literature." *Victorian Stud* 27 (1984), 198–200.

Selig, Robert L. *George Gissing,* 82–86.

Workers in the Dawn, 1880

Argyle, Gisela. *German Elements,* 91–97.

De Stasio, Clotilde. *Lo Scrittore,* 104–106.

Grylls, David. "Determinism and Determination," 76–78.

Hoyas Solis, José Antonio. "Speech and Character," 12–17.

Kropholler, P. F. "Notes on *Workers in the Dawn.*" *Gissing Newsl* 17:3 (1981), 19–28.

Mitchell, Sally. *The Fallen Angel,* 133–134.

Rataboul, Louis J. *Le pasteur anglican,* 400–402.

Selig, Robert L. *George Gissing,* 23–27.

Wright, T. R. "George Gissing," 1–14.

FRANCIS GODWIN

The Man in the Moone, 1638

Janssen, Anke. *Francis Godwins "The Man in the Moone."*

Janssen, Anke. "Wirkung eines Romans als Inspirationsquelle: Francis Godwins *The Man in the Moone.*" *Arcadia* 20 (1985), 20–46.

WILLIAM GODWIN

Caleb Williams, 1794

Barfoot, C. C. *The Thread*, 134–136.

Barker, Gerard A. "Ferdinando Falkland's Fall: Grandison in Disarray." *Papers on Lang & Lit* 16 (1980), 376–386.

Barker, Gerard A. *Grandison's Heirs*, 127–143.

Butler, Marilyn. "Godwin, Burke, and *Caleb Williams*." *Essays in Criticism* 32 (1982), 237–256.

Coleman, William Emmet. *On the Discrimination*, 197–199.

Day, William Patrick. *In the Circles*, 137–139.

DePorte, Michael. "The Consolations of Fiction: Mystery in *Caleb Williams*." *Papers on Lang & Lit* 20 (1984), 154–164.

Drexler, Peter. " 'An unconquerable spirit of curiosity': William Godwins *Caleb Williams* in der Vorgeschichte des Detektivromans." *Braunschweiger Anglistische Arbeiten* 7 (1981), 67–89.

Everest, Kevin, and Gavin Edwards. "William Godwin's *Caleb Williams*: Truth and 'Things as They Are'," in Francis Barker et al., eds , *1789*, 129–146.

Gordon, Jan B. "Narrative Enclosure as Textual Ruin: An Archaeology of Gothic Consciousness." *Dickens Stud Annual* 11 (1983), 209–211.

Graham, Kenneth W. "The Gothic Unity of Godwin's *Caleb Williams*." *Papers on Lang & Lit* 20 (1984), 47–59.

Harvey, A. D. "*Frankenstein* and *Caleb Williams*." *Keats-Shelley J* 29 (1980), 21–27.

Jackson, Rosemary. *Fantasy*, 97–99.

Lamoine, Georges. "*Caleb Williams*, le mythe de Faust, et l'intention morale." *Bull de la Société d'Etudes Anglo-Américaines des XVIIe et XVIIIe Siècles* 9 (1979), 91–110.

MacAndrew, Elizabeth. *The Gothic Tradition*, 96–98, 141–143.

Powers, Katherine Richardson. *The Influence*, 38–41, 82–83, 101–106, 113–124.

Punter, David. "Fictional Representation of the Law in the Eighteenth Century." *Eighteenth-Century Stud* 16 (1982–83), 64–66.

Punter, David. *The Literature of Terror*, 135–141.

Reddin, Chitra Pershad. *Forms of Evil*, 49–51, 100, 127–128, 156–158, 162–163, 173–174, 207–208, 222, 242–243, 263–264, 272.

Scheiber, Andrew. "Falkland's Story: *Caleb Williams'* Other Voice." *Stud in the Novel* 17 (1985), 255–265.

Scheuermann, Mona. *Social Protest*, 143–168.

Cloudesly, 1830

Powers, Katherine Richardson. *The Influence*, 76–78.

Damon and Delia, 1784

Kelly, Gary. "Convention and Criticism in William Godwin's Early Novels." *Keats-Shelley J* 33 (1984), 53–60.

Deloraine, 1833

Powers, Katherine Richardson. *The Influence*, 62, 68–70.

Fleetwood, 1805

Powers, Katherine Richardson. *The Influence*, 42–43, 88.
Scheuermann, Mona. "The Study of Mind: The Later Novels of William Godwin." *Forum for Mod Lang Stud* 19 (1983), 17–23.
Shore, Elizabeth M. "Godwin's Fleetwood and the Hero of Meredith's *The Amazing Marriage*." *Engl Stud in Canada* 8 (1982), 38–47.

Imogen, 1784

Kelly, Gary. "Convention and Criticism," 65–69.

Italian Letters, 1783

Kelly, Gary. "Convention and Criticism," 60–65.

Mandeville, 1817

Powers, Katherine Richardson. *The Influence*, 44–50.
Scheuermann, Mona. "The Study of Mind," 22–29.

St. Leon, 1799

Coleman, William Emmet. *On the Discrimination*, 199–202.
Powers, Katherine Richardson. *The Influence*, 41–42.
Reddin, Chitra Pershad. *Forms of Evil*, 51–52, 128–129, 161–162, 272–274.
Tracy, Ann Blaisdell. *Patterns of Fear*, 280–286.

WILLIAM GOLDING

Darkness Visible, 1979

Baranger, Colette. "Quelques aspects des modes d'écriture comparés dans *Earthly Powers* d'Anthony Burgess et dans *Darkness Visible* de William Golding." *Etudes Anglaises* 36 (1983), 159–167.
Cleve, Gunnel. "Some Elements of Mysticism in William Golding's Novel *Darkness Visible*." *Neuphilologische Mitteilungen* 83 (1982), 457–470.
Clews, Hetty. "Darkness Visible: William Golding's *Parousia*." *Engl Stud in Canada* 10 (1984), 317–327.
Crompton, Don. *A View from the Spire*, 94–126.
Crompton, Donald W. "Biblical and Classical Metaphor in *Darkness Visible*." *Twentieth Century Lit* 28 (1982), 195–214.
Davies, Cecil. " 'The Burning Bird': Golding's *Poems* and the Novels." *Stud in the Liter Imagination* 13:1 (1980), 113–117.
Gregor, Ian, and Mark Kinkead-Weekes. "The Later Golding." *Twentieth Century Lit* 28 (1982), 119–128.
Johnston, Arnold. *Of Earth and Darkness*, 98–110.
Mills, John. "William Golding: *Darkness Visible*." *West Coast R* 15:3 (1981), 70–72.

Nelson, William. "The Grotesque in *Darkness Visible* and *Rites of Passage*." *Twentieth Century Lit* 28 (1982), 182–188.

Redpath, Philip. "Tricks of the Light: William Golding's *Darkness Visible*." *Ariel* 17:1 (1986), 3–15.

Stalhammar, Mall. "William Golding's Oeuvre: 'the most excellent work of an ideal spirit'." *Moderna Sprak* 77 (1983), 323.

Free Fall, 1959

Atkins, John. "Two Views of Life: William Golding and Graham Greene." *Stud in the Liter Imagination* 13:1 (1980), 86–88.

Clews, Hetty. *The Only Teller*, 181–189.

Daleski, H. M. *Unities*, 189–207.

Davies, Cecil. " 'The Burning Bird'," 103–106.

Johnston, Arnold. *Of Earth and Darkness*, 50–66.

O'Donnell, Patrick. "Journeying to the Center: Time, Pattern, and Transcendence in William Golding's *Free Fall*." *Ariel* 11:3 (1980), 83–97.

Regard, Frédéric. "Sublimation et sublime: le problème de la psychanalyse chez W. Golding." *Etudes Anglaises* 38 (1985), 417–421.

Sander, Hans-Jochen. " 'Menschliche Natur' und Individualität in Fieldings *Tom Jones* und im spätbürgerlichen englischen Roman." *Zeitschrift für Anglistik und Amerikanistik* 28 (1980), 241–242.

Stalhammar, Mall. "William Golding's Oeuvre," 322–323.

The Inheritors, 1955

Atkins, John. "Two Views of Life," 83–84.

Davies, Cecil. " 'The Burning Bird'," 98–100.

Halliday, Michael A. K. "Sprachfunktion und literarischer Stil: Eine Untersuchung über die Sprache von William Goldings *The Inheritors*," in Ernest W. B. Hess-Lüttich, ed., *Literatur und Konversation*, 311–340.

Harrison, James. "Golding's *The Inheritors*." *Explicator* 43:2 (1985), 47–48.

Hassler, Donald M. *Comic Tones*, 96–99.

Henighan, Tom. *Natural Space*, 83–85.

Johnston, Arnold. *Of Earth and Darkness*, 21–35.

Leech, Geoffrey N., and Michael H. Short. *Style in Fiction*, 31–36.

Redpath, Philip. "The Resolution of Antithesis in *Lord of the Flies* and *The Inheritors*." *English* 33 (1984), 43–51.

Regard, Frédéric. "Sublimation et sublime," 413–416.

Stalhammar, Mall. "William Golding's Oeuvre," 322.

Walker, Jeanne Murray. "Reciprocity and Exchange in William Golding's *The Inheritors*." *Science-Fiction Stud* 8 (1981), 297–310.

Lord of the Flies, 1954

Atkins, John. "Two Views of Life," 81–83.

Beem, Jane A. "Golding as a Key to Conrad," in *Literature*, 3–6.

Boyum, Joy Gould. *Double Exposure*, 169–175.

Davies, Cecil. " 'The Burning Bird'," 97–98.

Galvan Reula, J. F. "El misterio en la estructura de *Lord of the Flies*." *Revista Canaria de Estudios Ingleses* 3 (1981), 66–73.

Hadomi, Leah. "Imagery as a Source of Irony in Golding's *Lord of the Flies*." *Hebrew Univ Stud in Lit* 9 (1981), 126–138.

Johnston, Arnold. *Of Earth and Darkness*, 8–20.

Klaus, Gérard. "Jeu et sacré dans *Lord of the Flies* de William Golding." *Etudes Anglaises* 37 (1984), 424–436.

McEwan, Neil. *The Survival of the Novel*, 147–161.

Mafud Haye, Hilda. "*El senor de las moscas*: William Golding." *Nueva Revista del Pacifico* 13–14 (1979), 98–114.

Redpath, Philip. "The Resolution of Antithesis," 43–51.

Regard, Frédéric. "Sublimation et sublime," 411–413.

Sander, Hans-Jochen. " 'Menschliche Natur' und Individualität," 241–242.

Selby, Keith. "Golding's *Lord of the Flies*." *Explicator* 41:3 (1983), 57–59.

Stalhammar, Mall. "William Golding's Oeuvre," 321–322.

Weiand, Hermann J. "*Lord of the Flies*," in Weiand, ed., *Insight V*, 90–105.

Woodward, Kathleen. "On Aggression: William Golding's *Lord of the Flies*," in Eric S. Rabkin et al., eds., *No Place Else*, 199–220.

The Paper Men, 1984

Bufkin, E. C. "The Nobel Prize and the Paper Men: The Fixing of William Golding." *Georgia R* 39 (1985), 60–65.

Crompton, Don. *A View from the Spire*, 157–184.

Pincher Martin, 1956

Atkins, John. "Two Views of Life," 84–86.

Davies, Cecil. " 'The Burning Bird'," 100–103.

Johnston, Arnold. *Of Earth and Darkness*, 36–49.

Lakshmi, Vijay. "Entering the Whirlpool: The Movement towards Self-Awareness in William Golding's *Pincher Martin*." *Liter Criterion* 17:3 (1982), 25–36.

Regard, Frédéric. "Sublimation et sublime," 416.

The Pyramid, 1967

Atkins, John. "Two Views of Life," 89–91.

Crompton, Don. *A View from the Spire*, 52–72.

Davies, Cecil. " 'The Burning Bird'," 111–113.

Johnston, Arnold. *Of Earth and Darkness*, 83–97.

Kelly, Rebecca S. "The Tragicomic Mode: William Golding's *The Pyramid*." *Perspectives on Contemp Lit* 7 (1981), 110–116.

Rites of Passage, 1980

Crompton, Don. *A View from the Spire*, 127–156.

Gregor, Ian, and Mark Kinkead-Weekes. "The Later Golding," 111–118.

Krahé, Peter. "Die Linientaufe und ihre Folgen in William Goldings *Rites of Passage.*" *Literatur in Wissenschaft und Unterricht* 18 (1985), 13–28.

Nelson, William. "The Grotesque in . . . *Rites of Passage*," 188–194.

Sinclair, Andrew. "William Golding's The Sea, The Sea." *Twentieth Century Lit* 28 (1982), 178–179.

Stalhammar, Mall. "William Golding's Oeuvre," 323–324.

Tiger, Virginia. "William Golding's 'Wooden World': Religious Rites in *Rites of Passage.*" *Twentieth Century Lit* 28 (1982), 216–230.

The Scorpion God, 1971

Crompton, Don. *A View from the Spire*, 73–93.

The Spire, 1964

Atkins, John. "Two Views of Life," 88–89.

Birmann, Marie-Claude. *"The Spire" de William Golding*, 17–171.

Crompton, Don. *A View from the Spire*, 28–51.

Davies, Cecil. " 'The Burning Bird'," 106–110.

Dickson, L. L. "Modern Allegory: The Cathedral Motif in William Golding's *The Spire.*" *West Virginia Univ Philol Papers* 27 (1981), 98–105.

Johnston, Arnold. *Of Earth and Darkness*, 67–82.

Lerner, Laurence. "Jocelin's Folly; or, Down with the Spire." *Crit Q* 24:3 (1982), 3–15.

Regard, Frédéric. "Sublimation et sublime," 417–421.

Stalhammar, Mall. "William Golding's Oeuvre," 323.

OLIVER GOLDSMITH

The Vicar of Wakefield, 1766

Davie, Donald. "Notes on Goldsmith's Politics," in Andrew Swarbrick, ed., *The Art*, 86–88.

Ferguson, Oliver W. "Goldsmith as Ironist." *Stud in Philology* 81 (1984), 213–216, 225–228.

Gilligan, Thomas Maher. "Goldsmith's *The Vicar of Wakefield.*" *Explicator* 40:4 (1982), 24–25.

Golden, Morris. *"Sidney Bidulph* and *The Vicar of Wakefield.*" *Mod Lang Stud* 9:2 (1979), 33–35.

Green, Mary Elizabeth. "Oliver Goldsmith and the Wisdom of the World." *Stud in Philology* 77 (1980), 208–212.

Hilliard, Raymond F. "The Redemption of Fatherhood in *The Vicar of Wakefield.*" *Stud in Engl Lit, 1500–1900* 23 (1983), 465–480.

Jefferson, D. W. *"The Vicar of Wakefield* and Other Prose Writings: A Reconsideration," in Andrew Swarbrick, ed., *The Art*, 23–32.

Lehmann, James H. *"The Vicar of Wakefield*: Goldsmith's Sublime, Oriental Job." *ELH* 46 (1979), 97–115.

Preston, Thomas R. "The Uses of Adversity: Worldly Detachment and Heavenly Treasure in *The Vicar of Wakefield*." *Stud in Philology* 81 (1984), 229–251.

Russell, Kenneth C. "The Devil's Contemplative and the Miracle Rabbi, Two Novels: Golding's *The Spire* and Wallant's *Human Season*." *Studia Mystica* 3:3 (1980), 52–64.

Sheriff, John K. *The Good-Natured Man*, 30–34.

Shroff, Homai J. *The Eighteenth Century Novel*, 193–204.

KENNETH GRAHAME

The Wind in the Willows, 1908

Lippman, Carlee. "All the Comforts of Home." *Antioch R* 41 (1983), 409–420.

Robson, William W. "On *The Wind in the Willows*." *Hebrew Univ Stud in Lit* 9 (1981), 76ff.

RICHARD GRAVES

The Spiritual Quixote, 1773

Milligan, Ian. *The Novel in English*, 31–36.

ROBERT GRAVES

The Antigua Stamp, 1936

Snipes, Katherine. *Robert Graves*, 130–131.

Claudius the God, 1935

Snipes, Katherine. *Robert Graves*, 173–188.

Count Belisarius, 1938

Snipes, Katherine. *Robert Graves*, 167–172.

I, Claudius, 1934

Snipes, Katherine. *Robert Graves*, 173–188.

My Head! My Head!, 1925

Snipes, Katherine. *Robert Graves*, 88–97.

No Decency Left, 1932

Snipes, Katherine. *Robert Graves*, 127–130.

Roger Lamb's America, 1940

Snipes, Katherine. *Robert Graves*, 163–166.

Watch the North Wind Rise, 1949

Snipes, Katherine. *Robert Graves*, 69–79.

HENRY GREEN

Back, 1946

Bassoff, Bruce. *Toward "Loving*," 127–133, 140–143.
Mengham, Rod. *The Idiom of the Time*, 157–180.
North, Michael. *Henry Green*, 123–137.
Wall, Carey. "Henry Green's Enchantments: Passage and the Renewal of Life." *Twentieth Century Lit* 29 (1983), 437–438.

Blindness, 1926

Bassoff, Bruce. *Toward "Loving*," 108–111.
Brothers, Barbara. "*Blindness*: The Eye of Henry Green." *Twentieth Century Lit* 29 (1983), 403–419.
Mengham, Rod. *The Idiom of the Time*, 1–12.
North, Michael. *Henry Green*, 16–24, 33–35.

Caught, 1943

Bassoff, Bruce. *Toward "Loving*," 80–83, 140–143.
Mengham, Rod. *The Idiom of the Time*, 68–108.
North, Michael. *Henry Green*, 103–123.
Swinden, Patrick. *The English Novel*, 76–83, 90–92.
Wall, Carey. "Henry Green's Enchantments," 434–435.

Concluding, 1948

Bassoff, Bruce. *Toward "Loving*," 73–81, 83–92.
Mengham, Rod. *The Idiom of the Time*, 181–206.
North, Michael. *Henry Green*, 169–193.
Swinden, Patrick. *The English Novel*, 61–66.
Wall, Carey. "Henry Green's Enchantments," 438–445.

Doting, 1952

Bassoff, Bruce. *Toward "Loving*," 104–106.
Mengham, Rod. *The Idiom of the Time*, 207–215.
North, Michael. *Henry Green*, 199–202.

Living, 1929

Bassoff, Bruce. *Toward "Loving*," 53–60.
Mengham, Rod. *The Idiom of the Time*, 12–30.
North, Michael. *Henry Green*, 55–79.
Ortega, Ramon Lopez. "The Language of the Working-Class Novel of the 1930s," in H. Gustav Klaus, ed., *The Socialist Novel*, 123–126.
Wall, Carey. "Henry Green's Enchantments," 432–434.

Loving, 1945

Bassoff, Bruce. *Toward "Loving*," 140–160.
Mengham, Rod. *The Idiom of the Time*, 109–156.
North, Michael. *Henry Green*, 142–166.
Swinden, Patrick. *The English Novel*, 83–92.
Wall, Carey. "Henry Green's Enchantments," 435–437.

Nothing, 1950

Bassoff, Bruce. *Toward "Loving,"* 104–107.
Mengham, Rod. *The Idiom of the Time*, 207–215.
North, Michael. *Henry Green*, 203–211.

Party Going, 1939

Bassoff, Bruce. *Toward "Loving,"* 50–54, 59–66, 94–100, 117–120, 134–139.
Mengham, Rod. *The Idiom of the Time*, 31–52.
North, Michael. *Henry Green*, 83–99.
Swinden, Patrick. *The English Novel*, 66–75.
Wall, Carey. "Henry Green's Enchantments," 438–442.

WILLIAM CHILD GREEN

The Abbot of Monserrat, 1826

Tracy, Ann Blaisdell. *Patterns of Fear*, 157–159.

Alibeg the Tempter, 1831

Tracy, Ann Blaisdell. *Patterns of Fear*, 67–68, 286–293.

GRAHAM GREENE

Brighton Rock, 1938

Atkins, John. "Two Views of Life: William Golding and Graham Greene." *Stud in the Liter Imagination* 13:1 (1980), 93.
Crawford, Fred D. *Mixing Memory*, 108–117.
Donaghy, Henry J. *Graham Greene*, 34–39.
Donaghy, Henry J. "Graham Greene's 'Virtue of Disloyalty'." *Christianity & Lit* 32:3 (1983), 33–34.
Falk, Quentin. *Travels in Greeneland*, 52–65.
Gaston, Georg M. A. *The Pursuit*, 18–26.
Green, Geoffrey. "Relativism and the Multiple Contexts for Contemporary Fiction," in Jackson I. Cope and Geoffrey Green, eds., *Novel vs. Fiction*, 40–41.
Hansen, N. Bugge. *Graham Greene*, 70–82.
Hoskins, Robert. "The Napoleonic Strategist of *Brighton Rock*." *Coll Lit* 12 (1985), 11–16.
Johnstone, Richard. *The Will to Believe*, 72–77.
Kelly, Richard. *Graham Greene*, 37–46.
Kulshrestha, J. P. *Graham Greene*, 56–73.
Kurismmootil, K. C. Joseph. *Heaven and Hell*, 31–57.
Panitz, Esther L. *The Alien*, 146–148.
Prasad, Keshava. *Graham Greene*, 103–108.
Rai, Gangeshwar. *Graham Greene*, 35–41.
Routh, Michael. " 'Kolley Kibber': Newspaper Promotion in *Brighton Rock*." *Coll Lit* 12 (1985), 80–83.

Sharrock, Roger. *Saints*, 79–101.
Weber, Antonie. *Die Erzählstruktur*, 39–70.
Wright, David G. "Greene's *Brighton Rock*." *Explicator* 41:4 (1983), 52–53.

A Burnt-Out Case, 1961

Donaghy, Henry J. *Graham Greene*, 79–87.
Gaston, Georg M. A. *The Pursuit*, 74–87.
Hansen, N. Bugge. *Graham Greene*, 163–178.
Kelly, Edward E. "Absurdity but Faith with Suffering in Greene's *Burnt-Out Case*." *Greyfriar* 21 (1980), 29–34.
Kelly, Richard. *Graham Greene*, 73–79.
Kulshrestha, J. P. *Graham Greene*, 131–141.
Kurismmootil, K. C. Joseph. *Heaven and Hell*, 167–198.
Palfrey, J. "Reading Graham Greene, *A Burnt-Out Case*." *Univ Voices/ Voix Universitaires* (Brazzaville) 1 (1976), 26–31.
Prasad, Keshava. *Graham Greene*, 145–148.
Rai, Gangeshwar. *Graham Greene*, 58–63.
Sharrock, Roger. *Saints*, 177–196.
Weiand, Hermann J. "*A Burnt-Out Case*," in Weiand, ed., *Insight V*, 108–118.

The Comedians, 1966

Atkins, John. "Two Views of Life," 94–95.
Donaghy, Henry J. *Graham Greene*, 88–93.
Falk, Quentin. *Travels in Greeneland*, 154–162.
Ferns, C. S. " 'Brown is not Greene': Narrative Role in *The Comedians*." *Coll Lit* 12 (1985), 60–66.
Gaston, Georg M. A. *The Pursuit*, 87–101.
Hansen, N. Bugge. *Graham Greene*, 179–190.
Kelly, Richard. *Graham Greene*, 79–86.
Kulshrestha, J. P. *Graham Greene*, 159–168.
Prasad, Keshava. *Graham Greene*, 158–162.
Sharrock, Roger. *Saints*, 222–237.
Snape, Ray. "The Political Novels of Graham Greene." *Durham Univ J* 75:1 (1982), 79–81.
Spurling, John. *Graham Greene*, 58–60.

The Confidential Agent, 1939

Calendrillo, Linda T. "Role Playing and 'Atmosphere' in Four Modern British Spy Novels." *Clues* 3:1 (1982), 111–119.
Falk, Quentin. *Travels in Greeneland*, 42–47.
Hansen, N. Bugge. *Graham Greene*, 98–100.
Kelly, Richard. *Graham Greene*, 124–127.
Kulshrestha, J. P. *Graham Greene*, 193–199.
Panek, LeRoy L. *The Special Branch*, 119–122.
Prasad, Keshava. *Graham Greene*, 109–116.

The End of the Affair, 1951

Daleski, H. M. *The Divided Heroine*, 133–150.

Donaghy, Henry J. *Graham Greene*, 62–66.

Donaghy, Henry J. "Graham Greene's 'Virtue of Disloyalty'," 34–35.

Falk, Quentin. *Travels in Greeneland*, 109–114.

Gaston, Georg M. A. *The Pursuit*, 43–48.

Hansen, N. Bugge. *Graham Greene*, 120–133.

Higdon, David Leon. " 'Betrayed Intentions': Graham Greene's *The End of the Affair*." *Library* 1 (1979), 70–77.

Higdon, David Leon. "Saint Catherine, Von Hügel, and Graham Greene's *The End of the Affair*." *Engl Stud* 62 (1981), 46–52.

Hoskins, Robert. "Through a Glass Darkly: Mirrors in *The End of the Affair*." *Notes on Contemp Lit* 9:3 (1979), 3–5.

Kelly, Richard. *Graham Greene*, 62–67.

Kulshrestha, J. P. *Graham Greene*, 113–131.

Kurismmootil, K. C. Joseph. *Heaven and Hell*, 137–166.

Pake, Lucy S. "Courtly Love in Our Own Time: Graham Greene's *The End of the Affair*." *Lamar J of the Hum* 8:2 (1982), 36–43.

Prasad, Keshava. *Graham Greene*, 140–144.

Rai, Gangeshwar. *Graham Greene*, 52–58, 101–109.

Schwab, Gweneth. "Graham Greene's Pursuit of God." *Bucknell R* 26:2 (1982), 45–57.

Sharrock, Roger. *Saints*, 156–176.

Snape, Ray. "Plaster Saints, Flesh and Blood Sinners: Graham Greene's *The End of the Affair*." *Durham Univ J* 74 (1981–82), 241–250.

Spurling, John. *Graham Greene*, 44–47.

Walker, Ronald G. "World without End: An Approach to Narrative Structure in Greene's *The End of the Affair*." *Texas Stud in Lit and Lang* 26 (1984), 218–239.

Weber, Antonie. *Die Erzählstruktur*, 71–113.

England Made Me, 1935

Donaghy, Henry J. *Graham Greene*, 27–33.

Falk, Quentin. *Travels in Greeneland*, 169–177.

Hansen, N. Bugge. *Graham Greene*, 53–62.

Kelly, Richard. *Graham Greene*, 31–37.

Kulshrestha, J. P. *Graham Greene*, 43–55.

Prasad, Keshava. *Graham Greene*, 82–92.

Rai, Gangeshwar. *Graham Greene*, 22–27.

Sharrock, Roger. *Saints*, 72–77.

A Gun for Sale, 1936

Brock, Robert R. "Robbe-Grillet's *Les Gommes* and Graham Greene's *This Gun for Hire*." *Mod Fiction Stud* 29 (1983), 688–694.

Crawford, Fred D. *Mixing Memory*, 105–108.

Falk, Quentin. *Travels in Greeneland*, 27–33.

Hansen, N. Bugge. *Graham Greene*, 63–69.

Kelly, Richard. *Graham Greene*, 119–124.

Kulshrestha, J. P. *Graham Greene*, 189–193.

Melada, Ivan. "Graham Greene and the Munitions Makers: The Historical Context of *A Gun for Sale*." *Stud in the Novel* 13 (1981), 311–320.

Panek, LeRoy L. *The Special Branch*, 115–119.

Panitz, Esther L. *The Alien*, 142–146.

Prasad, Keshava. *Graham Greene*, 98–103.

The Heart of the Matter, 1948

Atkins, John. "Two Views of Life," 93–94.

Donaghy, Henry J. *Graham Greene*, 55–61.

Donaghy, Henry J. "Graham Greene's 'Virtue of Disloyalty'," 32–33.

Falk, Quentin. *Travels in Greeneland*, 102–109.

Gaston, Georg M. A. *The Pursuit*, 35–44.

Hansen, N. Bugge. *Graham Greene*, 107–119.

Harkness, Bruce. "Greene's Old-Fashioned Remedy in *The Heart of the Matter*." *Am Notes and Queries* 20:7–8 (1982), 115–116.

Kelly, Richard. *Graham Greene*, 54–62.

Kulshrestha, J. P. *Graham Greene*, 93–112.

Kurismmootil, K. C. Joseph. *Heaven and Hell*, 93–135.

Maini, Irma. "The Theme of Grace in *The Heart of the Matter*." *Liter Criterion* 17:3 (1982), 51–59.

Milbury-Steen, Sarah L. *European and African Stereotypes*, 46–51.

Prasad, Keshava. *Graham Greene*, 133–140.

Rai, Gangeshwar. *Graham Greene*, 45–52.

Reynolds. Jerry D. "Oral Readings in Greene's Fiction." *Coll Lit* 12 (1985), 21.

Sharrock, Roger. "Graham Greene at the Heart of the Matter." *Essays & Stud 1983*, 56–78.

Sharrock, Roger. *Saints*, 130–156.

Spurling, John. *Graham Greene*, 40–44.

Tracy, Laura. "Passport to Greeneland." *Coll Lit* 12 (1985), 46–49.

Weber, Antonie. *Die Erzählstruktur*, 121–123.

The Honorary Consul, 1973

Donaghy, Henry J. *Graham Greene*, 98–103.

Gaston, Georg M. A. *The Pursuit*, 117–122.

Hansen, N. Bugge. *Graham Greene*, 191–203.

Kelly, Richard. *Graham Greene*, 89–93.

Kulshrestha, J. P. *Graham Greene*, 168–178.

Leigh, David J. "The Structures of Greene's *The Honorary Consul*." *Renascence* 38 (1985), 13–24.

Lenz, Bernd. "Graham Greene, *The Honorary Consul*," in Rainer Lengeler, ed., *Englische Literatur*, 201–215.

Panek, LeRoy L. *The Special Branch*, 131–134.

Rai, Gangeshwar. *Graham Greene*, 86–91.

Sharrock, Roger. *Saints*, 238–249.
Spurling, John. *Graham Greene*, 60–61.

The Human Factor, 1978

Atkins, John. *The British Spy Novel*, 195–199.
Donaghy, Henry J. *Graham Greene*, 104–111.
Donaghy, Henry J. "Graham Greene's 'Virtue of Disloyalty'," 35–37.
Duran, Leopoldo. "*El factor humano*, de Graham Greene." *Arbor* 413 (1980), 71–84.
Elizade, Ignacio. "Graham Greene y *The Human Factor*." *Letras de Deusto* 9:18 (1979), 145–164.
Falk, Quentin. *Travels in Greeneland*, 178–186.
Ferreira, A. M. Cabral. "*O Factor Humano* de Graham Greene." *Broteria* 109 (1979), 181–186.
Gaston, Georg M. A. *The Pursuit*, 123–130.
Hansen, N. Bugge. *Graham Greene*, 204–214.
Kelly, Richard. *Graham Greene*, 93–96.
Panek, LeRoy L. *The Special Branch*, 134–137.
Rai, Gangeshwar. *Graham Greene*, 91–97.
Seehase, Georg. "Horizonte des künstlerischen Bildes in Graham Greenes Roman *The Human Factor* (1978)." *Zeitschrift für Anglistik und Amerikanistik* 32 (1984), 19–30.
Sharrock, Roger. *Saints*, 249–259.
Spurling, John. *Graham Greene*, 66–70.
Storhoff, Gary. "To Choose a Different Loyalty: Graham Greene's Politics in *The Human Factor*." *Essays in Lit* (Macomb) 11 (1984), 59–65.
Tracy, Laura. "Passport to Greeneland," 49–52.

It's a Battlefield, 1934

Adinaryana, L. "A Reading of Greene's *It's a Battlefield*." *Liter Endeavour* 3:1–2 (1981), 54–64.
Hansen, N. Bugge. *Graham Greene*, 48–53.
Kelly, Richard. *Graham Greene*, 27–31.
Kulshrestha, J. P. *Graham Greene*, 31–43.
Poznar, Walter. "Graham Greene's *It's a Battlefield*: A Center That Will Not Hold." *Wascana R* 18:1 (1983), 3–12.
Prasad, Keshava. *Graham Greene*, 71–82.
Rai, Gangeshwar. *Graham Greene*, 15–22.
Sharrock, Roger. *Saints*, 58–70.

Loser Takes All, 1955

Falk, Quentin. *Travels in Greeneland*, 119–124.
Kelly, Richard. *Graham Greene*, 137–139.
Kulshrestha, J. P. *Graham Greene*, 209–210.

The Man Within, 1929

Donaghy, Henry J. *Graham Greene*, 21–26.
Donaghy, Henry J. "Graham Greene's 'Virtue of Disloyalty'," 31–32.
Falk, Quentin. *Travels in Greeneland*, 47–51.
Hansen, N. Bugge. *Graham Greene*, 34–42.
Kulshrestha, J. P. *Graham Greene*, 18–29.
Prasad, Keshava. *Graham Greene*, 50–59.
Rai, Gangeshwar. *Graham Greene*, 12–15.
Sharrock, Roger. *Saints*, 37–43.

The Ministry of Fear, 1943

Donaghy, Henry J. *Graham Greene*, 49–54.
Falk, Quentin. *Travels in Greeneland*, 33–41.
Hansen, N. Bugge. *Graham Greene*, 100–107.
Hoskins, Robert. "Greene and Wordsworth: *The Ministry of Fear*." *South Atlantic R* 48:4 (1983), 32–41.
Kelly, Richard. *Graham Greene*, 127–133.
Kulshrestha, J. P. *Graham Greene*, 199–206.
Panek, LeRoy L. *The Special Branch*, 122–126.
Prasad, Keshava. *Graham Greene*, 117–122.
Spurling, John. *Graham Greene*, 37–39.

Monsignor Quixote, 1982

Gaston, Georg M. A. *The Pursuit*, 135–138.
Henry, Patrick. "Doubt and Certitude in *Monsignor Quixote*." *Coll Lit* 12 (1985), 68–78.
Kelly, Richard. *Graham Greene*, 102–112.
Kelly, Richard. "Greene's Consuming Fiction." *Coll Lit* 12 (1985), 58–59.
Sharrock, Roger. *Saints*, 270–275.
Spurling, John. *Graham Greene*, 52–53.

The Name of Action, 1930

Johnstone, Richard. *The Will to Believe*, 64–66.
Prasad, Keshava. *Graham Greene*, 59–61.

Our Man in Havana, 1958

Crawford, Fred D. *Mixing Memory*, 120–123.
Donaghy, Henry J. *Graham Greene*, 73–78.
Falk, Quentin. *Travels in Greeneland*, 145–154.
Gaston, Georg M. A. *The Pursuit*, 72–74.
Hansen, N. Bugge. *Graham Greene*, 154–162.
Kelly, Richard. *Graham Greene*, 139–144.
Kelly, Richard. "Greene's Consuming Fiction," 54–56.
Kulshrestha, J. P. *Graham Greene*, 210–214.
Panek, LeRoy L. *The Special Branch*, 129–131.
Sharrock, Roger. *Saints*, 220–222.
Snape, Ray. "The Political Novels," 78.

The Power and the Glory, 1940

Brannon, Lil. "The Possibilities of Sainthood: A Study of the Moral Dilemma in Graham Greene's *The Power and the Glory* and T. S. Eliot's *Murder in the Cathedral*." *Publs of the Arkansas Philol Assoc* 4:3 (1978), 66–71.

Donaghy, Henry J. *Graham Greene*, 40–48.

Fetrow, Fred M. "The Function of Geography in *The Power and the Glory*." *Descant* 23:3 (1979), 40–48.

Gaston, Georg M. A. *The Pursuit*, 28–34.

Hansen, N. Bugge. *Graham Greene*, 83–95.

Janisch, Josandra. "*The Power and the Glory* by Graham Greene." *CRUX* 14:2 (1980), 30–37.

Kelly, Richard. *Graham Greene*, 46–54.

Kulshrestha, J. P. *Graham Greene*, 77–93.

Kurismmootil, K. C. Joseph. *Heaven and Hell*, 59–92.

O'Rourke, Brian. "Echoes of A. E.'s Poetry in *The Power and the Glory*." *Etudes Irlandaises* 7 (1982), 87–95.

Pearson, Sheryl S. " 'Is There Anybody There?': Graham Greene in Mexico." *J of Mod Lit* 9 (1982), 277–290.

Prasad, Keshava. *Graham Greene*, 122–129.

Rai, Gangeshwar. *Graham Greene*, 41–47.

Reynolds. Jerry D. "Oral Readings in Greene's Fiction," 18–20.

Sharrock, Roger. *Saints*, 101–129.

Veitch, Douglas W. *Lawrence, Greene and Lowry*, 58–110.

Weber, Antonie. *Die Erzählstruktur*, 132–136.

The Quiet American, 1955

Barley, Tony. *Taking Sides*, 119–124.

Donaghy, Henry J. *Graham Greene*, 67–72.

Falk, Quentin. *Travels in Greeneland*, 134–141.

Gaston, G. M. "The Structure of Salvation in *The Quiet American*." *Renascence* 31 (1979), 93–106.

Gaston, Georg M. A. *The Pursuit*, 55–70.

Hansen, N. Bugge. *Graham Greene*, 134–146.

Hansen, Niels Bugge. "The Unquiet Englishman: A Reading of Graham Greene's *The Quiet American*," in Graham D. Caie et al., eds., *Occasional Papers*, 188–201.

Kelly, Richard. *Graham Greene*, 67–72.

Kulshrestha, J. P. *Graham Greene*, 142–159.

Panek, LeRoy L. *The Special Branch*, 126–129.

Prasad, Keshava. *Graham Greene*, 151–156.

Rai, Gangeshwar. *Graham Greene*, 74–80.

Sharrock, Roger. *Saints*, 200–220.

Snape, Ray. "The Political Novels," 76–78.

Rumour at Nightfall, 1931

Johnstone, Richard. *The Will to Believe*, 64–66.

Prasad, Keshava. *Graham Greene*, 61–63.

Stamboul Train, 1932

Falk, Quentin. *Travels in Greeneland*, 19–21.
Hansen, N. Bugge. *Graham Greene*, 42–47.
Kelly, Richard. *Graham Greene*, 114–119.
Kulshrestha, J. P. *Graham Greene*, 181–187.
Panek, LeRoy L. *The Special Branch*, 112–115.
Prasad, Keshava. *Graham Greene*, 63–71.
Sharrock, Roger. *Saints*, 53–58.

The Third Man, 1950

Falk, Quentin. *Travels in Greeneland*, 75–93.
Kelly, Richard. *Graham Greene*, 133–137.
Kulshrestha, J. P. *Graham Greene*, 206–209.
Macleod, Norman. " 'This strange, rather sad story': The Reflexive Design of Graham Greene's *The Third Man*." *Dalhousie R* 63 (1983), 217–239.
Palmer, James W., and Michael M. Riley. "The Lone Rider in Vienna: Myth and Meaning in *The Third Man*." *Lit/Film Q* 8 (1980), 14–20.
Prasad, Keshava. *Graham Greene*, 156–162.
Sutherland, John. *Bestsellers*, 210–211.
Vineberg, Steve. "The Harry Lime Mystery: Greene's *Third Man* Screenplay." *Coll Lit* 12 (1985), 33–44.

Travels with My Aunt, 1969

Donaghy, Henry J. *Graham Greene*, 94–97.
Falk, Quentin. *Travels in Greeneland*, 165–169.
Gaston, Georg M. A. *The Pursuit*, 101–115.
Kelly, Richard. *Graham Greene*, 86–89.
Kelly, Richard. "Greene's Consuming Fiction," 56–58.
Kulshrestha, J. P. *Graham Greene*, 214–222.
Sharrock, Roger. *Saints*, 261–265.

ROBERT GREENE

Ciceronis Amor: Tullies Love, 1589

Crupi, Charles W. *Robert Greene*, 82–84.

Mamillia, 1580

Crupi, Charles W. *Robert Greene*, 39–44.

Menaphon, 1589

Crupi, Charles W. *Robert Greene*, 53–60.
Hamilton, A. C. "Elizabethan Romance: The Example of Prose Fiction." *ELH* 49 (1982), 288–292.

Pandosto, 1588

Coggins, Gordon. "Greene's *Pandosto*: A 'Ghost' of 1584." *Library* 2 (1980), 448–456.

Crupi, Charles W. *Robert Greene*, 80–81.
Cuvelier, Eliane. "Horror and Cruelty in the Works of Three Elizabethan Novelists." *Cahiers Elisabéthains* 19 (1981), 39–51.
Kinney, Arthur F. "Humanist Poetics and Elizabethan Fiction." *Renaissance Papers* 1978, 31–45.
Tanner, Tony. *Adultery in the Novel*, 48–51.

Philomela, 1592

Crupi, Charles W. *Robert Greene*, 94–96.

WALTER GREENWOOD

Love on the Dole, 1933

Constantine, Stephen. "*Love on the Dole* and Its Reception in the 1930s." *Lit and Hist* 8 (1982), 232–245.
Ortega, Ramon Lopez. "The Language of the Working-Class Novel of the 1930s," in H. Gustav Klaus, ed., *The Socialist Novel*, 127–129.
Paul, Ronald. *"Fire in Our Hearts,"* 28–36.

GERALD GRIFFIN

The Collegians, 1829

Cronin, John. *The Anglo-Irish Novel*, 64–81.
Davis, Robert. *Gerald Griffin*, 90–103.

The Duke of Monmouth, 1836

Davis, Robert. *Gerald Griffin*, 128–133.

The Invasion, 1832

Davis, Robert. *Gerald Griffin*, 115–121.

DURHAM GRIFFITH

An Arctic Eden, 1892

Christensen, Inger. "Ground Untrodden: Images of Norway in Nineteenth-Century English Fiction." *Edda*, 1985, 354–355.

NEIL M. GUNN

Butcher's Broom, 1934

Bold, Alan. *Modern Scottish Literature*, 149–151.
Watson, G. J. "The Novels of Neil Gunn," in David Hewitt and Michael Spiller, eds., *Literature*, 142–144.

The Green Isle of the Great Deep, 1944

Watson, G. J. "The Novels," 146–147.

Highland River, 1937

Bold, Alan. *Modern Scottish Literature*, 151–153.
Watson, G. J. "The Novels," 137–139.

The Lost Glen, 1937

Bold, Alan. *Modern Scottish Literature*, 145–148.

The Silver Darlings, 1941

Bold, Alan. *Modern Scottish Literature*, 154–157.
McCleery, Alistair M. "The Sources of *The Silver Darlings*." *Stud in Scottish Lit* 20 (1985), 177–193.
Watson, G. J. "The Novels," 142–144.

HENRY RIDER HAGGARD

Allan Quartermain, 1887

Etherington, Norman. *Rider Haggard*, 44–46.
Higgins, D. S. *Rider Haggard*, 79–83, 116–118.

Ayesha, 1905

Katz, Wendy R. "Rider Haggard and the Empire of the Imagination." *Engl Lit in Transition* 23 (1980), 116–120.

Beatrice, 1890

Etherington, Norman. *Rider Haggard*, 30–33.

Child of Storm, 1913

Etherington, Norman. *Rider Haggard*, 69–70, 72–73.

Colonel Quaritch, V. C., 1888

Etherington, Norman. *Rider Haggard*, 28–30.

Dawn, 1884

Etherington, Norman. *Rider Haggard*, 22–25.
Higgins, D. S. *Rider Haggard*, 59–68.

Eric Brighteyes, 1888

Vogelsberger, Hartwig A. *'King Romance'*, 48–54.

Finished, 1917

Etherington, Norman. *Rider Haggard*, 70–72.

Jess, 1887

Etherington, Norman. *Rider Haggard*, 27–28.

Joan Haste, 1895

Etherington, Norman. *Rider Haggard*, 32–33.

King Solomon's Mines, 1885

Bass, Jeff D. "The Romance as Rhetorical Dissociation: The Purification of Imperialism in *King Solomon's Mines*." *Q J of Speech* 67 (1981), 259–269.

Etherington, Norman. *Rider Haggard*, 39–48.
Higgins, D. S. *Rider Haggard*, 71–79, 82–86.
Mannsaker, Frances M. "The Dog that didn't Bark: The Subject Races in Imperial Fiction at the Turn of the Century," in David Dabydeen, ed., *The Black Presence*, 117–118.
Rabkin, David. "Ways of Looking: Origins of the Novel in South Africa." *J of Commonwealth Lit* 13:1 (1978), 37–39.
Vogelsberger, Hartwig A. *'King Romance'*, 135–153.

The Mahatma and the Hare, 1911

Vogelsberger, Hartwig A. *'King Romance'*, 162–171.

Marie, 1912

Etherington, Norman. *Rider Haggard*, 69–72.

Montezuma's Daughter, 1891

Vogelsberger, Hartwig A. *'King Romance'*, 41–47.

Nada the Lily, 1892

Etherington, Norman. *Rider Haggard*, 49–50.

People of the Mist, 1894

Etherington, Norman. *Rider Haggard*, 59–61.

She, 1887

Auerbach, Nina. *Woman and the Demon*, 36–38.
Crawford, Claudia. "*She*." *SubStance* 29 (1981), 83–96.
De Angelis, Maria Pia. "*She* di Rider Haggard: Il fascino degli archetipi." *Quaderni di Filologia Germanica* (Bologna) 2 (1982), 75–95.
Etherington, Norman. *Rider Haggard*, 46–47, 86–90.
Higgins, D. S. *Rider Haggard*, 91–107.
Katz, Wendy R. "Rider Haggard and the Empire," 116–123.
Showalter, Elaine. "Syphilis, Sexuality, and the Fiction of the Fin de Siècle," in Ruth Bernard Yeazell, ed., *Sex*, 109–111.
Vogelsberger, Hartwig A. *'King Romance'*, 82–109.

She and Allan, 1921

Etherington, Norman. *Rider Haggard*, 63–65.

Smith and the Pharaos, 1912

Vogelsberger, Hartwig A. *'King Romance'*, 171–176.

Swallow, 1899

Etherington, Norman. *Rider Haggard*, 67–70.

The Witch's Head, 1884

Etherington, Norman. *Rider Haggard*, 24–25.

The World's Desire, 1889

Vogelsberger, Hartwig A. *'King Romance'*, 55–61.

MARGUERITE RADCLYFFE HALL

Adam's Breed, 1926

Franks, Claudia Stillman. *Beyond "The Well of Loneliness,"* 77–96.

The Forge, 1924

Franks, Claudia Stillman. *Beyond "The Well of Loneliness,"* 60–67.

The Master of the House, 1932

Franks, Claudia Stillman. *Beyond "The Well of Loneliness,"* 115–121.

A Saturday Life, 1925

Franks, Claudia Stillman. *Beyond "The Well of Loneliness,"* 68–76.

The Sixth Beatitude, 1936

Franks, Claudia Stillman. *Beyond "The Well of Loneliness,"* 153–160.

The Unlit Lamp, 1924

Beauman, Nicola. *A Very Great Profession*, 51–53.
Franks, Claudia Stillman. *Beyond "The Well of Loneliness,"* 47–59.
Newton, Esther. "The Mythic Mannish Lesbian: Radclyffe Hall and the New Woman." *Signs* 9 (1984), 559–575.

The Well of Loneliness, 1928

Bernikow, Louise. *Among Women*, 177–181.
Brake, Mike. "The Image of the Homosexual in Contemporary English and American Fiction," in Diana Laurenson, ed., *The Sociology*, 181–182.
Fortunati, Vita. "Un feuilleton lesbico: *The Well of Loneliness* di Radclyffe Hall," in Paola Colaiacomo et al., eds., *Come nello specchio*, 51–71.
Franks, Claudia Stillman. *Beyond "The Well of Loneliness,"* 97–114.
Franks, Claudia Stillman. "Stephen Gordon, Novelist: A Re-evaluation of Radclyffe Hall's *The Well of Loneliness.*" *Tulsa Stud in Women's Lit* 1 (1982), 125–138.
Newton, Esther. "The Mythic Mannish Lesbian," 559–575.
Pratt, Annis. *Archetypal Patterns*, 102–103.
Stimpson, Catharine R. "Zero Degree Deviancy: The Lesbian Novel in English." *Crit Inquiry* 8 (1981), 367–372.

CICELY HAMILTON

William—An Englishman, 1919

Beauman, Nicola. *A Very Great Profession*, 28–31.

MARY AGNES HAMILTON

Follow My Leader, 1922

Klaus, H. Gustav. "Silhouettes of Revolution: Some Neglected Novels of the Early 1920s," in Klaus, ed., *The Socialist Novel*, 103–106.

GERALD HANLEY

Drinkers of Darkness, 1955

O'Rourke, Brian. *The Conscience of the Race*, 29, 39–40.

JAMES HANLEY

Boy, 1931

Worpole, Ken. *Dockers and Detectives*, 81–83.

Drift, 1930

Worpole, Ken. *Dockers and Detectives*, 80–81.

An End and a Beginning, 1957

O'Rourke, Brian. *The Conscience of the Race*, 29, 45.

The Furys, 1935

Worpole, Ken. *Dockers and Detectives*, 83–85.

THOMAS HARDY

Desperate Remedies, 1871

Casagrande, Peter J. *Unity*, 74–81.

Escuret, Annie. "Le macabre dans l'oeuvre romanesque de Thomas Hardy." *Cahiers Victoriens et Edouardiens* 15 (1982), 94–95.

Gibson, James. "Hardy and His Readers," in Norman Page, ed., *Thomas Hardy*, 192–195.

Hughes, Winifred. *The Maniac*, 172–175.

Jones, Lawrence. "*Tess of the d'Urbervilles* and the 'New Edition' of *Desperate Remedies*." *Colby Lib Q* 15 (1979), 194–200.

Kendrick, Walter M. "The Sensationalism of Thomas Hardy." *Texas Stud in Lit and Lang* 22 (1980), 484–499.

Mitchell, Sally. *The Fallen Angel*, 95–97.

Moore, Kevin Z. "The Poet within the Architect's Ring: *Desperate Remedies*, Hardy's Hybrid Detective-Gothic Narrative." *Stud in the Novel* 14 (1982), 31–41.

Ousby, Ian. "Class in *Desperate Remedies*." *Durham Univ J* 76 (1983–84), 217–222.

Salter, C. H. *Good Little Thomas Hardy*, 122–124.

Springer, Marlene. *Hardy's Use of Allusion*, 18–33.

Sumner, Rosemary. *Thomas Hardy*, 13–17.

Taylor, Richard H. *The Neglected Hardy*, 6–28.

Wickens, C. Glen. "Hardy's *Desperate Remedies*." *Explicator* 39:1 (1980), 12–14.

Wickens, C. Glen. "Romantic Myth and Victorian Nature in *Desperate Remedies*." *Engl Stud in Canada* 8 (1982), 154–172.

Wittenberg, Judith Bryant. "Early Hardy Novels and the Fictional Eye." *Novel* 16 (1983), 156–160.

Wittenberg, Judith Bryant. "Thomas Hardy's First Novel: Women and the Quest for Autonomy." *Colby Lib Q* 18 (1982), 47–54.

Wotton, George. *Thomas Hardy*, 127–130.

Far from the Madding Crowd, 1874

Benson, Michael. "Moving Bodies in Hardy and Beckett." *Essays in Criticism* 34 (1984), 241–242.

Casagrande, Peter J. "A New View of Bathsheba Everdene," in Dale Kramer, ed., *Critical Approaches*, 50–73.

Casagrande, Peter J. *Unity*, 97–114.

Costabile, Rita. "Hardy in Soft Focus," in Michael Klein and Gillian Parker, eds., *The English Novel*, 155–164.

Daleski, H. M. *Unities*, 225–230.

Dave, Jagdish Chandra. *The Human Predicament*, 71–75.

Escuret, Annie. "Le macabre dans l'oeuvre romanesque," 97–99.

Gatrell, Simon. "Hardy the Creator: *Far from the Madding Crowd*," in Dale Kramer, ed., *Critical Approaches*, 74–98.

Giordano, Frank R., Jr. *'I'd Have My Life Unbe'*, 101–115.

Gregor, Ian. "Reading a Story: Sequence, Pace, and Recollection," in Gregor, ed., *Reading the Victorian Novel*, 98–101.

Hardy, Barbara. *Forms of Feeling*, 174–178.

Hasan, Noorul. *Thomas Hardy*, 13–36.

Henighan, Tom. *Natural Space*, 108–115.

Horne, Lewis. "Passion and Flood in *Far from the Madding Crowd*." *Ariel* 13:3 (1982), 39–48.

Hunter, Shelagh. *Victorian Idyllic Fiction*, 202–208.

Jackson, Arlene M. *Illustration*, 32–37, 79–88.

Jacobus, Mary. "Hardy's Magian Retrospect." *Essays in Criticism* 32 (1982), 268–270.

Jones, Lawrence. "George Eliot and Pastoral Tragicomedy in Hardy's *Far from the Madding Crowd*." *Stud in Philology* 77 (1980), 402–425.

Milberg-Kaye, Ruth. *Thomas Hardy*, 7–8, 15–18, 30–32, 40–42.

Miles, Rosalind. "The Women of Wessex," in Anne Smith, ed., *The Novels*, 27–34.

Millar, A. R. "*Far from the Madding Crowd*: Let's Indulge in an Homeric Fallacy or Two." *CRUX* 13:3 (1979), 41–43.

Sénéchal, Janie. "Focalisation, regard et désir dans *Far from the Madding Crowd*." *Cahiers Victoriens et Edouardiens* 12 (1980), 73–83.

Shelston, Alan. "The Particular Pleasure of *Far from the Madding Crowd*." *Thomas Hardy Yearbook* 7 (1977), 31–39.

Springer, Marlene. *Hardy's Use of Allusion*, 53–78.

Stottlar, James F. "Hardy vs. Pinero: Two Stage Versions of *Far from the Madding Crowd*." *Theatre Survey* 18:2 (1977), 23–43.

Sumner, Rosemary. *Thomas Hardy*, 46–55.

Thomas, Denis W. "Drunkenness in Thomas Hardy's Novels." *Coll Lang Assoc J* 28 (1984), 190–193.

Thompson, Geoffrey. "Toller Whelme, Waterston House, and *Far from the Madding Crowd*." *Thomas Hardy Soc R* 1:6 (1980), 196–198.

Walters, Usha. *The Poetry*, 8–11, 18–19, 48–49, 57–59, 108–111, 147–148.

Welsh, James M. "Hardy and the Pastoral, Schlesinger and Shepherds: *Far from the Madding Crowd*." *Lit/Film Q* 9 (1981), 79–84.

Wickens, C. Glen. "Literature and Science: Hardy's Response to Mill, Huxley and Darwin." *Mosaic* 14:3 (1981), 63–79.

Winner, Anthony. *Characters in the Twilight*, 44–49.

Wittenberg, Judith Bryant. "Angles of Vision and Questions of Gender in *Far from the Madding Crowd*." *Centennial R* 30 (1986), 25–40.

The Hand of Ethelberta, 1876

Casagrande, Peter J. *Unity*, 118–125.

Dave, Jagdish Chandra. *The Human Predicament*, 141–149.

Gittings, Robert. "Findon and *The Hand of Ethelberta*." *Thomas Hardy Soc R* 1:10 (1984), 306–307.

Jackson, Arlene M. *Illustration*, 37–39, 120–122.

Springer, Marlene. *Hardy's Use of Allusion*, 78–81.

Taylor, Richard H. *The Neglected Hardy*, 56–75.

Jude the Obscure, 1895

Adewoye, Sam. "Human Responsibility in Thomas Hardy's *Jude the Obscure*." *Nigerian J of the Hum* 2 (1978), 87–101.

Alden, Patricia. "A Short Story Prelude to *Jude the Obscure*: More Light on the Genesis of Hardy's Last Novel." *Colby Lib Q* 19 (1983), 45–52.

Basham, Diana. "*Jude the Obscure* and *Idylls of the King*." *Thomas Hardy Soc R* 1:10 (1984), 311–315.

Beatty, C. J. P. "An Architectural Anomaly in *Jude the Obscure*." *Thomas Hardy Soc R* 1:10 (1984), 310–311.

Bennett, James R. "Plot Repetition: Theme and Variation of Narrative Macro-Episodes." *Papers on Lang & Lit* 17 (1981), 415.

Buckler, William E. "Thomas Hardy's Illusion of Letters: Narrative Consciousness as Imaginative Style in *The Dynasts*, *Tess*, and *Jude*." *Dickens Stud Annual* 8 (1980), 289–298.

Casagrande, Peter J. *Unity*, 199–218.

Childers, Mary. "Thomas Hardy, The Man Who 'Liked' Women." *Criticism* 23 (1981), 330–331.

Collins, Philip. "Hardy and Education," in Norman Page, ed., *Thomas Hardy*, 64–71.

Conroy, Christopher J. "Place and Movement in *Jude*." *Thomas Hardy Soc R* 1:5 (1979), 154–157.

Coulson, John. *Religion and Imagination*, 106–108.

Coustillas, P. "Thomas Hardy: *Jude the Obscure*," in Coustillas et al., eds., *Le roman anglais*, 258–270.

Daleski, H. M. *Unities*, 235–240.

Dave, Jagdish Chandra. *The Human Predicament*, 112–134, 166–169.

Eagleton, Mary, and David Pierce. *Attitudes to Class*, 88–92.

Edwards, Carol and Duane. "*Jude the Obscure*: A Psychoanalytic Study." *Univ of Hartford Stud in Lit* 13 (1981), 78–88.

Edwards, Lee R. *Psyche as Hero*, 109–112, 118–123.

Efron, Arthur. " 'A Bluer, Moister Atmosphere': Life Energy in *Jude the Obscure*." *Intl J of Life Energy* 1 (1979), 175–184.

Enstice, Andrew. "The Fruit of the Tree of Knowledge," in Anne Smith, ed., *The Novels*, 18–21.

Escuret, Annie. "Le macabre dans l'oeuvre romanesque," 101.

Fischler, Alexander. "An Affinity for Birds: Kindness in Hardy's *Jude the Obscure*." *Stud in the Novel* 13 (1981), 250–264.

Fischler, Alexander. "Gins and Spirits: The Letter's Edge in Hardy's *Jude the Obscure*." *Stud in the Novel* 16 (1984), 1–18.

Fischler, Alexander. "A Kinship with Job: Obscurity and Remembrance in Hardy's *Jude the Obscure*." *J of Engl and Germanic Philology* 84 (1985), 515–533.

Gallivan, Patricia. "Science and Art in *Jude the Obscure*," in Anne Smith, ed., *The Novels*, 126–143.

Gemmette, Elizabeth Villiers. "G. Eliot's *Mill on the Floss* and Hardy's *Jude the Obscure*." *Explicator* 42:3 (1984), 28–30.

Gibson, James. "Hardy and His Readers," 210–213.

Giordano, Frank R., Jr. *'I'd Have My Life Unbe'*, 116–134.

Goetz, William R. "The Felicity and Infelicity of Marriage in *Jude the Obscure*." *Nineteenth-Century Fiction* 38 (1983), 189–213.

Goode, John. "Sue Bridehead and the New Woman," in Mary Jacobus, ed., *Women Writing*, 100–113.

Günisik, Sema. "Thomas Hardy'nin *Jude the Obscure* Adli Romaninda 'Yabancilasma' Konusu." *Bati Edebiyatlari Arastirma Dergisi* 3 (1980), 64–75.

Hagen, June Steffensen. "Does Teaching Make a Difference in Ethical Reflection?: A Report on Teaching Hardy's *Jude the Obscure* with Attention to Marriage, Divorce, and Remarriage." *Christianity & Lit* 33:3 (1984), 23–35.

Hardy, Barbara. *Forms of Feeling*, 159–161, 178–180.

Hasan, Noorul. *Thomas Hardy*, 156–175.

Henighan, Tom. *Natural Space*, 140–144.

Horne, Lewis B. "The Gesture of Pity in *Jude the Obscure* and *Tender Is the Night*." *Ariel* 11:2 (1980), 53–61.

Hughes, Winifred. *The Maniac*, 179–182.

Humm, Maggie. "Gender and Narrative in Thomas Hardy." *Thomas Hardy Yearbook* 11 (1984), 41–48.

Jackson, Arlene M. *Illustration*, 114–120.

Labbé, Monique. "Symbolisme judéo-chrétien, mythe personnel et pessimisme à travers les figures féminines de *Jude the Obscure*." *Cahiers Victoriens et Edouardiens* 15 (1982), 119–128.

Langbaum, Robert. "Hardy and Lawrence." *Thomas Hardy Annual* 3 (1985), 29–35.

Langbaum, Robert. "Lawrence and Hardy," in Jeffrey Meyers, ed., *D. H. Lawrence*, 83–88.

Langland, Elizabeth. "A Perspective of One's Own: Thomas Hardy and the Elusive Sue Bridehead." *Stud in the Novel* 12 (1980), 12–26.

Leavis, L. R. "The Late Nineteenth Century Novel and the Change towards the Sexual: Gissing, Hardy and Lawrence." *Engl Stud* 66 (1985), 41–43.

Lodge, David. "*Jude the Obscure*: Pessimism and Fictional Form," in Dale Kramer, ed., *Critical Approaches*, 193–201.

McCormack, Peggy A. "The Syntax of Quest in *Jude the Obscure*." *New Orleans R* 8:1 (1981), 42–48.

Milberg-Kaye, Ruth. *Thomas Hardy*, 25–27, 31–34, 56–58, 67–69, 96–107.

Mulderig, Gerald P. "Darkness and Discord at Marygreen: A Note on the Opening Chapters of *Jude the Obscure*." *Colby Lib Q* 15 (1979), 201–202.

Murfin, Ross C. *Swinburne*, 142–149.

Ousby, Ian. "The Convergence of the Twain: Hardy's Alteration of Plato's Parable." *Mod Lang R* 77 (1982), 784–788, 793–796.

Peck, John. "Hardy's *Jude the Obscure*." *Explicator* 39:1 (1980), 6–7.

Phillips, Dauna. "Lawrence's Understanding of Miriam through Sue." *Recovering Lit* 7:1 (1979), 46–55.

Rabiger, Michael. "Tess and Saint Tryphena: Two Pure Women Faithfully Presented." *Thomas Hardy Annual* 3 (1985), 59–60.

Saldivar, Ramon. "*Jude the Obscure*: Reading and the Spirit of the Law." *ELH* 50 (1983), 607–622.

Salter, C. H. *Good Little Thomas Hardy*, 16–19, 39–42, 45–49, 80–82.

Salter, C. H. "*Jude* and Wessex." *Thomas Hardy Soc R* 1:3 (1977), 91–94.

Scheick, William J. "Fictional Structure and Ethics in the Edwardian, Modern and Contemporary Novel." *Philol Q* 63 (1984), 296–297.

Showalter, Elaine. "Syphilis, Sexuality, and the Fiction of the Fin de Siècle," in Ruth Bernard Yeazell, ed., *Sex*, 106–109.

Sonstroem, David. "Order and Disorder in *Jude the Obscure*." *Engl Lit in Transition* 24 (1981), 6–14.

Spivey, Ted R. *The Journey beyond Tragedy*, 51–53.

Springer, Marlene. *Hardy's Use of Allusion*, 146–172.

Stone, Donald D. "House and Home in Thomas Hardy." *Nineteenth-Century Fiction* 39 (1984), 300.

Stubbs, Patricia. *Women and Fiction*, 60–62, 81–82.

Sumner, Rosemary. "Hardy as Innovator: Sue Bridehead." *Thomas Hardy Soc R* 1:5 (1979), 151–154.

Sumner, Rosemary. *Thomas Hardy*, 99–101, 107–110, 119–122, 146–188.

Thomas, Denis W. "Drunkenness," 197–198, 206–208.

Van Tassel, Daniel E. " 'Gin-Drunk' and 'Creed-Drunk': Intoxication and Inspiration in *Jude the Obscure*." *Thomas Hardy Soc R* 1:7 (1981), 218–221.

Vichy, Thérèse. "Humanisme tragique et tragique de la démesure transhumaine dans *The Return of the Native, The Mayor of Casterbridge, Tess of the d'Urbervilles* et *Jude the Obscure*." *Cahiers Victoriens et Edouardiens* 15 (1982), 109–117.

Walters, Usha. *The Poetry*, 39–40, 70–71, 82–87, 119–120.

Weinstein, Philip M. *The Semantics of Desire*, 125–146.

Wheeler, Michael. *English Fiction*, 190–192.

Williams, Merryn. *Women in the English Novel*, 184–186.

Wing, George. "Hardy and Regionalism," in Norman Page, ed., *Thomas Hardy*, 87–89, 92–98.

Wotton, George. *Thomas Hardy*, 102–107.

A Laodicean, 1881

Hochstadt, Pearl R. "Hardy's Romantic Diptych: A Reading of *A Laodicean* and *Two on a Tower*." *Engl Lit in Transition* 26 (1983), 25–28.

Jackson, Arlene M. *Illustration*, 48–53.

Larkin, Peter. "Absences and Presences: Narrative Bifurcation in *A Laodicean*." *Thomas Hardy Soc R* 1:3 (1977), 81–86.

Milberg-Kaye, Ruth. *Thomas Hardy*, 25–27, 62–63.

Pettit, Charles C. "A Reassessment of *A Laodicean*." *Thomas Hardy Soc R* 1:9 (1983), 276–282.

Stone, Donald D. "House and Home," 297–298.

Taylor, Richard H. *The Neglected Hardy*, 96–120.

Ward, Paul. "A Laodicean." *Thomas Hardy Yearbook* 11 (1984), 28–30.

The Mayor of Casterbridge, 1886

Anderson, Wayne C. "The Rhetoric of Silence in Hardy's Fiction." *Stud in the Novel* 17 (1985), 58–63.

Aschkenasy, Nehama. "Biblical Substructures in the Tragic Form: Hardy, *The Mayor of Casterbridge*; Agnon, *And the Crooked Shall Be Made Straight*." *Mod Lang Stud* 13 (1983), 102–105, 108–109.

Awad, Ramses. "Some Reflections on Thomas Hardy's *Mayor of Casterbridge*." *J of Engl* (Sana'a Univ) 2 (1976), 110–119.

Bennett, James R. "Plot Repetition," 414.

Benson, Michael. "Moving Bodies," 235–236, 240–241.

Caless, Bryn. "Hardy's Humour." *Thomas Hardy Annual* 3 (1985), 116–118, 120–121.

Casagrande, P. J., and Charles Lock. "The Name 'Henchard'." *Thomas Hardy Soc R* 1:4 (1978), 115–118.

Casagrande, Peter J. *Unity*, 183–199.

Dave, Jagdish Chandra. *The Human Predicament*, 63–70.

Diffey, T. J. "Henchard and Falstaff: A Note Comparing Their Deaths." *Thomas Hardy Soc R* 1:9 (1983), 282–284.

Dollar, J. Gerard. "The 'Looped Orbit' of the Mayor of Casterbridge." *Papers on Lang & Lit* 19 (1983), 293–308.

Draper, R. P. *"The Mayor of Casterbridge."* *Cambridge Q* 25:1 (1983), 57–70.

Drew, Philip. *The Meaning of Freedom*, 263–266, 269–276.

Edmond, Rod. " 'The Past-marked Prospect': Reading *The Mayor of Casterbridge*," in Ian Gregor, ed., *Reading the Victorian Novel*, 111–126.

Giordano, Frank R., Jr. *'I'd Have My Life Unbe'*, 78–97.

Gregor, Ian. "Reading a Story," 102–104.

Grindle, Juliet M. "Compulsion and Choice in *The Mayor of Casterbridge*," in Anne Smith, ed., *The Novels*, 91–106.

Haig, Stirling. " 'By the Rivers of Babylon': Water and Exile in *The Mayor of Casterbridge*." *Thomas Hardy Yearbook* 11 (1984), 55–61.

Hardy, Barbara. *Forms of Feeling*, 166–170.

Hasan, Noorul. *Thomas Hardy*, 58–81.

Henighan, Tom. *Natural Space*, 123.

Higbie, Robert. "The Flight of the Swallow in *The Mayor of Casterbridge*." *Engl Lang Notes* 16 (1979), 311–312.

Irwin, Michael. *Picturing*, 149–152.

Irwin, Michael. "Readings of Melodrama," in Ian Gregor, ed., *Reading the Victorian Novel*, 24–26.

Jackson, Arlene M. *Illustration*, 53–55, 96–105.

Kendrick, Walter M. "The Sensationalism," 499–500.

Milberg-Kaye, Ruth. *Thomas Hardy*, 63–65.

Miles, Rosalind. "The Women," 34–39.

Murfin, Ross C. *Swinburne*, 128–133.

Narayanaswamy, K. R. *"The Mayor of Casterbridge*: A Reappraisal." *Liter Half-Yearly* 21:2 (1980), 68–77.

Potter, Jonathan, Peter Stringer, and Margaret Wetherell. *Social Texts and Context*, 31–41.

Salter, C. H. *Good Little Thomas Hardy*, 28–30.

Showalter, Elaine. "The Unmanning of the Mayor of Casterbridge," in Dale Kramer, ed., *Critical Approaches*, 99–115.

Siemens, Lloyd. "Wife-Selling in *The Mayor of Casterbridge*." *Thomas Hardy Soc R* 1:3 (1977), 86–88.

Solimine, Joseph. " 'The Turbid Ebb and Flow of Human Misery': 'Love among the Ruins' and *The Mayor of Casterbridge*." *Stud in Browning and His Circle* 8 (1980), 99–101.

Stone, Donald D. "House and Home," 298–299.
Taft, Michael. "Hardy's Manipulation of Folklore and Literary Imagination: The Case of the Wife-Sale in *The Mayor of Casterbridge*." *Stud in the Novel* 13 (1981), 399–406.
Thomas, Denis W. "Drunkenness," 202–206.
Vichy, Thérèse. "Humanisme tragique," 109–117.
Walters, Usha. *The Poetry*, 20–21, 45–46, 50–51, 60–62, 78–82, 114–115.
Winner, Anthony. *Characters in the Twilight*, 50–72.
Wotton, George. *Thomas Hardy*, 63–65.

A Pair of Blue Eyes, 1873

Benson, Michael. "Moving Bodies," 231–232.
Bolduc, Stevie Anne. "The Imperative for Individuation: Thomas Hardy's *A Pair of Blue Eyes*." *J of Evolutionary Psych* 4 (1983), 196–206.
Casagrande, Peter J. *Unity*, 85–95.
Childers, Mary. "Thomas Hardy," 331–334.
Clark, S. L., and J. N. Wasserman. *Thomas Hardy*, 11–15.
Cosslett, Tess. *The 'Scientific Movement'*, 140–152.
Halperin, John. "Leslie Stephen, Thomas Hardy, and *A Pair of Blue Eyes*." *Mod Lang R* 75 (1980), 738–745.
Henighan, Tom. *Natural Space*, 138–140.
Jackson, Arlene M. *Illustration*, 30–32, 73–79.
Jacobus, Mary. "Hardy's Magian Retrospect," 262–266.
Lamarca Margalef, Jordi. *Ciencia y literatura*, 159.
Milberg-Kaye, Ruth. *Thomas Hardy*, 30–31, 38–40, 77–79, 93–94.
Rabiger, Michael. "Tess and Saint Tryphena," 56–57.
Rataboul, Louis J. *Le pasteur anglican*, 260–261.
Springer, Marlene. *Hardy's Use of Allusion*, 37–52.
Sumner, Rosemary. *Thomas Hardy*, 119–129, 132–134.
Taylor, Richard H. *The Neglected Hardy*, 29–55.
Wittenberg, Judith Bryant. "Early Hardy Novels," 160–164.
Wotton, George. *Thomas Hardy*, 94–98.

The Return of the Native, 1878

Anderson, Wayne C. "The Rhetoric of Silence," 54–59.
Benson, Michael. "Moving Bodies," 233–234, 239.
Casagrande, Peter J. *Unity*, 126–143.
Cohen, Sandy. "Blind Clym, Unchristian Christian and the Redness of the Reddleman: Character Correspondences in Hardy's *The Return of the Native*." *Thomas Hardy Yearbook* 11 (1984), 49–54.
Collins, Philip. "Hardy and Education," 60–63.
Dave, Jagdish Chandra. *The Human Predicament*, 33–61.
Ebbatson, Roger. *The Evolutionary Self*, 41–56.
Enstice, Andrew. "The Fruit of the Tree," 13–15.
Fricker, Robert. *The Unacknowledged Legislators*, 132–170.

Garcès, Jean-Pierre. "Marginalité et Puritanisme: L'exemple de Thomas Hardy," in *La Marginalité*, 129–132.

Giordano, Frank R., Jr. "Eustacia Vye's Suicide." *Texas Stud in Lit and Lang* 22 (1980), 504–519.

Giordano, Frank R., Jr. *'I'd Have My Life Unbe'*, 55–77.

Hasan, Noorul. *Thomas Hardy*, 38–56.

Heilman, Robert B. *"The Return*: Centennial Observations," in Anne Smith, ed., *The Novels*, 58–80.

Henighan, Tom. *Natural Space*, 115–123.

Higgins, Elizabeth Jean. *Reading the Novel*, 241–245.

Hopkins, V. T. "Clym the Obscure." *Thomas Hardy Soc R* 1:9 (1983), 273–275.

Jackson, Arlene M. *Illustration*, 39–46, 88–96.

Jordan, Mary Ellen. "Thomas Hardy's *Return of the Native*: Clym Yeobright and Melancholia." *Am Imago* 39 (1982), 101–118.

Leech, Geoffrey N., and Michael H. Short. *Style in Fiction*, 198–200.

Meed, John. "Extended Metaphor in *The Return of the Native*." *Thomas Hardy Soc R* 1:8 (1982), 237–239.

Milberg-Kaye, Ruth. *Thomas Hardy*, 11–12, 37–38, 86–94.

Miles, Rosalind. "The Women," 28–34.

Miller, J. Hillis. "Topography in *The Return of the Native*." *Essays in Lit* (Macomb) 8 (1981), 119–134.

Murfin, Ross C. *Swinburne*, 117–119, 126–128.

Nadel, Ira Bruce. "From Fathers and Sons to Sons and Lovers." *Dalhousie R* 59 (1979), 233–234.

Salter, C. H. *Good Little Thomas Hardy*, 4–6, 59–61.

Springer, Marlene. *Hardy's Use of Allusion*, 98–120.

Stubbs, Patricia. *Women and Fiction*, 71–76.

Sumner, Rosemary. *Thomas Hardy*, 99–122.

Vichy, Thérèse. "Humanisme tragique," 109–117.

Walters, Usha. *The Poetry*, 37–38, 45–46, 52–54, 68–70, 103–108.

Wheeler, Michael. *English Fiction*, 183–185.

Winner, Anthony. *Characters in the Twilight*, 42–44.

Wotton, George. *Thomas Hardy*, 61–63, 112–121.

Wyatt, Bryant N. "Poetic Justice in *The Return of the Native*." *Mark Twain J* 21:4 (1983), 56–57.

Tess of the d'Urbervilles, 1891

Anderson, Wayne C. "The Rhetoric of Silence," 63–65.

Anonby, John A. "Hardy's Handling of Biblical Allusions in His Portrayal of Tess in *Tess of the d'Urbervilles*." *Christianity & Lit* 30:3 (1981), 13–25.

Auerbach, Nina. "The Rise of the Fallen Woman." *Nineteenth-Century Fiction* 35 (1980), 42–44.

Auerbach, Nina. *Woman and the Demon*, 171–174.

Beer, Gillian. "Origins and Oblivion in Victorian Narrative," in Ruth Bernard Yeazell, ed., *Sex*, 80–85.

Benson, Michael. "Moving Bodies," 234–235.

Bill, Judith R. "The 'Golden' World in *Tess of the d'Urbervilles*." *Thomas Hardy Soc R* 1:10 (1984), 307–310.

Blake, Kathleen. "Pure Tess: Hardy on Knowing a Woman." *Stud in Engl Lit, 1500–1900* 22 (1982), 689–705.

Bonica, Charlotte. "Nature and Paganism in Hardy's *Tess of the D'Urbervilles*." *ELH* 49 (1982), 849–861.

Boyum, Joy Gould. *Double Exposure*, 138–145.

Brown, Suzanne Hunter. " 'Tess' and *Tess*: An Experiment in Genre." *Mod Fiction Stud* 28 (1982), 25–44.

Buckler, William E. "Thomas Hardy's Illusion of Letters," 289–298.

Burns, Wayne. "The Panzaic Principle in Hardy's *Tess of the d'Urbervilles*." *Recovering Lit* 7:2–3 (1979), 19–41.

Caless, Bryn. "Hardy's Humour," 113–115.

Casagrande, Peter J. *Unity*, 199–218.

Childers, Mary. "Thomas Hardy," 328–330.

Clark, S. L., and J. N. Wasserman. "Tess and Iseult." *Thomas Hardy Soc R* 1:5 (1979), 160–163.

Clark, S. L., and J. N. Wasserman. *Thomas Hardy*, 9–10, 17–56.

Clark, S. L., and Julian Wasserman. "*Tess of the d'Urbervilles* as Arthurian Romance." *Stud in Medievalism* 1:1 (1979), 55–64.

Daleski, H. M. *The Divided Heroine*, 69–87.

Daleski, H. M. "*Tess of the d'Urbervilles*: Mastery and Abandon." *Essays in Criticism* 30 (1980), 326–344.

Dave, Jagdish Chandra. *The Human Predicament*, 150–166.

Eagleton, Mary, and David Pierce. *Attitudes to Class*, 84–88.

Eakins, Rosemary L. "Tess: The Pagan and Christian Traditions," in Anne Smith, ed., *The Novels*, 107–124.

Ebbatson, Roger. *Lawrence and the Nature Tradition*, 116–124.

Elbarbary, Samir. "*Tess* and Joyce's *Portrait*: A Possible Parallel." *Thomas Hardy Annual* 3 (1985), 74–77.

Enstice, Andrew. "The Fruit of the Tree," 16–18.

Ermarth, Elizabeth. "Fictional Consensus and Female Casualties," in Carolyn G. Heilbrun and Margaret R. Higonnet, eds., *The Representation of Women*, 12–15.

Escuret, Annie. "Le macabre dans l'oeuvre romanesque," 100–101.

Escuret, Annie. "*Tess des d'Urberville*: le Corps et le Signe." *Cahiers Victoriens et Edouardiens* 12 (1980), 85–132.

Fontane, Marilyn Stall. "The Devil in *Tess*." *Thomas Hardy Soc R* 1:8 (1982), 250–254.

Freeman, Janet. "Ways of Looking at *Tess*." *Stud in Philology* 79 (1982), 311–323.

Gibson, James. "Hardy and His Readers," 205–210.

Giordano, Frank R., Jr. *'I'd Have My Life Unbe'*, 159–181.

Grainville, Patrick. "Tess, l'hérétique." *Quinzaine Littéraire* 314 (1979), 14.

Grundy, Joan. "Hardy and Milton." *Thomas Hardy Annual* 3 (1985), 4–9.

Hardy, Barbara. *Forms of Feeling*, 161–166.

Harris, Margaret. "Reading Thomas Hardy: Reshaping *Tess of the d'Urbervilles*." *Sydney Stud in Engl* 2 (1976–77), 139–144.

Hasan, Noorul. *Thomas Hardy*, 129–154.

Henighan, Tom. *Natural Space*, 125–135.

Hughes, Winifred. *The Maniac*, 187–189.

Humm, Maggie. "Gender and Narrative," 41–48.

Irwin, Michael. *Picturing*, 30–37.

Jackson, Arlene M. *Illustration*, 56–58, 105–114.

Jones, Lawrence. "*Tess of the d'Urbervilles*," 194–200.

Kelly, Mary Ann. "Hardy's Reading in Schopenhauer: *Tess of the D'Urbervilles*." *Colby Lib Q* 18 (1982), 183–198.

Kishtainy, Khalid. *The Prostitute*, 43–44.

Kozloff, Sarah R. "Where Wessex Meets New England: Griffith's *Way Down East* and Hardy's *Tess of the d'Urbervilles*." *Lit/Film Q* 13 (1985), 35–40.

Kurata, Marilyn J. "Hardy's *Tess of the d'Urbervilles*." *Explicator* 42:1 (1983), 34–35.

Laird, J. T. "New Light on the Evolution of *Tess of the d'Urbervilles*." *R of Engl Stud* 31 (1980), 414–435.

Langbaum, Robert. "Hardy and Lawrence," 26–35.

Leech, Geoffrey N., and Michael H. Short. *Style in Fiction*, 341–342.

Milberg-Kaye, Ruth. *Thomas Hardy*, 28–29, 38–40, 57–58, 78–81.

Miles, Rosalind. "The Women," 41–44.

Miller, J. Hillis. *Fiction and Repetition*, 116–146.

Milligan, Ian. *The Novel in English*, 43–47, 108–131.

Morton, Peter. *The Vital Science*, 194–208.

Murfin, Ross C. *Swinburne*, 137–142.

Narayanaswamy, K. R. "Archetypal Myths in *Tess of the d'Urbervilles*." *Panjab Univ Res Bull* 13:2 (1982), 53–63.

Perry, P. J. "William Dewy, John Small and the Musical Bull." *Thomas Hardy Yearbook* 8 (1978), 34–35.

Platzner, Robert Leonard. *The Metaphysical Novel*, 216–284.

Poole, Adrian. " 'Men's Words' and Hardy's Women." *Essays in Criticism* 31 (1981), 328–345.

Rabiger, Michael. "Tess and Saint Tryphena," 58–59, 63–71.

Rataboul, Louis J. *Le pasteur anglican*, 191–192.

Robinson, Roger. "Hardy and Darwin," in Norman Page, ed., *Thomas Hardy*, 137–144, 147–149.

Salter, C. H. *Good Little Thomas Hardy*, 5–10, 15–17, 44–46, 55–57, 70–72, 74–77, 128–130.

Seltzer, Sandra. "Some Similarities between Three Heroines: Tess d'Urberville, Ellen Chesser, and Kristin Lavransdatter." *Kentucky Folklore Record* 24 (1978), 89–102.

Silverman, Kaja. "History, Figuration and Female Subjectivity in *Tess of the d'Urbervilles.*" *Novel* 18 (1984), 5–28.

Sommers, Jeffrey. "Hardy's Other *Bildungsroman: Tess of the d'Urbervilles.*" *Engl Lit in Transition* 25 (1982), 159–166.

Springer, Marlene. *Hardy's Use of Allusion*, 121–146.

Stone, Donald D. "House and Home," 300–303.

Stubbs, Patricia. *Women and Fiction*, 66–71, 82–86.

Sumner, Rosemary. *Thomas Hardy*, 107–109, 119–122, 129–146.

Thomas, Denis W. "Drunkenness," 195–196, 200–202.

Thompson, Charlotte. "Language and the Shape of Reality in *Tess of the d'Urbervilles.*" *ELH* 50 (1983), 729–760.

Vichy, Thérèse. "Humanisme tragique," 109–117.

Waldman, Nell Kozak. "All That She Is: Hardy's Tess and Polanski's." *Queen's Q* 88 (1981), 429–436.

Waldoff, Leon. "Psychological Determinism in *Tess of the d'Urbervilles*," in Dale Kramer, ed., *Critical Approaches*, 135–154.

Walters, Usha. *The Poetry*, 12–13, 33–36, 44–45, 66–70, 87–91, 96–103, 111–114.

Watt, George. *The Fallen Woman*, 147–167.

Weinstein, Philip M. *The Semantics of Desire*, 108–125.

Wickens, C. Glen. "Hardy and the Aesthetic Mythographers: The Myth of Demeter and Persephone in *Tess of the d'Urbervilles.*" *Univ of Toronto Q* 53 (1983), 85–104.

Williams, Merryn. *Women in the English Novel*, 182–184.

Wing, George. "Hardy and Regionalism," 88–92.

Winner, Anthony. *Characters in the Twilight*, 39–41.

Wotton, George. *Thomas Hardy*, 89–94.

The Trumpet-Major, 1880

Escuret, Annie. "*Le Trompette-Major* ou l'Histoire du Perroquet et de l'Agami." *Cahiers Victoriens et Edouardiens* 17 (1983), 1–15.

Hardy, Barbara. *Forms of Feeling*, 180–189.

Irwin, Michael. *Picturing*, 91–93, 115–117.

Jackson, Arlene M. *Illustration*, 122–124.

La Belle, Jenijoy. "Hardy's *The Trumpet-Major.*" *Explicator* 38:3 (1980), 10–11.

Rignall, J. M. "The Historical Double: *Waverley, Sylvia's Lovers, The Trumpet-Major.*" *Essays in Criticism* 34 (1984), 27–31.

Taylor, Richard H. *The Neglected Hardy*, 76–95.

Two on a Tower, 1882

Bayley, John. "The Love Story in *Two on a Tower.*" *Thomas Hardy Annual* 1 (1982), 60–70.

Casagrande, Peter J. *Unity*, 179–183.

Childers, Mary. "Thomas Hardy," 327–328.

Hochstadt, Pearl R. "Hardy's Romantic Diptych," 28–33.

Lamarca Margalef, Jordi. *Ciencia y literatura*, 155–156.

Summer, Rosemary. "The Experimental and the Absurd in *Two on a Tower*." *Thomas Hardy Annual* 1 (1982), 71–81.

Taylor, Richard H. *The Neglected Hardy*, 121–146.

Ward, Paul. "*Two on a Tower*: A Critical Revaluation." *Thomas Hardy Yearbook* 8 (1978), 29–34.

Wotton, George. *Thomas Hardy*, 107–111.

Under the Greenwood Tree, 1872

Casagrande, Peter J. *Unity*, 81–87.

Edwards, Duane. "The Ending of *Under the Greenwood Tree*." *Thomas Hardy Yearbook* 8 (1978), 21–22.

Escuret, Annie. "Le macabre dans l'oeuvre romanesque," 95–97.

Hardy, Barbara. *Forms of Feeling*, 171–173.

Hardy, Barbara. "*Under the Greenwood Tree*: A Novel about the Imagination," in Anne Smith, ed., *The Novels*, 45–57.

Henighan, Tom. *Natural Space*, 105–108.

Hunter, Shelagh. *Victorian Idyllic Fiction*, 169–178.

Springer, Marlene. *Hardy's Use of Allusion*, 32–37, 92–94.

Winner, Anthony. *Characters in the Twilight*, 33–35.

Wotton, George. *Thomas Hardy*, 85–87.

The Well-Beloved, 1892

Caless, Bryn. "Hardy's Humour," 119–120.

Casagrande, Peter J. *Unity*, 153–160.

Dave, Jagdish Chandra. *The Human Predicament*, 89–92.

Davidson, Arnold E. "Eros and Expectations in Thomas Hardy's *The Well-Beloved*." *Dalhousie R* 63 (1983), 504–514.

Fussell, D. H. " 'Do You Like Poe, Mr. Hardy'." *Mod Fiction Stud* 27 (1981), 218–221.

Jackson, Arlene M. *Illustration*, 127–129.

Jacobus, Mary. "Hardy's Magian Retrospect," 270–274.

Milberg-Kaye, Ruth. *Thomas Hardy*, 44–53.

Miller, J. Hillis. *Fiction and Repetition*, 147–175.

Ousby, Ian. "The Convergence of the Twain," 790–793.

Ryan, Michael. "One Name of Many Shapes: *The Well-Beloved*," in Dale Kramer, ed., *Critical Approaches*, 172–192.

Salter, C. H. *Good Little Thomas Hardy*, 124–126.

Sumner, Rosemary. *Thomas Hardy*, 32–45.

Takakuwa, Yoshiko. "*The Well-Beloved*: Hardy's 'Slight' Novel." *Stud in Engl Lit* (Japan), Engl Number 1983, 19–32.

Taylor, Richard H. *The Neglected Hardy*, 147–173.

Wotton, George. *Thomas Hardy*, 139–141.

The Woodlanders, 1887

Austin, Frances. "Dialogue in *The Woodlanders*." *Thomas Hardy Soc R* 1:5 (1979), 144–151.

Benson, Michael. "Moving Bodies," 230–231, 234–235.

Buckler, William E. "Toward a Poetics of Hardy's Novels: *The Woodlanders*." *Dickens Stud Annual* 14 (1985), 327–336.

Casagrande, Peter J. *Unity*, 143–153.

Chalfant, Fran C. "In Defence of Hardy's Gentleman from South Carolina." *Thomas Hardy Soc R* 1:5 (1979), 142–144.

Collins, Philip. "Hardy and Education," 56–59.

Cramer, Jeffrey S. "The Grotesque in Thomas Hardy's *The Woodlanders*." *Thomas Hardy Yearbook* 8 (1978), 25–29.

Daleski, H. M. *Unities*, 230–235.

Escuret, Annie. "Le macabre dans l'oeuvre romanesque," 99–100.

Essex, Ruth. "A New Sentimental Journey." *Thomas Hardy Soc R* 1:9 (1983), 285–286.

Fontane, Marilyn Stall. "Hardy's Best Story." *Thomas Hardy Yearbook* 11 (1984), 37–41.

Gibson, James. "Hardy and His Readers," 202–205.

Giordano, Frank R., Jr. *'I'd Have My Life Unbe'*, 137–158.

Gitter, Elisabeth G. "The Power of Women's Hair in the Victorian Imagination." *PMLA* 99 (1984), 945–946.

Hannaford, Richard. " 'A Forlorn Hope?' Grace Melbury and *The Woodlanders*." *Thomas Hardy Yearbook* 10 (1980), 72–76.

Hardy, Barbara. *Forms of Feeling*, 170–171.

Hasan, Noorul. *Thomas Hardy*, 82–103.

Henighan, Tom. *Natural Space*, 123–125.

Hunter, Shelagh. *Victorian Idyllic Fiction*, 179–202.

Jacobus, Mary. "Tree and Machine: *The Woodlanders*," in Dale Kramer, ed., *Critical Approaches*, 116–134.

Lamarca Margalef, Jordi. *Ciencia y literatura*, 176–177.

Milberg-Kaye, Ruth. *Thomas Hardy*, 23–27, 36–37, 74–75.

Murfin, Ross C. *Swinburne*, 133–137.

Peck, John. "Hardy's *The Woodlanders*: The Too Transparent Web." *Engl Lit in Transition* 24 (1981), 147–154.

Salter, C. H. *Good Little Thomas Hardy*, 20–22.

Stone, Donald D. "House and Home," 299–300.

Stubbs, Patricia. *Women and Fiction*, 62–63, 76–79.

Sumner, Rosemary. *Thomas Hardy*, 28–30, 82–97.

Thomas, Denis W. "Drunkenness," 193–194.

Walters, Usha. *The Poetry*, 4–5, 13–15, 74–78, 100–101.

Wheeler, Michael. *English Fiction*, 187–190.

Wotton, George. *Thomas Hardy*, 52–58, 98–102.

MARGARET HARKNESS

Captain Lobe, 1889

Goode, John. "Margaret Harkness and the Socialist Novel," in H. Gustav Klaus, ed., *The Socialist Novel*, 62–64.

A City Girl, 1887

> Goode, John. "Margaret Harkness," 53–57.

Out of Work, 1888

> Goode, John. "Margaret Harkness," 57–61.

L. P. HARTLEY

The Brickfield, 1964

> Curcuru, Monique. *Childhood and Adolescence*, 19–26, 45–47, 51–54.

The *Eustace and Hilda* Trilogy, 1944–1947

> Curcuru, Monique. *Childhood and Adolescence*, 26–41, 45–86, 93–114, 128–134.

Facial Justice, 1960

> Jones, Edward T. "Therapeutic Dystopia: A Szaszian Approach to Hawthorne's *The Blithedale Romance* and L. P. Hartley's *Facial Justice*," in M. E. Grenander, comp., *Proceedings of Asclepius*, 19–28.

The Go-Between, 1953

> Curcuru, Monique. *Childhood and Adolescence*, 17–26, 50–51, 54–56, 61–65, 91–93, 119–124, 149–152.
> McEwan, Neil. *The Survival of the Novel*, 129–145.
> Pritchard, R. E. "L. P. Hartley's *The Go-Between*." *Crit Q* 22:1 (1980), 45–55.

The Harness Room, 1971

> Curcuru, Monique. *Childhood and Adolescence*, 163–207, 215–216.

The Love-Adept, 1969

> Curcuru, Monique. *Childhood and Adolescence*, 157–159, 163–207.

My Sisters' Keeper, 1970

> Curcuru, Monique. *Childhood and Adolescence*, 163–207, 209–215.

The Will and the Way, 1973

> Curcuru, Monique. *Childhood and Adolescence*, 159–161, 163–207, 216–218.

JOHN MACDOUGALL HAY

Gillespie, 1963

> Bold, Alan. *Modern Scottish Literature*, 117–123.
> Mitchell, Jack. "Early Harvest: Three Anti-Capitalist Novels Published in 1914," in H. Gustav Klaus, ed., *The Socialist Novel*, 81–87.
> Ower, Patricia. "The Minor Characters in Hay's *Gillespie*." *Stud in Scottish Lit* 16 (1981), 50–60.

Spring, Ian. "Determinism in John MacDougall Hay's *Gillespie*." *Scottish Liter J* 6:2 (1979), 55–68.
Whyte, Christopher. "Myth and Realism in *Gillespie*." *Stud in Scottish Lit* 20 (1985), 34–48.

MARY HAYS

Memoirs of Emma Courtney, 1796

Suhr, Heidrun. *Englische Romanautorinnen*, 249–258.

ELIZA HAYWOOD

The Adventures of Eovaai, 1736

Schofield, Mary Anne. *Eliza Haywood*, 78–80.
Schofield, Mary Anne. *Quiet Rebellion*, 41–43.

The Agreeable Caledonian, 1728–29

Schofield, Mary Anne. *Quiet Rebellion*, 88–90.

Anti-Pamela, 1741

Schofield, Mary Anne. *Eliza Haywood*, 84–85.
Schofield, Mary Anne. *Quiet Rebellion*, 62–63.
Suhr, Heidrun. *Englische Romanautorinnen*, 87–90.

The Arragonian Queen, 1724

Schofield, Mary Anne. *Eliza Haywood*, 48–50.
Schofield, Mary Anne. *Quiet Rebellion*, 75–77.

Betsy Thoughtless, 1751

Schofield, Mary Anne. *Eliza Haywood*, 92–97.
Schofield, Mary Anne. *Quiet Rebellion*, 107–111.
Suhr, Heidrun. *Englische Romanautorinnen*, 90–103.

The British Recluse, 1722

Schofield, Mary Anne. *Eliza Haywood*, 22–24.
Schofield, Mary Anne. *Quiet Rebellion*, 49–52.

The City Jilt, 1726

Schofield, Mary Anne. " 'Descending Angels': Salubrious Sluts and Pretty Prostitutes in Haywood's Fiction," in Mary Anne Schofield and Cecilia Macheski, eds., *Fetter'd or Free?*, 193–194.
Schofield, Mary Anne. *Eliza Haywood*, 51–52.
Schofield, Mary Anne. *Quiet Rebellion*, 52–55.

Cleomelia, 1727

Schofield, Mary Anne. *Eliza Haywood*, 63–65.

Dalinda, 1749

Schofield, Mary Anne. *Eliza Haywood*, 90–91.

Life's Progress through the Passions, 1748

Schofield, Mary Anne. *Eliza Haywood*, 87–89.

Love in Excess, 1719–20

London, April. "Placing the Female: The Metonymic Garden in Amatory and Pious Narrative, 1700–1740," in Mary Anne Schofield and Cecilia Macheski, eds., *Fetter'd or Free?*, 109–112.
Schofield, Mary Anne. *Eliza Haywood*, 18–22.
Schofield, Mary Anne. *Quiet Rebellion*, 30–33.
Suhr, Heidrun. *Englische Romanautorinnen*, 32–34.

Love-Letters on All Occasions, 1730

Schofield, Mary Anne. *Quiet Rebellion*, 26–27.

The Masqueraders, 1724–25

Schofield, Mary Anne. *Eliza Haywood*, 44–46.

The Memoirs of a Certain Island Adjacent to the Kingdom of Utopia, 1724–25

Schofield, Mary Anne. *Quiet Rebellion*, 78–81.

The Padlock, 1728

Schofield, Mary Anne. *Quiet Rebellion*, 44–45.

The Perplex'd Dutchess, 1728

Schofield, Mary Anne. *Eliza Haywood*, 74–75.
Schofield, Mary Anne. *Quiet Rebellion*, 83–85.

Phildore and Placentia, 1727

Schofield, Mary Anne. "The Awakening of the Eighteenth-Century Heroine: Eliza Haywood's New Women." *CEA Critic* 43:3 (1981), 9–13.
Schofield, Mary Anne. *Eliza Haywood*, 70–74.
Schofield, Mary Anne. *Quiet Rebellion*, 38–41.

The Rash Resolve, 1724

Schofield, Mary Anne. *Eliza Haywood*, 29–30.
Schofield, Mary Anne. *Quiet Rebellion*, 74–75.

The Secret History of the Present Intrigues of the Court of Caramania, 1727

Schofield, Mary Anne. *Quiet Rebellion*, 81–83.

The Surprise, 1724

Schofield, Mary Anne. *Eliza Haywood*, 47–48.

HAROLD HESLOP

The Crime of Peter Ropner, 1934

Klaus, H. Gustav. *The Literature*, 102–103.

Last Cage Down, 1935

    Klaus, H. Gustav. *The Literature*, 103–104.

SUSAN HILL

The Bird of Night, 1972

    Jackson, Rosemary. "Cold Enclosures: The Fiction of Susan Hill," in Thomas F. Staley, ed., *Twentieth-Century Women Novelists*, 94–95.

A Change for the Better, 1969

    Jackson, Rosemary. "Cold Enclosures," 87–88.

Do Me a Favour, 1963

    Jackson, Rosemary. "Cold Enclosures," 84–86.

The Enclosure, 1961

    Jackson, Rosemary. "Cold Enclosures," 82–85.

Gentlemen and Ladies, 1968

    Jackson, Rosemary. "Cold Enclosures," 86–87.

I'm the King of the Castle, 1970

    Jackson, Rosemary. "Cold Enclosures," 88–90.

In the Springtime of the Year, 1974

    Butter, Peter H. *"In the Springtime of the Year,"* in Hermann J. Weiand, ed., *Insight V*, 120–124.
    Ireland, K. R. "Rite at the Center: Narrative Duplication in Susan Hill's *In the Springtime of the Year*." *J of Narrative Technique* 13 (1983), 172–179.
    Jackson, Rosemary. "Cold Enclosures," 97–100.

Strange Meeting, 1971

    Jackson, Rosemary. "Cold Enclosures," 92–93.

Strip Jack Naked, 1974

    Jackson, Rosemary. "Cold Enclosures," 101–103.

JAMES HILTON

Lost Horizon, 1933

    Heck, Francis S. "The Domain as a Symbol of a Paradise Lost: *Lost Horizon* and *Brideshead Revisited*." *Nassau R* 4:3 (1982), 24–29.

ARCHIE HIND

The Dear Green Place, 1966

    Bold, Alan. *Modern Scottish Literature*, 236–239.

BARRY HINES

Kes, 1969

Hermes, Liesel. *"Kes,"* in Hermann J. Weiand, ed., *Insight V*, 125–134.

A Kestrel for a Knave, 1968

Paul, Ronald. *"Fire in Our Hearts,"* 164–185.

WILLIAM HOPE HODGSON

The Night Land, 1912

Landow, George P. "And the World Became Strange: Realms of Literary Fantasy." *Georgia R* 33 (1979), 37–41.

Stableford, Brian. *Scientific Romance*, 98–100.

Wagar, W. Warren. "The Rebellion of Nature," in Eric S. Rabkin et al., eds., *The End of the World*, 150–151.

MARGARET HOLFORD HODSON

Warbeck of Wolfstein, 1820

Tracy, Ann Blaisdell. *Patterns of Fear*, 118–120, 140–142, 192–201.

JAMES HOGG

The Brownie of Bodsbeck, 1818

Reddin, Chitra Pershad. *Forms of Evil*, 92–95.

Smith, Nelson C. *James Hogg*, 109–110, 141–142.

The Private Memoirs and Confessions of a Justified Sinner, 1824

Bligh, John. "The Doctrinal Premises of Hogg's *Confessions of a Justified Sinner.*" *Stud in Scottish Lit* 19 (1984), 148–162.

Campbell, Ian. "Hogg's *Confessions* and the *Heart of Darkness.*" *Stud in Scottish Lit* 15 (1980), 187–199.

Campbell, Ian. "James Hogg and the Bible." *Scottish Liter J* 10:1 (1983), 22–27.

Glage, Liselotte, and Jörg Rublack. *Die gestörte Identität*, 1–26, 32–89.

Gordon, Jan B. "Narrative Enclosure as Textual Ruin: An Archaeology of Gothic Consciousness." *Dickens Stud Annual* 11 (1983), 218–221.

Groves, David. "Allusions to *Dr. Faustus* in James Hogg's *Justified Sinner.*" *Stud in Scottish Lit* 18 (1983), 157–164.

Groves, David. "James Hogg's 'Singular Dream' and the *Confessions.*" *Scottish Liter J* 10:1 (1983), 54–65.

Groves, David. "Other Prose Writings of James Hogg in Relation to *A Justified Sinner.*" *Stud in Scottish Lit* 20 (1985), 262–265.

Groves, David. "Parallel Narratives in Hogg's *Justified Sinner.*" *Scottish Liter J* 9:2 (1982), 37–44.

Harries, Elizabeth W. "Duplication and Duplicity: James Hogg's *Justified Sinner*." *Wordsworth Circle* 10 (1979), 187–195.

MacAndrew, Elizabeth. *The Gothic Tradition*, 98–100.

Mack, Douglas S. "The Devil's Pilgrim: A Note on Wringhim's Private Memoirs in James Hogg's *Confessions of a Justified Sinner*." *Scottish Liter J* 2:1 (1975), 36–40.

Mack, Douglas S. " 'The Rage of Fanaticism in Former Days': James Hogg's *Confessions of a Justified Sinner* and the Controversy over *Old Mortality*," in Ian Campbell, ed., *Nineteenth-Century Scottish Fiction*, 38–49.

Oakleaf, David. " 'Not the Truth': The Doubleness of Hogg's *Confessions* and the Eighteenth-Century Tradition." *Stud in Scottish Lit* 18 (1983), 59–71.

Punter, David. *The Literature of Terror*, 149–154.

Reddin, Chitra Pershad. *Forms of Evil*, 96–97, 115–116, 140–144, 183–184, 202–203, 213–214, 237–238, 283.

Redekop, Magdalene. "Beyond Closure: Buried Alive with Hogg's *Justified Sinner*." *ELH* 52 (1985), 159–182.

Smith, Nelson C. *James Hogg*, 145–166.

Tracy, Ann Blaisdell. *Patterns of Fear*, 90–91, 123–124, 168–169, 190–192.

Wilt, Judith. *Ghosts of the Gothic*, 73–79.

The Three Perils of Man, 1822

Reddin, Chitra Pershad. *Forms of Evil*, 95–96, 137–140, 201.

Smith, Nelson C. *James Hogg*, 68–69, 72–74.

Tracy, Ann Blaisdell. *Patterns of Fear*, 29–30, 69–70, 88–89, 110–111, 169–172.

The Three Perils of Woman, 1823

Groves, David. "Myth and Structure in James Hogg's *The Three Perils of Woman*." *Wordsworth Circle* 13 (1982), 193–197.

Smith, Nelson C. *James Hogg*, 71–72, 74–75.

THOMAS HOLCROFT

The Adventures of Hugh Trevor, 1797

Hamm, Jean-Jacques. "Stendhal et Holcroft: De *Hugh Trevor* à *Rouge et Noir*." *Stendhal-Club* 25:101 (1983), 45–61.

Scheuermann, Mona. *Social Protest*, 119–142.

Anna St. Ives, 1792

Barker, Gerard A. *Grandison's Heirs*, 105–124.

Reddin, Chitra Pershad. *Forms of Evil*, 126–127.

Scheuermann, Mona. "Redefining the Filial Tie: Eighteenth-Century English Novelists from Brooke to Bage." *Etudes Anglaises* 37 (1984), 392–395.

Scheuermann, Mona. *Social Protest*, 89–118.
Tracy, Ann Blaisdell. *Patterns of Fear*, 201–211, 222–223, 306–309.

VICTORIA HOLT

On the Night of the Seventh Moon, 1972
Bayer-Berenbaum, Linda. *The Gothic Imagination*, 131–142.

WINIFRED HOLTBY

The Crowded Street, 1924
Beauman, Nicola. *A Very Great Profession*, 54–56.

South Riding, 1936
Crosland, Margaret. *Beyond the Lighthouse*, 125–128.
Roberts, Helen. "Propaganda and Ideology in Women's Fiction," in Diana Laurenson, ed., *The Sociology*, 168–170.

THEODORE HOOK

The Parson's Daughter, 1833
Engel, Elliot, and Margaret F. King. *The Victorian Novel*, 125–127.

ANTHONY HOPE

The Prisoner of Zenda, 1894
McConnell, Frank. *Storytelling*, 94–98.
Zapponi, Niccolo. "Il fido monarca sostituto." *Calibano* 5 (1980), 44–51.

GEOFFREY HOUSEHOLD

Rogue Male, 1939
Bromley, Roger. "The Gentry, Bourgeois Hegemony and Popular Fiction." *Lit and Hist* 7 (1981), 177–183.

MATILDA CHARLOTTE HOUSTOUN

Recommended to Mercy, 1862
Mitchell, Sally. *The Fallen Angel*, 108–110.

WILLIAM HENRY HUDSON

A Crystal Age, 1887
Morton, Peter. *The Vital Science*, 70–80.

Green Mansions, 1904

Gilkes, Michael. *The West Indian Novel*, 132–142.
Shrubsall, Dennis. *W. H. Hudson*, 63–64.

The Purple Land, 1885

Carpenter, Richard. "How to Read *The Purple Land*: A Problem in Genre," in James Hogg, ed., *Essays*, 7–22.

RICHARD HUGHES

The Fox in the Attic, 1961

Dumbleton, Susanne M. "*The Fox in the Attic* and *The Wooden Shepherdess*: A Definition of the Human Predicament." *Anglo-Welsh R* 73 (1983), 38–48.
Savage, D. S. "Richard Hughes, Solipsist." *Anglo-Welsh R* 68 (1981), 36–50.

A High Wind in Jamaica, 1929

Dumbleton, Susanne M. "Animals and Humans in *A High Wind in Jamaica*." *Anglo-Welsh R* 68 (1981), 51–61.

The Human Predicament, 1961–

Swinden, Patrick. *The English Novel*, 25–56.

The Wooden Shepherdess, 1973

Ahrends, Günter. "Richard Hughes, *The Wooden Shepherdess*," in Rainer Lengeler, ed., *Englische Literatur*, 226–241.
Dumbleton, Susanne M. "*The Fox in the Attic*," 38–48.

THOMAS HUGHES

Tom Brown at Oxford, 1861

Vance, Norman. *The Sinews of the Spirit*, 151–165.

Tom Brown's School Days, 1857

Cordery, Gareth. "*Tom Brown's Schooldays* and *Foreskin's Lament*: The Alpha and Omega of Rugby Football." *J of Popular Culture* 19:2 (1985), 97–104.
Haley, Bruce. *The Healthy Body*, 145–155.
Harrington, Henry R. " 'Muscular Christianity' and Brutality: The Case of Tom Brown." *Victorian Newsl* 65 (1984), 26–29.
Mason, Philip. *The English Gentleman*, 163–166.
Musgrave, P. W. *From Brown to Bunter*, 47–65.
Quigly, Isabel. *The Heirs of Tom Brown*, 60–68.
Vance, Norman. *The Sinews of the Spirit*, 143–151.
Watson, Ian. "Victorian England, Colonialism and the Ideology of *Tom Brown's Schooldays*." *Zeitschrift für Anglistik und Amerikanistik* 29 (1981), 116–128.

Worth, George J. "Of Muscles and Manliness: Some Reflections on
Thomas Hughes," in James R. Kincaid and Albert J. Kuhn, eds.,
Victorian Literature, 300–312.
Wright, Terence. "Two Little Worlds of School: An Outline of a Dual
Tradition in Schoolboy Fiction." *Durham Univ J* 75 (1982), 59–71.

ALDOUS HUXLEY

After Many a Summer Dies the Swan, 1939

Abrash, Merritt. "Is There Life After Immortality?" in Carl B. Yoke
and Donald M. Hassler, eds., *Death and the Serpent*, 21–22.
Baker, Robert S. *The Dark Historic Page*, 132–135, 187–228.
Chakoo, B. L. *Aldous Huxley*, 191–210.
Ferns, C. S. *Aldous Huxley*, 133–139, 148–165.
Lamarca Margalef, Jordi. *Ciencia y literatura*, 35–36, 53–55.
Pfeiffer, John R. "Aldous Huxley," in E. F. Bleiler, ed., *Science Fiction
Writers*, 105.

Antic Hay, 1923

Baker, Robert S. *The Dark Historic Page*, 54–73.
Bode, Christoph. *Intellektualismus*, 58–142.
Cardoso, Olga Lana. "Similes e metaforas em *Antic Hay*, de Aldous
Huxley." *Estudos Anglo-Americanos* 2 (1978), 75–89.
Chakoo, B. L. *Aldous Huxley*, 26–33.
Crawford, Fred D. *Mixing Memory*, 35–37.
Ferns, C. S. *Aldous Huxley*, 67–77.
Lamarca Margalef, Jordi. *Ciencia y literatura*, 119–120.

Ape and Essence, 1949

Ferns, C. S. *Aldous Huxley*, 176–184.
Lamarca Margalef, Jordi. *Ciencia y literatura*, 75.
Pfeiffer, John R. "Aldous Huxley," 105–106.

Brave New World, 1932

Aldridge, Alexandria. "*Brave New World* and the Mechanist/Vitalist
Controversy." *Compar Lit Stud* 17 (1980), 116–131.
Baker, Robert S. *The Dark Historic Page*, 135–145.
Crawford, Fred D. *Mixing Memory*, 39–42.
Drew, Philip. *The Meaning of Freedom*, 364–366.
Ferns, C. S. *Aldous Huxley*, 133–148, 162–165.
Firchow, Peter Edgerly. *The End of Utopia*, 13–128.
Hoffecker, W. Andrew. "A Reading of *Brave New World*: Dystopianism
in Historical Perspective." *Christianity & Lit* 29:2 (1980), 46–61.
Ingle, Stephen. *Socialist Thought*, 149–157.
Lamarca Margalef, Jordi. *Ciencia y literatura*, 72–74.
Larsen, Peter M. "Synthetic Myths in Aldous Huxley's *Brave New
World*: A Note." *Engl Stud* 62 (1981), 506–508.

Lobb, Edward. "The Subversion of Drama in Huxley's *Brave New World*." *Intl Fiction R* 11 (1984), 94–101.

Matter, William. "On *Brave New World*," in Eric S. Rabkin et al., eds., *No Place Else*, 94–108.

Meckier, Jerome. "Boffin and Podsnap in Utopia." *Dickensian* 77:3 (1981), 154–161.

Meckier, Jerome. "A Neglected Huxley 'Preface': His Earliest Synopsis of *Brave New World*." *Twentieth Century Lit* 25 (1979), 1–17.

Pfeiffer, John R. "Aldous Huxley," 103–105.

Plank, William. "Orwell and Huxley: Social Control through Standardized Eroticism." *Recovering Lit* 12 (1984), 329–339.

Stableford, Brian. *Scientific Romance*, 254–256.

Thiel, Berthold. *Aldous Huxley's "Brave New World,"* 7–248.

Vitoux, Pierre. "Le Conflit idéologique dans *Brave New World*," in *Autour de l'idée*, 211–214.

Watt, Donald. "The Manuscript Revisions of *Brave New World*." *J of Engl and Germanic Philology* 77 (1978), 374–382.

Wells, Arvin R. "Huxley, Plato and the Just Society." *Centennial R* 24 (1980), 475–491.

Williams, Raymond. "Utopia and Science Fiction," in Patrick Parrinder, ed., *Science Fiction*, 60–62.

Crome Yellow, 1921

Baker, Robert S. *The Dark Historic Page*, 31–54.

Bode, Christoph. *Intellektualismus*, 15–57.

Chakoo, B. L. *Aldous Huxley*, 16–26.

Ferns, C. S. *Aldous Huxley*, 55–76.

Singh, Kirpal. "Denis Stone and the Problem of Integrated Living: An Essay on Aldous Huxley's *Crome Yellow*." *Liter Criterion* 20:2 (1985), 1–7.

Eyeless in Gaza, 1936

Aithal, S. Krishnamoorthy. "Huxley's *Eyeless in Gaza*." *Explicator* 42:3 (1984), 46–49.

Baker, Robert S. *The Dark Historic Page*, 128–130, 146–186.

Chakoo, B. L. *Aldous Huxley*, 140–167.

Crawford, Fred D. *Mixing Memory*, 42–45.

Ferns, C. S. *Aldous Huxley*, 103–116, 120–132.

Wasserman, Jerry. "Huxley's Either/Or: The Case for *Eyeless in Gaza*." *Novel* 13 (1980), 188–203.

The Genius and the Goddess, 1955

Ferns, C. S. *Aldous Huxley*, 184–193.

Island, 1962

Chakoo, B. L. *Aldous Huxley*, 264–290.

Crawford, John W. "Huxley's *Island*: A Contemporary Utopia," in his *Discourse*, 141–148.

Ferns, C. S. *Aldous Huxley*, 211–214, 219–234.
Pfeiffer, John R. "Aldous Huxley," 106–107.

Point Counter Point, 1928

Aronson, Alex. *Music and the Novel*, 76–77, 149–151.
Atkins, John. "*Point Counter Point* and the Uncongenital Novelist."
    Stud in the Liter Imagination 13:1 (1980), 69–80.
Baker, Robert S. *The Dark Historic Page*, 99–126, 130–132.
Bode, Christoph. *Intellektualismus*, 234–321.
Chakoo, B. L. *Aldous Huxley*, 49–87.
Crawford, Fred D. *Mixing Memory*, 37–39.
Ferns, C. S. *Aldous Huxley*, 93–104, 113–132.
Ghosh, Sisir Kumar. "*Point Counter Point*: Looking Back." *Aligarh J
    of Engl Stud* 6:1 (1981), 76–88.
Green, Carlanda. "Huxley's Cosmic Dandy." *Dalhousie R* 62 (1982),
    303–313.
Kellman, Steven G. *The Self-Begetting Novel*, 85–87.
Lamarca Margalef, Jordi. *Ciencia y literatura*, 120–121.
McCall, Raymond G. "Huxley's *Point Counter Point*." *Explicator* 42:1
    (1983), 49–50.
Meckier, Jerome. "Aldous Huxley and the Congenital Novelists: New
    Ideas about the Novel of Ideas." *Southern R* (Adelaide) 13 (1980),
    203–212, 214–216.
Morton, Peter R. "Huxley's *Point Counter Point*." *Explicator* 37:4
    (1979), 10–11.

Those Barren Leaves, 1925

Baker, Robert S. *The Dark Historic Page*, 73–98.
Bode, Christoph. *Intellektualismus*, 143–233.
Chakoo, B. L. *Aldous Huxley*, 33–48.
Ferns, C. S. *Aldous Huxley*, 77–93.

Time Must Have a Stop, 1944

Chakoo, B. L. *Aldous Huxley*, 220–235.
Ferns, C. S. *Aldous Huxley*, 166–176.

ELIZABETH INCHBALD

Nature and Art, 1796

Scheuermann, Mona. *Social Protest*, 169–202.
Suhr, Heidrun. *Englische Romanautorinnen*, 210–211.

A Simple Story, 1791

Barker, Gerard A. *Grandison's Heirs*, 85–103.
Hunt, Linda C. "A Woman's Portion: Jane Austen and the Female in
    Eighteenth-Century Literature," in Mary Anne Schofield and Cecilia
    Macheski, eds., *Fetter'd or Free?*, 12–13.

Kern, Jean B. "The Old Maid, or 'to grow old, and be poor, and laughed at'," in Mary Anne Schofield and Cecilia Macheski, eds., *Fetter'd or Free?*, 207–208.

Macheski, Cecilia. "Penelope's Daughters: Images of Needlework in Eighteenth-Century Literature," in Mary Anne Schofield and Cecilia Macheski, eds., *Fetter'd or Free?*, 95–96.

Rogers, Katharine M. "Dreams and Nightmares: Male Characters in the Feminine Novel of the Eighteenth Century." *Women & Lit* 2 (1981), 13–17.

Suhr, Heidrun. *Englische Romanautorinnen*, 205–210.

CHRISTOPHER ISHERWOOD

All the Conspirators, 1928

Finney, Brian. *Christopher Isherwood*, 69–75.
Johnstone, Richard. *The Will to Believe*, 102–105.
Piazza, Paul. *Christopher Isherwood*, 19–30, 172–173.
Summers, Claude J. *Christopher Isherwood*, 46–52.

Down There on a Visit, 1962

Adams, Stephen. *The Homosexual*, 145–148.
Finney, Brian. *Christopher Isherwood*, 235–246.
Piazza, Paul. *Christopher Isherwood*, 72–73, 102–106, 126–135, 183–185.
Poznar, Walter. "Christopher in *Down There on a Visit*: *Un jour sans lendemain*." *Wascana R* 16:1 (1981), 3–15.
Summers, Claude J. *Christopher Isherwood*, 93–106.

Goodbye to Berlin, 1939

Finney, Brian. *Christopher Isherwood*, 143–154.
Johnstone, Richard. *The Will to Believe*, 100–102.
Piazza, Paul. *Christopher Isherwood*, 123–126.
Summers, Claude J. *Christopher Isherwood*, 29–42.

Lions and Shadows, 1938

Finney, Brian. *Christopher Isherwood*, 129–135.
Johnstone, Richard. *The Will to Believe*, 10–12.
Summers, Claude J. *Christopher Isherwood*, 137–142.

A Meeting by the River, 1967

Finney, Brian. *Christopher Isherwood*, 256–266.
Piazza, Paul. *Christopher Isherwood*, 73–77, 161–169.
Summers, Claude J. *Christopher Isherwood*, 122–135.

The Memorial, 1932

Finney, Brian. *Christopher Isherwood*, 93–100.
Johnstone, Richard. *The Will to Believe*, 102–104.

Piazza, Paul. *Christopher Isherwood*, 30–40.
Summers, Claude J. *Christopher Isherwood*, 52–62.

Mr. Norris Changes Trains, 1935

Finney, Brian. *Christopher Isherwood*, 110–118.
Fussell, Paul. *Abroad*, 31–33.
Johnstone, Richard. *The Will to Believe*, 110–113.
Piazza, Paul. *Christopher Isherwood*, 120–123, 174–176.
Summers, Claude J. *Christopher Isherwood*, 17–29.

Prater Violet, 1946

Finney, Brian. *Christopher Isherwood*, 187–192.
Piazza, Paul. *Christopher Isherwood*, 60–72.
Summers, Claude J. *Christopher Isherwood*, 70–78.

A Single Man, 1964

Adams, Stephen. *The Homosexual*, 149–154.
Brake, Mike. "The Image of the Homosexual in Contemporary English and American Fiction," in Diana Laurenson, ed., *The Sociology*, 184–186.
Finney, Brian. *Christopher Isherwood*, 247–255.
Leech, Geoffrey N., and Michael H. Short. *Style in Fiction*, 189–191.
Piazza, Paul. *Christopher Isherwood*, 150–161, 183–190.
Summers, Claude J. *Christopher Isherwood*, 107–121.

The World in the Evening, 1954

Adams, Stephen. *The Homosexual*, 143–145.
Finney, Brian. *Christopher Isherwood*, 215–222.
Parker, Dorothy. "*The World in the Evening* and Christopher Isherwood." *Engl Stud in Canada* 9 (1983), 213–224.
Piazza, Paul. *Christopher Isherwood*, 43–52, 180–183.
Summers, Claude J. *Christopher Isherwood*, 79–92.

RICHARD JEFFERIES

The Dewy Morn, 1878
Ebbatson, Roger. *Lawrence and the Nature Tradition*, 154–161.

Greene Ferne Farm, 1880
Ebbatson, Roger. *Lawrence and the Nature Tradition*, 146–154.

ROBIN JENKINS

A Toast to the Lord, 1972
Bold, Alan. *Modern Scottish Literature*, 206–209.

GERALDINE JEWSBURY

The Half-Sisters, 1848

Foster, Shirley. *Victorian Women's Fiction*, 31–33.

Marian Withers, 1851

Foster, Shirley. *Victorian Women's Fiction*, 33–34.

Zoe, 1845

Foster, Shirley. *Victorian Women's Fiction*, 30–31.

B. S. JOHNSON

Albert Angelo, 1964

Davies, David John. "The Book as Metaphor: Artifice and Experiment in the Novels of B. S. Johnson." *R of Contemp Fiction* 5:2 (1985), 73–74.

Levitt, Morton P. "The Novels of B. S. Johnson: Against the War against Joyce." *Mod Fiction Stud* 27 (1981), 576–578.

Mackrell, Judith. "B. S. Johnson and the British Experimental Tradition: An Introduction." *R of Contemp Fiction* 5:2 (1985), 48–52.

Thielemans, Johan. "*Albert Angelo* or B. S. Johnson's Paradigm of Truth." *R of Contemp Fiction* 5:2 (1985), 81–87.

Tredell, Nicolas. "The Truths of Lying: *Albert Angelo*." *R of Contemp Fiction* 5:2 (1985), 64–69.

Christie Malry's Own Double-Entry, 1973

Levitt, Morton P. "The Novels," 581–583.

Mackrell, Judith. "B. S. Johnson," 58–61.

House Mother Normal, 1971

Levitt, Morton P. "The Novels," 580–581.

Mackrell, Judith. "B. S. Johnson," 56–58.

See the Old Lady Decently, 1975

Levitt, Morton P. "The Novels," 583–585.

Mackrell, Judith. "B. S. Johnson," 61–63.

Travelling People, 1963

Davies, David John. "The Book as Metaphor," 72–73.

Kanaganayakam, C. "Artifice and Paradise in B. S. Johnson's *Travelling People*." *R of Contemp Fiction* 5:2 (1985), 87–92.

Levitt, Morton P. "The Novels," 575–576.

Mackrell, Judith. "B. S. Johnson," 45–48.

Trawl, 1966

Davies, David John. "The Book as Metaphor," 74–75.

Levitt, Morton P. "The Novels," 578–579.

Mackrell, Judith. "B. S. Johnson," 52–54.

The Unfortunates, 1969

Davies, David John. "The Book as Metaphor," 75–76.
Levitt, Morton P. "The Novels," 579–580.
Mackrell, Judith. "B. S. Johnson," 54–56.
Tredell, Nicolas. "Telling Life, Telling Death: *The Unfortunates.*" *R of Contemp Fiction* 5:2 (1985), 35–41.

PAMELA HANSFORD JOHNSON

An Avenue of Stone, 1947

Lindblad, Ishrat. *Pamela Hansford Johnson*, 77–81.

Blessed Above Women, 1936

Lindblad, Ishrat. *Pamela Hansford Johnson*, 86–91.

Catherine Carter, 1952

Lindblad, Ishrat. *Pamela Hansford Johnson*, 115–120.
Stewart, Grace. *A New Mythos*. 64–66.

Cork Street, Next to the Hatter's, 1965

Lindblad, Ishrat. *Pamela Hansford Johnson*, 149–152.

An Error of Judgement, 1962

Lindblad, Ishrat. *Pamela Hansford Johnson*, 154–161.

The Family Pattern, 1942

Lindblad, Ishrat. *Pamela Hansford Johnson*, 60–63.

Girdle of Venus, 1939

Lindblad, Ishrat. *Pamela Hansford Johnson*, 56–60.

The Good Husband, 1978

Lindblad, Ishrat. *Pamela Hansford Johnson*, 169–173.

The Good Listener, 1975

Lindblad, Ishrat. *Pamela Hansford Johnson*, 164–169.

Here Today, 1937

Lindblad, Ishrat. *Pamela Hansford Johnson*, 32–39.

The Holiday Friend, 1972

Lindblad, Ishrat. *Pamela Hansford Johnson*, 98–107.

The Honours Board, 1970

Lindblad, Ishrat. *Pamela Hansford Johnson*, 161–164.

The Humbler Creation, 1959

Lindblad, Ishrat. *Pamela Hansford Johnson*, 133–140.

An Impossible Marriage, 1954

Lindblad, Ishrat. *Pamela Hansford Johnson*, 120–123.

The Last Resort, 1956
>   Lindblad, Ishrat. *Pamela Hansford Johnson*, 126–133.

The Monument, 1938
>   Lindblad, Ishrat. *Pamela Hansford Johnson*, 44–47.

Night and Silence, Who is Here?, 1963
>   Lindblad, Ishrat. *Pamela Hansford Johnson*, 146–149.

The Philistines, 1949
>   Lindblad, Ishrat. *Pamela Hansford Johnson*, 110–115.

A Summer to Decide, 1948
>   Lindblad, Ishrat. *Pamela Hansford Johnson*, 73–75, 78–84.

The Survival of the Fittest, 1968
>   Lindblad, Ishrat. *Pamela Hansford Johnson*, 47–50, 52–55.

This Bed Thy Centre, 1935
>   Lindblad, Ishrat. *Pamela Hansford Johnson*, 29–33.

Too Dear for My Possessing, 1940
>   Lindblad, Ishrat. *Pamela Hansford Johnson*, 68–71, 79–83.

The Trojan Brothers, 1944
>   Lindblad, Ishrat. *Pamela Hansford Johnson*, 91–98.

The Unspeakable Skipton, 1959
>   Lindblad, Ishrat. *Pamela Hansford Johnson*, 141–146.

Winter Quarters, 1943
>   Lindblad, Ishrat. *Pamela Hansford Johnson*, 64–67.

World's End, 1937
>   Lindblad, Ishrat. *Pamela Hansford Johnson*, 42–44.

SAMUEL JOHNSON

Rasselas, 1759

>   Broadhead, Glenn J. "The Journey and the Stream: Space and Time Imagery in Johnson's *Rasselas*." *Exploration* 8 (1980), 15–24.
>   Crossley, Robert. "Ethereal Ascents: Eighteenth-Century Fantasies of Human Flight." *Eighteenth-Century Life* 7:2 (1982), 55–64.
>   Damrosch, Leopold, Jr. "Johnson's *Rasselas*: Limits of Wisdom, Limits of Art," in Douglas Lane Patey and Timothy Keegan, eds., *Augustan Studies*, 205–213.
>   Ehrenpreis, Irvin. "*Rasselas* and Some Meanings of 'Structure' in Literary Criticism." *Novel* 14 (1981), 101–117.
>   Eversole, Richard. "Imlac and the Poets of Persia and Arabia." *Philol Q* 58 (1979), 155–166.

Gross, Gloria Sybil. "Sanity, Madness and the Family in Samuel Johnson's *Rasselas*." *Psychocultural R* 1 (1977), 152–160.

Hansen, Marlene R. "*Rasselas*, Milton, and Humanism." *Engl Stud* 60 (1979), 14–22.

Hansen, Marlene R. "Sex and Love, Marriage and Friendship: A Feminist Reading of the Quest for Happiness in *Rasselas*." *Engl Stud* 66 (1985), 513–525.

Hardy, J. P. *Samuel Johnson*, 127–148.

Hayden, Lucy K. "The Black Presence in Eighteenth-Century British Novels." *Coll Lang Assoc J* 24 (1981), 410–412.

Keener, Frederick M. *The Chain of Becoming*, 217–240.

Lin, Alan. "Toward a Theory of Common Sense: Beckford's *Vathek* and Johnson's *Rasselas*." *Texas Stud in Lit and Lang* 26 (1984), 183–211.

Mecziems, Jenny. "Utopia and 'the Thing which is not': More, Swift, and Other Lying Idealists." *Univ of Toronto Q* 52 (1982), 58–59.

New, Peter. *Fiction and Purpose*, 83–153.

Norman, Rose. "Fugal Technique in Johnson's *Rasselas*." *J of Narrative Technique* 15 (1985), 267–274.

Orr, Leonard. "The Structural and Thematic Importance of the Astronomer in *Rasselas*." *Recovering Lit* 9 (1981), 15–19.

Pierce, Charles E., Jr. *The Religious Life*, 124–130.

Sklenicka, Carol J. "Samuel Johnson and the Fiction of Activity." *South Atlantic Q* 78 (1979), 214–223.

Soupel, Serge. "Les Mouvements de *Rasselas*." *Etudes Anglaises* 38 (1985), 13–23.

Temmer, Mark J. "*Candide* and *Rasselas* Revisited." *Revue de Littérature Comparée* 222 (1982), 177–193.

Tomarken, Edward. "Travels into the Unknown: *Rasselas* and *A Journey to the Western Islands of Scotland*," in John J. Burke, Jr., and Donald Kay, eds., *The Unknown Samuel Johnson*, 150–159.

Vesterman, William. *The Stylistic Life*, 69–104.

Wharton, T. F. *Samuel Johnson*, 89–118.

Woodruff, James F. "*Rasselas* and the Traditions of 'Menippean Satire'," in Isobel Grundy, ed., *Samuel Johnson*, 158–181.

JENNIFER JOHNSTON

The Captains and the Kings, 1972

Benstock, Shari. "The Masculine World of Jennifer Johnston," in Thomas F. Staley, ed., *Twentieth-Century Women Novelists*, 211–217.

Burleigh, David. "Dead and Gone: The Fiction of Jennifer Johnston and Julia O'Faolain," in Masaru Sekine, ed., *Irish Writers*, 3–4.

The Christmas Tree, 1981

Burleigh, David. "Dead and Gone," 6–7.

The Gates, 1973

>   Benstock, Shari. "The Masculine World," 199–205.
>   Burleigh, David. "Dead and Gone," 2–3.

How Many Miles to Babylon?, 1974

>   Benstock, Shari. "The Masculine World," 193–199.
>   Burleigh, David. "Dead and Gone," 4–5.

The Old Jest, 1979

>   Benstock, Shari. "The Masculine World," 199–205.
>   Burleigh, David. "Dead and Gone," 5–6.

Shadows on Our Skin, 1977

>   Benstock, Shari. "The Masculine World," 205–211.
>   Burleigh, David. "Dead and Gone," 5.

CHARLES JOHNSTONE

Chrysal or the Adventures of a Guinea, 1760–65

>   Link, Viktor. *Die Tradition*, 110–117, 132–140.

ERNEST JONES

De Brassier, 1851

>   Vicinus, Martha. "Chartist Fiction and the Development of a Class-Based Literature," in H. Gustav Klaus, ed., *The Socialist Novel*, 16–19.

GWYN JONES

Times Like These, 1936

>   Ortega, Ramon Lopez. "The Language of the Working-Class Novel of the 1930s," in H. Gustav Klaus, ed., *The Socialist Novel*, 135–137.

JAMES JOYCE

Finnegans Wake, 1939

>   Atherton, James S. "The Paris Background of *Finnegans Wake*," in J. Aubert and M. Jolas, eds., *Joyce & Paris*, 27–30.
>   Attridge, Derek. "The Backbone of *Finnegans Wake*: Narrative, Digression, and Deconstruction." *Genre* 17 (1984), 375–395.
>   Beckman, E. M. *The Verbal Empires*, 30–35, 200–208.
>   Begnal, Michael H. "*Finnegans Wake* and the Nature of Narrative." *Mod Brit Lit* 5 (1980), 43–52.
>   Bekker, Pieter. "Reading *Finnegans Wake*," in W. J. McCormack and Alistair Stead, eds., *James Joyce*, 185–201.

Benstock, Bernard. *James Joyce*, 17–21, 143–187.

Benstock, Shari. "At the Margin of Discourse: Footnotes in the Fictional Text." *PMLA* 98 (1983), 211–220.

Benstock, Shari. "The Genuine Christine: Psychodynamics of Issy," in Suzette Henke and Elaine Unkeless, eds., *Women in Joyce*, 169–192.

Benstock, Shari. "The Letter of the Law: *La Carte Postale* in *Finnegans Wake*." *Philol Q* 63 (1984), 163–184.

Benstock, Shari. "Sexuality and Survival in *Finnegans Wake*," in Bernard Benstock, ed., *The Seventh of Joyce*, 247–254.

Ben-Zvi, Linda. "Mauthner's *Critique of Language*: A Forgotten Book at the Wake." *Compar Lit Stud* 19 (1982), 143–160.

Best, Nigel. *Dawn: A Study of the Present Age and "Finnegans Wake."*

Bolt, Sydney. *A Preface*, 152–163.

Bosinelli, Rosa Maria, and Diarmuid Maguire. "*La Calumnia è un Vermicelli:* Rumor and Noise in *Finnegans Wake*, 3–74." *Compar Lit Stud* 19 (1982), 175–193.

Boyle, Robert. "Joyce and Faith," in Richard F. Peterson et al., eds., *Work in Progress*, 133–135, 137–144.

Boyle, Robert. "Joyce's Consubstantiality: Woman as Creator," in Heyward Ehrlich, ed., *Light Rays*, 130–132.

Brivic, Sheldon. *Joyce between Freud and Jung*, 199–216.

Brivic, Sheldon. "Joycean Psychology," in Richard F. Peterson et al., eds., *Work in Progress*, 111–114.

Brivic, Sheldon. "The Mind Factory: Kabbalah in *Finnegans Wake*." *James Joyce Q* 21 (1983), 7–28.

Brown, Carole. "Will the Real Signor Foli Please Stand Up and Sing 'Mother Machree'?" *Wake Newslitter* 17:6 (1980), 99–100.

Brown, Richard. *James Joyce*, 41–42, 45–49, 59–60.

Carver, Craig. "An Inquiry into *Wake* Lexicology." *Wake Newslitter* 17:3 (1980), 33–45.

Cheng, Vincent J. "Shakespearean Reversals in *Finnegans Wake*." *Engl Lang Notes* 22:3 (1985), 58–61.

Cheng, Vincent John. *Shakespeare and Joyce*, 17–192.

Cope, Jackson I. *Joyce's Cities*, 110–124.

Cowley, Geoffrey N. "Harmonic Condenser Enginium: A Sentential Drama from *Finnegans Wake*." *Lang and Style* 15 (1982), 48–63.

Cumpiano, Marion. *Saint John of the Cross*, 1–20.

Cumpiano, Marion W. "Dolphins and Dolphin's Barn: The Womb of Youth in *Ulysses* and *Finnegans Wake*." *Dutch Q R of Anglo-American Letters* 11 (1981), 134–144.

Cumpiano, Marion W. "The Embattled Arch: A Study of One Paragraph in *Finnegans Wake*, 403.06–17." *Papers on Lang & Lit* 16 (1980), 417–429.

Cumpiano, Marion W. "The Flowerpot on the Pole: A Motif Approach to *Finnegans Wake*." *James Joyce Q* 21 (1983), 61–68.

Cumpiano, Marion W. "The Multifarious Cad in *Finnegans Wake*: Recurrent Elements in His Encounter with HCE." *Stud in the Novel* 16 (1984), 101–109.

Devlin, Kimberly. "Self and Other in *Finnegans Wake*: A Framework for Analyzing Versions of Shem and Shaun." *James Joyce Q* 21 (1983), 31–49.

DiBernard, Barbara. "Alchemical Number Symbolism in *Finnegans Wake*." *James Joyce Q* 16 (1979), 433–446.

DiBernard, Barbara. *Alchemy and "Finnegans Wake."*

Dilworth, Thomas. "Tarpey in *Finnegans Wake*." *James Joyce Q* 21 (1983), 51–57.

Eckley, Grace. *Children's Lore*, 1–219.

Epstein, Edmund L. "James Joyce and Language," in Richard F. Peterson et al., eds., *Work in Progress*, 65–71.

Faj, Attila. "Neuer Schlüssel zu *Finnegans Wake* von James Joyce." *Ural-Altaische Jahrbücher* 54 (1982), 97–107.

Fargnoli, A. Nicholas. "A-taufing in the *Wake*: Joyce's Baptismal Motif." *James Joyce Q* 20 (1983), 293–304.

Farrell, Thomas J. "Joyce's *Finnegans Wake*." *Explicator* 42:4 (1984), 32–33.

Ferrer, Daniel. "The Freudful Couchmare of d: Joyce's Notes on Freud and the Composition of Chapter XVI of *Finnegans Wake*." *James Joyce Q* 22 (1985), 367–381.

Firestone, Evan R. "James Joyce and the First Generation New York School," in Heyward Ehrlich, ed., *Light Rays*, 210–214.

Ford, Jane. "James Joyce and Those (K)nights of 'Ruful Continence'," in Bernard Benstock, ed., *The Seventh of Joyce*, 245–246.

Fredkin, Grace. "S in *Finnegans Wake*." *James Joyce Q* 23 (1985), 189–198.

Füger, Wilhelm. " 'Epistlemadethemology' (*FW* 374.17): ALP's Letter and the Tradition of Interpolated Letters." *James Joyce Q* 19 (1982), 405–413.

Gandelman, Claude. "*Finnegans Wake* and the Anthropomorphic Landscape." *J of Mod Lit* 7 (1979), 39–50.

Gandelman, Claude. "Le texte littéraire comme carte anthropomorphe: d'Opicinus de Canistris à *Finnegans Wake*." *Littérature* 53 (1984), 3–17.

Garvin, John. *James Joyce's Disunited Kingdom*, 121–219.

Gellerfelt, Mats. "To Have Confidence in One's Language . . .," in *Nordic Rejoycings*, 107–120.

Gillespie, Michael Patrick. "An Inquisition of Chapter Seven of *Finnegans Wake*." *Renascence* 35 (1983), 138–150.

Gluck, Barbara Reich. *Beckett and Joyce*, 54–56, 70–73, 135–137, 145–146.

Golden, Sean. "Parsing Rhetorics: The Cad As Prolegomena to the Readings of *Finnegans Wake*," in Bernard Benstock, ed., *The Seventh of Joyce*, 173–177.

Gordon, John. *James Joyce's Metamorphoses*, 4–12, 151–154, 157–178.

Gould, Eric. *Mythical Intentions*, 162–170.

Hall, Susan Grove. "The Grammar of *Finnegans Wake*." *Wake Newslitter* 17:4 (1980), 51–59.

Halper, Nathan. "The Narrative Thread in the Cad Episode," in Bernard Benstock, ed., *The Seventh of Joyce*, 171–172.

Halper, Nathan. *Studies in Joyce*, 9–67, 89–99.

Handwerk, Gary. "What Really Goes Before the Fall? Narrative Dynamics in *Finnegans Wake* III:4." *James Joyce Q* 20 (1983), 307–323.

Harrington, John P. "Swift through Le Fanu and Joyce." *Mosaic* 12:3 (1979), 49–58.

Hart, Clive. "Rhythm, Rule, and Resolution in *Finnegans Wake*," in Francisco Garcia Tortosa et al., eds., *James Joyce*, 243–252.

Hayman, David. "James Joyce, Paratactitian." *Contemp Lit* 26 (1985), 155–156, 173–178.

Hayman, David. "Joyce—Beckett/Joyce," in Bernard Benstock, ed., *The Seventh of Joyce*, 37–43.

Heath, Stephen. "Joyce in Language," in Colin MacCabe, ed., *James Joyce*, 129–145.

Henke, Suzette A. "James Joyce and Women: The Matriarchal Muse," in Richard F. Peterson et al., eds., *Work in Progress*, 126–129.

Hodgart, Matthew. *James Joyce*, 130–188.

Jackson, Selwyn. *The Poems of James Joyce*, 103–145.

Jacquet, Claude. "Bisquebasque: Le Basque dans le carnet VI.B.46 et dans *Finnegans Wake*." *Etudes Anglaises* 35 (1982), 311–316.

Jacquet, Claude. "Fonctions du langage dans *Finnegans Wake*: Néologismes et glossolalies," in *Autour de l'idée*, 253–266.

Knuth, A. M. L. *The Wink of the Word*, 44–65, 159–210.

Korg, Jacob. *Language*, 201–225.

Kuberski, Philip. "The Joycean Gaze: Lucia in the I of the Father." *SubStance* 46 (1985), 49–65.

Langdon, M. "Some Reflections of Physics in *Finnegans Wake*." *James Joyce Q* 17 (1980), 359–377.

Lernout, Geert. "Dutch in *Finnegans Wake*." *James Joyce Q* 23 (1985), 45–62.

MacCabe, Colin. "An Introduction to *Finnegans Wake*," in MacCabe, ed., *James Joyce*, 29–41.

MacCabe, Colin. *James Joyce*, 142–157.

McCarthy, Patrick A. "The Jeweleyed Harlots of His Imagination: Prostitution and Artistic Vision in Joyce." *Eire-Ireland* 17:4 (1982), 106–109.

McCarthy, Patrick A. "Joyce's *Finnegans Wake*, 3.18–21." *Explicator* 43:3 (1985), 26–27.

McCarthy, Patrick A. *The Riddles of "Finnegans Wake,"* 15–156.

McCarthy, Patrick A. " 'A Warping Process': Reading *Finnegans Wake*," in Richard F. Peterson et al., eds., *Work in Progress*, 47–55.

McHugh, Roland. *The "Finnegans Wake" Experience*, 1–110.

MacKillop, James. *Fionn mac Cumhaill*, 163–193.

Manganiello, Dominic. "Irish Family Names in *Finnegans Wake*." *Wake Newslitter* 16:2 (1979), 30–31.

Manganiello, Dominic. *Joyce's Politics*, 175–189, 223–234.

Norris, Margot. "Anna Livia Plurabelle: The Dream Woman," in Suzette Henke and Elaine Unkeless, eds., *Women in Joyce*, 197–213.

O'Dwyer, Riana. "Czarnowski and *Finnegans Wake*: A Study of the Cult of the Hero." *James Joyce Q* 17 (1980), 281–291.

O'Dwyer, Riana. "Ireland's 'long vicefreegal existence': A Context for *Finnegans Wake* 34–36," in Bernard Benstock, ed., *The Seventh of Joyce*, 178–181.

O'Hanlon, John. "In the Language of Flowers." *Wake Newslitter* 16:1 (1979), 9–12.

O'Hanlon, John. "Specific Use of Yeats' *A Vision* in *Finnegans Wake*." *Wake Newslitter* 16:3 (1979), 35–44.

Overstreet, David. "Oxymoronic Language and Logic in Quantum Mechanics and James Joyce." *SubStance* 28 (1981), 50–57.

Parrinder, Patrick. *James Joyce*, 10–13, 198–238.

Polhemus, Robert M. *Comic Faith*, 294–337.

Quick, Jonathan R. " 'Idiot': T. S. Eliot in *Finnegans Wake*." *Thalia* 1:3 (1978–79), 17–24.

Rabaté, Jean-Michel. "Alimentaire et vestimentaire dans *Finnegans Wake*." *Etudes Anglaises* 35 (1982), 268–279.

Rabaté, Jean-Michel. "Vers une approche de l'idiolecte de *Finnegans Wake*," in Patrick Rafroidi and Pierre Joannon, eds., *James Joyce*, 111–123.

Reynolds, Mary T. *Joyce and Dante*, 199–213.

Riquelme, John Paul. "Twists of the Teller's Tale: *Finnegans Wake*," in Suheil Badi Bushrui and Bernard Benstock, eds., *James Joyce*, 82–112.

Rose, Danis. *Chapters of Coming Forth*, 1–24.

Rose, Danis, and John O'Hanlon. "Finn MacCool and the Final Weeks of Work in Progress." *Wake Newslitter* 17:5 (1980), 69–87.

Rose, Danis, and John O'Hanlon. *Understanding Finnegans Wake*, 1–329.

Sandulesco, Georges. "Types of Information in *Finnegans Wake*," in Patrick Rafroidi and Pierre Joannon, eds., *James Joyce*, 125–132.

Scarry, John. "Mozart, Beethoven, and John McCormack in *Finnegans Wake*, III,ii," in Patrick Rafroidi and Pierre Joannon, eds., *James Joyce*, 101–109.

Scarry, John. "The Tenor of an Apologia in *Finnegans Wake* III,ii." *Cahiers du Centre d'Etudes Irlandaises* 6 (1981), 91–95.

Scott, Bonnie Kime. *Joyce and Feminism*, 184–200.

Senn, Fritz. "Foreign Readings," in Richard F. Peterson et al., eds., *Work in Progress*, 100–102.

Senn, Fritz. *Joyce's Dislocutions*, 69–71, 80–82, 85–95, 97–102, 111–116, 209–212.

Senn, Fritz. "Seeking a Sign." *Wake Newslitter* 16:2 (1979), 25–29.

Slattery, William C. "Some Dutch Elements in *Finnegans Wake*, 403.06–17." *Papers on Lang & Lit* 21 (1985), 443–447.

Smith, Sarah W. R. "The Word Made Celluloid: On Adapting Joyce's *Wake*," in Michael Klein and Gillian Parker, eds., *The English Novel*, 301–312.

Sörensen, Dolf. *James Joyce's Aesthetic Theory*, 67–80.

Spivey, Ted R. *The Journey beyond Tragedy*, 117–121.

Splitter, Randolph. "Watery Words: Language, Sexuality, and Motherhood in Joyce's Fiction." *ELH* 49 (1982), 197–201, 209–211.

Theall, Donald F. "Sendence of Sundance: Sense, Communication and Community in *Finnegans Wake*." *Canadian J of Irish Stud* 6:1 (1980), 2–13.

Walkiewicz, E. P. "Sanhydas!" *Wake Newslitter* 17:6 (1980), 101–102.

Warner, Alan. *A Guide*, 118–120.

Welch, Robert. "Some Thoughts on Writing a Companion to Irish Literature," in Masaru Sekine, ed., *Irish Writers*, 228–229.

White, David A. *The Grand Continuum*, 3–77, 133–184.

Wright, David G. *Characters of Joyce*, 104–117.

Wright, David G. "The Mystery of Himself: Joyce in His Own Wake." *Colby Lib Q* 18 (1982), 150–159.

Yee, Cordell D. K. "Metemsinopsychosis: Confucius and Ireland in *Finnegans Wake*." *Compar Lit Stud* 20 (1983), 115–122.

A Portrait of the Artist as a Young Man, 1917

Abernathy, F. E. "Stephen's Passage through the Wilderness." *New Orleans R* 1 (1979), 162–164.

Armour, Robert A. "The 'Whatness' of Joseph Strick's *Portrait*," in Michael Klein and Gillian Parker, eds., *The English Novel*, 279–290.

Aronson, Alex. *Music and the Novel*, 43–46.

Aschkenasy, Nehama. "Biblical Females in a Joycean Episode: The 'Strange Woman' Scene in James Joyce's *A Portrait of the Artist as a Young Man*." *Mod Lang Stud* 15:4 (1985), 28–39.

Bariou, Michel. "Le Vent paraclet: Quelques aspects de l'inspiration dans *Le Portrait*." *Cahiers du Centre d'Etudes Irlandaises* 7 (1982), 9–20.

Bazin, Nancy Topping. "The Moment of Revelation in *Martha Quest* and Comparable Moments by Two Modernists." *Mod Fiction Stud* 26 (1980), 90–93.

Beebe, Maurice. "The *Portrait* as Portrait: Joyce and Impressionism." *Irish Renaissance Annual* 1 (1980), 13–29.

Benstock, Bernard. *James Joyce*, 8–14, 49–72.

Bidwell, Bruce, and Linda Heffer. *The Joycean Way*, 9–58.

Billy, Ted. "Optics and Irony: Hoffmann's 'Sand-Man' and Joyce's *Portrait*." *Irish Renaissance Annual* 4 (1983), 110–117.

Bolt, Sydney. *A Preface*, 54–87.

Bowen, Zack. "Epiphanies, Stephen's Diary, and the Narrative Perspective of *A Portrait of the Artist as a Young Man*." *James Joyce Q* 16 (1979), 485–488.

Bowen, Zack. "Joyce and the Modern Coalescence," in Heyward Ehrlich, ed., *Light Rays*, 50–54.

Bowers, Rick. "Stephen's Practical Artistic Development." *James Joyce Q* 21 (1984), 231–234.

Boyle, Robert. "James Joyce and Ignatius of Loyola: *The Spiritual Exercises* in *A Portrait of the Artist*." *Christianity & Lit* 31:2 (1982), 48–57.

Bramsbäck, Birgit. "Allusions to Yeats in *Stephen Hero* and *A Portrait of the Artist as a Young Man*," in *Nordic Rejoycings*, 15–22.

Brivic, Sheldon. "The Father in Joyce," in Bernard Benstock, ed., *The Seventh of Joyce*, 74–80.

Brivic, Sheldon. *Joyce between Freud and Jung*, 17–83.

Butler, Christopher. "Joyce and the Displaced Author," in W. J. McCormack and Alistair Stead, eds., *James Joyce*, 56–73.

Byrd, Forrest M. "Unifying Factors in *A Portrait of the Artist as a Young Man*." *Publs of the Arkansas Philol Assoc* 1:3 (1975), 1–4.

Carens, James F. "The Motif of Hands in *A Portrait of the Artist as a Young Man*." *Irish Renaissance Annual* 2 (1981), 139–156.

Cervo, Nathan. " 'Seeing' as Being: The Blind Apotheosis of Stephen Dedalus." *Northern New England R* 10 (1983), 52–65.

Choi, Myung Kyoo. "Stephen's Aesthetic Awareness in *A Portrait of the Artist as a Young Man*." *Yonsei R* (Seoul) 5 (1978), 105–112.

Church, Margaret. "The Adolescent Point of View toward Women in Joyce's *A Portrait of the Artist as a Young Man*." *Irish Renaissance Annual* 2 (1981), 158–164.

Church, Margaret. *Structure and Theme*, 147–158.

Clews, Hetty. *The Only Teller*, 44–48.

Collinson, Diane. "The Aesthetic Theory of Stephen Dedalus." *Brit J of Aesthetics* 23:1 (1983), 61–73.

Connolly, Thomas E. "Kinesis and Stasis: Structural Rhythm in Joyce's *Portrait*." *Irish Renaissance Annual* 2 (1981), 166–183.

Cope, Jackson I. *Joyce's Cities*, 53–61.

Crespo Allue, Maria J., and Luisa F. Rodriguez Palomero. "*A Portrait of the Artist as a Young Man*: su traduccion y Rosa Chacel," in Francisco Garcia Tortosa et al., eds., *James Joyce*, 67–83.

Daleski, H. M. *Unities*, 171–188.

Di Giuseppe Trivellato, Rita. "James Joyce's *Portrait*: A Case of Applied Mythology." *Quaderni di Lingue e Letterature* 2 (1977), 59–67.

Di Giuseppe Trivellato, Rita. "The Mythos of Irony and Satire in Joyce's *Portrait*." *Quaderni di Lingue e Letterature* 6 (1981), 33–48.

Druff, James H., Jr. "The Romantic Complaint: The Logical Movement of Stephen's Aesthetics in *A Portrait of the Artist as a Young Man*." *Stud in the Novel* 14 (1982), 180–188.

Ellmann, Maud. "Disremembering Dedalus: *A Portrait of the Artist as a Young Man*," in Robert Young, ed., *Untying the Text*, 189–206.

Ellmann, Maud. "Polytropic Man: Paternity, Identity and Naming in *The Odyssey* and *A Portrait of the Artist as a Young Man*," in Colin MacCabe, ed., *James Joyce*, 73–103.

Epstein, Edmund L. "James Joyce and Language," 62–63.

Eruvbetine, Agwonorobo Enaeme. *Intellectualized Emotions*, 36–54, 60–64, 84–98.

Farrell, James T. *On Irish Themes*, 45–55.

Firestone, Evan R. "James Joyce and the First Generation," 214–218.

Ford, Jane. "James Joyce and Those (K)nights," 243.

Forkner, B. "Stephen's Esthetic Trinities in *Ulysses*." *Marginalia* 2 (1978), 7–18.

Forkner, Ben. "Stephen's Vision: First Steps toward an Aesthetic." *Cahiers du Centre d'Etudes Irlandaises* 4 (1979), 33–48.

Gifford, Don. *Joyce Annotated*, 129–287.

Gomez Lara, Manuel José. "Analisis textual de la epifania de Stephen en la playa," in Francisco Garcia Tortosa et al., eds., *James Joyce*, 87–93.

Gose, Elliott B., Jr. "Destruction and Creation in *A Portrait of the Artist as a Young Man*." *James Joyce Q* 22 (1985), 259–269.

Gould, Eric. *Mythical Intentions*, 143–152.

Grayson, Janet. " 'Do You Kiss Your Mother?' Stephen Dedalus' Sovereignty of Ireland." *James Joyce Q* 19 (1982), 119–126.

Green, Martin. *The English Novel*, 91–96.

Halper, Nathan. *Studies in Joyce*, 109–122.

Harkness, Marguerite. "The Separate Roles of *Language* and *Word* in James Joyce's *Portrait*." *Irish Renaissance Annual* 4 (1983), 94–108.

Hayman, David. "James Joyce, Paratactitian," 156–160.

Hayman, David. "The Joycean Inset." *James Joyce Q* 23 (1985), 137–154.

Henke, Suzette A. "James Joyce and Women," 120–121.

Henke, Suzette. "Stephen Dedalus and Women: A Portrait of the Artist as a Young Misogynist," in Suzette Henke and Elaine Unkeless, eds., *Women in Joyce*, 82–102.

Heusel, Barbara Stevens. "The Problems of Figure and Ground in *A Portrait of the Artist as a Young Man*." *Centennial R* 26 (1982), 180–198.

Hodgart, Matthew. *James Joyce*, 57–63.

Jackson, Selwyn. *The Poems of James Joyce*, 41–63.

Jauss, David. "Indirect Interior Monologue and Subjective Narration in *A Portrait of the Artist as a Young Man*." *Par Rapport* 3–4 (1980–81), 45–52.

Jeffares, A. Norman. "Anglo-Irish Literature: Treatment for Radio," in Masaru Sekine, ed., *Irish Writers*, 85–88.

Kellman, Steven G. *The Self-Begetting Novel*, 80–85.

Kenner, Hugh. *Joyce's Voices*, 16–18.

Kestner, Joseph A. *The Spatiality*, 139–145.

Kimball, Jean. "Freud, Leonardo, and Joyce: The Dimensions of a Childhood Memory," in Bernard Benstock, ed., *The Seventh of Joyce*, 60–68.

Knuth, A. M. L. *The Wink of the Word*, 102–116.

Korg, Jacob. *Language*, 95–99.

Kuder, Stephen R. "James Joyce and Ignatius of Loyola: *The Spiritual Exercises* in *A Portrait of the Artist*." *Christianity & Lit* 31:2 (1982), 48–57.

Lampkin, Loretta. "*Tristram Shandy* and *A Portrait of the Artist*: The Gestation of Identical Twins." *James Joyce Q* 21 (1984), 137–144.

Lanser, Susan Snider. "Stephen's Diary: The Hero Unveiled." *James Joyce Q* 16 (1979), 417–423.

Leech, Geoffrey N., and Michael H. Short. *Style in Fiction*, 27–28, 183–184.

Levenson, Michael. "Mode of Writing and Mode of Living: Stephen's Diary in Joyce's *Portrait*." *ELH* 52 (1985), 1017–1034.

Levitt, Morton P. "The Modernist Age: The Age of James Joyce," in Heyward Ehrlich, ed., *Light Rays*, 139–140.

Locatelli, Angela. *Una coscienza*, 90–95.

Lubbers, Klaus. " 'Ivy and Ivory': George Moore, Joyces *Portrait* und das verdrängte Irland," in Peter Erlebach et al., eds., *Geschichtlichkeit*, 221–238.

Lucente, Gregory L. "D'Annunzio's *Il fuoco* and Joyce's *Portrait of the Artist*: From Allegory to Irony." *Italica* 57 (1980), 19–33.

MacCabe, Colin. *James Joyce*, 52–68.

McCarthy, Patrick A. "The Jeweleyed Harlots," 94–100.

MacKillop, James. *Fionn mac Cumhaill*, 166–168.

Manganiello, Dominic. "Joyce's 'Third Gospel': The Earthbound Vision of *A Portrait of the Artist*." *Renascence* 35 (1983), 219–232.

Martin, Augustine. "Prose Fiction in the Irish Literary Renaissance," in Masaru Sekine, ed., *Irish Writers*, 142–143.

Martin, Augustine. "Sin and Secrecy in Joyce's Fiction," in Suheil Badi Bushrui and Bernard Benstock, eds., *James Joyce*, 143–145, 147–148.

Mills, Jerry Leath. "Joyce's *A Portrait of the Artist as a Young Man*." *Explicator* 42:4 (1984), 30–32.

Müller, Klaus Peter. *Epiphanie*, 124–351.

Olofsson, Tommy. "A Portrait of the Artist as a Flying Man." *Moderna Sprak* 76 (1982), 3–37. [Also in *Nordic Rejoycings*, 59–93.]

Overstreet, David. "Oxymoronic Language and Logic," 47–53.

Palmieri, Anthony F. R. "*Stephen Hero* and *A Portrait of the Artist as a Young Man*." *DeKalb Liter Arts J* 13:1–2 (1978–79), 93–98.

Palumbo, Donald. "Alone, Isolated, Betrayed, Banished: Similarities in the Social Alienation of Joyce's Stephen Dedalus and Leopold Bloom," in Patrick Rafroidi and Pierre Joannon, eds., *James Joyce*, 69–81.

Parrinder, Patrick. *James Joyce*, 71–105.

Paterson, Gary H. "Stephen and Alice: Not So Strange Bedfellows." *Interpretations* 15:1 (1983), 60–69.

Peterson, Richard F. "Stephen and the Narrative of *A Portrait of the Artist as a Young Man*," in Peterson et al., eds., *Work in Progress*, 15–27.

Pope, Deborah. "The Misprision of Vision: A Comparison of Stephen's Heaven and Hell in *A Portrait of the Artist as a Young Man*." *James Joyce Q* 17 (1980), 263–270.

Reid, B. L. "Gnomon and Order in Joyce's *Portrait*." *Sewanee R* 92 (1984), 397–420.

Reinhart, Tanya. "Reported Consciousness and Point of View: A Comparison between Joyce's *Stephen Hero* and *A Portrait of the Artist as a Young Man*." *PTL* 4 (1979), 63–75.

Restuccia, Frances L. "Molly in Furs: Deleuzean/Masochian Masochism in the Writing of James Joyce." *Novel* 18 (1985), 106–108.

Reynolds, Mary T. *Joyce and Dante*, 180–186, 193–199.

Rimmon-Kenan, Shlomith. "Identity and Identification: Joyce's *A Portrait of the Artist as a Young Man*." *Hebrew Univ Stud in Lit* 9 (1981), 107–125.

Riquelme, John Paul. "Pretexts for Reading and for Writing: Title, Epigraph, and Journal in *A Portrait of the Artist as a Young Man*." *James Joyce Q* 18 (1981), 301–321.

Rose, Ellen Cronan. "Dancing Daedalus: Another Source for Joyce's *Portrait*." *Mod Fiction Stud* 28 (1982), 596–603.

Rossman, Charles. "The Reader's Role in *A Portrait of the Artist as a Young Man*," in Suheil Badi Bushrui and Bernard Benstock, eds., *James Joyce*, 19–36.

Scheick, William J. "Fictional Structure and Ethics in the Edwardian, Modern and Contemporary Novel." *Philol Q* 63 (1984), 295–296.

Schenker, Daniel. "Stalking the Invisible Hero: Ibsen, Joyce, Kierkegaard, and the Failure of Modern Irony." *ELH* 51 (1984), 158–163.

Scott, Bonnie Kime. *Joyce and Feminism*, 15–17, 85–87, 94–96, 151–154.

Senn, Fritz. "Foreign Readings," 85–89.

Senn, Fritz. *Joyce's Dislocutions*, 42–44, 73–83.

Senn, Fritz. " 'Stately, plump', for example: Allusive Overlays and Widening Circles of Irrelevance." *James Joyce Q* 22 (1985), 347–348.

Smith, John B. *Imagery*, 13–207.

Sörensen, Dolf. *James Joyce's Aesthetic Theory*, 44–53.

Splitter, Randolph. "Watery Words," 194–197.

Steinberg, Erwin R. "The Bird-Girl in *A Portrait* as Synthesis: The Sacred Assimilated to the Profane." *James Joyce Q* 17 (1980), 149–163.

Taylor, Anne Robinson. *Male Novelists*, 193–195.

Usandizaga Sainz, Aranzazu. "James Joyce: de Dédalo a Telémaco," in Francisco Garcia Tortosa et al., eds., *James Joyce*, 159–165.

Vichy, Thérèse. "Rhétorique et crise du sujet dans *A Portrait of the Artist as a Young Man*." *Etudes Anglaises* 37 (1984), 283–292.

Warner, Alan. *A Guide*, 114–116.

Watson, G. J. *Irish Identity*, 179–198.

Watson, George J. " 'Words Alone are Certain Good'? James Joyce's Literary Scepticism," in Francisco Garcia Tortosa et al., eds., *James Joyce*, 17–18.

White, David A. *The Grand Continuum*, 81–102.

Wright, David G. *Characters of Joyce*, 30–48.

Yee, Cordell D. K. "St. Thomas Aquinas as Figura of James Joyce: A Medieval View of Literary Influence." *James Joyce Q* 22 (1984), 25–35.

Stephen Hero, 1944

Bolt, Sydney. *A Preface*, 54–58, 83–85.

Bramsbäck, Birgit. "Allusions to Yeats," 9–15.

Farrell, James T. *On Irish Themes*, 56–60.

Ford, Jane. "James Joyce and Those (K)nights," 242–243.

Kestner, Joseph A. *The Spatiality*, 139–146.

Levitt, Morton P. "The Modernist Age," 138–139.

Lubbers, Klaus. " 'Ivy and Ivory'," 221–238.

MacCabe, Colin. *James Joyce*, 52–68.

Manganiello, Dominic. *Joyce's Politics*, 75–82, 85–94.

Martin, Augustine. "Prose Fiction," 141–142.

Martinez-Duenas Espejo, José L. "Reconstruccion gramatical de *Stephen Hero*," in Francisco Garcia Tortosa et al., eds., *James Joyce*, 57–65.

Müller, Klaus Peter. *Epiphanie*, 51–123.

Palmieri, Anthony F. R. "*Stephen Hero* and *A Portrait*," 93–98.

Palumbo, Donald. "Alone, Isolated, Betrayed, Banished," 69–81.

Parrinder, Patrick. *James Joyce*, 32–40.

Reinhart, Tanya. "Reported Consciousness," 63–75.

Reynolds, Mary T. *Joyce and Dante*, 177–183.

Rossman, Charles. "The Reader's Role," 24–25.

Scott, Bonnie Kime. "Emma Clery in *Stephen Hero*: A Young Woman Walking Proudly through the Decayed City," in Suzette Henke and Elaine Unkeless, eds., *Women in Joyce*, 57–78.

Scott, Bonnie Kime. *Joyce and Feminism*, 29–32, 133–155.

Scott, Bonnie Kime. "The Woman in the Black Straw Hat: A Transitional Priestess in *Stephen Hero*." *James Joyce Q* 16 (1979), 407–416.

Wright, David G. *Characters of Joyce*, 30–37.

Ulysses, 1922

Aithal, S. Krishnamoorthy. "Allusions to the Buddha in *Ulysses*." *James Joyce Q* 16 (1979), 510–512.

Aithal, S. Krishnamoorthy. "Indian Allusions in *Ulysses*." *Eire-Ireland* 14:4 (1979), 141–144.

Almeida, Hermione de. *Byron and Joyce*, 5–189.

Aronson, Alex. *Music and the Novel*, 46–60.

Back, Anthony. *Constructing Reality*, 1–56.

Barrow, Craig Wallace. *Montage in James Joyce's "Ulysses,"* 22–199.

Barsam, Richard. "When in Doubt, Persecute Bloom," in Michael Klein and Gillian Parker, eds., *The English Novel*, 291–300.

Bassoff, Bruce. "Impotency and Artistic Omnipotence in *Ulysses*." *Etudes Anglaises* 38 (1985), 442–446.

Bassoff, Bruce. "Joyce's *Ulysses* and Plato's *Symposium*." *Explicator* 44:2 (1986), 34–36.

Bawer, Bruce. "The Last Three Words of *Ulysses*." *Engl Lang Notes* 21:1 (1983), 55–57.

Bazargan, Susan. "Oxen of the Sun: Maternity, Language, and History." *James Joyce Q* 22 (1985), 271–279.

Beckman, E. M. *The Verbal Empires*, 1–30.

Beja, Morris. "The Joyce of Sex: Sexual Relationships in *Ulysses*," in Bernard Benstock, ed., *The Seventh of Joyce*, 255–266. [Also in Heyward Ehrlich, ed., *Light Rays*, 186–196.]

Bell, Michael. "Modern Movements in Literature," in Bell, ed., *1900–1930*, 3–19.

Benko, Stephen E. "Joyce's *Ulysses*." *Explicator* 41:1 (1982), 43–44.

Benstock, Bernard. "Dateline *Ithaca*: The News from Eccles Street." *Mod Brit Lit* 5 (1980), 29–42.

Benstock, Bernard. *James Joyce*, 23–28, 95–142.

Benstock, Bernard. "On the Nature of Evidence in *Ulysses*," in Suheil Badi Bushrui and Bernard Benstock, eds., *James Joyce*, 46–63.

Benstock, Shari. "The Double Image of Modernism: Matisse's Etchings for *Ulysses*." *Contemp Lit* 21 (1980), 450–479. [Also in Heyward Ehrlich, ed., *Light Rays*, 186–196.]

Benstock, Shari. "The Dynamics of Narrative Performance: Stephen Dedalus as Storyteller." *ELH* 49 (1982), 707–736.

Benstock, Shari. "Is He a Jew or a Gentile or a Holy Roman?" *James Joyce Q* 16 (1979), 493–497.

Benstock, Shari. "The Printed Letters in *Ulysses*." *James Joyce Q* 19 (1982), 415–427.

Benstock, Shari. "Who Killed Cock Robin? The Sources of Free Indirect Style in *Ulysses*." *Style* 14 (1980), 259–271.

Benstock, Shari, and Bernard Benstock. "The Benstock Principle," in Bernard Benstock, ed., *The Seventh of Joyce*, 10–20.

Benstock, Shari, and Bernard Benstock. "Narrative Sources and the Problem of *Ulysses*." *J of Narrative Technique* 12 (1982), 24–33.

Benstock, Shari, and Bernard Benstock. "*Ulysses*: Narrative Movement and Place," in Richard F. Peterson et al., eds., *Work in Progress*, 30–46.

Bleikasten, André. "Bloom and Quentin," in Bernard Benstock, ed., *The Seventh of Joyce*, 100–107.

Bolt, Sydney. *A Preface*, 93–150.

Boone, Joseph Allen. "A New Approach to Bloom as 'Womanly Man': The Mixed Middling's Progress in *Ulysses*." *James Joyce Q* 20 (1982), 67–82.

Bowen, Zack. " 'Circe': Why, What and How—Circe and the Epiphany Concept," in J. Aubert and M. Jolas, eds., *Joyce & Paris*, 11–14.

Bowen, Zack. "Joyce and the Modern Coalescence," 40–49.

Bowers, Rick. "Stephen's Practical Artistic Development," 234–242.

Boyle, Robert. "Joyce's Consubstantiality," 127–129.

Brivic, Sheldon. *Joyce between Freud and Jung*, 3–10, 125–198.

Brivic, Sheldon. "Joyce's Sly Rhetoric: The Expanding Rhetoric of *Ulysses*," in J. Aubert and M. Jolas, eds., *Joyce & Paris*, 93–96.

Brown, Carole. "Omar Khayyam in Monto: A Reading of a Passage from James Joyce's *Ulysses*." *Neophilologus* 68 (1984), 623–633.

Brown, Carole, and Leo Knuth. *Bloomsday*, 1–14.

Brown, Richard. *James Joyce*, 19–22, 37–39, 60–62, 66–75, 86–88, 120–125, 131–135.

Bruns, Gerald L. *Inventions*, 160–174.

Bücking, Willem H. "Emma Clery in *Ulysses*." *James Joyce Q* 16 (1979), 508–510.

Burgan, Mary. "Androgynous Fatherhood in *Ulysses* and *Women in Love*." *Mod Lang Q* 44 (1983), 182–186, 191–197.

Bynum, Paige Matthey. "Joyce's *Ulysses*." *Explicator* 43:1 (1984), 50–51.

Cappio, James. "Aristotle, Berkeley, and Proteus: Joyce's Use of Philosophy." *Philos and Lit* 5 (1981), 21–31.

Card, James Van Dyck. "The Ups and Downs, Ins and Outs of Molly Bloom: Patterns of Words in 'Penelope'." *James Joyce Q* 19 (1982), 127–140.

Carens, James F. "Following a Suffix into the Maze," in Bernard Benstock, ed., *The Seventh of Joyce*, 153–155.

Church, Margaret. "Existential Absurdity and the Nostos of *Ulysses*." *James Joyce Q* 16 (1979), 355–357.

Church, Margaret. *Structure and Theme*, 158–165.

Clews, Hetty. *The Only Teller*, 48–51.

Cohen, Keith. *Film and Fiction*, 103–106, 111–114, 147–156, 162–164, 172–179, 188–192, 197–204.

Collins, R. G. "Questions Suspended and Vital: Criticism and Joyce's Catechism in 'Ithaca'." *Dalhousie R* 62 (1982), 70–85.

Cope, Jackson I. *Joyce's Cities*, 20–28, 62–102.

Cope, Jackson I. "Joyce's Waste Land." *Genre* 12 (1979), 527–532.

Crépu, Michel. "Pour Joyce: Dans les corridors de Babel." *Esprit 55–56* (1981), 3–21.

Cronin, Edward J. "Eliade, Joyce, and the 'Nightmare of History'." *J of the Am Acad of Religion* 50 (1982), 435–448.

Cronin, Edward J. "Of Mirrors and Maps and Houses with Gardens: Joyce's 'Wandering Rocks', Chapter X, *Ulysses.*" *North Dakota Q* 48:1 (1980), 40–52.

Cumpiano, Marion W. "Dolphins," 134–144.

Daghistani, Ann, and J. J. Johnson. "Romantic Irony, Spatial Form, and Joyce's *Ulysses*," in Jeffrey R. Smitten and Ann Daghistani, eds., *Spatial Form*, 48–60.

Dasenbrock, Reed Way. "*Omphalos*: Untying Joyce's Knot." *Engl Lang Notes* 23:1 (1985), 63–66.

Dasenbrock, Reed Way. "*Ulysses* and Joyce's Discovery of Vico's 'True Homer'." *Eire-Ireland* 20:1 (1985), 96–108.

David, Alain. "Kant avec Joyce." *Revue des Sciences Humaines* 1:185 (1982), 161–174.

Day, Robert Adams. "Deacon Dedalus: The Text of the *Exultet* and Its Implications for *Ulysses*," in Bernard Benstock, ed., *The Seventh of Joyce*, 157–165.

Deane, Seamus. "Joyce and Nationalism," in Colin MacCabe, ed., *James Joyce*, 176–183.

Debray-Ritzen, Pierre. "De la pensée sans langage au langage pensé," in Patrick Rafroidi and Pierre Joannon, eds., *James Joyce*, 65–67.

Devlin, Kimberly. "The Romance Heroine Exposed: 'Nausicaa' and *The Lamplighter.*" *James Joyce Q* 22 (1985), 383–396.

Diez, Enrique Garcia. "*Ulysses* y *Bouvard et Pécuchet*: la farsa de las ideas recibidas," in Francisco Garcia Tortosa et al., eds., *James Joyce*, 153–157.

Doody, Terrence. "*Don Quixote, Ulysses*, and the Idea of Realism." *Novel* 12 (1979), 197–214.

Doody, Terrence, and Wesley Morris. "Language and Value, Freedom and the Family in *Ulysses.*" *Novel* 15 (1982), 224–239.

Eagleton, Mary, and David Pierce. *Attitudes to Class*, 108–113.

Eakin, David B. " 'Safe!' Bloom's Peristaltic Journey to the National Library." *Cahiers du Centre d'Etudes Irlandaises* 8 (1983), 97–105.

Eddins, Dwight. "*Ulysses*: The Search for the Logos." *ELH* 47 (1980), 804–818.

Epstein, Edmund L. "James Joyce and Language," 63–65.

Epstein, Edmund L. "Joyce and Judaism," in Bernard Benstock, ed., *The Seventh of Joyce*, 221–224.

Eruvbetine, Agwonorobo Enaeme. *Intellectualized Emotions*, 36–54, 56–98.

Erzgräber, Willi. "Metamorphosen im Labyrinth: Zu James Joyces *Ulysses*," in Günter Schnitzler et al., eds., *Bild und Gedanke*, 365–384.

Erzgräber, Willi. "Spaziergang am Strand: Zur Proteus-Episode in James Joyces *Ulysses*." *Literaturwissenschaftliches Jahrbuch im Auftrage der Görres-Gesellschaft* 23 (1982), 151–171.

Esch, Arno. "James Joyce und Homer: Zur Frage der Odyssee-Korrespondenzen im *Ulysses*," in Therese Fischer-Seidel, ed., *James Joyces "Ulysses*," 213–227.

Fargion, Luisa. "La tela di Molly Bloom." *Acme* 34 (1981), 499–511.

Faris, Wendy B. "*Ulysses* in Mexico: Carlos Fuentes." *Compar Lit Stud* 19 (1982), 236–249.

Farrell, James T. *On Irish Themes*, 85–86.

Fernandez, Francisco Fernandez. " 'Oxen of the Sun': sintesis de la historia de la lengua y literatura inglesas?," in Francisco Garcia Tortosa et al., eds., *James Joyce*, 193–220.

Fiddian, Robin. "A Case of Literary Infection: *Palinuro de México* and *Ulysses*." *Compar Lit Stud* 19 (1982), 220–233.

Fiddian, Robin William. "*Palinuro de México* and *Ulysses*." *Estudos Anglo-Americanos* 5–6 (1981–82), 50–56.

Firestone, Evan R. "James Joyce and the First Generation," 209–210.

Fischer-Seidel, Therese. "Charakter als Mimesis und Rhetorik: Bewusstseinsdarstellung in Joyces *Ulysses*," in Fischer-Seidel, ed., *James Joyces "Ulysses*," 304–343.

Fludernik, Monika. "*Ulysses* and Joyce's Change of Artistic Aims: External and Internal Evidence." *James Joyce Q* 23 (1985), 173–186.

Fogel, Daniel Mark. "James Joyce, the Jews, and *Ulysses*." *James Joyce Q* 16 (1979), 498–501.

Fogel, Daniel Mark. "Symbol and Context in *Ulysses*: Joyce's 'Bowl of Bitter Waters' and Passover." *ELH* 46 (1979), 710–721.

Ford, Jane. "James Joyce and Those (K)nights," 244–245.

Foshay, Toby. "The Desire of Writing and the Writing of Desire in *Ulysses*." *Dalhousie R* 62 (1982), 87–103.

Foster, Thomas C. "Joyce's Grammar of Experience." *Eire-Ireland* 17:4 (1982), 19–40.

Friedman, Alan J. "*Ulysses* and Modern Science," in Bernard Benstock, ed., *The Seventh of Joyce*, 198–205.

Gabler, Hans Walter. "James Joyce as Author and Scribe: A Problem in Editing 'Eumaeus'," in *Nordic Rejoycings*, 98–105.

Gabler, Hans Walter. "Werkentstehung und Textsituation des *Ulysses*," in Therese Fischer-Seidel, ed., *James Joyces "Ulysses*," 58–79.

Galimberti, Ana. "Distancia y aproximacion al *Ulises* de Joyce." *Revista Universitaria de Letras* 1:2 (1979), 18–27.

Garvin, John. *James Joyce's Disunited Kingdom*, 11–118.

Georgi, Helen. "The Significance of the Date in *Ulysses*." *J of Mod Lit* 9 (1982), 311–312.

Gibson, Andrew. " 'Broken Down and Fast Breaking Up': Style, Technique and Vision in the 'Eumaeus' Episode in *Ulysses*." *Southern R* (Adelaide) 17 (1984), 256–268.

Gifford, Don. "A Memory at the Elbow: The Teaching of James Joyce's *Ulysses.*" *Bull of the Assoc of Depts of Engl* 76 (1983), 43–45.

Gilbert, Sandra M. "Costumes of the Mind: Transvestism as Metaphor in Modern Literature." *Crit Inquiry* 7 (1980), 394–399.

Gillespie, Michael Patrick. "Sources and the Independent Artist." *James Joyce Q* 20 (1983), 325–335.

Gillespie, Michael Patrick. "A Swift Reading of *Ulysses.*" *Texas Stud in Lit and Lang* 27 (1985), 178–188.

Gillespie, Michael Patrick. "Wagner in the Ormond Bar: Operatic Elements in the 'Sirens' Episode of *Ulysses.*" *Irish Renaissance Annual* 4 (1983), 157–172.

Glowka, Arthur W. "Stephen Dedalus, Poet of *Ulysses.*" *Gypsy Scholar* 7 (1980), 26–37.

Gluck, Barbara Reich. *Beckett and Joyce,* 50–51, 78–79, 117–118, 156–158.

Gomes, Aila de Oliveira. "Joyce's *Ulysses*: The Music of Chapter 11." *Estudos Anglo-Americanos* 5–6 (1981–82), 3–35.

Gonzalez, José Carnero. "Calipso y Penelope en *Ulysses,*" in Francisco Garcia Tortosa et al., eds., *James Joyce,* 167–173.

Gordon, John. *James Joyce's Metamorphoses,* 10–12, 29–155.

Gordon, John. "The Multiple Journeys of 'Oxen of the Sun'." *ELH* 46 (1979), 158–171.

Gordon, John. "The Orphic *Ulysses.*" *Texas Stud in Lit and Lang* 27 (1985), 191–206.

Gordon, John S. "The M'Intosh Mystery." *Mod Fiction Stud* 29 (1983), 671–679.

Gose, Elliott B., Jr. *The Transformation Process.*

Gottfried, Roy K. *The Art of Joyce's Syntax.*

Gottfried, Roy K. "A June Winter's Tale: Leopold, Leontes and Shakespeare Once Again." *James Joyce Q* 20 (1983), 411–426.

Gotzmann, Werner. "Wer war M'Intosh? James Joyce' Universalroman *Ulysses*: Eine Partitur." *Sprache im technischen Zeitalter* 86 (1983), 125–137.

Gould, Eric. "Condemned to Speak Excessively: Notes on the Novel, Mythic Form and James Joyce's *Ulysses.*" *SubStance* 22 (1979), 73–83.

Gould, Eric. *Mythical Intentions,* 139–143, 150–161, 253–257.

Green, Martin. *The English Novel,* 96–99.

Groden, Michael. *"Ulysses" in Progress,* 13–204.

Gulli Pugliatti, Paola. "Per un supplemento di studio della 'voce' in *Ulysses.*" *Spicilegio Moderno* 12 (1979), 107–120.

Hall, Vernon, and Burton A. Waisbren. "Syphilis as a Major Theme of James Joyce's *Ulysses.*" *Archives of Internal Medicine* 140 (1980), 963–965.

Halper, Nathan. *Studies in Joyce,* 101–107.

Hampson, R. G. "Joyce's Bed-Trick: A Note on Indeterminacy in *Ulysses.*" *James Joyce Q* 17 (1980), 445–448.

Hannay, John. "Coincidence and Analytic Reduction in the 'Ithaca' Episode in *Ulysses*." *J of Narrative Technique* 13 (1983), 141–152.

Hannay, John. "Coincidence and Converging Characters in *Ulysses*." *ELH* 51 (1984), 385–403.

Hannay, John. "Coincidence and Fables of Identity in 'Eumaeus'." *James Joyce Q* 21 (1984), 341–354.

Hannay, John. "The Throwaway of 'Wandering Rocks'." *James Joyce Q* 17 (1980), 434–439.

Harkness, Marguerite. "Gesture in 'Circe'," in J. Aubert and M. Jolas, eds., *Joyce & Paris*, 17–19.

Harrigan, Ursula A. "*Ulysses* as *Missal*: Another Structure in James Joyce's *Ulysses*." *Christianity & Lit* 33:4 (1984), 35–48.

Hatfield, Henry. "The Walpurgis Night: Themes and Variations." *J of European Stud* 13:1–2 (1983), 56–74.

Haule, James M. "Joyce's *Ulysses*." *Explicator* 41:3 (1983), 39–42.

Hawthorn, Jeremy. "*Ulysses*, Modernism, and Marxist Criticism," in W. J. McCormack and Alistair Stead, eds., *James Joyce*, 112–125.

Hayman, David. "James Joyce, Paratactitian," 160–173.

Heath, Stephen. "Joyce in Language," 131–137.

Henke, Suzette. "Gerty MacDowell: Joyce's Sentimental Heroine," in Suzette Henke and Elaine Unkeless, eds., *Women in Joyce*, 132–147.

Henke, Suzette A. "Gerty MacDowell: Nymph or Nun?," in J. Aubert and M. Jolas, eds., *Joyce & Paris*, 149–151.

Henke, Suzette A. "James Joyce and Joris-Karl Huysmans: What Was Leopold Bloom Doing with That Circus-Lady?" *Mod Brit Lit* 5 (1980), 68–72.

Henke, Suzette A. "James Joyce and Women," 123–126.

Herr, Cheryl. "Compound Words and Consubstantiality in *Ulysses*." *Lang and Style* 15 (1982), 33–45.

Herr, Cheryl. "Irish Censorship and 'Aeolus': The New Old Language of Ideology," in Francisco Garcia Tortosa et al., eds., *James Joyce*, 175–181.

Herr, Cheryl. "Irish Censorship and 'The Pleasure of the Text': The 'Aeolus' Episode of Joyce's *Ulysses*." *Irish Renaissance Annual* 3 (1982), 141–175.

Herr, Cheryl. "Nature and Culture in the 'Sirens' Episode in Joyce's *Ulysses*." *Essays in Lit* (Macomb) 11 (1984), 49–57.

Herr, Cheryl T. "Theosophy, Guilt, and 'That word known to all men' in Joyce's *Ulysses*." *James Joyce Q* 18 (1980), 45–54.

Herring, Phillip. "Joyce and Rimbaud: An Introductory Essay," in Suheil Badi Bushrui and Bernard Benstock, eds., *James Joyce*, 181–185.

Herring, Phillip F. "Toward an Historical Molly Bloom." *ELH* 45 (1978), 501–519.

Herring, Phillip F. "Zur Textgenese des *Ulysses*: Joyces Notizen und seine Arbeitsmethode," in Therese Fischer-Seidel, ed., *James Joyces "Ulysses,"* 80–104.

Heusel, Barbara Stevens. "Parallax as a Metaphor for the Structure of *Ulysses*." *Stud in the Novel* 15 (1983), 135–144.

Hodgart, Matthew. *James Joyce*, 69–129.

Holloway, Julia Bolton. "*Semus Sumus*: Joyce and Pilgrimage." *Thought* 56 (1981), 212–225.

Hylton, Sara. "Joyce's *Ulysses*." *Explicator* 39:4 (1981), 21–23.

Jackson, Selwyn. *The Poems of James Joyce*, 64–102.

Jameson, Fredric. "*Ulysses* in History," in W. J. McCormack and Alistair Stead, eds., *James Joyce*, 126–141.

Jimenez, Manuel Almagro. "*Ulysses* como epica: apuntes para una nueva perspectiva," in Francisco Garcia Tortosa et al., eds., *James Joyce*, 123–131.

Kawin, Bruce F. *The Mind of the Novel*, 17–19.

Kenner, Hugh. *Joyce's Voices*, 17–20, 35–38, 41–45, 91–97, 102–104.

Kenner, Hugh. "Who's He When He's At Home?," in Heyward Ehrlich, ed., *Light Rays*, 58–69.

Kestner, Joseph A. *The Spatiality*, 139–142.

Kiasaschwili, Niko. "Die 'Nestor'-Episode als Paradigma des *Ulysses*," in Helmut Brandt and Nodar Kakabadse, eds., *Erzählte Welt*, 320–336.

Kiberd, Declan. "The Vulgarity of Heroics: Joyce's *Ulysses*," in Suheil Badi Bushrui and Bernard Benstock, eds., *James Joyce*, 65–80.

Kimball, Jean. "Family Romance and Hero Myth: A Psychoanalytic Context for the Paternity Theme in *Ulysses*." *James Joyce Q* 20 (1983), 161–170.

Kimball, Jean. "Freud, Leonardo, and Joyce," 57–60, 63–69.

Kimball, Jean. "A Jungian Scenario for *Ulysses*." *Compar Lit Stud* 19 (1982), 195–205.

Kiremidjian, David. *A Study*, 115–179.

Klieneberger, H. R. *The Novel*, 205–206.

Knuth, A. M. L. *The Wink of the Word*, 29–39, 46–57, 64–70, 89–101, 121–150.

Korg, Jacob. *Language*, 99–109.

Kreutzer, Eberhard. "Das Wortspiel im *Ulysses*," in Therese Fischer-Seidel, ed., *James Joyces "Ulysses,"* 160–188.

Kunkel, Francis L. "Joyce's *Ulysses*." *Explicator* 43:3 (1985), 28.

Lawrence, Karen R. " 'Aeolus': Interruption and Inventory." *James Joyce Q* 17 (1980), 389–405.

Lawrence, Karen R. "Style and Narrative in the 'Ithaca' Chapter of Joyce's *Ulysses*." *ELH* 47 (1980), 559–572.

Le Brocquy, Louis. "Painting and Awareness." *Etudes Irlandaises* 4 (1979), 149–161.

Leech, Geoffrey N., and Michael H. Short. *Style in Fiction*, 187–189, 286–287, 301–302.

Lees, Heath. "The Introduction to 'Sirens' and the *Fuga per Canonem*." *James Joyce Q* 22 (1984), 39–52.

Levine, Jennifer. "Reading *Ulysses*," in Eleanor Cook et al., eds., *Centre and Labyrinth*, 264–283.

Levitt, Morton P. "The Humanity of Bloom, The Jewishness of Joyce," in Bernard Benstock, ed., *The Seventh of Joyce*, 225–228.

Levitt, Morton P. "Legitimate and False Correspondences," in Bernard Benstock, ed., *The Seventh of Joyce*, 150–152.

Link, Viktor. "Das 'Circe'-Kapitel: Die Elemente des Aufbaus und ihre Funktion," in Therese Fischer-Seidel, ed., *James Joyces "Ulysses,"* 228–254.

Litz, A. Walton. "The Author in *Ulysses*: The Zurich Chapters," in Francisco Garcia Tortosa et al., eds., *James Joyce*, 113–121.

Lopez-Santos, Antonio. "Funcion de las acotaciones en *Exiles* y en 'Circe'," in Francisco Garcia Tortosa et al., eds., *James Joyce*, 98–102.

Loss, Archie. "Painting and *Ulysses*," in J. Aubert and M. Jolas, eds., *Joyce & Paris*, 99–100.

Loss, Archie. "Everyman Blooms as Everybody," in J. Aubert and M. Jolas, eds., *Joyce & Paris*, 128–130.

Loss, Archie K. "Joyce's Use of Collage in 'Aeolus'." *J of Mod Lit* 9 (1982), 175–182.

Loux, Ann Kimble. " 'Am I father? If I were?': A Trinitarian Analysis of the Growth of Stephen Dedalus in *Ulysses*." *James Joyce Q* 22 (1985), 281–295.

Lyman, Stephany. "Revision and Intention in Joyce's 'Penelope'." *James Joyce Q* 20 (1983), 193–199.

McBride, Margaret. "Watchwords in *Ulysses*: The Stylistics of Suppression." *J of Engl and Germanic Philology* 77 (1978), 356–366.

MacCabe, Colin. *James Joyce*, 79–132, 139–141.

MacCabe, Colin. "The Voice of Esau: Stephen in the Library," in MacCabe, ed., *James Joyce*, 111–126.

McCarthy, Patrick A. "The Jeweleyed Harlots," 100–106.

McCarthy, Patrick A. "Joyce's Unreliable Catechist: Mathematics and the Narration of 'Ithaca'." *ELH* 51 (1984), 605–617.

McCarthy, Patrick A. "Non-Dramatic Illusion in 'Circe'," in J. Aubert and M. Jolas, eds., *Joyce & Paris*, 23–26.

McGann, Jerome J. "*Ulysses* as a Postmodern Text: The Gabler Edition." *Criticism* 27 (1985), 283–303.

McGrath, F. C. "*Ulysses* and the Pragmatic Semiotics of Modernism." *Compar Lit Stud* 19 (1982), 170–174.

McMahon, Dorothy E. "Joyce and Menippus." *Classical and Mod Lit* 4 (1983), 27–34.

McMichael, James. "Real, Schlemiel." *Crit Inquiry* 11 (1985), 474–485.

Madtes, Richard E. *The 'Ithaca' Chapter*, 65–107.

Manganiello, Dominic. *Joyce's Politics*, 98–114, 166–173.

Mantell, Deborah Byrd. "Leopold Bloom: Joyce's Loveless Irishman, or Everlasting Caricature of the Serious World?" *Irish Renaissance Annual* 2 (1981), 115–136.

Marcus, Hedda. "The Theme of Childbirth in *Ulysses*, as Seen through Stephen Dedalus, Leopold Bloom, and Molly Bloom." *Nassau R* 4:3 (1982), 16–21.

Mayer, Hans. *Outsiders*, 350–355.

Melnik, Daniel C. "Dissonant *Ulysses*: A Study of How To Read Joyce." *Twentieth Century Lit* 26 (1980), 45–62.

Mercier, Vivien. "John Eglinton as Socrates: A Study of 'Scylla and Charybdis'," in Suheil Badi Bushrui and Bernard Benstock, eds., *James Joyce*, 65–80.

Michels, James. "The Role of Language in Consciousness: A Structuralist Look at 'Proteus' in *Ulysses*." *Lang and Style* 15 (1982), 23–32.

Michels, James. " 'Scylla and Charybdis': Revenge in James Joyce's *Ulysses*." *James Joyce Q* 20 (1983), 175–190.

Mingorance, Leocadio Martin. "Motivacion ludica y creacion lexica en *Ulysses*: apuntes para un fragmento de una gramatica textual," in Francisco Garcia Tortosa et al., eds., *James Joyce*, 133–143.

Mobley, Jonnie P. "Joyce's *Ulysses*." *Explicator* 37:2 (1979), 31–32.

Morrow, Patrick D. "Joyce as Vaudeville: The Catholic Force of Nighttown," in his *Tradition*, 156–175.

Newman, Robert D. "Joyce's *Ulysses*." *Explicator* 42:4 (1984), 33–34.

Newman, Robert D. "The Shadow of Stephen Dedalus." *J of Evolutionary Psych* 2:3–4 (1981), 112–124.

Oded, Brenda. "The Maternal Ghost in Joyce." *Mod Lang Stud* 15:4 (1985), 40–46.

Orr, Leonard. "Joyce's *Ulysses*." *Explicator* 40:1 (1981), 42.

O'Shea, Michael J. "Catholic Liturgy in Joyce's *Ulysses*." *James Joyce Q* 21 (1984), 123–134.

Overstreet, David. "Oxymoronic Language and Logic," 47–53.

Palumbo, Donald. "Alone, Isolated, Betrayed, Banished," 69–81.

Palumbo, Donald. "Death and Rebirth, Sexuality, and Fantasy in Homer and Joyce." *Colby Lib Q* 20 (1984), 90–99.

Panitz, Esther L. *The Alien*, 129–142.

Parrinder, Patrick. *James Joyce*, 1–13, 114–196.

Patey, Caroline. "Note per una lettura della Telemachia: Capitoli I, II, III dell'*Ulysses* di James Joyce." *Acme* 35:1 (1982), 97–126.

Pearce, Richard. "From Joyce to Beckett: The Tale That Wags the Telling," in Bernard Benstock, ed., *The Seventh of Joyce*, 44–46.

Peck, John. "Hardy and Joyce: A Basis for Comparison." *Ariel* 12:2 (1981), 71–85.

Pérez Gallego, Candido. "*Ulises* y los mapas del subconsciente." *Cuadernos Hispanoamericanos* 384 (1982), 536–548.

Perlis, Alan David. "The Newtonian Nightmare of *Ulysses*," in Bernard Benstock, ed., *The Seventh of Joyce*, 191–196.

Pitavy, François L. "Joyce's and Faulkner's 'Twining Stresses': A Textual Comparison," in Bernard Benstock, ed., *The Seventh of Joyce*, 90–98.

Power, Mary. "The Discovery of *Ruby*." *James Joyce Q* 18 (1981), 115–121.

Pringle, M. B., and D. Ross, Jr. "Dialogue and Narration in Joyce's *Ulysses*," in Serge Lusignan and John S. North, eds., *Computing*, 73–84.

Pringle, Mary Beth. "Funfersum: Dialogue as Metafictional Technique in the Cyclops Episode of *Ulysses*." *James Joyce Q* 18 (1981), 397–416.

Rader, Ralph W. "The Logic of *Ulysses*; or, Why Molly Had to Live in Gibraltar." *Crit Inquiry* 10 (1984), 567–577.

Raleigh, John Henry. *The Chronicle of Leopold*, 11–272.

Raleigh, John Henry. "On the Way Home to Ithaca: The Functions of the 'Eumaeus' Section in *Ulysses*." *Irish Renaissance Annual* 2 (1981), 13–110.

Raleigh, John Henry. "*Ulysses* and Scott's *Ivanhoe*." *Stud in Romanticism* 22 (1983), 569–586.

Reizbaum, Marilyn. "The Jewish Connection, Cont'd," in Bernard Benstock, ed., *The Seventh of Joyce*, 229–236.

Renan, Yael. "Joyce's *Ulysses*." *Explicator* 42:3 (1984), 40–43.

Restuccia, Frances L. "Molly in Furs," 109–116.

Restuccia, Frances L. "Not Foreknowledge, Simply Knowledge: Secular Typology in *Ulysses*." *James Joyce Q* 20 (1983), 429–441.

Restuccia, Frances L. "Transubstantiating *Ulysses*." *James Joyce Q* 21 (1984), 329–339.

Reynolds, Mary T. *Joyce and Dante*, 35–44, 64–82, 92–106, 143–145, 180–183, 186–191.

Richards, Thomas Karr. "Gerty MacDowell and the Irish Common Reader." *ELH* 52 (1985), 755–774.

Richards, Thomas Karr. "Provisional Fixity in James Joyce's 'Proteus'." *James Joyce Q* 20 (1983), 385–398.

Rimo, Patricia A. " 'Proteus': From Thoughts to Things." *Stud in the Novel* 17 (1985), 296–302.

Riquelme, J. P. "Enjoying Invisibility: The Myth of Joyce's Impersonal Narrator," in Bernard Benstock, ed., *The Seventh of Joyce*, 22–24.

Rizzo, Patrick V. "Joyce's *Ulysses*." *Explicator* 38:1 (1979), 27–28.

Saldivar, Ramon. "Bloom's Metaphors and the Language of Flowers." *James Joyce Q* 20 (1983), 399–408.

Sandulesco, C. Georges. "The Polyvalency of Joyce's Characters." *Etudes Irlandaises* 9 (1984), 125–143.

Sawyer, Thomas. "Stephen Dedalus' Word." *James Joyce Q* 20 (1983), 201–207.

Schenker, Daniel. "Stalking the Invisible Hero," 176–182.

Schiffer, Paul S. " 'Homing, Upstream': Fictional Closure and the End of *Ulysses*." *James Joyce Q* 16 (1979), 283–298.

Schmuhl, Norbert. *Perspektivität und Aperspektivität*.

Schneider, Ulrich. "Alttestamentarische Anspielungen im *Ulysses*," in Therese Fischer-Seidel, ed., *James Joyces "Ulysses,"* 189–212.

Schöneich, Christoph. *Epos und Roman*, 9–204.

Schork, R. J. "Kennst Du das Haus Citrons, Bloom?" *James Joyce Q* 17 (1980), 407–418.

Schotz, Myra Glazer. "Parallax in *Ulysses*." *Dalhousie R* 59 (1979), 487–498.

Schutte, William M. "An Index of Recurrent Elements in *Ulysses*." *James Joyce Q* 16 (1979), 311–333, 455–472; 17 (1979), 67–80.

Schwab, Gabriele. "Mollyloquy," in Bernard Benstock, ed., *The Seventh of Joyce*, 81–85.

Scott, Bonnie Kime. *Joyce and Feminism*, 23–26, 93–96, 118–124, 156–183.

Senn, Fritz. "Bloom Among the Orators: The Why and the Wherefore and All the Codology." *Irish Renaissance Annual* 1 (1980), 168–189.

Senn, Fritz. "Dynamics of Corrective Unrest," in Francisco Garcia Tortosa et al., eds., *James Joyce*, 231–242.

Senn, Fritz. "Foreign Readings," 89–100.

Senn, Fritz. *Joyce's Dislocutions*, 121–212.

Senn, Fritz. "Odysseische Metamorphosen," in Therese Fischer-Seidel, ed., *James Joyces "Ulysses,"* 26–57.

Senn, Fritz. "Remodeling Homer," in Heyward Ehrlich, ed., *Light Rays*, 71–90.

Senn, Fritz. "Righting *Ulysses*," in Colin MacCabe, ed., *James Joyce*, 3–27.

Senn, Fritz. "*Scareotypes*: On Some Trenchant Renditions in *Ulysses*." *Mod Brit Lit* 5 (1980), 22–28.

Senn, Fritz. " 'Stately, plump', for example," 348–353.

Shanahan, Dennis M. "The Way of the Cross in *Ulysses*." *James Joyce Q* 20 (1983), 275–290.

Sicker, Philip. "Shades of Descartes: An Approach to Stephen's Dream in *Ulysses*." *James Joyce Q* 22 (1984), 7–22.

Sieburth, Stephanie. "James Joyce and Leopoldo Alas: Patterns of Influence." *Revista Canadiense de Estudios Hispanicos* 7 (1983), 401–406.

Singh, Amritjit. "Leopold Bloom as Son." *Liter Criterion* 16:2 (1981), 31–42.

Skene, Arlene E. "The Poetics of Science: The Bloomsday Myth." *Canadian J of Irish Stud* 7:2 (1981), 56–75.

Smith, Mack. "The Structural Rhythm in *Ulysses*: Dominant to Love to Return." *Twentieth Century Lit* 30 (1984), 404–418.

Sörensen, Dolf. *James Joyce's Aesthetic Theory*, 54–66.

Spector, Judith. "James Joyce's *Ulysses*: The Complete Masculine Aesthetic." *Coll Lang Assoc J* 28 (1985), 299–313.

Spilka, Mark. "Leopold Bloom as Jewish Pickwick: A Neo-Dickensian Perspective." *Novel* 13 (1979), 121–146.

Spivey, Ted R. *The Journey beyond Tragedy*, 110–113, 117–119.

Splitter, Randolph. "Watery Words," 201–202.

Staley, Thomas F. "James Joyce and One of His Ghosts: Edouard Dujardin." *Renascence* 35:2 (1983), 85–95.

Stead, Alistair. "Reflections on Eumaeus: Ways of Error and Glory in *Ulysses*," in W. J. McCormack and Alistair Stead, eds., *James Joyce*, 142–165.

Steinberg, Erwin R. "James Joyce and the Critics Notwithstanding, Leopold Bloom Is Not Jewish." *J of Mod Lit* 9 (1981–82), 27–49.

Steinberg, Erwin R. "Leopold Bloom and the Nineteenth-Century Fictional Stereotype of the Jew." *Cithara* 22:2 (1983), 48–61.

Steinberg, Erwin R. "Telemachus, Stephen, and the Paradigm of the Initiation Rite." *James Joyce Q* 19 (1982), 289–301.

Stevens, Kenneth R. "*Ulysses* on Trial." *Lib Chron of the Univ of Texas* 20–21 (1982), 90–105.

Stewart, James. "Three Anglo-Irish Notes: 3, a Passage in *Ulysses*," in Graham D. Caie et al., eds., *Occasional Papers*, 177–179.

Storey, Robert. "The Argument of *Ulysses*, Reconsidered." *Mod Lang Q* 40 (1979), 175–195.

Sultan, Stanley. "*Ulysses*," 11–75.

Swartzlanger, Susan. "Joyce's *Ulysses*." *Explicator* 43:3 (1985), 29–31.

Takashi, Suzuki. "The Unity of 'Circe'." *Stud in Engl Lit* (Tokyo) 58 (1981), 23–32.

Taylor, Anne Robinson. *Male Novelists*, 189–216.

Thomas, Brook. "Formal Re-creation: Re-reading and Re-joycing the Re-rightings of *Ulysses*." *Genre* 13 (1980), 337–353. [Also in Bernard Benstock, ed., *The Seventh of Joyce*, 5–9.]

Thomas, Brook. *James Joyce's "Ulysses*," 1–182.

Thomsen, Christian W. *Menschenfresser*, 32–33.

Thorn, Arline R. "A Mighty Maze: Word Games in *Ulysses*." *Perspectives on Contemp Lit* 6 (1980), 1–10.

Tolomeo, Diane. "Leopold Bloom and the Law of Falling Bodies: Joyce's Use of the Fall in *Ulysses*." *Engl Stud in Canada* 5 (1979), 301–310.

Torrance, Robert M. *The Comic Hero*, 240–254.

Tortosa, Francisco Garcia. "Interpretacion de las acotaciones de Shakespeare en," in Francisco Garcia Tortosa et al., eds., *James Joyce*, 145–151.

Tucker, Lindsey. *Stephen and Bloom*, 11–155.

Tymoczko, Maria. "Symbolic Structures in *Ulysses* from Early Irish Literature." *James Joyce Q* 21 (1984), 215–228.

Unkeless, Elaine. "The Conventional Molly Bloom," in Suzette Henke and Elaine Unkeless, eds., *Women in Joyce*, 150–165.

Usandizaga Sainz, Aranzazu. "James Joyce," 159–165.

Van Caspel, P. P. J. "Father and Son in the Lotus-Eaters Episode of Joyce's *Ulysses*." *Engl Stud* 60 (1979), 593–602.

Van Caspel, Paul. *Bloomers on the Liffy*.

Venegas Lagüéns, Maria Luisa. "Father Conmee, A Criticism of the Clergy: A Contextual Approach," in Francisco Garcia Tortosa et al., eds., *James Joyce*, 183–188.

Vesterman, William. "Poldy's Potence Preserved." *Essays in Lit* (Macomb) 10 (1983), 111–118.

Voelker, Joseph C. "Molly Bloom and the Rhetorical Tradition." *Compar Lit Stud* 16 (1979), 146–164.

Vors, Marie-Danièle. " 'Ah si ce thé aux fesses teint': La Nourriture dans *Ulysses*," in Patrick Rafroidi and Pierre Joannon, eds., *James Joyce*, 85–97.

Walker, Nancy. "Stephen and Quentin," in Bernard Benstock, ed., *The Seventh of Joyce*, 109–113.

Walkley, R. Barrie. "The Bloom of Motherhood: Couvade as Structural Device in *Ulysses*." *James Joyce Q* 18 (1980), 55–67.

Warner, Alan. *A Guide*, 116–118.

Waters, Maureen. *The Comic Irishman*, 97–109.

Watson, G. J. *Irish Identity*, 198–244.

Watson, George J. " 'Words Alone are Certain Good'?," 18–25.

Weinstein, Norman. "The 'Ithaca' Chapter of *Ulysses*: Notes on Science, Number and Poetic Structure." *Southern R* (Adelaide) 12 (1979), 3–22.

Weinstein, Philip M. *The Semantics of Desire*, 252–287.

Wenke, John. "Charity: The Measure of Morality in 'Wandering Rocks'." *Eire-Ireland* 15:1 (1980), 100–113.

White, David A. *The Grand Continuum*, 103–129.

White, Michacl C. " 'Cyclops': Beyond Parody," in Francisco Garcia Tortosa et al., eds., *James Joyce*, 189–192.

Witkowsky, Paul. "Poldy's Moly: Bloom's Reassertion of Manhood in 'Circe'," in Francisco Garcia Tortosa et al., eds., *James Joyce*, 223–229.

Winters, Kirk. "Joyce's *Ulysses* as Poem: Rhythm, Rhyme, and Color in 'Wandering Rocks'." *Emporia State Res Stud* 31:3 (1983), 5–44.

Woolmer, J. Howard. "*Ulysses* at Auction with a Preliminary Census." *James Joyce Q* 17 (1980), 141–148.

Wright, David G. *Characters of Joyce*, 66–103.

Wright, David G. "Joyce's *Ulysses*." *Explicator* 42:3 (1984), 39–40.

Zimmerman, Michael. "Leopold Paula Bloom: The New Womanly Man." *Lit and Psych* 29 (1979), 176–184.

ANNA KAVAN

Ice, 1967

Byrne, Janet. "Moving toward Entropy: Anna Kavan's Science Fiction Mentality." *Extrapolation* 23:1 (1982), 5–11.

JULIA KAVANAGH

Rachel Gray, 1856
  Kestner, Joseph. *Protest and Reform*, 187–192.

PATRICK KAVANAGH

The Green Fool, 1938
  Karrer, Wolfgang. "Patrick Kavanagh: Dichter und literarischer
  Markt," in J. Kornelius et al., eds., *Einführung*, 199–200.
  Waters, Maureen. *The Comic Irishman*, 138–141.

Tarry Flynn, 1948
  Karrer, Wolfgang. "Patrick Kavanagh," 203–204.
  Kavanagh, Peter. *Sacred Keeper*, 174–178, 241–242.
  O'Rourke, Brian. *The Conscience of the Race*, 14–15.
  Warner, Alan. *A Guide*, 92–94.
  Waters, Maureen. *The Comic Irishman*, 138–148.

JAMES KENNAWAY

Silence, 1972
  Bold, Alan. *Modern Scottish Literature*, 254–256.

MARGARET KENNEDY

Together and Apart, 1936
  Beauman, Nicola. *A Very Great Profession*, 213–215.

CHARLES KICKHAM

Knocknagow, 1879
  Cronin, John. *The Anglo-Irish Novel*, 103–112.

BENEDICT KIELY

Call for a Miracle, 1950
  O'Rourke, Brian. *The Conscience of the Race*, 44–45.

CHARLES KINGSLEY

Alton Locke, 1850
  Bergmann, Helena. *Between Obedience and Freedom*, 47–48, 62–65,
  152–155.
  Cross, Nigel. *The Common Writer*, 152–154.

Dawson, Carl. *Victorian Noon*, 194–204.
Gallagher, Catherine. *The Industrial Reformation*, 89–110.
Kestner, Joseph. *Protest and Reform*, 139–141.
Lamarca Margalef, Jordi. *Ciencia y literatura*, 145–147.
Landow, George P. *Victorian Types*, 208–210.
Muller, C. H. "The Standard Victorian Novel of Charles Kingsley and Its Relevance Today." *Communique* (Pietersburg) 5:2 (1980), 37–46.
Rataboul, Louis J. *Le pasteur anglican*, 252–260.
Tarantelli, Carole Beebe. *Ritratto di ignoto*, 119–135.
Vance, Norman. "Heroic Myth and Women in Victorian Literature." *Yearbook of Engl Stud* 12 (1982), 184–185.
Vance, Norman. *The Sinews of the Spirit*, 81–84.

Hereward the Wake, 1866

Haley, Bruce. *The Healthy Body*, 216–220.
Vance, Norman. "Heroic Myth and Women," 183–184.
Vance, Norman. *The Sinews of the Spirit*, 109–111.
Wijesinha, Rajiva. *The Androgynous Trollope*, 140–141, 252–254.
Young, Michael. "History as Myth: Charles Kingsley's *Hereward the Wake*." *Stud in the Novel* 17 (1985), 174–188.

Hypatia, 1853

Dorman, Susann. "*Hypatia* and *Callista*: The Initial Skirmish between Kingsley and Newman." *Nineteenth-Century Fiction* 34 (1979), 175–193.
Vance, Norman. "Heroic Myth and Women," 180–182.
Wijesinha, Rajiva. *The Androgynous Trollope*, 143–145, 159–160.

Two Years Ago, 1857

Haley, Bruce. *The Healthy Body*, 183–188.
Lamarca Margalef, Jordi. *Ciencia y literatura*, 147–149.
Muller, C. H. "Poetics and Providence in Kingsley's *Two Years Ago*." *Unisa Engl Stud* 17:2 (1979), 29–39.
Rataboul, Louis J. *Le pasteur anglican*, 264–267.
Vance, Norman. *The Sinews of the Spirit*, 90–95.
Wijesinha, Rajiva. *The Androgynous Trollope*, 145–146, 248–252.

The Water-Babies, 1863

Babbitt, Natalie. "Saying What You Think." *Q J of the Lib of Congress* 39 (1982), 80–89.
Cunningham, Valentine. "Soiled Fairy: *The Water-Babies* in its Time." *Essays in Criticism* 35 (1985), 121–145.
Ison, Mary M. "Things Nobody Ever Heard Of: Jessie Wilcox Smith Draws the Water-Babies." *Q J of the Lib of Congress* 39 (1982), 90–101.
Jackson, Rosemary. *Fantasy*, 151–153.
Prickett, Stephen. *Victorian Fantasy*, 150–173.
Vance, Norman. *The Sinews of the Spirit*, 95–98.

Westward Ho!, 1855

Vance, Norman. *The Sinews of the Spirit*, 86–90.

Yeast, 1848

Kestner, Joseph. *Protest and Reform*, 135–139.
Rataboul, Louis J. *Le pasteur anglican*, 186–187, 252–260, 330–333.
Watt, George. *The Fallen Woman*, 183–185.
Wijesinha, Rajiva. *The Androgynous Trollope*, 142–143.

RUDYARD KIPLING

Captains Courageous, 1897

Harrison, James. *Rudyard Kipling*, 66–67.
Watson, Fiona. "*Captains Courageous* and the Hispanic World."
Kipling J 57:227 (1983), 10–20.

Kim, 1901

Alam, Qamar. "Form and Pattern of Kipling's *Kim*." *Osmania J of Engl Stud* 15 (1979), 11–14.
Batchelor, John. *The Edwardian Novelists*, 12–13.
Blackburn, William. "Internationalism and Empire: *Kim* and the Art of Rudyard Kipling," in Priscilla A. Ord, ed., *Proceedings*, 78–85.
Feeley, Margaret Peller. "The *Kim* that Nobody Reads." *Stud in the Novel* 13 (1981), 266–281.
Gorchov, Robert D. " 'The Little Friend of All the World': A Note on Rudyard Kipling's *Kim*." *Osmania J of Engl Stud* 15 (1979), 1–10.
Gournay, Jean-François. "Esquisse d'une lecture anthropologique de *Kim*." *Etudes Anglaises* 35 (1982), 385–395.
Harrison, James. *Rudyard Kipling*, 47–57.
McClure, John. "Problematic Presence: The Colonial Other in Kipling and Conrad," in David Dabydeen, ed., *The Black Presence*, 165–166.
McClure, John A. *Kipling & Conrad*, 70–81.
Rabkin, David. "Ways of Looking: Origins of the Novel in South Africa." *J of Commonwealth Lit* 13:1 (1978), 35–37.
Scheerer, Constance. "The Lost Paradise of Rudyard Kipling." *Dalhousie R* 61 (1981), 27–36.
Stewart, D. H. "Kipling's *Kim*: Rehearsals and Echoes." *J of Narrative Technique* 15 (1985), 52–65.
Stewart, David H. "Aspects of Language in *Kim*." *Kipling J* 57:226 (1983), 25–39.
Stewart, David H. "Orality in Kipling's *Kim*." *J of Narrative Technique* 13 (1983), 47–55.
Stewart, David H. "Structure in Kipling's *Kim*." *Victorian Newsl* 58 (1980), 24–26.

The Light That Failed, 1890

Coustillas, Pierre. "*The Light that Failed*; or, Artistic Bohemia as Self-Revelation." *Engl Lit in Transition* 29 (1986), 127–138.

Green, Martin. *The English Novel*, 26–32.
Harrison, James. *Rudyard Kipling*, 76–82.

The Man Who Would Be King, 1888

Beckerman, Jim. "On Adapting 'The Most Audacious Thing in Fiction'," in Michael Klein and Gillian Parker, eds., *The English Novel*, 180–186.
Draudt, Manfred. "Reality or Delusion? Narrative Technique and Meaning in Kipling's *The Man Who Would Be King*." *Engl Stud* 65 (1984), 316–326.

Stalky & Co., 1899

Musgrave, P. W. *From Brown to Bunter*, 168–181.

FRANCIS KIRKMAN

The Counterfeit Lady Unveiled, 1673

Pache, Walter. *Profit and Delight*, 60–66.

ARTHUR KOESTLER

The Age of Longing, 1951

Levene, Mark. *Arthur Koestler*, 113–130.

Arrival and Departure, 1943

Levene, Mark. *Arthur Koestler*, 78–95.

The Call-Girls, 1971

Lamarca Margalef, Jordi. *Ciencia y literatura*, 77–78, 122–124.
Levene, Mark. *Arthur Koestler*, 133–143.

Darkness at Noon, 1940

Drew, Philip. *The Meaning of Freedom*, 371–374.
Ingle, Stephen. *Socialist Thought*, 102–105.
Levene, Mark. *Arthur Koestler*, 55–77.
Wilding, Michael. *Political Fictions*, 192–215.

The Gladiators, 1939

Levene, Mark. *Arthur Koestler*, 33–54.

Thieves in the Night, 1946

Levene, Mark. *Arthur Koestler*, 96–112.

LADY CAROLINE LAMB

Glenarvon, 1816

Clubbe, John. "*Glenarvon* Revised—and Revisited." *Wordsworth Circle* 10 (1979), 205–215.
Garver, Joseph. "Gothic Ireland: Lady Caroline Lamb's *Glenarvon*." *Irish Univ R* 10 (1980), 213–227.

Kelly, Gary. "Amelie Opie, Lady Caroline Lamb, and Maria Edge-
worth: Official and Unofficial Ideology." *Ariel* 12:4 (1981), 12–18.
Kelsall, Malcolm. "The Byronic Hero and Revolution in Ireland: The
Politics of *Glenarvon*." *Byron J* 9 (1981), 4–19.

EDWARD WILSON LANDOR

Lofoden, 1849

Christensen, Inger. "Ground Untrodden: Images of Norway in Nineteenth-Century English Fiction." *Edda*, 1985, 353–354.

PHILIP LARKIN

A Girl in Winter, 1947

Domnarski, William. "Wishing for More: Philip Larkin's Novels."
Critique (Atlanta) 22:1 (1980), 5–6, 12–19.

Jill, 1946

Coates, Paul. *The Realist Fantasy*, 186–188.
Domnarski, William. "Wishing for More," 6–12.

MARY LAVIN

The House in Clewe Street, 1945

Koenig, Marianne. "Mary Lavin: The Novels and the Stories." *Irish
Univ R* 9 (1979), 244–248.
Peterson, Richard F. *Mary Lavin*, 46–63.

Mary O'Grady, 1950

Koenig, Marianne. "Mary Lavin," 248–250.
Peterson, Richard F. *Mary Lavin*, 63–75.

D. H. LAWRENCE

Aaron's Rod, 1922

Aronson, Alex. *Music and the Novel*, 96–98.
Baker, Paul G. *A Reassessment*, 1–148.
Becker, George J. *D. H. Lawrence*, 101–104.
Clark, L. D. *The Minoan Distance*, 224–231.
Kiely, Robert. "Accident and Purpose: 'Bad Form' in Lawrence's
Fiction," in Peter Balbert and Phillip L. Marcus, eds., *D. H. Law-
rence*, 95–96.
Meyers, Jeffrey. *D. H. Lawrence*, 112–116.
Niven, Alastair. *D. H. Lawrence*, 61–64.
Perloff, Marjorie. "Lawrence's Lyric Theater: *Birds, Beasts and
Flowers*," in Peter Balbert and Phillip L. Marcus, eds., *D. H.
Lawrence*, 108–110, 127–128.

Prasad, Madhusudan. *D. H. Lawrence*, 85–94.
Ruderman, Judith. *D. H. Lawrence*, 90–103.
Ruderman, Judith. "The 'Trilogy' That Never Was: *The Rainbow*, *Women in Love*, and *Aaron's Rod.*" *Papers of the Bibliographical Soc of America* 74 (1980), 76–80.
Scheckner, Peter. *Class, Politics*, 92–111.
Schneider, Daniel J. *D. H. Lawrence*, 193–210.
Simpson, Hilary. *D. H. Lawrence and Feminism*, 105–118.
Tristram, Philippa. "Eros and Death (Lawrence, Freud and Women)," in Anne Smith, ed., *Lawrence*, 151–155.
Worthen, John. *D. H. Lawrence*, 118–135.

The Boy in the Bush, 1924

Burgess, Anthony. *Flame Into Being*, 130–134.
Rossman, Charles. "*The Boy in the Bush* in the Lawrence Canon," in Robert B. Partlow, Jr., and Harry T. Moore, eds., *D. H. Lawrence*, 185–194.

John Thomas and Lady Jane, 1972

Britton, Derek. "Henry Moat, Lady Ida Sitwell, and *John Thomas and Lady Jane.*" *D. H. Lawrence R* 15 (1982), 69–75.
Clark, L. D. *The Minoan Distance*, 365–368.
Sagar, Keith. *D. H. Lawrence*, 293–295.
Scheckner, Peter. *Class, Politics*, 151–159, 163–165.
Weinstein, Philip M. *The Semantics of Desire*, 233–240.

Kangaroo, 1923

Becker, George J. *D. H. Lawrence*, 104–107.
Burgess, Anthony. *Flame Into Being*, 136–146.
Clark, L. D. *The Minoan Distance*, 258–265.
Daalder, Joost. "Dogs and Foxes in D. H. Lawrence and W. H. Auden." *Zeitschrift für Anglistik und Amerikanistik* 32 (1984), 330–332.
Darroch, Robert. *D. H. Lawrence*, 22–26, 46–57, 61–71, 75–79, 84–98.
Dervin, Daniel. *A 'Strange Sapience'*, 57–60.
Humma, John B. "Of Bits, Beasts, and Bush: The Interior Wilderness in D. H. Lawrence's *Kangaroo.*" *South Atlantic R* 51:1 (1986), 83–99.
Meyers, Jeffrey. *D. H. Lawrence*, 116–123.
Niven, Alastair. *D. H. Lawrence*, 64–68.
Peek, Andrew. "Tim Burstall's *Kangaroo.*" *Westerly* 25:4 (1980), 39–42.
Pollak, Paulina S. "Anti-Semitism in the Works of D. H. Lawrence: Search for and Rejection of the Father." *Lit and Psych* 32:1 (1986), 25–28.
Prasad, Madhusudan. *D. H. Lawrence*, 94–112.
Ruderman, Judith. *D. H. Lawrence*, 104–114.
Scheckner, Peter. *Class, Politics*, 113–127, 134–136.
Schneider, Daniel J. *D. H. Lawrence*, 90–94, 100–102, 209–223.

Schneider, Daniel J. "Psychology and Art in Lawrence's *Kangaroo*." *D. H. Lawrence R* 14 (1981), 156–171.

Spivey, Ted R. *The Journey beyond Tragedy*, 79–81.

Widmer, Kingsley. "Lawrence and the Nietzschean Matrix," in Jeffrey Meyers, ed., *D. H. Lawrence*, 123–126.

Wilding, Michael. *Political Fictions*, 150–191.

Worthen, John. *D. H. Lawrence*, 136–151.

Lady Chatterley's Lover, 1928

Arellano Salgado, Olga. "El sentido del amor en *El amante de Lady Chatterley*." *Nueva Revista del Pacifico* 9 (1978), 1–4.

Balbert, Peter H. "The Loving of Lady Chatterley: D. H. Lawrence and the Phallic Imagination," in Robert B. Partlow, Jr., and Harry T. Moore, eds., *D. H. Lawrence*, 143–158.

Becker, George J. *D. H. Lawrence*, 79–91.

Bevan, D. G. "The Sensual and the Cerebral: The Mating of D. H. Lawrence and André Malraux." *Canadian R of Compar Lit* 9 (1982), 200–207.

Burgess, Anthony. *Flame Into Being*, 179–191.

Burns, Aidan. *Nature and Culture*, 101–111.

Clark, L. D. *The Minoan Distance*, 368–377.

Clausson, Nils. "*Lady Chatterley's Lover* and the Condition-of-England Novel." *Engl Stud in Canada* 8 (1982), 296–309.

Cowan, James C. "D. H. Lawrence and the Resurrection of the Body," in Robert B. Partlow, Jr., and Harry T. Moore, eds., *D. H. Lawrence*, 99–102.

Crawford, Fred D. *Mixing Memory*, 30–32.

Davies, Rosemary Reeves. "The Eighth Love Scene: The Real Climax of *Lady Chatterley's Lover*." *D. H. Lawrence R* 15 (1982), 167–175.

Dervin, Daniel. *A 'Strange Sapience'*, 138–147, 190–199.

Doherty, Gerald. "Connie and the Chakras: Yogic Patterns in D. H. Lawrence's *Lady Chatterley's Lover*." *D. H. Lawrence R* 13 (1980), 79–92.

Edwards, Duane. "Mr. Mellors' Lover: A Study of Lady Chatterley." *Southern Hum R* 19 (1985), 117–130.

Gordon, David J. "Sex and Language in D. H. Lawrence." *Twentieth Century Lit* 27 (1981), 369–374.

Gutierrez, Donald. "The Ancient Imagination of D. H. Lawrence." *Twentieth Century Lit* 27 (1981), 192–194.

Gutierrez, Donald. "The Hylozoistic Vision of *Lady Chatterley's Lover*." *North Am Mentor Mag* 19:1 (1981), 25–34.

Gutierrez, Donald. " 'The Impossible Notation': The Sodomy Scene in *Lady Chatterley's Lover*." *Sphinx* 4:2 (1982), 109–125.

Hanlon, Lindley. "Sensuality and Simplification," in Michael Klein and Gillian Parker, eds., *The English Novel*, 268–278.

Hinz, Evelyn J. "Pornography, Novel, Mythic Narrative: The Three Versions of *Lady Chatterley's Lover*." *Modernist Stud* 3 (1979), 35–47.

Holderness, Graham. *D. H. Lawrence*, 223–227.

Humma, John B. "The Interpenetrating Metaphor: Nature and Myth in *Lady Chatterley's Lover*." *PMLA* 98 (1983), 77–85.

Jackson, Dennis. "Lady Chatterley's Color." *Interpretations* 15:1 (1983), 39–52.

Kim, Dong-son. "D. H. Lawrence: *Lady Chatterley's Lover*—Phallic Tenderness vs. Industrialism." *Phoenix* (Seoul) 23 (1981), 101–119.

King, Dixie. "The Influence of Forster's *Maurice* on *Lady Chatterley's Lover*." *Contemp Lit* 23 (1982), 76–82.

Leith, Richard. "Dialogue and Dialect in D. H. Lawrence." *Style* 14 (1980), 253–257.

Marcus, Phillip L. "Lawrence, Yeats, and 'the Resurrection of the Body'," in Peter Balbert and Phillip L. Marcus, eds., *D. H. Lawrence*, 230–231.

Meyers, Jeffrey. *D. H. Lawrence*, 156–164.

Niven, Alastair. *D. H. Lawrence*, 74–81.

Oates, Joyce Carol. " 'At Least I Have Made a Woman of Her': Images of Women in Twentieth-Century Literature." *Georgia R* 37 (1983), 23–24.

Prasad, Madhusudan. *D. H. Lawrence*, 115–125.

Ross, Michael L. " 'Carrying On the Human Heritage': From *Lady Chatterley's Lover* to *Nineteen Eighty-Four*." *D. H. Lawrence R* 17 (1984), 5–27.

Ruderman, Judith. *D. H. Lawrence*, 159–164.

Sagar, Keith. *D. H. Lawrence*, 292–295.

Saunders, David. "The Trial of *Lady Chatterley's Lover*: Limiting Cases and Literary Canons." *Southern R* (Adelaide) 15 (1982), 161–176.

Scheckner, Peter. *Class, Politics*, 137–140, 144–170.

Schneider, Daniel J. *D. H. Lawrence*, 237–243.

Schotz, Myra Glazer. "For the Sexes: Blake's Hermaphrodite in *Lady Chatterley's Lover*." *Bucknell R* 24:1 (1978), 17–25.

Simpson, Hilary. *D. H. Lawrence and Feminism*, 130–140.

Spilka, Mark. "Lawrence versus Peeperkorn on Abdication; or, *What Happens to a Pagan Vitalist When the Juice Runs Out?*" in Robert B. Partlow, Jr., and Harry T. Moore, eds., *D. H. Lawrence*, 111–120.

Spilka, Mark. "On Lawrence's Hostility to Wilful Women: The Chatterley Solution," in Anne Smith, ed., *Lawrence*, 198–210.

Squires, Michael. *The Creation of "Lady Chatterley's Lover."*

Sullivan, J. P. "Lady Chatterley in Rome." *Pacific Coast Philology* 15:1 (1980), 53–62.

Urang, Sarah. *Kindled in the Flame*, 93–121.

Voelker, Joseph C. "The Spirit of No-Place: Elements of the Classical Ironic Utopia in D. H. Lawrence's *Lady Chatterley's Lover.*" *Mod Fiction Stud* 25 (1979), 223–239.

Wasson, Richard. "Class and the Vicissitudes of the Male Body in Works by D. H. Lawrence." *D. H. Lawrence R* 14 (1981), 300–304.

Weinstein, Philip M. "Choosing Between the Quick and the Dead: Three Versions of *Lady Chatterley's Lover.*" *Mod Lang Q* 43 (1982), 267–290.

Weinstein, Philip M. *The Semantics of Desire*, 224–250.

Worthen, John. *D. H. Lawrence*, 168–182.

Yanada, Noriyuki. "On *Lady Chatterley's Lover*: Uncertainty of the Opposition." *Essays in Foreign Langs & Lit* (Hokkaido Univ) 24 (1978), 145–163. [In Japanese.]

Yoshida, Tetsuo. "On the Rebirth of Connie in the Second Version of *Lady Chatterley.*" *Stud in Engl Lang and Lit* (Fukuoka, Japan) 29 (1979), 83–104. [In Japanese.]

The Lost Girl, 1920

Becker, George J. *D. H. Lawrence*, 97–101.

Clark, L. D. *The Minoan Distance*, 214–222.

Herring, Phillip. "Caliban in Nottingham: D. H. Lawrence's *The Lost Girl.*" *Mosaic* 12:4 (1979), 9–19.

Kiely, Robert. "Accident and Purpose," 95–96.

Meyers, Jeffrey. *D. H. Lawrence*, 94–104.

Niven, Alastair. *D. H. Lawrence*, 56–60.

Prasad, Madhusudan. *D. H. Lawrence*, 77–85.

Ruderman, Judith. *D. H. Lawrence*, 37–47.

Ruderman, Judith. "Rekindling the 'Father-Spark': Lawrence's Ideal of Leadership in *The Lost Girl* and *The Plumed Serpent.*" *D. H. Lawrence R* 13 (1980), 240–248.

Simpson, Hilary. *D. H. Lawrence and Feminism*, 73–78.

Worthen, John. *D. H. Lawrence*, 105–117.

The Plumed Serpent, 1926

Apter, T. E. "Let's Hear What the Male Chauvinist is Saying: *The Plumed Serpent*," in Anne Smith, ed., *Lawrence*, 156–176.

Ballin, Michael. "Lewis Spence and the Myth of Quetzalcoatl in D. H. Lawrence's *The Plumed Serpent.*" *D. H. Lawrence R* 13 (1980), 63–75.

Baron, C. E. "Forster on Lawrence," in G. K. Das and John Beer, eds., *E. M. Forster*, 186–195.

Becker, George J. *D. H. Lawrence*, 107–112.

Böker, Uwe. "D. H. Lawrence' transpolitischer Antirassismus: *The Plumed Serpent.*" *Anglistik & Englischunterricht* 16 (1982), 31–50.

Burgess, Anthony. *Flame Into Being*, 152–158.

Clark, L. D. *The Minoan Distance*, 288–292, 321–322.

Clarke, Bruce. "The Eye and the Soul: A Moment of Clairvoyance in *The Plumed Serpent.*" *Southern R* (Baton Rouge) 19 (1983), 298–301.

Comellini, Carla. "D. H. Lawrence: Il mito infranto in *The Plumed Serpent.*" *Spicilegio Moderno* 11 (1979), 106–122.

Humma, John. "The Imagery of *The Plumed Serpent*: The Going-Under of Organicism." *D. H. Lawrence R* 15 (1982), 197–216.

Marcus, Phillip L. "Lawrence, Yeats," 225–226.

Meyers, Jeffrey. *D. H. Lawrence*, 124–129.

Moore, Harry T. "The Prose of D. H. Lawrence," in Robert B. Partlow, Jr., and Harry T. Moore, eds., *D. H. Lawrence*, 252–253.

Niven, Alastair. *D. H. Lawrence*, 69–74.

Prasad, Madhusudan. *D. H. Lawrence*, 112–114.

Ramey, Frederick. "Words in the Service of Silence: Preverbal Language in Lawrence's *The Plumed Serpent.*" *Mod Fiction Stud* 27 (1981), 613–621.

Rossman, Charles. "D. H. Lawrence and Mexico," in Peter Balbert and Phillip L. Marcus, eds., *D. H. Lawrence*, 192–198.

Ruderman, Judith. *D. H. Lawrence*, 142–153.

Ruderman, Judith. "Rekindling the 'Father-Spark'," 248–258.

Sagar, Keith. *D. H. Lawrence*, 283–286, 299–300.

Scheckner, Peter. *Class, Politics*, 92–94, 123–136.

Schneider, Daniel J. *D. H. Lawrence*, 91–94, 225–237.

Simpson, Hilary. *D. H. Lawrence and Feminism*, 113–117.

Stewart, Jack F. "Lawrence and Gauguin." *Twentieth Century Lit* 26 (1980), 393–398.

Urang, Sarah. *Kindled in the Flame*, 69–92.

Veitch, Douglas W. *Lawrence, Greene and Lowry*, 14–57.

Widmer, Kingsley. "Lawrence and the Nietzschean Matrix," 126–127.

Wilt, Judith. *Ghosts of the Gothic*, 290–292.

Worthen, John. *D. H. Lawrence*, 152–167.

The Rainbow, 1915

Balbert, Peter. " 'Logic of the Soul': Prothalamic Pattern in *The Rainbow.*" *Papers on Lang & Lit* 19 (1983), 309–325. [Also in Peter Balbert and Phillip L. Marcus, eds., *D. H. Lawrence*, 45–66.]

Becker, George J. *D. H. Lawrence*, 43–59.

Bell, Elizabeth S. "Slang Associations of D. H. Lawrence's Image Patterns in *The Rainbow.*" *Modernist Stud* 4 (1982), 77–86.

Bell, Michael. "Modern Movements in Literature," in Bell, ed., *1900–1930*, 22–26.

Ben-Ephraim, Gavriel. *The Moon's Dominion*, 129–172.

Blanchard, Lydia. "Mothers and Daughters in D. H. Lawrence: *The Rainbow* and Selected Shorter Works," in Anne Smith, ed., *Lawrence*, 75–98.

Burgess, Anthony. *Flame Into Being*, 70–76.

Burns, Aidan. *Nature and Culture*, 46–71.

Clark, L. D. *The Minoan Distance*, 97–105.

Dervin, Daniel. *A 'Strange Sapience'*, 50–53.

Eagleton, Mary, and David Pierce. *Attitudes to Class*, 104–106.

Ebbatson, Roger. *The Evolutionary Self*, 76–95.

Eggert, Paul. "The Half-Structured Rainbow." *Critical R* (Canberra) 23 (1981), 89–97.

Ford, George H. "The Eternal Moment: D. H. Lawrence's *The Rainbow* and *Women in Love*," in J. T. Fraser, ed., *The Study of Time III*, 512–539.

Gutierrez, Donald. *Lapsing Out*, 34–36.

Henighan, Tom. *Natural Space*, 182–195.

Herzinger, Kim A. *D. H. Lawrence*, 91–99.

Hinz, Evelyn J. "*Ancient Art and Ritual* and *The Rainbow*." *Dalhousie R* 58 (1978–79), 617–637.

Holderness, Graham. *D. H. Lawrence*, 174–189.

Hyde, Virginia. "Toward 'the Earth's New Architecture': Triads, Arches, and Angles in *The Rainbow*." *Modernist Stud* 4 (1982), 7–35.

Ingersoll, Earl G. "*The Rainbow*'s Winifred Inger." *D. H. Lawrence R* 17 (1984), 67–69.

Joshi, Rita. "The Dissent Tradition: The Relation of Mark Rutherford to D. H. Lawrence." *Engl Lang Notes* 22:3 (1985), 66–67.

Kennedy, Andrew. "After Not So Strange Gods in *The Rainbow*." *Engl Stud* 63 (1982), 220–230.

Kestner, Joseph A. *The Spatiality*, 98–105.

Klieneberger, H. R. *The Novel*, 213–215.

Kondo, Kyoko. "The Rainbow in Focus: A Study of the Form of *The Rainbow* by D. H. Lawrence." *Stud in Engl Lit* (Japan), Engl Number 1985, 53–69.

Landow, George P. "Lawrence and Ruskin: The Sage as Word-Painter," in Jeffrey Meyers, ed., *D. H. Lawrence*, 40–42.

Leith, Richard. "Dialogue and Dialect," 251–253.

McLaughlin, Ann L. "The Clenched and Knotted Horses in *The Rainbow*." *D. H. Lawrence R* 13 (1980), 179–185.

Manicom, David. "An Approach to the Imagery: A Study of Biblical Analogues in D. H. Lawrence's *The Rainbow*." *Engl Stud in Canada* 11 (1985), 474–483.

Milligan, Ian. *The Novel in English*, 160–164.

Moore, Harry T. "The Prose," 255–257.

Murfin, Ross C. *Swinburne*, 198–207.

Niven, Alastair. *D. H. Lawrence*, 42–49.

Nixon, Cornelia. "To Procreate Oneself: Ursula's Horses in *The Rainbow*." *ELH* 49 (1982), 123–141.

Oates, Joyce Carol. " 'At Least I Have Made a Woman of Her'," 20–23.

Otte, George. "The Loss of History in the Modern Novel: The Case of *The Rainbow*." *Pacific Coast Philology* 16 (1981), 67–76.

Prasad, Madhusudan. *D. H. Lawrence*, 57–67.

Rosenzweig, Paul. "A Defense of the Second Half of *The Rainbow*: Its Structure and Characterization." *D. H. Lawrence R* 13 (1980), 150–159.

Ross, Charles L. *The Composition of "The Rainbow."*
Ross, Michael L. " 'More or Less a Sequel': Continuity and Disconti-
nuity in Lawrence's Brangwensaga." *D. H. Lawrence R* 14 (1981),
263–285.
Ruderman, Judith. "The 'Trilogy'," 76–80.
Ruffolo, Lara R. "Lawrence's Borrowed Bird: The Flight of Bede's
Sparrow through *The Rainbow*." *Antigonish R* 53 (1983), 127–132.
Sagar, Keith. *D. H. Lawrence*, 110–146.
Salgado, Gamini. *A Preface*, 108–121.
Scheckner, Peter. *Class, Politics*, 15–17, 39–57, 91–96.
Schleifer, Ronald. "Lawrence's Rhetoric of Vision: The Ending of *The
Rainbow*." *D. H. Lawrence R* 13 (1980), 161–177.
Schneider, Daniel J. *D. H. Lawrence*, 145–169.
Schug, Charles. *The Romantic Genesis*, 228–230.
Schwarz, Daniel R. "Lawrence's Quest in *The Rainbow*." *Ariel* 11:3
(1980), 43–65.
Sharma, R. S. *"The Rainbow": A Study of Symbolic Mode.*
Simpson, Hilary. *D. H. Lawrence and Feminism*, 37–41.
Spivey, Ted R. *The Journey beyond Tragedy*, 76–78.
Stewart, Jack F. "Expressionism in *The Rainbow*." *Novel* 13 (1980),
296–315.
Stewart, Jack F. "Lawrence and Gauguin," 390–393.
Thomas, Marlin. "Somewhere under *The Rainbow*: D. H. Lawrence
and the Typology of Hermeneutics." *Mid-Hudson Lang Stud* 6
(1983), 57–65.
Tobin, Patricia Drechsel. *Time and the Novel*, 81–106.
Torgovnick, Marianna. *The Visual Arts*, 142–152.
Tristram, Philippa. "Eros and Death," 136–155.
Twitchell, James. "Lawrence's Lamias: Predatory Women in *The Rain-
bow* and *Women in Love*." *Stud in the Novel* 11 (1979), 23–33.
Twitchell, James B. *The Living Dead*, 195–200.
Urang, Sarah. *Kindled in the Flame*, 11–31.
Wilding, Michael. *Political Fictions*, 127–149.
Wilt, Judith. *Ghosts of the Gothic*, 235–237, 251–257, 264–270.
Worthen, John. *D. H. Lawrence*, 45–82.
Wright, Terence. "Rhythm in the Novel." *Mod Lang R* 80 (1985), 4–8.
Wussow, Helen M. "Lawrence's *The Rainbow*." *Explicator* 41:1 (1982),
44–45.

Sons and Lovers, 1913

Adamowski, T. H. "The Father of All Things: The Oral and the Oedipal
in *Sons and Lovers*." *Mosaic* 14:4 (1981), 69–88.
Adamowski, T. H. "Intimacy at a Distance: Sexuality and Orality in
Sons and Lovers." *Mosaic* 13:2 (1980), 71–89.
Baudino, Mario. "L'anima e il sole: La biografia esemplare in *Figli e
amanti*." *Il Verri* 17 (1980), 133–152.

264 LAWRENCE

Bazin, Nancy Topping. "The Moment of Revelation in *Martha Quest* and Comparable Moments by Two Modernists." *Mod Fiction Stud* 26 (1980), 87–90.

Becker, George J. *D. H. Lawrence*, 25–42.

Ben-Ephraim, Gavriel. *The Moon's Dominion*, 84–122.

Bonds, Diane S. "Miriam, the Narrator, and the Reader of *Sons and Lovers*." *D. H. Lawrence R* 14 (1981), 143–154.

Brunsdale, Mitzi M. *The German Effect*, 254–264.

Burgess, Anthony. *Flame Into Being*, 39–52.

Burns, Aidan. *Nature and Culture*, 35–45.

Clark, L. D. *The Minoan Distance*, 57–61.

D'Avanzo, Mario L. "On the Naming of Paul Morel and the Ending of *Sons and Lovers*." *Southern R* (Adelaide) 12 (1979), 103–107.

Delavenay, Emile. "Lawrence's Major Work," in Robert B. Partlow, Jr., and Harry T. Moore, eds., *D. H. Lawrence*, 139–142.

Denitto, Dennis. "All Passion Spent," in Michael Klein and Gillian Parker, eds., *The English Novel*, 235–247.

Dervin, Daniel. "Play, Creativity and Matricide: The Implications of Lawrence's 'Smashed Doll' Episode." *Mosaic* 14:3 (1981), 81–94.

Dervin, Daniel. *A 'Strange Sapience'*, 112–117, 127–130, 182–185.

Gillespie, Michael Patrick. "Lawrence's *Sons and Lovers*." *Explicator* 40:4 (1982), 36–38.

Green, Martin. *The English Novel*, 61–63.

Gutierrez, Donald. "The Ancient Imagination," 182–186.

Gutierrez, Donald. *Lapsing Out*, 33–34.

Henighan, Tom. *Natural Space*, 178–182.

Herzinger, Kim A. *D. H. Lawrence*, 87–89.

Holderness, Graham. *D. H. Lawrence*, 130–158.

Holmes, Brenda. " 'Gypsy' in *Sons and Lovers*: A Student Paper." *Recovering Lit* 8 (1980), 43–46.

Leith, Richard. "Dialogue and Dialect," 248–251.

Longmire, Samuel E. "Lawrence's *Sons and Lovers*." *Explicator* 42:3 (1984), 3–4.

Mitchell, Giles. "*Sons and Lovers* and the Oedipal Project." *D. H. Lawrence R* 13 (1980), 209–219.

Moore, Harry T. "The Prose," 248–249.

Nadel, Ira Bruce. "From Fathers and Sons to Sons and Lovers." *Dalhousie R* 59 (1979), 234–236.

Nash, Thomas. " 'Bleeding at the Roots': The Folklore of Plants in *Sons and Lovers*." *Kentucky Folklore Record* 27:1–2 (1981), 20–32.

Newmarch, David. " 'Death of a Young Man in London': Ernest Lawrence and William Morel in *Sons and Lovers*." *Durham Univ J* 76 (1983–84), 73–79.

Niven, Alastair. *D. H. Lawrence*, 32–42.

Phillips, Danna. "Lawrence's Understanding of Miriam through Sue." *Recovering Lit* 7:1 (1979), 46–56.

Prasad, Madhusudan. *D. H. Lawrence*, 30–56.

Pullin, Faith. "Lawrence's Treatment of Women in *Sons and Lovers*," in Anne Smith, ed., *Lawrence*, 49–73.

Sagar, Keith. *D. H. Lawrence*, 77–101.

Salgado, Gamini. *A Preface*, 99–107.

Scheckner, Peter. *Class, Politics*, 26–40.

Schneider, Daniel J. *D. H. Lawrence*, 132–143.

Shrubb, E. P. "Reading *Sons and Lovers.*" *Sydney Stud in Engl* 6 (1980–81), 87–104.

Simpson, Hilary. *D. H. Lawrence and Feminism*, 26–37.

Spilka, Mark. "For Mark Schorer with Combative Love: The *Sons and Lovers* Manuscript," in Peter Balbert and Phillip L. Marcus, eds., *D. H. Lawrence*, 29–44.

Spivey, Ted R. *The Journey beyond Tragedy*, 75–77.

Templeton, Wayne. "The Drift Towards Life: Paul Morel's Search for a Place." *D. H. Lawrence R* 15 (1982), 177–193.

Unrue, Darlene Harbour. "The Symbolism of Names in *Sons and Lovers.*" *Names* 28 (1980), 131–140.

Wilt, Judith. *Ghosts of the Gothic*, 249–252.

Worthen, John. *D. H. Lawrence*, 26–44.

The Trespasser, 1912

Becker, George J. *D. H. Lawrence*, 96–97.

Ben-Ephraim, Gavriel. *The Moon's Dominion*, 61–80.

Brunsdale, Mitzi M. *The German Effect*, 241–253.

Burgess, Anthony. *Flame Into Being*, 27–31.

Clark, L. D. *The Minoan Distance*, 20–23.

Dervin, Daniel. *A 'Strange Sapience'*, 148–150, 162–165.

Ebbatson, Roger. *Lawrence*, 44–60.

Holderness, Graham. *D. H. Lawrence*, 116–129.

Nakanishi, Yoshihiro. "On *The Freshwater Diary*, Helen Corke's Memoirs, and *The Trespasser*, the Second Long Novel by D. H. Lawrence: The Distance between Creation and Reflexion." *Bull for Langs and Lits* (Tenri Univ, Japan) 111, 50–67.

Niven, Alastair. *D. H. Lawrence*, 27–32.

Prasad, Madhusudan. *D. H. Lawrence*, 21–30.

Pullin, Faith. "Lawrence's Treatment of Women," 54–55.

Schneider, Daniel J. *D. H. Lawrence*, 118–132.

Worthen, John. *D. H. Lawrence*, 15–25.

The White Peacock, 1911

Becker, George J. *D. H. Lawrence*, 93–96.

Ben-Ephraim, Gavriel. *The Moon's Dominion*, 31–57.

Brown, Christopher. "As Cyril Likes It: Pastoral Reality and Illusion in *The White Peacock.*" *Essays in Lit* (Macomb) 6 (1979), 187–192.

Brunsdale, Mitzi M. *The German Effect*, 165–177.

Burgess, Anthony. *Flame Into Being*, 12–26.

Burns, Aidan. *Nature and Culture*, 30–35.

Daleski, H. M. *The Divided Heroine*, 89–109.

Daleski, H. M. "Lawrence and George Eliot: The Genesis of *The White Peacock*," in Jeffrey Meyers, ed., *D. H. Lawrence*, 51–68.

Daleski, H. M. *Unities*, 83–98.

Ebbatson, Roger. *Lawrence*, 44–60.

Herzinger, Kim A. *D. H. Lawrence*, 76–86.

Holderness, Graham. *D. H. Lawrence*, 95–115.

Modiano, Marko. "Symbolism, Characterization, and Setting in *The White Peacock*, by D. H. Lawrence." *Moderna Sprak* 77 (1983), 345–352.

Murfin, Ross C. *Swinburne*, 187–198.

Nakanishi, Yoshihiro. "Concerning the Transition of the Maiden Novel by D. H. Lawrence from *Laetitia* and *Nethermere* to *The White Peacock*." *Bull for Langs and Lits* (Tenri Univ, Japan) 109, 85–105.

Niven, Alastair. *D. H. Lawrence*, 23–27.

Prasad, Madhusudan. *D. H. Lawrence*, 6–21.

Pullin, Faith. "Lawrence's Treatment of Women," 55–59.

Sagar, Keith. *D. H. Lawrence*, 5–8, 14–20.

Salgado, Gamini. *A Preface*, 97–98.

Schneider, Daniel J. *D. H. Lawrence*, 111–119.

Simpson, Hilary. *D. H. Lawrence and Feminism*, 51–53.

Verhoeven, W. M. "D. H. Lawrence's Duality Concept in *The White Peacock*." *Neophilologus* 69 (1985), 294–316.

Worthen, John. *D. H. Lawrence*, 1–14.

Women in Love, 1920

Ananthamurthy, U. R. "D. H. Lawrence as an Indian Writer Sees Him." *Liter Criterion* 16:2 (1981), 10–17.

Balbert, Peter. "Ursula Brangwen and 'The Essential Criticism': The Female Corrective in *Women in Love*." *Stud in the Novel* 17 (1985), 267–283.

Becker, George J. *D. H. Lawrence*, 61–78.

Ben-Ephraim, Gavriel. *The Moon's Dominion*, 179–232.

Benson, Michael. "Moving Bodies in Hardy and Beckett." *Essays in Criticism* 34 (1984), 229–230.

Blanchard, Lydia. "The 'Real Quartet' of *Women in Love*: Lawrence on Brothers and Sisters," in Robert B. Partlow, Jr., and Harry T. Moore, eds., *D. H. Lawrence*, 199–206.

Blanchard, Lydia. "*Women in Love*: Mourning Becomes Narcissism." *Mosaic* 15:1 (1982), 105–118.

Bonds, Diane S. "Going into the Abyss: Literalization in *Women in Love*." *Essays in Lit* (Macomb) 8 (1981), 189–202.

Boyum, Joy Gould. *Double Exposure*, 124–131.

Bradshaw, Graham. " 'Lapsing Out' in *Women in Love*." *English* 32 (1983), 17–32.

Burgan, Mary. "Androgynous Fatherhood in *Ulysses* and *Women in Love*." *Mod Lang Q* 44 (1983), 186–191, 193–197.

Burgess, Anthony. *Flame Into Being*, 87–100.

Burns, Aidan. *Nature and Culture*, 72–100.

Cain, William E. "Lawrence's 'Purely Destructive' Art in *Women in Love*." *South Carolina R* 13:1 (1980), 38–47.

Clark, L. D. *The Minoan Distance*, 145–179.

Coates, Paul. *The Realist Fantasy*, 89–96.

Cox, Gary D. "D. H. Lawrence and F. M. Dostoevsky: Mirror Images of Murderous Aggression." *Mod Fiction Stud* 29 (1983), 180–182.

DiBattista, Maria. "*Women in Love*: D. H. Lawrence's Judgment Book," in Peter Balbert and Phillip L. Marcus, eds., *D. H. Lawrence*, 67–90.

Dillon, M. C. "Love in *Women in Love*: A Phenomenological Analysis." *Philos and Lit* 2 (1978), 190–207.

Doherty, Gerald. "The Darkest Source: D. H. Lawrence, Tantric Yoga, and *Women in Love*." *Essays in Lit* (Macomb) 11 (1984), 211–221.

Doherty, Gerald. "The Salvator Mundi Touch: Messianic Typology in D. H. Lawrence's *Women in Love*." *Ariel* 13:3 (1982), 53–69.

Ebbatson, Roger. *The Evolutionary Self*, 96–112.

Farber, Lauren. "An Assemblage of Christians and Heathens: An Exploration into D. H. Lawrence's Sources for *Women in Love*." *Cresset*, Sept.-Oct. 1977, 10–14.

Ford, G. H. "The Eternal Moment," 512–536.

French, A. L. " 'The Whole Pulse of Social England': *Women in Love*." *Crit R* 21 (1979), 57–71.

Gomez, Joseph A. "Russell's Images of Lawrence's Vision," in Michael Klein and Gillian Parker, eds., *The English Novel*, 248–256.

Gordon, David J. "Sex and Language," 364–369.

Gordon, William A. "D. H. Lawrence and the Two Truths," in Mary Lynn Johnson and Seraphia D. Leyda, eds., *Reconciliations*, 202–205, 213–215.

Green, Martin. *The English Novel*, 51–55, 66–69.

Gutierrez, Donald. "The Ancient Imagination," 186–188.

Gutierrez, Donald. *Lapsing Out*, 29–31.

Henighan, Tom. *Natural Space*, 195–216.

Hinz, Evelyn J., and John J. Teunissen. "*Women in Love* and the Myth of Eros and Psyche," in Robert B. Partlow, Jr., and Harry T. Moore, eds., *D. H. Lawrence*, 207–220.

Holderness, Graham. *D. H. Lawrence*, 190–219.

Hughes, Cameron. "On *Women in Love*." *Spectrum* (Santa Barbara) 23 (1981), 70–74.

Journet, Debra. "Symbol and Allegory in *Women in Love*." *South Atlantic R* 49:2 (1984), 42–58.

Kestner, Joseph A. *The Spatiality*, 101–105.

Kiely, Robert. "Accident and Purpose," 97–107.

Klieneberger, H. R. *The Novel*, 213–215.

Langbaum, Robert. "Lawrence and Hardy," in Jeffrey Meyers, ed., *D. H. Lawrence*, 77–82, 88–90.

Leavis, L. R. "The Late Nineteenth Century Novel and the Change towards the Sexual: Gissing, Hardy and Lawrence." *Engl Stud* 66 (1985), 43–46.

McVeagh, John. *Tradefull Merchants*, 167–168.

Moore, Harry T. "The Prose," 253–255.

Morris, Inez R. "African Sculpture Symbols in *Women in Love*." *D. H. Lawrence R* 15 (1982), 177–193. [Also in *Publs of the Mississippi Philol Assoc* 1 (1982), 8–17; and *Coll Lang Assoc J* 28 (1985), 263–280.]

New, Peter. *Fiction and Purpose*, 231–302.

Niven, Alastair. *D. H. Lawrence*, 49–56.

O'Hara, Daniel. "The Power of Nothing in *Women in Love*." *Bucknell R* 28:2 (1983), 151–163.

Pitre, David. "The Mystical Lawrence: Rupert Birkin's Taoist Quest." *Stud in Mystical Lit* 3:1 (1983), 43–64.

Pollak, Paulina S. "Anti-Semitism," 25.

Prasad, Madhusudan. *D. H. Lawrence*, 67–76.

Ross, Charles L. *The Composition of . . . "Women in Love."*

Ross, Charles L. "Homoerotic Feeling in *Women in Love*: Lawrence's 'struggle for verbal consciousness' in the Manuscripts," in Robert B. Partlow, Jr., and Harry T. Moore, eds., *D. H. Lawrence*, 168–182.

Ross, Michael L. " 'More or Less a Sequel'," 263–285.

Ruderman, Judith. "The 'Trilogy'," 76–80.

Sagar, Keith. *D. H. Lawrence*, 108–114, 147–193.

Scheckner, Peter. *Class, Politics*, 56–69, 151–153.

Schneider, Daniel J. *D. H. Lawrence*, 51–53, 171–190.

Schneider, Daniel J. "The Laws of Action and Reaction in *Women in Love*." *D. H. Lawrence R* 14 (1981), 238–261.

Simpson, Hilary. *D. H. Lawrence and Feminism*, 59–60.

Smailes, T. A. "Plato's 'Great Life of Ideals': Function in *Women in Love*," in Brian Green, ed., *Generous Converse*, 133–135.

Spilka, Mark. "On Lawrence's Hostility," 192–195.

Spivey, Ted R. *The Journey beyond Tragedy*, 77–80.

Stewart, Jack F. "Primitivism in *Women in Love*." *D. H. Lawrence R* 13 (1980), 45–58.

Stewart, Jack F. "Rhetoric and Image in Lawrence's 'Moony'." *Stud in the Hum* 8:1 (1980), 33–37.

Torgovnick, Marianna. "Closure and the Shape of Fictions: The Example of *Women in Love*," in J. T. Fraser, ed., *The Study of Time IV*, 147–158.

Torgovnick, Marianna. "Pictorial Elements in *Women in Love*: The Uses of Insinuation and Visual Rhyme." *Contemp Lit* 21 (1980), 420–434.

Torgovnick, Marianna. *The Visual Arts*, 192–213.

Tristram, Philippa. "Eros and Death," 142–155.
Twitchell, James. "Lawrence's Lamias," 33–38.
Twitchell, James B. *The Living Dead*, 200–205.
Urang, Sarah. *Kindled in the Flame*, 33–67.
Vichy, Thérèse. "Symbolisme et structures dans *Women in Love*."
    Etudes Anglaises 33 (1980), 400–413.
Vitoux, Pierre. "*Women in Love*: From Typescripts into Print." *Texas
    Stud in Lit and Lang* 23 (1981), 577–592.
Walsh, Sylvia. "Women in Love." *Soundings* 15 (1982), 353–366.
Weinstein, Philip M. *The Semantics of Desire*, 204–223.
Widmer, Kingsley. "Lawrence and the Nietzschean Matrix," 118–120.
Wilt, Judith. *Ghosts of the Gothic*, 237–239, 257–264, 270–274.
Worthen, John. *D. H. Lawrence*, 83–104.
Zapf, Hubert. "Taylorism in D. H. Lawrence's *Women in Love*." *D. H.
    Lawrence R* 15 (1982), 129–138.

GEORGE ALFRED LAWRENCE

Guy Livingstone, 1857

Terry, R. C. *Victorian Popular Fiction*, 19–22.

JOHN LE CARRÉ

Call for the Dead, 1961

Monaghan, David. *The Novels*, 107–110, 127–133.
Sauerberg, Lars Ole. *Secret Agents*, 54–58, 132–135, 189–192, 194–196.

The Honourable Schoolboy, 1977

Barley, Tony. *Taking Sides*, 105–126.
Monaghan, David. "John le Carré and England: A Spy'e-Eye View."
    Mod Fiction Stud 29 (1983), 572–581.
Monaghan, David. *The Novels*, 14–16, 20–28, 64–66, 136–138, 148–154,
    162–166.
Sauerberg, Lars Ole. *Secret Agents*, 58–63, 175–178, 193–196.

The Little Drummer Girl, 1983

Barley, Tony. *Taking Sides*, 146–166.
Monaghan, David. *The Novels*, 172–202.

The Looking-Glass War, 1965

Barley, Tony. *Taking Sides*, 48–65.
Monaghan, David. "John le Carré," 572–580.
Monaghan, David. *The Novels*, 44–47.

A Murder of Quality, 1962

Monaghan, David. *The Novels*, 148–153.

The Naive and Sentimental Lover, 1971

Monaghan, David. *The Novels*, 67–70.

A Small Town in Germany, 1968

> Barley, Tony. *Taking Sides*, 66–83.
> Monaghan, David. "John le Carré," 571–580.
> Monaghan, David. *The Novels*, 54–56.
> Sauerberg, Lars Ole. *Secret Agents*, 171–175, 180–182, 195–197.

Smiley's People, 1980

> Barley, Tony. *Taking Sides*, 127–145.
> Monaghan, David. "John le Carré," 572–582.
> Monaghan, David. *The Novels*, 45–47, 167–171.
> Sauerberg, Lars Ole. *Secret Agents*, 58–60, 123–125, 186–188, 202–206.

The Spy Who Came in from the Cold, 1963

> Barley, Tony. *Taking Sides*, 27–47.
> Calendrillo, Linda T. "Role Playing and 'Atmosphere' in Four Modern British Spy Novels." *Clues* 3:1 (1982), 111–119.
> Monaghan, David. "John le Carré," 572–580.
> Sauerberg, Lars Ole. *Secret Agents*, 54–57, 94–96, 192–196.

Tinker, Tailor, Soldier, Spy, 1974

> Barley, Tony. *Taking Sides*, 84–104.
> Monaghan, David. "John le Carré," 571–577.
> Monaghan, David. *The Novels*, 14–23, 44–54 73–76, 154–162.
> Sauerberg, Lars Ole. *Secret Agents*, 58–60, 122–124, 129–131, 197–201.

SOPHIA LEE

The Recess, 1785

> Punter, David. *The Literature of Terror*, 56–59.
> Roberts, Bette B. *The Gothic Romance*, 84–115.
> Sandy, Stephen. *The Raveling*, 55–66.

JOSEPH SHERIDAN LEFANU

All in the Dark, 1866

> Peterson, Audrey. *Victorian Masters*, 150–152.

Carmilla, 1872

> Day, William Patrick. *In the Circles*, 86–89.
> Foust, Ronald. "Rite of Passage: The Vampire Tale as Cosmogonic Myth," in William Coyle, ed., *Aspects of Fantasy*, 75–76.
> Lozes, Jean. "Joseph Shéridan LeFanu, prince de l'invisible au 'grand siècle' des vampires." *Caliban* 16 (1979), 59–63.
> Sullivan, Jack. *Elegant Nightmares*, 60–66.
> Twitchell, James B. *The Living Dead*, 129–132.
> Veeder, William. "*Carmilla*: The Arts of Repression." *Texas Stud in Lit and Lang* 22 (1980), 197–220.

The Fortunes of Colonel Torlogh O'Brien, 1847

    Cahalan, James M. *Great Hatred*, 74–77.

The House by the Churchyard, 1863

    Peterson, Audrey. *Victorian Masters*, 127–130.

Uncle Silas, 1864

    Bayer-Berenbaum, Linda. *The Gothic Imagination*, 107–119.

    Day, William Patrick. *In the Circles*, 109–114.

    Nalecz-Wojtczak, Jolanta. "*Uncle Silas*: A Link between the Gothic Romance and the Detective Novel in England." *Studia Anglica Posnaniensia* 12 (1980), 157–167.

    Peterson, Audrey. *Victorian Masters*, 141–149.

    Punter, David. *The Literature of Terror*, 233–237.

Wylder's Hand, 1864

    Peterson, Audrey. *Victorian Masters*, 131–141.

ROSAMOND LEHMANN

The Ballad and the Source, 1944

    Coopman, Tony. "Character and Narrative in Rosamond Lehmann's *The Ballad and the Source*," in Jacques Lerot and Rudolf Kern, eds., *Mélanges de linguistique*, 165–173.

    Haule, James M. "Moral Obligation and Social Responsibility in the Novels of Rosamond Lehmann." *Critique* (Atlanta) 26 (1985), 199–200.

    Kaplan, Sydney Janet. "Rosamond Lehmann's *The Ballad and the Source*: A Confrontation with 'The Great Mother'." *Twentieth Century Lit* 27 (1981), 127–143.

Dusty Answer, 1927

    Haule, James M. "Moral Obligation," 195–196.

The Echoing Grove, 1953

    Codaccioni, Marie-José. "La marginalité chez Rosamond Lehmann: la rupture du code," in *La marginalité*, 138–146.

    Crosland, Margaret. *Beyond the Lighthouse*, 75–76.

    Haule, James M. "Moral Obligation," 197–199.

Invitation to the Waltz, 1932

    Haule, James M. "Moral Obligation," 197.

A Note in Music, 1930

    Haule, James M. "Moral Obligation," 196–197.

A Sea-Grape Tree, 1976

    Gindin, James. "Three Recent British Novels and an American Response." *Michigan Q R* 17 (1978), 223–246.

    Haule, James M. "Moral Obligation," 200–202.

The Weather in the Streets, 1936

> Beauman, Nicola. *A Very Great Profession*, 126–127, 155–157.
> Codaccioni, Marie-José. "La marginalité," 138–146.
> Haule, James M. "Moral Obligation," 197.

THOMAS LELAND

Longsword, Earl of Salisbury, 1762

> Harp, Richard L. "Goldsmith's College Tutor: The Malicious Monk in Leland's *Longsword, Earl of Salisbury*." *Moderna Sprak* 76 (1982), 241–242.

CHARLOTTE LENNOX

The Female Quixote, 1752

> Chiesa, Clara. "*The Female Quixote* di Charlotte Lennox: Tra *romance* e *novel*." *Lettore di Provincia* 39 (1979), 33–46.
> Langbauer, Laurie. "Romance Revised: Charlotte Lennox's *The Female Quixote*." *Novel* 18 (1984), 29–49.
> Müller, Wolfgang G. "Charlotte Lennox' *The Female Quixote* und die Geschichte des englischen Romans." *Poetica* 11 (1979), 369–393.
> Suhr, Heidrun. *Englische Romanautorinnen*, 129–133.
> Warren, Leland E. "Of the Conversation of Women: *The Female Quixote* and the Dream of Perfection." *Stud in Eighteenth-Century Culture* 11 (1982), 367–380.

Henrietta, 1758

> Suhr, Heidrun. *Englische Romanautorinnen*, 134–142.

Sophia, 1762

> Macheski, Cecilia. "Penelope's Daughters: Images of Needlework in Eighteenth-Century Literature," in Mary Anne Schofield and Cecilia Macheski, eds., *Fetter'd or Free?*, 92–93.
> Spacks, Patricia Meyer. "Sisters," in Mary Anne Schofield and Cecilia Macheski, eds., *Fetter'd or Free?*, 138–146.

DORIS LESSING

Briefing for a Descent into Hell, 1971

> Bazin, Nancy Topping. "Androgyny or Catastrophe: The Vision of Doris Lessing's Later Novels." *Frontiers* 5:3 (1980), 11–12.
> Füger, Wilhelm. "Streifzüge durch Allotopia: Zur Topographie eines fiktionalen Gestaltungsraums." *Anglia* 102 (1984), 377–382.
> Fuoroli, Caryn. "Doris Lessing's 'Game': Referential Language and Fictional Form." *Twentieth Century Lit* 27 (1981), 156–164.

Galbreath, Robert. "Ambiguous Apocalypse: Transcendental Versions of the End," in Eric S. Rabkin et al., eds., *The End of the World*, 71–72.

Kaplan, Sydney Janet. "Passionate Portrayal of Things to Come: Doris Lessing's Recent Fiction," in Thomas F. Staley, ed., *Twentieth-Century Women Novelists*, 2–5.

Knapp, Mona. *Doris Lessing*, 104–113.

Kuns, Guido. "Structuring the Reader's Response: *Briefing for a Descent into Hell*." *Dutch Q R of Anglo-American Letters* 11 (1981), 197–208.

Marder, Herbert. "Borderline Fantasies: The Two Worlds of *Briefing for a Descent into Hell*." *Papers on Lang & Lit* 19 (1983), 427–448.

Sage, Lorna. *Doris Lessing*, 68–69.

Spiegel, Rotraut. *Doris Lessing*, 102–146.

Canopus in Argos, 1979–1983

Khanna, Lee Cullen. "*Canopus* in the Classroom." *Doris Lessing Newsl* 7:1 (1983), 9–10.

Knapp, Mona. *Doris Lessing*, 130–165.

Levy, Jette Lundbo. *Lessing-perspektiver*, 75–89.

Oumhani, Cécile. "Doris Lessing et le soufisme (*Shikasta* et *The Marriages between Zones Three, Four and Five*)." *Revue de Littérature Comparée* 225 (1983), 82–93.

Wilson, Raymond J., III. "Doris Lessing's Symbolic Motifs: The Canopus Novels." *Doris Lessing Newsl* 6:1 (1982), 1, 9–11.

Children of Violence, 1952–1969

Fishburn, Katherine. "The Nightmare Repetition: The Mother-Daughter Conflict in Doris Lessing's *Children of Violence*," in Cathy N. Davidson and E. M. Broner, eds., *The Lost Tradition*, 207–215.

Gurr, Andrew. *Writers in Exile*, 126–132.

Hartveit, Lars. "Commitment and the Novelist's Craft: The Racial Issue in the African Volumes of Doris Lessing's *Children of Violence*," in Daniel Massa, ed., *Individual*, 28–35.

Holmquist, Ingrid. *From Society to Nature*.

Jouve, Nicole Ward. "Of Mud and Other Matter: *The Children of Violence*," in Jenny Taylor, ed., *Notebooks/Memoirs/Archives*, 75–130.

Knapp, Mona. *Doris Lessing*, 36–47, 86–103.

Levy, Jette Lundbo. *Lessing-perspektiver*, 48–62.

Pickering, Jean. "Marxism and Madness: The Two Faces of Doris Lessing's Myth." *Mod Fiction Stud* 26 (1980), 17–30.

Rosen, Ellen I. "Martha's 'Quest' in Lessing's *Children of Violence*." *Frontiers* 3:2 (1978), 54–58.

Scanlan, Margaret. "Memory and Continuity in the Series Novel: The Example of *Children of Violence*." *Mod Fiction Stud* 26 (1980), 75–85.

Swingewood, Alan. "Structure and Ideology in the Novels of Doris Lessing," in Diana Laurenson, ed., *The Sociology*, 42–43.

Thorpe, Michael. *Doris Lessing's Africa*, 6–9, 49–86.

The Four-Gated City, 1969

Abel, Elizabeth. "(E)Merging Identities: The Dynamics of Female Friendship in Contemporary Fiction by Women." *Signs* 6 (1981), 418–421.

Hogeland, Lisa Maria. "Coda to 'An Edge of History': The Implicit Feminism of Doris Lessing's *The Four-Gated City*." *Doris Lessing Newsl* 7:2 (1983), 11–12.

Hogeland, Lisa Maria. *An Edge of History*, 1–30.

Jouve, Nicole Ward. "Of Mud and Other Matter," 83–86, 112–114.

Kaplan, Carey. "A Womb with a View: The House on Radlett Street in *The Four-Gated City*." *Doris Lessing Newsl* 7:1 (1983), 3–4.

Kaplan, Sydney Janet. "Passionate Portrayal," 1–5.

Knapp, Mona. *Doris Lessing*, 86–103.

Levy, Jette Lundbo. *Lessing-perspektiver*, 55–62.

Pratt, Annis. *Archetypal Patterns*, 161–166.

Sage, Lorna. *Doris Lessing*, 59–68.

Scott, Ann. "The More Recent Writings: Sufism, Mysticism and Politics," in Jenny Taylor, ed., *Notebooks/Memoirs/Archives*, 180–181, 183–186.

Sizemore, Christine W. "Reading the City as Palimpsest: The Experiential Perception of the City in Doris Lessing's *The Four-Gated City*," in Susan Merrill Squier, ed., *Women Writers*, 176–188.

Sprague, Claire. " 'Without Contraries is no Progression': Lessing's *The Four-Gated City*." *Mod Fiction Stud* 26 (1980), 99–116.

Thorpe, Michael. *Doris Lessing's Africa*, 80–86.

Walker, Melissa G. "Doris Lessing's *The Four-Gated City*: Consciousness and Community—A Different History." *Southern R* (Baton Rouge) 17 (1981), 97–120.

The Golden Notebook, 1962

Abel, Elizabeth. "(E)Merging Identities," 429–432.

Brownstein, Rachel M. *Becoming a Heroine*, 26–29.

Bugliani, Francesca. "Nuove tendenze del romanzo inglese contemporaneo: *The Golden Notebook* di Doris Lessing." *Studi dell'Istituto Linguistico* 4 (1981), 147–176.

Byatt, A. S. "People in Paper Houses: Attitudes to 'Realism' and 'Experiment' in English Postwar Fiction," in Malcolm Bradbury and David Palmer, eds., *The Contemporary English Novel*, 38–41.

Crosland, Margaret. *Beyond the Lighthouse*, 102–106.

Draine, Betsy. "Nostalgia and Irony: The Postmodern Order of *The Golden Notebook*." *Mod Fiction Stud* 26 (1980), 31–48.

Fuoroli, Caryn. "Doris Lessing's 'Game'," 146–156.

Green, Martin. *The English Novel*, 184–188.

Gurr, Andrew. "The Freedom of Exile in Naipaul and Doris Lessing." *Ariel* 13:4 (1982), 7–8, 14–18.

Henke, Suzette A. "Lessing's *Golden Notebook* and Engels' *Origin of the Family*." *Doris Lessing Newsl* 7:2 (1983), 6.

Kawin, Bruce F. *The Mind of the Novel*, 307–311.

Kellman, Steven G. *The Self-Begetting Novel*, 97–100.

Knapp, Mona. *Doris Lessing*, 52–67.

Lemon, Lee T. *Portraits of the Artist*, 52–69.

Leonard, Vivien. " 'Free Women' as Parody: Fun Games in *The Golden Notebook*." *Perspectives on Contemp Lit* 6 (1980), 20–27.

Levy, Jette Lundbo. *Lessing-perspektiver*, 39–47.

McCormick, Kathleen. "What Happened to Anna Wulf: Naivety in *The Golden Notebook*." *Massachusetts Stud in Engl* 8:3 (1982), 56–62.

McCrindle, Jean. "Reading *The Golden Notebook* in 1962," in Jenny Taylor, ed., *Notebooks/Memoirs/Archives*, 43–56.

Marder, Herbert. "The Paradox of Form in *The Golden Notebook*." *Mod Fiction Stud* 26 (1980), 49–54.

Perrakis, Phyllis Sternberg. "Doris Lessing's *The Golden Notebook*: Separation and Symbiosis." *Am Imago* 38 (1981), 407–428.

Sage, Lorna. *Doris Lessing*, 49–58.

Schweickart, Patrocinio P. "Reading a Worthless Statement: The Structure of Doris Lessing's *The Golden Notebook*." *Mod Fiction Stud* 31 (1985), 263–279.

Spiegel, Rotraut. *Doris Lessing*, 59–92.

Sprague, Claire. "Doubletalk and Doubles Talk in *The Golden Notebook*." *Papers on Lang & Lit* 18 (1982), 181–197.

Stewart, Grace. *A New Mythos*, 35–38, 84–89, 136–146.

Stimpson, Catharine R. "Ad/d Feminam: Women, Literature, and Society," in Edward W. Said, ed., *Literature and Society*, 183–185.

Swingewood, Alan. "Structure and Ideology," 43–44, 46–52.

Taylor, Jenny. "Introduction: Situating Reading," in Taylor, ed., *Notebooks/Memoirs/Archives*, 7–12.

Thorpe, Michael. *Doris Lessing's Africa*, 87–100.

Tiger, Virginia. "The Female Novel of Education and the Confessional Heroine." *Dalhousie R* 60 (1980), 472–485.

Wilson, Elizabeth. "Yesterday's Heroines: On Rereading Lessing and de Beauvoir," in Jenny Taylor, ed., *Notebooks/Memoirs/Archives*, 61–65, 69–72.

Zeman, Anthea. *Presumptuous Girls*, 172–174.

The Grass Is Singing, 1950

Crosland, Margaret. *Beyond the Lighthouse*, 96–99.

Kay, Helen. " 'Realities . . . rooted in geography': An Analysis of *The Grass is Singing* in Relation to *Going Home*." *Doris Lessing Newsl* 6:1 (1982), 3–4, 11.

Knapp, Mona. *Doris Lessing*, 19–28.

Marion, Eileen. " 'Not about the Colour Problem': Doris Lessing's Portrayal of the Colonial Order." *World Lit Written in Engl* 21 (1982), 434–455.

Marquard, Jean. "The Farm: A Concept in the Writing of Olive Schreiner, Pauline Smith, Doris Lessing, Nadine Gordimer and Bessie Head." *Dalhousie R* 59 (1979), 294–295, 298–301.

Morphet, Fionna. "The Narrowing Horizon: Two Chapter Openings in *The Grass is Singing.*" *Doris Lessing Newsl* 9:2 (1985), 14–15.

Sage, Lorna. *Doris Lessing*, 24–28.

Sarvan, Charles and Liebetraut. "D. H. Lawrence and Doris Lessing's *The Grass Is Singing.*" *Mod Fiction Stud* 24 (1978), 533–537.

Thorpe, Michael. *Doris Lessing's Africa*, 11–18.

Landlocked, 1965

Jouve, Nicole Ward. "Of Mud and Other Matter," 108–111.

Knapp, Mona. *Doris Lessing*, 44–47.

Levy, Jette Lundbo. *Lessing-perspektiver*, 56–57.

Sage, Lorna. *Doris Lessing*, 58–59.

Thorpe, Michael. *Doris Lessing's Africa*, 53–54, 76–79.

Wienhold, Christa. "Doris Lessing und Afrika: Zum Widerstand gegen den britischen Kolonialismus im ehemaligen Südrhodesien." *Zeitschrift für Anglistik und Amerikanistik* 32 (1984), 135–137.

The Making of the Representative for Planet 8, 1982

Sage, Lorna. *Doris Lessing*, 84–85.

The Marriages between Zones Three, Four, and Five, 1980

Cleary, Rochelle. "What's in a Name? Lessing's Message in *The Marriages Between Zones Three, Four, and Five.*" *Doris Lessing Newsl* 6:2 (1982), 8–9.

Knapp, Mona. *Doris Lessing*, 155–163.

Levy, Jette Lundbo. *Lessing-perspektiver*, 79–85.

Oumhani, Cécile. "Doris Lessing et le soufisme," 82–93.

Peel, Ellen. "Communicating Differently: Doris Lessing's *Marriages Between Zones Three, Four, and Five.*" *Doris Lessing Newsl* 6:2 (1982), 11–13.

Pohl, Joy. "*The Marriages Between Zones Three, Four, and Five*: Doris Lessing's Alchemical Allegory." *Extrapolation* 24 (1983), 201–213.

Rowe, Marsha. " 'If You Mate a Swan and a Gander, Who Will Ride'?," in Jenny Taylor, ed., *Notebooks/Memoirs/Archives*, 194–204.

Sage, Lorna. *Doris Lessing*, 80–82.

Sprague, Claire. "Naming in *Marriages*: Another View." *Doris Lessing Newsl* 7:1 (1983), 13.

Martha Quest, 1952

Bazin, Nancy Topping. "The Moment of Revelation in *Martha Quest* and Comparable Moments by Two Modernists." *Mod Fiction Stud* 26 (1980), 94–98.

Green, Martin. *The English Novel*, 177–183.

Knapp, Mona. *Doris Lessing*, 36–41.

Levy, Jette Lundbo. *Lessing-perspektiver*, 48–52.

Mandl, Betty. "*Martha Quest*: The Dynamics of Mood." *Doris Lessing Newsl* 5:2 (1981), 3–4.

Sage, Lorna. *Doris Lessing*, 30–34.

Spiegel, Rotraut. *Doris Lessing*, 33–49.

Swingewood, Alan. "Structure and Ideology," 44–46.

Thorpe, Michael. *Doris Lessing's Africa*, 60–65.

The Memoirs of a Survivor, 1974

Bazin, Nancy Topping. "Androgyny or Catastrophe," 13–15.

Carter, Nancy Corson. "Journey toward Wholeness: A Meditation on Doris Lessing's *The Memoirs of a Survivor*." *J of Evolutionary Psych* 2:1–2 (1981), 33–47.

Castillo, Debra A. *The Translated World*, 280–283, 291–294, 304–312.

Cederstrom, Lorelei. " 'Inner Space' Landscape: Doris Lessing's *Memoirs of a Survivor*." *Mosaic* 13:3–4 (1980), 115–132.

Draine, Betsy. "Changing Frames: Doris Lessing's *Memoirs of a Survivor*." *Stud in the Novel* 11 (1979), 51–61.

Duyfhuizen, Bernard. "On the Writing of Future-History: Beginning the Ending in Doris Lessing's *The Memoirs of a Survivor*." *Mod Fiction Stud* 26 (1980), 147–156.

Edwards, Lee R. *Psyche as Hero*, 271–283.

Green, Martin. "The Doom of Empire: *Memoirs of a Survivor*." *Doris Lessing Newsl* 6:2 (1982), 6–7, 10.

Green, Martin. *The English Novel*, 184–202.

Hoffeld, Laura, and Roni Natov. "*The Summer Before the Dark* and *The Memoirs of a Survivor*: Lessing's New Female Bondings." *Doris Lessing Newsl* 3:2 (1979), 11–12.

Knapp, Mona. *Doris Lessing*, 121–129.

Kuns, Guido. "Apocalypse and Utopia in Doris Lessing's *The Memoirs of a Survivor*." *Intl Fiction R* 7 (1980), 79–84.

Levy, Jette Lundbo. *Lessing-perspektiver*, 68–72.

Sage, Lorna. *Doris Lessing*, 73–77.

Scott, Ann. "The More Recent Writings," 182–183.

Sullivan, Alvin. "*The Memoirs of a Survivor*: Lessing's Notes toward a Supreme Fiction." *Mod Fiction Stud* 26 (1980), 157–162.

A Proper Marriage, 1954

Knapp, Mona. *Doris Lessing*, 41–44.

Levy, Jette Lundbo. *Lessing-perspektiver*, 53–54.

Morrow, Patrick D. "Fortunes of War, Fortunes of Love: Theme and Artistry in Doris Lessing's *A Proper Marriage*," in his *Tradition*, 176–225.

Sage, Lorna. *Doris Lessing*, 34–36.

Stitzel, Judith G. " 'That's Not Funny': Attitudes toward Humor in Doris Lessing's *A Proper Marriage* and *A Ripple from the Storm*." *Bull of the West Virginia Assoc of Coll Engl Teachers* 5:1–2 (1979), 40–46.

Swingewood, Alan. "Structure and Ideology," 44–46.

Wienhold, Christa. "Doris Lessing und Afrika," 132–134.

Retreat to Innocence, 1956

Fishburn, Katherine. "The Dialectics of Perception in Doris Lessing's *Retreat to Innocence*." *World Lit Written in Engl* 21 (1982), 416–433.

Knapp, Mona. *Doris Lessing*, 48–52.

Levy, Jette Lundbo. *Lessing-perspektiver*, 54–55.

Sage, Lorna. *Doris Lessing*, 41–42.

A Ripple from the Storm, 1958

Brown, Ruth Christiani. "Peace at Any Price: *A Ripple from the Storm*." *Doris Lessing Newsl* 7:2 (1983), 7–8, 10.

Sage, Lorna. *Doris Lessing*, 36–38.

Stitzel, Judith G. " 'That's Not Funny'," 40–46.

Swingewood, Alan. "Structure and Ideology," 44–46.

Wienhold, Christa. "Doris Lessing und Afrika," 130–132, 134–135.

The Sentimental Agents, 1983

Knapp, Mona. *Doris Lessing*, 148–155.

Shikasta, 1979

Frost, Cheryl. "Breakdown and Regeneration: Some Major Themes in Doris Lessing's Latest Fiction." *LiN Q* 8:3 (1980), 128–133.

Gray, Stephen. "Circular Imperial History and Zimbabwe in *Shikasta*." *Doris Lessing Newsl* 9:2 (1985), 11, 16.

Jouve, Nicole Ward. "Of Mud and Other Matter," 123–125.

Knapp, Mona. *Doris Lessing*, 133–139.

Levy, Jette Lundbo. *Lessing-perspektiver*, 75–78.

Mooney, Jane. "*Shikasta*: Vision or Reality?" *Doris Lessing Newsl* 8:1 (1984), 12–14.

Oumhani, Cécile. "Doris Lessing et le soufisme," 82–93.

Sage, Lorna. *Doris Lessing*, 77–80.

The Sirian Experiments, 1981

Knapp, Mona. *Doris Lessing*, 139–143.

Levy, Jette Lundbo. *Lessing-perspektiver*, 85–89.

Sage, Lorna. *Doris Lessing*, 82–84.

The Summer Before the Dark, 1973

Barets, Ralph. "A Jungian Interpretation of the Dream Sequence in Doris Lessing's *The Summer Before the Dark*." *Mod Fiction Stud* 26 (1980), 117–129.

Bazin, Nancy Topping. "Androgyny or Catastrophe," 12–13.

Campbell, Elaine. "The Life Passages of Kate Brown: Doris Lessing's Neglected Novel." *World Lit Written in Engl* 21 (1982), 411–415.

Cederstrom, Lorelei. "Doris Lessing's Use of Satire in *The Summer Before the Dark*." *Mod Fiction Stud* 26 (1980), 131–145.

Hoffeld, Laura, and Roni Natov. "*The Summer Before the Dark*," 11–12.

Hovet, Grace Ann, and Barbara Lounsberry. "The Affirmation of Signs in Doris Lessing's *The Summer Before the Dark*." *Wascana R* 16:2 (1981), 41–52.

Kaplan, Sydney Janet. "Passionate Portrayal," 4–15.

Knapp, Mona. *Doris Lessing*, 113–121.

Levy, Jette Lundbo. *Lessing-perspektiver*, 63–67.

Poznar, Walter. "Crisis of Identity in Doris Lessing's *The Summer before the Dark*: Who Is 'Kate Brown'?" *Texas R* 4:1–2 (1983), 55–61.

Sage, Lorna. *Doris Lessing*, 69–71.

Verleun, Jan. "The World of Doris Lessing's *The Summer before the Dark*." *Neophilologus* 69 (1985), 620–638.

Zeman, Anthea. *Presumptuous Girls*, 134–138.

CHARLES LEVER

Charles O'Malley, 1841

Christie, N. M. B. "Lever's *Charles O'Malley*: A Book to Recommend to a Friend?" *Etudes Irlandaises* 4 (1979), 33–54.

The O'Donoghue, 1845

Rix, Walter T. "Charles James Lever: The Irish Dimension of a Cosmopolitan," in Heinz Kosok, ed., *Studies*, 59–63.

AMY LEVY

Reuben Sachs; A Sketch, 1888

Zatlin, Linda Gertner. *The Nineteenth-Century Anglo-Jewish Novel*, 90–97.

C. S. LEWIS

The Chronicles of Narnia

Bailey, Mark. "The Honour and Glory of a Mouse: Reepicheep of Narnia." *Mythlore* 5:2 (1978), 35–36.

Bernhard, Wendy. "Personhood in Narnia." *Lamp-Post* 3:1 (1979), 3–6.

Ford, Paul F. *Companion to Narnia*.

Glover, Donald E. *C. S. Lewis*, 131–187.

Howard, Thomas. *The Achievement*, 21–52.

Huttar, Charles A. "The Heresy of Allegorizing Narnia: A Rejoinder." *Bull of the New York C. S. Lewis Soc* 11:3 (1980), 1–3.

Morrison, John. "The Idea of Covenant in Narnia." *Bull of the New York C. S. Lewis Soc* 10:12 (1979), 1–7.

Murphy, Brian. *C. S. Lewis*, 72–78.

Nagakura, Reiko. "Aslan the Lion in C. S. Lewis' *Narnia*." *Sophia Engl Stud* 4 (1979), 23–33.

Nakao, Bernadette Setsuko. "Salvation Theme in the Fiction of C. S. Lewis." *Stud in Engl Lit* (Japan) 56 (1979), 73–77.

Patterson, Nancy-Lou. "*Guardaci Ben*: The Visionary Woman in C. S. Lewis' Chronicles of Narnia and *That Hideous Strength*." *Mythlore* 6:3 (1979), 6–10; 6:4 (1979), 20–24.

Presley, Horton. "C. S. Lewis: Mythmaker," in Thomas D. Clareson and Thomas L. Wymer, eds., *Voices for the Future*, 130–149.

Rossi, Lee D. *The Politics of Fantasy*, 51–55.

Schakel, Peter J. *Reading with the Heart*.

Stock, R. D. "Dionysus, Christ, and C. S. Lewis." *Christianity & Lit* 34:2 (1985), 9–11.

Swinfen, Ann. *In Defence*, 19–23, 79–93, 148–159.

Tixier, Elaine. "Les Chroniques de Narnia de C. S. Lewis: nouveaux contes merveilleux pour notre temps?" *Caliban* 16 (1979), 27–39.

Walsh, Chad. *The Literary Legacy*, 123–157.

The Horse and His Boy, 1954

Gibson, Evan K. *C. S. Lewis*, 146–155.

Rossi, Lee D. *The Politics of Fantasy*, 68–70.

The Last Battle, 1956

Gibson, Evan K. *C. S. Lewis*, 207–218.

Hart, Dabney Adams. *Through the Open Door*, 132–134.

Murphy, Brian. *C. S. Lewis*, 77–88.

Phelps, Russ A. "*Mother Hubberds Tale* and *The Last Battle*." *Bull of the New York C. S. Lewis Soc* 11:6 (1980), 9–10.

Rossi, Lee D. *The Politics of Fantasy*, 76–78.

Walsh, Chad. *The Literary Legacy*, 147–157.

The Lion, the Witch, and the Wardrobe, 1950

Collings, Michael R. "Of Lions and Lamp-Posts: C. S. Lewis' *The Lion, The Witch, and The Wardrobe* as Response to Olaf Stapledon's *Sirius*." *Christianity & Lit* 32:4 (1983), 33–38.

Gibson, Evan K. *C. S. Lewis*, 131–146.

Rossi, Lee D. *The Politics of Fantasy*, 55–58.

Swinfen, Ann. *In Defence*, 156–158.

Walsh, Chad. *The Literary Legacy*, 138–147.

The Magician's Nephew, 1955

Gibson, Evan K. *C. S. Lewis*, 194–207.

Rossi, Lee D. *The Politics of Fantasy*, 71–75.

Walsh, Chad. *The Literary Legacy*, 132–138.

Out of the Silent Planet, 1938

Clute, John. "C. S. Lewis," in E. F. Bleiler, ed., *Science Fiction Writers*, 245–246.

Elgin, Don D. *The Comedy*, 66–69, 82–84.

Fisher, Judith L. "Trouble in Paradise: The Twentieth-Century Utopian Ideal." *Extrapolation* 24 (1983), 330–332.

Gibson, Evan K. *C. S. Lewis*, 25–45.

Glover, Donald E. *C. S. Lewis*, 74–84, 93–97.

Hart, Dabney Adams. *Through the Open Door*, 33–34.

Howard, Thomas. *The Achievement*, 53–87.

Murphy, Brian. *C. S. Lewis*, 25–43.

Nardo, A. K. "Decorum in the Fields of Arbol: Interplanetary Genres in C. S. Lewis's Space Trilogy." *Extrapolation* 20 (1979), 118–128.

O'Hare, Colman. "The Hero in C. S. Lewis's Space Novels." *Renascence* 31 (1979), 142–153.

Presley, Horton. "C. S. Lewis: Mythmaker," 129–149.

Rossi, Lee D. *The Politics of Fantasy*, 39–44.

Sammons, Martha C. *A Guide*, 27–127.

Stableford, Brian. *Scientific Romance*, 291–293.

Walsh, Chad. *The Literary Legacy*, 83–96.

Willis, John. "The Eldila in the Space Trilogy." *Bull of the New York C. S. Lewis Soc* 11:4 (1980), 1–5.

Perelandra, 1943

Brown, Robert F. "Temptation and Freedom in *Perelandra*." *Renascence* 37 (1984), 52–68.

Carnell, Corbin Scott. "Ransom in C. S. Lewis' *Perelandra* as Hero in Transformation: Notes toward a Jungian Reading of the Novel." *Stud in the Liter Imagination* 14:2 (1981), 67–71.

Clute, John. "C. S. Lewis," 247–248.

Elgin, Don D. *The Comedy*, 69–71, 84–85.

Fisher, Judith L. "Trouble in Paradise," 330–332.

Gibson, Evan K. *C. S. Lewis*, 46–68.

Glover, Donald E. *C. S. Lewis*, 91–105, 113–116.

Hart, Dabney Adams. *Through the Open Door*, 34–35.

Hodgens, Richard. "Some Aspects of Perelandra." *Bull of the New York C. S. Lewis Soc* 10:5 (1979), 1–6.

Howard, Thomas. *The Achievement*, 89–118.

Murphy, Brian. *C. S. Lewis*, 45–55.

Nardo, A. K. "Decorum in the Fields of Arbol," 118–128.

O'Hare, Colman. "The Hero," 142–153.

Presley, Horton. "C. S. Lewis: Mythmaker," 129–149.

Sammons, Martha C. *A Guide*, 27–127.

Stableford, Brian. *Scientific Romance*, 293–295.

Walsh, Chad. *The Literary Legacy*, 98–109.

Willis, John. "The Eldila in the Space Trilogy," 1–5.

Prince Caspian, 1951

> Gibson, Evan K. *C. S. Lewis*, 156–166.
> Rossi, Lee D. *The Politics of Fantasy*, 58–61.
> Swinfen, Ann. *In Defence*, 155–157.

The Silver Chair, 1953

> Gibson, Evan K. *C. S. Lewis*, 182–193.
> Rossi, Lee D. *The Politics of Fantasy*, 28–30, 64–67.
> Swinfen, Ann. *In Defence*, 150–152, 156–159.

That Hideous Strength, 1945

> Clute, John. "C. S. Lewis," 246–247.
> Collings, Michael. "Science and Scientism in C. S. Lewis's *That Hideous Strength*," in George E. Slusser and Eric S. Rabkin, eds., *Hard Science Fiction*, 131–140.
> Elgin, Don D. *The Comedy*, 72–79, 85–86, 90–91.
> Gibson, Evan K. *C. S. Lewis*, 69–97.
> Glover, Donald E. *C. S. Lewis*, 105–123.
> Hart, Dabney Adams. *Through the Open Door*, 36–38, 127–128.
> Howard, Thomas. *The Achievement*, 119–154.
> Murphy, Brian. *C. S. Lewis*, 57–69.
> Nakao, Setsuko. "Salvation Theme in C. S. Lewis's *That Hideous Strength*." *Bull of Seisen Women's Coll* 27 (1979), 1–16.
> Nardo, A. K. "Decorum in the Fields of Arbol," 118–128.
> Neuleib, Janice. "Love's Alchemy: Jane in *That Hideous Strength*." *Mythlore* 7:1 (1980), 16–17.
> Neuleib, Janice Witherspoon. "Comic Grotesques: The Means of Revelation in *Wise Blood* and *That Hideous Strength*." *Christianity & Lit* 30:4 (1981), 27–35.
> Nolan, Charles J., Jr. "*That Hideous Strength*: Antidote to Modernism." *Bull of the New York C. S. Lewis Soc* 11:9 (1980), 5–6.
> O'Hare, Colman. "The Hero," 142–153.
> Parrinder, Patrick. "Science Fiction and the Scientific World-View," in Parrinder, ed., *Science Fiction*, 79–80.
> Patterson, Nancy-Lou. "*Guardaci Ben*," 6–10; 20–24.
> Presley, Horton. "C. S. Lewis: Mythmaker," 129–149.
> Rossi, Lee D. *The Politics of Fantasy*, 46–49.
> Sammons, Martha C. *A Guide*, 27–127.
> Stableford, Brian. *Scientific Romance*, 295–297.
> Stewart, D. H. "What Lewis Really Did in *That Hideous Strength*." *Mod Fiction Stud* 26 (1980), 248–254.
> Stock, R. D. "Dionysus, Christ, and C. S. Lewis," 9.
> Walsh, Chad. *The Literary Legacy*, 109–122.
> Willis, John. "The Eldila in the Space Trilogy," 1–5.

Till We Have Faces, 1956

> Chard, Jean Marie. "Some Elements of Myth and Mysticism in C. S. Lewis' Novel *Till We Have Faces*." *Mythlore* 5:2 (1978), 15–18.

Elgin, Don D. *The Comedy*, 79–82, 86–87.
Elgin, Don D. "True and False Myth in C. S. Lewis' *Till We Have Faces*." *South Central Bull* 41 (1981), 98–101.
Fitzgerald, Dorothy Hobson. "Themes of Joy and Substitution in the Works of C. S. Lewis and Charles Williams." *Bull of the New York C. S. Lewis Soc* 12:3 (1981), 1–9.
Gibson, Evan K. *C. S. Lewis*, 221–255.
Glover, Donald E. *C. S. Lewis*, 187–199.
Hart, Dabney Adams. *Through the Open Door*, 38–39.
Howard, Thomas. *The Achievement*, 155–193.
Murphy, Brian. *C. S. Lewis*, 78–81.
Nakao, Bernadette Setsuko. "Salvation Theme," 77–81.
Reddy, Albert F. "*Till We Have Faces*: 'An Epistle to the Greeks'." *Mosaic* 13:3–4 (1980), 153–164.
Rossi, Lee D. *The Politics of Fantasy*, 78–84.
Sammons, Martha. "Christian Doctrines 'Transposed' in C. S. Lewis' *Till We Have Faces*." *Mythlore* 7:1 (1980), 31–35.
Schakel, Peter J. *Reason and Imagination*, 2–182.
Stock, R. D. "Dionysus, Christ, and C. S. Lewis," 11–13.
Walsh, Chad. *The Literary Legacy*, 159–178.

The Voyage of the "Dawn Treader," 1952

Gibson, Evan K. *C. S. Lewis*, 166–182.
Rossi, Lee D. *The Politics of Fantasy*, 61–65.
Swinfen, Ann. *In Defence*, 149–151, 155–157.

MATTHEW GREGORY LEWIS

The Monk, 1796

Allen, Virginia M. *The Femme Fatale*, 39–41.
Anderson, Howard. "Gothic Heroes," in Robert Folkenflik, ed., *The English Hero*, 212–217.
Coleman, William Emmet. *On the Discrimination*, 177–192.
Daleski, H. M. *The Divided Heroine*, 16–18.
Day, William Patrick. *In the Circles*, 121–124.
Fongaro, Antoine. "Baudelaire, *L'Aminta* et *Le Moine*." *Bull Baudelairien* 17:1–2 (1982), 5–8.
Gordon, Jan B. "Narrative Enclosure as Textual Ruin: An Archaeology of Gothic Consciousness." *Dickens Stud Annual* 11 (1983), 227–229.
Haggerty, George E. "Fact and Fancy in the Gothic Novel." *Nineteenth-Century Fiction* 39 (1985), 384–387.
Hennessy, Brendan. *The Gothic Novel*, 24–27.
Howells, Coral Ann. *Love, Mystery*, 62–79.
Le Tellier, Robert Ignatius. *An Intensifying Vision*, 21–26, 41–43, 54–57, 71–74, 80, 85–86, 103–109, 126–132, 144–146, 152–153, 157–158, 177–179, 191–194, 202–205, 211–214, 231–235.

Le Tellier, Robert Ignatius. *Kindred Spirits*, 71–85, 141–145, 170–173, 191–194.

Lewis, Paul. "Fearful Lessons: The Didacticism of the Early Gothic Novel." *Coll Lang Assoc J* 23 (1980), 476–484.

MacAndrew, Elizabeth. *The Gothic Tradition*, 86–93, 137–139.

Platzner, Robert Leonard. *The Metaphysical Novel*, 29–43.

Punter, David. *The Literature of Terror*, 68–70, 90–93.

Reddin, Chitra Pershad. *Forms of Evil*, 74–78, 124–126, 150–151, 221–222, 241–242, 261–263, 270–271.

Reno, Robert Princeton. *The Gothic Visions*, 98–154.

Sedgwick, Eve Kosofsky. "The Character in the Veil: Imagery of the Surface in the Gothic Novel." *PMLA* 96 (1981), 256–260.

Tracy, Ann Blaisdell. *Patterns of Fear*, 148–152, 164–166, 274–276.

Van Luchene, Stephen Robert. *Essays in Gothic Fiction*, 111–148.

Weiss, Fredric. *The Antic Spectre*, 159–192.

Wilt, Judith. *Ghosts of the Gothic*, 42–48.

WYNDHAM LEWIS

The Apes of God, 1930

Chapman, Robert T. *Wyndham Lewis*, 99–109.

Edwards, Paul. "*The Apes of God*: Form and Meaning," in Jeffrey Meyers, ed., *Wyndham Lewis*, 133–148.

Kush, Thomas. *Wyndham Lewis's Pictorial Integer*, 100–114.

Lake, Steve. "Wyndham Lewis." *Akzente* 32 (1985), 311–312.

Messerli, Douglas. "The Role of Voice in Nonmodernist Fiction." *Contemp Lit* 25 (1984), 286–289.

Munton, Alan. "Wyndham Lewis: The Transformations of Carnival," in Giovanni Cianci, ed., *Wyndham Lewis*, 154–157.

The Childermass, 1928

Chapman, Robert T. *Wyndham Lewis*, 165–176.

Jameson, Fredric. *Fables of Aggression*, 52–55, 69–75, 108–110.

Kush, Thomas. *Wyndham Lewis's Pictorial Integer*, 91–100.

Lake, Steve. "Wyndham Lewis," 318–319.

Munton, Alan. "A Reading of *The Childermass*," in Jeffrey Meyers, ed., *Wyndham Lewis*, 120–132.

The Human Age, 1955

Bridson, D. G. "*The Human Age* in Retrospect," in Jeffrey Meyers, ed., *Wyndham Lewis*, 238–251.

Chapman, Robert T. *Wyndham Lewis*, 165–182.

Fox, C. J. "Wyndham Lewis and 'the Schoolmaster of Manslaughter': The Machiavellian Presence," in Giovanni Cianci, ed., *Wyndham Lewis*, 199–202.

Jameson, Fredric. *Fables of Aggression*, 118–121, 148–164.

Mrs. Dukes' Million, 1977

Cianci, Giovanni. "Un futurismo in panni neoclassici: sul primo Wyndham Lewis vorticista," in Cianci, ed., *Wyndham Lewis*, 29–30.

Duncan, Ian. "Towards a Modernist Poetic: Wyndham Lewis's Early Fiction," in Giovanni Cianci, ed., *Wyndham Lewis*, 68–74.

Kenner, Hugh. "*Mrs. Dukes' Million*: The Stunt of an Illusionist," in Jeffrey Meyers, ed., *Wyndham Lewis*, 85–91.

Munton, Alan. "Wyndham Lewis," 141–143.

The Revenge for Love, 1937

Jameson, Fredric. *Fables of Aggression*, 82–86, 145–148.

Meyers, Jeffrey. "Van Gogh and Lewis' *Revenge for Love*." *Mod Fiction Stud* 29 (1983), 235–239.

Self Condemned, 1954

Chapman, Robert T. *Wyndham Lewis*, 153–164.

Jameson, Fredric. *Fables of Aggression*, 138–145.

Meyers, Jeffrey. "*Self Condemned*," in Meyers, ed., *Wyndham Lewis*, 226–237.

Snooty Baronet, 1932

Chapman, Robert T. *Wyndham Lewis*, 109–116.

Smith, Rowland. "*Snooty Baronet*: Satire and Censorship," in Jeffrey Meyers, ed., *Wyndham Lewis*, 181–195.

Tarr, 1918

Chapman, Robert T. *Wyndham Lewis*, 68–82.

Cianci, Giovanni. "Un futurismo in panni neoclassici," 43–56.

Currie, Robert. "Wyndham Lewis, E. T. A. Hoffmann, and *Tarr*." *R of Engl Stud* 30 (1979), 169–181.

Davies, Alistair. "*Tarr*: A Nietzschean Novel," in Jeffrey Meyers, ed., *Wyndham Lewis*, 107–119.

Jameson, Fredric. *Fables of Aggression*, 42–49, 64–67, 90–104.

Kush, Thomas. *Wyndham Lewis's Pictorial Integer*, 63–78.

Starr, Alan. "*Tarr* and Wyndham Lewis." *ELH* 49 (1982), 179–188.

Tamone, Sara. "Il vivisezionatore della propria risata: *Tarr* tra decadentismo e avanguardia," in Giovanni Cianci, ed., *Wyndham Lewis*, 129–140.

The Vulgar Streak, 1941

Chapman, Robert T. *Wyndham Lewis*, 131–139.

DAVID LINDSAY

The Adventures of Monsieur de Mailly, 1926

Sellin, Barnard. *The Life and Works*, 28–30.

Devil's Tor, 1932

McClure, J. Derrick. "*Devil's Tor*: A Rehabilitation of David Lindsay's 'Monster'." *Extrapolation* 21 (1980), 367–378.
Sellin, Barnard. *The Life and Works*, 30–34, 60–80, 88–97, 103–116, 120–126, 131–136, 175–181, 190–216.
Wilson, Colin. *The Haunted Man*, 46–53.

The Haunted Woman, 1922

Punter, David. *The Literature of Terror*, 340–345.
Sellin, Barnard. *The Life and Works*, 25–27, 57–63, 69–97, 108–122, 198–203, 212–217.
Wilson, Colin. *The Haunted Man*, 33–39.

Sphinx, 1923

Sellin, Barnard. *The Life and Works*, 26–28, 69–94, 100–105, 107–114, 118–120, 123–126, 200–206, 210–214.
Wilson, Colin. *The Haunted Man*, 39–46.

The Violet Apple, 1976

Sellin, Barnard. *The Life and Works*, 210–221.

A Voyage to Arcturus, 1920

Bold, Alan. *Modern Scottish Literature*, 193–198.
Hume, Kathryn. "Visionary Allegory in David Lindsay's *A Voyage to Arcturus*." *J of Engl and Germanic Philology* 77 (1978), 72–91.
McClure, J. D. "Language and Logic in *A Voyage to Arcturus*." *Scottish Liter J* 1:1 (1974), 29–38.
Pohl, Joy. "Dualities in David Lindsey's *A Voyage to Arcturus*." *Extrapolation* 22 (1981), 164–169.
Raff, Melvin. "The Structure of *A Voyage to Arcturus*." *Stud in Scottish Lit* 15 (1980), 262–268.
Sellin, Barnard. *The Life and Works*, 22–25, 41–52, 56–59, 61–76, 90–92, 127–129, 138–173, 190–193, 198–202, 221–226, 230–233.
Wilson, Colin. *The Haunted Man*, 14–33.

The Witch, 1976

Sellin, Barnard. *The Life and Works*, 221–230.

ERIC LINKLATER

Private Angelo, 1946

Rutherford, Andrew. "Eric Linklater as Comic Novelist," in David Hewitt and Michael Spiller, eds., *Literature*, 157–160.

ELIZA LINTON

The True History of Joshua Davidson, 1872

Rataboul, Louis J. *Le pasteur anglican*, 261–262.

Rignall, J. M. "Between Chartism and the 1880s: J. W. Overton and E. Lynn Linton," in H. Gustav Klaus, ed., *The Socialist Novel*, 36–40.

Under Which Lord?, 1879

Rataboul, Louis J. *Le pasteur anglican*, 356–358.

THOMAS HENRY LISTER

Arlington, 1832

Hart, Francis Russell. "The Regency Novel of Fashion," in Samuel I. Mintz et al., eds., *From Smollett to James*, 127–129.

Granby, 1826

Hart, Francis Russell. "The Regency Novel," 124–127.

JOHN GIBSON LOCKHART

Adam Blair, 1822

Richardson, Thomas C. "Character and Craft in Lockhart's *Adam Blair*," in Ian Campbell, ed., *Nineteenth-Century Scottish Fiction*, 51–67.

DAVID LODGE

The British Museum Is Falling Down, 1965

Burden, Robert. "The Novel Interrogates Itself: Parody as Self-Consciousness in Contemporary English Fiction," in Malcolm Bradbury and David Palmer, eds., *The Contemporary English Novel*, 138–143.

How Far Can You Go?, 1980

Streichsbier, Beata. "Irony in David Lodge's *How Far Can You Go?*," in Siegfried Korninger, ed., *A Yearbook*, 97–109.

THOMAS LODGE

Euphues Shadow, 1592

Addison, James Clyde. *An Old-Spelling Critical Edition*, 23–27.

Forbonius and Prisceria, 1584

Addison, James Clyde. *An Old-Spelling Critical Edition*, 16–18.

A Margarite of America, 1596

Addison, James Clyde. *An Old-Spelling Critical Edition*, 27–38.

Robert, Second Duke of Normandy, 1591

Addison, James Clyde. *An Old-Spelling Critical Edition*, 20–23.

Robin the Devil, 1591

Selzer, John L. "The Achievement of Lodge's *Robin the Devil.*" *Texas Stud in Lit and Lang* 26 (1984), 19–31.

Rosalynde, 1590

Addison, James Clyde. *An Old-Spelling Critical Edition*, 18–20.

Couton, Marie. "Variations arcadiennes dans le roman pastoral élisabéthain," in *Le Genre pastoral*, 151–159.

Cuvelier, Eliane. "Horror and Cruelty in the Works of Three Elizabethan Novelists." *Cahiers Elisabéthains* 19 (1981), 39–51.

Paran, Janice. "The Amorous Girl-Boy: Sexual Ambiguity in Thomas Lodge's *Rosalynde.*" *Assays* 1 (1981), 91–97.

SAMUEL LOVER

Handy Andy, 1842

Sloan, Barry. "Samuel Lover's Irish Novels." *Etudes Irlandaises* 7 (1982), 31–32, 36–37, 41.

Waters, Maureen. " 'No Divarshin': Samuel Lover's *Handy Andy.*" *Eire-Ireland* 14:4 (1979), 54–64.

Rory O'More, 1837

Sloan, Barry. "Samuel Lover's Irish Novels," 32–36, 38–41.

MALCOLM LOWRY

Dark as the Grave Wherein My Friend Is Laid, 1968

Bareham, Tony. "The Title of *Dark as the Grave Wherein My Friend Is Laid.*" *Malcolm Lowry Newsl* 1 (1977), 5–6.

Cross, Richard K. *Malcolm Lowry*, 68–75.

Falk, David. "Beyond the Volcano: The Religious Vision of Malcolm Lowry's Late Fiction." *Religion & Lit* 16:3 (1984), 26–34.

Grace, Sherrill E. *The Voyage*, 61–73.

Rankin, Elizabeth D. "Writer as Metaphor in Malcolm Lowry's *Dark as the Grave.*" *Twentieth Century Lit* 28 (1982), 319–333.

Veitch, Douglas W. *Lawrence, Greene and Lowry*, 175–177.

Lunar Caustic, 1968

Cross, Richard K. *Malcolm Lowry*, 17–25.

Grace, Sherrill E. "Malcolm Lowry and the Expressionist Vision," in Anne Smith, ed., *The Art of Malcolm Lowry*, 104–105.

Grace, Sherrill E. *The Voyage*, 29–33.

October Ferry to Gabriola, 1970

Binns, Ronald. "Beckett, Lowry and the Anti-Novel," in Malcolm Bradbury and David Palmer, eds., *The Contemporary English Novel*, 109–110.

Bradbrook, M. C. "Intention and Design in *October Ferry to Gabriola*," in Anne Smith, ed., *The Art of Malcolm Lowry*, 144–154.
Cross, Richard K. *Malcolm Lowry*, 75–84.
Grace, Sherrill E. *The Voyage*, 74–98.
Harrison, Keith. "Malcolm Lowry's *October Ferry to Gabriola*: Balancing Time." *Stud in Canadian Lit* 7 (1982), 115–121.
MacDonald, R. D. "Canada in Lowry's Fiction." *Mosaic* 14:2 (1981), 35–53.

Ultramarine, 1933

Cross, Richard K. *Malcolm Lowry*, 3–13.
Grace, Sherrill E. *The Voyage*, 24–29.
Rankin, Elizabeth D. "Beyond Autobiography: Art and Life in Malcolm Lowry's *Ultramarine*." *Stud in Canadian Lit* 6 (1981), 53–64.
Woodcock, George. "The Own Place of the Mind: An Essay in Lowrian Topography," in Anne Smith, ed., *The Art of Malcolm Lowry*, 115–116.

Under the Volcano, 1947

Ackerley, C. J. "Lowry's Tlaxcala." *Malcolm Lowry Newsl* 13 (1983), 17–30.
Ackerley, C. J. "Malcolm Lowry's Quauhnahuac." *Malcolm Lowry Newsl* 12 (1982), 14–29.
Ackerley, C. J. "Some Notes towards *Under the Volcano*." *Canadian Lit* 95 (1982), 185–190.
Ackerley, C. J. "*Under the Volcano*: Four Notes." *Malcolm Lowry Newsl* 11 (1982), 13–16.
Ackerley, Chris. "Strange Comfort." *Malcolm Lowry Newsl* 9 (1981), 31–33.
Ackerley, Chris, and Lawrence J. Clipper. *A Companion*, 3–446.
Binns, Ronald. "Beckett, Lowry," 102–105.
Binns, Ronald. "The Q-Ship Incident: The Historical Source." *Malcolm Lowry Newsl* 8 (1981), 5–7.
Boyd, Wendy. "Malcolm Lowry's *Under the Volcano*: La despedida." *Am Imago* 37 (1980), 49–64.
Boyum, Joy Gould. *Double Exposure*, 205–212.
Cailloux, Bernd G. "Die letzte Bestellung." *Akzente* 28 (1981), 229–234.
Champan, Marilyn. " 'Alastor': The Spirit of *Under the Volcano*." *Stud in Canadian Lit* 6 (1981), 256–272.
Coates, Paul. *The Realist Fantasy*, 188–190.
Cope, Jackson I. "Generic Geographies." *Genre* 14 (1981), 156–159. [Also in Jackson I. Cope and Geoffrey Green, eds., *Novel vs. Fiction*, 156–159.]
Costa, Richard Hauer. "The Grisly Graphics of Malcolm Lowry." *Coll Lit* 11 (1984), 250–256.
Costa, Richard Hauer. "*Under the Volcano*: A 'New' Charting of the Way It Was." *Malcolm Lowry Newsl* 4 (1979), 2–3.

Costa, Richard Hauer. "*Under the Volcano*—The Way It Was: A Thirty-Year Perspective," in Anne Smith, ed., *The Art of Malcolm Lowry*, 29–43.

Cripps, Michael. "Lost in the Wilderness: The Puritan Theme in *Under the Volcano*." *Engl Stud in Canada* 10 (1984), 457–473.

Cripps, Michael. "*Under the Volcano*: The Politics of the Imperial Self." *Canadian Lit* 95 (1982), 85–101.

Cross, Richard K. *Malcolm Lowry*, 26–64.

De Zordo, Ornella. "*Under the Volcano* e i due tempi del modernismo di Malcolm Lowry." *Lettore di Provincia* 13:51 (1982), 71–83.

Falk, David. "Self and Shadow: The Brothers Firmin in *Under the Volcano*." *Texas Stud in Lit and Lang* 27 (1985), 209–222.

Garnett, George Rhys. "*Under the Volcano*: The Myth of the Hero." *Canadian Lit* 84 (1980), 31–40.

Gilmore, Thomas B. "The Place of Hallucinations in *Under the Volcano*." *Contemp Lit* 23 (1982), 285–305.

Grace, Sherrill. "The Consul's 'Contiguity' Disorder." *Malcolm Lowry Newsl* 13 (1983), 31–34.

Grace, Sherrill E. "Malcolm Lowry," 97–109.

Grace, Sherrill E. *The Voyage*, 34–58.

Harrison, Keith. "The Myth of Oedipus in *Under the Volcano*." *Malcolm Lowry Newsl* 11 (1982), 16–19.

Harrison, Keith. " 'Objectivisation' in *Under the Volcano*: The Modernism of Eliot, Joyce, and Pound." *Malcolm Lowry Newsl* 10 (1982), 14–17.

Harrison, Keith. "The Philoctetes Myth in *Under the Volcano*." *Malcolm Lowry Newsl* 10 (1982), 3–5.

Huddleston, Joan. "From Short Story to Novel: The Language of *Under the Volcano*." *ACLALS Bull* (Mysore) 5:2 (1979), 80–90.

Jakobsen, Arnt Lykke. *Introduction and Notes.*

Jakobsen, Arnt Lykke. "Malcolm Lowry's *Under the Volcano*," in Stig Johansson and Bjorn Tysdahl, eds., *Papers*, 83–94.

Longo, Joseph A. "*Under the Volcano*: Geoffrey Firmin's Tragic Epiphany." *Notre Dame Engl J* 12 (1979), 15–23.

MacDonald, R. D. "Canada in Lowry's Fiction," 35–53.

Middlebro', Tom. "The Political Strand in Malcolm Lowry's *Under the Volcano*." *Stud in Canadian Lit* 7 (1982), 122–126.

Moon, Kenneth. "Lowry's *Under the Volcano* and Coleridge's *Kubla Khan*." *Explicator* 44:2 (1986), 44–46.

O'Kill, Brian. "Aspects of Language in *Under the Volcano*," in Anne Smith, ed., *The Art of Malcolm Lowry*, 72–90.

Thornton, Lawrence. *Unbodied Hope*, 35–37.

Tifft, Stephen. "Tragedy as a Meditation on Itself: Reflexiveness in *Under the Volcano*," in Anne Smith, ed., *The Art of Malcolm Lowry*, 46–69.

Veitch, Douglas W. *Lawrence, Greene and Lowry*, 112–177.

Walker, Ronald G. " 'The Weight of the Past': Toward a Chronology of *Under the Volcano.*" *Malcolm Lowry Newsl* 9 (1981), 3–23.
Woodcock, George. "The Own Place," 116–123.
York, Thomas. "The Post-Mortem Point of View in Malcolm Lowry's *Under the Volcano.*" *Canadian Lit* 99 (1983), 35–46.

E. V. LUCAS

Over Bemerton's, 1908
  Hunter, Jefferson. *Edwardian Fiction*, 185–188.

ARNOLD LUNN

The Harrovians, 1913
  Quigly, Isabel. *The Heirs of Tom Brown*, 155–163.

JOHN LYLY

Euphues, 1578
  Henderson, Judith Rice. "Euphues and His Erasmus." *Engl Liter Renaissance* 12 (1982), 135–161.
  Leech, Geoffrey N., and Michael H. Short. *Style in Fiction*, 16–18.
  Lo, Ch'ing-che. "Ssu-ma Hsiang-ju's *Fu* and John Lyly's Euphuism." *Tamkang R* 10 (1980), 385–413.
  McCabe, Richard A. "Wit, Eloquence, and Wisdom in *Euphues: The Anatomy of Wit.*" *Stud in Philology* 81 (1984), 299–324.
  Stephanson, Raymond. "John Lyly's Prose Fiction: Irony, Humor and Anti- Humanism." *Engl Liter Renaissance* 11 (1981), 3–21.

ROSE MACAULAY

Dangerous Ages, 1921
  Crosland, Margaret. *Beyond the Lighthouse*, 47–49.
Potterism, 1920
  Crosland, Margaret. *Beyond the Lighthouse*, 42–47.

GEORGE MACDONALD

Alec Forbes of Howglen, 1865
  Hein, Rolland. " 'If You Would But Write Novels, Mr MacDonald'." *Seven* 1 (1980), 16–17.
  Manlove, Colin. "George MacDonald's Early Scottish Novels," in Ian Campbell, ed., *Nineteenth-Century Scottish Fiction*, 71–86.

Annals of a Quiet Neighbourhood, 1867

    Rataboul, Louis J. *Le pasteur anglican*, 244–245.

At the Back of the North Wind, 1871

    McGillis, Roderick F. "Language and Secret Knowledge in *At the Back of the North Wind*." *Durham Univ J* 73 (1981), 191–198.

David Elginbrod, 1863

    Manlove, Colin. "George MacDonald's Early Scottish Novels," 70–86.

Guild Court, 1868

    Hein, Rolland. *The Harmony Within*, 117–121.
    Hein, Rolland. " 'If You Would But Write Novels'," 14–16, 17–18.

Lilith, 1895

    Hein, Rolland. *The Harmony Within*, 85–111.
    Jackson, Rosemary. *Fantasy*, 147–150.
    Jackson, Rosemary. "Narcissism and Beyond: A Psychoanalytic Reading of *Frankenstein* and Fantasies of the Double," in William Coyle, ed., *Aspects of Fantasy*, 50–51.
    McGillis, Roderick F. "George MacDonald and the Lilith Legend in the XIX Century." *Mythlore* 6:1 (1979), 3–11.
    Manlove, C. N. *The Impulse*, 71–92.
    Manlove, Colin. "The Circle of the Imagination: George MacDonald's *Phantastes* and *Lilith*." *Stud in Scottish Lit* 17 (1982), 55–76.
    Mendelson, Michael. "George MacDonald's *Lilith* and the Conventions of Ascent." *Stud in Scottish Lit* 20 (1985), 197–214.
    Prickett, Stephen. *Victorian Fantasy*, 87–88, 180–182, 189–193.

Malcolm, 1875

    Manlove, Colin. "George MacDonald's Early Scottish Novels," 72–86.

Paul Faber, Surgeon, 1879

    Hein, Rolland. *The Harmony Within*, 129–132.
    Hein, Rolland. " 'If You Would But Write Novels'," 22–24.

Phantastes, 1858

    Hein, Rolland. *The Harmony Within*, 54–84.
    Jackson, Rosemary. *Fantasy*, 147–150.
    Landow, George P. "And the World Became Strange: Realms of Literary Fantasy." *Georgia R* 33 (1979), 25–29.
    Manlove, C. N. *The Impulse*, 71–92.
    Manlove, Colin. "The Circle of the Imagination," 55–76.
    Robb, David S. "The Fiction of George MacDonald," in David Hewitt and Michael Spiller, eds., *Literature*, 71–73, 76–77.
    Wilson, Keith. "The Quest for 'The Truth': A Reading of George MacDonald's *Phantastes*." *Etudes Anglaises* 34 (1981), 141–152.

The Princess and the Goblin, 1872

McGillis, Roderick. " 'If You Call Me Grandmother, That Will Do'." *Mythlore* 6:3 (1979), 27–28.
Robb, David S. "The Fiction of George MacDonald," 74–76.
Willis, Leslie. " 'Born Again': The Metamorphosis of Irene in George MacDonald's *The Princess and the Goblin*." *Scottish Liter J* 12:1 (1985), 24–38.

Robert Falconer, 1868

Boaden, Ann. "Falcons and Falconers: Vision in the Novels of George MacDonald." *Christianity & Lit* 31:1 (1981), 11–17.
Manlove, Colin. "George MacDonald's Early Scottish Novels," 71–86.

The Seaboard Parish, 1868

Rataboul, Louis J. *Le pasteur anglican*, 245–246.

Thomas Wingfold, Curate, 1876

Hein, Rolland. " 'If You Would But Write Novels'," 19–20.
Rataboul, Louis J. *Le pasteur anglican*, 388–390.

Wilfrid Cumbermede, 1872

Rataboul, Louis J. *Le pasteur anglican*, 190–191.

TOM MACDONALD

The Albannach, 1932

McClure, J. Derrick. "Fionn Mac Colla: Unity through Trilingualism," in David Hewitt and Michael Spiller, eds., *Literature*, 170–174.

And the Cock Crew, 1945

Bold, Alan. *Modern Scottish Literature*, 200–203.
McClure, J. Derrick. "Fionn Mac Colla," 163–167.

IAN MCEWAN

The Cement Garden, 1978

Duperray, Max. "Insolite modernité: *The Cement Garden* (1978) d'Ian McEwan, chef-d'oeuvre d'une nouvelle littérature de l'angoisse." *Etudes Anglaises* 35 (1982), 420–429.

JOHN MCGAHERN

The Barracks, 1963

O'Rourke, Brian. *The Conscience of the Race*, 22–24.
Schwartz, Karlheinz. "John McGahern's Point of View." *Eire-Ireland* 19:3 (1984), 93–98.
Warner, Alan. *A Guide*, 247–249.

The Dark, 1965

O'Rourke, Brian. *The Conscience of the Race*, 15–16.
Schwartz, Karlheinz. "John McGahern's Point of View," 98–102.
Toolan, Michael J. "John McGahern: The Historian and the Pornographer." *Canadian J of Irish Stud* 7:2 (1981), 39–55.

Leavetaking, 1974

Schwartz, Karlheinz. "John McGahern's Point of View," 102–106.

The Pornographer, 1979

Berlind, Bruce. "*The Pornographer.*" *New Letters* 47:4 (1981), 140–141.
Schwartz, Karlheinz. "John McGahern's Point of View," 106–110.
Toolan, Michael J. "John McGahern," 39–55.

P. MACGILL

Children of the Dead End, 1914

Mitchell, Jack. "Early Harvest: Three Anti-Capitalist Novels Published in 1914," in H. Gustav Klaus, ed., *The Socialist Novel*, 75–81.

ARTHUR MACHEN

The Hill of Dreams, 1907

Punter, David. *The Literature of Terror*, 265–267.

WILLIAM MCILVANNEY

Docherty, 1975

Bold, Alan. *Modern Scottish Literature*, 239–241.

J. T. MCINTOSH

The Fittest, 1955

Wagar, W. Warren. "The Rebellion of Nature," in Eric S. Rabkin et al., eds., *The End of the World*, 139–141.

WALTER MACKEN

The Bogman, 1952

Kohl, Stephan. "Zur Tyrannei irischer Lebensart: Walter Mackens Gesellschaftsromane *The Bogman* und *Brown Lord of the Mountain*," in J. Kornelius et al., eds., *Einführung*, 140–148.

Brown Lord of the Mountain, 1967

Kohl, Stephan. "Zur Tyrannei irischer Lebensart," 141–148.

The Scorching Wind, 1964

    Cahalan, James M. *Great Hatred*, 160–164.

Seek the Fair Land, 1959

    Cahalan, James M. *Great Hatred*, 160–164.

The Silent People, 1962

    Cahalan, James M. *Great Hatred*, 160–164.

COMPTON MACKENZIE

The Four Winds of Love, 1937–1945

    Bold, Alan. *Modern Scottish Literature*, 177–180.

Sinister Street, 1913–1914

    Bold, Alan. *Modern Scottish Literature*, 174–176.

GEORGE MACKENZIE

Aretina, 1660

    Spiller, Michael. "The First Scots Novel: Sir George Mackenzie's *Aretina* (1660)." *Scottish Literary J*, Supplement 11 (1979), 1–20.

    Spiller, Michael. "Pioneers of Prose: Sir Thomas Urquhart and Sir George Mackenzie," in David Hewitt and Michael Spiller, eds., *Literature*, 38–40.

HENRY MACKENZIE

Julia de Roubigné, 1777

    MacAndrew, Elizabeth. *The Gothic Tradition*, 114–117.

The Man of Feeling, 1771

    Barker, Gerard A. "*David Simple*: The Novel of Sensibility in Embryo." *Mod Lang Stud* 12:2 (1982), 69–80.

    Burnham, R. Peter. "The Social Ethos of Mackenzie's *The Man of Feeling*." *Stud in Scottish Lit* 18 (1983), 123–135.

    Bystrom, Valerie Ann. "The Abyss of Sympathy: The Conventions of Pathos in Eighteenth and Nineteenth Century British Novels." *Criticism* 23 (1981), 213–214, 220.

    MacAndrew, Elizabeth. *The Gothic Tradition*, 54–58.

    McGuirk, Carol. "Sentimental Encounter in Sterne, Mackenzie, and Burns." *Stud in Engl Lit, 1500–1900* 20 (1980), 507–509.

    Punter, David. *The Literature of Terror*, 28–30.

    Sheriff, John K. *The Good-Natured Man*, 82–91.

    Shroff, Homai J. *The Eighteenth Century Novel*, 204–210.

The Man of the World, 1773

   Shroff, Homai J. *The Eighteenth Century Novel*, 77–80, 209–211, 215–217.

ELIZABETH MACKINTOSH

The Daughter of Time, 1951

   Bakerman, Jane S. "Advice Unheeded: Shakespeare in Some Modern Mystery Novels." *Armchair Detective* 14 (1981), 134–139.
   Rollyson, Carl E., Jr. "The Detective as Historian: Josephine Tey's *The Daughter of Time*." *Iowa State J of Res* 53:1 (1978), 21–30.

FRANCIS MACMANUS

Candle for the Proud, 1936

   Cahalan, James M. *Great Hatred*, 127–130.

The Fire in the Dust, 1951

   O'Rourke, Brian. *The Conscience of the Race*, 20–21, 46.

Flow On, Lovely River, 1941

   O'Rourke, Brian. *The Conscience of the Race*, 21–22.

Men Withering, 1939

   Cahalan, James M. *Great Hatred*, 127–130.

Stand and Give Challenge, 1934

   Cahalan, James M. *Great Hatred*, 127–130.

WILLIAM H. MALLOCK

The Heart of Life, 1895

   Rataboul, Louis J. *Le pasteur anglican*, 271–274.

The New Paul and Virginia, 1878

   Lamarca Margalef, Jordi. *Ciencia y literatura*, 92–93, 112–113.
   Rataboul, Louis J. *Le pasteur anglican*, 398–399.

The New Republic, 1877

   Jaudel, Philippe. "*The New Republic* de William Hurrell Mallock: Dialogue de mandarins dans la bonne société victorienne," in *Essais sur le dialogue*, 139–155.
   Lamarca Margalef, Jordi. *Ciencia y literatura*, 110–112.
   Rataboul, Louis J. *Le pasteur anglican*, 366–367.

THOMAS MALORY

Le Morte Darthur, 1485

Allen, Judson B. "Malory's Diptych *Distinctio*: The Closing Books of His Work," in James W. Spisak, ed., *Studies*, 237–252.

Allen, Judson Boyce. "The Medieval Unity of Malory's *Morte Darthur*." *Mediaevalia* 6 (1980), 279–309.

Annunziata, Anthony W. "The *Pas d'Armes* and Its Occurrences in Malory." *Stud in Medieval Culture* 14 (1980), 39–48.

Atkinson, Stephen C. B. "Malory's 'Healing of Sir Urry': Lancelot, the Earthly Fellowship, and the World of the Grail." *Stud in Philology* 78 (1981), 341–352.

Atkinson, Stephen C. B. "Malory's Lancelot and the Quest of the Grail," in James W. Spisak, ed., *Studies*, 129–149.

Barron, W. R. J. "Knighthood on Trial: The Acid Test of Irony." *Forum for Mod Lang Stud* 17 (1981), 181–197.

Benson, C. David. "Gawain's Defence of Lancelot in Malory's *Death of Arthur*." *Mod Lang R* 78 (1983), 267–272.

Brewer, Derek. *English Gothic Literature*, 264–276.

Brewer, Derek. "Malory: The Traditional Writer and the Archaic Mind," in Richard Barber, ed., *Arthurian Literature I*, 94–120.

Brink, Jeanie R. "The Design of Malory's 'Tale of Balin': Narrative and Dialogue Counterpoint." *Stud in Short Fiction* 17 (1980), 1–7.

Dillon, Bert. *A Malory Handbook*, 5–165.

Evans, Murray J. "Camelot or Corbenic? Malory's New Blend of Secular and Religious Chivalry in the 'Tale of the Holy Grail'." *Engl Stud in Canada* 8 (1982), 249–261.

Evans, Murray J. "*Ordinatio* and Narrative Links: The Impact of Malory's Tales as a 'hoole book'," in James W. Spisak, ed., *Studies*, 29–46.

Field, P. J. C. "Time and Elaine of Astolat," in James W. Spisak, ed., *Studies*, 231–235.

Fries, Maureen. "Indiscreet Objects of Desire: Malory's 'Tristram' and the Necessity of Deceit," in James W. Spisak, ed., *Studies*, 87–107.

Gibson, James M. "*The Book of Sir Tristrem* and the Chronology in Malory's *Le Morte Darthur*." *Tristania* 5 (1979), 22–38.

Hoffman, Donald L. "The Conflict from Within: The 'Timeliness' of Malory." *Fifteenth-Century Stud* 7 (1983), 179–202.

Holbrook, Sue Ellen. "Malory's Identification of Camelot as Winchester," in James W. Spisak, ed., *Studies*, 13–23.

Hynes-Berry, Mary. "A Tale 'Breffly Drawyne oute of Freynshe'," in Toshiyuki Takamiya and Derek Brewer, eds., *Aspects*, 93–106.

Jesmok, Janet. " 'A knyght wyveles': The Young Lancelot in Malory's *Morte Darthur*." *Mod Lang Q* 42 (1981), 315–330.

Kashiwagi, Hideo. "Natsume Soseki's Lancelot and Guinevere: A Comparative Study of 'Kairoko'." *Essays in Foreign Langs & Lit* (Hokkaido Univ) 24 (1978), 33–81. [In Japanese.]

Kelly, Robert L. "Wounds, Healing, and Knighthood in Malory's Tale of Lancelot and Guenevere," in James W. Spisak, ed., *Studies*, 173–192.

Kirk, Elizabeth. " 'Clerkes, Poetes and Historiographs': The *Morte Darthur* and Caxton's 'Poetics' of Fiction," in James W. Spisak, ed., *Studies*, 286–292.

Knight, Stephen. *Arthurian Literature*, 105–147.

Kurent, Tine. "The Mochlar Composition of King Arthur's Table Round." *Acta Neophilologica* 13 (1980), 3–20.

McCarthy, Terence. "Malory and the Alliterative Tradition," in James W. Spisak, ed., *Studies*, 53–81.

McCarthy, Terence. "The Sequence of Malory's Tales," in Toshiyuki Takamiya and Derek Brewer, eds., *Aspects*, 107–124.

Maclean, Madi. "The Patterned Presentation of Lancelot and Gawain in Malory's 'Tale of Gareth'." *Parergon* 27 (1980), 33–37.

Magister, Karl-Heinz. "Zur Kontinuität höfisch-epischer Literatur in England: Das Prosawerk Thomas Malorys." *Zeitschrift für Anglistik und Amerikanistik* 27 (1979), 108–120.

Mahoney, Dhira B. "Narrative Treatment of Name in Malory's *Morte D'Arthur*." *ELH* 47 (1980), 646–655.

Mahoney, Dhira B. "The Truest and Holiest Tale: Malory's Transformation of *La Queste del Saint Graal*," in James W. Spisak, ed., *Studies*, 109–124.

Mandel, Jerome. "Constraint and Motivation in Malory's 'Lancelot and Elaine'." *Papers on Lang & Lit* 20 (1984), 243–258.

Mann, Jill. " 'Taking the Adventure': Malory and the *Suite du Merlin*," in Toshiyuki Takamiya and Derek Brewer, eds., *Aspects*, 71–91.

Noguchi, Shunichi. "Englishness in Malory," in Toshiyuki Takamiya and Derek Brewer, eds., *Aspects*, 17–26.

O'Malley, Jerome F. "Sir Galahad: Malory's Healthy Hero." *Annuale Mediaevale* 20 (1981), 33–51.

Pickering, James D. "Malory's *Morte Darthur*: The Shape of Tragedy." *Fifteenth-Century Stud* 7 (1983), 307–328.

Plummer, John F. "*Tunc se Coeperunt non Intelligere*: The Image of Language in Malory's Last Books," in James W. Spisak, ed., *Studies*, 153–168.

Rivers, Bryan. "Malory's Lamerake and the Perils of 'Prouesse'." *Engl Stud in Canada* 7 (1981), 15–26.

Ruff, Joseph R. "Malory's Gareth and Fifteenth-Century Chivalry." *Stud in Medieval Culture* 14 (1980), 101–116.

Saycell, K. J. "Organic Unity and Interlace: Some Aspects of Malory's *Morte Darthur*." *Unisa Engl Stud* 17:2 (1979), 1–7.

Scott, Mary Etta. "The Good, the Bad, and the Ugly: A Study of Malory's Women." *Mid-Hudson Lang Stud* 5 (1982), 21–29.

Shichtman, Martin B. "Malory's Gawain Reconsidered." *Essays in Lit* (Macomb) 11 (1984), 159–171.

Spisak, James W. "Malory's 'Lost' Source," in Spisak, ed., *Studies*, 227–229.

Stiller, Nikki. *Eve's Orphans*, 128–132.

Vinaver, Eugène. "Landmarks in Arthurian Romance," in Nathaniel B. Smith and Joseph T. Snow, eds., *The Expansion*, 26–29.

Vinaver, Eugène. "A Note on Malory's Prose," in Toshiyuki Takamiya and Derek Brewer, eds., *Aspects*, 9–15.

Walsh, John Michael. "Malory's Arthur and the Plot of Agravain." *Texas Stud in Lit and Lang* 23 (1981), 517–531.

Walsh, John Michael. "Malory's Characterization of Elaine of Astolat." *Philol Q* 59 (1980), 140–148.

Walsh, John Michael. "Malory's 'Very Mater of La Cheualer du Charyot': Characterization and Structure," in James W. Spisak, ed., *Studies*, 199–222.

Whitaker, Muriel. "Christian Iconography in *The Quest of the Holy Grail*." *Ariel* 12:2 (1979), 11–19.

Wilson, Robert H. "Fate and Choice in Malory's Arthurian Tragedy," in Mohammad Ali Jazayery et al., eds., *Linguistic and Literary Studies*, 185–190.

Wright, Thomas L. "On the Genesis of Malory's *Gareth*." *Speculum* 57 (1982), 569–582.

Ziegler, Georgianna. "The Hunt as Structural Device in Malory's *Morte Darthur*." *Tristania* 5 (1979), 15–21.

MARY DELARIVIERE MANLEY

The New Atalantis, 1709

Beasley, Jerry C. "Politics and Moral Idealism: The Achievement of Some Early Women Novelists," in Mary Anne Schofield and Cecilia Macheski, eds., *Fetter'd or Free?*, 223–224.

London, April. "Placing the Female: The Metonymic Garden in Amatory and Pious Narrative, 1700–1740," in Mary Anne Schofield and Cecilia Macheski, eds., *Fetter'd or Free?*, 103–107.

Pache, Walter. *Profit and Delight*, 73–78.

Suhr, Heidrun. *Englische Romanautorinnen*, 27–29.

The Secret History of Queen Zarah and the Zarazians, 1705

Beasley, Jerry C. "Politics and Moral Idealism," 222–224.

OLIVIA MANNING

Friends and Heroes, 1965

Mooney, Harry J., Jr. "Olivia Manning: Witness to History," in Thomas F. Staley, ed., *Twentieth-Century Women Novelists*, 54–58.

The Great Fortune, 1960

Mooney, Harry J., Jr. "Olivia Manning," 39–48.

The Spoilt City, 1962

   Mooney, Harry J., Jr. "Olivia Manning," 48–54.

FREDERICK MARRYAT

Mr. Midshipman Easy, 1836

   Engel, Elliot, and Margaret F. King. *The Victorian Novel*, 36–38.
   Jean, Dominique. "Avatars du picaresque à l'époque victorienne."
   Caliban 20 (1983), 48–49.

Peter Simple, 1833–1834

   Jean, Dominique. "Avatars du picaresque," 48–49.

Snarleyyow, 1837

   Engel, Elliot, and Margaret F. King. *The Victorian Novel*, 27–28, 88–91.

HARRIET MARTINEAU

Deerbrook, 1842

   Figes, Eva. *Sex and Subterfuge*, 114–119.
   Pichanik, Valerie Kossew. *Harriet Martineau*, 114–119.
   Sanders, Valerie. " 'No Ordinary Case of a Village Apothecary': The
   Doctor as Hero in Harriet Martineau's *Deerbrook*." *Notes and Que-
   ries* 30 (1983), 293–294.
   Thomas, Gillian. *Harriet Martineau*, 94–100.

The Hour and the Man, 1841

   Pichanik, Valerie Kossew. *Harriet Martineau*, 125–126.
   Thomas, Gillian. *Harriet Martineau*, 92–94.

A. E. W. MASON

The Broken Road, 1908

   Hunter, Jefferson. *Edwardian Fiction*, 101–103.

CHARLES ROBERT MATURIN

The Albigenses, 1824

   D'Amico, Diane. "Feeling and Conception of Character in the Novels
   of Charles Robert Maturin." *Massachusetts Stud in Engl* 9:3 (1984),
   46–48.
   Harris, John B. *Charles Robert Maturin*, 297–317.
   Reddin, Chitra Pershad. *Forms of Evil*, 87–91, 136–137, 160, 181–183,
   212–213, 246.
   Tracy, Ann Blaisdell. *Patterns of Fear*, 107–109, 219–221.

Fatal Revenge, 1807

D'Amico, Diane. "Feeling and Conception of Character," 42–45.
Harris, John B. *Charles Robert Maturin*, 29–62.
Reddin, Chitra Pershad. *Forms of Evil*, 82–83, 130–132, 151–152, 158–159, 165–166, 176–179, 210–211, 227, 244–245, 264–265, 278–280.
Tracy, Ann Blaisdell. *Patterns of Fear*, 44–50, 80–86, 101–103, 302–304.

Melmoth the Wanderer, 1820

Auerbach, Nina. *Romantic Imprisonment*, 11–14.
Bayer-Berenbaum, Linda. *The Gothic Imagination*, 75–106.
Coleman, William Emmet. *On the Discrimination*, 217–226.
D'Amico, Diane. "Feeling and Conception of Character," 49–52.
Day, William Patrick. *In the Circles*, 64–65.
Ehlers, Leigh A. "The 'Incommunicable Condition' of Melmoth." *Res Stud* 49 (1981), 171–182.
Gordon, Jan B. "Narrative Enclosure as Textual Ruin: An Archaeology of Gothic Consciousness." *Dickens Stud Annual* 11 (1983), 229–230.
Haggerty, George E. "Fact and Fancy in the Gothic Novel." *Nineteenth-Century Fiction* 39 (1985), 387–391.
Harris, John B. *Charles Robert Maturin*, 251–296.
Hennelly, Mark M., Jr. "*Melmoth the Wanderer* and Gothic Existentialism." *Stud in Engl Lit, 1500–1900* 21 (1981), 665–679.
Hennessy, Brendan. *The Gothic Novel*, 27–30.
Howells, Coral Ann. *Love, Mystery*, 131–158.
Jackson, Rosemary. *Fantasy*, 104–107.
Le Tellier, Robert Ignatius. *An Intensifying Vision*, 35–38, 47–49, 61–68, 76–77, 81–82, 86–87, 114–118, 137–140, 147–148, 174–175, 189–191, 196–201, 214–221.
Le Tellier, Robert Ignatius. *Kindred Spirits*, 124–126, 131–132, 178–180.
Lloyd, Rosemary. "*Melmoth the Wanderer*: The Code of Romanticism," in Malcolm Bowie et al., eds., *Baudelaire*, 80–94.
MacAndrew, Elizabeth. *The Gothic Tradition*, 163–165.
Moynahan, Julian. "The Politics of Anglo-Irish Gothic: Maturin, Le Fanu and 'The Return of the Regressed'," in Heinz Kosok, ed., *Studies*, 48–49.
Platzner, Robert Leonard. *The Metaphysical Novel*, 43–57.
Punter, David. *The Literature of Terror*, 141–149.
Reddin, Chitra Pershad. *Forms of Evil*, 83–87, 132–136, 166–168, 179–181, 196–200, 211–212, 227–229, 245–246, 265–267, 280–282.
Soldati, Joseph Arthur. *Configurations of Faust*, 75–108.
Teyssandier, Hubert. *Les formes de la création*, 357–389.
Tracy, Ann Blaisdell. *Patterns of Fear*, 293–301.
Weiss, Fredric. *The Antic Spectre*, 220–223.
Wilt, Judith. *Ghosts of the Gothic*, 48–61.

The Milesian Chief, 1812

D'Amico, Diane. "Feeling and Conception of Character," 45–46.
Fiérobe, Claude. "C. R. Maturin: Nationalisme et fantastique." *Etudes Irlandaises* 9 (1984), 43–55.
Fiérobe, Claude. "Quelques images de la nature irlandaise dans l'oeuvre de C. R. Maturin," in *Autour de l'idée*, 117–124.
Harris, John B. *Charles Robert Maturin*, 97–139.
Tracy, Ann Blaisdell. *Patterns of Fear*, 177–179.

The Wild Irish Boy, 1808

D'Amico, Diane. "Feeling and Conception of Character," 48–49.
Fiérobe, Claude. "Quelques images," 117–124.
Harris, John B. *Charles Robert Maturin*, 63–96.

Women, 1818

D'Amico, Diane. "Feeling and Conception of Character," 49.
Fiérobe, Claude. "Quelques images," 117–124.
Harris, John B. *Charles Robert Maturin*, 191–226.

WILLIAM SOMERSET MAUGHAM

Cakes and Ale, 1930

Burt, Forrest D. *W. Somerset Maugham*, 115–133.
Curtis, Anthony. *Somerset Maugham*, 34–36.
Palmer, R. Barton. "Artists and Hacks: Maugham's *Cakes and Ale*." *South Atlantic R* 46:4 (1981), 54–62.

Liza of Lambeth, 1897

Burt, Forrest D. *W. Somerset Maugham*, 42–51.
Peschel, Enid Rhodes. "Callousness or Caring: Portraits of Doctors by Somerset Maugham and Richard Selzer." *Mosaic* 15:1 (1982), 77–88.

The Making of a Saint, 1898

Burt, Forrest D. *W. Somerset Maugham*, 52–54.

The Merry-Go-Round, 1904

Curtis, Anthony. *Somerset Maugham*, 26–27.

Mrs. Craddock, 1902

Burt, Forrest D. *W. Somerset Maugham*, 54–56.

The Moon and Sixpence, 1919

Burt, Forrest D. *W. Somerset Maugham*, 97–101.
Curtis, Anthony. *Somerset Maugham*, 30–33.

Of Human Bondage, 1915

Braendlin, Bonnie Hoover. "The Prostitute as Scapegoat: Mildred Rogers in Somerset Maugham's *Of Human Bondage*," in Pierre L. Horn and Mary Beth Pringle, eds., *The Image*, 9–18.

Burt, Forrest D. *W. Somerset Maugham*, 30–35, 72–93.
Curran, Trisha. "Variations on a Theme," in Michael Klein and Gillian
   Parker, eds., *The English Novel*, 228–234.
Curtis, Anthony. *Somerset Maugham*, 28–30.

The Razor's Edge, 1944

Burt, Forrest D. *W. Somerset Maugham*, 137–139.

HENRY MAYHEW

1851; or The Adventures of Mr. and Mrs. Sandboys, 1851
   Humpherys, Anne. *Henry Mayhew*, 50–52.

The Fear of the World, 1850
   Humpherys, Anne. *Henry Mayhew*, 49–50.

The Greatest Plague of Life, 1847
   Humpherys, Anne. *Henry Mayhew*, 45–46.

The Image of His Father, 1848
   Humpherys, Anne. *Henry Mayhew*, 47–49.

Whom to Marry and How to Get Married!, 1848
   Humpherys, Anne. *Henry Mayhew*, 46–47.

FANNY MAYNE

Jane Rutherford, 1854
   Kestner, Joseph. *Protest and Reform*, 177–182.

WILLIAM MAYNE

A Game of Dark, 1971
   Swinfen, Ann. *In Defence*, 63–67.

GEORGE MEREDITH

The Adventures of Harry Richmond, 1871
   Moses, Joseph. *The Novelist*, 113–129.
   Shaheen, Mohammad. *George Meredith*, 30–52.

The Amazing Marriage, 1895
   Argyle, Gisela. *German Elements*, 176–191.
   Morgan, Susan. "Dumbly a Poet: Lost Harmonies in Meredith's Later
      Fiction." *Huntington Lib Q* 47 (1984), 116–117, 123–125.
   Moses, Joseph. *The Novelist*, 61–64.
   Shaheen, Mohammad. *George Meredith*, 89–103.

Shore, Elizabeth M. "Godwin's Fleetwood and the Hero of Meredith's *The Amazing Marriage*." *Engl Stud in Canada* 8 (1982), 38–47.

Beauchamp's Career, 1875

Harris, Margaret. "The Epistle of Dr. Shrapel to Commander Beauchamp in Meredith's *Beauchamp's Career*." *Notes and Queries* 29 (1982), 317–320.

Moses, Joseph. *The Novelist*, 132–142.

Shaheen, Mohammad. *George Meredith*, 53–69.

Stone, Donald D. *The Romantic Impulse*, 309–315.

Wilding, Michael. "George Meredith's *Beauchamp's Career*: Politics, Romance and Realism." *Sydney Stud in Engl* 8 (1982–83), 46–69.

Diana of the Crossways, 1885

Argyle, Gisela. *German Elements*, 175–191.

Brownstein, Rachel M. *Becoming a Heroine*, 198–202.

Courow, Margaret. "Meredith's Ideal of Purity." *Essays in Lit* (Macomb) 10 (1983), 199–206.

Deis, Elizabeth J. "Marriage as Crossways: George Meredith's Victorian-Modern Compromise," in Anne C. Hargrove and Maurine Magliocco, eds., *Portraits of Marriage*, 18–24.

Milberg-Kaye, Ruth. "Meredith's *Diana of the Crossways* and Moore's *Irish Melodies*." *Explicator* 37:2 (1979), 27–29.

Morgan, Susan. "Dumbly a Poet," 117–122.

The Egoist, 1879

Argyle, Gisela. *German Elements*, 173–191.

Brownstein, Rachel M. *Becoming a Heroine*, 183–198.

Courow, Margaret. "Meredith's Ideal of Purity," 199–206.

Emerson, Sheila. "Imagery as Countercurrent in *The Egoist*." *Ariel* 12:1 (1981), 21–27.

Foster, David. "The 'Golden Key': Imagination and Reason in *The Egoist*." *J of Engl and Germanic Philology* 79 (1980), 541–554.

Goss, Marjorie H. "Language and Sir Willoughby in Meredith's *The Egoist*." *Interpretations* 13:1 (1981), 18–23.

Haley, Bruce. *The Healthy Body*, 240–251.

Handwerk, Gary J. "Linguistic Blindness and Ironic Vision in *The Egoist*." *Nineteenth-Century Fiction* 39 (1984), 163–185.

Miller, J. Hillis. " 'Herself Against Herself': The Clarification of Clara Middleton," in Carolyn G. Heilbrun and Margaret R. Higonnet, eds., *The Representation of Women*, 98–122.

Morgan, Susan. "Dumbly a Poet," 114–115.

Moses, Joseph. *The Novelist*, 164–183.

Ogunsanwo, O. "Meredith's Use of Narrative Personae and Offstage Incidents in *The Egoist*." *Lagos R of Engl Stud* 1:1 (1979), 71–93.

Polhemus, Robert M. *Comic Faith*, 204–244.

Rataboul, Louis J. *Le pasteur anglican*, 163–165.

Stewart, Maaja A., and Elvira Casal. "Clara Middleton: Wit and Pattern in *The Egoist*." *Stud in the Novel* 12 (1980), 210–226.
Stubbs, Patricia. *Women and Fiction*, 97–103.
Wheeler, Michael. *English Fiction*, 148–150.
Williams, Carolyn. "Natural Selection and Narrative Form in *The Egoist*." *Victorian Stud* 27 (1983), 53–79.
Williams, Merryn. *Women in the English Novel*, 170–172.

Evan Harrington, 1861

Mason, Philip. *The English Gentleman*, 175–180.
Moses, Joseph. *The Novelist*, 148–163.
Wheeler, Michael. *English Fiction*, 141–143.
White, Allon. *The Uses of Obscurity*, 82–85.

Harry Richmond, 1871

Stone, Donald D. *The Romantic Impulse*, 303–310.

Lord Ormont and His Aminta, 1894

Moses, Joseph. *The Novelist*, 64–66.

One of Our Conquerors, 1891

Moses, Joseph. *The Novelist*, 192–197, 200–208.
Shaheen, Mohammad. *George Meredith*, 70–88.
White, Allon. *The Uses of Obscurity*, 104–107.

The Ordeal of Richard Feverel, 1859

DeEulis, Marilyn David. "Meredith's *The Ordeal of Richard Feverel*." *Explicator* 38:4 (1980), 29–30.
DeGraaff, Robert M. "The Trouble with *Richard Feverel*." *J of Narrative Technique* 9 (1979), 81–89.
Ebbatson, Roger. *Lawrence and the Nature Tradition*, 80–86.
Haley, Bruce. *The Healthy Body*, 229–240.
Higgins, Elizabeth Jean. *Reading the Novel*, 316–323.
Jeffers, Thomas L. "Meredith's Concept of Nature: Beyond the Ironies of *Richard Feverel*." *ELH* 47 (1980), 121–146.
Moses, Joseph. *The Novelist*, 225–234.
Nadel, Ira Bruce. "From Fathers and Sons to Sons and Lovers." *Dalhousie R* 59 (1979), 222–224.
Raimond, J. "George Meredith: *The Ordeal of Richard Feverel*," in Pierre Coustillas et al., eds., *Le roman anglais*, 234–246.
Shaheen, Mohammad. *George Meredith*, 14–29.
Simon, Richard Keller. *The Labyrinth*, 138–177.
Smirlock, Daniel. "The Models of *Richard Feverel*." *J of Narrative Technique* 11 (1981), 91–107.
Stone, Donald D. *The Romantic Impulse*, 298–303.
Wheeler, Michael. *English Fiction*, 144–148.

Rhoda Fleming, 1865

Mitchell, Sally. *The Fallen Angel*, 93–95.

Sandra Belloni, 1886

> Moses, Joseph. *The Novelist*, 52–60, 69–85.

The Shaving of Shagpat, 1856

> Landow, George P. "And the World Became Strange: Realms of Literary Fantasy." *Georgia R* 33 (1979), 29–32.
> Moses, Joseph. *The Novelist*, 95–112.
> Moses, Joseph. "Shaving the Shaggy Dog: Ironies of Narrative and Meaning in Meredith's *Shagpat*." *Forum* (Houston) 16:3 (1978), 14–23.

The Tragic Comedians, 1880

> Argyle, Gisela. *German Elements*, 175–191.
> Moses, Joseph. *The Novelist*, 90–92.

A. A. MILNE

Winnie-the-Pooh, 1926

> Low, Anthony. "Religious Myth in *Winnie-the-Pooh*." *Greyfriar* 22 (1981), 13–16.

JAMES LESLIE MITCHELL

Cloud Howe, 1933

> Norquay, Glenda. "Voices in Time: *A Scots Quair*." *Scottish Liter J* 11:1 (1984), 59–61.

Gay Hunter, 1934

> Malcolm, William K. *A Blasphemer & Reformer*, 111–115.

Grey Granite, 1934

> Norquay, Glenda. "Voices in Time," 61–68.
> Paul, Ronald. *"Fire in Our Hearts,"* 36–43.
> Scobie, Brian. "Lewis Grassic Gibbon," in Francis Barker et al., eds., *Practices*, 134–142.

Image and Superscription, 1933

> Malcolm, William K. *A Blasphemer & Reformer*, 96–100.

The Lost Trumpet, 1932

> Malcolm, William K. *A Blasphemer & Reformer*, 106–111.

A Scots Quair, 1932–34

> Bold, Alan. *Modern Scottish Literature*, 129–139.
> Malcolm, William K. *A Blasphemer & Reformer*, 127–184.
> Morton, Brian. "Lewis Grassic Gibbon and the Heroine of *A Scots Quair*." *Edda*, 1980, 193–203.
> Murray, Isobel. "Action and Narrative Stance in *A Scots Quair*," in David Hewitt and Michael Spiller, eds., *Literature*, 109–120.

Norquay, Glenda. "Voices in Time," 57–68.

Ortega, Ramon Lopez. "Language and Point of View in Lewis Grassic Gibbon's *A Scots Quair.*" *Stud in Scottish Lit* 16 (1981), 148–156.

Ortega, Ramon Lopez. "The Language of the Working-Class Novel of the 1930s," in H. Gustav Klaus, ed., *The Socialist Novel,* 137–141.

Roskies, D. M. "Lewis Grassic Gibbon and *A Scots Quair*: Ideology, Literary Form, and Social History." *Southern R* (Adelaide) 15 (1982), 178–201.

Roskies, D. M. E. "Language, Class and Radical Perspective in *A Scots Quair.*" *Zeitschrift für Anglistik und Amerikanistik* 29 (1981), 142–152.

Wilson, Patricia J. "Freedom and God: Some Implications of the Key Speech in *A Scots Quair.*" *Scottish Liter J* 7:2 (1980), 55–78.

Spartacus, 1933

Bold, Alan. *Modern Scottish Literature,* 126–128.

Campbell, Ian. "James Leslie Mitchell's *Spartacus*: A Novel of Rebellion." *Scottish Liter J* 5:1 (1978), 53–60.

Malcolm, William K. *A Blasphemer & Reformer,* 115–126.

Stained Radiance, 1930

Malcolm, William K. *A Blasphemer & Reformer,* 82–92.

Sunset Song, 1932

Carter, Ian. "Burns, Scott, and the Scottish Peasantry," in Kathleen Parkinson and Martin Priestman, eds., *Peasants and Countrymen,* 118–120.

Norquay, Glenda. "Voices in Time," 58–59.

The Thirteenth Disciple, 1931

Bold, Alan. *Modern Scottish Literature,* 125–126.

Malcolm, William K. *A Blasphemer & Reformer,* 92–96.

Three Go Back, 1932

Malcolm, William K. *A Blasphemer & Reformer,* 102–106.

MARY RUSSELL MITFORD

Our Village, 1824–1832

Hunter, Shelagh. *Victorian Idyllic Fiction,* 68–76.

NANCY MITFORD

The Pursuit of Love, 1945

Beauman, Nicola. *A Very Great Profession,* 198–201.

EDWARD MONTAGUE

Demon of Sicily, 1807

    Tracy, Ann Blaisdell. *Patterns of Fear*, 159–162.

MICHAEL MOORCOCK

Behold the Man, 1968

    Greenland, Colin. *The Entropy Exhibition*, 129–134.

Breakfast in the Ruins, 1972

    Greenland, Colin. *The Entropy Exhibition*, 134–139.

The Condition of Muzak, 1977

    Greenland, Colin. *The Entropy Exhibition*, 152–156.

A Cure for Cancer, 1971

    Greenland, Colin. *The Entropy Exhibition*, 143–147.

The Dancers at the End of Time, 1972–1976

    Wagar, W. Warren. "Round Trips to Doomsday," in Eric S. Rabkin et al., eds., *The End of the World*, 95–96.

The English Assassin, 1972

    Greenland, Colin. *The Entropy Exhibition*, 147–151.

The Final Programme, 1965

    Glover, David. "Utopia and Fantasy in the Late 1960s: Burroughs, Moorcock, Tolkien," in Christopher Pawling, ed., *Popular Fiction*, 201–203.

    Greenland, Colin. *The Entropy Exhibition*, 140–143.

Gloriana, 1978

    Nicholls, Peter. "Michael Moorcock," in E. F. Bleiler, ed., *Science Fiction Writers*, 455–456.

GEORGE MOORE

Confessions of a Young Man, 1888

    Guillot-McGarry, Pascale. "Les Miniatures dans *Confessions of a Young Man.*" *Cahiers du Centre d'Etudes Irlandaises* 8 (1983), 7–15.

    Noël, Jean C. "George Moore's Pluridimensional Autobiography: Remarks on His *Confessions of a Young Man.*" *Cahiers du Centre d'Etudes Irlandaises* 4 (1979), 49–66.

A Drama in Muslin, 1886

    Cronin, John. *The Anglo-Irish Novel*, 120–133.

    Gonzalez, Alexander G. "Paralysis and Exile in George Moore's *A Drama in Muslin.*" *Colby Lib Q* 20 (1984), 152–163.

Mitchell, Judith. "*A Drama in Muslin*: George Moore's Victorian
Novel." *Engl Lit in Transition* 25 (1982), 211–223.
Stubbs, Patricia. *Women and Fiction*, 90–91, 94–96.
Warner, Alan. *A Guide*, 63–65.

Esther Waters, 1894

Bennett, James R. "Plot Repetition: Theme and Variation of Narrative
Macro-Episodes." *Papers on Lang & Lit* 17 (1981), 415–416.
Hall, Wayne. "*Esther Waters*: An Irish Story." *Irish Renaissance
Annual* 1 (1980), 137–155.
Stubbs, Patricia. *Women and Fiction*, 92–94.
Watt, George. *The Fallen Woman*, 182–222.

"*Hail and Farewell*," 1911–1914

O'Murchadha, Tomas. "A Naked Gael Screaming 'Brian Boru'," in
Robert Welch, ed., *The Way Back*, 64–65, 72, 78.
Schleifer, Ronald. "George Moore's Turning Mind: Digression and
Autobiographical Art in *Hail and Farewell*." *Genre* 12 (1979), 473–
503.
Warner, Alan. *A Guide*, 69–71.
Welch Robert. "Moore's Way Back: *The Untilled Field* and *The Lake*,"
in Welch, ed., *The Way Back*, 43–44.

The Lake, 1905

Hart, Clive. "The Continous Melody of *The Lake*," in Robert Welch,
ed., *The Way Back*, 83–92.
Martin, Augustine. "Prose Fiction in the Irish Literary Renaissance,"
in Masaru Sekine, ed., *Irish Writers*, 150–151.
Noël, Jean C. "Rambling Round *The Lake* with George Moore."
Cahiers du Centre d'Etudes Irlandaises 5 (1980), 71–88.
O'Leary, Joseph Stephen. "Father Bovary," in Robert Welch, ed., *The
Way Back*, 105–118.
O'Murchadha, Tomas. "A Naked Gael Screaming," 75–77.
Thomas, Sue. "The Influence of Ivan Turgenev on George Moore with
Special Reference to *A House of Gentlefolk* and *The Lake*." *Irish
Univ R* 12 (1982), 157–172.
Thomas, Sue. "A Study of George Moore's Revisions of *The Lake*."
Engl Lit in Transition 24 (1981), 174–183.
Warner, Alan. *A Guide*, 67–68.
Welch Robert. "Moore's Way Back," 39–44.

A Mummer's Wife, 1885

Watt, George. *The Fallen Woman*, 172–174.

JOHN MOORE

Edward, 1796

Bystrom, Valerie Ann. "The Abyss of Sympathy: The Conventions of
Pathos in Eighteenth and Nineteenth Century British Novels." *Criticism* 23 (1981), 213–214, 220.

HANNAH MORE

Coelebs in Search of a Wife, 1809

   Figes, Eva. *Sex and Subterfuge*, 93–95.

LADY MORGAN

The Wild Irish Girl, 1806

   Tracy, Robert. "Maria Edgeworth and Lady Morgan: Legality versus
   Legitimacy." *Nineteenth-Century Fiction* 40 (1985), 7–9.

WILLIAM MORRIS

A Dream of John Ball, 1888

   Mann, Nancy D. "Eros and Community in the Fiction of William
   Morris." *Nineteenth-Century Fiction* 34 (1979), 317–318.
   Silver, Carole. "Eden and Apocalypse: William Morris' Marxist Vision
   in the 1880s." *Univ of Hartford Stud in Lit* 13 (1981), 70–71.

The House of the Wolfings, 1889

   Boos, Florence. "Morris's German Romances as Socialist History."
   Victorian Stud 27 (1984), 322–342.
   Mathews, Richard. "William Morris's *Roots*: History into Metaphor."
   Cahiers Victoriens et Edouardiens 16 (1982), 69–76.
   Silver, Carole. "Eden and Apocalypse," 71–72.

News from Nowhere, 1890

   Faulkner, Peter. *Against the Age*, 133–144.
   Frye, Northrop. "The Meeting of Past and Future in William Morris."
   Stud in Romanticism 21 (1982), 307–313.
   Holzman, Michael. "Anarchism and Utopia: William Morris's *News
   from Nowhere*." *ELH* 51 (1984), 589–603.
   Ingle, Stephen. *Socialist Thought*, 82–87, 137–149.
   Khouri, Nadia. "The Clockwork and Eros: Models of Utopia in Edward
   Bellamy and William Morris." *Coll Lang Assoc J* 24 (1981), 390–399.
   Mecziems, Jenny. "Utopia and 'the Thing which is not': More, Swift,
   and Other Lying Idealists." *Univ of Toronto Q* 52 (1982), 58–59.
   Menichelli, Alfredo. "Utopia e desiderio in *News from Nowhere*," in
   Agostino Lombardo, ed., *Studi inglesi*, 165–188.
   Poston, Lawrence. "Three Versions of Victorian Pastoral." *Genre* 13
   (1980), 314–320.
   Seehase, Georg. "Überwindung der Utopie: Versuch über William
   Morris (1834–1896)." *Zeitschrift für Anglistik und Amerikanistik* 33
   (1985), 227–232.
   Sharratt, Bernard. "*News from Nowhere*: Detail and Desire," in Ian
   Gregor, ed., *Reading the Victorian Novel*, 288–304.

Silver, Carole. "Eden and Apocalypse," 73–75.

Sussman, Herbert. "The Language of the Future in Victorian Science Fiction," in George E. Slusser and Eric S. Rabkin, eds., *Hard Science Fiction*, 121–130.

Sypher, Eileen. "The 'Production' of William Morris' *News from Nowhere.*" *Minnesota R* 22 (1984), 84–101.

Wheeler, Michael. *English Fiction*, 163–165.

Wilding, Michael. *Political Fictions*, 48–90.

The Roots of the Mountains, 1889

Boos, Florence. "Morris's German Romances," 322–342.

Mathews, Richard. "William Morris's *Roots*," 69–76.

Silver, Carole. "Eden and Apocalypse," 72–73.

The Water of the Wondrous Isles, 1897

Bennett, James R. "Plot Repetition: Theme and Variation of Narrative Macro-Episodes." *Papers on Lang & Lit* 17 (1981), 416–417.

Landow, George P. "And the World Became Strange: Realms of Literary Fantasy." *Georgia R* 33 (1979), 33–35.

Manlove, C. N. *The Impulse*, 130–131.

Mann, Nancy D. "Eros and Community," 319–321.

The Well at the World's End, 1896

Faulkner, Peter. *Against the Age*, 169–173.

Hillgärtner, Rüdiger. "Freiheit und Brüderlichkeit in der Klassengesellschaft: Von der Möglichkeit des Unmöglichen in William Morris' Romanze *The Well at the World's End.*" *Zeitschrift für Anglistik und Amerikanistik* 33 (1985), 235–243.

Mann, Nancy D. "Eros and Community," 321–324.

The Wood Beyond the World, 1894

Faulkner, Peter. *Against the Age*, 166–169.

Manlove, C. N. *The Impulse*, 127–129.

Mann, Nancy D. "Eros and Community," 320–321.

Wolfshohl, Clarence. "William Morris's *The Wood Beyond the World*: The Victorian World vs. The Mythic Eternities." *Mythlore* 6:3 (1979), 29–32.

ARTHUR MORRISON

A Child of the Jago, 1896

De Stasio, Clotilde. *Lo Scrittore*, 153–156.

Paul, Ronald. *"Fire in Our Hearts,"* 19–26.

Rataboul, Louis J. *Le pasteur anglican*, 279–282.

DINAH MARIA MULOCK

Agatha's Husband, 1853

Mitchell, Sally. *Dinah Mulock Craik*, 34–36.

A Brave Lady, 1869

>Mitchell, Sally. *Dinah Mulock Craik*, 69–73.
>Mitchell, Sally. *The Fallen Angel*, 117–118.

Christian's Mistake, 1865

>Mitchell, Sally. *Dinah Mulock Craik*, 61–64.

Hannah, 1871

>Mitchell, Sally. *Dinah Mulock Craik*, 73–75.
>Mitchell, Sally. *The Fallen Angel*, 118–120.

The Head of the Family, 1852

>Mitchell, Sally. *Dinah Mulock Craik*, 31–34.

John Halifax, Gentleman, 1856

>Gilmour, Robin. *The Idea of the Gentleman*, 101–102.
>Kestner, Joseph. *Protest and Reform*, 182–187.
>Mitchell, Sally. *Dinah Mulock Craik*, 39–53.
>Mitchell, Sally. *The Fallen Angel*, 113–115.

A Life for a Life, 1859

>Foster, Shirley. *Victorian Women's Fiction*, 64–67.
>Mitchell, Sally. *Dinah Mulock Craik*, 56–58.
>Mitchell, Sally. *The Fallen Angel*, 115–117.

Mistress and Maid, 1862

>Mitchell, Sally. *Dinah Mulock Craik*, 59–61.

A Noble Life, 1866

>Mitchell, Sally. *Dinah Mulock Craik*, 64–66.

The Ogilvies, 1849

>Mitchell, Sally. *Dinah Mulock Craik*, 26–29.

Olive, 1850

>Foster, Shirley. *Victorian Women's Fiction*, 62–64.
>Mitchell, Sally. *Dinah Mulock Craik*, 29–31.

The Woman's Kingdom, 1869

>Mitchell, Sally. *Dinah Mulock Craik*, 68–69.

Young Mrs. Jardine, 1879

>Mitchell, Sally. *Dinah Mulock Craik*, 75–77.

IRIS MURDOCH

An Accidental Man, 1971

>Dipple, Elizabeth. *Iris Murdoch*, 197–212.
>Hague, Angela. *Iris Murdoch's Comic Vision*, 70–90.
>Todd, Richard. *Iris Murdoch*, 44–49, 89–92.

Widmer, Kingsley. "The Wages of Intellectuality . . . and the Fictional Wages of Iris Murdoch," in Thomas F. Staley, ed., *Twentieth-Century Women Novelists*, 31–33.

Zirker, Herbert. "Iris Murdoch, *An Accidental Man*," in Rainer Lengeler, ed., *Englische Literatur*, 288–300.

The Bell, 1958

Adams, Stephen. *The Homosexual*, 166–170.

Dipple, Elizabeth. *Iris Murdoch*, 102–104, 145–147, 242–251.

McEwan, Neil. *The Survival of the Novel*, 39–45.

Roxman, Susanna. "Contingency and the Image of the Net in Iris Murdoch, Novelist and Philosopher." *Edda*, 1983, 67–69.

Stewart, Jack F. "Dialectics in Murdoch's *The Bell*." *Res Stud* 48 (1980), 210–217.

Winsor, Dorothy A. "Iris Murdoch and the Uncanny: Supernatural Events in *The Bell*." *Lit and Psych* 30 (1980), 147–153.

Winsor, Dorothy A. "Solipsistic Sexuality in Iris Murdoch's Gothic Novels." *Renascence* 34 (1981), 53–57.

The Black Prince, 1973

Byatt, A. S. "People in Paper Houses: Attitudes to 'Realism' and 'Experiment' in English Postwar Fiction," in Malcolm Bradbury and David Palmer, eds., *The Contemporary English Novel*, 34–36.

Cohan, Steven. "From Subtext to Dream Text: The Brutal Egoism of Iris Murdoch's Male Narrators." *Women & Lit* 2 (1981), 226–228.

Dipple, Elizabeth. *Iris Murdoch*, 42–46, 109–132.

Hague, Angela. *Iris Murdoch's Comic Vision*, 95–118.

Lamarque, Peter. "Truth and Art in Iris Murdoch's *The Black Prince*." *Philos and Lit* 2 (1978), 209–222.

Roxman, Susanna. "Contingency," 65–67.

Slaymaker, William. "Myths, Mystery and the Mechanisms of Determinism: The Aesthetics of Freedom in Iris Murdoch's Fiction." *Papers on Lang & Lit* 18 (1982), 173–180.

Todd, Richard. *Iris Murdoch*, 29–42.

Widmer, Kingsley. "The Wages of Intellectuality," 35–37.

Bruno's Dream, 1969

Dipple, Elizabeth. *Iris Murdoch*, 168–181.

Todd, Richard. *Iris Murdoch*, 57–66.

Widmer, Kingsley. "The Wages of Intellectuality," 28.

A Fairly Honourable Defeat, 1970

Adams, Stephen. *The Homosexual*, 175–181.

Burling, Valerie. "*A Fairly Honourable Defeat*: Jeux formels," in *Rencontres*, 37–43.

Dipple, Elizabeth. *Iris Murdoch*, 17–22, 181–196.

Todd, Richard. *Iris Murdoch*, 10–14.

Widmer, Kingsley. "The Wages of Intellectuality," 28–31.

The Flight from the Enchanter, 1956

Dipple, Elizabeth. *Iris Murdoch*, 136–142.

Henry and Cato, 1976

Dipple, Elizabeth. *Iris Murdoch*, 22–27, 242–245, 252–264.
McEwan, Neil. *The Survival of the Novel*, 55–59.
Widmer, Kingsley. "The Wages of Intellectuality," 27–28.

The Italian Girl, 1964

Bruni, Valerio. "La doppia funzione dell' 'ingranaggio' in *The Italian Girl* di Iris Murdoch." *Spicilegio Moderno* 9 (1978), 121–135.
Widmer, Kingsley. "The Wages of Intellectuality," 19.

The Nice and the Good, 1968

Ashworth, Ann M. " 'Venus, Cupid, Folly, and Time': Bronzino's Allegory and Murdoch's Fiction." *Critique* (Atlanta) 23:1 (1981), 18–24.
Crosland, Margaret. *Beyond the Lighthouse*, 219–220.
Dipple, Elizabeth. *Iris Murdoch*, 9–14, 155–166.
McEwan, Neil. *The Survival of the Novel*, 45–53.
Todd, Richard. *Iris Murdoch*, 85–88, 114–118.
Widmer, Kingsley. "The Wages of Intellectuality," 25–27.

Nuns and Soldiers, 1980

Conradi, Peter J. "Useful Fictions: Iris Murdoch." *Crit Q* 23:3 (1981), 63–69.
Dipple, Elizabeth. *Iris Murdoch*, 306–347.

The Red and the Green, 1965

Cahalan, James M. *Great Hatred*, 165–169.
Charpentier, Colette. "The Critical Reception of Iris Murdoch's Irish Novels (1963–1976) II: *The Red and the Green*." *Etudes Irlandaises* 6 (1981), 87–97.
DeSalvo, Louise A. " 'This Should Not Be': Iris Murdoch's Critique of English Policy Towards Ireland in *The Red and the Green*." *Colby Lib Q* 19 (1983), 113–124.
Scanlan, Margaret. "Fiction and the Fictions of History in Iris Murdoch's *The Red and the Green*." *CLIO* 9 (1980), 365–376.

The Sacred and Profane Love Machine, 1974

Dipple, Elizabeth. *Iris Murdoch*, 226–241.
Ganner-Rauth, H. "Iris Murdoch and the Brontë Heritage." *Stud in Engl Lit* (Japan) 58 (1981), 62–68.
Lloyd, Genevieve. "Iris Murdoch on the Ethical Significance of Truth." *Philos and Lit* 6 (1982), 68–73.
Todd, Richard. *Iris Murdoch*, 92–95.
Widmer, Kingsley. "The Wages of Intellectuality," 33–34.
Winsor, Dorothy A. "Iris Murdoch's Conflicting Ethical Demands: Separation versus Passivity in *The Sacred and Profane Love Machine*." *Mod Lang Q* 44 (1983), 394–409.

The Sandcastle, 1957

Dipple, Elizabeth. *Iris Murdoch*, 15–17, 142–146.
Widmer, Kingsley. "The Wages of Intellectuality," 21.

The Sea, the Sea, 1978

Cohan, Steven. "From Subtext to Dream Text," 233–241.
Dipple, Elizabeth. *Iris Murdoch*, 265–267, 274–305.
Hague, Angela. *Iris Murdoch's Comic Vision*, 119–142.

A Severed Head, 1961

Castillo, Debra A. *The Translated World*, 297–304.
Cohan, Steven. "From Subtext to Dream Text," 229–231.
Conradi, Peter. "The Metaphysical Hostess: The Cult of Personal Relations in the Modern English Novel." *ELH* 48 (1981), 430–432.
Dipple, Elizabeth. *Iris Murdoch*, 148–150.
Fletcher, John. *Novel and Reader*, 42–44.
Reckwitz, Erhard. "Der notwendige Zufall: Die Romane von Iris Murdoch." *Germanisch-Romanische Monatsschrift* 31 (1981), 342–348.
Smithson, Isaiah. "Iris Murdoch's *A Severed Head*: The Revolution of Human Consciousness." *Southern R* (Adelaide) 11 (1978), 133–153.
Widmer, Kingsley. "The Wages of Intellectuality," 21–24.

A Time of the Angels, 1966

Dipple, Elizabeth. *Iris Murdoch*, 62–78.
Widmer, Kingsley. "The Wages of Intellectuality," 19–20.
Winsor, Dorothy A. "Solipsistic Sexuality," 59–62.

Under the Net, 1954

Conradi, Peter. "The Metaphysical Hostess," 429–430.
Dipple, Elizabeth. *Iris Murdoch*, 53–57.
Fletcher, John. "Reading Beckett with Iris Murdoch's Eyes." *AUMLA* 55 (1981), 7–14.
Fontane, Marilyn Stall. "Under the Net of a Mid-Summer Night's Dream." *Publs of the Arkansas Philol Assoc* 9:1 (1983), 43–54.
Kellman, Steven G. *The Self-Begetting Novel*, 87–93.
Roxman, Susanna. "Contingency," 65–70.
Sander, Hans-Jochen. " 'Menschliche Natur' und Individualität in Fieldings *Tom Jones* und im spätbürgerlichen englischen Roman." *Zeitschrift für Anglistik und Amerikanistik* 28 (1980), 240–241.
Sander, Hans-Jochen. "Zum Verhältnis von philosophisch-literarischer Theoriebildung und Romanpraxis bei Iris Murdoch." *Zeitschrift für Anglistik und Amerikanistik* 30 (1982), 38–41.
Widmer, Kingsley. "The Wages of Intellectuality," 20–21.

The Unicorn, 1963

Bertrandias, Bernadette. "Vision fantastique et vision mythique dans *The Unicorn* d'Iris Murdoch." *Confluents* 2 (1975), 13–37.

Charpentier, Colette. "The Critical Reception of Iris Murdoch's Irish Novels (1963–1976) I: *The Unicorn.*" *Etudes Irlandaises* 5 (1980), 94–99.

Charpentier, Colette. "L'Etrange dans *The Unicorn* d'Iris Murdoch." *Etudes Irlandaises* 9 (1984), 89–93.

Dipple, Elizabeth. *Iris Murdoch*, 265–274.

Dutruch, Suzanne. "*The Unicorn*: art et artifice." *Etudes Anglaises* 36 (1983), 57–66.

Ganner-Rauth, H. "Iris Murdoch and the Brontë Heritage," 68–73.

Sander, Hans-Jochen. " 'Menschliche Natur' und Individualität," 240–241.

Widmer, Kingsley. "The Wages of Intellectuality," 17–19.

Winsor, Dorothy A. "Solipsistic Sexuality," 57–59.

An Unofficial Rose, 1962

Dipple, Elizabeth. *Iris Murdoch*, 57–60.

Todd, Richard. *Iris Murdoch*, 82–85.

Widmer, Kingsley. "The Wages of Intellectuality," 24–25.

A Word Child, 1975

Cohan, Steven. "From Subtext to Dream Text," 228–229, 231–232.

Dipple, Elizabeth. *Iris Murdoch*, 212–226.

MacPhail, Fiona, and Jean-Louis Chevalier. "*A Word Child* ou *L'Héautontimorouménos*," in *Rencontres*, 19–36.

Todd, Richard. *Iris Murdoch*, 49–57.

Widmer, Kingsley. "The Wages of Intellectuality," 34–35.

V. S. NAIPAUL

A Bend in the River, 1979

Campbell, Elaine. "A Refinement of Rage: V. S. Naipaul's *A Bend in the River.*" *World Lit Written in Engl* 18 (1979), 394–406.

Jama, Virginia. "The Image of the African Leader in Recent Western Fiction." *Horn of Africa* 3:1 (1980), 43–45.

McSweeney, Kerry. *Four Contemporary Novelists*, 190–194.

Prescott, Lynda. "Past and Present Darkness: Sources for V. S. Naipaul's *A Bend in the River.*" *Mod Fiction Stud* 30 (1984), 547–559.

Smyer, Richard I. "Experience as Drama in the Works of V. S. Naipaul." *Kunapipi* 3:2 (1981), 38–40.

Guerillas, 1975

Hemenway, Robert. "Sex and Politics in V. S. Naipaul." *Stud in the Novel* 14 (1982), 193–201.

McSweeney, Kerry. *Four Contemporary Novelists*, 187–190.

Swinden, Patrick. *The English Novel*, 246–251.

Wirth-Nesher, Hana. "The Curse of Marginality: Colonialism in Naipaul's *Guerillas.*" *Mod Fiction Stud* 30 (1984), 531–545.

A House for Mr. Biswas, 1961

Belitt, Ben. "The Heraldry of Accommodation: A House for Mr. Naipaul." *Salmagundi* 54 (1981), 23–42.

Carthew, John. "Adapting to Trinidad: Mr Biswas and Mr Polly Revisited." *J of Commonwealth Lit* 13:1 (1978), 58–64.

Garebian, Keith. "The Grotesque Satire of *A House for Mr Biswas*." *Mod Fiction Stud* 30 (1984), 487–496.

Gilkes, Michael. *The West Indian Novel*, 94–98.

Gurr, Andrew. "The Freedom of Exile in Naipaul and Doris Lessing." *Ariel* 13:4 (1982), 9–10.

Gurr, Andrew. *Writers in Exile*, 72–82.

McSweeney, Kerry. *Four Contemporary Novelists*, 166–173.

Robinson, Fred Miller. "Comic Realism and V. S. Naipaul's *A House for Mr Biswas*." *Thalia* 5:2 (1982–83), 14–23.

Verut, Annie. "Aliénation et délimitation de l'espace dans *A House for Mr. Biswas* de V. S. Naipaul," in *L'Autre dans la sensibilité*, 119–127.

Miguel Street, 1959

St. Omer, Garth. "The Writer as Naive Colonial: V. S. Naipaul and *Miguel Street*." *Carib* 1 (1979), 7–17.

Swinden, Patrick. *The English Novel*, 212–215.

Thieme, John. "Calypso Allusions in Naipaul's *Miguel Street*." *Kunapipi* 3:2 (1981), 18–30.

The Mimic Men, 1967

Gilkes, Michael. *The West Indian Novel*, 99–102.

Gurr, Andrew. *Writers in Exile*, 83–88.

Lindroth, James R. "The Figure of Performance in Naipaul's *The Mimic Men*." *Mod Fiction Stud* 30 (1984), 519–529.

McSweeney, Kerry. *Four Contemporary Novelists*, 176–181.

Swinden, Patrick. *The English Novel*, 236–246.

Thieme, John. "A Hindu Castaway: Ralph Singh's Journey in *The Mimic Men*." *Mod Fiction Stud* 30 (1984), 505–518.

Mr. Stone and the Knights Companion, 1963

McSweeney, Kerry. *Four Contemporary Novelists*, 173–176.

Thieme, John. "Naipaul's English Fable: *Mr Stone and the Knights Companion*." *Mod Fiction Stud* 30 (1984), 497–503.

The Mystic Masseur, 1957

McSweeney, Kerry. *Four Contemporary Novelists*, 163–165.

Mann, Harveen Sachdeva. "Variations on the Theme of Mimicry: Naipaul's *The Mystic Masseur* and *The Suffrage of Elvira*." *Mod Fiction Stud* 30 (1984), 469–476.

Naik, M. K. "Irony as Stance and as Vision: A Comparative Study of V. S. Naipaul's *The Mystic Masseur* and R. K. Narayan's *The Guide*." *J of Indian Writing in Engl* 6:1 (1978), 1–13.

Swinden, Patrick. *The English Novel*, 215–217.

The Suffrage of Elvira, 1958

Crew, Gary. "V. S. Naipaul's *The Suffrage of Elvira*," in Brian Green, ed., *Generous Converse*, 47–57.

McSweeney, Kerry. *Four Contemporary Novelists*, 163–165.

Mann, Harveen Sachdeva. "Variations," 476–485.

THOMAS NASHE

The Unfortunate Traveller, 1594

Cuvelier, Eliane. "Horror and Cruelty in the Works of Three Elizabethan Novelists." *Cahiers Elisabéthains* 19 (1981), 39–51.

Ferguson, Margaret. "Nashe's *The Unfortunate Traveller*: The 'Newes of the Maker' Game." *Engl Liter Renaissance* 11 (1981), 165–182.

Jones, Ann R. "Inside the Outsider: Nashe's *Unfortunate Traveller* and Bakhtin's Polyphonic Novel." *ELH* 50 (1983), 61–78.

McGinn, Donald J. *Thomas Nashe*, 87–103.

Maillard, Jean-François. *Essai sur l'esprit*, 128–141.

Morrow, Patrick D. "The Brazen World of Thomas Nashe and *The Unfortunate Traveller*," in his *Tradition*, 68–92.

Stephanson, Raymond. "The Epistemological Challenge of Nashe's *The Unfortunate Traveller*." *Stud in Engl Lit, 1500–1900* 23 (1983), 21–36.

Sulfridge, Cynthia. "*The Unfortunate Traveller*: Nashe's Narrative in a 'Cleane Different Vaine'." *J of Narrative Technique* 10 (1980), 1–14.

Suzuki, Mihoko. " 'Signiorie ouer the Pages': The Crisis of Authority in Nashe's *The Unfortunate Traveller*." *Stud in Philology* 81 (1984), 348–371.

Wenke, John. "The Moral Aesthetic of Thomas Nashe's *The Unfortunate Traveller*." *Renascence* 34 (1981), 17–32.

BILL NAUGHTON

Alfie, 1966

Paul, Ronald. *"Fire in Our Hearts,"* 62–64.

JOHN HENRY NEWMAN

Callista, 1856

Dorman, Susann. "*Hypatia* and *Callista*: The Initial Skirmish between Kingsley and Newman." *Nineteenth-Cent Fiction* 34 (1979), 175–193.

Loss and Gain, 1848

Rataboul, Louis J. *Le pasteur anglican*, 314–328, 365–366.

CAROLINE NORTON

Lost and Saved, 1863

Mitchell, Sally. *The Fallen Angel*, 105–107.

EDNA O'BRIEN

August is a Wicked Month, 1965

Gnutzmann, Rita. "Die Romane Edna O'Briens," in J. Kornelius et al., eds., *Einführung*, 154–155.

The Country Girls, 1960

Gnutzmann, Rita. "Die Romane," 150–152.

The Girl with Green Eyes, 1962

Gnutzmann, Rita. "Die Romane," 152–153.
Zeman, Anthea. *Presumptuous Girls*, 39–41.

Girls in Their Married Bliss, 1964

Gnutzmann, Rita. "Die Romane," 153.

Night, 1972

Gnutzmann, Rita. "Die Romane," 157–158.

A Pagan Place, 1970

Gnutzmann, Rita. "Die Romane," 156.
O'Rourke, Brian. *The Conscience of the Race*, 15–16.

FLANN O'BRIEN

At Swim-Two-Birds, 1939

Benstock, Bernard. "A Flann for All Seasons." *Irish Renaissance Annual* 3 (1982), 15–29.
Brooke-Rose, Christine. "The Readerhood of Man," in Susan R. Suleiman and Inge Crosman, eds., *The Reader*, 131–134.
Brooke-Rose, Christine. *A Rhetoric*, 112–116.
Castillo, Debra A. *The Translated World*, 56–60, 73–75.
De Selby, Nicholas, and Alf MacLochlainn. "De Selby Discovered," in Rüdiger Imhof, ed., *Alive-Alive O!*, 190–194.
Imhof, Rüdiger. "Flann O'Brien," in J. Kornelius et al., eds., *Einführung*, 164–170.
Imhof, Rüdiger. "Two Meta-Novelists: Sternesque Elements in Novels by Flann O'Brien." *Anglo-Irish Stud* 4 (1979), 61–90. [Also in Imhof, ed., *Alive-Alive O!*, 162–190.]
Jacquin, Danielle. "Le langage, R2JE favorite de Flann O'Brien." *Etudes Irlandaises* 4 (1979), 107–121.
Lanters, José. "Fiction within Fiction: The Role of the Author in Flann O'Brien's *At Swim-Two-Birds* and *The Third Policeman*." *Dutch Q R of Anglo-American Letters* 13 (1983), 267–281.
MacKillop, James. *Fionn mac Cumhaill*, 133–143.
Peterson, Richard F. "Flann O'Brien's Timefoolery." *Irish Renaissance Annual* 3 (1982), 42–45.
Voelker, Joseph C. " 'Doublends Jined': The Fiction of Flann O'Brien." *J of Irish Lit* 12:1 (1983), 87–95.

Wäppling, Eva. *Four Irish Legendary Figures*, 28–101.
Warner, Alan. *A Guide*, 153–157.
Waters, Maureen. *The Comic Irishman*, 89–91, 127–137.

The Dalkey Archive, 1964

Dietrich, Julia. "Flann O'Brien's Parody of Transubstantiation in *The Dalkey Archive*." *Notes on Contemp Lit* 10:5 (1980), 5–6.
Imhof, Rüdiger. "Flann O'Brien," 176–178.
Jacquin, Danielle. "Le langage," 107–121.
Peterson, Richard F. "Flann O'Brien's Timefoolery," 32–39.
Voelker, Joseph C. " 'Doublends Jined'," 87–95.
Warner, Alan. *A Guide*, 163–165.

The Hard Life, 1961

Imhof, Rüdiger. "Flann O'Brien," 175–176.
Jacquin, Danielle. "Le langage," 107–121.
Power, Mary. "The Figure of the Magician in *The Third Policeman* and *The Hard Life*." *Canadian J of Irish Stud* 8:1 (1982), 55–63.
Voelker, Joseph C. " 'Doublends Jined'," 87–95.
Warner, Alan. *A Guide*, 162–165.

The Third Policeman, 1967

Imhof, Rüdiger. "Flann O'Brien," 170–174.
Imhof, Rüdiger. "Two Meta-Novelists," 77–88 [178–189].
Jacquin, Danielle. "Le langage," 107–121.
Kemnitz, Charles. "Beyond the Zone of Middle Dimensions: A Relativistic Reading of *The Third Policeman*." *Irish Univ R* 15 (1985), 56–72.
Lanters, José. "Fiction within Fiction," 267–281.
McGuire, Jerry L. "Teasing after Death: Metatextuality in *The Third Policeman*." *Eire-Ireland* 16:2 (1981), 107–121.
Peterson, Richard F. "Flann O'Brien's Timefoolery," 39–42.
Petro, Peter. "Four Eccentrics: The Eccentric Character in the Novels of Céline, O'Brien, Gombrowicz and Solzenicyn." *Canadian R of Compar Lit* 8 (1981), 51–54.
Power, Mary. "The Figure of the Magician," 55–63.
Voelker, Joseph C. " 'Doublends Jined'," 87–95.
Warner, Alan. *A Guide*, 157–160.

KATE O'BRIEN

The Land of Spices, 1941

Ryan, Joan. "Women in the Novels of Kate O'Brien: The Mellick Novels," in Heinz Kosok, ed., *Studies*, 327–331.

Pray for the Wanderer, 1938

Ryan, Joan. "Women in the Novels of Kate O'Brien," 322–326.

FRANK O'CONNOR

Dutch Interior, 1940
>Tomory, William M. *Frank O'Connor*, 46–51.

The Saint and Mary Kate, 1932
>Farrell, James T. *On Irish Themes*, 95–96.
>Matthews, James H. "Women, War, and Words: Frank O'Connor's First Confessions." *Irish Renaissance Annual* 1 (1980), 103–111.
>Tomory, William M. *Frank O'Connor*, 43–46.

JULIA O'FAOLAIN

No Country for Young Men, 1980
>Burleigh, David. "Dead and Gone: The Fiction of Jennifer Johnston and Julia O'Faolain," in Masaru Sekine, ed., *Irish Writers*, 10–13.

The Obedient Wife, 1982
>Burleigh, David. "Dead and Gone," 13.

Women in the Wall, 1975
>Burleigh, David. "Dead and Gone," 9–10.

SEAN O'FAOLAIN

A Nest of Simple Folk, 1933
>Cahalan, James M. *Great Hatred*, 116–121.

LIAM O'FLAHERTY

Famine, 1937
>Cahalan, James M. *Great Hatred*, 140–147.

Insurrection, 1950
>Cahalan, James M. *Great Hatred*, 150–153.

Land, 1946
>Cahalan, James M. *Great Hatred*, 147–150.

STANDISH JAMES O'GRADY

The Flight of the Eagle, 1897
>Cahalan, James M. *Great Hatred*, 94–100.

Ulrick the Ready, 1896
>Cahalan, James M. *Great Hatred*, 100–102.

MARGARET OLIPHANT

The Curate in Charge, 1876

> Rataboul, Louis J. *Le pasteur anglican*, 230–231.

Miss Marjoribanks, 1866

> Stubbs, Patricia. *Women and Fiction*, 40–46.
> Terry, R. C. *Victorian Popular Fiction*, 88–94.

The Perpetual Curate, 1864

> Rataboul, Louis J. *Le pasteur anglican*, 242–243, 333–334.
> Terry, R. C. *Victorian Popular Fiction*, 83–88.

Phoebe Junior, 1876

> Terry, R. C. *Victorian Popular Fiction*, 95–101.

Salem Chapel, 1863

> Terry, R. C. *Victorian Popular Fiction*, 78–83.
> Trodd, Anthea. "The Policeman and the Lady: Significant Encounters in Mid-Victorian Fiction." *Victorian Stud* 27 (1984), 435–446.

A Son of the Soil, 1866

> Colby, Robert and Vineta. "Mrs. Oliphant's Scotland: The Romance of Reality," in Ian Campbell, ed., *Nineteenth-Century Scottish Fiction*, 97–100.

GEORGE ORWELL

Burmese Days, 1934

> Bal, Sant Singh. *George Orwell*, 61–70.
> Bolton, W. F. *The Language of 1984*, 110–114, 144–146.
> Bonifas, Gilbert. *George Orwell*, 41–52.
> Hammond, J. R. *A George Orwell Companion*, 89–98.
> Hunter, Lynette. *George Orwell*, 22–27.
> Jolicoeur, C. "Marginalité chez Orwell," in *La Marginalité*, 150–152.
> Jurgensen, Jean-Daniel. *Orwell*, 58–64.
> Knapp, John V. "Orwell's Fiction: Funny, But Not Vulgar!" *Mod Fiction Stud* 27 (1981), 297–298.
> Lewis, Peter. *George Orwell*, 41–43.
> Manferlotti, Stefano. *George Orwell*, 17–25.
> Matthews, Brian. "The Orwellian Fat Men." *Southern R* (Adelaide) 13 (1980), 102–103.
> Patai, Daphne. *The Orwell Mystique*, 21–52.
> Reilly, Patrick. *George Orwell*, 97–118.
> Shamsul Islam. *Chronicles of the Raj*, 73–82.

A Clergyman's Daughter, 1935

> Bal, Sant Singh. *George Orwell*, 85–90.
> Bonifas, Gilbert. *George Orwell*, 34–35, 70–73.

Hammond, J. R. *A George Orwell Companion*, 99–106.
Hunter, Lynette. *George Orwell*, 28–35.
Jolicoeur, C. "Marginalité," 154–155.
Manferlotti, Stefano. *George Orwell*, 28–34.
Matthews, Brian. "The Orwellian Fat Men," 103–104.
Patai, Daphne. *The Orwell Mystique*, 96–109.
Reilly, Patrick. *George Orwell*, 118–132.

Coming Up for Air, 1939

Atkins, John. "Orwell in 1984." *Coll Lit* 11 (1984), 39–41.
Crawford, Fred D. *Mixing Memory*, 68–70.
Green, Martin. *The English Novel*, 144–147.
Hammond, J. R. *A George Orwell Companion*, 146–157.
Hunter, Jefferson. "Orwell, Wells, and *Coming Up for Air*." *Mod Philology* 78 (1980), 38–47.
Hunter, Lynette. *George Orwell*, 95–105.
Jurgensen, Jean-Daniel. *Orwell*, 95–102.
Knapp, John V. "Orwell's Fiction," 299–301.
Lewis, Peter. *George Orwell*, 68–70.
Manferlotti, Stefano. *George Orwell*, 60–70.
Marroni, Francesco. "Retorica e struttura topologica in *Coming Up for Air*." *Trimestre* 13–14 (1980–81), 115–125.
Matthews, Brian. "The Orwellian Fat Men," 105–118.
Patai, Daphne. *The Orwell Mystique*, 159–200.
Poznar, Walter. "Orwell's George Bowling: How to Be." *Wascana R* 14:2 (1979), 80–90.
Reilly, Patrick. *George Orwell*, 217–135.

Down and Out in Paris and London, 1933

Bal, Sant Singh. *George Orwell*, 85–98.
Bolton, W. F. *The Language of 1984*, 84–87.
Bonifas, Gilbert. *George Orwell*, 35–40.
Hammond, J. R. *A George Orwell Companion*, 79–88.
Hunter, Lynette. *George Orwell*, 14–22.
Jolicoeur, C. "Marginalité," 152–154.
Lewis, Peter. *George Orwell*, 18–28.
Manferlotti, Stefano. *George Orwell*, 25–27.
Matthews, Brian. "The Orwellian Fat Men," 101–102.
Patai, Daphne. *The Orwell Mystique*, 53–69.
Reilly, Patrick. *George Orwell*, 133–148.

Homage to Catalonia, 1938

Bal, Sant Singh. *George Orwell*, 106–113.
Bonifas, Gilbert. *George Orwell*, 262–354.
Cowley, Malcolm. "No Homage to Catalonia: A Memory of the Spanish Civil War." *Southern R* (Baton Rouge) 18 (1982), 131–140.
Hammond, J. R. *A George Orwell Companion*, 130–145.

Hunter, Lynette. *George Orwell*, 70–95.
Ingle, Stephen. *Socialist Thought*, 91–94.
Israel, Joachim. "Orwell and the Intellectuals," in Shlomo Giora Shoham and Francis Posenstiel, eds., *And He Loved*, 82–89.
Jurgensen, Jean-Daniel. *Orwell*, 66–87.
Lewis, Peter. *George Orwell*, 65–67.
Manferlotti, Stefano. *George Orwell*, 53–60.
Patai, Daphne. *The Orwell Mystique*, 123–159.
Reilly, Patrick. *George Orwell*, 169–196.

Keep the Aspidistra Flying, 1936

Bal, Sant Singh. *George Orwell*, 90–97.
Bonifas, Gilbert. *George Orwell*, 54–66.
Crawford, Fred D. *Mixing Memory*, 65–68.
Hammond, J. R. *A George Orwell Companion*, 107–114.
Hunter, Lynette. *George Orwell*, 35–40.
Ingle, Stephen. *Socialist Thought*, 51–53.
Jolicoeur, C. "Marginalité," 150–152.
Knapp, John V. "Orwell's Fiction," 298–299.
Manferlotti, Stefano. *George Orwell*, 34–40.
Matthews, Brian. "The Orwellian Fat Men," 104–105.
Patai, Daphne. *The Orwell Mystique*, 109–122.
Reilly, Patrick. *George Orwell*, 197–217.
Woodcock, George. *Orwell's Message*, 64–66.

Nineteen Eighty-Four, 1948

Abrahams, William. "*Nineteen Eighty-Four*: The Book," in Peter Stansky, ed., *On Nineteen Eight-Four*, 2–8.
Adelson, Joseph. "The Self and Memory in *Nineteen Eighty-Four*," in Ejner J. Jensen, ed., *The Future*, 111–118.
Aldiss, Brian W. "The Downward Journey: Orwell's *1984*." *Extrapolation* 25 (1984), 5–11.
Aldiss, Brian W. "Die Reise in den Abgrund: Orwells *1984*," in Dieter Hasselblatt, ed., *Orwells Jahr*, 50–59.
Allen, Francis A. "*Nineteen Eighty-Four* and the Eclipse of Private Worlds." *Michigan Q R* 22 (1983), 517–540. [Also in Ejner J. Jensen, ed., *The Future*, 151–169.]
Arrow, Kenneth J. "The Economics of *Nineteen Eighty-Four*," in Peter Stansky, ed., *On Nineteen Eight-Four*, 43–47.
Aubrey, Crispin. "The Making of 1984," in Paul Chilton and Crispin Aubrey, eds., *"Nineteen Eighty-Four,"* 7–14.
Avishai, Bernard. "Orwell and the English Language," in Irving Howe, ed., *"1984" Revisited*, 57–71.
Babcock, Barbara Allen. "Lawspeak and Doublethink," in Peter Stansky, ed., *On Nineteen Eight-Four*, 86–91.
Bailey, Richard W. "George Orwell and the English Language," in Ejner J. Jensen, ed., *The Future*, 23–43.

Bal, Sant Singh. *George Orwell*, 36–38, 132–150, 172–174, 218–221.

Barnsley, John H. " 'The Last Man in Europe': A Comment on George Orwell's *1984*." *Contemp R* 239 (1981), 30–34.

Baruch, Elaine Hoffman. " 'The Golden Country': Sex and Love in *1984*," in Irving Howe, ed., *"1984" Revisited*, 47–56.

Beauchamp, Gorman. "From Bingo to Big Brother: Orwell on Power and Sadism," in Ejner J. Jensen, ed., *The Future*, 65–82.

Beauchamp, Gorman. "*1984*: Oceania as an Ideal State." *Coll Lit* 11 (1984), 1–9.

Behrend, Hanna. "George Orwell: *1984*—The Vital Factor." *Zeitschrift für Anglistik und Amerikanistik* 32 (1984), 234–240.

Bieler, Manfred. "Visionäres am Rande," in Dieter Hasselblatt, ed., *Orwells Jahr*, 29–30.

Bolton, W. F. *The Language of 1984*, 15–18, 35–37, 46–49, 185–187.

Bonifas, Gilbert. *George Orwell*, 373–377.

Brown, Edward J. "Zamyatin's *We* and *Nineteen Eighty-Four*," in Peter Stansky, ed., *On Nineteen Eight-Four*, 159–169.

Carpenter, Luther P. "*1984* on Staten Island," in Irving Howe, ed., *"1984" Revisited*, 72–85.

Carrier, Hervé. "The Parable of Anticulture: George Orwell—1984," in Shlomo Giora Shoham and Francis Rosenstiel, eds., *And He Loved*, 127–132.

Chilton, Paul. "Newspeak: It's The Real Thing," in Paul Chilton and Crispin Aubrey, eds., *"Nineteen Eighty-Four,"* 36–41.

Clayton, Raymond B. "The Biomedical Revolution and Totalitarian Control," in Peter Stansky, ed., *On Nineteen Eight-Four*, 76–84.

Comfort, Alex. "1939 and 1984: George Orwell and the Vision of Judgment," in Peter Stansky, ed., *On Nineteen Eight-Four*, 15–22.

Conquest, Robert. "Totaliterror," in Peter Stansky, ed., *On Nineteen Eight-Four*, 177–187.

Cooley, Mike, and Mike Johnson. "The Robots' Return?" in Paul Chilton and Crispin Aubrey, eds., *"Nineteen Eighty-Four,"* 71–78.

Corrigan, Philip. "Hard Machines, Soft Messages," in Paul Chilton and Crispin Aubrey, eds., *"Nineteen Eighty-Four,"* 98–104.

Craig, Gordon A. "Triangularity and International Violence," in Peter Stansky, ed., *On Nineteen Eight-Four*, 24–32.

Crick, Bernard. "*Nineteen Eighty-Four*: Satire or Prophecy?" *Dutch Q R of Anglo-American Letters* 13 (1983), 90–102. [Also in Ejner J. Jensen, ed., *The Future*, 7–19.]

Crick, Bernard. "The Reception of *Nineteen Eighty-Four*," in *George Orwell*, 97–103.

Currie, Robert. "The 'Big Truth' in *Nineteen Eighty-Four*." *Essays in Criticism* 34 (1984), 56–69.

Cutileiro, José-Pires. "Winston Smith in Africa," in Shlomo Giora Shoham and Francis Rosenstiel, eds., *And He Loved*, 25–29.

Dallin, Alexander. "Big Brother is Watching You," in Peter Stansky, ed., *On Nineteen Eight-Four*, 188–196.

Dilworth, Thomas. " 'The Village Blacksmith' in *Nineteen Eight-Four.*" *Intl Fiction R* 8 (1981), 63–65.

Dittmar, Kurt. "Die Fiktionalisierung der Wirklichkeit als antiutopische Fiktion: Manipulative Realitätskontrolle in George Orwells *Nineteen Eighty-Four.*" *Deutsche Vierteljahrsschrift für Literaturwissenschaft und Geistesgeschichte* 58 (1984), 679–712.

Djilas, Milovan. "The Disintegration of Leninist Totalitarianism," in Irving Howe, ed., *"1984" Revisited*, 136–148.

Donoghue, Denis. "*Nineteen Eighty-Four*: Politics and Fable," in *George Orwell*, 57–69.

Dorfman, Gerald A. "The Proles of Airstrip One," in Peter Stansky, ed., *On Nineteen Eight-Four*, 170–176.

Drell, Sidney D. "Newspeak and Nukespeak," in Peter Stansky, ed., *On Nineteen Eight-Four*, 33–42.

Ehrlich, Paul R., and Anne H. Ehrlich. "1984: Population and Environment," in Peter Stansky, ed., *On Nineteen Eight-Four*, 49–55.

Elkins, Charles L. "George Orwell," in E. F. Bleiler, ed., *Science Fiction Writers*, 234–235, 238–240.

Esslin, Martin. "Television and Telescreen," in Peter Stansky, ed., *On Nineteen Eight-Four*, 126–138.

Feder, Lillian. "Selfhood, Language, and Reality: George Orwell's *Nineteen Eighty-Four.*" *Georgia R* 37 (1983), 392–409.

Ferrarotti, Franco. "Science, Applied Science and Conscience: Preliminary Remarks on the Crisis in Scientific Rationality in Tomorrow's World," in Shlomo Giora Shoham and Francis Rosenstiel, eds., *And He Loved*, 137–144.

Flechtheim, Ossip K. "Von Thomas Morus zu Orwell," in Dieter Hasselblatt, ed., *Orwells Jahr*, 25–28.

Franke, Herbert W. "Das Gespenst des Großen Bruders," in Dieter Hasselblatt, ed., *Orwells Jahr,* 172–177.

Freedman, Carl. "Antinomies of *Nineteen Eighty-Four.*" *Mod Fiction Stud* 30 (1984), 601–620.

Freund, Julien. "The Only Child and the Little Brothers: An Interpretation of George Orwell," in Shlomo Giora Shoham and Francis Rosenstiel, eds., *And He Loved*, 145–151.

Fyvel, Tosco R. "*1984* as a Satire on the Relations between Rulers and Ruled," in Shlomo Giora Shoham and Francis Rosenstiel, eds., *And He Loved*, 73–80.

Good, Graham. " 'Ingsoc in Relation to Chess': Reversible Opposites in Orwell's *1984.*" *Novel* 18 (1984), 50–63.

Gulati, Basia Miller. "Orwell's *Nineteen Eighty-Four*: Escape from Doublethink." *Intl Fiction R* 12 (1985), 79–83.

Hammond, J. R. *A George Orwell Companion*, 169–183.

Hasselblatt, Dieter. "Genaueres Zwiedenken," in Hasselblatt, ed., *Orwells Jahr*, 103–109.

Hoffmann, Stanley. "Policies and Strategies," in Shlomo Giora Shoham and Francis Rosenstiel, eds., *And He Loved*, 31–38.

Holmes, John W. "With the Best of Intentions: Interdependence and Freedom," in Shlomo Giora Shoham and Francis Rosenstiel, eds., *And He Loved*, 39–46.

Howe, Irving. "1984: Enigmas of Power," in Howe, ed., *"1984" Revisited*, 3–18.

Hunter, Lynette. *George Orwell*, 191–224.

Ingle, Stephen. *Socialist Thought*, 173–182.

Jensen, Ejner J. *"1984*: The Language and Ideas of Orwell's Book Have Fixed Themselves in Our Awareness." *Horizon*, Jan./Feb. 1984, 14–15.

John, George. "Towards a Stylistic Analysis of Orwell's *1984*." *Rajasthan Univ Stud in Engl* 11 (1978), 57–65.

Jolicoeur, C. "Marginalité," 156–159.

Jurgensen, Jean-Daniel. *"1984*," in Shlomo Giora Shoham and Francis Rosenstiel, eds., *And He Loved*, 91–95.

Jurgensen, Jean-Daniel. *Orwell*, 163–203.

Jurgensen, Jean-Daniel. "Vers *1984*: Orwell et la liberté." *Nouvelle Revue des Deux Mondes*, August 1981, 285–292.

Kazin, Alfred. " 'Not One of Us': George Orwell and *Nineteen Eighty-Four*," in *George Orwell*, 70–78.

Khouri, Nadia. "Reaction and Nihilism: The Political Genealogy of Orwell's *1984*." *Science-Fiction Stud* 12 (1985), 136–146.

Kibel, Alvin C. "1984," in Shlomo Giora Shoham and Francis Rosenstiel, eds., *And He Loved*, 97–105.

Köberl, Johann. "Der sprachphilosophische Hintergrund von Newspeak: Ein Beitrag zum 100. Geburtstag von Albert Einstein." *Arbeiten aus Anglistik und Amerikanistik* 4 (1979), 171–183.

Kolakowski, Leszek. "Totalitarianism and the Virtue of the Lie," in Irving Howe, ed., *"1984" Revisited*, 122–135.

Koser, Michael. *"1984*—alternativ," in Dieter Hasselblatt, ed., *Orwells Jahr*, 138–142.

Kunert, Günter. "Was Orwell nicht ahnte," in Dieter Hasselblatt, ed., *Orwells Jahr*, 80–85.

Lashmar, Paul. "Information as Power," in Paul Chilton and Crispin Aubrey, eds., *"Nineteen Eighty-Four,"* 79–88.

Leech, Geoffrey N., and Michael H. Short. *Style in Fiction*, 187–189.

Lewenstein, Marion. "Smokey Bear as Big Brother," in Peter Stansky, ed., *On Nineteen Eight-Four*, 139–145.

Lewis, Florence, and Peter Moss. "The Tyranny of Language," in Paul Chilton and Crispin Aubrey, eds., *"Nineteen Eighty-Four,"* 45–57.

Lewis, Peter. *George Orwell*, 112–115.

Macey, Samuel L. "George Orwell's *1984*: The Future that Becomes the Past." *Engl Stud in Canada* 11 (1985), 450–457.

McGinn, Robert E. "The Politics of Technology and the Technology of Politics," in Peter Stansky, ed., *On Nineteen Eight-Four*, 67–75.

Manferlotti, Stefano. *George Orwell*, 87–107.

Markus, Manfred. "Orwells *1984* aus der Sicht der Linguistik, die Linguistik 1984 aus der Sicht Orwells." *Literatur in Wissenschaft und Unterricht* 17 (1984), 305–316.

Mellor, Anne. " 'You're Only a Rebel from the Waist Downwards': Orwell's View of Women," in Peter Stansky, ed., *On Nineteen Eight-Four*, 115–125.

Meyer, Alfred G. "The Political Theory of Pessimism: George Orwell and Herbert Marcuse," in Ejner J. Jensen, ed., *The Future*, 121–134.

Meyers, Jeffrey. "*Nineteen Eighty-Four*: A Novel of the 1930s," in *George Orwell*, 79–88.

Meyers, Walter E. *Aliens and Linguists*, 163–165.

Miller, Mark Crispin. "Big Brother Is You, Watching." *Georgia R* 38 (1984), 695–719.

Miller, Mark Crispin. "The Fate of *1984*," in Irving Howe, ed., *"1984" Revisited*, 19–46.

Nisbet, Robert. "*1984* and the Conservative Imagination," in Irving Howe, ed., *"1984" Revisited*, 180–206.

Patai, Daphne. "Gamesmanship and Androcentrism in Orwell's *1984*." *PMLA* 97 (1982), 856–869.

Patai, Daphne. *The Orwell Mystique*, 219–263.

Pearson, Scott R. "Economic Doublethink: Food and Politics," in Peter Stansky, ed., *On Nineteen Eight-Four*, 56–65.

Plank, Robert. "One Grand Inquisitor and Some Lesser Ones." *Gamut* (Cleveland State Univ) 4 (1981), 29–38.

Plank, Robert. "Science Fiction and Psychology," in Jack Williamson, ed. *Teaching Science Fiction*, 161–167.

Plank, William. "Orwell and Huxley: Social Control through Standardized Eroticism." *Recovering Lit* 12 (1984), 329–339.

Reaves, R. B. "Orwell's 'Second Thoughts on James Burnham' and *1984*." *Coll Lit* 11 (1984), 13–20.

Reilly, Patrick. *George Orwell*, 269–297.

Reilly, Patrick. "*Nineteen Eighty-Four*: The Failure of Humanism." *Crit Q* 24 (1982), 19–30.

Robinson, Paul. "For the Love of Big Brother: The Sexual Politics of *Nineteen Eight-Four*," in Peter Stansky, ed., *On Nineteen Eight-Four*, 148–158.

Roper, Christopher. "Taming the Universal Machine," in Paul Chilton and Crispin Aubrey, eds., *"Nineteen Eighty-Four,"* 58–70.

Ross, Michael L. " 'Carrying On the Human Heritage': From *Lady Chatterley's Lover* to *Nineteen Eighty-Four*." *D. H. Lawrence R* 17 (1984), 5–27.

Rottensteiner, Franz. "1984 und die Science-Fiction," in Dieter Hasselblatt, ed., *Orwells Jahr*, 61–66.

Rule, James B. "*1984*—The Ingredients of Totalitarianism," in Irving Howe, ed., *"1984" Revisited*, 166–179.

Scott, Nathan A., Jr. "Orwell's Legacy," in *George Orwell*, 104–114.

Sharrock, Roger. "*1984* and the Rupture of Desire." *Essays in Criticism* 34 (1984), 319–337.

Sheldon, Leslie E. "Newspeak and Nadsat: The Disintegration of Language in *1984* and *A Clockwork Orange*." *Stud in Contemp Satire* 6 (1979), 7–13.

Shoham, Shlomo Giora. "Alienation and Apocalypse," in Shoham and Francis Rosenstiel, eds., *And He Loved*, 113–117.

Siganos, André. "Métamorphoses 'noires' chez Lautréamont, F. Kafka et G. Orwell." *Arquipélago* 3 (1981), 23–39.

Sperber, Murray. " 'Gazing into the Glass Paperweight': The Structure and Psychology of Orwell's *1984*." *Mod Fiction Stud* 26 (1980), 213–226.

Stableford, Brian. *Scientific Romance*, 318–320.

Stafford, Tim. "*1984*: Can Orwell's Nightmare Still Become Reality?" *Christianity Today*, 13 Jan. 1984, 22–26.

Stansky, Peter. "Orwell: The Man," in Stansky, ed., *On Nineteen Eight-Four*, 9–13.

Steinhoff, William. "Utopia Reconsidered: Comments on *1984*," in Eric S. Rabkin et al., eds., *No Place Else*, 147–160.

Steinhoff, William R. "Afterword: The Inner Heart," in Ejner J. Jensen, ed., *The Future*, 201–208.

Stewart, Ralph. "Orwell's Waste Land." *Intl Fiction R* 8 (1981), 150–152.

Strasser, Johanno. "*1984*: Decade of the Experts?," in Irving Howe, ed., *"1984" Revisited*, 149–165.

Sussman, Bernard J. "Orwell's *1984*." *Explicator* 38:4 (1980), 32–33.

Taylor, Jenni. "Desire is Thoughtcrime," in Paul Chilton and Crispin Aubrey, eds., *"Nineteen Eighty-Four,"* 24–32.

Tentler, Leslie. " 'I'm Not Literary, Dear': George Orwell on Women and the Family," in Ejner J. Jensen, ed., *The Future*, 47–62.

Traugott, Elizabeth Closs. "Newspeak: Could It Really Work?" in Peter Stansky, ed., *On Nineteen Eight-Four*, 92–102.

Tucker, Robert C. "Does Big Brother Really Exist?," in Irving Howe, ed., *"1984" Revisited*, 89–102.

Veil, Simone. "*1984*: A European Perspective," in Shlomo Giora Shoham and Francis Rosenstiel, eds., *And He Loved*, 47–51.

Verut, Annie. "*1984*: De dieu à 'Big Brother'," in *Aspects du sacré*, 93–105.

Wagar, W. Warren. "George Orwell as Political Secretary of the Zeitgeist," in Ejner J. Jensen, ed., *The Future*, 182–196.

Wagschal, Peter H. "*1984*: A Second Look." *World Futures* 18 (1982), 285–290.

Walzer, Michael. "On 'Failed Totalitarianism'," in Irving Howe, ed., *"1984" Revisited*, 103–121.

Ward, Colin. "Big Brother Drives a Bulldozer," in Paul Chilton and Crispin Aubrey, eds., *"Nineteen Eighty-Four,"* 89–97.

Watt, Ian. "Winston Smith: The Last Humanist," in Peter Stansky, ed., *On Nineteen Eight-Four*, 103–113.

Weatherly, Joan. "The Death of Big Sister: Orwell's Tragic Message." *Coll Lit* 11 (1984), 22–31.

Westphal, Gert. "Mit Winston Smith auf 'eines langen Tages Reise in die Nacht'," in Dieter Hasselblatt, ed., *Orwells Jahr*, 125–129.

Whellens, Arthur. "Anthony Burgess's *1985*." *Studi dell'Istituto Linguistico* 5 (1982), 223–244.

Widgery, David. "Reclaiming Orwell," in Paul Chilton and Crispin Aubrey, eds., *"Nineteen Eighty-Four,"* 15–23.

Wilding, Michael. "Orwell's *1984*: Rewriting the Future." *Sydney Stud in Engl* 2 (1976–77), 38–63.

Wilding, Michael. *Political Fictions*, 216–246.

Woodcock, George. *Orwell's Message*, 1–4, 10–12, 15–21, 38–47, 50–56, 66–68, 83–85, 98–105, 110–114, 133–142.

Wright, Patrick. "The Conscription of History," in Paul Chilton and Crispin Aubrey, eds., *"Nineteen Eighty-Four,"* 105–114.

Zehr, David Morgan. "Orwell and the Proles: Revolutionary or Middle-Class Voyeur?" *Centennial R* 27 (1983), 35–40.

Zimbardo, Philip G. "Mind Control: Political Fiction and Psychological Reality," in Peter Stansky, ed., *On Nineteen Eight-Four*, 197–215.

Zinoviev, Alexandre. "*1984* and 1984," in Shlomo Giora Shoham and Francis Rosenstiel, eds., *And He Loved*, 63–69.

Zwerdling, Alex. "Orwell's Psychopolitics," in Ejner J. Jensen, ed., *The Future*, 87–108.

The Road to Wigan Pier, 1937

Bal, Sant Singh. *George Orwell*, 98–104, 154–156, 193–196.

Bolton, W. F. *The Language of 1984*, 87–92, 157–159.

Bonifas, Gilbert. "Le Chapitre douze de *The Road to Wigan Pier*: Notes sur la pensée anti-utopique de George Orwell," in *Hommage à Emile Gasquet*, 171–179.

Bonifas, Gilbert. *George Orwell*, 68–70, 78–253.

Hammond, J. R. *A George Orwell Companion*, 115–129.

Hunter, Jefferson. "Orwell's Prose: Discovery, Communion, Separation." *Sewanee R* 87 (1979), 439–451.

Hunter, Lynette. *George Orwell*, 45–69.

Ingle, Stephen. *Socialist Thought*, 33–35.

Klaus, H. Gustav. *The Literature*, 153–155.

Lewis, Peter. *George Orwell*, 23–26, 50–54.

Manferlotti, Stefano. *George Orwell*, 42–52.

Marroni, Francesco. "*The Road to Wigan Pier*: Fallimento di uno ricerca," in Agostino Lombardo, ed., *Studi inglesi*, 245–260.

Patai, Daphne. *The Orwell Mystique*, 69–94.

Reilly, Patrick. *George Orwell*, 149–168.

Woodcock, George. *Orwell's Message*, 43–45, 117–119.

'OUIDA'

The Massarenes, 1925

Reed, John R. "A Friend to Mammon: Speculation in Victorian Literature." *Victorian Stud* 27 (1984), 200–201.

Moths, 1880

Mitchell, Sally. *The Fallen Angel*, 140–142.

JOHN W. OVERTON

Harry Hartley, 1859

Rignall, J. M. "Between Chartism and the 1880s: J. W. Overton and E. Lynn Linton," in H. Gustav Klaus, ed., *The Socialist Novel*, 27–31.

Saul of Mitre Court, 1879

Rignall, J. M. "Between Chartism," 31–36.

ROBERT PALTOCK

The Life and Adventures of Peter Wilkins, 1751

Crossley, Robert. "Ethereal Ascents: Eighteenth-Century Fantasies of Human Flight." *Eighteenth-Century Life* 7:2 (1982), 55–64.

Lamoine, Georges. "Deux utopies du dix-huitième siècle chez les hommes volants: Quelques aspects." *Littératures* 5 (1982), 7–18.

Lamoine, Georges. "*Peter Wilkins*: bonheur et religion au pays des hommes volants." *Etudes Anglaises* 35 (1982), 129–138.

MOLLIE PANTER-DOWNES

One Fine Day, 1947

Beauman, Nicola. *A Very Great Profession*, 231–235.

ELIZA PARSONS

The Mysterious Warning, 1796

Roberts, Bette B. *The Gothic Romance*, 207–223.

WALTER HORATIO PATER

Gaston de Latour, 1896

Monsman, Gerald. "*Gaston de Latour* and Pater's Art of Autobiography." *Nineteenth-Century Fiction* 33 (1979), 411–433.

Monsman, Gerald. "Narrative Design in Pater's *Gaston de Latour*." *Victorian Stud* 23 (1980), 347–367.

Murray, Isobel. "*Gaston de Latour*: Pater's Unfinished Business." *Durham Univ J* 75:2 (1983), 73–76.

Marius the Epicurean, 1885

Bassett, Sharon. "*Marius* and the Varieties of Stoic Will: 'Can the Will Itself be an Organ of Knowledge, of Vision?" *Engl Lit in Transition* 27 (1984), 52–61.

Buckler, William E. "*Déjà vu* Inverted: The Imminent Future in Walter Pater's *Marius the Epicurean*." *Victorian Newsl* 55 (1979), 1–4.

Bump, Jerome. "Seeing and Hearing in *Marius the Epicurean*." *Nineteenth-Century Fiction* 37 (1982), 188–206.

Conlon, John J. *Walter Pater*, 97–103.

Johnson, Lee McKay. *The Metaphor of Painting*, 198–200, 212–215, 224–226.

Levey, Michael. *The Case of Walter Pater*, 162–168.

Maekawa, Yuichi. "*Epicurean Marius*: Walter Pater." *Eigo Seinen* (Tokyo) 126 (1981), 521–523, 577–579, 614–616.

Meisel, Perry. *The Absent Father*, 126–136.

Monsman, Gerald. " 'Definite History and Dogmatic Interpretation': The 'White-nights' of Pater's *Marius the Epicurean*." *Criticism* 26 (1984), 171–191.

Monsman, Gerald. "Pater Redivivus," in Richard A. Levine, ed., *The Victorian Experience*, 206–212, 228–231.

Monsman, Gerald. "The White Bird in the Marketplace: *Animula Vagula, Anima Christiana*." *Engl Lit in Transition* 27 (1984), 41–50.

Morioka, Shin. "The Fate of Personality in Walter Pater." *Stud in Engl Lit* (Japan) 61 (1984), 66–70.

Nadel, Ira B. "Autobiography as Fiction: The Example of Pater's *Marius*." *Engl Lit in Transition* 27 (1984), 34–39.

Ramel, Annie. "*John Inglesant* et *Marius l'Epicurien*." *Confluents* 4:1 (1978), 163–185.

Richards, Bernard. "Stopping the Press in *Marius*." *Engl Lit in Transition* 27 (1984), 90–98.

Scott, Nathan A., Jr. "Pater's Imperative: To Dwell Poetically." *New Liter Hist* 15 (1983), 93–118.

Small, Ian. "The 'Fictional' and the 'Real' in *Marius*." *Engl Lit in Transition* 27 (1984), 140–146.

Williams, Carolyn. "Typology as Narrative Form: The Temporal Logic of *Marius*." *Engl Lit in Transition* 27 (1984), 11–30.

JAMES PAYN

By Proxy, 1878

Peterson, Audrey. *Victorian Masters*, 180–182.
Terry, R. C. *Victorian Popular Fiction*, 162–164.

The Clyffards of Clyffe, 1866

Terry, R. C. *Victorian Popular Fiction*, 157–159.

A Confidential Agent, 1880

  Peterson, Audrey. *Victorian Masters*, 182–186.

Like Father, Like Son, 1871

  Peterson, Audrey. *Victorian Masters*, 178–180.

Lost Sir Massingberd, 1864

  Peterson, Audrey. *Victorian Masters*, 175–177.
  Terry, R. C. *Victorian Popular Fiction*, 151–154.

Married Beneath Him, 1865

  Terry, R. C. *Victorian Popular Fiction*, 154–156.

THOMAS LOVE PEACOCK

Crotchet Castle, 1831

  Burns, Bryan. *The Novels*, 165–190.
  Butler, Marilyn. *Peacock Displayed*, 183–230.
  Mulvihill, James D. "Thomas Love Peacock's *Crotchet Castle*: Reconciling the Spirits of the Age." *Nineteenth-Century Fiction* 38 (1983), 253–270.

Gryll Grange, 1860

  Burns, Bryan. *The Novels*, 191–218.
  Butler, Marilyn. *Peacock Displayed*, 235–272.
  Crabbe, John K. "The Emerging Heroine in the Works of Thomas Love Peacock." *Zeitschrift für Anglistik und Amerikanistik* 27 (1979), 121–132.

  Rataboul, Louis J. *Le pasteur anglican*, 159–163.

Headlong Hall, 1816

  Burns, Bryan. *The Novels*, 15–41.
  Butler, Marilyn. *Peacock Displayed*, 40–57.
  Crabbe, John K. "The Emerging Heroine," 121–132.
  Garside, Peter. "*Headlong Hall* Revisited." *Trivium* 14 (1979), 107–126.
  Lamarca Margalef, Jordi. *Ciencia y literatura*, 103–105.
  Mulvihill, James D. "Peacock and Perfectibility in *Headlong Hall*." *CLIO* 13 (1984), 227–243.
  Teyssandier, Hubert. *Les formes de la création*, 200–220.

Maid Marian, 1822

  Burns, Bryan. *The Novels*, 110–137.
  Butler, Marilyn. *Peacock Displayed*, 140–155.

Melincourt, 1817

  Burns, Bryan. *The Novels*, 42–75.
  Butler, Marilyn. *Peacock Displayed*, 58–101.
  Crabbe, John K. "The Emerging Heroine," 121–132.
  Teyssandier, Hubert. *Les formes de la création*, 221–250.

The Misfortunes of Elphin, 1829

> Burns, Bryan. *The Novels*, 138–164.
> Butler, Marilyn. *Peacock Displayed*, 155–182.

Nightmare Abbey, 1818

> Burns, Bryan. *The Novels*, 76–109.
> Butler, Marilyn. *Peacock Displayed*, 102–139.
> Hennessy, Brendan. *The Gothic Novel*, 32–33.
> Lamarca Margalef, Jordi. *Ciencia y literatura*, 96–98.
> May, Leland Chandler. *Parodies of the Gothic Novel*, 45–72.
> Polhemus, Robert M. *Comic Faith*, 60–87.
> Weiss, Fredric. *The Antic Spectre*, 212–218.

MERVYN PEAKE

Gormenghast, 1950

> Binna, Ronald. "Situating Gormenghast." *Crit Q* 21:1 (1979), 21–33.
> Blignaut, E. A. "Mervyn Peake: From Artist as Entertainer to Artist as Philosopher and Moralist in the 'Titus' Books." *Engl Stud in Africa* 24 (1981), 109–112.
> Edwards, Malcolm, and Robert Holdstock. *Realms of Fantasy*, 33–43.
> Gunnell, Bryn. "The Fantasy of Mervyn Peake." *Malahat R* 58 (1981), 17–35.
> Hunt, Bruce. "*Gormenghast*: Psychology of the *Bildungsroman*." *Mervyn Peake R* 6 (1978), 10–17.
> Leech, Geoffrey N., and Michael H. Short. *Style in Fiction*, 140–145.
> Little, Edmund. *The Fantasts*, 54–73.
> Manlove, C. N. *The Impulse*, 115–126.
> Manlove, C. N. "A World in Fragments: Peake and the Titus Books." *Mervyn Peake R* 11 (1980), 9–16.
> Ochoki, Margaret. "*Gormenghast*: Fairytale Gone Wrong?" *Mervyn Peake R* 15 (1982), 11–17.
> Sanders, Joseph L. " 'The Passions in the Clay': Mervyn Peake's Titus Stories," in Thomas D. Clareson and Thomas L. Wymer, eds., *Voices for the Future*, 87–99.
> Sutton, David. "The Religion of Gormenghast: A Note." *Mervyn Peake R* 9 (1979), 11–13.

Titus Alone, 1959

> Blignaut, E. A. "Mervyn Peake," 112–114.
> Bristow-Smith, Laurence. "A Critical Conclusion: The End of *Titus Alone*." *Mervyn Peake R* 12 (1981), 10–13.
> Greenland, Colin. "From Beowulf to Kafka: The Difficulty of *Titus Alone*." *Mervyn Peake R* 12 (1981), 4–9.
> Gunnell, Bryn. "The Fantasy," 17–35.
> Manlove, C. N. *The Impulse*, 115–126.

Manlove, C. N. "A World in Fragments," 9–16.
Sanders, Joseph L. " 'The Passions in the Clay'," 99–104.

Titus Groan, 1946

Blignaut, E. A. "Mervyn Peake," 107–109.
Edwards, Malcolm, and Robert Holdstock. *Realms of Fantasy*, 33–43.
Gunnell, Bryn. "The Fantasy," 17–35.
Little, Edmund. *The Fantasts*, 54–73.
Manlove, C. N. *The Impulse*, 115–126.
Manlove, C. N. "A World in Fragments," 9–16.
Mason, Desmond. *"Titus Groan*: Errors and Flaws." *Mervyn Peake R* 5 (1977), 12–16.
Punter, David. *The Literature of Terror*, 376–378.
Sanders, Joseph L. " 'The Passions in the Clay'," 76–87.
Winnington, G. Peter. "The Reader Takes Over." *Mervyn Peake R* 10 (1980), 5–16.

JIM PHELAN

Ten-A-Penny-People, 1938

Warpole, Ken. *Dockers and Detectives*, 88–90.

JAMES PLUNKETT

Farewell Companions, 1977

Behrend, Hanna. "James Plunkett's Contribution to Democratic and Socialist Culture." *Zeitschrift für Anglistik und Amerikanistik* 27 (1979), 314–322.

Strumpet City, 1969

Behrend, Hanna. "James Plunkett's Contribution," 312–314.
Cahalan, James M. *Great Hatred*, 179–190.

ANNA MARIA PORTER

The Recluse of Norway, 1814

Christensen, Inger. "Ground Untrodden: Images of Norway in Nineteenth-Century English Fiction." *Edda*, 1985, 352–353.

JANE PORTER

The Scottish Chiefs, 1810

Sandy, Stephen. *The Raveling*, 159–164.

Thaddeus of Warsaw, 1803

Sandy, Stephen. *The Raveling*, 140–159, 165–170.

ANTHONY POWELL

At Lady Molly's, 1957

McEwan, Neil. *The Survival of the Novel*, 100–103.

Books Do Furnish a Room, 1971

Schäfer, Jürgen. "Anthony Powell, *Books Do Furnish a Room*," in Rainer Lengeler, ed., *Englische Literatur*, 241–256.

A Dance to the Music of Time, 1951–1975

Bader, Rudolf. *Anthony Powell's "Music of Time,"* 14–164.

Birns, Margaret Boe. "Anthony Powell's Secret Harmonies: Music in a Jungian Key." *Liter R* 25:1 (1981), 80–92.

Crawford, Fred D. *Mixing Memory*, 76–78.

Eaton, Marcia Muelder. "Anthony Powell and the Aesthetic Life." *Philos and Lit* 9 (1985), 166–182.

Gutierrez, Donald. "The Doubleness of Anthony Powell: Point of View in *A Dance to the Music of Time.*" *Univ of Dayton R* 14:2 (1980), 15–27.

Gutierrez, Donald. "Exemplary Punishment: Anthony Powell's Dance as Comedy." *Greyfriar* 22 (1981), 27–44.

Harrington, Henry R. "Anthony Powell, Nicolas Poussin, and the Structure of Time." *Contemp Lit* 24 (1983), 431–448.

Lindemann, M. D. "Nicholas Jenkins's Bonfire." *Engl Stud in Africa* 26 (1983), 27–36.

McEwan, Neil. *The Survival of the Novel*, 98–119.

McVeagh, John. *Tradefull Merchants*, 191–192.

Swinden, Patrick. *The English Novel*, 93–129.

Tapscott, Stephen J. "The Epistemology of Gossip: Anthony Powell's *Dance to the Music of Time.*" *Texas Q* 21:1 (1978), 104–116.

Wilson, Keith. "Pattern and Process: The Narrative Strategies of Anthony Powell's *A Dance to the Music of Time.*" *Engl Stud in Canada* 11 (1985), 214–222.

The Soldier's Art, 1966

Swinden, Patrick. *The English Novel*, 118–121.

Temporary Kings, 1973

Swinden, Patrick. *The English Novel*, 106–108.

JOHN COWPER POWYS

After My Fashion, 1980

Coates, C. A. *John Cowper Powys*, 21–28.

All or Nothing, 1960

Krissdottir, Morine. *John Cowper Powys*, 182–183.

Atlantis, 1954

Coates, C. A. *John Cowper Powys*, 156–158.
Krissdottir, Morine. *John Cowper Powys*, 175–178.

The Brazen Head, 1956

Krissdottir, Morine. *John Cowper Powys*, 178–180.

Ducdame, 1925

Coates, C. A. *John Cowper Powys*, 28–39.
Krissdottir, Morine. *John Cowper Powys*, 57–63.

A Glastonbury Romance, 1932

Coates, C. A. *John Cowper Powys*, 90–118.
Krissdottir, Morine. *John Cowper Powys*, 80–99.
Thompson, Raymond H. *The Return from Avalon*, 27–31.

The Inmates, 1952

Krissdottir, Morine. *John Cowper Powys*, 174–175.

Maiden Castle, 1936

Krissdottir, Morine. *John Cowper Powys*, 111–120.

Morwyn, 1937

Jaworski, Philippe. "Histoire et procès du Mal." *Quinzaine Littéraire*
  293 (1979), 12.
Krissdottir, Morine. *John Cowper Powys*, 117–121.
Lamarca Margalef, Jordi. *Ciencia y literatura*, 47–49.

Owen Glendower, 1940

Coates, C. A. *John Cowper Powys*, 133–137.
Krissdottir, Morine. *John Cowper Powys*, 121–126.

Porius, 1951

Coates, C. A. *John Cowper Powys*, 137–156.
Krissdottir, Morine. *John Cowper Powys*, 127–170.
Lane, Denis. "Elementalism in John Cowper Powys' *Porius*." *Papers
  on Lang & Lit* 17 (1981), 381–404.

Real Wraiths, 1974

Coates, C. A. *John Cowper Powys*, 160–161.

Rodmoor, 1916

Krissdottir, Morine. *John Cowper Powys*, 50–56.

Weymouth Sands, 1935

Coates, C. A. *John Cowper Powys*, 119–124.
Crawford, Fred D. *Mixing Memory*, 80–82.
Krissdottir, Morine. *John Cowper Powys*, 102–111.
Lamarca Margalef, Jordi. *Ciencia y literatura*, 33–35.

Wolf Solent, 1929

>   Coates, C. A. *John Cowper Powys*, 40–62.
>   Krissdottir, Morine. *John Cowper Powys*, 64–79.
>   Lukacher, Ned. "Notre-Homme-des-Fleurs: *Wolf Solent*'s Metaphoric Legends." *Powys R* 2:2 (1979–80), 64–73.

Wood and Stone, 1915

>   Coates, C. A. *John Cowper Powys*, 10–18.
>   Krissdottir, Morine. *John Cowper Powys*, 48–50.

HILDA F. M. PRESCOTT

The Man on a Donkey, 1952

>   Raleigh, John Henry. "The Historical Novel as Work of Art and Tragedy: H. F. M. Prescott's *The Man on a Donkey*." *Novel* 12 (1979), 149–168.

J. B. PRIESTLEY

Adam in Moonshine, 1927

>   DeVitis, A. A., and Albert E. Kalson. *J. B. Priestley*, 39–43.

Angel Pavement, 1930

>   Atkins, John. *J. B. Priestley*, 47–51.
>   DeVitis, A. A., and Albert E. Kalson. *J. B. Priestley*, 48–50.

Benighted, 1927

>   DeVitis, A. A., and Albert E. Kalson. *J. B. Priestley*, 43–44.

Black-Out in Gretley, 1942

>   DeVitis, A. A., and Albert E. Kalson. *J. B. Priestley*, 67–69.

Bright Day, 1946

>   DeVitis, A. A., and Albert E. Kalson. *J. B. Priestley*, 73–76.

Daylight on Saturday, 1943

>   DeVitis, A. A., and Albert E. Kalson. *J. B. Priestley*, 69–72.

The Doomsday Men, 1938

>   DeVitis, A. A., and Albert E. Kalson. *J. B. Priestley*, 59–63.

Faraway, 1932

>   DeVitis, A. A., and Albert E. Kalson. *J. B. Priestley*, 51–54.

Festival at Farbridge, 1951

>   DeVitis, A. A., and Albert E. Kalson. *J. B. Priestley*, 79–82.

The Good Companions, 1929

>   Atkins, John. *J. B. Priestley*, 205–209.
>   DeVitis, A. A., and Albert E. Kalson. *J. B. Priestley*, 45–48.

The Image Men, 1968

    Atkins, John. *J. B. Priestley*, 195–201.
    DeVitis, A. A., and Albert E. Kalson. *J. B. Priestley*, 102–109.

It's an Old Country, 1967

    DeVitis, A. A., and Albert E. Kalson. *J. B. Priestley*, 99–102.

Jenny Villiers, 1967

    DeVitis, A. A., and Albert E. Kalson. *J. B. Priestley*, 77–79.

Let the People Sing, 1939

    DeVitis, A. A., and Albert E. Kalson. *J. B. Priestley*, 65–67.

Lost Empires, 1965

    DeVitis, A. A., and Albert E. Kalson. *J. B. Priestley*, 97–99.

Low Notes on a High Level, 1954

    DeVitis, A. A., and Albert E. Kalson. *J. B. Priestley*, 82–84.

The Magicians, 1954

    DeVitis, A. A., and Albert E. Kalson. *J. B. Priestley*, 84–86.

Salt is Leaving, 1966

    DeVitis, A. A., and Albert E. Kalson. *J. B. Priestley*, 92–94.

Saturn over the Water, 1961

    DeVitis, A. A., and Albert E. Kalson. *J. B. Priestley*, 88–90.

The Shapes of Sleep, 1962

    DeVitis, A. A., and Albert E. Kalson. *J. B. Priestley*, 90–92.

Sir Michael and Sir George, 1964

    DeVitis, A. A., and Albert E. Kalson. *J. B. Priestley*, 95–97.

They Walk in the City, 1964

    DeVitis, A. A., and Albert E. Kalson. *J. B. Priestley*, 58–59.

Three Men in New Suits, 1945

    DeVitis, A. A., and Albert E. Kalson. *J. B. Priestley*, 72–73.

Wonder Hero, 1933

    DeVitis, A. A., and Albert E. Kalson. *J. B. Priestley*, 56–58.

BARBARA PYM

Excellent Women, 1952

    Brothers, Barbara. "Women Victimised by Fiction: Living and Loving in the Novels by Barbara Pym," in Thomas F. Staley, ed., *Twentieth-Century Women Novelists*, 61–79.
    Nardin, Jane. *Barbara Pym*, 71–82.

A Few Green Leaves, 1980

> Nardin, Jane. *Barbara Pym*, 134–142.

A Glass of Blessings, 1958

> Brothers, Barbara. "Women Victimised," 61–79.
> Nardin, Jane. *Barbara Pym*, 103–113.

Jane and Prudence, 1953

> Brothers, Barbara. "Women Victimised," 61–79.
> Nardin, Jane. *Barbara Pym*, 82–91.

Less Than Angels, 1955

> Brothers, Barbara. "Women Victimised," 61–79.
> Nardin, Jane. *Barbara Pym*, 91–103.

No Fond Return of Love, 1961

> Brothers, Barbara. "Women Victimised," 61–79.

Quartet in Autumn, 1977

> Brothers, Barbara. "Women Victimised," 61–79.
> Nardin, Jane. *Barbara Pym*, 124–134.
> Stetz, Margaret Diane. "*Quartet in Autumn*: New Light on Barbara Pym as a Modernist." *Arizona Q* 41 (1985), 24–37.

Some Tame Gazelle, 1950

> Brothers, Barbara. "Women Victimised," 61–79.
> Nardin, Jane. *Barbara Pym*, 63–71.

The Sweet Dove Died, 1978

> Brothers, Barbara. "Women Victimised," 61–79.
> Nardin, Jane. *Barbara Pym*, 114–124.

ANN RADCLIFFE

The Castles of Athlin and Dunbayne, 1789

> Lewis, Paul. "Fearful Lessons: The Didacticism of the Early Gothic Novel." *Coll Lang Assoc J* 23 (1980), 471–472.
> Reno, Robert Princeton. *The Gothic Visions*, 11–25.

Gaston de Blondeville, 1826

> Reddin, Chitra Pershad. *Forms of Evil*, 71–72, 124, 221.

The Italian, 1797

> Anderson, Howard. "Gothic Heroes," in Robert Folkenflik, ed., *The English Hero*, 217–220.
> Coleman, William Emmet. *On the Discrimination*, 163–177.
> Day, William Patrick. *In the Circles*, 107–109.
> Hennessy, Brendan. *The Gothic Novel*, 22–24.
> Le Tellier, Robert Ignatius. *An Intensifying Vision*, 27–29, 43–44, 57–59, 74–75, 100–102, 123–126, 159–161.

Le Tellier, Robert Ignatius. *Kindred Spirits*, 312–316.

MacAndrew, Elizabeth. *The Gothic Tradition*, 139–141.

Novak, Maximillian E. "The Extended Moment: Time, Dream, History, and Perspective in Eighteenth-Century Fiction," in Paula R. Backscheider, ed., *Probability*, 145–146, 161–163.

Punter, David. "Fictional Representation of the Law in the Eighteenth Century." *Eighteenth-Century Stud* 16 (1982–83), 67–68.

Punter, David. *The Literature of Terror*, 70–73, 93–96.

Reddin, Chitra Pershad. *Forms of Evil*, 70–71, 123–124, 220–221.

Reno, Robert Princeton. *The Gothic Visions*, 155–209.

Rogers, Katharine M. "Dreams and Nightmares: Male Characters in the Feminine Novel of the Eighteenth Century." *Women & Lit* 2 (1981), 18–20.

Sedgwick, Eve Kosofsky. "The Character in the Veil: Imagery of the Surface in the Gothic Novel." *PMLA* 96 (1981), 260–267.

Thomson, John. "Seasonal and Lighting Effects in Ann Radcliffe's Fiction." *AUMLA* 56 (1981), 197–199.

Todd, Janet M. "Posture and Imposture: The Gothic Manservant in Ann Radcliffe's *The Italian*." *Women & Lit* 2 (1982), 25–37.

Wilt, Judith. *Ghosts of the Gothic*, 31–42.

The Mysteries of Udolpho, 1794

Anderson, Howard. "Gothic Heroes," 205–206, 209–212.

Arnaud, Pierre. "Les Jardins dans les romans de Mrs. Radcliffe," in *Autour de l'idée*, 83–89.

Butler, Marilyn. "The Woman at the Window: Ann Radcliffe in the Novels of Mary Wollstonecraft and Jane Austen." *Women & Lit* 1 (1980), 141–142.

Coleman, William Emmet. *On the Discrimination*, 122–124, 135–163.

Day, William Patrick. *In the Circles*, 105–107.

Durant, David S. "Aesthetic Heroism in *The Mysteries of Udolpho*." *Eighteenth Century* 22 (1981), 175–188.

Fawcett, Mary Laughlin. "*Udolpho*'s Primal Mystery." *Stud in Engl Lit, 1500–1900* 23 (1983), 481–494.

Figes, Eva. *Sex and Subterfuge*, 68–75.

Flaxman, Rhoda L. "Radcliffe's Dual Modes of Vision," in Mary Anne Schofield and Cecilia Macheski, eds., *Fetter'd or Free?*, 125–132.

Haggerty, George E. "Fact and Fancy in the Gothic Novel." *Nineteenth-Century Fiction* 39 (1985), 383–384.

Hennessy, Brendan. *The Gothic Novel*, 23–24.

Howells, Coral Ann. *Love, Mystery*, 29–61.

Le Tellier, Robert Ignatius. *An Intensifying Vision*, 17–19, 40–41, 51–54, 70–71, 79, 84–85, 95–100, 150–152, 158–161.

Le Tellier, Robert Ignatius. *Kindred Spirits*, 182–188, 229–236.

Lewis, Paul. "Fearful Lessons," 474–476.

MacAndrew, Elizabeth. *The Gothic Tradition*, 131–137.

Morrow, Patrick D. "Sublime or Sensible: *The Mysteries of Udolpho* and *Northanger Abbey*," in his *Tradition*, 93–106.
Novak, Maximillian E. "The Extended Moment," 159–161.
Platzner, Robert Leonard. *The Metaphysical Novel*, 16–29.
Punter, David. *The Literature of Terror*, 66–68, 86–90.
Reddin, Chitra Pershad. *Forms of Evil*, 68–70, 72–73, 121–123, 219–220, 240.
Reno, Robert Princeton. *The Gothic Visions*, 58–97.
Roberts, Bette B. *The Gothic Romance*, 147–183.
Sandy, Stephen. *The Raveling*, 80–126.
Schroeder, Natalie. "*The Mysteries of Udolpho* and *Clermont*: The Radcliffean Encroachment on the Art of Regina Maria Roche." *Stud in the Novel* 12 (1980), 131–143.
Sedgwick, Eve Kosofsky. "The Character," 260–267.
Tatu, Chantal. "Cris et chuchotements dans *Les Mystères d'Udolphe* d'Anne Radcliffe: mais à quoi sert le fantastique?" *Caliban* 16 (1979), 87–97.
Thomson, John. "Seasonal and Lighting Effects," 193–197.
Van Luchene, Stephen Robert. *Essays in Gothic Fiction*, 73–110.
Weiss, Fredric. *The Antic Spectre*, 123–158.
Wilt, Judith. *Ghosts of the Gothic*, 124–141.

The Romance of the Forest, 1791

Arnaud, Pierre. "Les Jardins," 83–89.
Butler, Marilyn. "The Woman at the Window," 130–132.
Reno, Robert Princeton. *The Gothic Visions*, 39–57.
Thomson, John. "Seasonal and Lighting Effects," 191–193.

A Sicilian Romance, 1790

Arnaud, Pierre. "Les Jardins," 83–89.
Lewis, Paul. "Fearful Lessons." 472–474.
Nollen, Elizabeth. "Ann Radcliffe's *A Sicilian Romance*: A New Source for Jane Austen's *Sense and Sensibility*." *Engl Lang Notes* 22:2 (1984), 30–37.
Reddin, Chitra Pershad. *Forms of Evil*, 189–191.
Reno, Robert Princeton. *The Gothic Visions*, 25–39.

MARY-ANNE RADCLIFFE

Manfroné, or The One-Handed Monk, 1809
Howells, Coral Ann. *Love, Mystery*, 100–113.

ROBERT S. RATTRAY

The Leopard Priestess, 1934
Milbury-Steen, Sarah L. *European and African Stereotypes*, 66–71.

ERNEST RAYMOND

Tell England, 1922

   Quigly, Isabel. *The Heirs of Tom Brown*, 241–245.

HERBERT READ

The Green Child, 1935

   Barker, Robert. "Sources of Herbert Read's *The Green Child*, II."
      Notes and Queries 27 (1980), 531–533.
   Murayama, Mariko. "Irony in Herbert Read's *The Green Child*." *J of
      the Engl Inst* 11 (1980), 1–26. [In Japanese.]

CHARLES READE

Griffith Gaunt, 1865

   Hughes, Winifred. *The Maniac*, 101–104.

Hard Cash, 1863

   Hughes, Winifred. *The Maniac*, 86–98.
   Nobuhiro, Shinji. "*Eikoku Koshi no Den* to *Hard Cash*." *Bungaku* 47:2
      (1979), 52–75.

It Is Never Too Late to Mend, 1856

   Hughes, Winifred. *The Maniac*, 77–86.
   Rataboul, Louis J. *Le pasteur anglican*, 267–270.

A Terrible Temptation, 1871

   Mitchell, Sally. *The Fallen Angel*, 127–129.

CLARA REEVE

The Old English Baron, 1778

   Coleman, William Emmet. *On the Discrimination*, 56–59, 62–64.
   Ehlers, Leigh. "A Striking Lesson to Posterity: Providence and Charac-
      ter in Clara Reeve's *The Old English Baron*." *Enlightenment Essays* 9
      (1978), 62–76.
   Le Tellier, Robert Ignatius. *An Intensifying Vision*, 89–90, 119–121.
   MacAndrew, Elizabeth. *The Gothic Tradition*, 127–129.
   Punter, David. *The Literature of Terror*, 53–56.
   Roberts, Bette B. *The Gothic Romance*, 59–83.
   Sandy, Stephen. *The Raveling*, 47–54.
   Van Luchene, Stephen Robert. *Essays in Gothic Fiction*, 42–72.

FORREST REID

Peter Waring, 1937

Martin, Augustine. "Prose Fiction in the Irish Literary Renaissance," in Masaru Sekine, ed., *Irish Writers*, 149–150.

MARY RENAULT

The Bull from the Sea, 1962

Crosland, Margaret. *Beyond the Lighthouse*, 166–168.

JEAN RHYS

After Leaving Mr. Mackenzie, 1931

Davidson, Arnold E. "The Art and Economics of Destitution in Jean Rhys's *After Leaving Mr. Mackenzie*." *Stud in the Novel* 16 (1984), 215–226.

Kraf, Elaine. "Jean Rhys: The Men in Her Novels (Hugh Heidler, 'The Gigolo', and Mr. Mackenzie)." *R of Contemp Fiction* 5:2 (1985), 124–127.

Lindroth, Colette. "Whispers Outside the Room: The Haunted Fiction of Jean Rhys." *R of Contemp Fiction* 5:2 (1985), 136–137.

Mossin, Henrik. "The Existentialist Dimension in the Novels of Jean Rhys." *Kunapipi* 3:1 (1981), 145–146.

Nebeker, Helen. *Jean Rhys*, 14–38.

Staley, Thomas F. *Jean Rhys*, 67–83.

Wolfe, Peter. *Jean Rhys*, 84–102.

Good Morning, Midnight, 1939

Borinsky, Alicia. "Jean Rhys: Poses of a Woman as Guest." *Poetics Today* 6:1–2 (1985), 231, 242–243.

Byrne, Jack. "Jean Rhys's *Good Morning, Midnight*: The Boulevard of Broken Dreams." *R of Contemp Fiction* 5:2 (1985), 151–158.

Davidson, Arnold E. "The Dark is Light Enough: Affirmation from Despair in Jean Rhys's *Good Morning, Midnight*." *Contemp Lit* 24 (1983), 349–364.

Emery, Mary Lou. "The Paradox of Style: Metaphor and Ritual in *Good Morning, Midnight*." *R of Contemp Fiction* 5:2 (1985), 145–150.

Gardiner, Judith Kegan. "Good Morning, Midnight; Good Night, Modernism." *Boundary 2* 11:1–2 (1982–83), 233–249.

Kraf, Elaine. "Jean Rhys: The Men in Her Novels," 121–124.

Mossin, Henrik. "The Existentialist Dimension," 147–148.

Nebeker, Helen. *Jean Rhys*, 85–121.

Staley, Thomas F. *Jean Rhys*, 84–99.

Thompson, Irene. "The Left Bank Apéritifs of Jean Rhys and Ernest Hemingway." *Georgia R* 35 (1981), 99–101.

Wolfe, Peter. *Jean Rhys*, 121–136.

Quartet, 1928

Berger, Gertrude. "Rhys, de Beauvoir, and the Woman in Love." *R of Contemp Fiction* 5:2 (1985), 139–145.

Borinsky, Alicia. "Jean Rhys," 231–235.

Gardiner, Judith Kegan. "Rhys Recalls Ford: *Quartet* and *The Good Soldier*." *Tulsa Stud in Women's Lit* 1 (1982), 67–81.

Kraf, Elaine. "Jean Rhys: The Men in Her Novels," 118–121.

Mossin, Henrik. "The Existentialist Dimension," 144–145.

Nebeker, Helen. *Jean Rhys*, 1–13.

Nebeker, Helen E. "Jean Rhys's *Quartet*: The Genesis of Myth." *Intl J of Women's Stud* 2 (1979), 257–267.

Staley, Thomas F. *Jean Rhys*, 35–54.

Wolfe, Peter. *Jean Rhys*, 67–83.

Voyage in the Dark, 1934

Borinsky, Alicia. "Jean Rhys," 235–243.

Campbell, Elaine. "Reflections of Obeah in Jean Rhys' Fiction." *Kunapipi* 4:2 (1982), 45–46.

Emery, Mary Lou. "The Politics of Form: Jean Rhys's Social Vision in *Voyage in the Dark* and *Wide Saragasso Sea*." *Twentieth Century Lit* 28 (1982), 419–424.

Gurr, Andrew. *Writers in Exile*, 123–124.

James, Selma. *The Ladies*, 59–60.

Kloepfer, Deborah Kelly. "*Voyage in the Dark*: Jean Rhys's Masquerade for the Mother." *Contemp Lit* 26 (1985), 443–459.

Lindroth, Colette. "Whispers Outside the Room," 135–136.

Mossin, Henrik. "The Existentialist Dimension," 146–147.

Nebeker, Helen. *Jean Rhys*, 39–84.

Nudd, Donna Marie. "The Uneasy *Voyage* of Jean Rhys and Selma Vaz Dias." *Lit in Performance* 4:2 (1984), 23–31.

Staley, Thomas F. *Jean Rhys*, 59–67.

Wolfe, Peter. *Jean Rhys*, 103–120.

Wide Saragasso Sea, 1966

Berger, Gertrude. "Jean Rhys's 'Tree of Life'." *R of Contemp Fiction* 5:2 (1985), 114–117.

Bon, Adriano. "Jean Rhys: Dominatori e devianti." *Uomini e Libri* 16 (1980), 28.

Campbell, Elaine. "Reflections of Obeah," 46–50.

Emery, Mary Lou. "The Politics of Form," 424–429.

Ganner-Rauth, Heidi. "To Be Continued? Sequels and Continuations of Nineteenth-Century Novels and Novel Fragments." *Engl Stud* 64 (1983), 138–142.

Harris, Wilson. "Carnival of Psyche: Jean Rhys's *Wide Saragasso Sea*." *Kunapipi* 2:2 (1980), 142–150.

James, Selma. *The Ladies*, 62–75.

Lindroth, Colette. "Whispers Outside the Room," 137–139.

Mossin, Henrik. "The Existentialist Dimension," 149–150.
Nebeker, Helen. *Jean Rhys*, 122–194.
Nunez-Harrell, Elizabeth. "The Paradoxes of Belonging: The White West Indian Woman in Fiction." *Mod Fiction Stud* 31 (1985), 281–282, 286–292.
Scharfman, Ronnie. "Mirroring and Mothering in Simone Schwarz-Bart's *Pluie et vent sur Télumée Miracle* and Jean Rhys' *Wide Saragasso Sea*." *Yale French Stud* 62 (1981), 88–106.
Staley, Thomas F. *Jean Rhys*, 100–120.
Tarozzi, Bianca. "La verità del sogno: Jean Rhys e *Wide Saragasso Sea*," in Paola Colaiacomo et al., eds., *Come nello specchio*, 91–117.
Wolfe, Peter. *Jean Rhys*, 137–158.

DOROTHY RICHARDSON

Pilgrimage, 1915–1967

Beauman, Nicola. *A Very Great Profession*, 151–155.
Fromm, Gloria G. "What Are Men to Dorothy Richardson?" *Women & Lit* 2 (1981), 168–187.
Gubar, Susan. "The Birth of the Artist as Heroine: (Re)production, the *Künstlerroman* Tradition, and the Fiction of Katherine Mansfield," in Carolyn G. Heilbrun and Margaret R. Higonnet, eds., *The Representation of Women*, 40–42.
Hanscombe, Gillian E. *The Art of Life*, 26–36, 39–59, 62–92, 95–129, 133–166.
Henke, Suzette A. "Male and Female Consciousness in Dorothy Richardson's *Pilgrimage*." *J of Women's Stud in Lit* 1 (1979), 51–60.
McLaurin, Allen. " 'Siamese Twins': The Verbal and the Visual in Dorothy Richardson's *Pilgrimage*." *Trivium* 18 (1983), 73–85.
Stewart, Grace. *A New Mythos*, 21–28, 56–61, 112–120.
Thorn, Arline R. " 'Feminine' Time in Dorothy Richardson's *Pilgrimage*." *Intl J of Women's Stud* 1 (1978), 211–219.

SAMUEL RICHARDSON

Clarissa, 1748

Altman, Janet Gurkin. *Epistolarity*, 22–26.
Barker, Gerard A. *Grandison's Heirs*, 53–55.
Bell, Michael. *The Sentiment of Reality*, 15–39.
Bigges, Penelope. "Hunt, Conquest, Trial: Lovelace and the Metaphors of the Rake." *Stud in Eighteenth-Century Culture* 11 (1982), 51–64.
Bredsdorff, Thomas. "Whatever Happened to Women's Lust?," in Michael Chesnutt et al., eds., *Essays*, 175–180.
Brownstein, Rachel M. *Becoming a Heroine*, 40–58, 62–77.
Butler, Janet. "The Garden: Early Symbol of Clarissa's Complicity." *Stud in Engl Lit, 1500–1900* 24 (1984), 527–544.

Castle, Terry. *Clarissa's Ciphers*, 32–187.

Coates, Paul. *The Realist Fantasy*, 23–49.

Connaughton, Michael E. "Richardson's Familiar Quotations: *Clarissa* and Bysshe's *Art of English Poetry*." *Philol Q* 60 (1981), 183–194.

Cox, Stephen D. *'The Stranger Within Thee'*, 59–81.

Denton, Ramona. "Anna Howe and Richardson's Ambivalent Artistry in *Clarissa*." *Philol Q* 58 (1979), 53–60.

Doederlein, Sue Warrick. "Clarissa in the Hands of the Critics." *Eighteenth-Century Stud* 16 (1983), 401–414.

Donaldson, Ian. "Fielding, Richardson, and the Ends of the Novel." *Essays in Criticism* 32 (1982), 34–40.

Dussinger, John A. "Love and Consanguinity in Richardson's Novels." *Stud in Engl Lit, 1500–1900* 24 (1984), 520–521.

Duthie, Elizabeth. "The Genuine Man of Feeling." *Mod Philology* 78 (1981), 284–285.

Eagleton, Terry. *The Rape of Clarissa*, 40–94.

Edwards, Lee R. *Psyche as Hero*, 29–48.

Eldredge, Patricia Reid. "Karen Horney and *Clarissa*: The Tragedy of Neurotic Pride." *Am J of Psychoanalysis* 42 (1982), 51–59.

Faiola Neri, Simonetta. "Pamela a Clarissa: Due donne in conflitto con la società del settecento." *Engl Miscellany* 28–29 (1979–80), 227–250.

Flynn, Carol Houlihan. *Samuel Richardson*, 76–96, 107–112, 128–144, 170–185, 202–208, 243–258, 267–277.

Furber, Donald, and Anne Callahan. *Erotic Love*, 118–128.

Furst, Lilian R. "The Man of Sensibility and the Woman of Sense." *Jahrbuch für Internationale Germanistik* 14 (1982), 13–26.

Garber, Frederick. *The Anatomy of the Self*, 3–32.

Gillis, Christina Marsden. *The Paradox of Privacy*, 17–136.

Gillis, Christine Marsden. "Private Room and Public Space: The Paradox of Form in *Clarissa*." *Stud on Voltaire and the Eighteenth Century* 176 (1979), 153–168.

Golden, Morris. "Public Context and Imagining Self in *Clarissa*." *Stud in Engl Lit, 1500–1900* 25 (1985), 575–598.

Hagstrum, Jean H. *Sex and Sensibility*, 195–213.

Hardy, Barbara. *Forms of Feeling*, 25–31.

Higbie, Robert. *Character & Structure*, 60–82.

Johnson, Glen M. "Richardson's 'Editor' in *Clarissa*." *J of Narrative Technique* 10 (1980), 99–114.

Kawin, Bruce F. *The Mind of the Novel*, 234–240.

Konigsberg, Ira. *Narrative Technique*, 50–99.

Leech, Geoffrey N., and Michael H. Short. *Style in Fiction*, 270–272.

Lenta, Margaret. "Comedy, Tragedy and Feminism: The Novels of Richardson and Fielding." *Engl Stud in Africa* 26 (1983), 15–25.

Lindley, Arthur. "Richardson's Lovelace and the Self-dramatizing Hero of the Restoration," in Robert Folkenflik, ed., *The English Hero*, 195–203.

Loesberg, Jonathan. "Allegory and Narrative in *Clarissa*." *Novel* 15 (1981), 39–59.

Macey, Samuel L. *Money and the Novel*, 105–114, 168–169.

Maddox, James H., Jr. "Lovelace and the World of Ressentiment in *Clarissa*." *Texas Stud in Lit and Lang* 24 (1982), 271–291.

Miller, Nancy K. *The Heroine's Text*, 83–95.

Moon, Elaine. " 'Sacrific'd to my sex': The Marriages of Samuel Richardson's Pamela and Mr. B., and Mr. and Mrs. Harlowe." *AUMLA* 63 (1985), 19–32.

Morgan, Susan. *In the Meantime*, 45–49.

Novak, Maximillian E. *Eighteenth-Century English Literature*, 122–124.

Novak, Maximillian E. "The Extended Moment: Time, Dream, History, and Perspective in Eighteenth-Century Fiction," in Paula R. Backscheider, ed., *Probability*, 150–158.

Panitz, Esther L. *The Alien*, 95–97.

Perry, Ruth. *Women*, 163–165.

Price, John Valdimir. "Patterns of Sexual Behaviour in Some Eighteenth- Century Novels," in Paul-Gabriel Boucé, ed., *Sexuality*, 162–166.

Robins, Ross. "Richardson's Development." *Spectrum* (Santa Barbara) 21 (1979), 144–150.

Rogers, Katharine M. "Creative Variation: *Clarissa* and *Les Liaisons dangereuses*." *Compar Lit* 38 (1986), 36–52.

Rudnik-Smalbraak, Marijke. *Samuel Richardson*, 87–137.

Runte, Roseann. "Dying Words: The Vocabulary of Death in Three Eighteenth-Century English and French Novels." *Canadian R of Compar Lit* 6 (1979), 361–368.

Shroff, Homai J. *The Eighteenth Century Novel*, 30–32, 98–108.

Smith, Grahame. *The Novel & Society*, 72–91.

Stevenson, John Allen. "The Courtship of the Family: Clarissa and the Harlowes Once More." *ELH* 48 (1981), 757–775.

Stuber, Florian. "On Fathers and Authority in *Clarissa*." *Stud in Engl Lit, 1500–1900* 25 (1985), 557–574.

Tanner, Tony. *Adultery in the Novel*, 101–112.

Taylor, Anne Robinson. *Male Novelists*, 60–88.

Todd, Janet. *Women's Friendship*, 9–68.

Traugott, John. "Molesting *Clarissa*." *Novel* 15 (1982), 163–170.

Trotter, W. A. "Richardson and the 'New Lights': *Clarissa* among Victorians." *English* 33 (1984), 117–125.

Vaid, Sudesh. *The Divided Mind*, 162–213.

Vargish, Thomas. *The Providential Aesthetic*, 44–46.

Williams, Ioan. *The Idea of the Novel*, 174–185.

Wilson, Bruce L. " 'Sex and the Single Girl' in the Eighteenth Century: An Essay on Marriage and the Puritan Myth." *J of Women's Stud in Lit* 1 (1979), 195–219.

Yeazell, Ruth Bernard. "Podsnappery, Sexuality, and the English Novel." *Crit Inquiry* 9 (1982), 351–353.

Pamela, 1740

Altman, Janet Gurkin. *Epistolarity*, 103–106.

Backscheider, Paula R. " 'I Died for Love': Esteem in Eighteenth-Century Novels by Women," in Mary Anne Schofield and Cecilia Macheski, eds., *Fetter'd or Free?*, 163–164.

Belyea, Barbara. "Romance and Richardson's *Pamela*." *Engl Stud in Canada* 10 (1984), 407–414.

Berg, Temma F. "From Pamela to Jane Grey; or, How Not to Become the Heroine of Your Own Text." *Stud in the Novel* 17 (1985), 116–123.

Berger, Dieter A. "Aspekte der Anrede in Samuel Richardsons *Pamela*." *Germanisch-Romanische Monatsschrift* 32 (1982), 174–188.

Bini, Benedetta. "*Pamela*, o il panciotto che divenne giovedì." *Calibano* 1 (1977), 95–114.

Blondel, Jacques. "L'Amour dans *Pamela*: De l'affrontement à la découverte de soi," in *Etudes sur le XVIIIe siècle*, 15–30.

Brady, Jennifer. "Readers in Richardson's *Pamela*." *Engl Stud in Canada* 9 (1983), 164–176.

Castle, Terry J. "P/B: *Pamela* as Sexual Fiction." *Stud in Engl Lit, 1500–1900* 22 (1982), 469–489.

Chaber, Lois A. "Art and Artistry in *Pamela*." *Revista Canaria de Estudios Ingleses* 7 (1983), 73–86.

Davis, Lennard J. "A Social History of Fact and Fiction: Authorial Disavowal in the Early English Novel," in Edward W. Said, ed., *Literature and Society*, 135–145.

Donaldson, Ian. "Fielding, Richardson," 29–34.

Dussinger, John A. "Love and Consanguinity," 515–519.

Eagleton, Terry. *The Rape of Clarissa*, 29–39.

Faiola Neri, Simonetta. "Pamela a Clarissa," 227–250.

Flynn, Carol Houlihan. *Samuel Richardson*, 136–139, 157–167, 214–218, 235–245.

Fortuna, James Louis, Jr. *'The Unsearchable Wisdom of God'*, 59–113.

Hagstrum, Jean H. *Sex and Sensibility*, 191–195.

Hughes, Peter. "Wars within Doors: Erotic Heroism in Eighteenth-Century Literature," in Robert Folkenflik, ed., *The English Hero*, 185–188.

Indyk, Ivor. "Interpretative Relevance, and Richardson's *Pamela*." *Southern R* (Adelaide) 16 (1983), 31–42.

Koretsky, Allen C. "Poverty, Wealth, and Virtue: Richardson's Social Outlook in *Pamela*." *Engl Stud in Canada* 9 (1983), 36–55.

Larson, Kerry. " 'Naming the Writer': Exposure, Authority, and Desire in *Pamela*." *Criticism* 23 (1981), 126–140.

Laurence-Anderson, Judith. "Changing Affective Life in Eighteenth-Century England and Samuel Richardson's *Pamela*." *Stud in Eighteenth-Century Culture* 10 (1981), 445–456.

Lenta, M. "From *Pamela* to *Joseph Andrews*: An Investigation of the Relationship between Two Originals." *Engl Stud in Africa* 23 (1980), 63–74.

Lenta, Margaret. "Comedy, Tragedy and Feminism," 17–25.

McDermott, M. Hubert. "*Vertue Rewarded: Or, The Irish Princess*: A Source for *Pamela*." *Durham Univ J* 77 (1984–85), 195–201.

Macey, Samuel L. *Money and the Novel*, 99–102, 105–107, 111–114, 121–123.

Macheski, Cecilia. "Penelope's Daughters: Images of Needlework in Eighteenth-Century Literature," in Mary Anne Schofield and Cecilia Macheski, eds., *Fetter'd or Free?*, 89–90.

McKee, Patricia. "Corresponding Freedoms: Language and the Self in *Pamela*." *ELH* 52 (1985), 621–647.

Miller, Nancy K. *The Heroine's Text*, 37–50.

Moon, Elaine. " 'Sacrific'd to my sex'," 19–32.

Novak, Maximillian E. *Eighteenth-Century English Literature*, 120–122.

Perry, Ruth. *Women*, 22–23, 58–59, 165–166.

Peters, Dolores. "The Pregnant Pamela: Characterization and Popular Medical Attitudes in the Eighteenth Century." *Eighteenth-Century Stud* 14 (1981), 432–451.

Pickering, Samuel, Jr. "The 'Ambiguous Circumstances of a *Pamela*': Early Children's Books and the Attitude Towards *Pamela*." *J of Narrative Technique* 14 (1984), 153–169.

Plaisant, Michèle. "Passion, sexualité et violence dans *Pamela*." *Bull de la Société d'Etudes Anglo-Américaines des XVIIe et XVIIIe Siècles* 6 (1978), 37–59.

Robins, Ross. "Richardson's Development," 144–150.

Roussel, Roy. *The Conversation*, 67–93.

Rudnik-Smalbraak, Marijke. *Samuel Richardson*, 39–83.

Sciullo, Luciana. "*Pamela* da Richardson a Goldoni." *Quaderni di Lingue e Letterature* 1 (1976), 117–121.

Shroff, Homai J. *The Eighteenth Century Novel*, 27–30.

Sturrock, June. "The Completion of *Pamela*." *Durham Univ J* 74 (1981–82), 227–232.

Suleiman, Susan Rubin. "Of Readers and Narratees: The Experience of *Pamela*." *L'Esprit Créateur* 21:2 (1981), 89–97.

Suzuki, Kenzo. "*Pamela* saiho." *Eigo Seinen* (Tokyo) 126 (1980), 68–70.

Usaily, Mohammad Awad al-. "Richardson's Sentimentalism: A Study of *Pamela*." *J of Engl* (Sana'a Univ) 1 (1975), 37–50.

Vaid, Sudesh. *The Divided Mind*, 152–162, 211–213.

Sir Charles Grandison, 1754

Barker, Gerard A. "Ferdinando Falkland's Fall: Grandison in Disarray." *Papers on Lang & Lit* 16 (1980), 376–386.

Barker, Gerard A. *Grandison's Heirs*, 13–49, 146–150.

Crabtree, Paul R. "Propriety, *Grandison*, and the Novel of Manners." *Mod Lang Q* 41 (1980), 151–161.

Doody, Margaret Anne. "George Eliot and the Eighteenth-Century Novel." *Nineteenth-Century Fiction* 35 (1980), 264–265.

Dussinger, John A. "Love and Consanguinity," 521–526.

Fergus, Jan. *Jane Austen*, 72–86.

Figes, Eva. *Sex and Subterfuge*, 15–20.

Flynn, Carol Houlihan. *Samuel Richardson*, 45–49, 72–76, 96–98, 130–132, 185–189, 231–234, 258–262.

Gilmour, Robin. *The Idea of the Gentleman*, 30–32.

Hagstrum, Jean H. *Sex and Sensibility*, 214–218.

Harris, Jocelyn. " 'As if they had been living friends': *Sir Charles Grandison* into *Mansfield Park*." *Bull of Res in the Hum* 83 (1980), 360–403.

Macey, Samuel L. *Money and the Novel*, 91–92, 102–105, 114–121, 136–137, 146–148, 168–169.

Novak, Maximillian E. *Eighteenth-Century English Literature*, 124–125.

Panitz, Esther L. *The Alien*, 95–97.

Rudnik-Smalbraak, Marijke. *Samuel Richardson*, 141–197.

Sabor, Peter. "*Amelia* and *Sir Charles Grandison*: The Convergence of Fielding and Richardson." *Wascana R* 17:2 (1982), 3–18.

Shroff, Homai J. *The Eighteenth Century Novel*, 107–121, 247–249.

Trickett, Rachel. " 'Curious Eye': Some Aspects of Visual Description in Eighteenth-Century Literature," in Douglas Lane Patey and Timothy Keegan, eds., *Augustan Studies*, 247–249.

Yates, Mary V. "The Christian Rake in *Sir Charles Grandison*." *Stud in Engl Lit, 1500–1900* 24 (1984), 545–561.

REGINA MARIA ROCHE

The Children of the Abbey, 1796

Howells, Coral Ann. *Love, Mystery*, 82–100.

Roberts, Bette B. *The Gothic Romance*, 184–207.

Clermont, 1798

Schroeder, Natalie. "*The Mysteries of Udolpho* and *Clermont*: The Radcliffean Encroachment on the Art of Regina Maria Roche." *Stud in the Novel* 12 (1980), 131–143.

FREDERICK ROLFE

Hadrian the Seventh, 1904

Weeks, Donald. "Frederick Rolfe and the Gleeson Whites." *J of the Eighteen Nineties Soc* 10 (1979), 9–12.

Nicholas Crabbe, 1958

>   Jones, G. P. "The Date of Composition of Frederick Rolfe's *Nicholas Crabbe*." *Engl Lit in Transition (1880–1920)* 23 (1980), 125–130.

CHRISTINA GEORGINA ROSSETTI

Maude, 1897

>   D'Amico, Diane. "Christina Rossetti's *Maude*: A Reconsideration." *Univ of Dayton R* 15:1 (1981), 129–142.

VITA SACKVILLE-WEST

All Passion Spent, 1931

>   DeSalvo, Louise A. "Every Woman Is an Island: Vita Sackville-West, the Image of the City, and the Pastoral Idyll," in Susan Merrill Squier, ed., *Women Writers*, 97–112.

DOROTHY L. SAYERS

Busman's Honeymoon, 1937

>   Epperson, William R. "The Repose of Very Delicate Balance: Postulants and Celebrants of the Sacrament of Marriage in the Detective Fiction of Dorothy L. Sayers." *Mythlore* 6:4 (1979), 33–36.
>   Gaillard, Dawson. *Dorothy L. Sayers*, 83–87, 96–97.
>   Hall, Trevor H. *Dorothy L. Sayers*, 104–118.
>   Hannay, Margaret P. "Harriet's Influence on the Characterization of Lord Peter Whimsey," in Hannay, ed., *As Her Whimsey*, 44–45.
>   Reaves, R. B. "Crime and Punishment in the Detective Fiction of Dorothy L. Sayers," in Margaret P. Hannay, ed., *As Her Whimsey*, 12–13.
>   Roberts, Helen. "Propaganda and Ideology in Women's Fiction," in Diana Laurenson, ed., *The Sociology*, 171–172.
>   Tischler, Nancy M. *Dorothy L. Sayers*, 87–92.

Clouds of Witness, 1926

>   Gaillard, Dawson. *Dorothy L. Sayers*, 29–31, 34–35, 37–39.
>   Hone, Ralph E. *Dorothy L. Sayers*, 49–50.
>   Tischler, Nancy M. *Dorothy L. Sayers*, 56–58.

The Documents in the Case, 1930

>   Gaillard, Dawson. *Dorothy L. Sayers*, 46–49.
>   Gregory, E. R. "Wilkie Collins and Dorothy L. Sayers," in Margaret P. Hannay, ed., *As Her Whimsey*, 58–64.
>   Hall, Trevor H. *Dorothy L. Sayers*, 62–78.
>   Morris, Virginia B. "Arsenic and Blue Lace: Sayers' Criminal Women." *Mod Fiction Stud* 29 (1983), 487–489.

Stock, R. D., and Barbara Stock. "The Agents of Evil and Justice in the Novels of Dorothy L. Sayers," in Margaret P. Hannay, ed., *As Her Whimsey*, 17–18.

The Five Red Herrings, 1931

Gaillard, Dawson. *Dorothy L. Sayers*, 55–58, 62–65.

Gaudy Night, 1936

Auerbach, Nina. *Romantic Imprisonment*, 184–194.

Brody, Miriam. "The Haunting of *Gaudy Night*: Misreadings in a Work of Detective Fiction." *Style* 19 (1985), 94–115.

Campbell, SueEllen. "The Detective Heroine and the Death of Her Hero: Dorothy Sayers to P. D. James." *Mod Fiction Stud* 29 (1983), 498–502, 509–510.

Craig, Patricia, and Mary Cadogan. *The Lady Investigates*, 191–195.

Dunn, Robert Paul. " 'The Laughter of the Universe': Dorothy L. Sayers and the Whimsical Vision," in Margaret P. Hannay, ed., *As Her Whimsey*, 204–208.

Edwards, Lee R. *Psyche as Hero*, 161–168, 184–187.

Epperson, William R. "The Repose of Very Delicate Balance," 33–36.

Gaillard, Dawson. *Dorothy L. Sayers*, 1–3, 71–79, 82–84, 97–98.

Hannay, Margaret P. "Harriet's Influence," 46–49.

Hannay, Margaret P. "Head versus Heart in Dorothy L. Sayers' *Gaudy Night*." *Mythlore* 6:3 (1979), 33–37.

Heldreth, Lillian M. "Breaking the Rules of the Game: Shattered Patterns in Dorothy L. Sayers' *Gaudy Night*." *Clues* 3:1 (1982), 120–127.

Hone, Ralph E. *Dorothy L. Sayers*, 74–77.

Morris, Virginia B. "Arsenic and Blue Lace," 489–495.

Reaves, R. B. "Crime and Punishment," 11–12.

Roberts, Helen. "Propaganda and Ideology," 170–171.

Tischler, Nancy M. *Dorothy L. Sayers*, 15–20, 84–88.

Have His Carcase, 1932

Gaillard, Dawson. *Dorothy L. Sayers*, 58–61, 95–96.

Tischler, Nancy M. *Dorothy L. Sayers*, 83–86.

Murder Must Advertise, 1933

Gaillard, Dawson. *Dorothy L. Sayers*, 61–65.

Hannay, Margaret P. "Harriet's Influence," 42–43.

Hone, Ralph E. *Dorothy L. Sayers*, 65–67.

Reaves, R. B. "Crime and Punishment," 3–5.

Stock, R. D., and Barbara Stock. "The Agents of Evil," 19–21.

Tischler, Nancy M. *Dorothy L. Sayers*, 28–33.

The Nine Tailors, 1934

Basney, Lionel. "*The Nine Tailors* and the Complexity of Innocence," in Margaret P. Hannay, ed., *As Her Whimsey*, 23–35.

Gaillard, Dawson. *Dorothy L. Sayers*, 65–69, 80–82, 90–94.
Hall, Trevor H. *Dorothy L. Sayers*, 36–39.
Hone, Ralph E. *Dorothy L. Sayers*, 67–69.
Reaves, R. B. "Crime and Punishment," 5–6.

Strong Poison, 1930

Gaillard, Dawson. *Dorothy L. Sayers*, 49–53, 55–56.
Hall, Trevor H. *Dorothy L. Sayers*, 119–123.
Hannay, Margaret P. "Harriet's Influence," 46.
Morris, Virginia B. "Arsenic and Blue Lace," 486–488.

Unnatural Death, 1927

Gaillard, Dawson. *Dorothy L. Sayers*, 31–33, 39–41.
Hannay, Margaret P. "Harriet's Influence," 43–44.
Hone, Ralph E. *Dorothy L. Sayers*, 51–54.
Morris, Virginia B. "Arsenic and Blue Lace," 488–489.
Reaves, R. B. "Crime and Punishment," 2–3.

The Unpleasantness at the Bellona Club, 1928

Gaillard, Dawson. *Dorothy L. Sayers*, 33–36, 41–43.
Hannay, Margaret P. "Harriet's Influence," 39–40.
Hone, Ralph E. *Dorothy L. Sayers*, 55–56.
Stock, R. D., and Barbara Stock. "The Agents of Evil," 16–17.

Whose Body?, 1923

Gaillard, Dawson. *Dorothy L. Sayers*, 28–30, 36–37.
Hannay, Margaret P. "Harriet's Influence," 38–39, 41–42.
Hone, Ralph E. *Dorothy L. Sayers*, 41–44.
Stock, R. D., and Barbara Stock. "The Agents of Evil," 15–16.
Tischler, Nancy M. *Dorothy L. Sayers*, 40–41.

OLIVE SCHREINER

From Man to Man, 1926

First, Ruth, and Ann Scott. *Olive Schreiner*, 172–178.
Lerner, Laurence. "Olive Schreiner and the Feminists," in Cherry Clayton, ed., *Olive Schreiner*, 189–191.
Showalter, Elaine. *A Literature*, 201–203.

The Story of an African Farm, 1883

Blake, Kathleen. "Olive Schreiner: A Note on Sexist Language and the Feminist Writer." *Women & Lit* 1 (1980), 81–85.
First, Ruth, and Ann Scott. *Olive Schreiner*, 92–107.
Goode, John. "Sue Bridehead and the New Woman," in Mary Jacobus, ed., *Women Writing*, 109–111.
Gray, Stephen. "An Approach to Schreiner's Realism in *The Story of an African Farm*." *Standpunte* 138 (1978), 38–49.

Green, Robert. "Stability and Flux: The Allotropic Narrative of *An African Farm*," in Cherry Clayton, ed., *Olive Schreiner*, 158–168.

Haynes, R. D. "Elements of Romanticism in *The Story of an African Farm*." *Engl Lit in Transition* 24 (1981), 59–78.

Hofmeyr, Isabel. "South African Liberalism and the Novel," in Cherry Clayton, ed., *Olive Schreiner*, 155–157.

Katzorke, Heidrun. "Die Widerspiegelung der britischen Kolonialherrschaft in Südafrika im Schaffen von Olive Schreiner." *Zeitschrift für Anglistik und Amerikanistik* 32 (1984), 115–122.

Lenta, Margaret. "Independence as the Creative Choice in Two South African Fictions." *Ariel* 17:1 (1986), 35–51.

Lerner, Laurence. "Olive Schreiner and the Feminists," 181–189.

Marquard, Jean. "The Farm: A Concept in the Writing of Olive Schreiner, Pauline Smith, Doris Lessing, Nadine Gordimer and Bessie Head." *Dalhousie R* 59 (1979), 296–297.

Marquard, Jean. "Hagar's Child: A Reading of *The Story of an African Farm*." *Standpunte* 121 (1976), 35–47. [Also in Cherry Clayton, ed., *Olive Schreiner*, 143–153.]

Rive, Richard. *The Story of an African Farm*, Introduction.

Showalter, Elaine. *A Literature*, 199–201.

Stubbs, Patricia. *Women and Fiction*, 112–114.

Voss, A. E. " 'Not a Word or a Sound in the World about Him that is not Modifying Him': Learning, Lore and Language in *The Story of an African Farm*," in Cherry Clayton, ed., *Olive Schreiner*, 170–178.

Trooper Peter Halket, 1897

First, Ruth, and Ann Scott. *Olive Schreiner*, 226–231.

Gray, Stephen. "The Trooper at the Hanging Tree," in Cherry Clayton, ed., *Olive Schreiner*, 198–207.

Katzorke, Heidrun. "Die Widerspiegelung," 123–126.

Sarvan, C. P. "Olive Schreiner's *Trooper Halket*: An Altered Awareness." *Intl Fiction R* 11 (1984), 45–47.

Wilhelm, Peter. "*Peter Halket*, Rhodes and Colonialism," in Cherry Clayton, ed., *Olive Schreiner*, 208–212.

Undine, 1929

First, Ruth, and Ann Scott. *Olive Schreiner*, 84–92.

PAUL SCOTT

The Alien Sky, 1953

Rao, K. Bhaskara. *Paul Scott*, 43–47.

Swinden, Patrick. *Paul Scott*, 19–25.

The Bender, 1963

Rao, K. Bhaskara. *Paul Scott*, 29–33.

The Birds of Paradise, 1962

Rao, K. Bhaskara. *Paul Scott*, 56–62.
Swinden, Patrick. *Paul Scott*, 47–57.

The Chinese Love Pavilion, 1960

Rao, K. Bhaskara. *Paul Scott*, 47–52.
Swinden, Patrick. *Paul Scott*, 41–47.

The Corrida at San Feliu, 1964

Rao, K. Bhaskara. *Paul Scott*, 34–42.
Swinden, Patrick. *Paul Scott*, 57–64.

The Day of the Scorpion, 1968

Rao, K. Bhaskara. *Paul Scott*, 74–82.
Tedesco, Janis, and Janet Popham. *Introduction*, 57–109.

A Division of Spoils, 1975

Rao, K. Bhaskara. *Paul Scott*, 88–96.
Tedesco, Janis, and Janet Popham. *Introduction*, 195–237.

The Jewel in the Crown, 1966

Rao, K. Bhaskara. *Paul Scott*, 64–74.
Tedesco, Janis, and Janet Popham. *Introduction*, 1–49.

Johnnie Sahib, 1952

Rao, K. Bhaskara. *Paul Scott*, 22–24.
Swinden, Patrick. *Paul Scott*, 11–19.

A Male Child, 1956

Rao, K. Bhaskara. *Paul Scott*, 26–29.
Swinden, Patrick. *Paul Scott*, 25–30.

The Mark of the Warrior, 1958

Rao, K. Bhaskara. *Paul Scott*, 52–55.
Swinden, Patrick. *Paul Scott*, 30–40.

The Raj Quartet, 1976

Hoffmann, Barbara. *Paul Scotts "Raj Quartet,"* 18–273.
Mahood, M. M. "Paul Scott's Guardians." *Yearbook of Engl Stud* 13 (1983), 244–258.
Pollard, Arthur. "Twilight of Empire: Paul Scott's *Raj Quartet*," in Daniel Massa, ed., *Individual*, 169–176.
Rao, K. Bhaskara. *Paul Scott*, 63–144.
Swinden, Patrick. *Paul Scott*, 65–102.
Tedesco, Janis, and Janet Popham. *Introduction*, 1–237.
Weinbaum, Francine S. "Psychological Defenses and Thwarted Union in *The Raj Quartet*." *Lit and Psych* 31:2 (1981), 75–86.

Staying On, 1977

Swinden, Patrick. *Paul Scott*, 103–118.

The Towers of Silence, 1971

Kim, Suzanne. "Histoire et roman." *Etudes Anglaises* 36 (1983), 171–174.

Rao, K. Bhaskara. *Paul Scott*, 82–88.

Tedesco, Janis, and Janet Popham. *Introduction*, 129–177.

SARAH SCOTT AND LADY BARBARA MONTAGU

A Description of Millenium Hall, 1762

Kern, Jean B. "The Old Maid, or 'to grow old, and be poor, and laughed at'," in Mary Anne Schofield and Cecilia Macheski, eds., *Fetter'd or Free?*, 206–207.

Todd, Janet. *Women's Friendship*, 342–345.

WALTER SCOTT

The Abbot, 1820

Crawford, Thomas. *Scott*, 70–71, 79–80.

Wilson, A. N. *The Laird*, 98–104.

Wilt, Judith. *Secret Leaves*, 92–95, 111–115.

Anne of Geierstein, 1829

Dale, Thomas R. "*Anne of Geierstein*: A Political Testament." *Scottish Liter J* 7:1 (1980), 193–201.

Engel, Wilson F., III. "Scott's *Anne of Geierstein*." *Explicator* 40:4 (1982), 28–30.

McMaster, Graham. *Scott*, 193–200.

Wilson, A. N. *The Laird*, 159–162.

The Antiquary, 1816

Anderson, James. *Sir Walter Scott*, 44–48.

Brown, David. *Walter Scott*, 47–67.

Engel, Wilson F., III. "Scott's *The Antiquary*." *Explicator* 40:4 (1982), 26–28.

Garside, Peter. "Scott, the Eighteenth Century and the New Man of Sentiment." *Anglia* 103 (1985), 84–86.

McMaster, Graham. *Scott*, 152–156, 163–165.

Millgate, Jane. *Walter Scott*, 85–105.

Reed, James. *Sir Walter Scott*, 89–99.

Wilson, A. N. *The Laird*, 68–74.

Wilt, Judith. *Secret Leaves*, 156–160, 164–170.

The Black Dwarf, 1816

McMaster, Graham. *Scott*, 168–170.

Millgate, Jane. *Walter Scott*, 110–114.

The Bride of Lammermoor, 1819

Anderson, James. *Sir Walter Scott*, 69–72.
Brown, David. *Walter Scott*, 129–150.
Coleman, William Emmet. *On the Discrimination*, 211–217.
Daleski, H. M. *The Divided Heroine*, 6–7.
Edwards, Simon. "Producing Voices: The Discursive Art of Walter Scott," in Kathleen Parkinson and Martin Priestman, eds., *Peasants and Countrymen*, 128–135.
Farrell, John P. *Revolution as Tragedy*, 114–128.
Garside, Peter Dignus. "Union and *The Bride of Lammermoor*." *Stud in Scottish Lit* 19 (1984), 72–89.
Hollingworth, Brian. "The Tragedy of Lucy Ashton, the Bride of Lammermoor." *Stud in Scottish Lit* 19 (1984), 94–105.
Klieneberger, H. R. *The Novel*, 49–51.
Lamont, Claire. "Scott as Story-Teller: *The Bride of Lammermoor*." *Scottish Liter J* 7:1 (1980), 113–124.
Levine, George. "Sir Walter Scott: The End of Romance." *Wordsworth Circle* 10 (1979), 152–153.
McMaster, Graham. *Scott*, 165–178.
Millgate, Jane. *Walter Scott*, 169–185.
Punter, David. *The Literature of Terror*, 162–165.
Reed, James. *Sir Walter Scott*, 122–134.
Shaw, Harry E. "Scott, Mackenzie, and Structure in *The Bride of Lammermoor*." *Stud in the Novel* 13 (1981), 349–364.
Walker, Eric G. *Scott's Fiction*, 27–55, 60–68.
Williams, Merryn. *Women in the English Novel*, 53–55.
Wilson, A. N. *The Laird*, 135–140.

Count Robert of Paris, 1832

Gamerschlag, Kurt. "The Making and Un-Making of Sir Walter Scott's *Count Robert of Paris*." *Stud in Scottish Lit* 15 (1980), 95–115.
Hobsbaum, Philip. "Scott's 'Apoplectic' Novels," in J. H. Alexander and David Hewitt, eds., *Scott and His Influence*, 153–155.
McMaster, Graham. *Scott*, 207–215.
Wilt, Judith. *Secret Leaves*, 176–179.

The Fair Maid of Perth, 1828

Brown, David. *Walter Scott*, 188–190.
Hobsbaum, Philip. "Scott's 'Apoplectic' Novels," 150–152.
McMaster, Graham. *Scott*, 200–207.

Guy Mannering, 1815

Brown, David. *Walter Scott*, 31–46.
Davis, Jana. "Landscape Images and Epistemology in *Guy Mannering*," in J. H. Alexander and David Hewitt, eds., *Scott and His Influence*, 119–128.
Garside, Peter. "Scott, the Eighteenth Century," 81–84.

Hart, Francis Russell. "Scott and the Idea of Adventure," in Alan Bold, ed., *Sir Walter Scott*, 173–190.

McMaster, Graham. *Scott*, 155–162.

Millgate, Jane. "The Structure of *Guy Mannering*," in J. H. Alexander and David Hewitt, eds., *Scott and His Influence*, 109–117.

Millgate, Jane. *Walter Scott*, 59–84.

Reed, James. *Sir Walter Scott*, 69–88.

The Heart of Mid-Lothian, 1818

Anderson, James. *Sir Walter Scott*, 61–65, 84–85.

Blake, N. F. *Non-Standard Language*, 138–143.

Brown, David. *Walter Scott*, 112–128.

Carter, Ian. "Burns, Scott, and Scottish Peasantry," in Kathleen Parkinson and Martin Priestman, eds., *Peasants and Countrymen*, 116–118.

Crawford, Thomas. *Scott*, 91–114.

Criscuola, Margaret Movshin. "The Porteous Mob: Fact and Truth in *The Heart of Midlothian*." *Engl Lang Notes* 22:1 (1984), 43–50.

Dale, Thomas. "The Jurists, the Dominie, and Jeanie Deans." *Scottish Liter J* 11:1 (1984), 36–44.

D'Arcy, Julian Meldon. "Davie Deans and Bothwell Bridge: A Re-evaluation." *Scottish Liter J* 12:2 (1985), 23–33.

Davies, Rick A. "The Demon Lover Motif in *The Heart of Midlothian*." *Stud in Scottish Lit* 16 (1981), 91–96.

Edwards, Simon. "Producing Voices," 140–144.

Farrell, John P. *Revolution as Tragedy*, 100–114.

Gifford, Douglas. "Scott's Fiction and the Search for Mythic Regeneration," in J. H. Alexander and David Hewitt, eds., *Scott and His Influence*, 180–188.

Hayden, John O. "Jeanie Deans: The Big Lie (and a Few Small Ones)." *Scottish Liter J* 6:1 (1979), 34–42.

Lascelles, Mary. *The Story-Teller*, 84–102.

Millgate, Jane. *Walter Scott*, 151–167.

Raimond, Jean. "Walter Scott: *The Heart of Midlothian*," in Pierre Coustillas et al., eds., *Le roman anglais*, 139–149.

Reed, James. *Sir Walter Scott*, 100–121.

Tulloch, Graham. "Scott and the Creation of Dialogue in Scots," in Alan Bold, ed., *Sir Walter Scott*, 151–157.

Ward, Nicole. "The Prison-House of Language: *The Heart of Midlothian* and *La Chartreuse de Parme*." *Compar Criticism* 2 (1980), 93–107.

Williams, Merryn. *Women in the English Novel*, 59–61.

Wilson, A. N. *The Laird*, 119–130.

Wilt, Judith. *Secret Leaves*, 123–126, 129–142.

Ivanhoe, 1819

Brown, Cedric C. "Sir Walter Scott, Robert Belt, and *Ivanhoe*." *Scottish Liter J* 8:2 (1981), 38–42.

Brown, David. *Walter Scott*, 173–186.

Crawford, Thomas. *Scott*, 60–61.

Matamoro, Blas. "El lugar del héroe." *Cuadernos Hispanoamericanos* 386 (1982), 407–416.

Naman, Anne Aresty. *The Jew*, 18–30.

Panitz, Esther L. *The Alien*, 96–100.

Raleigh, John Henry. "*Ulysses* and Scott's *Ivanhoe*." *Stud in Romanticism* 22 (1983), 569–586.

Salari, Marinella. "Ivanhoe's Middle Ages," in Piero Boitani and Anna Torti, eds., *Medieval . . . Literature*, 149–160.

Scribner, Margo. "*Daniel Deronda* and *Ivanhoe*: The Dark Lady and the Knight." *Graduate Engl Papers* 9:1 (1979), 3–8.

Sroka, Kenneth M. "The Function of Form: *Ivanhoe* as Romance." *Stud in Engl Lit, 1500–1900* 19 (1979), 645–660.

Whitmore, Daniel. "Scott's Indebtedness to German Romantics: *Ivanhoe* Recondsidered." *Wordsworth Circle* 15 (1984), 72–73.

Williams, Merryn. *Women in the English Novel*, 55–58.

Wilson, A. N. *The Laird*, 145–158.

Wilt, Judith. *Secret Leaves*, 18–26, 37–50.

Kenilworth, 1821

Engel, Wilson F., III. "Scott's *Kenilworth*." *Explicator* 39:3 (1981), 11–12.

Wilson, A. N. *The Laird*, 142–144.

The Legend of Montrose, 1819

Anderson, James. *Sir Walter Scott*, 66–69.

Millgate, Jane. *Walter Scott*, 185–190.

The Monastery, 1820

Harkin, Patricia. "The Fop, the Fairy, and the Genres of Scott's *Monastery*." *Stud in Scottish Lit* 19 (1984), 177–191.

McMaster, Graham. *Scott*, 178–181.

Wilson, A. N. *The Laird*, 93–98.

Wilt, Judith. *Secret Leaves*, 89–92, 105–110.

Old Mortality, 1816

Anderson, James. *Sir Walter Scott*, 49–57.

Barrett, Deborah J. "Balfour of Burley: The Evil Energy in Scott's *Old Mortality*." *Stud in Scottish Lit* 17 (1982), 248–253.

Besses, Pierre. "Le Héros solaire et les emblèmes de la raison dans *Old Mortality* de Walter Scott: Métaphore, réalisme épique et idéologie," in *Le Mythe du héros*, 77–95.

Brown, David. *Walter Scott*, 68–91.

Carnie, Robert Hay. "Scottish Presbyterian Eloquence and *Old Mortality*." *Scottish Liter J* 3:2 (1976), 51–61.

Crawford, Thomas. *Scott*, 72–73, 81–82.

Cullinan, Mary. "The Possibilities of History: Scott's *Old Mortality*." *Philol Q* 58 (1979), 321–334.

de Groot, H. B. "Scott and Galt: *Old Mortality* and *Ringan Gilhaize*," in J. H. Alexander and David Hewitt, eds., *Scott and His Influence*, 321–329.

Edwards, Owen Dudley. "Scott as a Contemporary Historian," in Alan Bold, ed., *Sir Walter Scott*, 72–74.

Edwards, Simon. "Producing Voices," 145–148.

Farrell, John P. *Revolution as Tragedy*, 85–100.

Fleischner, Jennifer B. "Class, Character and Landscape in *Old Mortality*." *Scottish Liter J* 9:2 (1982), 21–36.

Garside, Peter D. "*Old Mortality*'s Silent Minority." *Scottish Liter J* 7:1 (1980), 127–143.

Gifford, Douglas. "Scott's Fiction," 183–185.

Gordon, Robert C. "Scott, Racine, and the Future of Honor," in J. H. Alexander and David Hewitt, eds., *Scott and His Influence*, 258–259.

Hewitt, David. "Scott's Art and Politics," in Alan Bold, ed., *Sir Walter Scott*, 58–63.

Humma, John B. "The Narrative Framing Apparatus of Scott's *Old Mortality*." *Stud in the Novel* 12 (1980), 301–314.

Klepetar, Steven F. "Levels of Narration in *Old Mortality*." *Wordsworth Circle* 13 (1982), 38–44.

Lascelles, Mary. *The Story-Teller*, 21–24.

Millgate, Jane. *Walter Scott*, 114–130.

Milligan, Ian. *The Novel in English*, 68–70.

Priestman, Donald G. "Old Battles Fought Anew: The Religious and Political Ramifications of Scott's *Old Mortality*." *Wordsworth Circle* 12 (1981), 117–121.

Sroka, Kenneth M. "Echoes of *Old Mortality* in Dickens and Katherine Anne Porter," in J. H. Alexander and David Hewitt, eds., *Scott and His Influence*, 351–358.

Sroka, Kenneth M. "Scott's Aesthetic Parable: A Study of *Old Mortality*'s Two-Part Structure." *Essays in Lit* (Macomb) 10 (1983), 183–195.

Teyssandier, Hubert. *Les formes de la création*, 291–324.

Thurber, Barton. "Scott and the Sublime," in J. H. Alexander and David Hewitt, eds., *Scott and His Influence*, 87–90.

Wilson, A. N. *The Laird*, 106–119.

Wilt, Judith. *Secret Leaves*, 86–89, 95–105.

Peveril of the Peake, 1822

Burwick, Frederick. "Scott and Dryden's Ironic Reconciliation," in J. H. Alexander and David Hewitt, eds., *Scott and His Influence*, 268–269, 273–276.

McMaster, Graham. *Scott*, 129–147.

The Pirate, 1821

> McMaster, Graham. *Scott*, 182–192.
> Reed, James. *Sir Walter Scott*, 135–147.
> Wilt, Judith. *Secret Leaves*, 119–123, 143–146.

Quentin Durward, 1823

> Hart, Francis Russell. "Scott and the Idea," 173–190.
> Johnson, R. V. "An Assurance of Continuity: Scott's Model of Past and Present in *Quentin Durward.*" *Southern R* (Adelaide) 13 (1980), 79–96.
> Rollyson, Carl E., Jr. "Quentin Durward and Quentin Compson: The Romantic Standardbearers of Scott and Faulkner." *Massachusetts Stud in Engl* 7:3 (1980), 34–38.
> Wilt, Judith. *Secret Leaves*, 49–60, 70–79.

Redgauntlet, 1824

> Anderson, James. *Sir Walter Scott*, 72–75.
> Brown, David. *Walter Scott*, 151–172.
> Coleman, William Emmet. *On the Discrimination*, 90–93.
> Criscuola, Margaret M. "Constancy and Change: The Process of History in Scott's *Redgauntlet.*" *Stud in Scottish Lit* 20 (1985), 123–135.
> Elbers, Joan S. "A Contrast of Fictional Worlds: *Redgauntlet* and *St. Ronan's Well.*" *Scottish Liter J* 7:1 (1980), 155–165.
> Hart, Francis Russell. "Scott and the Idea," 173–190.
> Lascelles, Mary. *The Story-Teller*, 114–119.
> Levine, George. "Sir Walter Scott," 156–158.
> McMaster, Graham. *Scott*, 17–48, 201–204, 224–226.
> Reed, James. *Sir Walter Scott*, 148–164.
> Sosnoski, Patricia H. "Reading *Redgauntlet.*" *Scottish Liter J* 7:1 (1980), 145–154.
> Tulloch, Graham. "Scott and the Creation," 143–151.
> Weinstein, Mark A. "Law, History, and the Nightmare of Romance in *Redgauntlet*," in J. H. Alexander and David Hewitt, eds., *Scott and His Influence*, 140–147.
> Wilson, A. N. *The Laird*, 76–87.
> Wilt, Judith. *Secret Leaves*, 126–129, 146–152.
> Wright, Terence. "The Imperfect Ideal of the Novel." *Mod Lang R* 73 (1978), 5–8.

Rob Roy, 1817

> Anderson, James. *Sir Walter Scott*, 57–61, 85.
> Brown, David. *Walter Scott*, 92–111.
> Gilmour, Robin. "Scott and the Victorian Novel: The Case of *Wuthering Heights*," in J. H. Alexander and David Hewitt, eds., *Scott and His Influence*, 368–371.
> Hewitt, David. "*Rob Roy* and First Person Narratives," in J. H. Alexander and David Hewitt, eds., *Scott and His Influence*, 372–381.

McClure, J. Derrick. "Linguistic Characterization in *Rob Roy*," in J. H. Alexander and David Hewitt, eds., *Scott and His Influence*, 129–139.

Millgate, Jane. "*Rob Roy* and the Limits of Frankness." *Nineteenth-Century Fiction* 34 (1980), 379–396.

Millgate, Jane. *Walter Scott*, 131–150.

Ruddick, William. "Sir Walter Scott's Northumberland," in J. H. Alexander and David Hewitt, eds., *Scott and His Influence*, 26–29.

Tulloch, Graham. "Scott and the Creation," 157–164.

Williams, Ioan. *The Idea of the Novel*, 201–203.

Wilson, A. N. *The Laird*, 48–53.

Wilt, Judith. *Secret Leaves*, 49–70.

St. Ronan's Well, 1824

Elbers, Joan S. "A Contrast of Fictional Worlds," 155–165.

McMaster, Graham. *Scott*, 215–220.

Sroka, Kenneth M. "Wealth and Illth in *St. Ronan's Well*." *Scottish Liter J* 7:1 (1980), 167–183.

The Talisman, 1825

Wilt, Judith. *Secret Leaves*, 162–164, 176–184.

The Two Drovers, 1827

Lascelles, Mary. *The Story-Teller*, 151–153.

Waverley, 1814

Alexander, J. H. " 'Only Connect': The Passionate Style of Walter Scott." *Scottish Liter J* 6:2 (1979), 47–53.

Anderson, James. *Sir Walter Scott*, 39–44.

Brown, David. *Walter Scott*, 6–30.

Carter, Ian. "Burns, Scott, and Scottish Peasantry," 114–116.

Crawford, Thomas. *Scott*, 64–65, 73–74, 82–83.

Daiches, David. "Scott's *Waverley*: The Presence of the Author," in Ian Campbell, ed., *Nineteenth-Century Scottish Fiction*, 7–16.

Edwards, Simon. "Producing Voices," 135–140.

Ferris, Ina. "The Reader in the Rhetoric of Realism: Scott, Thackeray and Eliot," in J. H. Alexander and David Hewitt, eds., *Scott and His Influence*, 384–386.

Gifford, Douglas. "Scott's Fiction," 180–185.

Harkin, Patricia. "Romance and Real History: The Historical Novel as Literary Innovation," in J. H. Alexander and David Hewitt, eds., *Scott and His Influence*, 157–167.

Hartveit, Lars. "Affinity or Influence? Sir Walter Scott and J. G. Farrell as Historical Novelists," in J. H. Alexander and David Hewitt, eds., *Scott and His Influence*, 414–420.

Lascelles, Mary. *The Story-Teller*, 36–41.

Levine, George. "Sir Walter Scott," 147–151.

McMaster, Graham. *Scott*, 9–17.

Meisel, Martin. "*Waverley*, Freud, and Topographical Metaphor." *Univ of Toronto Q* 48 (1979), 226–244.

Millgate, Jane. "Scott and the Dreaming Boy: A Context for *Waverley*." *R of Engl Stud* 32 (1981), 286–293.

Millgate, Jane. *Walter Scott*, 35–57.

Nicolaisen, W. F. H. "Literary Names as Text: Personal Names in Sir Walter Scott's *Waverley*." *Nomina* 3 (1979), 29–39.

Omasreiter, Ria. *Travels*, 185–212.

Raleigh, John Henry. "Scott and Pushkin," in Samuel I. Mintz et al., eds., *From Smollet to James*, 73–77.

Reed, James. *Sir Walter Scott*, 50–68.

Reilly, Pamela. "The Influence of *Waverley* on Maria Edgeworth's *Ormond*," in J. H. Alexander and David Hewitt, eds., *Scott and His Influence*, 290–297.

Rignall, J. M. "The Historical Double: *Waverley, Sylvia's Lovers, The Trumpet-Major*." *Essays in Criticism* 34 (1984), 15–22.

Ross, Alexander M. "*Waverley* and the Picturesque," in J. H. Alexander and David Hewitt, eds., *Scott and His Influence*, 99–108.

Sandy, Stephen. *The Raveling*, 175–183, 197–239.

Sroka, Kenneth M. "Education in Walter Scott's *Waverley*." *Stud in Scottish Lit* 15 (1980), 139–160.

Teyssandier, Hubert. *Les formes de la création*, 261–291.

Wilson, A. N. *The Laird*, 42–48.

Wilt, Judith. *Secret Leaves*, 18–37.

Wright, Terence. "The Imperfect Ideal," 3–5.

Waverley Novels

Anderson, James. *Sir Walter Scott*, 169–189.

Berger, Dieter A. " 'Damn the Mottoe': Scott and the Epigraph." *Anglia* 100 (1982), 373–396.

Cottom, Daniel. "Violence and Law in the Waverley Novels." *Stud in Romanticism* 20 (1981), 65–84.

Cottom, Daniel. "The Waverley Novels: Superstition and the Enchanted Reader." *ELH* 47 (1980), 80–101.

Gamerschlag, Kurt. *Die Korrektur der Waverley Novels*.

Gamerschlag, Kurt. *Sir Walter Scott und die Waverley Novels*.

Mewton, R. J. "Scott and a Romantic Difficulty, as Illustrated by the Function of Power in the Fictional Development of Three of the *Waverley Novels*," in *Le Pouvoir*, 57–69.

Mitchell, Jerome. "Scott's Use of the Tristan-Story in the Waverley Novels." *Tristania* 6:1 (1980), 19–27.

Morgan, Susan. "Old Heroes and a New Heroine in the Waverley Novels." *ELH* 50 (1983), 559–583.

Müllenbrock, Heinz-Joachim. "Die Entstehung des Scottschen historischen Romans als Problem der Literaturgeschichtsschreibung." *Anglia* 99 (1981), 355–378.

Nicolaisen, W. F. H. "Sir Walter Scott: The Folklorist as Novelist," in J. H. Alexander and David Hewitt, eds., *Scott and His Influence*, 171–178.

Nicolaisen, W. F. H. "What Is Your Name? The Question of Identity in Some of the Waverley Novels." *Names* 28 (1980), 255–266.

Waswo, Richard. "Story as Historiography in the Waverley Novels." *ELH* 47 (1980), 304–326.

Woodstock, 1826

Crawford, Thomas. *Scott*, 56–57, 85.

Hobsbaum, Philip. "Scott's 'Apoplectic' Novels," 150–152.

McMaster, Graham. *Scott*, 127–129.

Wilt, Judith. *Secret Leaves*, 170–176.

ELIZABETH SEWELL

The Experience of Life, 1853

Foster, Shirley. *Victorian Women's Fiction*, 130–133.

Katherine Ashton, 1854

Foster, Shirley. *Victorian Women's Fiction*, 123–124, 126–128.

Margaret Percival, 1847

Foster, Shirley. *Victorian Women's Fiction*, 121–123, 125–126.

Ursula, 1858

Foster, Shirley. *Victorian Women's Fiction*, 128–130.

GEORGE BERNARD SHAW

Cashel Byron's Profession, 1886

Amalric, Jean-Claude. *Bernard Shaw*, 80–102.

Immaturity, 1930

Amalric, Jean-Claude. *Bernard Shaw*, 78–102.

Sidhu, C. D. *The Pattern of Tragicomedy*, 102–103.

The Irrational Knot, 1905

Amalric, Jean-Claude. *Bernard Shaw*, 79–102.

Sidhu, C. D. *The Pattern of Tragicomedy*, 103–107.

Love Among the Artists, 1914

Amalric, Jean-Claude. *Bernard Shaw*, 80–102.

Sidhu, C. D. *The Pattern of Tragicomedy*, 105–107.

An Unsocial Socialist, 1887

Amalric, Jean-Claude. *Bernard Shaw*, 81–102.

Sidhu, C. D. *The Pattern of Tragicomedy*, 107–109.

MARY SHELLEY

Falkner, 1837

El-Shater, Safaa. *The Novels*, 156–164.
Neumann, Bonnie Rayford. *The Lonely Muse*, 236–246.
Poovey, Mary. "Fathers and Daughters: The Trauma of Growing Up Female." *Women & Lit* 2 (1981), 47–57.
Powers, Katherine Richardson. *The Influence*, 64.

Frankenstein, 1818

Aldiss, Brian W. "Mary Wollstonecraft Shelley," in E. F. Bleiler, ed., *Science Fiction Writers*, 5–8.
Aldridge, Alexandra. "Science Fiction and Emerging Values," in Robert E. Myers, ed., *The Intersection*, 17–18.
Bayer-Berenbaum, Linda. *The Gothic Imagination*, 131–142.
Bowerbank, Sylvia. "The Social Order *vs* the Wretch: Mary Shelley's Contradictory-Mindedness in *Frankenstein*." *ELH* 46 (1979), 418–429.
Brunkhorst, Martin. " 'The castled crag of Drachenfels': Funktionswechsel eines Landschaftsbildes." *Arcadia* 17 (1982), 137–140.
Cantor, Paul A. *Creature and Creator*, 103–132.
Cleridge, Laura P. "Parent-Child Tensions in *Frankenstein*: The Search for Communion." *Stud in the Novel* 17 (1985), 14–24.
Coleman, William Emmet. *On the Discrimination*, 256–259.
Cosslett, Tess. *The 'Scientific Movement'*, 5–8.
Cottom, Daniel. "*Frankenstein* and the Monster of Representation." *SubStance* 28 (1981), 60–70.
Day, William Patrick. *In the Circles*, 139–143.
El-Shater, Safaa. *The Novels*, 4–33.
Figes, Eva. *Sex and Subterfuge*, 152–154.
Foust, R. E. "Monstrous Image: Theory of Fantasy Antagonists." *Genre* 13 (1980), 441–453.
Friedman, Lester D. "The Blasted Tree," in Michael Klein and Gillian Parker, eds., *The English Novel*, 52–66.
Gilbert, Sandra M., and Susan Gubar. *The Madwoman*, 221–247.
Harvey, A. D. "*Frankenstein* and *Caleb Williams*." *Keats-Shelley J* 29 (1980), 21–27.
Hennessy, Brenda. *The Gothic Novel*, 18–22.
Hodges, Devon. "*Frankenstein* and the Feminine Subversion of the Novel." *Tulsa Stud in Women's Lit* 2 (1983), 155–163.
Jackson, Rosemary. *Fantasy*, 99–104.
Jackson, Rosemary. "Narcissism and Beyond: A Psychoanalytic Reading of *Frankenstein* and Fantasies of the Double," in William Coyle, ed., *Aspects of Fantasy*, 44–51.

Jacobus, Mary. "Is There a Woman in This Text?" *New Liter Hist* 14 (1982), 117–154.

Johnson, Barbara. "My Monster/My Self." *Diacritics* 12:2 (1982), 2–10.

Kawin, Bruce F. *The Mind of the Novel*, 194–201.

Kestner, Joseph. "Narcissism as Symptom and Structure: The Case of Mary Shelley's *Frankenstein*," in William Weathers, ed., *The Nature of Identity*, 15–25.

Ketterer, David. *Frankenstein's Creation*, 9–106.

Ketterer, David. "Metaphoric Matrix: Magnetism in *Frankenstein*," in Thomas J. Remington, ed., *Selected Proceedings*, 55–67.

Lamarca Margalef, Jordi. *Ciencia y literatura*, 26–30.

Laszlo, Pierre. "Extase sublime et déclin de la nature: Note sur le *Frankenstein* de Mary Shelley." *Revue des Sciences Humaines* 4:188 (1982), 89–92.

Le Tellier, Robert Ignatius. *An Intensifying Vision*, 30–34, 45–46, 59–60, 81, 110–114, 133–136, 146–147, 161–166, 187–189, 199–200.

MacAndrew, Elizabeth. *The Gothic Tradition*, 74–79, 100–106, 144–146, 173–175.

McInerney, Peter. "*Frankenstein* and the Godlike Science of Letters." *Genre* 13 (1980), 455–473.

McInerney, Peter. "Satanic Conceits in *Frankenstein* and *Wuthering Heights*." *Milton and the Romantics* 4 (1980), 1–15.

Markus, Manfred. "Erscheinungsformen des Feminismus in Mary Shelleys *Frankenstein*." *Literatur in Wissenschaft und Unterricht* 16 (1983), 1–17.

Moretti, Franco. "Dialettica della paura." *Calibano* 2 (1978), 77–103.

Murray, E. B. "Shelley's Contribution to Mary's *Frankenstein*." *Keats-Shelley Memorial Bull* 29 (1978), 50–68.

Neumann, Bonnie Rayford. *The Lonely Muse*, 44–67.

Oates, Joyce Carol. "Frankenstein's Fallen Angel." *Crit Inquiry* 10 (1984), 543–553.

Ocasio, Blanca. "Mary Shelley's *Frankenstein*: SF Paradigm," in Madeleine F. Marshall, ed., *Science Fiction Miscellany*, 19–27.

O'Flinn, Paul. "Production and Reproduction: The Case of *Frankenstein*." *Lit and Hist* 9 (1983), 194–210.

Parrinder, Patrick. *Science Fiction . . . Teaching*, 5–6.

Paulson, Ronald. "Gothic Fiction and the French Revolution." *ELH* 48 (1981), 545–552.

Platzner, Robert Leonard. *The Metaphysical Novel*, 155–174.

Poovey, Mary. "My Hideous Progeny: Mary Shelley and the Feminization of Romanticism." *PMLA* 95 (1980), 332–346.

Powers, Katherine Richardson. *The Influence*, 50–54, 72–74, 124–129.

Preston, John. "The Silence of the Novel." *Mod Lang R* 74 (1979), 263–264.

Prickett, Stephen. *Victorian Fantasy*, 75–79.

Punter, David. *The Literature of Terror*, 121–128.

Randel, Fred V. "*Frankenstein*, Feminism, and the Intertextuality of Mountains." *Stud in Romanticism* 23 (1984), 515–532.

Reddin, Chitra Pershad. *Forms of Evil*, 78–79, 129–130, 163–165, 174–175, 222–223, 243, 274–276.

Reed, John R. "Will and Fate in *Frankenstein*." *Bull of Res in the Hum* 83 (1980), 319–338.

Roberts, Bette B. *The Gothic Romance*, 230–234.

Schopf, Sue Weaver. " 'Of what strange nature is knowledge!': Hartleian Psychology and the Creature's Arrested Moral Sense in Mary Shelley's *Frankenstein*." *Romanticism Past and Present* 5:1 (1981), 33–52.

Schug, Charles. *The Romantic Genesis*, 59–73.

Seed, David. "*Frankenstein*—Parable of Spectacle?" *Criticism* 24 (1982), 327–340.

Sherwin, Paul. "*Frankenstein*: Creation as Catastrophe." *PMLA* 96 (1981), 883–902.

Sherwin, Paul. "A Psychoaesthetic Reading of Mary Shelley's *Frankenstein*." *CUNY Engl Forum* 1 (1985), 199–210.

Soldati, Joseph Arthur. *Configurations of Faust*, 39–69.

Spector, Judith A. "Science Fiction and the Sex War: A Womb of One's Own." *Lit and Psych* 31:1 (1981), 21–22.

Teyssandier, Hubert. *Les formes de la création*, 333–357.

Thurber, Bart. "Toward a Technological Sublime," in Robert E. Myers, ed., *The Intersection*, 215–217.

Twitchell, James B. "*Frankenstein* and the Anatomy of Horror." *Georgia R* 37 (1983), 41–78.

Van Luchene, Stephen Robert. *Essays in Gothic Fiction*, 149–221.

Vasbinder, Samuel Holmes. *Scientific Attitudes*, 5–84.

Veeder, William. "The Negative Oedipus: Father, *Frankenstein*, and the Shelleys." *Crit Inquiry* 12 (1986), 365–386.

Vlasopolos, Anca. "*Frankenstein*'s Hidden Skeleton: The Psycho-Politics of Oppression." *Science-Fiction Stud* 10 (1983), 125–134.

Warrick, Patricia. *The Cybernetic Imagination*, 35–39.

Weiss, Fredric. *The Antic Spectre*, 219–220.

Wexelblatt, Robert. "The Ambivalence of *Frankenstein*." *Arizona Q* 36 (1980), 101–117.

Wilt, Judith. *Ghosts of the Gothic*, 62–73.

Ziolkowski, Theodore. "Science, Frankenstein, and Myth." *Sewanee R* 89 (1981), 38–53.

The Last Man, 1826

Aldiss, Brian W. "Mary Wollstonecraft Shelley," 8.

El-Shater, Safaa. *The Novels*, 67–110.

Franci, Giovanna. "Lo specchio del futuro: Visione e apocalisse in *The Last Man* di Mary Shelley." *Quaderni di Filologia Germanica* (Bologna) 1 (1980), 75–84.

Neumann, Bonnie Rayford. *The Lonely Muse*, 173–194.

Powers, Katherine Richardson. *The Influence*, 58–60, 79–82, 97–101.
Reddin, Chitra Pershad. *Forms of Evil*, 80–81, 175–176, 209–210, 225–227, 244, 277–278.

Lodore, 1835

El-Shater, Safaa. *The Novels*, 127–155.
Neumann, Bonnie Rayford. *The Lonely Muse*, 227–235.
Powers, Katherine Richardson. *The Influence*, 62–64, 74–76.

Mathilda, 1959

Neumann, Bonnie Rayford. *The Lonely Muse*, 108–119.
Reddin, Chitra Pershad. *Forms of Evil*, 154–155, 223–224, 276–277.

Perkin Warbeck, 1830

El-Shater, Safaa. *The Novels*, 111–126.
Neumann, Bonnie Rayford. *The Lonely Muse*, 215–227.
Powers, Katherine Richardson. *The Influence*, 60–62, 71–72.

Valperga, 1823

El-Shater, Safaa. *The Novels*, 34–66.
Neumann, Bonnie Rayford. *The Lonely Muse*, 121–139.
Powers, Katherine Richardson. *The Influence*, 54–58.
Reddin, Chitra Pershad. *Forms of Evil*, 79–80.

PERCY BYSSHE SHELLEY

St. Irvyne, 1811

Hogle, Jerrold E. "Shelley's Fiction: The 'Stream of Fate'." *Keats-Shelley J* 30 (1981), 86–88.
Seed, David. "Shelley's 'Gothick' in *St. Irvyne* and After," in Miriam Allott, ed., *Essays on Shelley*, 39–70.
Tracy, Ann Blaisdell. *Patterns of Fear*, 50–52.

Zastrozzi, 1810

Hogle, Jerrold E. "Shelley's Fiction," 83–86.
Zimansky, Curt R. "*Zastrozzi* and *The Bravo of Venice*: Another Shelley Borrowing." *Keats-Shelley J* 30 (1981), 15–17.

FRANCES SHERIDAN

The History of Nourjahad, 1767

Doody, Margaret Anne. "Frances Sheridan: Morality and Annihilated Time," in Mary Anne Schofield and Cecilia Macheski, eds., *Fetter'd or Free?*, 351–356.

The Memoirs of Miss Sidney Bidulph, 1761–67

Barker, Gerard A. *Grandison's Heirs*, 53–68.
Doody, Margaret Anne. "Frances Sheridan," 326–351.

M. P. SHIEL

The Lord of the Sea, 1901

> Bleiler, E. F. "M. P. Shiel," in Bleiler, ed., *Science Fiction Writers*, 33–34.

The Purple Cloud, 1901

> Bleiler, E. F. "M. P. Shiel," 32–33.
> Stableford, Brian. *Scientific Romance*, 78–80.

J. H. SHORTHOUSE

John Ingelsant, 1880

> Hutchinson, Joanne. "John Inglesant, Victorian Cavalier: History as Faith in the 1880s." *Univ of Hartford Stud in Lit* 13:1 (1981), 1–16.
> Ramel, Annie. "*John Inglesant* et *Marius l'Epicurien*." *Confluents* 4:1 (1978), 163–185.

MRS. ALFRED SIDGWICK

The Devil's Cradle, 1918

> Zatlin, Linda Gertner. *The Nineteenth-Century Anglo-Jewish Novel*, 42–43, 45–46.

PHILIP SIDNEY

Arcadia, 1598

> Astell, Ann W. "Sidney's Didactic Method in the *Old Arcadia*." *Stud in Engl Lit, 1500–1900* 24 (1984), 39–51.
> Bergbusch, Martin. "The 'Subalterne Magistrate' in Sir Philip Sidney's *Arcadia*: A Study of the Character of Philanax." *Engl Stud in Canada* 7 (1981), 27–36.
> Chaudhuri, Sukanta. "The Eclogues in Sidney's *New Arcadia*." *R of Engl Stud* 35 (1984), 185–202.
> Couton, Marie. "Variations arcadiennes dans le roman pastoral élisabéthain," in *Le genre pastoral*, 151–159.
> Craft, William. "Remaking the Heroic Self in the *New Arcadia*." *Stud in Engl Lit, 1500–1900* 25 (1985), 45–67.
> Craft, William. "The Shaping Picture of Love in Sidney's *New Arcadia*." *Stud in Philology* 81 (1984), 395–418.
> Desvignes, Lucette. "De l'*Arcadie* de Sidney à *La Cour bergère*, ou du roman pastoral à la tragi-comédie," in *Le genre pastoral*, 311–318.
> Dorangeon, Simone. "Tensions et ambiguïtés dans l'*Arcadie* de Sidney en rapport avec l'idée de nature," in *Rhétorique et communication*, 11–24.

Green, Paul D. "Doors to the House of Death: The Treatment of Suicide in Sidney's *Arcadia.*" *Sixteenth Century J* 10:3 (1979), 17–27.

Greenfield, Thelma N. *The Eye of Judgment.*

Hannay, Margaret P. " 'Faining Notable Images of Vertue': Sidney's *New Arcadia* as *Legenda Sanctorum.*" *Univ of Hartford Stud in Lit* 15:3–16:1 (1983/84), 80–88.

Jehenson, Myriam Yvonne. *The Golden World of the Pastoral.*

Kinney, Arthur F. "Humanist Poetics and Elizabethan Fiction." *Renaissance Papers* 1978, 31–45.

Lindenbaum, Peter. "The Geography of Sidney's *Arcadia.*" *Philol Q* 63 (1984), 524–530.

Lindheim, Nancy. *The Structures*, 13–167.

Loring, Katherine M. "Sidney's *Arcadia.*" *Explicator* 39:1 (1980), 27–28.

McCanles, Michael. "Oracular Prediction and the Fore-Conceit of Sidney's *Arcadia.*" *ELH* 50 (1983), 233–243.

McCanles, Michael. "Reading Description in Sidney's New *Arcadia*: A Differential Analysis." *Univ of Toronto Q* 53 (1983), 36–50.

McCanles, Michael. "The Rhetoric of Character Portrayal in Sidney's *New Arcadia.*" *Criticism* 25 (1983), 123–138.

McCoy, Richard C. *Sir Philip Sidney*, 36–68, 110–217.

Magister, Karl-Heinz. "Philip Sidneys *Arcadia*: Ein höfisch-humanistischer Renaissance-Roman." *Shakespeare-Jahrbuch* 117 (1981), 109–126.

Moore, Dennis. "Philisides and Mira: Autobiographical Allegory in the *Old Arcadia.*" *Spenser Stud* 3 (1982), 125–137.

Oliveira e Silva, J. de. "Recurrent Onomastic Textures in the *Diana* of Jorge de Montemayor and the *Arcadia* of Sir Philip Sidney." *Stud in Philology* 79 (1982), 30–31, 35–40.

Patterson, Annabel M. " 'Under . . . Pretty Tales': Intention in Sidney's *Arcadia.*" *Stud in the Liter Imagination* 15:1 (1982), 5–21.

Raitière, Martin N. "Amphialus' Rebellion: Sidney's Use of History in *New Arcadia.*" *J of Medieval and Renaissance Stud* 12 (1982), 113–131.

Rees, Joan. *Exploring "Arcadia,"* 1–14.

Roberts, Josephine A. "Herculean Love in Sir Philip Sidney's Two Versions of *Arcadia.*" *Explorations in Renaissance Culture* 4 (1978), 43–54.

Scanlon, Patrick M. "Emblematic Narrative and the Argument of Love in Sidney's *New Arcadia.*" *J of Narrative Technique* 15 (1985), 219–232.

Sinfield, Alan. "Power and Ideology: An Outline Theory and Sidney's *Arcadia.*" *ELH* 52 (1985), 259–275.

Skretkowicz, Victor. "Symbolic Architecture in Sidney's *New Arcadia.*" *R of Engl Stud* 33 (1982), 175–180.

Stillman, Robert E. "The Perils of Fancy: Poetry and Self-Love in *The Old Arcadia.*" *Texas Stud in Lit and Lang* 26 (1984), 1–14.

Stillman, Robert E. "The Politics of Sidney's Pastoral: Mystification and Mythology in *The Old Arcadia*." *ELH* 52 (1985), 795–811.

Stump, Donald V. "Sidney's Concept of Tragedy in the *Apology* and in the *Arcadia*." *Stud in Philology* 79 (1982), 41–61.

Thrasher-Smith, Shelley. *The Luminous Globe*, 1–224.

Turner, Myron. " 'Disguised Passion' and the Psychology of Suicide in Sidney's Old *Arcadia*." *Papers on Lang & Lit* 15 (1979), 17–37.

Weiner, Andrew D. *Sir Philip Sidney*, 51–185.

Williams, Kent F. "Theme and Structure in the Third Eclogues of Sidney's *Old Arcadia*." *Selected Papers from the West Virginia Shakespeare and Renaissance Assoc* 4 (1979), 1–9.

ALAN SILLITOE

Key to the Door, 1961

Paul, Ronald. *"Fire in Our Hearts,"* 134–151.

Roskies, D. M. "Alan Sillitoe's Anti-Pastoral." *J of Narrative Technique* 10 (1980), 170–183.

Saturday Night and Sunday Morning, 1958

Eagleton, Mary, and David Pierce. *Attitudes to Class*, 134–136.

Schlüter, Kurt. "The Time and Life of Arthur Seaton in Alan Sillitoe's *Saturday Night and Sunday Morning*." *Anglia* 101 (1983), 99–116.

Wilson, Keith. "Arthur Seaton Twenty Years On: A Reappraisal of Sillitoe's *Saturday Night and Sunday Morning*." *Engl Stud in Canada* 7 (1981), 414–425.

MAY SINCLAIR

Arnold Waterlow, 1924

Gillespie, Diane F. " 'The Muddle of the Middle': May Sinclair on Women." *Tulsa Stud in Women's Lit* 4 (1985), 248–249.

Audrey Craven, 1897

Gillespie, Diane F. " 'The Muddle of the Middle'," 245–246.

The Creators, 1910

Gillespie, Diane F. " 'The Muddle of the Middle'," 246–248.

Mary Olivier, 1919

Beauman, Nicola. *A Very Great Profession*, 160–162.

Gillespie, Diane F. " 'The Muddle of the Middle'," 244–245.

Stewart, Grace. *A New Mythos*, 50–56, 123–129.

Superseded, 1906

Gillespie, Diane F. " 'The Muddle of the Middle'," 241–243.

ANNE SKINN

The Old Maid, 1771

Staves, Susan. "Matrimonial Discord in Fiction and in Court: The Case of Ann Masterman," in Mary Anne Schofield and Cecilia Macheski, eds., *Fetter'd or Free?*, 169–184.

CHARLOTTE SMITH

The Banished Man, 1794

Fry, Carroll Lee. *Charlotte Smith*, 136–137, 160–165.

Celestina, 1791

Fry, Carroll Lee. *Charlotte Smith*, 39–59, 89–90, 95–97, 119–120, 147–149.

Desmond, 1792

Bowstead, Diana. "Charlotte Smith's *Desmond*: The Epistolary Novel as Ideological Argument," in Mary Anne Schofield and Cecilia Macheski, eds., *Fetter'd or Free?*, 237–261.
Fry, Carroll Lee. *Charlotte Smith*, 59–64, 120–122, 149–158.
Reddin, Chitra Pershad. *Forms of Evil*, 54–56, 117, 215–216.

Emmeline, 1788

Figes, Eva. *Sex and Subterfuge*, 62–68.
Fry, Carroll Lee. *Charlotte Smith*, 38–59, 86–87, 94–95, 115–118.
Macheski, Cecilia. "Penelope's Daughters: Images of Needlework in Eighteenth-Century Literature," in Mary Anne Schofield and Cecilia Macheski, eds., *Fetter'd or Free?*, 94–95.
Suhr, Heidrun. *Englische Romanautorinnen*, 212–216.

Ethelinde, 1789

Fry, Carroll Lee. *Charlotte Smith*, 39–59, 88–89, 95–97, 118–119.
Sandy, Stephen. *The Raveling*, 67–76.

Marchmont, 1796

Fry, Carroll Lee. *Charlotte Smith*, 174–176, 192–194.

Montalbert, 1795

Fry, Carroll Lee. *Charlotte Smith*, 129–132.

The Old Manor House, 1793

Fry, Carroll Lee. *Charlotte Smith*, 122–124, 168–169, 172–174.
Reddin, Chitra Pershad. *Forms of Evil*, 56–58, 117, 216–217.
Roberts, Bette B. *The Gothic Romance*, 116–146.
Rogers, Katharine M. "Dreams and Nightmares: Male Characters in the Feminine Novel of the Eighteenth Century." *Women & Lit* 2 (1981), 11–12.

The Wanderings of Warwick, 1794

    Fry, Carroll Lee. *Charlotte Smith*, 169–170.

The Young Philosopher, 1798

    Fry, Carroll Lee. *Charlotte Smith*, 180–192, 194–196.

TOBIAS SMOLLETT

Ferdinand Count Fathom, 1753

    Beasley, Jerry C. "Smollett's Novels: *Ferdinand Count Fathom* for the Defense." *Papers on Lang & Lit* 20 (1984), 165–184.

    Boucé, Paul-Gabriel. "The Thematic Structure of *Ferdinand Count Fathom*," in Alan Bold, ed., *Smollett*, 170–191.

    Coleman, William Emmet. *On the Discrimination*, 69–75, 95–98.

    Daiches, David. "Smollett Reconsidered," in Alan Bold, ed., *Smollett*, 40–45. [Also in Samuel I. Mintz et al., eds., *From Smollett to James*, 40–46.]

    Day, Robert Adams. "Sex, Scatology, Smollett," in Paul-Gabriel Boucé, ed., *Sexuality*, 230–241.

    Grant, Damian. *Tobias Smollett*, 24–31, 49–52, 195–199.

    Hambridge, Roger A. " 'Empiricomany, or an Infatuation in Favour of *Empiricism* or Quackery': The Socio-economics of Eighteenth-Century Quackery," in Serge Soupel and R. A. Hambridge, eds., *Literature and Science*, 55–62.

    Punter, David. *The Literature of Terror*, 45–49.

    Sena, John F. "Fathoming Fathom: Smollett's Count as Malevolent Artist." *Forum for Mod Lang Stud* 16 (1980), 1–9.

    Simpson, K. G. "Tobias Smollett: The Scot as English Novelist," in Alan Bold, ed., *Smollett*, 82–84, 92–102.

The History and Adventures of an Atom, 1769

    Day, Robert Adams. "The Authorship of the *Atom*." *Philol Q* 59 (1980), 187–191.

    Day, Robert Adams. "Sex, Scatology, Smollett," 229–241.

    Douglass, Wayne J. "Done After the Dutch Taste: Political Prints and Smollett's *Atom*." *Essays in Lit* (Macomb) 9 (1982), 170–178.

    Douglass, Wayne J. "Smollett's Authorship of the *Atom*." *Engl Lang Notes* 17 (1980), 183–184.

    Grant, Damian. *Tobias Smollett*, 56–59, 80–82, 175–177.

    Link, Viktor. *Die Tradition*, 128–132.

Humphry Clinker, 1771

    Altman, Janet Gurkin. *Epistolarity*, 172–176.

    Anderson, Earl R. "Footnotes More Pedestrian Than Sublime: A Historical Background for the Foot-Races in *Evelina* and *Humphry Clinker*." *Eighteenth-Century Stud* 14 (1980), 56–68.

    Blake, N. F. *Non-Standard Language*, 120–123.

Daiches, David. "Smollett Reconsidered," 18–21 [20–22].

Day, Robert Adams. "Sex, Scatology, Smollett," 229–241.

Giddings, Robert. "Matthew Bramble's Bath: Smollett and the West Indian Connection," in Alan Bold, ed., *Smollett*, 60–63.

Graham-Campbell, David. "The Original of Mr. Paunceford in *Humphry Clinker*." *Scottish Liter J* 4:1 (1977), 17–35.

Grant, Damian. *Tobias Smollett*, 59–61, 87–90, 95–98, 108–114, 146–148, 163–170, 182–185, 201–203.

Jack, R. D. S. "Appearance and Reality in *Humphry Clinker*," in Alan Bold, ed., *Smollett*, 209–226.

Konigsberg, Ira. *Narrative Technique*, 184–212.

Miles, Peter. "Platonic Topography and the Locations of *Humphry Clinker*." *Trivium* 16 (1981), 81–98.

Nemoianu, Virgil. "The Semantics of Bramble's Hypochondria: A Connection between Illness and Style in the Eighteenth Century." *CLIO* 9 (1979), 39–51.

Omasreiter, Ria. *Travels*, 148–165.

Panitz, Esther L. *The Alien*, 92–94.

Preston, Thomas R. "Smollett Among the Indians." *Philol Q* 61 (1982), 231–239.

Punter, David. "Fictional Representation of the Law in the Eighteenth Century." *Eighteenth-Century Stud* 16 (1982–83), 63–64.

Rothstein, Eric. "Scotophilia and *Humphry Clinker*: The Politics of Beggary, Bugs, and Buttocks." *Univ of Toronto Q* 52 (1982), 63–76.

Scott, Tom. "The Note of Protest in Smollett's Novels," in Alan Bold, ed., *Smollett*, 118–124.

Sena, John F. "Ancient Designs and Modern Folly: Architecture in *The Expedition of Humphry Clinker*." *Harvard Lib Bull* 27 (1979), 86–113.

Sheriff, John K. *The Good-Natured Man*, 46–48.

Shroff, Homai J. *The Eighteenth Century Novel*, 166–170, 179–181, 184–191.

Peregrine Pickle, 1751

Collins, R. G. "The Hidden Bastard: A Question of Illegitimacy in Smollett's *Peregrine Pickle*." *PMLA* 94 (1979), 91–105.

Daiches, David. "Smollett Reconsidered," 32–37.

Day, Robert Adams. "Sex, Scatology, Smollett," 230–241.

Grant, Damian. *Tobias Smollett*, 47–49, 140–144.

Price, John Valdimir. "Patterns of Sexual Behaviour in Some Eighteenth-Century Novels," in Paul-Gabriel Boucé, ed., *Sexuality*, 165–166, 169–171.

Punter, David. "Fictional Representation of the Law," 62–63.

Ross, Ian Campbell. " 'With Dignity and Importance': Peregrine Pickle as Country Gentleman," in Alan Bold, ed., *Smollett*, 148–167.

Shroff, Homai J. *The Eighteenth Century Novel*, 161–169, 171–179.

Speck, W. A. *Society and Literature*, 177–185.

Roderick Random, 1748

Beasley, Jerry C. "*Roderick Random*: The Picaresque Transformed."
Coll Lit 6 (1979), 211–220.

Blake, N. F. *Non-Standard Language*, 113–120.

Boucé, Paul-Gabriel. " 'Snakes in Iceland': The 'Picaresque' in Smollett's *Roderick Random*." *Caliban* 20 (1983), 29–39.

Bunn, James H. "Signs of Randomness in *Roderick Random*." *Eighteenth-Century Stud* 14 (1981), 452–469.

Bystrom, Valerie Ann. "The Abyss of Sympathy: The Conventions of
Pathos in Eighteenth and Nineteenth Century British Novels." *Criticism* 23 (1981), 219–220.

Daiches, David. "Smollett Reconsidered," 23–24, 26–28.

Day, Robert Adams. "Sex, Scatology, Smollett," 230–241.

Grant, Damian. "*Roderick Random*: Language as Projectile," in Alan
Bold, ed., *Smollett*, 129–146.

Grant, Damian. *Tobias Smollett*, 18–20, 43–47, 116–119, 122–124, 127–
130, 136–138.

Haywood, Ian. "Dreams in Pregnancy: The Opening of Defoe's *Memoirs of a Cavalier* and Smollett's *Roderick Random*." *Am Notes and
Queries* 20 (1982), 71–73.

Jeffrey, David K. "*Roderick Random*: The Form and Structure of a
Romance." *Revue Belge de Philologie et d'Histoire* 58 (1980), 604–
614.

Lévy, Maurice. "Roderick Random, héros mythique?," in *Le Mythe du
héros*, 57–66.

Morvan, Alain. " 'Fraud, Perjury and Oppression': La Justice et les
hommes de loi dans *Roderick Random*." *Bull de la Société d'Etudes
Anglo-Américaines des XVIIe et XVIIIe Siècles* 13 (1981), 121–139.

Morvan, Alain. "*Roderick Random* et la rhétorique du suicide," in
Rhétorique, 143–156.

Moss, Harold Gene. "The Surgeon's Mate: Tobias Smollett and *The
Adventures of Roderick Random*," in Enid Rhodes Peschel, ed.,
Medicine and Literature, 35–38.

Scott, Tom. "The Note of Protest," 111–114.

Shroff, Homai J. *The Eighteenth Century Novel*, 161–172.

Simpson, K. G. "*Roderick Random* and the Tory Dilemma." *Scottish
Liter J* 2:2 (1975), 5–17.

Speck, W. A. *Society and Literature*, 172–177.

Weinsheimer, Joel. "Impedance as Value: *Roderick Random* and *Pride
and Prejudice*." *PTL* 3 (1978), 139–166.

Sir Lancelot Greaves, 1762

Bourgeois, Susan. "The Domestication of the Launcelot Legend in
Smollett's *Sir Launcelot Greaves*." *Publs of the Missouri Philol
Assoc* 8 (1983), 45–50.

Briden, Earl F. "Topical Satire in Smollett's *Sir Launcelot Greaves*."
Notes and Queries 27 (1980), 404–405.

Daiches, David. "Smollett Reconsidered," 14–18.
Grant, Damian. *Tobias Smollett*, 52–54, 93–95, 133–135.
Price, John Valdimir. "Smollett and the Reader in *Sir Launcelot Greaves*," in Alan Bold, ed., *Smollett*, 193–207.
Shroff, Homai J. *The Eighteenth Century Novel*, 181–184.

C. P. SNOW

The Conscience of the Rich, 1958

Levin, Gerald. "The Sadic Heroes of C. P. Snow." *Twentieth Century Lit* 26 (1980), 34–36.

The Malcontents, 1972

Graves, Nora Calhoun. "A Different Set of Malcontents in Snow's *The Malcontents*." *Notes on Contemp Lit* 10:1 (1980), 6–7.

New Lives for Old, 1933

Lamarca Margalef, Jordi. *Ciencia y literatura*, 52–53.

The New Men, 1954

Levin, Gerald. "The Sadic Heroes," 28–34.

SOMERVILLE AND ROSS

The Big House of Inver, 1925

Huppertsberg, Carla. *Das Irland-Bild*, 138–147, 184–213.
Martin, David. "The 'Castle Rackrent' of Somerville and Ross: A Tragic 'Colonial' Tale." *Etudes Irlandaises* 7 (1982), 47–53.
Robinson, Hilary. *Somerville & Ross*, 177–194.
Warner, Alan. *A Guide*, 54–55.

Dan Russel the Fox, 1911

Huppertsberg, Carla. *Das Irland-Bild*, 85–90.
Robinson, Hilary. *Somerville & Ross*, 139–146.

An Enthusiast, 1921

Martin, David. "The 'Castle Rackrent' of Somerville and Ross," 46–47.
Robinson, Hilary. *Somerville & Ross*, 165–176.

French Leave, 1928

Robinson, Hilary. *Somerville & Ross*, 194–200.

An Irish Cousin, 1889

Huppertsberg, Carla. *Das Irland-Bild*, 95–97.
Robinson, Hilary. *Somerville & Ross*, 57–69.

Mount Music, 1919

Huppertsberg, Carla. *Das Irland-Bild*, 82–84.
Martin, David. "The 'Castle Rackrent' of Somerville and Ross," 44–46.
Robinson, Hilary. *Somerville & Ross*, 147–165.

Naboth's Vineyard, 1891

    Robinson, Hilary. *Somerville & Ross*, 69–72.

The Real Charlotte, 1894

    Cronin, John. *The Anglo-Irish Novel*, 139–152.
    Huppertsberg, Carla. *Das Irland-Bild*, 91–92.
    Robinson, Hilary. *Somerville & Ross*, 85–117.
    Tuohy, Frank. "Five Fierce Ladies," in Masaru Sekine, ed., *Irish Writers*, 202–203.
    Warner, Alan. *A Guide*, 52–54.

Sarah's Youth, 1938

    Robinson, Hilary. *Somerville & Ross*, 201–204.

The Silver Fox, 1898

    Huppertsberg, Carla. *Das Irland-Bild*, 84–86.
    Robinson, Hilary. *Somerville & Ross*, 118–125.

JOHN SOMMERFIELD

May Day, 1936

    Klaus, H. Gustav. *The Literature*, 116–120.
    Laing, Stuart. "Presenting 'Things as They Are': John Sommerfield's *May Day* and Mass Observation," in Frank Gloversmith, ed., *Class*, 142–160.

ARTHUR E. SOUTHON

Napoleon, 1928

    Milbury-Steen, Sarah L. *European and African Stereotypes*, 40–46.

MURIEL SPARK

The Abbess of Crewe, 1974

    Codaccioni, Marie-José. "La Recherche du pouvoir chez Muriel Spark ou l'art de manipuler autrui," in *Le Pouvoir*, 111–122.
    Greene, George. "*Du Côté de Chez Disaster*: The Novels of Muriel Spark." *Papers on Lang & Lit* 16 (1980), 307–310.
    Haslag, Josef. "Muriel Spark, *The Abbess of Crewe*," in Rainer Lengeler, ed., *Englische Literatur*, 215–226.
    Little, Judy. *Comedy and the Woman Writer*, 165–168.
    McBrien, William. "Muriel Spark: The Novelist as Dandy," in Thomas F. Staley, ed., *Twentieth-Century Women Novelists*, 172–173.
    Massie, Allan. *Muriel Spark*, 81–85.
    Richmond, Velma Bourgeois. *Muriel Spark*, 133–139.
    Whittaker, Ruth. *The Faith and Fiction*, 103–106.

The Bachelors, 1960

Little, Judy. *Comedy and the Woman Writer*, 123–127.
McBrien, William. "Muriel Spark," 164.
Massie, Allan. *Muriel Spark*, 31–43.
Richmond, Velma Bourgeois. *Muriel Spark*, 79–85.
Whittaker, Ruth. *The Faith and Fiction*, 45–46, 60–62, 100–101.

The Ballad of Peckham Rye, 1960

Bold, Alan. *Modern Scottish Literature*, 221–223.
Little, Judy. *Comedy and the Woman Writer*, 119–123.
McBrien, William. "Muriel Spark," 163–164.
Massie, Allan. *Muriel Spark*, 30–31.
Richmond, Velma Bourgeois. *Muriel Spark*, 73–79.
Whittaker, Ruth. *The Faith and Fiction*, 147–148.

The Comforters, 1957

Little, Judy. *Comedy and the Woman Writer*, 107–110.
McBrien, William. "Muriel Spark," 155–159.
Massie, Allan. *Muriel Spark*, 21–24.
Pullin, Faith. "Autonomy and Fabulation in the Fiction of Muriel Spark," in Alan Bold, ed., *Muriel Spark*, 77–79.
Richmond, Velma Bourgeois. *Muriel Spark*, 29–37.
Shaw, Valerie. "Fun and Games with Life-stories," in Alan Bold, ed., *Muriel Spark*, 49–50.
Whittaker, Ruth. " 'Angels Dining at the Ritz': The Faith and Fiction of Muriel Spark," in Malcolm Bradbury and David Palmer, eds., *The Contemporary English Novel*, 171–174.
Whittaker, Ruth. *The Faith and Fiction*, 49–50, 91–93, 142–143.

The Driver's Seat, 1970

Bold, Alan. *Modern Scottish Literature*, 224–226.
Greene, George. "*Du Côté de Chez Disaster*," 299–302.
Little, Judy. *Comedy and the Woman Writer*, 153–157.
Massie, Allan. *Muriel Spark*, 73–76.
Pullin, Faith. "Autonomy and Fabulation," 74–77.
Rankin, Ian. "Surface and Structure: Reading Muriel Spark's *The Driver's Seat*." *J of Narrative Technique* 15 (1985), 146–155.
Richmond, Velma Bourgeois. *Muriel Spark*, 111–117.
Whittaker, Ruth. " 'Angels Dining at the Ritz'," 174–178.
Whittaker, Ruth. *The Faith and Fiction*, 9–10, 96–97, 117–119, 140–142.

The Girls of Slender Means, 1963

Little, Judy. *Comedy and the Woman Writer*, 136–140.
McBrien, William. "Muriel Spark," 166–167.
Massie, Allan. "Calvinism and Catholicism in Muriel Spark," in Alan Bold, ed., *Muriel Spark*, 104–105.
Massie, Allan. *Muriel Spark*, 52–58.
Richmond, Velma Bourgeois. *Muriel Spark*, 86–92.

Shaw, Valerie. "Fun and Games with Life-stories," 50–55.
Whittaker, Ruth. *The Faith and Fiction*, 65–70, 93–94, 98–99, 110–111.

The Hothouse by the East River, 1973

Greene, George. "*Du Côté de Chez Disaster*," 304–307.
Little, Judy. *Comedy and the Woman Writer*, 161–165.
McBrien, William. "Muriel Spark," 171–173.
Massie, Allan. *Muriel Spark*, 77–81.
Perrie, Walter. "Mrs. Spark's Verse," in Alan Bold, ed., *Muriel Spark*, 195–197.
Richmond, Velma Bourgeois. *Muriel Spark*, 124–133.

Loitering with Intent, 1981

Hart, Francis Russell. "Ridiculous Demons," in Alan Bold, ed., *Muriel Spark*, 24–25.
Little, Judy. *Comedy and the Woman Writer*, 175–177.
Pullin, Faith. "Autonomy and Fabulation," 79–84.
Richmond, Velma Bourgeois. *Muriel Spark*, 156–166.
Shaw, Valerie. "Fun and Games with Life-stories," 47–69.
Whittaker, Ruth. *The Faith and Fiction*, 121–125.

The Mandelbaum Gate, 1965

Hart, Francis Russell. "Ridiculous Demons," 32–33.
Little, Judy. *Comedy and the Woman Writer*, 140–146.
McBrien, William. "Muriel Spark," 167–168.
Massie, Allan. "Calvinism and Catholicism," 98–99, 105–107.
Massie, Allan. *Muriel Spark*, 61–73.
Richmond, Velma Bourgeois. *Muriel Spark*, 93–105.
Whittaker, Ruth. *The Faith and Fiction*, 70–79.

Memento Mori, 1959

Leonard, Joan. " 'Loitering with Intent': Muriel Spark's Parabolic Technique." *Stud in the Liter Imagination* 18:1 (1985), 69–71.
Little, Judy. *Comedy and the Woman Writer*, 116–119.
McBrien, William. "Muriel Spark," 161–163.
Massie, Allan. *Muriel Spark*, 24–30.
Richmond, Velma Bourgeois. *Muriel Spark*, 45–57.
Whittaker, Ruth. *The Faith and Fiction*, 53–58, 137–138, 144–145.

Not to Disturb, 1971

Greene, George. "*Du Côté de Chez Disaster*," 302–304.
Little, Judy. *Comedy and the Woman Writer*, 158–161.
McBrien, William. "Muriel Spark," 170–171.
Richmond, Velma Bourgeois. *Muriel Spark*, 117–123.
Whittaker, Ruth. *The Faith and Fiction*, 119–121, 130–131.

The Only Problem, 1984

Richmond, Velma Bourgeois. *Muriel Spark*, 166–176.

The Prime of Miss Jean Brodie, 1961

Bold, Alan. *Modern Scottish Literature*, 221–223.
Dorenkamp, J. H. "Moral Vision in Muriel Spark's *The Prime of Miss Jean Brodie*." *Renascence* 33 (1980), 3–9.
Hart, Francis Russell. "Ridiculous Demons," 35–36.
Leonard, Joan. " 'Loitering with Intent'," 71–76.
Little, Judy. *Comedy and the Woman Writer*, 128–136.
McBrien, William. "Muriel Spark," 164–166.
Massie, Allan. "Calvinism and Catholicism," 101–104.
Massie, Allan. *Muriel Spark*, 45–52.
Pullin, Faith. "Autonomy and Fabulation," 84–91.
Richmond, Velma Bourgeois. *Muriel Spark*, 16–23.
Royle, Trevor. "Spark and Scotland," in Alan Bold, ed., *Muriel Spark*, 154–163.
Whittaker, Ruth. *The Faith and Fiction*, 106–110, 131–133, 138–139.

The Public Image, 1968

Greene, George. "*Du Côté de Chez Disaster*," 296–299.
Little, Judy. *Comedy and the Woman Writer*, 148–153.
McBrien, William. "Muriel Spark," 168–170.
Pullin, Faith. "Autonomy and Fabulation," 71–74.
Richmond, Velma Bourgeois. *Muriel Spark*, 106–111.
Stewart, Grace. *A New Mythos*, 34–35.
Whittaker, Ruth. *The Faith and Fiction*, 101–102, 111–116.

Robinson, 1958

Little, Judy. *Comedy and the Woman Writer*, 110–116.
McBrien, William. "Muriel Spark," 159–160.
Richmond, Velma Bourgeois. *Muriel Spark*, 37–44.
Whittaker, Ruth. *The Faith and Fiction*, 28–29, 48–49, 52–53.

The Takeover, 1976

Greene, George. "*Du Côté de Chez Disaster*," 310–315.
Little, Judy. *Comedy and the Woman Writer*, 168–171.
McBrien, William. "Muriel Spark," 173–175.
Massie, Allan. *Muriel Spark*, 85–89.
Richmond, Velma Bourgeois. *Muriel Spark*, 140–149.
Whittaker, Ruth. *The Faith and Fiction*, 82–86.

Territorial Rights, 1979

Codaccioni, Marie-José. "La Recherche du pouvoir," 111–122.
Little, Judy. *Comedy and the Woman Writer*, 171–175.
McBrien, William. "Muriel Spark," 175–176.
Richmond, Velma Bourgeois. *Muriel Spark*, 149–155.
Whittaker, Ruth. *The Faith and Fiction*, 86–90.

OLAF STAPLEDON

Darkness and the Light, 1942

Crossley, Robert. "Politics and the Artist: The Aesthetic of *Darkness and the Light*." *Science-Fiction Stud* 9 (1982), 294–305.
McCarthy, Patrick A. *Olaf Stapledon*, 96–104.

Death into Life, 1946

McCarthy, Patrick A. *Olaf Stapledon*, 104–110.

The Flames, 1947

McCarthy, Patrick A. *Olaf Stapledon*, 110–115.
Stableford, Brian. *Scientific Romance*, 275–278.

4 Encounters, 1976

McCarthy, Patrick A. *Olaf Stapledon*, 128–130.

Last and First Men, 1930

Campbell, James L., Sr. "Olaf Stapledon," in E. F. Bleiler, ed., *Science Fiction Writers*, 95–98.
Goodheart, Eugene. "Olaf Stapledon's *Last and First Men*," in Eric S. Rabkin et al., eds., *No Place Else*, 78–93.
Huntington, John. "Olaf Stapledon and the Novel about the Future." *Contemp Lit* 22 (1981), 350–362.
Huntington, John. "Remembrance of Things to Come: Narrative Technique in *Last and First Men*." *Science-Fiction Stud* 9 (1982), 257–264.
McCarthy, Patrick A. *Olaf Stapledon*, 32–47.
Smith, Curtis C. "Olaf Stapledon and the Immortal Spirit," in Carl B. Yoke and Donald M. Hassler, eds., *Death and the Serpent*, 107–109.
Stableford, Brian. *Scientific Romance*, 200–203.
Wagar, W. Warren. "Round Trips to Doomsday," in Eric S. Rabkin et al., eds., *The End of the World*, 93–94.

Last Men in London, 1932

McCarthy, Patrick A. *Olaf Stapledon*, 48–53.
Smith, Curtis C. "Olaf Stapledon and the Immortal Spirit," 106.
Stableford, Brian. *Scientific Romance*, 203–206.

A Man Divided, 1950

McCarthy, Patrick A. *Olaf Stapledon*, 116–124.

Odd John, 1935

Campbell, James L., Sr. "Olaf Stapledon," 94–95.
McCarthy, Patrick A. *Olaf Stapledon*, 54–65, 68–74.
Swanson, Roy Arthur. "The Spiritual Factor in *Odd John* and *Sirius*." *Science-Fiction Stud* 9 (1982), 284–293.

Sirius, 1944

Campbell, James L., Sr. "Olaf Stapledon," 94–95.
Collings, Michael R. "Of Lions and Lamp-Posts: C. S. Lewis' *The Lion, The Witch, and The Wardrobe* as Response to Olaf Stapledon's *Sirius.*" *Christianity & Lit* 32:4 (1983), 33–38.
McCarthy, Patrick A. *Olaf Stapledon*, 65–74.
Smith, Curtis C. "Olaf Stapledon and the Immortal Spirit," 109–110.
Stableford, Brian. *Scientific Romance*, 213–215.
Swanson, Roy Arthur. "The Spiritual Factor," 284–293.

The Star Maker, 1937

Crossley, Robert. "Famous Mythical Beasts: Olaf Stapledon and H. G. Wells." *Georgia R* 36 (1982), 629–635.
Huntington, John. "Olaf Stapledon," 362–364.
McCarthy, Patrick A. *Olaf Stapledon*, 75–95.
Rutledge, Amelia A. "*Star Maker*: The Agnostic Quest." *Science-Fiction Stud* 9 (1982), 274–283.
Smith, Curtis C. "Olaf Stapledon and the Immortal Spirit," 109.
Stableford, Brian. *Scientific Romance*, 209–212.
Tremaine, Louis. "Olaf Stapledon's Note on Magnitude." *Extrapolation* 23 (1982), 243–253.

JAMES STEPHENS

The Charwoman's Daughter, 1912

Achilles, Jochen. "*The Charwoman's Daughter* and the Emergence of National Psychology." *Irish Univ R* 11 (1981), 185–197.
Huber, Werner. "James Stephens: His Philosophy of Composition," in Heinz Kosok, ed., *Studies*, 182–188.
McFate, Patricia. *The Writings*, 23–33.
Martin, Augustine. *James Stephens*, 1–13.
Warner, Alan. *A Guide*, 125–127.

The Crock of Gold, 1912

Boyer, Gary M. "*The Crock of Gold.*" *Antigonish R* 44 (1980), 91–99.
Bramsbäck, Birgit. "The Philosophical Quest in *The Crock of Gold*," in Heinz Kosok, ed., *Studies*, 190–197.
Dyer, Joyce Coyne. "Desire in the Prose of James Stephens, 1920–1928." *Eire-Ireland* 19:4 (1984), 120–124.
Huber, Werner. "James Stephens," 182–188.
McFate, Patricia. *The Writings*, 33–47.
Martin, Augustine. *James Stephens*, 38–55.
Martin, Augustine. "Prose Fiction in the Irish Literary Renaissance," in Masaru Sekine, ed., *Irish Writers*, 152–153.
Warner, Alan. *A Guide*, 127–129.

The Demi-Gods, 1914

Huber, Werner. "James Stephens," 182–188.

McFate, Patricia. *The Writings*, 47–57.

Martin, Augustine. *James Stephens*, 73–88.

LAURENCE STERNE

A Sentimental Journey, 1768

Bethune, John. "*A Sentimental Journey*: A Fragment." *Massachusetts Stud in Engl* 8:3 (1982), 9–15.

Dussinger, John A. "The Sensorium in the World of *A Sentimental Journey*." *Ariel* 13:2 (1982), 3–14.

Hall, Vernon. "The Secret Structure of *A Sentimental Journey*," in *Studies in Three Literary Periods*, 47–66.

Hardy, Barbara. *Forms of Feeling*, 36–43.

Harries, Elizabeth W. "Sterne's Novels: Gathering Up the Fragments." *ELH* 49 (1982), 35–48.

Lamb, Jonathan. "Language and Hartleian Associationism in *A Sentimental Journey*." *Eighteenth-Century Stud* 13 (1980), 285–312.

McGuirk, Carol. "Sentimental Encounter in Sterne, Mackenzie, and Burns." *Stud in Engl Lit, 1500–1900* 20 (1980), 505–506, 510–511.

Niehus, Edward L. "Quixote Figures in the Novels of Sterne." *Essays in Lit* (Macomb) 12 (1985), 41–57.

Novak, Maximillian E. *Eighteenth-Century English Literature*, 156–157.

Parke, Catherine. "Vision and Revision: A Model for Reading the Eighteenth-Century Novel of Education." *Eighteenth-Century Stud* 16 (1982–83), 162–165.

Plank, Jeffrey. "On Explaining Generic Change in Late Eighteenth-Century English Literature." *Genre* 16 (1983), 237–239.

Richter, David H. "The Reader as Ironic Victim." *Novel* 14 (1981), 138–143.

Sedgwick, Eve Kosofsky. "Sexualism and the Citizen of the World: Wycherley, Sterne, and Male Homosocial Desire." *Crit Inquiry* 11 (1984), 238–244.

Seidel, Michael. "Narrative Crossings: Sterne's *A Sentimental Journey*." *Genre* 18 (1985), 1–20.

Shroff, Homai J. *The Eighteenth Century Novel*, 222–226.

Smitten, Jeffrey R. "Gesture and Expression in Eighteenth-Century Fiction: *A Sentimental Journey*." *Mod Lang Stud* 9 (1979), 85–97.

Tristram Shandy, 1760–1767

Allen, Dennis W. "Sexuality/Textuality in *Tristram Shandy*." *Stud in Engl Lit, 1500–1900* 25 (1985), 651–670.

Beck, Hamilton H. H. "*Tristram Shandy* and Hippel's *Lebensläufe nach aufsteigender Linie*." *Stud in Eighteenth-Century Culture* 10 (1981), 261–278.

Bell, Robert H. "Sterne's Etristramology." *Thalia* 4:2 (1981–82), 3–9.

Benstock, Shari. "At the Margin of Discourse: Footnotes in the Fictional Text." *PMLA* 98 (1983), 207–211.

Berthoud, Jacques. "Shandeism and Sexuality," in Valerie Grosvenor Myer, ed., *Laurence Sterne*, 24–38.

Bloom, Edward A., and Lillian D. Bloom. " 'This Fragment of Life': From Process to Mortality," in Valerie Grosvenor Myer, ed., *Laurence Sterne*, 57–71.

Bony, Alain. "La Couture et le gond: la page marbrée dans *Tristram Shandy*." *Etudes Anglaises* 37 (1984), 14–27.

Briggs, Peter M. "Locke's *Essay* and the Tentativeness of *Tristram Shandy*." *Stud in Philology* 82 (1985), 493–520.

Brooks-Davies, Douglas. "The Mythology of Love: Venerean (and Related) Iconography in Pope, Fielding, Cleland and Sterne," in Paul-Gabriel Boucé, ed., *Sexuality*, 187–189.

Byrd, Max. *Tristram Shandy*, 1–136.

Cash, Arthur H. "The Birth of Tristram Shandy: Sterne and Dr Burton," in Paul-Gabriel Boucé, ed., *Sexuality*, 198–220.

Christensen, Inger. *The Meaning of Metafiction*, 15–36.

Davidson, Arnold E. "Locke, Hume, and Hobby-Horses in *Tristram Shandy*." *Intl Fiction R* 8 (1981), 17–21.

Day, W. G. "*Tristram Shandy*: Locke May Not Be the Key," in Valerie Grosvenor Myer, ed., *Laurence Sterne*, 75–82.

DeGraaff, Robert. "Sterne's *Tristram Shandy*." *Explicator* 42:3 (1984), 20–22.

Dowling, William C. "Tristram Shandy's Phantom Audience." *Novel* 13 (1980), 284–295.

Dupas, Jean-Claude. "*The Life and Opinions of Tristram Shandy*: Une Rhapsodie grotesque." *Bull de la Société d'Etudes Anglo-Américaines des XVIIe et XVIIIe Siècles* 6 (1978), 61–75.

Ehlers, Leigh A. "Mr. Shandy's 'Lint and Basilicon': The Importance of Women in *Tristram Shandy*." *South Atlantic R* 46:1 (1981), 61–73.

Flego, Fabio. "Equazione di significato nella definizione di romanzo del Tristram Shandy." *Studi dell'Istituto Linguistico* 5 (1982), 75–90.

Flego, Fabio. "Policentrismo e unità narrativa nel *Tristram Shandy*." *Studi dell'Istituto Linguistico* 6 (1983), 67–82.

Gottlieb, Sidney. "A Borrowing from Francis Bacon in *Tristram Shandy*." *Engl Lang Notes* 23:2 (1985), 43–45.

Gottlieb, Sidney. "*Tristram Shandy* and the Compulsion to Repeat." *Mid-Hudson Lang Stud* 4 (1981), 69–81.

Graves, Lila. "Sterne's *Tristram Shandy*." *Explicator* 40:3 (1982), 18.

Graves, Lila V. "Locke's Changeling and the Shandy Bull." *Philol Q* 60 (1981), 257–264.

Graves, Lila V. "Locke's *Essay* and Sterne's 'Work Itself'." *J of Narrative Technique* 12 (1982), 36–45.

Gysin, Fritz. *Model as Motif*, 7–153.

Hagstrum, Jean H. *Sex and Sensibility*, 253–259.

Hamlin, Cyrus. "The Conscience of Narrative: Toward a Hermeneutics of Transcendence." *New Liter Hist* 13 (1982), 205–230.

Harries, Elizabeth W. "Sterne's Novels," 35–48.

Hayden, Lucy K. "The Black Presence in Eighteenth-Century British Novels." *Coll Lang Assoc J* 24 (1981), 412–414.

Howes, Alan B. "Laurence Sterne, Rabelais and Cervantes: The Two Kinds of Laughter in *Tristram Shandy*," in Valerie Grosvenor Myer, ed., *Laurence Sterne*, 39–55.

Imhof, Rüdiger. "Two Meta-Novelists: Sternesque Elements in Novels by Flann O'Brien." *Anglo-Irish Stud* 4 (1979), 61–90. [Also in Imhof, ed., *Alive-Alive O!*, 162–190.]

Kawin, Bruce F. *The Mind of the Novel*, 242–247.

Khazoum, Violet. "The Inverted Comedy of *Tristram Shandy*." *Hebrew Univ Stud in Lit* 7 (1979), 139–160.

Konigsberg, Ira. *Narrative Technique*, 157–183.

Lamb, Jonathan. "The Comic Sublime and Sterne's Fiction." *ELH* 48 (1981), 132–141.

Lamb, Jonathan. "Sterne's System of Imitation." *Mod Lang R* 76 (1981), 794–810.

Lamb, Jonathan. "Sterne's Use of Montaigne." *Compar Lit* 32 (1980), 1–41.

Lampkin, Loretta. "*Tristram Shandy* and *A Portrait of the Artist*: The Gestation of Identical Twins." *James Joyce Q* 21 (1984), 137–144.

Loveridge, Mark. "Liberty in *Tristram Shandy*," in Valerie Grosvenor Myer, ed., *Laurence Sterne*, 126–140.

McMaster, Juliet and Rowland. *The Novel from Sterne to James*, 1–17.

Marco, Sergio de. "Alcune funzioni dell'*hobby-horse*." *Studi dell'Istituto Linguistico* 4 (1981), 41–58.

Markley, Robert. "*Tristram Shandy* and 'Narrative Middles': Hillis Miller and the Style of Deconstructive Criticism." *Genre* 17 (1984), 184–187.

Miller, J. Hillis. "Narrative Middle: A Preliminary Outline." *Genre* 11 (1978), 375–387.

Monkman, Kenneth. "*Tristram* in Dublin." *Transactions of the Cambridge Bibliographical Soc* 7 (1979), 343–368.

Moss, Roger B. "Sterne's Punctuation." *Eighteenth-Century Stud* 15 (1981–82), 179–200.

Myer, Valerie Grosvenor. "Tristram and the Animal Spirits," in Myer, ed., *Laurence Sterne*, 99–110.

Nänny, Max. "Similarity and Contiguity in *Tristram Shandy*." *Engl Stud* 60 (1979), 422–435.

New, Melvyn. " 'At the backside of the door of purgatory': A Note on Annotating *Tristram Shandy*," in Valerie Grosvenor Myer, ed., *Laurence Sterne*, 15–22.

New, Melvyn. "Sterne, Warburton, and the Burden of Exuberant Wit."
    Eighteenth-Century Stud 15 (1982), 245–274.

Niehus, Edward L. "Quixote Figures," 41–57.

Novak, Maximillian E. *Eighteenth-Century English Literature*, 153–
    156.

Pattison, Robert. *The Child Figure*, 37–42.

Peterfreund, Stuart. "Sterne and Late Eighteenth-Century Ideas of
    History." *Eighteenth-Century Life* 7:1 (1981), 25–50.

Porter, Roy. "Against the Spleen," in Valerie Grosvenor Myer, ed.,
    Laurence Sterne, 84–94.

Reed, Walter L. *An Exemplary History*, 137–161.

Richter, David H. "The Reader as Ironic Victim," 138–143.

Riggan, William. *Picaros*, 84–89.

Rivers, William E. "The Importance of Tristram's 'Dear, Dear *Jenny*'."
    Interpretations 13 (1981), 1–9.

Rodgers, James S. " 'Life' in the Novel: *Tristram Shandy* and Some
    Aspects of Eighteenth-Century Physiology." *Eighteenth-Century
    Life* 6:1 (1980), 1–17.

Rogers, Pat. "Tristram Shandy's Polite Conversation." *Essays in Criti-
    cism* 32 (1982), 305–320.

Rohrberger, Mary, and Samuel H. Woods, Jr. "Alchemy of the Word:
    Surrealism in *Tristram Shandy*." *Interpretations* 11 (1979), 24–34.

Schulze, Martin. "Do You Know the Meaning of *****? Die markierte
    Aussparung als Indiz für die planvolle Komposition des *Tristram
    Shandy*," in Gerd Rohmann, ed., *Laurence Sterne*, 394–436.

Schwanitz, Dietrich. "Der Unfall und die Weltgeschichte: Zur Themati-
    sierung der Alltagswelt in Laurence Sternes *Tristram Shandy*," in
    Hans-Heinrich Freitag and Peter Hühn, eds., *Literarische Ansichten*,
    143–172.

Sheriff, John K. *The Good-Natured Man*, 51–58.

Shroff, Homai J. *The Eighteenth Century Novel*, 217–235.

Simpson, K. G. "At this Moment in Space: Time, Space and Values in
    Tristram Shandy," in Valerie Grosvenor Myer, ed., *Laurence Sterne*,
    142–157.

Snow, Kathleen R. "Homunculus in Paracelsus, *Tristram Shandy*, and
    Faust." *J of Engl and Germanic Philology* 79 (1980), 67–74.

Sokolyansky, Mark G. "The Rhythmical Pattern of *Tristram Shandy*."
    Durham Univ J 73 (1980–81), 23–26.

Soupel, Serge. "*Tristram Shandy*, roman piégé." *Bull de la Société
    d'Etudes Anglo-Américaines des XVIIe et XVIIIe Siècles* 17 (1983),
    129–138.

Speck, Paul Surgi. "Frustration, Curiosity and Rumor: Sterne's Use of
    Women to Define Impotence in *Tristram Shandy*." *Publs of the
    Arkansas Philol Assoc* 5:2–3 (1979), 30–35.

Steele, Peter. "Sterne's Script: The Performing of *Tristram Shandy*," in
    Douglas Lane Patey and Timothy Keegan, eds., *Augustan Studies*,
    193–204.

Stovel, Bruce. "*Tristram Shandy* and the Art of Gossip," in Valerie Grosvenor Myer, ed., *Laurence Sterne*, 115–124.

Suzuki, Kenzo. "The World of *Tristram Shandy* Revisited." *Eigo Seinen* (Tokyo) 125 (1979), 398–400.

Toulmin, Stephen. "The Inwardness of Mental Life." *Crit Inquiry* 6 (1979), 1–16.

Tripodi, Vincenzo. *Studi su Laurence Sterne*, 22–37, 40–54, 56–88, 90–149, 151–166, 168–179.

Tyson, Gerald P. "The Rococo Style of *Tristram Shandy*." *Bucknell R* 24:2 (1978), 38–55.

Weisgerber, Jean. *L'espace romanesque*, 171–196.

Weisgerber, Jean. "Formes rococo: Littérature et beaux-arts." *Revue de Littérature Comparée* 218 (1981), 141–167.

Welsh, Alexander. *Reflections*, 13–35, 102–105.

Wendell, Elizabeth M. *Der Leser als Protagonist*.

Williams, Ioan. *The Idea of the Novel*, 220–233.

ROBERT LOUIS STEVENSON

The Black Arrow, 1888

Hammond, J. R. *A Robert Louis Stevenson Companion*, 142–147.

Catriona, 1891

Gannon, Susan R. "Repetition and Meaning in Stevenson's David Balfour Novels." *Stud in the Liter Imagination* 18:2 (1985), 21–33.

Dr. Jekyll and Mr. Hyde, 1886

Apter, T. E. *Fantasy Literature*, 48–53.

Auerbach, Nina. *Woman and the Demon*, 102–105.

Block, Ed, Jr. "James Sully, Evolutionist Psychology, and Late Victorian Gothic Fiction." *Victorian Stud* 25 (1982), 452–458.

Bold, Alan. *Modern Scottish Literature*, 102–104.

Daleski, H. M. *The Divided Heroine*, 20–23.

Day, William Patrick. *In the Circles*, 89–92.

Fraustino, Daniel V. "*Dr. Jekyll and Mr. Hyde*: Anatomy of Misperception." *Arizona Q* 38 (1982), 235–240.

Hammond, J. R. *A Robert Louis Stevenson Companion*, 115–126.

Harvie, Christopher. "The Politics of Stevenson," in Jenni Calder, ed., *Stevenson*, 121–122.

Hennelly, Mark M., Jr. "Stevenson's 'Silent Symbols' of the 'Fatal Cross Roads' in *Dr. Jekyll and Mr. Hyde*." *Gothic* 1 (1979), 10–15.

Jackson, Rosemary. *Fantasy*, 114–116.

Lamarca Margalef, Jordi. *Ciencia y literatura*, 86–88.

MacAndrew, Elizabeth. *The Gothic Tradition*, 223–229.

Oates, Joyce Carol. "Wonderlands." *Georgia R* 38 (1984), 500–503.

Parrinder, Patrick. *Science Fiction . . . Teaching*, 9–10.

Prawer, S. S. "Book into Film: *Dr. Jekyll and Mr. Hyde.*" *Times Liter Suppl*, 21 Dec. 1979, 161–164.

Punter, David. *The Literature of Terror*, 240–245.

Scheick, William J. "Fictional Structure and Ethics in the Edwardian, Modern and Contemporary Novel." *Philol Q* 63 (1984), 291.

Showalter, Elaine. "Syphilis, Sexuality, and the Fiction of the Fin de Siècle," in Ruth Bernard Yeazell, ed., *Sex*, 100–102.

Welsch, Janice R. "The Horrific and the Tragic," in Michael Klein and Gillian Parker, eds., *The English Novel*, 165–179.

Wheeler, Michael. *English Fiction*, 176–178.

Wilt, Judith. *Ghosts of the Gothic*, 79–85.

The Ebb-Tide, 1894

Fowler, Alistair. "Parables of Adventure: The Debatable Novels of Robert Louis Stevenson," in Ian Campbell, ed., *Nineteenth-Century Scottish Fiction*, 115–126.

Kidnapped, 1886

Gannon, Susan R. "Repetition and Meaning," 21–33.

Hammond, J. R. *A Robert Louis Stevenson Companion*, 127–135.

Lascelles, Mary. *The Story-Teller*, 46–50.

Robson, W. W. "On *Kidnapped*," in Jenni Calder, ed., *Stevenson*, 88–106.

Stewart, Ralph. "The Unity of *Kidnapped*." *Victorian Newsl* 64 (1983), 30–32.

The Master of Ballantrae, 1889

Craig, David M. "The Closed Form of *The Master of Ballantrae*." *Interpretations* 12 (1980), 40–52.

Gifford, Douglas. "Stevenson and Scottish Fiction: The Importance of *The Master of Ballantrae*," in Jenni Calder, ed., *Stevenson*, 62–86.

Hammond, J. R. *A Robert Louis Stevenson Companion*, 148–161.

Lascelles, Mary. *The Story-Teller*, 67–71, 73–78.

Prince Otto, 1885

Hammond, J. R. *A Robert Louis Stevenson Companion*, 110–114.

Harvie, Christopher. "The Politics of Stevenson," 116–118.

St. Ives, 1897

Hammond, J. R. *A Robert Louis Stevenson Companion*, 185–192.

Treasure Island, 1883

Fowler, Alistair. "Parables of Adventure," 108–115.

Hammond, J. R. *A Robert Louis Stevenson Companion*, 101–109.

Harvie, Christopher. "The Politics of Stevenson," 119–121.

Mckenzie, Mary Louise. "The Toy Theatre, Romance, and *Treasure Island*: The Artistry of R. L. S." *Engl Stud in Canada* 8 (1982), 409–421.

Mann, David D., and William H. Hardesty. "Stevenson's Method in *Treasure Island*: 'The Old Romance, Retold'." *Essays in Lit* (Macomb) 9 (1982), 180–192.

Osborn, Marijane. "Stevenson's Heavenly Island." *Scottish Liter J* 3:1 (1976), 43–50.

Pickering, Sam. "Stevenson's 'Elementary Novel of Adventure'." *Res Stud* 49 (1981), 99–106.

Rose, Jacqueline. *The Case of Peter Pan*, 79–80.

Weir of Hermiston, 1896

Bold, Alan. *Modern Scottish Literature*, 104–105.

Hammond, J. R. *A Robert Louis Stevenson Companion*, 193–207.

Harvie, Christopher. "The Politics of Stevenson," 122–124.

Lascelles, Mary. *The Story-Teller*, 79–83, 103–111.

BRAM STOKER

Dracula, 1897

Astle, Richard. "Dracula as Totemic Monster: Lacan, Freud, Oedipus and History." *SubStance* 25 (1980), 98–103.

Auerbach, Nina. "Magi and Maidens: The Romance of the Victorian Freud." *Crit Inquiry* 8 (1981), 289–292.

Auerbach, Nina. *Woman and the Demon*, 22–24.

Blinderman, Charles S. "Vampurella: Darwin and Count Dracula." *Massachusetts R* 21 (1980), 411–428.

Block, Ed, Jr. "James Sully, Evolutionist Psychology, and Late Victorian Gothic Fiction." *Victorian Stud* 25 (1982), 462–463.

Byers, Thomas B. "Good Men and Monsters: The Defenses of *Dracula*." *Lit and Psych* 31:4 (1981), 24–30.

Clements, William M. "Formula as Genre in Popular Horror Literature." *Res Stud* 49 (1981), 116–123.

Day, William Patrick. *In the Circles*, 143–149.

Fontana, Ernest. "Lambroso's Criminal Man and Stoker's *Dracula*." *Victorian Newsl* 66 (1984), 25–27.

Foust, Ronald. "Rite of Passage: The Vampire Tale as Cosmogonic Myth," in William Coyle, ed., *Aspects of Fantasy*, 76–83.

Gordon, Jan B. "Narrative Enclosure as Textual Ruin: An Archaeology of Gothic Consciousness." *Dickens Stud Annual* 11 (1983), 230–231.

Griffin, Gail B. " 'Your Girls That You All Love Are Mine': *Dracula* and the Victorian Male Sexual Imagination." *Intl J of Women's Stud* 3 (1980), 454–465.

Hatlen, Burton. "The Return of the Repressed/Oppressed in Bram Stoker's *Dracula*." *Minnesota R* 15 (1980), 80–96.

Jackson, Rosemary. *Fantasy*, 118–122.

Murphy, Brian. "The Nightmare of the Dark: The Gothic Legacy of Count Dracula." *Odyssey* 1:2 (1976), 9–15.

Oates, Joyce Carol. "Wonderlands." *Georgia R* 38 (1984), 490–492.

Punter, David. *The Literature of Terror*, 256–263.

Roth, Lane. "Dracula Meets the *Zeitgeist*: *Nosferatu* (1922) as Film Adaptation." *Lit/Film Q* 7 (1979), 309–313.

Roth, Phyllis A. *Bram Stoker*, 87–126.

Seed, David. "The Narrative Method of *Dracula*." *Nineteenth-Century Fiction* 40 (1985), 61–75.

Senf, Carol A. "*Dracula*: Stoker's Response to the New Woman." *Victorian Stud* 26 (1982), 33–49.

Senf, Carol A. "*Dracula*: The Unseen Face in the Mirror." *J of Narrative Technique* 9 (1979), 160–168.

Showalter, Elaine. "Syphilis, Sexuality, and the Fiction of the Fin de Siècle," in Ruth Bernard Yeazell, ed., *Sex*, 98–100.

Todd, Janet M. "The Class-ic Vampire," in Michael Klein and Gillian Parker, eds., *The English Novel*, 197–210.

Twitchell, James B. *The Living Dead*, 132–140.

Wall, Geoffrey. " 'Different from Writing': *Dracula* in 1897." *Lit and Hist* 10 (1984), 15–22.

Walsh, Thomas P. "*Dracula*: Logos and Myth." *Res Stud* 47 (1979), 229–237.

Wilt, Judith. *Ghosts of the Gothic*, 85–95.

The Jewel of Seven Stars, 1903

Roth, Phyllis A. *Bram Stoker*, 66–74.

The Lady of the Shroud, 1909

Roth, Phyllis A. *Bram Stoker*, 74–80.

The Lair of the White Worm, 1911

Roth, Phyllis A. *Bram Stoker*, 80–86.

The Man, 1905

Roth, Phyllis A. *Bram Stoker*, 38–51.

Miss Betty, 1898

Roth, Phyllis A. *Bram Stoker*, 34–38.

The Mystery of the Sea, 1902

Roth, Phyllis A. *Bram Stoker*, 103–106.

The Snake's Pass, 1890

Roth, Phyllis A. *Bram Stoker*, 23–33.

ELIZABETH STONE

William Langshawe, 1842

Kestner, Joseph. "The Manchester Magnate in Elizabeth Stone's *William Langshawe, the Cotton Lord*." *Papers on Lang & Lit* 19 (1983), 61–71.

Kestner, Joseph. "Men in Female Condition of England Novels." *Women & Lit* 2 (1981), 88–92.

Kestner, Joseph. *Protest and Reform*, 70–81.

The Young Milliner, 1843

Fryckstedt, Monica Correa. *Elizabeth Gaskell's "Mary Barton,"* 182–184.

Kestner, Joseph. *Protest and Reform*, 81–90.

DAVID STOREY

Pasmore, 1972

Eagleton, Mary, and David Pierce. *Attitudes to Class*, 142–146.

Saville, 1976

Olsson, Barbara. "Pitman and Poet: The Divided Self in Storey's *Saville*," in Siegfried Korninger, ed., *A Yearbook*, 39–51.

JAN STRUTHER

Mrs. Miniver, 1939

Beauman, Nicola. *A Very Great Profession*, 114–117.

FRANCIS STUART

Black List, Section H, 1971

Riley, Kathryn. "Autobiography and Fiction: Francis Stuart's *Black List, Section H*." *Critique* (Atlanta) 25 (1984), 115–123.

The Pillar of Cloud, 1948

O'Rourke, Brian. *The Conscience of the Race*, 60–61.

Warner, Alan. *A Guide*, 230–231.

Redemption, 1949

Warner, Alan. *A Guide*, 231–234.

ROBERT SMITH SURTEES

Jorrocks' Jaunts and Jollities, 1838

Engel, Elliot, and Margaret F. King. *The Victorian Novel*, 121–122, 128–130.

Mr. Sponge's Sporting Tour, 1853

Mason, Philip. *The English Gentleman*, 99–103.

JONATHAN SWIFT

Gulliver's Travels, 1726

Abrash, Merritt. "Is There Life After Immortality?," in Carl B. Yoke and Donald M. Hassler, eds., *Death and the Serpent*, 20–21.

el-Ajroud, Habib. "Lumières de l'ironie: Lecture des *Voyages de Gulliver*." *Bull de la Société d'Etudes Anglo-Américaines des XVIIe et XVIIIe Siècles* 12 (1981), 81–96.

Albert, B. "The Fourth Part of *Gulliver's Travels*." *J of Engl Stud* 2 (1979), 1–5.

Anderson, William S. "Paradise Regained by Horace, Lost by Gulliver." *Yearbook of Engl Stud* 14 (1984), 158–166.

Basu, Anjana. "The Apology of Jonathan Swift." *J of the Dept of Engl* (Calcutta Univ) 18:1 (1982–83), 22–32.

Brink, J. R. "From the Utopians to the Yahoos: Thomas More and Jonathan Swift." *J of the Rutgers Univ Libraries* 42 (1980), 59–66.

Castle, Terry J. "Why the Houyhnhnms Don't Write: Swift, Satire and the Fear of the Text." *Essays in Lit* (Macomb) 7 (1980), 31–43.

Cook, Terry. " 'Dividing the Swift Mind': A Reading of *Gulliver's Travels*." *Crit Q* 22:3 (1980), 35–47.

Donovan, Susan G., and George Walton Williams. "Swift's *Gulliver's Travels*." *Explicator* 42:3 (1984), 18–19.

Doody, Margaret Anne. "Insects, Vermin, and Horses: *Gulliver's Travels* and Virgil's *Georgics*," in Douglas Lane Patey and Timothy Keegan, eds., *Augustan Studies*, 151–173.

Downie, J. A. *Jonathan Swift*, 262–287.

Drew, Philip. *The Meaning of Freedom*, 138–140.

Ducroq, Jean. "Relations de voyages et récits symboliques: *Robinson et Gulliver*." *Stud on Voltaire and the Eighteenth Century* 215 (1982), 1–8.

Felsky, Martin. "Swift's *Gulliver's Travels*." *Explicator* 40:1 (1981), 23–24.

Fink, Ernst O. "Skizze der illusionsbildenden Kunstgriffe in Swifts *Gulliver's Travels* und Wells' *Time Machine*," in Hans-Heinrich Freitag and Peter Hühn, eds., *Literarische Ansichten*, 123–141.

Fitzgerald, Robert P. "Ancients and Moderns in Swift's Brobdingnag." *Literatur in Wissenschaft und Unterricht* 18 (1985), 89–98.

Fitzgerald, Robert P. "Swift's Immortals: The Satiric Point." *Stud in Engl Lit, 1500–1900* 24 (1984), 483–495.

Gill, James E. "Man and Yahoo: Dialectic and Symbolism in Gulliver's 'Voyage to the Country of the Houyhnhnms'," in Robert B. White, Jr., ed., *The Dress*, 67–90.

Hammond, Eugene R. "Nature-Reason-Justice in *Utopia* and *Gulliver's Travels*." *Stud in Engl Lit, 1500–1900* 22 (1982), 445–468.

Hartman, Jay H. "*Gulliver's Travels*: An Oblique Approach to Christianity." *Cresset* 43:3 (1980), 9–13.

Hassall, Anthony J. "Discontinuities in *Gulliver's Travels*." *Sydney Stud in Engl* 5 (1979–80), 3–14.

Higgins, Ian. "Swift and Sparta: The Nostalgia of *Gulliver's Travels*." *Mod Lang R* 78 (1983), 513–531.

Hunter, J. Paul. "Fielding and the Disappearance of Heroes," in Robert Folkenflik, ed., *The English Hero*, 120–121.

Jansen, F. J. Billeskov. "*Gulliver's Travels*: A Study in the Aesthetics of the roman à thèse." *Orbis Litterarum* 38 (1983), 13–23.

Keener, Frederick M. *The Chain of Becoming*, 89–126.

Koon, William. "Jonathan Swift, Lemuel Gulliver, and the English Tongue." *Coll Lang Assoc J* 24 (1980), 68–75.

Kuczynski, Michael P. "Swift's *Gulliver's Travels*." *Explicator* 41:4 (1983), 21–23.

Landa, Louis. "The Dismal Science in Houyhnhnmland." *Novel* 13 (1979), 38–49.

Lapraz, Françoise. "Les Métamorphoses de la mort dans les *Voyages de Gulliver*," in *Hommage à Emile Gasquet*, 133–147.

Leigh, David Joseph. "Wollaston and Swift: A Source for the Houyhnhnms?" *Philos and Lit* 4 (1980), 92–104.

Leonard, David Charles. "Swift, Whiston, and the Comet." *Engl Lang Notes* 16 (1979), 284–287.

Lock, F. P. *The Politics*, 4–149.

Lock, F. P. *Swift's Tory Politics*, 168–178.

Lock, F. P. "The Text of *Gulliver's Travels*." *Mod Lang R* 76 (1981), 513–526.

Louis, Frances Deutsch. *Swift's Anatomy*, 123–167.

Mecziems, Jenny. "Gulliver and Other Heroes," in Clive T. Probyn, ed., *The Art*, 189–208.

Mecziems, Jenny. "Swift's Praise of Gulliver: Some Renaissance Background to the *Travels*," in Claude Rawson, ed., *The Character*, 245–278.

Mecziems, Jenny. "Utopia and 'the Thing which is not': More, Swift, and Other Lying Idealists." *Univ of Toronto Q* 52 (1982), 45–46, 48–54, 57–58.

Metscher, Thomas. "The Radicalism of Swift: *Gulliver's Travels* and the Irish Point of View." *Zeitschrift für Anglistik und Amerikanistik* 30 (1982), 293–308. [Also in Heinz Kosok, ed., *Studies*, 13–21.]

Nath, Vishwanadha H. H. " 'The Wisdom of the Ancients is the Folly of the Moderns': A Reading of *Gulliver's Travels*, Book III." *Publs of the Arkansas Philol Assoc* 6:2 (1980), 61–76.

Nokes, David. *Jonathan Swift*, 317–329.

Novak, Maximillian E. *Eighteenth-Century English Literature*, 85–92.

Oakleaf, David. "*Trompe l'Oeil*: Gulliver and the Distortions of the Observing Eye." *Univ of Toronto Q* 53 (1983/84), 166–178.

Pache, Walter. *Profit and Delight*, 114–116.

Palomo, Dolores J. "The Dutch Connection: The University of Leiden and Swift's Academy of Lagado." *Huntington Lib Q* 41 (1977), 27–35.

Probyn, Clive T. "Swift and the Human Predicament," in Probyn, ed., *The Art*, 57–80.

Quintana, Ricardo. "*Gulliver's Travels*: Some Structural Properties and Certain Questions of Critical Approach and Interpretation," in Claude Rawson, ed., *The Character*, 282–301.

Rawson, Claude. "The Character of Swift's Satire: Reflections on Swift, Johnson, and Human Restlessness," in Rawson, ed., *The Character*, 33–36, 53–56.

Real, Hermann J., and Heinz J. Vienken. "Swift's *Gulliver's Travels*, I.ii." *Explicator* 42:1 (1983), 18–19.

Reilly, Patrick. *Jonathan Swift*, 16–21, 146–153, 159–173, 184–189, 195–199.

Renaker, David. "Swift's Laputians as a Caricature of the Cartesians." *PMLA* 94 (1979), 936–944.

Rogers, Pat. "Classics and Chapbooks," in Isabel Rivers, ed., *Books and Their Readers*, 41–44.

Rogers, Pat. *Eighteenth Century Encounters*, 1–9, 11–25.

Rothman, Irving N. "The Execution Scene in *Gulliver's Travels*." *J of Evolutionary Psych* 3:1–2 (1982), 56–75.

Rothstein, Eric. "In Brobdingnag: Captain Gulliver, Dr. Derham, and Master Tom Thumb." *Etudes Anglaises* 37 (1984), 129–141.

Schnackertz, Hermann Josef. "*Gulliver's Travels*: Swifts aufklärerisches Spiel mit der Fiktion." *Poetica* 14 (1982), 45–69.

Sena, John F. "The Language of Gestures in *Gulliver's Travels*." *Papers on Lang & Lit* 19 (1983), 145–166.

Smith, Frederik N. "The Danger of Reading Swift: The Double Binds of *Gulliver's Travels*." *Stud in the Liter Imagination* 17:1 (1984), 35–47.

Smith, Frederik N. "Vexing Voices: The Telling of Gulliver's Story." *Papers on Lang & Lit* 21 (1985), 383–398.

Smith, Frederik N., and Karen K. Dudra. "Gulliver and Niagara." *Scriblerian* 13 (1981), 116–118.

Socorro Suarez Lafuente, Maria. "Jonathan Swift y el 'Viaje al pais de los caballos parlantes'." *Arbor* 108 (1981), 111–117.

Speck, W. A. *Society and Literature*, 66–71.

Starkman, Miriam K. "Satirical Onomastics: Lemuel Gulliver and King Solomon." *Philol Q* 60 (1981), 41–49.

Sullivan, E. E. "Houyhnhnms and Yahoos: From Technique to Meaning." *Stud in Engl Lit, 1500–1900* 24 (1984), 497–511.

Swearington, James E. "Time and Technique in Gulliver's Third Voyage." *Philos and Lit* 6 (1982), 45–60.

Takase, Fumiko. "The Houyhnhnms and the Eighteenth-Century Goût Chinois." *Engl Stud* 61 (1980), 408–417.

Traugott, John. "The Yahoo in the Doll's House: *Gulliver's Travels* the Children's Classic." *Yearbook of Engl Stud* 14 (1984), 127–150.

Treadwell, Michael. "Swift, Richard Coleire, and the Origins of *Gulliver's Travels*." *R of Engl Stud* 34 (1983), 304–311.

Tucker, Bernard. *Jonathan Swift*, 68–73, 87–110.

Watt, Ian. "The Ironic Tradition in Augustan Prose from Swift to Johnson," in Claude Rawson, ed., *The Character*, 315–318.

Wyrick, Deborah Baker. "Life Interminable: Swift's Struldbruggs and Capek's Elina Makropoulos." *Comparatist* 7 (1983), 48–56.

ALGERNON CHARLES SWINBURNE

The Children of the Chapel, 1864

Lougy, Robert E. "Swinburne's *The Children of the Chapel*: A Historical Novel for Young Victorian Readers." *CLIO* 12 (1983), 123–135.

Lesbia Brandon, 1952

Northey, Margot. "Control and Freedom: Swinburne's Novels." *Engl Stud in Canada* 6 (1980), 300–306.

Silver, Carole. "Dreamers of Dreams: Toward a Definition of Literary Pre-Raphaelitism," in Carole G. Silver, ed., *The Golden Chain*, 39–41.

Thomas, Donald. *Swinburne*, 100–101.

Love's Cross Currents, 1901

Northey, Margot. "Control and Freedom," 293–300.

Thomas, Donald. *Swinburne*, 101–104.

ELIZABETH TAYLOR

Angel, 1957

Leclerq, Florence. *Elizabeth Taylor*, 43–53.

At Mrs. Lippincote's, 1945

Leclerq, Florence. *Elizabeth Taylor*, 10–20.

Blaming, 1976

Leclerq, Florence. *Elizabeth Taylor*, 102–109.

A Game of Hide and Seek, 1951

Leclerq, Florence. *Elizabeth Taylor*, 59–67.

In a Summer Season, 1961

Leclerq, Florence. *Elizabeth Taylor*, 67–75.

Mrs. Palfrey at the Claremont, 1961

Leclerq, Florence. *Elizabeth Taylor*, 95–102.

Palladian, 1946

Leclerq, Florence. *Elizabeth Taylor*, 20–25.

The Sleeping Beauty, 1953

Leclerq, Florence. *Elizabeth Taylor*, 53–58.

The Soul of Kindness, 1964

> Leclerq, Florence. *Elizabeth Taylor*, 76–85.

A View of the Harbour, 1947

> Leclerq, Florence. *Elizabeth Taylor*, 26–34.

The Wedding Group, 1968

> Leclerq, Florence. *Elizabeth Taylor*, 85–94.

A Wreath of Roses, 1949

> Leclerq, Florence. *Elizabeth Taylor*, 34–42.

WILLIAM MAKEPEACE THACKERAY

Catherine, 1840

> Ferris, Ina. *William Makepeace Thackeray*, 14–17.

Denis Duval, 1864

> Ferris, Ina. *William Makepeace Thackeray*, 117–119.
> Sinha, S. K. *Thackeray*, 160–161.

Henry Esmond, 1852

> Auerbach, Nina. *Woman and the Demon*, 89–101.
> Bennett, James R. "Plot Repetition: Theme and Variation of Narrative Macro-Episodes." *Papers on Lang & Lit* 17 (1981), 416.
> Carlisle, Janice. *The Sense of an Audience*, 143–155.
> Daleski, H. M. *Unities*, 151–170.
> Ferris, Ina. "Realism and the Discord of Ending: The Example of Thackeray." *Nineteenth-Century Fiction* 38 (1983), 298–299.
> Ferris, Ina. *William Makepeace Thackeray*, 59–74.
> Fisher, Judith Law. "Siren and Artist: Contradiction in Thackeray's Aesthetic Ideal." *Nineteenth-Century Fiction* 39 (1985), 402–403, 408–410.
> Garrett-Goodyear, Joan. "Stylized Emotions, Unrealized Selves: Expressive Characterization in Thackeray." *Victorian Stud* 22 (1979), 176–179, 188–190.
> Garson, Marjorie. "Henry Esmond's Love of Children." *Nineteenth-Century Fiction* 36 (1982), 387–406.
> Garson, Marjorie. " 'Knowledge of Good and Evil': Henry and Rachel in *The History of Henry Esmond*." *Engl Stud in Canada* 9 (1983), 418–432.
> Gilmour, Robin. *The Idea of the Gentleman*, 29–30.
> Harden, Edgar F. "The Writing and Publication of *Henry Esmond*." *Stud in the Novel* 13 (1981), 79–92.
> Hardy, Barbara. *Forms of Feeling*, 90–95.
> Lascelles, Mary. *The Story-Teller*, 153–157.
> Lindley, Dwight N. "Clio and Three Historical Novels." *Dickens Stud Annual* 10 (1982), 83–85.

Manning, Sylvia. "Incest and the Structure of *Henry Esmond*." *Nineteenth-Century Fiction* 34 (1979), 194–213.

Miller, J. Hillis. *Fiction and Repetition*, 73–115.

Phillips, K. C. *The Language of Thackeray*, 148–175.

Rosner, Mary. "Perspectives on *Henry Esmond*." *Victorian Newsl* 56 (1979), 26–31.

Schulze, Wolfgang. "*François le champi*: Vorbild für *Henry Esmond*?" *Archiv für das Studium der Neueren Sprachen und Literaturen* 216 (1979), 2–8.

Sinha, S. K. *Thackeray*, 138–155.

Wheeler, Michael. *English Fiction*, 43–47, 52–55.

Wijesinha, Rajiva. *The Androgynous Trollope*, 84–86, 152–154.

Wilt, Judith. "Steamboat Surfacing: Scott and the English Novelists." *Nineteenth-Century Fiction* 35 (1981), 467–468.

Lovel the Widower, 1860

Ferris, Ina. *William Makepeace Thackeray*, 117–118.

The Luck of Barry Lyndon, 1844

Bluestone, George. "*Barry Lyndon*: The Book, the Film." *Sphinx* 9 (1979), 16–27.

Connelly, Joseph F. "Transparent Poses: *Castle Rackrent* and *The Memoirs of Barry Lyndon*." *Eire-Ireland* 14:2 (1979), 37–43.

Ferris, Ina. "Realism and the Discord of Ending," 291–292.

Ferris, Ina. *William Makepeace Thackeray*, 17–20.

Gilmour, Robin. *The Idea of the Gentleman*, 43–45.

Hardy, Barbara. *Forms of Feeling*, 78–83.

Jean, Dominique. "Avatars du picaresque à l'époque victorienne." *Caliban* 20 (1983), 46–47.

Klein, Michael. "Narrative and Discourse in Kubrick's Modern Tragedy," in Michael Klein and Gillian Parker, eds., *The English Novel*, 95–107.

McCarthy, Terence. "Chronological Inconsistencies in *Barry Lyndon*." *Engl Lang Notes* 21:2 (1983), 29–37.

Nelson, Thomas Allen. "*Barry Lyndon*: Kubrick's Cinema of Disparity." *Rocky Mountain R of Lang and Lit* 33 (1979), 39–51.

Sinha, S. K. *Thackeray*, 1–4, 12–14, 92–98.

The Newcomes, 1854–1855

Canham, Stephen. "Art and the Illustrations of *Vanity Fair* and *The Newcomes*." *Mod Lang Q* 43 (1982), 52–66.

Carlisle, Janice. *The Sense of an Audience*, 119–141.

Ferris, Ina. "Realism and the Discord of Ending," 292–293.

Ferris, Ina. *William Makepeace Thackeray*, 75–99.

Fisher, Judith Law. "Siren and Artist," 393–397, 408–410.

Garrett, Peter K. *The Victorian Multiplot Novel*, 129–134.

Garrett-Goodyear, Joan. "Stylized Emotions," 179–184.

Gilmour, Robin. *The Idea of the Gentleman*, 76–82.

Lund, Michael. "Reading Serially Published Novels: Old Stories in Thackeray's *The Newcomes*." *Philol Q* 60 (1981), 205–220.

McMaster, Juliet and Rowland. *The Novel from Sterne to James*, 127–145.

Mason, Philip. *The English Gentleman*, 115–118.

Olmsted, John C. "Richard Doyle's Illustrations to *The Newcomes*." *Stud in the Novel* 13 (1981), 93–107.

Rataboul, Louis J. *Le pasteur anglican*, 146–148, 187–188.

Sinha, S. K. "Mythic Archetypes in Thackeray's Novels," in *Studies in Nineteenth Century Literature* (1), 42–45.

Sinha, S. K. *Thackeray*, 46–48, 126–137.

Stetz, Margaret Diane. "Thackeray's *The Newcomes* and the Artist's World." *J of Pre-Raphaelite Stud* 3:2 (1983), 80–95.

Stewart, Garrett. "Signing Off: Dickens and Thackeray, Woolf and Beckett," in William E. Cain, ed., *Philosophical Approaches*, 120–125.

Wijesinha, Rajiva. *The Androgynous Trollope*, 37–45.

Winner, Viola Hopkins. "Thackeray and Richard Doyle, the 'Wayward Artist' of *The Newcomes*." *Harvard Lib Bull* 26 (1978), 193–211.

Pendennis, 1849–1850

Auerbach, Nina. *Woman and the Demon*, 90–93.

Chrétien, Maurice. "La relation mère-fils dans *Pendennis*." *Confluents* 1975:1, 129–151.

Coates, John. "Handling Change: A Study of Thackeray's Techniques of Presenting Social and Personal Change in *Pendennis*." *Durham Univ J* 75:1 (1982), 43–51.

Ferris, Ina. "The Demystification of Laura Pendennis." *Stud in the Novel* 13 (1981), 122–131.

Ferris, Ina. *William Makepeace Thackeray*, 43–58.

Fisher, Judith Law. "Siren and Artist," 392–397, 406–407.

Garrett, Peter K. *The Victorian Multiplot Novel*, 96–104.

Garrett-Goodyear, Joan. "Stylized Emotions," 184–185.

Gilmour, Robin. *The Idea of the Gentleman*, 71–76.

Hardy, Barbara. *Forms of Feeling*, 87–90.

Lund, Michael. "Growing Up in Fiction and in Fact: Protagonist and Reader in Thackeray's *Pendennis*." *Dickens Stud Annual* 12 (1983), 285–299.

MacKay, Carol Hanbery. "Surrealization and the Redoubled Self: Fantasy in *David Copperfield* and *Pendennis*." *Dickens Stud Annual* 14 (1985), 241–261.

Nadel, Ira Bruce. "Thackeray and Clough." *Stud in the Novel* 13 (1981), 70–77.

Qualls, Barry V. *The Secular Pilgrims*, 190–192.

Rataboul, Louis J. *Le pasteur anglican*, 142–144.

Shillingsburg, Peter L. "*Pendennis* Revisited." *Etudes Anglaises* 34 (1981), 432–442.

Sinha, S. K. "Mythic Archetypes," 35–41.

Sinha, S. K. *Thackeray*, 72–80, 85–89, 118–126.

Thomas, Deborah A. "Bondage and Freedom in Thackeray's *Pendennis.*" *Stud in the Novel* 17 (1985), 138–155.

Vega-Ritter, Max. "Essai d'analyse psychocritique de *Pendennis.*" *Cahiers Victoriens et Edouardiens* 13 (1981), 53–78.

Wijesinha, Rajiva. *The Androgynous Trollope*, 86–90, 135–137.

Williams, Merryn. *Women in the English Novel*, 122–124.

Wilt, Judith. "Steamboat Surfacing," 465–466.

Philip, 1862

Ferris, Ina. "Narrative Strategy in Thackeray's *The Adventues of Philip.*" *Engl Stud in Canada* 5 (1979), 448–456.

Ferris, Ina. "Realism and the Discord of Ending," 293–294, 296–297.

Ferris, Ina. *William Makepeace Thackeray*, 107–116.

Fisher, Judith Law. "Siren and Artist," 411–419.

McMaster, Juliet. "Funeral Baked Meats: Thackeray's Last Novel." *Stud in the Novel* 13 (1981), 133–153.

Rataboul, Louis J. *Le pasteur anglican*, 148–149.

Wijesinha, Rajiva. *The Androgynous Trollope*, 137–140.

Rebecca and Rowena, 1850

Wilt, Judith. "Steamboat Surfacing," 463–466.

The Rose and the Ring, 1854

Prickett, Stephen. *Victorian Fantasy*, 66–72.

Vanity Fair, 1848

Bledsoe, Robert T. "*Vanity Fair* and Singing." *Stud in the Novel* 13 (1981), 51–60.

Brunkhorst, Martin. " 'The castled crag of Drachenfels': Funktionswechsel eines Landschaftsbildes." *Arcadia* 17 (1982), 143–146.

Burch, Mark H. " 'The world is a looking-glass': *Vanity Fair* as Satire." *Genre* 15 (1982), 265–278.

Bystrom, Valerie Ann. "The Abyss of Sympathy: The Conventions of Pathos in Eighteenth and Nineteenth Century British Novels." *Criticism* 23 (1981), 225–226.

Canham, Stephen. "Art and the Illustrations," 46–52.

Carlisle, Janice. *The Sense of an Audience*, 35–38, 54–60.

Carroll, Noel. "Becky Sharp Takes Over," in Michael Klein and Gillian Parker, eds., *The English Novel*, 108–120.

Cleall, Charles. *A Guide*, 1–143.

Cohen, Edward H. "George IV and Jos Sedley in *Vanity Fair.*" *Engl Lang Notes* 19 (1981), 122–130.

Colby, Robert A. " 'Scenes of All Sorts': *Vanity Fair* on Stage and Screen." *Dickens Stud Annual* 9 (1981), 163–189.

Daleski, H. M. *Unities*, 3–26.

DiBattista, Maria. "The Triumph of Clytemnestra: The Charades in *Vanity Fair*." *PMLA* 95 (1980), 827–836.

Ferris, Ina. "The Reader in the Rhetoric of Realism: Scott, Thackeray and Eliot," in J. H. Alexander and David Hewitt, eds., *Scott and His Influence*, 387–389.

Ferris, Ina. "Realism and the Discord of Ending," 292.

Ferris, Ina. *William Makepeace Thackeray*, 25–42.

Fisher, Judith Law. "Siren and Artist," 397–400.

Frazee, John P. "George IV and Jos Sedley in *Vanity Fair*." *Engl Lang Notes* 19 (1981), 122–128.

Garrett, Peter K. *The Victorian Multiplot Novel*, 104–127.

Gilmour, Robin. *The Idea of the Gentleman*, 55–71.

Gilmour, Robin. *Thackeray*, 8–61.

Hardy, Barbara. *Forms of Feeling*, 84–87.

Higgins, Elizabeth Jean. *Reading the Novel*, 167–173.

James, Louis. "The View from Brick Lane: Contrasting Perspectives in Working-Class and Middle-Class Fiction of the Early Victorian Period." *Yearbook of Engl Stud* 11 (1981), 95–101.

Kinkead-Weekes, Mark. "The Voicing of Fictions," in Ian Gregor, ed., *Reading the Victorian Novel*, 183–190.

Lund, Michael. "Beyond the Text of *Vanity Fair*." *Stud in the Novel* 11 (1979), 147–159.

Mandel, Oscar. *Annotations to "Vanity Fair."*

Mason, Philip. *The English Gentleman*, 108–114.

Maynor, Natalie. "Punctuation and Style in *Vanity Fair*: Thackeray versus His Compositors." *Engl Lang Notes* 22:2 (1984), 48–55.

Möller, Joachim. "Buchschmuck oder Verständnishilfe: Text und Illustration in *Vanity Fair* am Beispiel des *husband-hunting*." *Literatur in Wissenschaft und Unterricht* 13 (1980), 89–100.

Musselwhite, David. "Notes on a Journey to Vanity Fair." *Lit and Hist* 7 (1981), 62–89.

Nadel, Ira Bruce. "Becky Sharp and the Three Per Cent Solution." *Victorian Newsl* 58 (1980), 20–23.

Nesteby, James R. "Portraits of Blacks in Thackeray's *Vanity Fair*." *J of Engl* (Sana'a Univ) 8 (1980), 126–158.

Petit, J.-P. "William M. Thackeray: *Vanity Fair*," in Pierre Coustillas et al., eds., *Le roman anglais*, 179–186.

Polhemus, Robert M. *Comic Faith*, 124–165.

Rataboul, Louis J. *Le pasteur anglican*, 144–146.

Reed, Walter L. *An Exemplary History*, 188–196.

Rogers, Henry N. "*Vanity Fair* as Satiric Myth." *Publs of the Arkansas Philol Assoc* 8:2 (1982), 49–65.

Scarry, Elaine. "Enemy and Father: Comic Equilibrium of Number
Fourteen of *Vanity Fair*." *J of Narrative Technique* 10 (1980), 145–
154.

Shillingsburg, Peter L. "Final Touches and Patches in *Vanity Fair*: The
First Edition." *Stud in the Novel* 13 (1981), 40–49.

Simon, Richard Keller. *The Labyrinth*, 117–137.

Sinha, S. K. "Mythic Archetypes," 32–35.

Sinha, S. K. *Thackeray*, 19–24, 34–36, 44–46, 49–56, 63–72, 83–85, 98–
117.

Smith, Grahame. *The Novel & Society*, 147–172.

Wheeler, Michael. *English Fiction*, 47–52.

Wijesinha, Rajiva. *The Androgynous Trollope*, 90–100, 156–158.

Williams, Merryn. *Women in the English Novel*, 120–123.

The Virginians, 1858–1859

Carlisle, Janice. *The Sense of an Audience*, 142–149, 154–163.

Ferris, Ina. *William Makepeace Thackeray*, 102–107.

Fisher, Judith Law. "Siren and Artist," 411–419.

Sinha, S. K. "Mythic Archetypes," 38–39, 41–42, 45–46.

Sinha, S. K. *Thackeray*, 156–160.

Sorensen, Gerald C. "Beginning and Ending: *The Virginians* as a
Sequel." *Stud in the Novel* 13 (1981), 109–119.

Wijesinha, Rajiva. *The Androgynous Trollope*, 78–84, 154–156.

J. R. R. TOLKIEN

The Hobbit, 1937

Crabbe, Katharyn F. *J. R. R. Tolkien*, 28–65.

Giddings, Robert, and Elizabeth Holland. *J. R. R. Tolkien*, 7–9.

Hieatt, Constance. "The Text of *The Hobbit*: Putting Tolkien's Notes in
Order." *Engl Stud in Canada* 7 (1981), 212–222.

Hodge, James L. "Tolkien's Mythological Calendar in *The Hobbit*," in
William Coyle, ed., *Aspects of Fantasy*, 141–148.

Kendall, Douglas. "A Trip through Middle-Earth: A Chronology of *The
Hobbit* and *The Lord of the Rings*," in Alida Becker, ed., *The Tolkien
Scrapbook*, 56–73.

King, Roger. "Recovery, Escape, Consolation: Middle-Earth and the
English Fairy Tale," in Robert Giddings, ed., *J. R. R. Tolkien*, 42–54.

Kuznets, Lois R. "Tolkien and the Rhetoric of Childhood," in Neil D.
Isaacs and Rose A. Zimbardo, eds., *Tolkien*, 150–161.

Mathews, Richard. *Lightning*, 7–18.

Nitzsche, J. C. "The King under the Mountain: Tolkien's *The Hobbit*."
North Dakota Q 47:1 (1979), 5–18.

Nitzsche, Jane Chance. *Tolkien's Art*, 31–48.

Noel, Ruth S. *The Languages*, 3–207.

Palusci, Oriana. *John R. R. Tolkien*, 66–96.

Petty, Anne C. *One Ring*, 17–28.

Rogers, Deborah Webster, and Ivor A. Rogers. *J. R. R. Tolkien*, 64–77.

Rossi, Lee D. *The Politics of Fantasy*, 95–106.

Shippey, T. A. *The Road*, 48–50, 52–80.

Tabbert, Reinbert. "Bedürfnis nach Mythen: Zur Produktion der Hobbit Presse." *Merkur* 32 (1978), 1034–1046.

The Lord of the Rings, 1966

Basney, Lionel. "Myth, History, and Time in *The Lord of the Rings*," in Neil D. Isaacs and Rose A. Zimbardo, eds., *Tolkien*, 8–18.

Borgmeier, Raimund. "*No Message?*—Zur Deutung von Tolkiens *Lord of the Rings*." *Anglia* 100 (1982), 397–412.

Boyd, Heather. "*The Lord of the Rings*." *Standpunte* 142 (1979), 52–60.

Brooke-Rose, Christine. "The Evil Ring: Realism and the Marvelous." *Poetics Today* 1:4 (1980), 67–90.

Brooke-Rose, Christine. *A Rhetoric*, 233–255.

Bryce, Lynn. "The Influence of Scandinavian Mythology on the Works of J. R. R. Tolkien." *Edda*, 1983, 113–118.

Bryce, Lynn. "The Use of Christian Iconography in Selected Marginalia of J. R. R. Tolkien's Lothlorien Chapters." *Extrapolation* 25 (1984), 51–58.

Burger, Douglas A. "The Shire: A Tolkien Version of Pastoral," in William Coyle, ed., *Aspects of Fantasy*, 149–154.

Cornaro, Franz. "Karl-May-Ähnliches in J. R. R. Tolkiens Dichtung *Der Herr der Ringe*." *Jahrbuch der Karl-May-Gesellschaft*, 1981, 207–226.

Crabbe, Katharyn F. *J. R. R. Tolkien*, 66–111.

Downing, Angela. "From Quenya to the Common Speech: Linguistic Diversification in J. R. R. Tolkien's *The Lord of the Rings*." *Revista Canaria de Estudios Ingleses* 4 (1982), 23–31.

Dubs, Kathleen E. "Providence, Fate, and Chance: Boethian Philosophy in *The Lord of the Rings*." *Twentieth Century Lit* 27 (1981), 34–41.

Edwards, Malcolm, and Robert Holdstock. *Realms of Fantasy*, 11–22.

Elgin, Don D. *The Comedy*, 31–59.

Flieger, Verlyn. "Frodo and Aragorn: The Concept of the Hero," in Neil D. Isaacs and Rose A. Zimbardo, eds., *Tolkien*, 40–61.

Flieger, Verlyn. *Splintered Light*, 109–116, 135–145.

Fricker, Robert. *The Unacknowledged Legislators*, 202–231.

Friedman, Barton. "Tolkien and David Jones: The Great War and the War of the Ring." *CLIO* 11 (1982), 115–134.

Giddings, Robert, and Elizabeth Holland. *J. R. R. Tolkien*, 35–255.

Glover, David. "Utopia and Fantasy in the Late 1960s: Burroughs, Moorcock, Tolkien," in Christopher Pawling, ed., *Popular Fiction*, 203–207.

Grant, Patrick. "Tolkien: Archetype and Word," in Neil D. Isaacs and Rose A. Zimbardo, eds., *Tolkien*, 87–104.

Gray, Thomas. "Bureaucratization in *The Lord of the Rings*." *Mythlore*
    7:2 (1980), 3–5.

Green, William H. "The Four-Part Structure of Bilbo's Education."
    Children's Lit 8 (1979), 133–140.

Helms, Randel. *Tolkien*, 76–79.

Hennelly, Mark M., Jr. "The Dream of Fantasy: 'There and Back
    Again'—A Hobbit's Holiday." *Sphinx* 10 (1979), 29–43.

Hughes, Daniel. "Pieties and Giant Forms in *The Lord of the Rings*," in
    Neil D. Isaacs and Rose A. Zimbardo, eds., *Tolkien*, 72–86.

Jeffrey, David L. "Recovery: The Name in *The Lord of the Rings*," in
    Neil D. Isaacs and Rose A. Zimbardo, eds., *Tolkien*, 106–115.

Jeffrey, David Lyle. "Tolkien as Philologist." *Seven* 1 (1980), 47–57.

Jones, Diana Wynne. "The Shape of the Narrative in *The Lord of the
    Rings*," in Robert Giddings, ed., *J. R. R. Tolkien*, 87–107.

Keutsch, Wilfried. "Kult und Allegorie: J. R. R. Tolkiens *Lord of the
    Rings*." *Literatur in Wissenschaft und Unterricht* 15 (1982), 43–59.

King, Roger. "Recovery," 42–54.

Kocher, Paul. "Middle-Earth: An Imaginary World?," in Neil D. Isaacs
    and Rose A. Zimbardo, eds., *Tolkien*, 117–131.

Little, Edmund. *The Fantasts*, 13–38.

Lobdell, Jared. *England and Always: Tolkien's World of the Rings*.

Lynch, James. "The Literary Banquet and the Eucharistic Feast:
    Tradition in Tolkien." *Mythlore* 5:2 (1978), 13–14.

Mack, H. C. "A Parametric Analysis of Antithetical Conflict and Irony:
    Tolkien's *The Lord of the Rings*." *WORD* 31 (1980), 121–149.

McLeish, Kenneth. "The Rippingest Yarn of All," in Robert Giddings,
    ed., *J. R. R. Tolkien*, 125–136.

Marchesani, Diane. "Tolkien's Lore: The Songs of Middle Earth."
    Mythlore 7:1 (1980), 3–5.

Mathews, Richard. *Lightning*, 18–55.

Menzies, Janet. "Middle-Earth and the Adolescent," in Robert Gid-
    dings, ed., *J. R. R. Tolkien*, 57–71.

Meyers, Walter E. *Aliens and Linguists*, 148–156.

Miller, Miriam Y. "The Green Sun: A Study of Color in J. R. R.
    Tolkien's *The Lord of the Rings*." *Mythlore* 7:4 (1981), 3–11.

Nitzsche, Jane Chance. *Tolkien's Art*, 97–127.

Noel, Ruth S. *The Languages*, 3–207.

Noel, Ruth S. *The Mythology*, 15–173.

Otty, Nick. "The Structuralist's Guide to Middle-Earth," in Robert
    Giddings, ed., *J. R. R. Tolkien*, 156–177.

Palusci, Oriana. *John R. R. Tolkien*, 96–129.

Partridge, Brenda. "No Sex Please—We're Hobbits: The Construction
    of Female Sexuality in *The Lord of the Rings*," in Robert Giddings,
    ed., *J. R. R. Tolkien*, 179–195.

Petty, Anne C. *One Ring*, 9–106.

Poyet, Françoise. "Merveilleux et fantastique (?) dans *The Lord of the
    Rings*." *Caliban* 16 (1979), 41–52.

Purtill, Richard L. *J. R. R. Tolkien*, 8–141.

Robinson, Derek. "The Hasty Stroke Goes Oft Astray: Tolkien and Humour," in Robert Giddings, ed., *J. R. R. Tolkien*, 108–124.

Rogers, Deborah Webster, and Ivor A. Rogers. *J. R. R. Tolkien*, 94–120.

Rosenberg, Jerome. "The Humanity of Sam Gamgee." *Mythlore* 5:1 (1978), 10–11.

Rossi, Lee D. *The Politics of Fantasy*, 119–134.

St. Clair, Gloriana. "*The Lord of the Rings* as Saga." *Mythlore* 6:2 (1979), 11–16.

Scafella, Frank. "Tolkien, the Gospel, and the Fairy Story." *Soundings* 14 (1981), 319–325.

Schaafsma, Karen. "Wondrous Vision: Transformation of the Hero in Fantasy through Encounter with the Other," in William Coyle, ed., *Aspects of Fantasy*, 65–68.

Shippey, T. A. *The Road*, 76–168.

Simpson, Dale W. "Names and Moral Character in J. R. R. Tolkien's *The Lord of the Rings.*" *Publs of the Missouri Philol Assoc* 6 (1981), 1–5.

Swinfen, Ann. *In Defence*, 78–99.

Walker, Steven C. "The Making of a Hobbit: Tolkien's Tantalizing Narrative Technique." *Mythlore* 7:3 (1980), 6–7.

Zimbardo, Rose A. "The Medieval-Renaissance Vision of *The Lord of the Rings*," in Neil D. Isaacs and Rose A. Zimbardo, eds., *Tolkien*, 63–70.

Silmarillion, 1977

Adams, Robert M. "The Hobbit Habit," in Neil D. Isaacs and Rose A. Zimbardo, eds., *Tolkien*, 168–175.

Crabbe, Katharyn F. *J. R. R. Tolkien*, 112–144.

Crossley, Robert. "A Long Day's Dying: The Elves of J. R. R. Tolkien and Sylvia Townsend Warner," in Carl B. Yoke and Donald M. Hassler, eds., *Death and the Serpent*, 58–63.

Davis, Howard. "The Ainulindale: Music of Creation." *Mythlore* 9:2 (1982), 6–8.

Flieger, Verlyn. "Barfield's *Poetic Diction* and Splintered Light." *Stud in the Liter Imagination* 14:2 (1981), 47–66.

Flieger, Verlyn. *Splintered Light*, 93–107, 120–131.

Giddings, Robert, and Elizabeth Holland. *J. R. R. Tolkien*, 19–20, 170–173.

Helms, Randel. *Tolkien*, 1–90.

Kocher, Paul H. *A Reader's Guide*, 1–264.

McLellan, Joseph. "Frodo and the Cosmos: Reflections on *The Silmarillion*," in Neil D. Isaacs and Rose A. Zimbardo, eds., *Tolkien*, 163–167.

Mathews, Richard. *Lightning*, 56–59.

Nitzsche, Jane Chance. *Tolkien's Art*, 128–134.

Noel, Ruth S. *The Languages*, 3–207.

Palusci, Oriana. *John R. R. Tolkien*, 45–66.
Purtill, Richard L. *J. R. R. Tolkien*, 88–101.
Rogers, Deborah Webster, and Ivor A. Rogers. *J. R. R. Tolkien*, 78–93.
Shippey, T. A. *The Road*, 174–202.
Sommavilla, Guido. "*Il Silmarillion*: Una genesi dall'alto, dell'uomo, e del bene e del male." *Letture* 34 (1979), 274–284.

H. M. TOMLINSON

All Hands!, 1937

Crawford, Fred D. *H. M. Tomlinson*, 196–206.

All Our Yesterdays, 1930

Crawford, Fred D. *H. M. Tomlinson*, 181–189.

The Day Before, 1939

Crawford, Fred D. *H. M. Tomlinson*, 208–214.

Gallions Reach, 1927

Crawford, Fred D. *H. M. Tomlinson*, 174–181.

Morning Light, 1946

Crawford, Fred D. *H. M. Tomlinson*, 215–220.

The Snows of Helicon, 1933

Crawford, Fred D. *H. M. Tomlinson*, 190–196.

The Trumpet Shall Sound, 1957

Crawford, Fred D. *H. M. Tomlinson*, 220–226.

CHARLOTTE ELIZABETH TONNA

Combination, 1844

Kestner, Joseph. "Men in Female Condition of England Novels." *Women & Lit* 2 (1981), 86–88.

Helen Fleetwood, 1841

Bergmann, Helena. *Between Obedience and Freedom*, 26–28, 65–67.
Fryckstedt, Monica Correa. *Elizabeth Gaskell's "Mary Barton,"* 175–179.
Kestner, Joseph. "Men in Female . . . Novels," 83–86.
Kestner, Joseph. *Protest and Reform*, 58–65.
Tarantelli, Carole Beebe. *Ritratto di ignoto*, 69–80.

The Wrongs of Woman, 1843

Kestner, Joseph. "Charlotte Elizabeth Tonna's *The Wrongs of Woman*: Female Industrial Protest." *Tulsa Stud in Women's Lit* 2 (1983), 193–214.

ROBERT TRESSELL

The Ragged Trousered Philanthropists, 1914

Eagleton, Mary, and David Pierce. *Attitudes to Class*, 79–84.

Ingle, Stephen. *Socialist Thought*, 28–30.

Mitchell, Jack. "Early Harvest: Tree Anti-Capitalist Novels Published in 1914," in H. Gustav Klaus, ed., *The Socialist Novel*, 67–75.

Raby, Roger. "Propaganda où est ta victoire? Dialogue didactique manifeste et dialogues latents dans *The Ragged-Trousered Philanthropists* de Robert Tressell," in *Essais sur le dialogue*, 165–179.

Roskies, D. M. "Robert Tressell's Revolutionary Art." *Cahiers Victoriens et Edouardiens* 16 (1982), 51–68.

ANTHONY TROLLOPE

The American Senator, 1877

Hughes, Robert. "Trollope and Fox-Hunting." *Essays in Lit* (Macomb) 12 (1985), 81–82.

Wijesinha, Rajiva. *The Androgynous Trollope*, 112–116.

Ayala's Angel, 1881

Kendrick, Walter M. *The Novel-Machine*, 103–105.

Lansbury, Coral. *The Reasonable Man*, 182–189.

McMaster, Juliet. "Trollope's Country Estates," in John Halperin, ed., *Trollope Centenary Essays*, 75–76, 81–82.

Metz, Nancy Aycock. "*Ayala's Angel*: Trollope's Late Fable of Change and Choice." *Dickens Stud Annual* 9 (1981), 217–231.

Wright, Andrew. *Anthony Trollope*, 141–147.

Barchester Towers, 1857

Coustillas, P. "Anthony Trollope: *Barchester Towers*," in Coustillas et al., eds., *Le roman anglais*, 199–209.

Crawford, John W. " 'Victorian' Women in *Barchester Towers*," in his *Discourse*, 116–123.

Edwards, Owen Dudley. "Anthony Trollope, the Irish Writer." *Nineteenth-Century Fiction* 38 (1983), 12–14.

Emmerich, Janet. *Anthony Trollope*, 5–28.

Faulkner, Karen. "Anthony Trollope's Apprenticeship." *Nineteenth-Century Fiction* 38 (1983), 182–185.

Gilmour, Robin. *The Idea of the Gentleman*, 163–165.

Harvey, Geoffrey. *The Art*, 43–46, 48–50.

Higgins, Elizabeth Jean. *Reading the Novel*, 273–278.

Jacobs, Naomi. "Of Grace and Grease: Two Oily Clergymen." *Dickens Stud Newsl* 12 (1981), 47–48.

Langland, Elizabeth. "Society as Formal Protagonist: The Examples of *Nostromo* and *Barchester Towers*." *Crit Inquiry* 9 (1982), 359–378.

Lansbury, Coral. *The Reasonable Man*, 196–199.

Letwin, Shirley Robin. *The Gentleman*, 231–246.

Miller, D. A. "The Novel as Usual: Trollope's *Barchester Towers*," in Ruth Bernard Yeazell, ed., *Sex*, 1–37.

Polhemus, Robert M. *Comic Faith*, 166–203.

Polhemus, Robert M. "Trollope's Dialogue," in John Halperin, ed., *Trollope Centenary Essays*, 105–107.

Rataboul, Louis J. *Le pasteur anglican*, 344–345.

Sibley, Gay. "The Spectrum of 'Taste' in *Barchester Towers*." *Stud in the Novel* 17 (1985), 38–51.

Wiesenfarth, Joseph. "Dialectics in *Barchester Towers*," in Tony Bareham, ed., *Anthony Trollope*, 36–52.

Wright, Andrew. *Anthony Trollope*, 37–45.

The Belton Estate, 1866

Lansbury, Coral. *The Reasonable Man*, 107–109.

Letwin, Shirley Robin. *The Gentleman*, 107–112.

Wright, Andrew. "Trollope Revises Trollope," in John Halperin, ed., *Trollope Centenary Essays*, 120–121.

The Bertrams, 1859

Lansbury, Coral. *The Reasonable Man*, 53–55.

Wijesinha, Rajiva. *The Androgynous Trollope*, 321–323.

Can You Forgive Her?, 1864

Garrett, Peter K. *The Victorian Multiplot Novel*, 181–190.

Gilmour, Robin. *The Idea of the Gentleman*, 169–172.

Hendricks, Susan E. "Henry James as Adapter: *The Portrait of a Lady* and *Can You Forgive Her?*" *Rocky Mountain R of Lang and Lit* 38 (1984), 35–43.

Letwin, Shirley Robin. *The Gentleman*, 142–144.

Mason, Philip. *The English Gentleman*, 140–144.

Wijesinha, Rajiva. *The Androgynous Trollope*, 48–51, 184–186, 302–305.

Williams, Merryn. *Women in the English Novel*, 128–130.

Wright, Andrew. *Anthony Trollope*, 79–85.

Castle Richmond, 1860

Hynes, John G. "Anthony Trollope and the 'Irish Question': 1844–1882." *Etudes Irlandaises* 8 (1983), 216–222.

Tracy, Robert. " 'The Unnatural Ruin': Trollope and Nineteenth-Century Irish Fiction." *Nineteenth-Century Fiction* 37 (1982), 368–371.

The Claverings, 1867

Harvey, Geoffrey. *The Art*, 110–124.

McMaster, Juliet. "Trollope's Country Estates," 72–73.

Overton, Bill. *The Unofficial Trollope*, 157–164.

Wijesinha, Rajiva. *The Androgynous Trollope*, 173–175.

Wright, Andrew. *Anthony Trollope*, 128–135.

Cousin Henry, 1879

Lansbury, Coral. *The Reasonable Man*, 144–157.

Doctor Thorne, 1858

Edwards, Owen Dudley. "Anthony Trollope," 10, 30–33.
Gilmour, Robin. "A Lesser Thackeray? Trollope and the Victorian Novel," in Tony Bareham, ed., *Anthony Trollope*, 183–186.
Lansbury, Coral. *The Reasonable Man*, 199–203.
Letwin, Shirley Robin. *The Gentleman*, 123–127.
Overton, Bill. *The Unofficial Trollope*, 123–134.
Rataboul, Louis J. *Le pasteur anglican*, 345–346.
Wright, Andrew. *Anthony Trollope*, 45–53.

Dr. Wortle's School, 1881

Letwin, Shirley Robin. *The Gentleman*, 225–231.

The Duke's Children, 1880

Lansbury, Coral. *The Reasonable Man*, 222–224.
Letwin, Shirley Robin. *The Gentleman*, 86–91.
Overton, Bill. *The Unofficial Trollope*, 77–80.
Wijesinha, Rajiva. *The Androgynous Trollope*, 172–173.
Wright, Andrew. *Anthony Trollope*, 113–119.
Wright, Andrew. "Trollope Revises Trollope," 121–129.

The Eustace Diamonds, 1872

Halperin, John. "*The Eustace Diamonds* and Politics," in Tony Bareham, ed., *Anthony Trollope*, 138–158.
Hughes, Robert. "Trollope and Fox-Hunting," 79–81.
Hughes, Winifred. *The Maniac*, 168–171.
Irwin, Michael. *Picturing*, 16–21.
Kendrick, Walter M. "*The Eustace Diamonds*: The Truth of Trollope's Fiction." *ELH* 46 (1979), 136–156.
Letwin, Shirley Robin. *The Gentleman*, 96–105.
Naman, Anne Aresty. *The Jew*, 117–125.
Overton, Bill. *The Unofficial Trollope*, 164–177.
Stone, Donald D. *The Romantic Impulse*, 68–71.
Wijesinha, Rajiva. *The Androgynous Trollope*, 56–60, 102–106.
Wright, Andrew. *Anthony Trollope*, 92–99.

An Eye for an Eye, 1879

Harvey, Geoffrey. *The Art*, 83–88.
Watt, George. *The Fallen Woman*, 58–95.
White, Gertrude M. "Truth or Consequences: The Real World of Trollope's Melodrama." *Engl Stud* 64 (1983), 491–502.

The Fixed Period, 1882

Letwin, Shirley Robin. *The Gentleman*, 179–183.

Framley Parsonage, 1861

Harvey, Geoffrey. *The Art*, 10–13, 107–110.
Lansbury, Coral. *The Reasonable Man*, 203–207.
Overton, Bill. *The Unofficial Trollope*, 61–64.
Wijesinha, Rajiva. *The Androgynous Trollope*, 295–297, 332–334.
Wright, Andrew. *Anthony Trollope*, 53–60.

He Knew He Was Right, 1869

Garrett, Peter K. *The Victorian Multiplot Novel*, 203–216.
Gatrell, Simon. "Jealousy, Mastery, Love and Madness: A Brief Read-
ing of *He Knew He Was Right*," in Tony Bareham, ed., *Anthony
Trollope*, 95–115.
Herbert, Christopher. "*He Knew He Was Right*, Mrs. Lynn Linton, and
the Duplicities of Victorian Marriage." *Texas Stud in Lit and Lang* 25
(1983), 448–466.
Kendrick, Walter M. *The Novel-Machine*, 79–80, 110–140.
Letwin, Shirley Robin. *The Gentleman*, 166–172.
McMaster, Juliet and Rowland. *The Novel from Sterne to James*, 195–
212.
Nardin, Jane. "Tragedy, Farce, and Comedy in Trollope's *He Knew He
Was Right*." *Genre* 15 (1982), 303–313.
Overton, Bill. *The Unofficial Trollope*, 91–94.
Riffaterre, Michael. "Trollope's Metonymies." *Nineteenth-Century Fic-
tion* 37 (1982), 285–288.
Stone, Donald D. *The Romantic Impulse*, 66–68.
Wijesinha, Rajiva. *The Androgynous Trollope*, 119–120, 315–319.
Wright, Andrew. *Anthony Trollope*, 135–141.

Is He Popenjoy?, 1878

Letwin, Shirley Robin. *The Gentleman*, 253–257.
McMaster, Juliet. "Trollope's Country Estates," 77–78.
Wijesinha, Rajiva. *The Androgynous Trollope*, 51–53, 311–313.

John Caldigate, 1879

Letwin, Shirley Robin. *The Gentleman*, 113–115, 216–219.

The Kellys and the O'Kellys, 1848

Cronin, John. "Trollope and the Matter of Ireland," in Tony Bareham,
ed., *Anthony Trollope*, 26–28.
Edwards, Owen Dudley. "Anthony Trollope," 10–12, 29–30.
Faulkner, Karen. "Anthony Trollope's Apprenticeship," 168–174.
Overton, Bill. *The Unofficial Trollope*, 19–22.
Tracy, Robert. " 'The Unnatural Ruin'," 367–368.

Lady Anna, 1874

Harvey, Geoffrey. *The Art*, 29–32.
Letwin, Shirley Robin. *The Gentleman*, 123–125.
Wijesinha, Rajiva. *The Androgynous Trollope*, 52–56.

The Landleaguers, 1883

Cronin, John. "Trollope and the Matter of Ireland," 31–34.
Hynes, John G. "Anthony Trollope and the 'Irish Question'," 224–226.
Tracy, Robert. "Instant Replay: Trollope's *The Landleaguers*." *Eire-Ireland* 15:2 (1980), 30–46.
Tracy, Robert. " 'The Unnatural Ruin'," 372–375.

The Last Chronicle of Barset, 1867

Allen, Walter. "The Last Chronicle of Barset," in Tony Bareham, ed., *Anthony Trollope*, 81–94.
Emmerich, Janet. *Anthony Trollope*, 6–28, 41–52.
Garrett, Peter K. *The Victorian Multiplot Novel*, 190–203.
Gilead, Sarah. "Trollope's Orphans and the 'Power of Adequate Performance'." *Texas Stud in Lit and Lang* 27 (1985), 100–103.
Gilmour, Robin. *The Idea of the Gentleman*, 167–169.
Harvey, Geoffrey. *The Art*, 54–73.
King, Margaret F. "The Place of Lucius Mason in Trollope's Studies of Perversity." *South Atlantic Bull* 45:4 (1980), 43–44.
Lansbury, Coral. *The Reasonable Man*, 80–81, 207–211.
Overton, Bill. *The Unofficial Trollope*, 95–99, 109–120.
Polhemus, Robert M. "Trollope's Dialogue," 104–105.
Wijesinha, Rajiva. *The Androgynous Trollope*, 296–299, 329–332.
Wright, Andrew. *Anthony Trollope*, 70–77.

Linda Tressel, 1868

Wijesinha, Rajiva. *The Androgynous Trollope*, 60–62.

The Macdermotts of Ballycloran, 1847

Cronin, John. "Trollope and the Matter of Ireland," 14–24.
Faulkner, Karen. "Anthony Trollope's Apprenticeship," 163–168.
Johnston, Conor. "*The Macdermotts of Ballycloran*: Trollope as Conservative-Liberal." *Eire-Ireland* 16:2 (1981), 71–92.
Lansbury, Coral. *The Reasonable Man*, 112–130.
Overton, Bill. *The Unofficial Trollope*, 17–19.
Tracy, Robert. " 'The Unnatural Ruin'," 365–367, 378–379.
Wijesinha, Rajiva. *The Androgynous Trollope*, 162–165.

Miss Mackenzie, 1865

Harvey, Geoffrey. *The Art*, 24–26.
Riffaterre, Michael. "Trollope's Metonymies," 284.
Wijesinha, Rajiva. *The Androgynous Trollope*, 123–125.

Mr. Scarborough's Family, 1883

Gilmour, Robin. *The Idea of the Gentleman*, 179–181.
Harvey, Geoffrey. "A Parable of Justice: Drama and Rhetoric in *Mr. Scarborough's Family*." *Nineteenth-Century Fiction* 37 (1982), 419–429.
Hughes, Robert. "Trollope and Fox-Hunting," 78–79.

Lansbury, Coral. *The Reasonable Man*, 173–183.

Letwin, Shirley Robin. *The Gentleman*, 91–95.

McMaster, R. D. "Trollope and the Terrible Meshes of the Law: *Mr. Scarborough's Family*." *Nineteenth-Century Fiction* 36 (1981), 135–156.

Overton, Bill. *The Unofficial Trollope*, 177–193.

Wright, Andrew. *Anthony Trollope*, 147–154.

Wright, Andrew. "Trollope Revises Trollope," 129–132.

Nina Balatka, 1867

Harvey, Geoffrey. *The Art*, 74–83.

Naman, Anne Aresty. *The Jew*, 99–105.

Stern, Sheila. "The Spirit of the Place," in J. P. Stern, ed., *The World of Franz Kafka*, 44–46.

An Old Man's Love, 1884

Tracy, Robert. "*Lana Medicata Fuco*: Trollope's Classicism," in John Halperin, ed., *Trollope Centenary Essays*, 18–20.

Orley Farm, 1862

Gilead, Sarah. "Trollope's Orphans," 96–99.

Hapke, Laura. "The Lady as Criminal: Contradiction and Resolution in Trollope's *Orley Farm*." *Victorian Newsl* 66 (1984), 18–21.

Harvey, Geoffrey. *The Art*, 40–42, 90–107.

King, Margaret F. "The Place of Lucius Mason," 44–53.

Lansbury, Coral. *The Reasonable Man*, 156–171.

Overton, Bill. *The Unofficial Trollope*, 69–77, 134–151.

Wijesinha, Rajiva. *The Androgynous Trollope*, 100–102, 334–337.

Wright, Andrew. *Anthony Trollope*, 121–128.

Wright, Andrew. "Trollope Revises Trollope," 115–118.

Phineas Finn, 1869

Edwards, Owen Dudley. "Anthony Trollope," 15–27.

Lansbury, Coral. *The Reasonable Man*, 216–218.

Letwin, Shirley Robin. *The Gentleman*, 74–81, 144–154, 207–215.

Naman, Anne Aresty. *The Jew*, 106–116.

Polhemus, Robert M. "Being in Love in *Phineas Finn/Phineas Redux*: Desire, Devotion, Consolation." *Nineteenth-Century Fiction* 37 (1982), 383–395.

Polhemus, Robert M. "Trollope's Dialogue," 98–103.

Wijesinha, Rajiva. *The Androgynous Trollope*, 165–172, 319–321.

Wright, Andrew. *Anthony Trollope*, 85–92.

Phineas Redux, 1874

Edwards, Owen Dudley. "Anthony Trollope," 16–27.

Hughes, Robert. "Trollope and Fox-Hunting," 82–84.

Letwin, Shirley Robin. *The Gentleman*, 148–154, 187–203.

Naman, Anne Aresty. *The Jew*, 116–117, 125–128.

Overton, Bill. *The Unofficial Trollope*, 97–99.
Polhemus, Robert M. "Being in Love," 383–395.
Polhemus, Robert M. "Trollope's Dialogue," 96–98.
Wijesinha, Rajiva. *The Androgynous Trollope*, 165–172.
Wright, Andrew. *Anthony Trollope*, 99–105.

The Prime Minister, 1876

Gilmour, Robin. *The Idea of the Gentleman*, 172–178.
Harvey, Geoffrey. *The Art*, 33–37, 143–160.
Lansbury, Coral. *The Reasonable Man*, 219–222.
Letwin, Shirley Robin. *The Gentleman*, 81–85, 203–207, 211–215, 248–252, 265–269.
Naman, Anne Aresty. *The Jew*, 148–159.
Reed, John R. "A Friend to Mammon: Speculation in Victorian Literature." *Victorian Stud* 27 (1984), 189–190.
Wijesinha, Rajiva. *The Androgynous Trollope*, 304–310, 323–326.
Wright, Andrew. *Anthony Trollope*, 106–112.

Rachel Ray, 1863

Letwin, Shirley Robin. *The Gentleman*, 116–118, 216–218.
Riffaterre, Michael. "Trollope's Metonymies," 275–276, 280–283.

Ralph the Heir, 1871

Harvey, Geoffrey. *The Art*, 26–29.
Letwin, Shirley Robin. *The Gentleman*, 183–187.
Riffaterre, Michael. "Trollope's Metonymies," 279–280.
Wijesinha, Rajiva. *The Androgynous Trollope*, 66–69.

Sir Harry Hotspur, 1870

Gilmour, Robin. *The Idea of the Gentleman*, 160–163.
Halperin, John. "Trollope, Jones, and 'The Retribution of Time'." *Southern Hum R* 19 (1985), 301–308.
Pearson, David. " 'The Letter Killeth': Epistolary Purposes and Techniques in *Sir Harry Hotspur of Humblethwaite*." *Nineteenth-Century Fiction* 37 (1982), 396–418.

The Small House at Allington, 1864

Emmerich, Janet. *Anthony Trollope*, 29–41.
Gilead, Sarah. "Trollope's *The Small House at Allington*." *Explicator* 42:2 (1984), 12–14.
Gilead, Sarah. "Trollope's Orphans," 100–103.
Gilmour, Robin. *The Idea of the Gentleman*, 165–167.
Lansbury, Coral. *The Reasonable Man*, 86–88.
Riffaterre, Michael. "Trollope's Metonymies," 274–275.
Wijesinha, Rajiva. *The Androgynous Trollope*, 107–109, 326–328.
Wright, Andrew. *Anthony Trollope*, 60–70.
Wright, Andrew. "Trollope Revises Trollope," 119.

The Three Clerks, 1858

> Bareham, Tony. "Patterns of Excellence: Theme and Structure in *The Three Clerks*," in Bareham, ed., *Anthony Trollope*, 54–80.
> Faulkner, Karen. "Anthony Trollope's Apprenticeship," 186–188.
> Harvey, Geoffrey. *The Art*, 19–24.
> Wijesinha, Rajiva. *The Androgynous Trollope*, 293–295.

La Vendée, 1850

> Faulkner, Karen. "Anthony Trollope's Apprenticeship," 175–177.

The Vicar of Bullhampton, 1870

> Letwin, Shirley Robin. *The Gentleman*, 219–225.
> Mitchell, Sally. *The Fallen Angel*, 124–126.
> Watt, George. *The Fallen Woman*, 42–58.
> Wijesinha, Rajiva. *The Androgynous Trollope*, 121–123.

The Warden, 1855

> Edwards, Owen Dudley. "Anthony Trollope," 38–40.
> Faulkner, Karen. "Anthony Trollope's Apprenticeship," 177–182.
> Gilead, Sarah. "Trollope's Orphans," 92–96.
> Lansbury, Coral. *The Reasonable Man*, 128–143.
> McEwan, Neil. *The Survival of the Novel*, 155–157.
> Meckier, Jerome. "The Cant of Reform: Trollope Rewrites Dickens in *The Warden*." *Stud in the Novel* 15 (1983), 202–222.
> Murfin, Ross C. "The Gap in Trollope's Fiction: *The Warden* as Example." *Stud in the Novel* 14 (1982), 17–29.
> Overton, Bill. *The Unofficial Trollope*, 26–46.
> Riffaterre, Michael. "Trollope's Metonymies," 288–292.
> Saldivar, Ramon. "Trollope's *The Warden* and the Fiction of Realism." *J of Narrative Technique* 11 (1981), 166–179.
> Wheeler, Michael. *English Fiction*, 112–114.
> Wright, Andrew. *Anthony Trollope*, 29–37.
> Wright, Andrew. "Trollope Transformed, or The Disguises of Mr Harding and Others," in James R. Kincaid and Albert J. Kuhn, eds., *Victorian Literature*, 317–330.

The Way We Live Now, 1875

> Coates, J. D. "Moral Patterns in *The Way We Live Now*." *Durham Univ J* 71 (1978), 55–65.
> Gilmour, Robin. *The Idea of the Gentleman*, 157–158, 173–176.
> Gilmour, Robin. "A Lesser Thackeray?", 187–202.
> Harvey, Geoffrey. *The Art*, 125–144.
> Letwin, Shirley Robin. *The Gentleman*, 258–265.
> McMaster, R. D. "Women in *The Way We Live Now*." *Engl Stud in Canada* 7 (1981), 68–80.
> Nadel, Ira Bruce. "From Fathers and Sons to Sons and Lovers." *Dalhousie R* 59 (1979), 230–232.

Naman, Anne Aresty. *The Jew*, 128–148.
Panitz, Esther L. *The Alien*, 119–121.
Reed, John R. "A Friend to Mammon," 188–189.
Sutherland, John A. "Trollope at Work on *The Way We Live Now*."
   Nineteenth-Century Fiction 37 (1982), 472–493.
Wheeler, Michael. *English Fiction*, 117–119.
Wijesinha, Rajiva. *The Androgynous Trollope*, 62–66, 109–112, 175–177.
Williams, Merryn. *Women in the English Novel*, 130–132.

FRANCES TROLLOPE

The Abbess, 1833
   Heineman, Helen. *Mrs. Trollope*, 107–109.

The Barnabys in America, 1843
   Heineman, Helen. *Mrs. Trollope*, 161–165.

The Blue Belles of England, 1842
   Heineman, Helen. *Frances Trollope*, 106–108.
   Heineman, Helen. *Mrs. Trollope*, 198–203.

Charles Chesterfield, 1841
   Heineman, Helen. *Frances Trollope*, 101–106.
   Heineman, Helen. *Mrs. Trollope*, 198–203.

Fashionable Life, 1856
   Heineman, Helen. *Frances Trollope*, 130–133.

Jessie Phillips, 1843
   Heineman, Helen. *Frances Trollope*, 76–81.
   Heineman, Helen. *Mrs. Trollope*, 211–219.
   Kestner, Joseph. *Protest and Reform*, 104–109.
   Mitchell, Sally. *The Fallen Angel*, 23–25.

Jonathan Jefferson Whitlaw, 1836
   Heineman, Helen. *Frances Trollope*, 59–63.
   Heineman, Helen. *Mrs. Trollope*, 143–150.

The Laurringtons, 1844
   Heineman, Helen. *Frances Trollope*, 110–112.

The Life and Adventures of a Clever Woman, 1854
   Heineman, Helen. *Mrs. Trollope*, 246–248.

The Lottery of Marriage, 1849
   Heineman, Helen. *Frances Trollope*, 115–117.

Michael Armstrong, 1840
   Bergmann, Helena. *Between Obedience and Freedom*, 24–26, 67–70,
   78–79.

Heineman, Helen. *Frances Trollope*, 65–76.
Heineman, Helen. *Mrs. Trollope*, 169–186.
Kestner, Joseph. "Men in Female Condition of England Novels."
  Women & Lit 2 (1981), 78–83.
Kestner, Joseph. *Protest and Reform*, 51–58.
Tarantelli, Carole Beebe. *Ritratto di ignoto*, 81–94.

Mrs. Mathews, 1851

Heineman, Helen. *Frances Trollope*, 124–126.

One Fault, 1840

Heineman, Helen. *Frances Trollope*, 85–87.
Heineman, Helen. *Mrs. Trollope*, 188–192.

The Refugee in America, 1832

Heineman, Helen. *Frances Trollope*, 39–43.
Heineman, Helen. *Mrs. Trollope*, 102–106.

The Three Cousins, 1847

Heineman, Helen. *Mrs. Trollope*, 222–224.

Tremordyn Cliff, 1835

Heineman, Helen. *Frances Trollope*, 83–85.

Uncle Walter, 1852

Heineman, Helen. *Mrs. Trollope*, 242–246.

The Vicar of Wrexhill, 1837

Heineman, Helen. *Frances Trollope*, 63–65.
Heineman, Helen. *Mrs. Trollope*, 150–153.
Rataboul, Louis J. *Le pasteur anglican*, 178–185.

The Widow Barnaby, 1839

Heineman, Helen. *Frances Trollope*, 88–91.
Heineman, Helen. *Mrs. Trollope*, 156–168.

The Widow Married, 1840

Heineman, Helen. *Frances Trollope*, 91–93.

HORACE ANNESLEY VACHELL

The Hill, 1905

Quigly, Isabel. *The Heirs of Tom Brown*, 136–142.

JOHN WAIN

The Contenders, 1958

Salwak, Dale. *John Wain*, 48–53.

Hurry on Down, 1953

> Douglass, Wayne J., and Robert G. Walker. " 'A Moralist Perchance Appears': John Wain's *Hurry on Down*." *Renascence* 31 (1978), 43–50.
> Salwak, Dale. *John Wain*, 33–42.

Living in the Present, 1955

> Salwak, Dale. *John Wain*, 43–47.

The Pardoner's Tale, 1978

> Salwak, Dale. *John Wain*, 95–106.

The Smaller Sky, 1967

> Salwak, Dale. *John Wain*, 78–83.

Strike the Father Dead, 1962

> Salwak, Dale. *John Wain*, 59–70.

A Travelling Woman, 1959

> Salwak, Dale. *John Wain*, 53–57.

A Winter in the Hills, 1970

> Salwak, Dale. *John Wain*, 85–94.

The Young Visitors, 1965

> Salwak, Dale. *John Wain*, 71–78.

HORACE WALPOLE

The Castle of Otranto, 1765

> Anderson, Howard. "Gothic Heroes," in Robert Folkenflik, ed., *The English Hero*, 207–209.
> Coleman, William Emmet. *On the Discrimination*, 54–56, 60–62, 65–68, 99–104.
> Conger, Syndy McMillen. "Faith and Doubt in *The Castle of Otranto*." *Gothic* 1 (1979), 51–58.
> Ehlers, Leigh A. "The Gothic World as Stage: Providence and Character in *The Castle of Otranto*." *Wascana R* 14:2 (1979), 17–30.
> Gordon, Jan B. "Narrative Enclosure as Textual Ruin: An Archaeology of Gothic Consciousness." *Dickens Stud Annual* 11 (1983), 221–222.
> Harfst, Betsy Perteit. *Horace Walpole*, 22–107.
> Hennessy, Brendan. *The Gothic Novel*, 9–14.
> Le Tellier, Robert Ignatius. *An Intensifying Vision*, 6–7, 16–17, 39–40, 50–51, 78, 83–84, 88–89, 119–121, 149–150.
> Lévy, Maurice. "Lecture plurielle du *Chateau d'Otrante*," in *La Mort*, 149–153.
> Lewis, Paul. "Mysterious Laughter: Humor and Fear in Gothic Fiction." *Genre* 14 (1981), 313–315.

MacAndrew, Elizabeth. *The Gothic Tradition*, 9–18, 84–86, 119–121.
Palmer, Jerry. *Thrillers*, 122–125.
Punter, David. *The Literature of Terror*, 49–53.
Reddin, Chitra Pershad. *Forms of Evil*, 53–54, 116, 188–189, 193–194.
Sandy, Stephen. *The Raveling*, 21–42.
Van Luchene, Stephen Robert. *Essays in Gothic Fiction*, 4–41.
Weiss, Fredric. *The Antic Spectre*, 51–83.
Wilt, Judith. *Ghosts of the Gothic*, 25–31.

HUGH WALPOLE

Maradick at Forty, 1910

Hunter, Jefferson. *Edwardian Fiction*, 180–182.

Mr. Perrin and Mr. Traill, 1911

Quigly, Isabel. *The Heirs of Tom Brown*, 174–185.

MRS. HUMPHRY WARD

Canadian Born, 1910

Smith, Esther Marian Greenwell. *Mrs. Humphry Ward*, 99–101.

The Case of Richard Meynell, 1911

Smith, Esther Marian Greenwell. *Mrs. Humphry Ward*, 53–55.

The Coryston Family, 1913

Smith, Esther Marian Greenwell. *Mrs. Humphry Ward*, 104–108.

Cousin Philip, 1919

Smith, Esther Marian Greenwell. *Mrs. Humphry Ward*, 127–131.

Daphne, 1909

Smith, Esther Marian Greenwell. *Mrs. Humphry Ward*, 72–76.

David Grieve, 1892

Collister, Peter. "The Heritage of George Sand: Mrs Humphry Ward's
The History of David Grieve." *R of Engl Stud* 36 (1985), 501–521.
Collister, Peter. "Marie Bashkirtseff in Fiction: Edmond de Goncourt
and Mrs. Humphry Ward." *Mod Philology* 82 (1984), 58–67.
Smith, Esther Marian Greenwell. *Mrs. Humphry Ward*, 43–48, 62–64.

Delia Blanchflower, 1914

Smith, Esther Marian Greenwell. *Mrs. Humphry Ward*, 76–78.

Eleanor, 1900

Collister, Peter. "Mrs Humphry Ward's *Eleanor*: A Late Victorian
Portrait of Chateaubriand and Pauline de Beaumont." *Neophilologus*
65 (1981), 622–638.
Smith, Esther Marian Greenwell. *Mrs. Humphry Ward*, 82–88.

Eltham House, 1915

Smith, Esther Marian Greenwell. *Mrs. Humphry Ward*, 107–108.

Fenwick's Career, 1906

Smith, Esther Marian Greenwell. *Mrs. Humphry Ward*, 94–97.

Harvest, 1920

Smith, Esther Marian Greenwell. *Mrs. Humphry Ward*, 131–137.

Helbeck of Bannisdale, 1898

Smith, Esther Marian Greenwell. *Mrs. Humphry Ward*, 48–53.

Lady Connie, 1916

Smith, Esther Marian Greenwell. *Mrs. Humphry Ward*, 110–113.

Lady Rose's Daughter, 1903

Roberts, Helen. "Propaganda and Ideology in Women's Fiction," in Diana Laurenson, ed., *The Sociology*, 166–167.
Smith, Esther Marian Greenwell. *Mrs. Humphry Ward*, 88–90.

Marcella, 1894

Collister, Peter. "Portraits of 'Audacious Youth': George Eliot and Mrs Humphry Ward." *Engl Stud* 64 (1983), 296–311.
Smith, Esther Marian Greenwell. *Mrs. Humphry Ward*, 56–64.

The Marriage of William Ashe, 1905

Smith, Esther Marian Greenwell. *Mrs. Humphry Ward*, 90–94.

The Mating of Lydia, 1913

Smith, Esther Marian Greenwell. *Mrs. Humphry Ward*, 101–104.

Miss Bretherton, 1884

Smith, Esther Marian Greenwell. *Mrs. Humphry Ward*, 79–82.

Missing, 1917

Rives, Françoise. "Une romancière victorienne face à la Grande Guerre: Mrs Humphry Ward de 1914 à 1918." *Caliban* 19 (1982), 63–65.

Robert Elsmere, 1888

Collister, Peter. "Marie Bashkirtseff," 59–60.
Culp, Mildred L. "Literary Dimensions of *Robert Elsmere*: Idea, Character, and Form." *Intl Fiction R* 9 (1982), 35–40.
Rataboul, Louis J. *Le pasteur anglican*, 243–244, 409–432.
Smith, Esther Marian Greenwell. *Mrs. Humphry Ward*, 33–43.

Sir George Tressady, 1896

Collister, Peter. "Portraits of 'Audacious Youth'," 311–317.
Smith, Esther Marian Greenwell. *Mrs. Humphry Ward*, 65–69.

The Story of Bessie Costrell, 1895

Smith, Esther Marian Greenwell. *Mrs. Humphry Ward*, 69–72.

The Testing of Diana Mallory, 1908

    Smith, Esther Marian Greenwell. *Mrs. Humphry Ward*, 97–99.

The War and Elizabeth, 1918

    Rives, Françoise. "Une romancière victorienne," 63–65.

    Smith, Esther Marian Greenwell. *Mrs. Humphry Ward*, 123–127.

ROBERT WARD

Tremaine, or the Man of Refinement, 1825

    Hart, Francis Russell. "The Regency Novel of Fashion," in Samuel I.
Mintz et al., eds., *From Smollett to James*, 121–123.

REX WARNER

The Aerodrome, 1941

    Johnstone, Richard. *The Will to Believe*, 55–58.

The Wild Goose Chase, 1937

    Johnstone, Richard. *The Will to Believe*, 47–55.

SYLVIA TOWNSEND WARNER

Lolly Willowes, 1926

    Marcus, Jane. "A Wilderness of One's Own: Feminist Fantasy Novels
of the Twenties—Rebecca West and Sylvia Townsend Warner," in
Susan Merrill Squier, ed., *Women Writers*, 136–141, 148–157.

Mr. Fortune's Maggot, 1927

    Binding, Paul. "Sylvia Townsend Warner and *Mr. Fortune's Maggot*."
PN R 8:3 (1981), 51–52.

KEITH WATERHOUSE

Billy Liar, 1959

    Nash, Walter. *The Language of Humour*, 79–82.

    Paul, Ronald. *"Fire in Our Hearts,"* 59–62.

IAN WATSON

The Embedding, 1973

    Hunt, Robert. "Visionary States and the Search for Transcendence in
Science Fiction," in George E. Slusser et al., eds., *Bridges*, 66–69.

    Meyers, Walter E. *Aliens and Linguists*, 185–191.

ALEC WAUGH

The Loom of Youth, 1917

Musgrave, P. W. *From Brown to Bunter*, 181–194.

EVELYN WAUGH

Black Mischief, 1932

Kaplan, Stanley R. "Circularity and Futility in *Black Mischief.*" *Evelyn Waugh Newsl* 15:3 (1981), 1–4.

Lane, Calvin W. *Evelyn Waugh*, 62–70.

Littlewood, Ian. *The Writings*, 38–41, 44–45.

Montgomery, Robert L. "The Case of *Black Mischief*: Evelyn Waugh vs. *The Tablet.*" *Lib Chron of the Univ of Texas* 16 (1981), 42–61.

Brideshead Revisited, 1945

Brailow, David G. " 'My Theme is Memory': The Narrative Structure of *Brideshead Revisited.*" *Evelyn Waugh Newsl* 14:3 (1980), 1–4.

Davis, Robert Murray. "*Brideshead Revisited* and *All the King's Men*: Towards a Definition of Forties Sensibility." *Evelyn Waugh Newsl* 14:2 (1980), 1–4.

Green, Martin. *The English Novel*, 123–126.

Greene, Donald. "Peerage Nomenclature in *Brideshead Revisited.*" *Evelyn Waugh Newsl* 16:2 (1982), 5–6.

Heck, Francis S. "The Domain as a Symbol of a Paradise Lost: *Lost Horizon* and *Brideshead Revisited.*" *Nassau R* 4:3 (1982), 24–29.

Johnstone, Richard. *The Will to Believe*, 92–95.

Lane, Calvin W. *Evelyn Waugh*, 91–102.

Littlewood, Ian. *The Writings*, 114–116, 131–137, 190–192.

O'Hare, Colman. "The Sacred and Profane Memories of Evelyn Waugh's Men at War." *Papers on Lang & Lit* 20 (1984), 301–311.

Powell, Roberts. "Uncritical Perspective: Belief and Art in *Brideshead Revisited.*" *Crit Q* 22:3 (1980), 53–67.

Rauchbauer, Otto. "The Presentation and Function of Space in Evelyn Waugh's *Brideshead Revisited,*" in Siegfried Korninger, ed., *A Yearbook*, 61–76.

Walker, Julia M. "Being and Becoming: A Comment on Religion in *Vile Bodies* and *Brideshead Revisited.*" *Evelyn Waugh Newsl* 16:2 (1982), 4–5.

Crazy Pavements, 1927

Davis, Robert Murray. "A Dim Novel about Bright Young People." *Evelyn Waugh Newsl* 15:1 (1981), 4–5.

Decline and Fall, 1928

Anand, Shahla. *Choice Ruminations*, 135–140.

Crawford, Fred D. *Mixing Memory*, 50–52.

Heath, Jeffrey. "Intellect, Appetite, and Example in the Novels of Evelyn Waugh." *Engl Stud in Canada* 11 (1985), 53–67.

Johnstone, Richard. *The Will to Believe*, 85–89.

Lane, Calvin W. *Evelyn Waugh*, 45–53.

Littlewood, Ian. *The Writings*, 185–187.

A Handful of Dust, 1934

Crawford, Fred D. *Mixing Memory*, 53–56.

Johnstone, Richard. *The Will to Believe*, 88–92.

Kolek, Lezek. " 'Uncinematic Devices' in Evelyn Waugh's *A Handful of Dust*." *Literatur in Wissenschaft und Unterricht* 15 (1982), 353–365.

Lane, Calvin W. *Evelyn Waugh*, 70–77.

Littlewood, Ian. *The Writings*, 94–98, 146–148.

Meckier, Jerome. "Why the Man Who Liked Dickens Read Dickens Instead of Conrad: Waugh's *A Handful of Dust*." *Novel* 13 (1980), 171–187.

Slater, Ann Pasternak. "Waugh's *A Handful of Dust*: Right Things in Wrong Places." *Essays in Criticism* 32 (1982), 48–66.

Helena, 1950

Lane, Calvin W. *Evelyn Waugh*, 107–110.

Littlewood, Ian. *The Writings*, 155–157.

Love Among the Ruins, 1953

Miles, Peter. "Improving Culture: The Politics of Illustration in Evelyn Waugh's *Love among the Ruins*." *Trivium* 18 (1983), 7–38.

The Loved One, 1948

Barnard, Robert. "What the Whispering Glades Whispered: Dennis Barlow's Quest in *The Loved One*." *Engl Stud* 60 (1979), 176–182.

Doyle, Paul A. "That Poem in *The Loved One*." *Evelyn Waugh Newsl* 15:3 (1981), 6–7.

Lane, Calvin W. *Evelyn Waugh*, 103–107.

Lepage, John Louis. "Waugh's *The Loved One*." *Explicator* 42:3 (1984), 51–52.

Littlewood, Ian. *The Writings*, 56–59.

Lynch, James J. "*The Loved One* and the *Art Guide to Forest Lawn*." *Evelyn Waugh Newsl* 17:3 (1983), 1–5.

McCaffrey, Donald W. "*The Loved One*: An Irreverant, Invective, Dark Film Comedy." *Lit/Film Q* 11 (1983), 83–87.

Men at Arms, 1952

Green, Martin. *The English Novel*, 127–129.

Littlewood, Ian. *The Writings*, 59–62, 99–101.

Officers and Gentlemen, 1955

Littlewood, Ian. *The Writings*, 29–32, 193–195.

The Ordeal of Gilbert Pinfold, 1957

Hurst, Mary Jane, and Daniel Hurst. "Bromide Poisoning in *The Ordeal of Gilbert Pinfold*." *Evelyn Waugh Newsl* 16:2 (1982), 1–4.
Lane, Calvin W. *Evelyn Waugh*, 111–117.
Littlewood, Ian. *The Writings*, 219–230.

Put Out More Flags, 1942

Gorra, Michael. "Waugh in Transition: *Put Out More Flags*." *Evelyn Waugh Newsl* 14:3 (1980), 6–8.
Hopley, Claire. "The Significance of Exhilaration and Silence in *Put Out More Flags*." *Mod Fiction Stud* 30 (1984), 84–97.
Lane, Calvin W. *Evelyn Waugh*, 82–88.
Littlewood, Ian. *The Writings*, 27–29.

Scoop, 1938

Lane, Calvin W. *Evelyn Waugh*, 77–82.

Sword of Honour, 1965

Crawford, Fred D. *Mixing Memory*, 58–63.
Gribble, Thomas A. "The Nature of a Trimmer." *Evelyn Waugh Newsl* 15:2 (1981), 1–3.
Lane, Calvin W. *Evelyn Waugh*, 118–142.
Nemoianu, Virgil. "Evelyn Waugh and the Motley Society." *CLIO* 12 (1983), 233–242.
O'Hare, Colman. "The Sacred and Profane Memories," 301–311.

Unconditional Surrender, 1961

Crawford, Fred D. *Mixing Memory*, 59–62.
Davis, Robert Murray. "Evelyn Waugh and the Sword of Stalingrad." *Evelyn Waugh Newsl* 15:2 (1981), 3–4.
Littlewood, Ian. *The Writings*, 62–63, 102–104.

Vile Bodies, 1930

Johnstone, Richard. *The Will to Believe*, 87–89.
Lane, Calvin W. *Evelyn Waugh*, 53–62.
Littlewood, Ian. *The Writings*, 11–23, 187–189.
Stovel, Nora Foster. "The Aerial View of Modern Britain: The Airplane as a Vehicle for Idealism and Satire." *Ariel* 15:3 (1984), 28–29.
Walker, Julia M. "Being and Becoming," 4–5.

FAY WELDON

Female Friends, 1974

Crosland, Margaret. *Beyond the Lighthouse*, 204–207.

Praxis, 1978

Crosland, Margaret. *Beyond the Lighthouse*, 208–209.

Remember Me, 1976

Crosland, Margaret. *Beyond the Lighthouse*, 206–208.

H. G. WELLS

Ann Veronica, 1909

> Batchelor, John. *H. G. Wells*, 80–88.
> Beauman, Nicola. *A Very Great Profession*, 66–69.
> Costa, Richard Hauer. *H. G. Wells*, 69–72.
> Hammond, J. R. *An H. G. Wells Companion*, 153–157.
> Lamarca Margalef, Jordi. *Ciencia y literatura*, 178–180.
> Norton, David. "Lawrence, Wells and Bennett: Influence and Tradition." *AUMLA* 54 (1980), 181–184.
> Stubbs, Patricia. *Women and Fiction*, 183–184.

Apropos of Dolores, 1938

> Hammond, J. R. *An H. G. Wells Companion*, 214–217.
> Reed, John R. *The Natural History*, 80–82.

Babes in the Darkling Wood, 1940

> Costa, Richard Hauer. *H. G. Wells*, 126–128.
> Hammond, J. R. *An H. G. Wells Companion*, 219–222.

Bealby, 1915

> Hammond, J. R. *An H. G. Wells Companion*, 171–173.

Boon, 1915

> Batchelor, John. *H. G. Wells*, 113–122.
> Costa, Richard Hauer. *H. G. Wells*, 84–85.
> Hammond, J. R. *An H. G. Wells Companion*, 176–180.

Brynhild, 1937

> Batchelor, John. *H. G. Wells*, 153–154.
> Hammond, J. R. *An H. G. Wells Companion*, 209–212.
> Scheick, William J. "Schopenhauer, Maori Symbolism, and Wells's *Brynhild*." *Stud in the Liter Imagination* 13:1 (1980), 17–29.

The Bulpington of Blup, 1932

> Batchelor, John. *H. G. Wells*, 145–153.
> Hammond, J. R. *An H. G. Wells Companion*, 207–209.

The Camford Visitation, 1937

> Batchelor, John. *H. G. Wells*, 142–143.
> Scheick, William J. "Exorcising the Ghost Story: Wells's *The Croquet Player* and *The Camford Visitation*." *Cahiers Victoriens et Edouardiens* 17 (1983), 59–61.

Christina Alberta's Father, 1925

> Batchelor, John. *H. G. Wells*, 134–135.
> Hammond, J. R. *An H. G. Wells Companion*, 196–198.

The Croquet Player, 1936

> Batchelor, John. *H. G. Wells*, 143–145.
> Scheick, William J. "Exorcising the Ghost Story," 54–59.

The Dream, 1924

> Batchelor, John. *H. G. Wells*, 138–140.
> Hammond, J. R. *An H. G. Wells Companion*, 193–196.

The First Men in the Moon, 1901

> Batchelor, John. *H. G. Wells*, 52–58.
> Costa, Richard Hauer. *H. G. Wells*, 24–28.
> Hammond, J. R. *An H. G. Wells Companion*, 96–99.
> Henighan, Tom. *Natural Space*, 162–173.
> Hunter, Jefferson. *Edwardian Fiction*, 117–120.
> Huntington, John. *The Logic of Fantasy*, 87–97.
> Huntington, John. "The Science Fiction of H. G. Wells," in Patrick Parrinder, ed., *Science Fiction*, 45–47.
> Morton, Peter. *The Vital Science*, 133–135.
> Pagetti, Carlo. "H. G. Wells: *The First Men in the Moon*," in Agostino Lombardo, ed., *Studi inglesi*, 189–210.
> Simmons, Harvey G. "H. G. Wells as Futurologist." *Engl Stud in Canada* 6 (1980), 220–221.

The Food of the Gods, 1904

> Batchelor, John. *H. G. Wells*, 66–68.
> Hammond, J. R. *An H. G. Wells Companion*, 102–104.
> Huntington, John. *The Logic of Fantasy*, 129–132.
> Simmons, Harvey G. "H. G. Wells as Futurologist," 223.

The History of Mr. Polly, 1910

> Batchelor, John. *The Edwardian Novelists*, 137–142.
> Batchelor, John. *H. G. Wells*, 86–93.
> Carthew, John. "Adapting to Trinidad: Mr Biswas and Mr Polly Revisited." *J of Commonwealth Lit* 13:1 (1978), 58–64.
> Costa, Richard Hauer. *H. G. Wells*, 46–47.
> Eagleton, Mary, and David Pierce. *Attitudes to Class*, 76–78.
> Hammond, J. R. *An H. G. Wells Companion*, 157–159.

The Holy Terror, 1939

> Batchelor, John. *H. G. Wells*, 142–143.
> Hammond, J. R. *An H. G. Wells Companion*, 217–219.

In the Days of the Comet, 1906

> Hammond, J. R. *An H. G. Wells Companion*, 104–107.

The Invisible Man, 1897

> Beiderwell, Bruce. "The Grotesque in Wells's *The Invisible Man*." *Extrapolation* 24 (1983), 301–309.
> Costa, Richard Hauer. *H. G. Wells*, 19–21.
> Hammond, J. R. *An H. G. Wells Companion*, 87–90.
> Lake, David J. "The Whiteness of Griffin and H. G. Wells's Images of Death, 1897–1914." *Science-Fiction Stud* 8 (1981), 12–18.

Stableford, Brian. *Scientific Romance*, 61–63.

Walker, Jeanne Murray. "Exchange Short-Circuited: The Isolated Scientist in H. G. Wells's *The Invisible Man*." *J of Narrative Technique* 15 (1985), 156–167.

The Island of Dr. Moreau, 1896

Batchelor, John. *H. G. Wells*, 17–21.

Beauchamp, Gorman. "*The Island of Dr. Moreau* as Theological Grotesque." *Papers on Lang & Lit* 15 (1979), 408–417.

Block, Ed, Jr. "James Sully, Evolutionist Psychology, and Late Victorian Gothic Fiction." *Victorian Stud* 25 (1982), 465–467.

Costa, Richard Hauer. *H. G. Wells*, 16–19.

Hammond, J. R. *An H. G. Wells Companion*, 84–87.

Haynes, R. D. "Wells's Debt to Huxley and the Myth of Dr. Moreau." *Cahiers Victoriens et Edouardiens* 13 (1981), 31–40.

Henighan, Tom. *Natural Space*, 153–162.

Hennelly, Mark M., Jr. "Reader Vivisection in *The Island of Dr. Moreau*." *Essays in Arts and Sciences* 9 (1980), 217–233.

Huntington, John. *The Logic of Fantasy*, 63–70.

Jones, Myrddin. "Orwell, Wells and the Animal Fable." *English* 33 (1984), 127–132.

Lamarca Margalef, Jordi. *Ciencia y literatura*, 65–68.

Levine, Susan Jill. "Science versus the Library in *The Island of Dr. Moreau, La invencion de Morel*, and *Plan de evasion*." *Latin American Liter R* 9 (1981), 17–26.

Philmus, Robert M. "The Satiric Ambivalence of *The Island of Dr. Moreau*." *Science-Fiction Stud* 8 (1981), 2–11.

Platzner, Robert Leonard. *The Metaphysical Novel*, 174–204.

Punter, David. *The Literature of Terror*, 249–256.

Simmons, Harvey G. "H. G. Wells as Futurologist," 221–223.

Stableford, Brian. *Scientific Romance*, 59–61.

Joan and Peter, 1918

Hammond, J. R. *An H. G. Wells Companion*, 185–188.

Reed, John R. *The Natural History*, 129–131.

The King Who Was a King, 1929

Hammond, J. R. *An H. G. Wells Companion*, 114–116.

Kipps, 1905

Batchelor, John. *The Edwardian Novelists*, 131–136.

Batchelor, John. *H. G. Wells*, 43–52.

Costa, Richard Hauer. *H. G. Wells*, 41–46.

Hammond, J. R. *An H. G. Wells Companion*, 144–148.

Love and Mr. Lewisham, 1900

Batchelor, John. *The Edwardian Novelists*, 126–131.

Batchelor, John. *H. G. Wells*, 37–43.

Hammond, J. R. *An H. G. Wells Companion*, 142–144.
Huntington, John. *The Logic of Fantasy*, 111–114.

Marriage, 1912

Batchelor, John. *H. G. Wells*, 102–104.
Costa, Richard Hauer. *H. G. Wells*, 72–73.
Hammond, J. R. *An H. G. Wells Companion*, 163–166.

Meanwhile, 1927

Hammond, J. R. *An H. G. Wells Companion*, 203–205.

Men Like Gods, 1923

Costa, Richard Hauer. *H. G. Wells*, 115–117.
Hammond, J. R. *An H. G. Wells Companion*, 111–114.
Klaus, H. Gustav. "Silhouettes of Revolution: Some Neglected Novels of the Early 1920s," in Klaus, ed., *The Socialist Novel*, 101–103.
Simmons, Harvey G. "H. G. Wells as Futurologist," 228–230.

Mr. Blettsworthy on Rampole Island, 1928

Batchelor, John. *H. G. Wells*, 130–134.
Hammond, J. R. *An H. G. Wells Companion*, 205–207.
Reed, John R. *The Natural History*, 76–78.

Mr. Britling Sees It Through, 1916

Batchelor, John. *H. G. Wells*, 108–113.
Butler, Colin. "*Mr. Britling Sees It Through*: A View from the Other Side," in Charles N. Genno and Heinz Wetzel, eds., *The First World War*, 118–137.
Costa, Richard Hauer. *H. G. Wells*, 87–94.
Hammond, J. R. *An H. G. Wells Companion*, 180–183.
McDorman, Kathryne S. "Tarnished Brass: The Imperial Heroes of John Galsworthy and H. G. Wells." *North Dakota Q* 50:1 (1982), 37–45.

A Modern Utopia, 1905

Batchelor, John. *H. G. Wells*, 63–64.
Bleich, David. *Utopia*, 82–99.
Costa, Richard Hauer. *H. G. Wells*, 110–113.
Hughes, David Y. "The Mood of *A Modern Utopia*." *Extrapolation* 19 (1977), 59–67.
Huntington, John. *The Logic of Fantasy*, 167–170.
Ingle, Stephen. *Socialist Thought*, 159–173.
Parrinder, Patrick. "Utopia and Meta-Utopia in H. G. Wells." *Science-Fiction Stud* 12 (1985), 115–126.
Parrinder, Patrick. "Wells and the Aesthetics of Utopia." *Caliban* 22 (1985), 21–27.
Roemer, Kenneth M. "H. G. Wells and the 'Momentary Voices' of a Modern Utopia." *Extrapolation* 23 (1982), 117–135.

The New Machiavelli, 1910

Batchelor, John. *H. G. Wells,* 99–102.
Costa, Richard Hauer. *H. G. Wells,* 64–69.
Hammond, J. R. *An H. G. Wells Companion,* 159–163.
Ingle, Stephen. *Socialist Thought,* 66–70.
Norton, David. "Lawrence, Wells and Bennett," 171–177.

New Worlds for Old, 1908

Huntington, John. *The Logic of Fantasy,* 121–123.

The Passionate Friends, 1913

Costa, Richard Hauer. *H. G. Wells,* 73–74.
Hammond, J. R. *An H. G. Wells Companion,* 166–169.
Reed, John R. *The Natural History,* 56–58.

The Research Magnificent, 1915

Batchelor, John. *H. G. Wells,* 105–106.
Hammond, J. R. *An H. G. Wells Companion,* 173–176.

The Sea Lady, 1902

Batchelor, John. *H. G. Wells,* 64–66.
Hammond, J. R. *An H. G. Wells Companion,* 99–101.
Reed, John R. *The Natural History,* 213–215.

The Secret Places of the Heart, 1922

Hammond, J. R. *An H. G. Wells Companion,* 191–193.

The Shape of Things to Come, 1933

Bjornson, Richard. "The Future History: The Rhetoric of Utopian Narrative in H. G. Wells' *Things to Come,*" in Patricia Warrick et al., eds., *Science Fiction,* 31–36.
Hammond, J. R. *An H. G. Wells Companion,* 118–121.
Parrinder, Patrick. *Science Fiction . . . Teaching,* 83–84.

The Soul of a Bishop, 1917

Batchelor, John. *H. G. Wells,* 107–108.
Hammond, J. R. *An H. G. Wells Companion,* 183–185.

Star Begotten, 1937

Scheick, William J. "Towards the Ultra-Science-Fiction Novel: H. G. Wells's *Star Begotten.*" *Science-Fiction Stud* 8 (1981), 19–25.

The Time Machine, 1895

Batchelor, John. *H. G. Wells,* 8–17.
Begiebing, Robert J. "The Mythic Hero in H. G. Wells's *The Time Machine.*" *Essays in Lit* (Macomb) 11 (1984), 201–209.
Bengels, Barbara. "Flights into the Unknown: Structural Similarities in Two Works by H. G. Wells and Henry James." *Extrapolation* 21 (1980), 361–366.

Costa, Richard Hauer. *H. G. Wells*, 12–17.

De Stasio, Clotilde. *Lo Scrittore*, 143–162.

Fink, Ernst O. "Skizze der illusionsbildenden Kunstgriffe in Swifts *Gulliver's Travels* und Wells' *Time Machine*," in Hans-Heinrich Freitag and Peter Hühn, eds., *Literarische Ansichten*, 123–141.

Hammond, J. R. *An H. G. Wells Companion*, 79–82.

Henighan, Tom. *Natural Space*, 145–153.

Hennelly, Mark M., Jr. "*The Time Machine*: A Romance of 'The Human Heart'." *Extrapolation* 20 (1979), 154–167.

Hollow, John. *Against the Night*, 2–5.

Huntington, John. *The Logic of Fantasy*, 41–55, 71–73.

Huntington, John. "The Science Fiction," 38–42.

Lake, David J. "Wells's Time Traveller: An Unreliable Narrator?" *Extrapolation* 22 (1981), 117–126.

Lake, David J. "The White Sphinx and the Whitened Lemur: Images of Death in *The Time Machine*." *Science-Fiction Stud* 6 (1979), 77–84.

Mackerness, E. D. "Zola, Wells, and 'the Coming Beast'." *Science-Fiction Stud* 8 (1981), 143–148.

Morton, Peter. *The Vital Science*, 102–112.

Parrinder, Patrick. "Science Fiction as Truncated Epic," in George E. Slusser et al., eds., *Bridges*, 96–99.

Parrinder, Patrick. *Science Fiction . . . Teaching*, 94–97.

Parrinder, Patrick. "Wells," 19–20.

Scafella, Frank. "The White Sphinx and *The Time Machine*." *Science-Fiction Stud* 8 (1981), 255–265.

Showalter, Elaine. "Syphilis, Sexuality, and the Fiction of the Fin de Siècle," in Ruth Bernard Yeazell, ed., *Sex*, 104.

Simmons, Harvey G. "H. G. Wells as Futurologist," 217–220.

Wasson, Richard. "Myth and the Ex-Nomination of Class in *The Time Machine*." *Minnesota R* 15 (1980), 112–122.

Wasson, Richard. "Myths of the Future," in Michael Klein and Gillian Parker, eds., *The English Novel*, 187–196.

Wolfe, Gary K. *The Known and the Unknown*, 94–98.

Tono-Bungay, 1909

Anderson, Linda R. "Self and Society in H. G. Wells's *Tono-Bungay*." *Mod Fiction Stud* 26 (1980), 199–212.

Batchelor, John. *The Edwardian Novelists*, 119–126.

Batchelor, John. *H. G. Wells*, 68–80.

Costa, Richard Hauer. *H. G. Wells*, 53–60.

Hammond, J. R. *An H. G. Wells Companion*, 148–153.

Hunter, Jefferson. *Edwardian Fiction*, 115–117, 245–251, 253–255.

Ingle, Stephen. *Socialist Thought*, 118–122.

McVeagh, John. *Tradefull Merchants*, 165–166.

Norton, David. "Lawrence, Wells and Bennett," 181–184.

Sommers, Jeffrey. "Wells's *Tono-Bungay*: The Novel Within the Novel." *Stud in the Novel* 17 (1985), 69–77.

Storm, Melvin G., Jr. "Thematic Parallelism in *Tono-Bungay*: 'Night & the Open Sea' as Structural Device." *Extrapolation* 18 (1977), 181–185.

The Undying Fire, 1919

Costa, Richard Hauer. *H. G. Wells*, 94–98.
Hammond, J. R. *An H. G. Wells Companion*, 188–191.

The War in the Air, 1908

Hammond, J. R. *An H. G. Wells Companion*, 107–109.

The War of the Worlds, 1898

Batchelor, John. *H. G. Wells*, 23–29.
Costa, Richard Hauer. *H. G. Wells*, 21–24.
Hammond, J. R. *An H. G. Wells Companion*, 90–94.
Hume, Kathryn. "The Hidden Dynamics of *The War of the Worlds*." *Philol Q* 62 (1983), 279–290.
Huntington, John. *The Logic of Fantasy*, 74–84.
Rose, Mark. "Filling the Void: Verne, Wells, and Lem." *Science-Fiction Stud* 8 (1981), 121–142.
Wagar, W. Warren. "The Rebellion of Nature," in Eric S. Rabkin et al., eds., *The End of the World*, 165–166.

The Wealth of Mr. Waddy, 1969

Batchelor, John. *H. G. Wells*, 44–46.

The Wheels of Chance, 1896

Ballard, Michel. "Dualité et duplicité dans *The Wheels of Chance* (1896)." *Etudes Anglaises* 34 (1981), 153–164.
Hammond, J. R. *An H. G. Wells Companion*, 139–142.

When the Sleeper Wakes, 1899

Costa, Richard Hauer. *H. G. Wells*, 108–110.
Hammond, J. R. *An H. G. Wells Companion*, 94–96.
Huntington, John. *The Logic of Fantasy*, 143–148.
Simmons, Harvey G. "H. G. Wells as Futurologist," 227–228.
Wolfe, Gary K. *The Known and the Unknown*, 99–101.

The Wife of Sir Isaac Harman, 1914

Hammond, J. R. *An H. G. Wells Companion*, 169–171.

The Wonderful Visit, 1895

Hammond, J. R. *An H. G. Wells Companion*, 82–84.

The World of William Clissold, 1926

Batchelor, John. *H. G. Wells*, 140–141.
Costa, Richard Hauer. *H. G. Wells*, 121–122.
Hammond, J. R. *An H. G. Wells Companion*, 198–203.

The World Set Free, 1914

    Costa, Richard Hauer. *H. G. Wells*, 113–115.
    Hammond, J. R. *An H. G. Wells Companion*, 109–111.

You Can't Be Too Careful, 1941

    Costa, Richard Hauer. *H. G. Wells*, 128–129.
    Hammond, J. R. *An H. G. Wells Companion*, 222–224.

JAMES C. WELSH

The Underworld, 1920

    Klaus, H. Gustav. "Silhouettes of Revolution: Some Neglected Novels of the Early 1920s," in Klaus, ed., *The Socialist Novel*, 91–94.

JANE WEST

A Gossip's Story, 1796

    Figes, Eva. *Sex and Subterfuge*, 89–93.
    Spacks, Patricia Meyer. "Sisters," in Mary Anne Schofield and Cecilia Macheski, eds., *Fetter'd or Free?*, 137–146.

REBECCA WEST

The Birds Fall Down, 1966

    Deakin, Motley F. *Rebecca West*, 159–165.
    Orel, Harold. *The Literary Achievement*, 156–162.

The Fountain Overflows, 1956

    Deakin, Motley F. *Rebecca West*, 152–159.
    Orel, Harold. *The Literary Achievement*, 151–156.

Harriet Hume, 1929

    Deakin, Motley F. *Rebecca West*, 140–145.
    Marcus, Jane. "A Wilderness of One's Own: Feminist Fantasy Novels of the Twenties—Rebecca West and Sylvia Townsend Warner," in Susan Merrill Squier, ed., *Women Writers*, 136–148.
    Orel, Harold. *The Literary Achievement*, 132–137.

The Harsh Voice, 1935

    Orel, Harold. *The Literary Achievement*, 137–145.

The Judge, 1922

    Deakin, Motley F. *Rebecca West*, 134–140.
    Ferguson, Moira. "Feminist Manicheanism: Rebecca West's Unique Fusion." *Minnesota R* 15 (1980), 55–59.
    Orel, Harold. *The Literary Achievement*, 121–124, 127–132.

The Return of the Soldier, 1918

  Deakin, Motley F. *Rebecca West*, 131–134.
  Orel, Harold. *The Literary Achievement*, 124–127.

The Thinking Reed, 1936

  Deakin, Motley F. *Rebecca West*, 148–152.
  Orel, Harold. *The Literary Achievement*, 145–151.

THOMAS MARTIN WHEELER

Sunshine and Shadow, 1850

  Vicinus, Martha. "Chartist Fiction and the Development of a Class-Based Literature," in H. Gustav Klaus, ed., *The Socialist Novel*, 19–21.

THERESA WHISTLER

The River Boy, 1955

  Swinfen, Ann. *In Defence*, 109–116.

T. H. WHITE

The Once and Future King, 1958

  Gallix, François. "T. H. White et la legende du roi Arthur: De la fantaisie animale au moralisme politique." *Etudes Anglaises* 34 (1981), 192–203.
  Manlove, C. N. *The Impulse*, 96–114.
  Mitchell, Judith N. "The Boy Who Would Be King." *J of Popular Culture* 17:4 (1984), 134–137.

The Sword in the Stone, 1938

  Swinfen, Ann. *In Defence*, 21–30.

WILLIAM HALE WHITE

The Autobiography of Mark Rutherford, 1881

  Ebbatson, Roger. *Lawrence and the Nature Tradition*, 183–186.
  Joshi, Rita. "The Dissent Tradition: The Relation of Mark Rutherford to D. H. Lawrence." *Engl Lang Notes* 22:3 (1985), 63–65.

Catharine Furze, 1893

  Ebbatson, Roger. *Lawrence and the Nature Tradition*, 197–201.

Clara Hopgood, 1896

  Ebbatson, Roger. *Lawrence and the Nature Tradition*, 201–206.
  Joshi, Rita. "The Dissent Tradition," 67–69.

Mark Rutherford's Deliverance, 1885

>   Ebbatson, Roger. *Lawrence and the Nature Tradition*, 186–190.

Michael Trevanion, 1890

>   Ebbatson, Roger. *Lawrence and the Nature Tradition*, 195–197.

Miriam's Schooling, 1890

>   Ebbatson, Roger. *Lawrence and the Nature Tradition*, 192–195.

The Revolution in Tanner's Lane, 1887

>   Ebbatson, Roger. *Lawrence and the Nature Tradition*, 190–192.
>   Joshi, Rita. "The Dissent Tradition," 65–66.

OSCAR WILDE

The Picture of Dorian Gray, 1891

>   Cervo, Nathan. "Wilde's Closet Self: A Solo at One Remove." *Victorian Newsl* 67 (1985), 18–19.
>   Clark, Bruce B. "A Burnt Child Loves the Fire: Oscar Wilde's Search for Ultimate Meanings in Life." *Ultimate Reality & Meaning* 4 (1981), 225–247.
>   Day, William Patrick. *In the Circles*, 89–92.
>   Dickson, Donald R. " 'In a mirror that mirrors the soul': Masks and Mirrors in *Dorian Gray*." *Engl Lit in Transition* 26 (1983), 5–13.
>   Drew, Philip. *The Meaning of Freedom*, 333–342.
>   Elimimian, Isaac. " 'Preface' to *The Picture of Dorian Gray* in Light of Wilde's Literary Criticism." *Mod Fiction Stud* 26 (1980), 625–628.
>   Garber, Frederick. *The Anatomy of the Self*, 293–295.
>   Jackson, Rosemary. *Fantasy*, 112–114.
>   Klieneberger, H. R. *The Novel*, 185–187.
>   Kohl, Norbert. *Oscar Wilde*, 225–286.
>   Leblans, Anne. "Oscar Wilde: Komediant uit verlangen naar moederliefde: Vergelijkende interpretatie tussen 'The Picture of Dorian Gray' en 'De Profundis'." *Restant* 10 (1982), 145–163.
>   MacAndrew, Elizabeth. *The Gothic Tradition*, 220–223.
>   Magnan, Jean-Marie. "Jean Cocteau et le double peint de Dorian Gray." *Cahiers Jean Cocteau* 8 (1979), 185–192.
>   Martin, Robert K. "Parody and Homage: The Presence of Pater in *Dorian Gray*." *Victorian Newsl* 63 (1983), 15–18.
>   Mayer, Hans. *Outsiders*, 223–229.
>   Monneyron, Frédéric. "Une lecture nietzschéenne de *Dorian Gray*." *Cahiers Victoriens et Edouardiens* 16 (1982), 139–145.
>   Oates, Joyce Carol. "*The Picture of Dorian Gray*: Wilde's Parable of the Fall." *Crit Inquiry* 7 (1980), 419–428.
>   Powell, Kerry. "Hawthorne, Arlo Bates, and *The Picture of Dorian Gray*." *Papers on Lang & Lit* 16 (1980), 403–416.

Powell, Kerry. "Massinger, Wilde, and *The Picture of Dorian Gray*." *Engl Lang Notes* 16 (1979), 312–315.

Powell, Kerry. "The Mesmerizing of Dorian Gray." *Victorian Newsl* 65 (1984), 10–15.

Powell, Kerry. "Tom, Dick, and Dorian Gray: Magic-Picture Mania in Late Victorian Fiction." *Philol Q* 62 (1983), 147–166.

Punter, David. *The Literature of Terror*, 245–249.

Roberts, Randy. "Oscar Wilde and Sherlock Holmes: A Literary Mystery." *Clues* 1:1 (1980), 41–45.

Scheick, William J. "Fictional Structure and Ethics in the Edwardian, Modern and Contemporary Novel." *Philol Q* 63 (1984), 291–293.

Showalter, Elaine. "Syphilis, Sexuality, and the Fiction of the Fin de Siècle," in Ruth Bernard Yeazell, ed., *Sex*, 102–104.

Spivey, Ted R. *The Journey beyond Tragedy*, 58–62.

Twitchell, James B. *The Living Dead*, 171–178.

CHARLES WILLIAMS

All Hallows' Eve, 1945

Elgin, Don D. *The Comedy*, 105–109.

Hadfield, Alice Mary. *Charles Williams*, 227–228.

Howard, Thomas. *The Novels*, 151–180.

Manlove, C. N. *The Impulse*, 17–26.

Sibley, Agnes. *Charles Williams*, 83–89.

Descent into Hell, 1937

Elgin, Don D. *The Comedy*, 113–118.

Fitzgerald, Dorothy Hobson. "Themes of Joy and Substitution in the Works of C. S. Lewis and Charles Williams." *Bull of the New York C. S. Lewis Soc* 12:3 (1981), 1–9.

Hadfield, Alice Mary. *Charles Williams*, 141–142.

Howard, Thomas. *The Novels*, 181–211.

Manlove, C. N. *The Impulse*, 16–28.

Purdy, Margaret R. "Battle Hill: Places of Transition in Charles Williams' *Descent into Hell*." *Mythlore* 7:2 (1980), 11–12.

Sibley, Agnes. *Charles Williams*, 77–83.

The Greater Trumps, 1932

Elgin, Don D. *The Comedy*, 118–122.

Hadfield, Alice Mary. *Charles Williams*, 99–101.

Howard, Thomas. *The Novels*, 122–150.

Manlove, C. N. *The Impulse*, 17–25.

Sibley, Agnes. *Charles Williams*, 70–77.

Many Dimensions, 1931

Elgin, Don D. *The Comedy*, 118–122.

Hadfield, Alice Mary. *Charles Williams*, 96–97, 101–103.

Howard, Thomas. *The Novels*, 74–95.
Sibley, Agnes. *Charles Williams*, 54–63.

The Place of the Lion, 1931

Elgin, Don D. *The Comedy*, 109–113.
Hadfield, Alice Mary. *Charles Williams*, 97–99.
Haykin, Michael. "A Note on Charles Williams' *The Place of the Lion*."
   Mythlore 5:2 (1978), 37–38.
Howard, Thomas. *The Novels*, 96–121.
Manlove, C. N. *The Impulse*, 17–25.
Sibley, Agnes. *Charles Williams*, 63–70.

Shadows of Ecstasy, 1933

Elgin, Don D. *The Comedy*, 122–124.
Hadfield, Alice Mary. *Charles Williams*, 92–95.
Howard, Thomas. *The Novels*, 22–50.
Howard, Thomas. "*Shadows of Ecstasy*." *Stud in the Liter Imagination*
   14:2 (1981), 73–94.
Sibley, Agnes. *Charles Williams*, 42–46.

War in Heaven, 1930

Elgin, Don D. *The Comedy*, 100–105.
Hadfield, Alice Mary. *Charles Williams*, 92–93, 95–96.
Howard, Thomas. *The Novels*, 51–73.
Schrader, Richard J. "*Sehnsucht* and the Varieties of Religious Experi-
   ence in Charles Williams' *War in Heaven*." *Renascence* 30 (1978), 99–
   110.
Sibley, Agnes. *Charles Williams*, 47–54.

RAYMOND WILLIAMS

Border Country, 1960

Eagleton, Mary, and David Pierce. *Attitudes to Class*, 143–147.

Second Generation, 1964

Eagleton, Mary, and David Pierce. *Attitudes to Class*, 145–147.

HENRY WILLIAMSON

A Chronicle of Ancient Sunlight, 1951–1969

Mortimore, Roger. "Henry Williamson and *A Chronicle of Ancient
   Sunlight*," in *Henry Williamson*, 118–137.
Sewell, Brocard. "Thomas Hardy and G. K. Chesterton: A Footnote."
   Chesterton R 7 (1981), 323–328.

The Flax of Dream, 1921–1928

Blench, J. W. "Henry Williamson's *The Flax of Dream*: A Reappraisal." *Durham Univ J* 76 (1983–84), 81–96.
Hoyle, David. "*The Flax of Dream*," in *Henry Williamson*, 106–117.

ANGUS WILSON

Anglo-Saxon Attitudes, 1956

Drabble, Margaret. " 'No Idle Rentier': Angus Wilson and the Nourished Literary Imagination." *Stud in the Liter Imagination* 13:1 (1980), 120–121. [Also in Jay L. Halio, ed., *Critical Essays*, 184–185.]

Faulkner, Peter. *Angus Wilson*, 54–75.

Gardner, Averil. *Angus Wilson*, 56–67.

Hahn, Thomas. "Medievalism, Make-Believe, and Real Life in Wilson's *Anglo-Saxon Attitudes*." *Mosaic* 12:4 (1979), 115–134.

McSweeney, Kerry. *Four Contemporary Novelists*, 15–18.

Swinden, Patrick. *The English Novel*, 149–160.

Wilson, Angus. "The Genesis of *Anglo-Saxon Attitudes*." *Books at Iowa* 34 (1981), 3–8.

As If by Magic, 1973

Adams, Stephen. *The Homosexual*, 170–175.

Byatt, A. S. "People in Paper Houses: Attitudes to 'Realism' and 'Experiment' in English Postwar Fiction," in Malcolm Bradbury and David Palmer, eds., *The Contemporary English Novel*, 36–38.

Dev, Jai. "The Function of *The Idiot* Motifs in *As If by Magic*." *Twentieth Century Lit* 29 (1983), 223–230. [Also in Jay L. Halio, ed., *Critical Essays*, 176–181.

Drabble, Margaret. " 'No Idle Rentier'," 128–129 [191–192].

Faulkner, Peter. *Angus Wilson*, 191–204.

Gardner, Averil. *Angus Wilson*, 102–109.

McDowell, Frederick P. W. "An Exchange of Letters and Some Reflections on *As If by Magic*." *Twentieth Century Lit* 29 (1983), 231–235.

McSweeney, Kerry. *Four Contemporary Novelists*, 45–50.

Rauter, Herbert. "Angus Wilson, *As If by Magic*," in Rainer Lengeler, ed., *Englische Literatur*, 191–201.

Sage, Lorna. "Taking Risks." *Twentieth Century Lit* 29 (1983), 191–194.

Swinden, Patrick. *The English Novel*, 174–179.

Hemlock and After, 1952

Adams, Stephen. *The Homosexual*, 160–166.

Drabble, Margaret. " 'No Idle Rentier'," 120–121 [184–185].

Faulkner, Peter. *Angus Wilson*, 30–46.

Gardner, Averil. *Angus Wilson*, 36–46.

McSweeney, Kerry. *Four Contemporary Novelists*, 11–14.

Swinden, Patrick. *The English Novel*, 139–149.

Late Call, 1964

Bailey, Paul. "Meg and Sylvia." *Twentieth Century Lit* 29 (1983), 219–222.

Drabble, Margaret. " 'No Idle Rentier'," 124–125 [187–188].

Faulkner, Peter. *Angus Wilson*, 133–151.

Gardner, Averil. *Angus Wilson*, 86–94.
McSweeney, Kerry. *Four Contemporary Novelists*, 31–37.

The Middle Age of Mrs. Eliot, 1958

Bailey, Paul. "Meg and Sylvia," 219–222.
Drabble, Margaret. " 'No Idle Rentier'," 121–123 [185–186].
Faulkner, Peter. *Angus Wilson*, 87–101.
Gardner, Averil. *Angus Wilson*, 67–74.
McSweeney, Kerry. *Four Contemporary Novelists*, 19–24.
Swinden, Patrick. *The English Novel*, 149–160.

No Laughing Matter, 1967

Burden, Robert. "The Novel Interrogates Itself: Parody as Self-Consciousness in Contemporary English Fiction," in Malcolm Bradbury and David Palmer, eds., *The Contemporary English Novel*, 143–147.
Drabble, Margaret. " 'No Idle Rentier'," 125–128 [188–191].
Faulkner, Peter. *Angus Wilson*, 162–183.
Gardner, Averil. *Angus Wilson*, 94–101.
McEwan, Neil. *The Survival of the Novel*, 62–77.
McSweeney, Kerry. *Four Contemporary Novelists*, 37–46.
Swinden, Patrick. *The English Novel*, 170–174.

Old Men at the Zoo, 1961

Drabble, Margaret. " 'No Idle Rentier'," 123–124 [186–187].
Faulkner, Peter. *Angus Wilson*, 110–126.
Gardner, Averil. *Angus Wilson*, 75–85.
McSweeney, Kerry. *Four Contemporary Novelists*, 27–31.
Swinden, Patrick. *The English Novel*, 160–169.

Setting the World on Fire, 1980

Billy, Ted. "*Setting the World on Fire*: Phaethon's Fall and Wilson's Redemption," in Jay L. Halio, ed., *Critical Essays*, 192–202.
Gardner, Averil. *Angus Wilson*, 109–117.
Hanle, James M. "*Setting the World on Fire*: Angus Wilson and the Problem of Evil." *Twentieth Century Lit* 28 (1982), 453–465.
McDowell, Frederick P. W. "Chaos and the Forms of Order in *Setting the World on Fire*." *Twentieth Century Lit* 29 (1983), 236–248.
McSweeney, Kerry. *Four Contemporary Novelists*, 51–53.
O'Shea, Michael. "Sources and Analogues in Angus Wilson's *Setting the World on Fire*," in Jay L. Halio, ed., *Critical Essays*, 203–216.
Sage, Lorna. "Taking Risks," 191–194.

COLIN WILSON

Adrift in Soho, 1961

Bendau, Clifford P. *Colin Wilson*, 34–35.
Tredell, Nicolas. *The Novels*, 60–65.

The Black Room, 1971

    Bendau, Clifford P. *Colin Wilson*, 51–52.
    Bergström, K. Gunnar. *An Odyssey to Freedom*, 139–143.
    Tredell, Nicolas. *The Novels*, 130–137.

The Glass Cage, 1966

    Bendau, Clifford P. *Colin Wilson*, 42–43.
    Bergström, K. Gunnar. *An Odyssey to Freedom*, 54–57, 72–78, 100–105.
    Tredell, Nicolas. *The Novels*, 90–95.

The God of the Labyrinth, 1970

    Bendau, Clifford P. *Colin Wilson*, 49–50.
    Bergström, K. Gunnar. *An Odyssey to Freedom*, 112–120.
    Tredell, Nicolas. *The Novels*, 123–129.

The Killer, 1970

    Bendau, Clifford P. *Colin Wilson*, 47–48.
    Bergström, K. Gunnar. *An Odyssey to Freedom*, 94–100.
    Tredell, Nicolas. *The Novels*, 117–123.

The Mind Parasites, 1968

    Bendau, Clifford P. *Colin Wilson*, 43–44.
    Bergström, K. Gunnar. *An Odyssey to Freedom*, 79–88.
    Tredell, Nicolas. *The Novels*, 97–106.

Necessary Doubt, 1964

    Tredell, Nicolas. *The Novels*, 79–90.

The Philosopher's Stone, 1969

    Bendau, Clifford P. *Colin Wilson*, 46–47.
    Bergström, K. Gunnar. *An Odyssey to Freedom*, 122–139.
    Tredell, Nicolas. *The Novels*, 97–101, 106–115.

Ritual in the Dark, 1960

    Bendau, Clifford P. *Colin Wilson*, 32–34.
    Bergström, K. Gunnar. *An Odyssey to Freedom*, 59–67.
    Tredell, Nicolas. *The Novels*, 48–59.

The Sex Diary of Gerard Sorme, 1963

    Bendau, Clifford P. *Colin Wilson*, 37–38.
    Bergström, K. Gunnar. *An Odyssey to Freedom*, 107–112.
    Tredell, Nicolas. *The Novels*, 70–77.

The Space Vampires, 1976

    Bendau, Clifford P. *Colin Wilson*, 57–59.
    Tredell, Nicolas. *The Novels*, 139–140.

The World of Violence, 1963

    Tredell, Nicolas. *The Novels*, 65–70.

NICHOLAS WISEMAN

Fabiola, 1855

Durand, Michel. "*Les Martyrs, Les Derniers Jours de Pompei* et *Fabiola*, ou les romans des premiers siècles chrétiens en France et en Angleterre de 1809 à 1854." *Confluents* 1 (1975), 73–89.

P. G. WODEHOUSE

Psmith in the City, 1910

Ginestet, Evelyne. "Wodehouse amuseur édouardien?" *Cahiers Victoriens et Edouardiens* 19 (1984), 84–86.

MARY WOLLSTONECRAFT

Maria, or The Wrongs of Woman, 1798

Auerbach, Nina. *Romantic Imprisonment*, 16–18.
Butler, Marilyn. "The Woman at the Window: Ann Radcliffe in the Novels of Mary Wollstonecraft and Jane Austen." *Women & Lit* 1 (1980), 133–135.
Ferguson, Moira, and Janet Todd. *Mary Wollstonecraft*, 104–116.
Myers, Mitzi. "Unfinished Business: Wollstonecraft's *Maria*." *Wordsworth Circle* 11 (1980), 107–113.
Poovey, Mary. "Mary Wollstonecraft: The Gender of Genres in Late Eighteenth-Century England." *Novel* 15 (1982), 111–126.
Suhr, Heidrun. *Englische Romanautorinnen*, 266–277.
Todd, Janet. "Reason and Sensibility in Mary Wollstonecraft's *The Wrongs of Woman*." *Frontiers* 5:3 (1980), 17–20.
Todd, Janet. *Women's Friendship*, 208–226.

Mary, A Fiction, 1787

Ferguson, Moira, and Janet Todd. *Mary Wollstonecraft*, 31–38.
Pénigault-Duhet, Paule. "Passion, raison et déraison chez les héroines de Mary Wollstonecraft," in *La Passion*, 131–141.
Suhr, Heidrun. *Englische Romanautorinnen*, 259–266.
Todd, Janet. *Women's Friendship*, 191–208.

MRS. HENRY WOOD

East Lynne, 1861

Goubert, Denis. "Did Tolstoy Read *East Lynne*?" *Slavonic and East European R* 58 (1980), 22–39.
Hughes, Winifred. *The Maniac*, 112–116.
Mitchell, Sally. *The Fallen Angel*, 79–81.

Showalter, Elaine. "Family Secrets and Domestic Subversion: Rebellion in the Novels of the 1860s," in Anthony S. Wohl, ed., *The Victorian Family*, 109–111.

Mildred Arkell, 1865

Auerbach, Nina. *Woman and the Demon*, 131–135.

Verner's Pride, 1863

Hughes, Winifred. *The Maniac*, 116–119.

LEONARD SIDNEY WOOLF

The Village in the Jungle, 1913

Gooneratne, Yasmine. *Diverse Inheritance*, 142–152.
Meyerowitz, Selma S. *Leonard Woolf*, 40–44.

The Wise Virgins, 1914

Meyerowitz, Selma S. *Leonard Woolf*, 55–60.

VIRGINIA WOOLF

Between the Acts, 1941

Boyd, Mari. "The Art Theme in *Between the Acts*." *Stud in Engl Lit* (Japan), Engl Number 1983, 49–64.
DiBattista, Maria. *Virginia Woolf's Major Novels*, 190–234.
Dowling, David. *Bloomsbury Aesthetics*, 203–215.
Fourtina, Hervé. "*Between the Acts*: l'impossible entre-pris." *Etudes Anglaises* 35 (1982), 139–151.
Fromm, Harold. "*Between the Acts*: The Demiurge Made Flesh." *Southern Hum R* 15 (1981), 209–217.
Fussell, B. H. "Woolf's Peculiar Comic World: *Between the Acts*," in Ralph Freedman, ed., *Virginia Woolf*, 263–283.
Grundy, Isobel. " 'Words Without Meaning—Wonderful Words': Virginia Woolf's Choice of Names," in Patricia Clements and Isobel Grundy, eds., *Virginia Woolf*, 209–210.
Haller, Evelyn. "The Anti-Madonna in the Work and Thought of Virginia Woolf," in Elaine K. Ginsberg and Laura Moss Gottlieb, eds., *Virginia Woolf*, 101–104.
Kapur, Vijay. *Virginia Woolf's Vision*, 93–99.
Leblans, Anne. "*Between the Acts* als poging tot kommunikatie." *Restant* 10 (1982), 347–385.
Little, Judy. *Comedy and the Woman Writer*, 92–98.
Lyon, George Ella. "Virginia Woolf and the Problem of the Body," in Elaine K. Ginsberg and Laura Moss Gottlieb, eds., *Virginia Woolf*, 120–124.
Marcus, Jane. "Liberty, Sorority, Misogyny," in Carolyn G. Heilbrun and Margaret R. Higonnet, eds., *The Representation of Women*, 61–64, 89–91.

Meisel, Perry. *The Absent Father*, 211–216.

Mendez, Charlotte Walker. "Virginia Woolf and the Voices of Silence." *Lang and Style* 13 (1980), 107–111.

Miller, J. Hillis. *Fiction and Repetition*, 203–231.

Mittal, S. P. *The Aesthetic Venture*, 119–138.

Neuman, Shirley. "*Heart of Darkness*, Virginia Woolf and the Spectre of Domination," in Patricia Clements and Isobel Grundy, eds., *Virginia Woolf*, 69–74.

Poole, Roger. *The Unknown Virginia Woolf*, 219–227, 232–245.

Poresky, Louise A. *The Elusive Self*, 243–264.

Schneider, Daniel J. "The Returning Angel: Rebellion, Guilt and Expiation in Virginia Woolf's Novels." *South Atlantic R* 49:1 (1984), 36–37.

Swingle, L. J. "Virginia Woolf and Romantic Prometheanism." *Bucknell R* 25:2 (1980), 95–105.

Velicu, Adrian. *Unifying Strategies*, 96–111.

Wilde, Alan. "Touching Earth: Virginia Woolf and the Prose of the World," in William E. Cain, ed., *Philosophical Approaches*, 148–162.

Jacob's Room, 1922

Blain, Virginia. "Narrative Voice and the Female Perspective in Virginia Woolf's Early Novels," in Patricia Clements and Isobel Grundy, eds., *Virginia Woolf*, 130–135.

Church, Margaret. *Structure and Theme*, 169–176.

Dick, Susan. "The Tunnelling Process: Some Aspects of Virginia Woolf's Use of Memory and the Past," in Patricia Clements and Isobel Grundy, eds., *Virginia Woolf*, 184–185.

Dowling, David. *Bloomsbury Aesthetics*, 124–136.

Dowling, David. "Virginia Woolf's Own *Jacob's Room*." *Southern R* (Adelaide) 15 (1982), 60–71.

Freedman, Ralph. "The Form of Fact and Fiction: *Jacob's Room* as Paradigm," in Freedman, ed., *Virginia Woolf*, 123–140.

Gordon, Lyndall. "Our Silent Life: Virginia Woolf and T. S. Eliot," in Patricia Clements and Isobel Grundy, eds., *Virginia Woolf*, 83–85.

Koutsoudaki, Mary. "The 'Greek' Jacob: Greece in Virginia Woolf's *Jacob's Room*." *Papers in Romance* 2:Suppl 1 (1980), 67–75.

Little, Judy. *Comedy and the Woman Writer*, 39–48.

McCluskey, Kathleen. *Reverberations*, 31–53.

Meisel, Perry. *The Absent Father*, 190–194.

Mepham, John. "Mourning and Modernism," in Patricia Clements and Isobel Grundy, eds., *Virginia Woolf*, 139–140, 145–148, 151–154.

Mittal, S. P. *The Aesthetic Venture*, 52–54.

Poresky, Louise A. *The Elusive Self*, 74–97.

Schneider, Daniel J. "The Returning Angel," 30–31.

Velicu, Adrian. *Unifying Strategies*, 29–39.

Zwerdling, Alex. "*Jacob's Room*: Woolf's Elegy." *ELH* 48 (1981), 894–912.

Mrs. Dalloway, 1925

Armstrong, Nancy. "A Language of One's Own: Communication-Modeling Systems in *Mrs. Dalloway*." *Lang and Style* 16 (1983), 343–358.

Blunt, Katherine K. "Jay and Hawk: Their Song, and Echoes in *Mrs. Dalloway*." *Virginia Woolf Q* 2 (1980), 313–337.

Brownstein, Rachel M. *Becoming a Heroine*, 276–291.

Church, Margaret. *Structure and Theme*, 176–183.

Clements, Patricia. " 'As in the rough stream of a glacier': Virginia Woolf's Art of Narrative Fusion," in Patricia Clements and Isobel Grundy, eds., *Virginia Woolf*, 18–30.

Clews, Hetty. *The Only Teller*, 55–58.

Collins, Alexandra. "The Art of Self-Perception in Virginia Woolf's *Mrs. Dalloway* and Edith Wharton's *The Reef*." *Atlantis* 7:2 (1982), 47–58.

Conradi, Peter. "The Metaphysical Hostess: The Cult of Personal Relations in the Modern English Novel." *ELH* 48 (1981), 445–446.

Daleski, H. M. *The Divided Heroine*, 111–132.

DiBattista, Maria. "Joyce, Woolf and the Modern Mind," in Patricia Clements and Isobel Grundy, eds., *Virginia Woolf*, 100–102, 105–110.

DiBattista, Maria. *Virginia Woolf's Major Novels*, 22–63.

Dick, Susan. "The Tunnelling Process," 185–189.

Dowling, David. *Bloomsbury Aesthetics*, 136–148.

Dufour, Françoise. "Harmonie et sacré dans deux romans de Virginia Woolf: *To the Lighthouse* et *Mrs. Dalloway*," in *Visages de l'harmonie*, 127–144.

Eagleton, Mary, and David Pierce. *Attitudes to Class*, 123–125.

Ebert, Teresa L. "Metaphor, Metonymy, and Ideology: Language and Perception in *Mrs. Dalloway*." *Lang and Style* 18 (1985), 152–163.

Edwards, Lee R. *Psyche as Hero*, 254–271.

Elert, Kerstin. *Portraits of Women*, 66–68.

Erzgräber, Willi. "Zur Ästhetik des Augenblicks bei Virginia Woolf." *Germanisch-Romanische Monatsschrift* 34 (1984), 139–143.

Frazer, June M. "*Mrs. Dalloway*: Virginia Woolf's Greek Novel." *Res Stud* 47 (1979), 221–228.

Frye, Joanne S. "*Mrs. Dalloway* as Lyrical Paradox." *Ball State Univ Forum* 23:1 (1982), 42–56.

Haring-Smith, Tori. "Private and Public Consciousness in *Mrs. Dalloway* and *To the Lighthouse*," in Elaine K. Ginsberg and Laura Moss Gottlieb, eds., *Virginia Woolf*, 143–160.

Henke, Suzette A. " 'The Prime Minister': A Key to *Mrs. Dalloway*," in Elaine K. Ginsberg and Laura Moss Gottlieb, eds., *Virginia Woolf*, 127–139.

Henke, Suzette A. "Virginia Woolf's Septimus Smith: An Analysis of 'Paraphrenia' and the Schizophrenic Use of Language." *Lit and Psych* 31:4 (1981), 13–22.

Hessler, John G. "Moral Accountability in *Mrs. Dalloway.*" *Renascence* 30 (1978), 126–136.

Higgins, Elizabeth Jean. *Reading the Novel*, 351–357.

Kapur, Vijay. *Virginia Woolf's Vision*, 61–65.

Kuhlmann, Deborah. "Woolf's *Mrs. Dalloway.*" *Explicator* 43:2 (1985), 30–32.

Leech, Geoffrey N., and Michael H. Short. *Style in Fiction*, 299–300, 333–335, 340–341.

Little, Judy. *Comedy and the Woman Writer*, 48–56.

Locatelli, Angela. *Una coscienza*, 43–47.

Lyon, George Ella. "Virginia Woolf," 117–120.

McKeon, Zahava Karl. *Novels and Arguments*, 93–96.

Meisel, Perry. *The Absent Father*, 171–183.

Mepham, John. "Mourning and Modernism," 140–141, 148–153.

Miller, J. Hillis. *Fiction and Repetition*, 176–202.

Mittal, S. P. *The Aesthetic Venture*, 70–84.

Moon, Kenneth. "Where is Clarissa? Doris Kilman and Recoil from the Flesh in Virginia Woolf's *Mrs. Dalloway.*" *Coll Lang Assoc J* 23 (1980), 273–286.

Neuman, Shirley. "*Heart of Darkness*, Virginia Woolf," 58–62, 64–69.

Oltean, Stefan. "Textual Functions of Free Indirect Discourse in the Novel *Mrs. Dalloway* by Virginia Woolf." *Revue Roumaine de Linguistique* 26 (1981), 533–547.

Poole, Roger. *The Unknown Virginia Woolf*, 138–147, 161–172, 176–197.

Poresky, Louise A. *The Elusive Self*, 98–125.

Renaux, Sigrid. "The Interplay of Selves in *Mrs Dalloway.*" *Estudos Anglo-Americanos* 2 (1978), 5–12.

Richter, Harvena. "The Canonical Hours in *Mrs. Dalloway.*" *Mod Fiction Stud* 28 (1982), 236–240.

Rigney, Barbara Hill. "Objects of Vision: Women as Art in the Novels of Virginia Woolf," in Morris Beja, ed., *Critical Essays*, 245–246.

Ruotolo, Lucio. "*Mrs. Dalloway*: The Unguarded Moment," in Ralph Freedman, ed., *Virginia Woolf*, 141–160.

Schug, Charles. *The Romantic Genesis*, 198–211.

Showalter, Elaine. *A Literature*, 276–278.

Spilka, Mark. *Virginia Woolf's Quarrel*, 47–74.

Squier, Susan. "Mirroring and Mothering: Reflections on the Mirror Encounter Metaphor in Virginia Woolf's Works." *Twentieth Century Lit* 27 (1981), 281–282.

Squier, Susan M. *Virginia Woolf*, 91–121.

Trombley. Stephen. *All that Summer*, 35–37, 43–46, 66–68, 95–106.

Velicu, Adrian. *Unifying Strategies*, 42–56.

Viswanathan, Jacqueline. "Echanger sa vie pour une autre: Focalisation multiple dans *Mrs. Dalloway* et *Le Sourd dans la ville.*" *Arcadia* 20 (1985), 179–194.

Wade, Michael. "Mrs. Dalloway's Affirmation of Value." *Hebrew Univ Stud in Lit* 7 (1979), 245–270.

Wilde, Alan. "Touching Earth," 142–145.
Zeman, Anthea. *Presumptuous Girls*, 83–85.

Night and Day, 1919

Blain, Virginia. "Narrative Voice and the Female Perspective," 127–130.
Dick, Susan. "The Tunnelling Process," 179–182.
Dowling, David. *Bloomsbury Aesthetics*, 117–124.
Elert, Kerstin. *Portraits of Women*, 62–66, 107–113.
Erzgräber, Willi. "Zur Ästhetik des Augenblicks," 135–139.
Kapur, Vijay. *Virginia Woolf's Vision*, 52–56.
Little, Judy. *Comedy and the Woman Writer*, 34–38.
Marcus, Jane. "Enchanted Organs, Magic Bells: *Night and Day* as Comic Opera," in Ralph Freedman, ed., *Virginia Woolf*, 97–122.
Meisel, Perry. *The Absent Father*, 186–190.
Poole, Roger. *The Unknown Virginia Woolf*, 41–42, 46–49, 67–70.
Poresky, Louise A. *The Elusive Self*, 48–73.
Squier, Susan M. *Virginia Woolf*, 71–90.
Squier, Susan Merrill. "Tradition and Revision: The Classic City Novel and Virginia Woolf's *Night and Day*," in Squier, ed., *Women Writers*, 114–131.
Trombley. Stephen. *All that Summer*, 37–42.

Orlando, 1928

Bell, Barbara Currier. "*Orlando*: Mockery with a Grin or with a Vengeance?" *Modernist Stud* 4 (1982), 207–217.
Bisanz, Adam J. "Virginia Woolfs Literaturkritiker Nicholas Greene auf dem Hintergrund der geschichts-philosophischen Kulturzyklen-Theorie," in Peter Erlebach et al., eds., *Geschichtlichkeit*, 239–246.
Bovi-Guerra, Pedro. "*El mundo alucinante*: Ecos de *Orlando* y otros ecos." *Romanica* 15 (1978–79), 97–107.
Clements, Patricia. " 'As in the rough stream of a glacier'," 12–18.
DeSalvo, Louise A. "Every Woman Is an Island: Vita Sackville-West, the Image of the City, and the Pastoral Idyll," in Susan Merrill Squier, ed., *Women Writers*, 103–106.
DiBattista, Maria. "Joyce, Woolf and the Modern Mind," 110–112.
DiBattista, Maria. *Virginia Woolf's Major Novels*, 111–145.
Doody, Terrence. *Confession and Community*, 188–190.
Dowling, David. *Bloomsbury Aesthetics*, 162–170.
Gilbert, Sandra M. "Costumes of the Mind: Transvestism as Metaphor in Modern Literature." *Crit Inquiry* 7 (1980), 404–407.
Kapur, Vijay. *Virginia Woolf's Vision*, 74–77.
Kushen, Betty. " 'Dreams of Golden Domes': Manic Fusion in Virginia Woolf's *Orlando*." *Lit and Psych* 29 (1979), 25–32.
Lewis, Thomas S. W. "Combining 'The Advantages of Fact and Fiction': Virginia Woolf's Biographies of Vita Sackville-West, Flush, and Roger Fry," in Elaine K. Ginsberg and Laura Moss Gottlieb, eds., *Virginia Woolf*, 298–303.

Little, Judy. *Comedy and the Woman Writer*, 67–74.

Love, Jean O. "*Orlando* and Its Genesis: Venturing and Experimenting in Art, Love, and Sex," in Ralph Freedman, ed., *Virginia Woolf*, 189–218.

Pomeroy, Elizabeth W. "Garden and Wilderness: Virginia Woolf Reads the Elizabethans." *Mod Fiction Stud* 24 (1978), 505–508.

Poresky, Louise A. *The Elusive Self*, 154–184.

Skulsky, Harold. *Metamorphosis*, 195–222.

Snider, Clifton. " 'A Single Self': A Jungian Interpretation of Virginia Woolf's *Orlando*." *Mod Fiction Stud* 25 (1979), 263–268.

Stewart, Grace. *A New Mythos*, 28–31, 129–132.

To the Lighthouse, 1927

Adams, Kate. "Root and Branch: Mrs. Ramsay and Lily Briscoe in *To the Lighthouse*." *San Jose Stud* 9 (1983), 93–109.

Bassoff, Bruce. "Tables in Trees: Realism in *To the Lighthouse*." *Stud in the Novel* 16 (1984), 424–434.

Beer, Gillian. "Hume, Stephen, and Elegy in *To the Lighthouse*." *Essays in Criticism* 34 (1984), 33–55.

Bell, Michael. "Modern Movements in Literature," in Bell, ed., *1900–1930*, 73–75.

Burling, William J. "Virginia Woolf's *Lighthouse*: An Allusion to Shelley's 'Queen Mab'?" *Engl Lang Notes* 22:2 (1984), 62–65.

Burt, John. "Irreconcilable Habits of Thought in *A Room of One's Own* and *To the Lighthouse*." *ELH* 49 (1982), 899–905.

Cohen, Keith. *Film and Fiction*, 128–132, 168–172, 195–197.

Conradi, Peter. "The Metaphysical Hostess," 443–445.

Corner, Martin. "Mysticism and Atheism in *To the Lighthouse*." *Stud in the Novel* 13 (1981), 408–423.

Crosland, Margaret. *Beyond the Lighthouse*, 24–26.

Daleski, H. M. *Unities*, 39–58.

Dash, Irene G., Deena Dash Kushner, and Deborah Dash Moore. " 'How Light a *Lighthouse* for Today's Women?," in Cathy N. Davidson and E. M. Broner, eds., *The Lost Tradition*, 176–188.

DeKoven, Marianne. "History as Suppressed Referent in Modernist Fiction." *ELH* 51 (1984), 149–151.

DiBattista, Maria. "*To the Lighthouse*: Virginia Woolf's Winter's Tale," in Ralph Freedman, ed., *Virginia Woolf*, 161–188.

DiBattista, Maria. *Virginia Woolf's Major Novels*, 64–110.

Dick, Susan. "The Tunnelling Process," 189–196.

Dowling, David. *Bloomsbury Aesthetics*, 148–162.

Dufour, Françoise. "Harmonie et sacré," 127–144.

Elert, Kerstin. *Portraits of Women*, 69–77, 113–117.

Elliott, Jean. "The Protean Image: The Role of Mr. Carmichael in *To the Lighthouse*." *Stud in the Novel* 12 (1980), 359–367.

Erzgräber, Willi. "Zur Ästhetik des Augenblicks," 143–144.

Fokkema, Donwe W. "An Interpretation of *To the Lighthouse*: With Reference to the Code of Modernism." *PTL* 4 (1979), 475–500.

Gliserman, Martin. "Virginia Woolf's *To the Lighthouse*: Syntax and the Female Center." *Am Imago* 40 (1983), 51–101.

Gregor, Ian. "Voices: Reading Virginia Woolf." *Sewanee R* 88 (1980), 572–579.

Gubar, Susan. "The Birth of the Artist as Heroine: (Re)production, the *Künstlerroman* Tradition, and the Fiction of Katherine Mansfield," in Carolyn G. Heilbrun and Margaret R. Higonnet, eds., *The Representation of Women*, 45–48.

Guth, Deborah. "Virginia Woolf: Myth and *To the Lighthouse*." *Coll Lit* 11 (1984), 233–248.

Haring-Smith, Tori. "Private and Public Consciousness," 143–160.

Harrington, Henry R. "The Central Line Down the Middle of *To the Lighthouse*." *Contemp Lit* 21 (1980), 363–382.

Henke, Suzette. "Virginia Woolf's *To the Lighthouse*: In Defense of the Woman Artist." *Virginia Woolf Q* 2 (1980), 39–47.

Hennelly, Mark M. "Romantic Symbol and Psyche in *To the Lighthouse*." *J of Evolutionary Psych* 4:3–4 (1983), 145–162.

Hoffman, Anne G. "Demeter and Poseidon: Fusion and Distance in *To the Lighthouse*." *Stud in the Novel* 16 (1984), 182–192.

Humma, John B. " 'Time Passes' in *To the Lighthouse*; 'Governor Pyncheon' in *The House of the Seven Gables*." *Ball State Univ Forum* 20:3 (1979), 54–59.

Kahane, Claire. "The Nuptials of Metaphor: Self and Other in Virginia Woolf." *Lit and Psych* 30 (1980), 73–81.

Kapur, Vijay. *Virginia Woolf's Vision*, 65–74.

Knoepflmacher, U. C. "Genre and the Integration of Gender: From Wordsworth to George Eliot to Virginia Woolf," in James R. Kincaid and Albert J. Kuhn, eds., *Victorian Literature*, 111–115.

Libertin, Mary. "Speech Acts in *To the Lighthouse*," in Elaine K. Ginsberg and Laura Moss Gottlieb, eds., *Virginia Woolf*, 163–179.

Little, Judy. *Comedy and the Woman Writer*, 56–65.

McCluskey, Kathleen. *Reverberations*, 79–118.

Matro, Thomas G. "Only Relations: Vision and Achievement in *To the Lighthouse*." *PMLA* 99 (1984), 212–223.

Meisel, Perry. *The Absent Father*, 194–200.

Mendez, Charlotte Walker. "Virginia Woolf," 99–102.

Mepham, John. "Mourning and Modernism," 148–152.

Mittal, S. P. *The Aesthetic Venture*, 86–101.

Parkes, Graham. "Imagination and Reality in *To the Lighthouse*." *Philos and Lit* 6 (1982), 33–43.

Poole, Roger. *The Unknown Virginia Woolf*, 7–20, 271–273.

Poresky, Louise A. *The Elusive Self*, 126–153.

Pratt, Annis. *Archetypal Patterns*, 143–153.

Rigney, Barbara Hill. "Objects of Vision," 241–245.

Schneider, Daniel J. "The Returning Angel," 21–26.

Schug, Charles. *The Romantic Genesis*, 211–225.

Schulz, Muriel R. "A Style of One's Own," in Douglas Butturff and Edmund L. Epstein, eds., *Women's Language*, 75–83.

Spilka, Mark. *Virginia Woolf's Quarrel*, 20–23, 75–109.

Squier, Susan. "Mirroring and Mothering," 282–284.

Stewart, Grace. *A New Mythos*, 69–76.

Strouse, Louise F. "Virginia Woolf: Her Voyage Back." *Am Imago* 38 (1981), 185–203.

Thiher, Allen. *Words in Reflection*, 3–6.

Torgovnick, Marianna. *The Visual Arts*, 117–122, 136–142.

Velicu, Adrian. *Unifying Strategies*, 60–76.

Wilt, Judith. "Steamboat Surfacing: Scott and the English Novelists." *Nineteenth-Century Fiction* 35 (1981), 479–483.

Wyatt, Jean. "The Celebration of Eros: Greek Concepts of Love and Beauty in *To the Lighthouse*." *Philos and Lit* 2 (1978), 160–173.

The Voyage Out, 1915

Bishop, E. L. "Toward the Far Side of Language: Virginia Woolf's *The Voyage Out*." *Twentieth Century Lit* 27 (1981), 343–359.

Blain, Virginia. "Narrative Voice and the Female Perspective," 121–127.

Claudio, Mario. "Virginia Woolf e Portugal: Lisboa, Porto, *The Voyage Out*." *Coloquio/Letras* 41 (1978), 19–25.

Crosland, Margaret. *Beyond the Lighthouse*, 20–22.

DeSalvo, Louise A. *Virginia Woolf's First Voyage*, 1–159.

Dick, Susan. "The Tunnelling Process," 177–179.

Dowling, David. *Bloomsbury Aesthetics*, 108–116.

Elert, Kerstin. *Portraits of Women*, 59–62, 106–113.

Erzgräber, Willi. "Zur Ästhetik des Augenblicks," 134–135.

Fox, Alice. "Virginia Woolf at Work: The Elizabethan *Voyage Out*." *Bull of Res in the Hum* 84 (1981), 65–84.

Fry, Joanne S. "*The Voyage Out*: Thematic Tensions and Narrative Techniques." *Twentieth Century Lit* 26 (1980), 402–421.

Gordon, Lyndall. "Our Silent Life," 80–83.

Grundy, Isobel. " 'Words Without Meaning—Wonderful Words'," 210–214.

Heine, Elizabeth. "The Earlier *Voyage Out*: Virginia Woolf's First Novel." *Bull of Res in the Hum* 82 (1979), 294–312.

Kapur, Vijay. *Virginia Woolf's Vision*, 50–52, 110–112.

Leaska, Mitchell A. "The Death of Rachel Vinrace." *Bull of Res in the Hum* 82 (1979), 65–84.

Little, Judy. *Comedy and the Woman Writer*, 28–34.

Lyon, George Ella. "Virginia Woolf," 113–117.

McDowell, Frederick P. W. " 'Surely Order Did Prevail': Virginia Woolf and *The Voyage Out*," in Ralph Freedman, ed., *Virginia Woolf*, 73–96.

Meisel, Perry. *The Absent Father*, 183–186.

Neuman, Shirley. "*Heart of Darkness*, Virginia Woolf," 62–64.

Poole, Roger. *The Unknown Virginia Woolf*, 8–9, 33–38, 42–46, 52–53, 118–119.

Poresky, Louise A. *The Elusive Self*, 23–47.

Schlack, Beverly Ann. "The Novelist's Voyage from Manuscripts to Text: Revisions of Literary Allusions in *The Voyage Out*." *Bull of Res in the Hum* 82 (1979), 317–327.

Schneider, Daniel J. "The Returning Angel," 26–30.

Trombley. Stephen. *All that Summer*, 13–17, 30–34, 88–95, 243–248.

The Waves, 1931

Back, Anthony. *Constructing Reality*, 1–56.

Barzilai, Shulamith. "The Knot of Consciousness in *The Waves*." *Hebrew Univ Stud in Lit* 7 (1979), 214–244.

Beaman, Darlene. " 'Like as the Waves Make toward the Pebbled Shore': Shakespeare's Influence in *The Waves*." *CCTE Proc* 48 (1983), 79–88.

Bell, Carolyn. "Parallelism and Contrast in Virginia Woolf's *The Waves*." *Philol Q* 58 (1979), 348–358.

Boone, Joseph Allen. "The Meaning of Elvedon in *The Waves*: A Key to Bernard's Experience and Woolf's Vision." *Mod Fiction Stud* 27 (1981), 629–637.

Clews, Hetty. *The Only Teller*, 60–70.

Crosland, Margaret. *Beyond the Lighthouse*, 26–29.

DiBattista, Maria. *Virginia Woolf's Major Novels*, 146–189.

Dowling, David. *Bloomsbury Aesthetics*, 170–189.

Eagleton, Mary, and David Pierce. *Attitudes to Class*, 121–123.

Eder, Doris L. "Louis Unmasked: T. S. Eliot in *The Waves*." *Virginia Woolf Q* 2 (1980), 13–27.

Erzgräber, Willi. "Zur Ästhetik des Augenblicks," 144–147.

Gordon, Lyndall. "Our Silent Life," 87–92.

Graham, J. W. "Manuscript Revision and the Heroic Theme of *The Waves*." *Twentieth Century Lit* 29 (1983), 312–331.

Gregor, Ian. "Voices: Reading Virginia Woolf," 579–584.

Grundy, Isobel. " 'Words Without Meaning—Wonderful Words'," 216–217.

Grünewald-Huber, Elisabeth. *Virginia Woolf*, 35–143.

Haring-Smith, Tori. "Private and Public Consciousness," 157–160.

Kapur, Vijay. *Virginia Woolf's Vision*, 78–80, 82–87.

Levin, Gerald. "The Musical Style of *The Waves*." *J of Narrative Technique* 13 (1983), 164–170.

Little, Judy. *Comedy and the Woman Writer*, 74–86.

Locatelli, Angela. *Una coscienza*, 75–79.

Lorsch, Susan E. "Structure and Rhythm in *The Waves*: The Ebb and Flow of Meaning." *Essays in Lit* (Macomb) 6 (1979), 195–205.

McCluskey, Kathleen. *Reverberations*, 55–78.

McGavran, James Holt, Jr. " 'Alone Seeking the Visible Wortld': The Wordsworths, Virginia Woolf, and *The Waves*." *Mod Lang Q* 42 (1981), 267–291.

McGavran, James Holt, Jr. "Shelley, Virginia Woolf, and *The Waves*: A Balcony of One's Own." *South Atlantic R* 48:4 (1983), 58–72.

Meisel, Perry. *The Absent Father*, 200–205.

Mendez, Charlotte Walker. "Creative Breakthrough: Sequence and the Blade of Consciousness in Virginia Woolf's *The Waves*," in Douglas Butturff and Edmund L. Epstein, eds., *Women's Language*, 84–98.

Mendez, Charlotte Walker. "Virginia Woolf," 102–103.

Mepham, John. "Mourning and Modernism," 148–149, 151–152, 154–155.

Mittal, S. P. *The Aesthetic Venture*, 55–57, 102–117.

Moore, Madeline. "Nature and Community: A Study of Cyclical Reality in *The Waves*," in Ralph Freedman, ed., *Virginia Woolf*, 219–240.

Poole, Roger. *The Unknown Virginia Woolf*, 195–216, 268–270.

Poresky, Louise A. *The Elusive Self*, 185–213.

Rigney, Barbara Hill. "Objects of Vision," 239–241.

Schneider, Mary W. "The Arnoldian Voice in Woolf's *The Waves*." *Arnoldian* 10:2 (1983), 7–20.

Stewart, Garrett. "Signing Off: Dickens and Thackeray, Woolf and Beckett," in William E. Cain, ed., *Philosophical Approaches*, 126–130.

Stewart, Jack F. "Spatial Form and Color in *The Waves*." *Twentieth Century Lit* 28 (1982), 86–102.

Swartz, Mary Ann. "Making the Waves Heard." *Virginia Woolf Q* 2 (1980), 304–312.

Sypher, Eileen B. "*The Waves*: A Utopia of Androgyny?," in Elaine K. Ginsberg and Laura Moss Gottlieb, eds., *Virginia Woolf*, 187–210.

Torgovnick, Marianna. *The Visual Arts*, 130–136.

Trombley. Stephen. *All that Summer*, 46–54, 70–73.

Velicu, Adrian. *Unifying Strategies*, 79–93.

Wasserman, Jerry. "Mimetic Form in *The Waves*." *J of Narrative Technique* 9 (1979), 41–51.

The Years, 1937

Crosland, Margaret. *Beyond the Lighthouse*, 29–31.

Dowling, David. *Bloomsbury Aesthetics*, 189–203.

Friedman, Sharon. "Virginia Woolf's *The Years*: The Feminine Tradition Recreated by Three Women Characters." *Mid-Hudson Lang Stud* 4 (1981), 107–118.

Gottlieb, Laura Moss. "*The Years*: A Feminist Novel," in Elaine K. Ginsberg and L. M. Gottlieb, eds., *Virginia Woolf*, 215–226.

Grundy, Isobel. " 'Words Without Meaning—Wonderful Words'," 208–209.

Henke, Suzette. "Virginia Woolf's *The Years*: Echoes of Joyce's *Ulysses*." *Mod Brit Lit* 4 (1979), 137–139.

Janardanan, N. "The Problem of Unity in Virginia Woolf's *The Years*." *J of Engl Stud* 3 (1980), 28–37.

Joseph, Gerhard. "The *Antigone* as Cultural Touchstone: Matthew Arnold, Hegel, George Eliot, Virginia Woolf, and Margaret Drabble." *PMLA* 96 (1981), 28–29.

Kapur, Vijay. *Virginia Woolf's Vision*, 89–93.

Little, Judy. *Comedy and the Woman Writer*, 86–92.

Mendez, Charlotte Walker. "Virginia Woolf," 103–107.

Naremore, James. "Nature and History in *The Years*," in Ralph Freedman, ed., *Virginia Woolf*, 241–262.

Poole, Roger. *The Unknown Virginia Woolf*, 36–38.

Poresky, Louise A. *The Elusive Self*, 214–242.

Radin, Grace. *Virginia Woolf's "The Years."*

Schneider, Daniel J. "The Returning Angel," 31–36.

Spilka, Mark. *Virginia Woolf's Quarrel*, 22–26, 115–118.

Squier, Susan M. *Virginia Woolf*, 138–179.

Vigne, Marie-Paule. "Les Lieux de la parole dans *The Years*." *Etudes Anglaises* 38 (1985), 49–59.

Warner, Eric. "Re-Considering *The Years*." *North Dakota Q* 48:2 (1980), 16–30.

Wilde, Alan. "Touching Earth," 145–148.

JOHN WYNDHAM

The Chrysalids, 1955

Scarborough, John. "John Wyndham," in E. F. Bleiler, ed., *Science Fiction Writers*, 221–222.

The Day of the Triffids, 1951

Wolfe, Gary K. *The Known and the Unknown*, 191–197.

Re-Birth, 1955

Wolfe, Gary K. *The Known and the Unknown*, 131–134.

CHARLOTTE YONGE

The Clever Woman of the Family, 1865

Foster, Shirley. *Victorian Women's Fiction*, 23–25.
Sandbach-Dahlström, Catherine. *Be Good*, 136–170.

The Daisy Chain, 1856

Foster, Shirley. *Victorian Women's Fiction*, 25–26.
Sandbach-Dahlström, Catherine. *Be Good*, 61–100.
Williams, Merryn. *Women in the English Novel*, 156–159.

Wilson, Anita C. "Charlotte M. Yonge's *The Daisy Chain*: Victorian Artifact or Classic?," in Priscilla A. Ord, ed., *Proceedings*, 98–105.

Heartsease, 1854

Sandbach-Dahlström, Catherine. *Be Good*, 111–135.

The Heir of Redclyffe, 1853

Engel, Elliot. "Heir of the Oxford Movement: Charlotte Mary Yonge's *The Heir of Redclyffe*." *Etudes Anglaises* 33 (1980), 132–141.
Sandbach-Dahlström, Catherine. *Be Good*, 28–58.
Williams, Merryn. *Women in the English Novel*, 156–159.

Hopes and Fears, 1860

Sandbach-Dahlström, Catherine. *Be Good*, 111–135.

Pillars of the House, 1873

Sandbach-Dahlström, Catherine. *Be Good*, 61–100.
Williams, Merryn. *Women in the English Novel*, 156–159.

ISRAEL ZANGWILL

Children of the Ghetto, 1892

Zatlin, Linda Gertner. *The Nineteenth-Century Anglo-Jewish Novel*, 116–119.

ANONYMOUS NOVELS

The Adventures of an Air Balloon, 1780

Link, Viktor. *Die Tradition*, 140–149.

The Adventures of a Hackney Coach, 1781

Link, Viktor. *Die Tradition*, 140–149.

The Generous Rivals, 1716

London, April. "Placing the Female: The Metonymic Garden in Amatory and Pious Narrative, 1700–1740," in Mary Anne Schofield and Cecilia Macheski, eds., *Fetter'd or Free?*, 108–109.

The Illegal Lovers, 1728

Perry, Ruth. *Women*, 97–99.

The Sedan, 1757

Link, Viktor. *Die Tradition*, 102–109.

The Travels of Mons. le Post-Chaise, 1753

Link, Viktor. *Die Tradition*, 117–126.

LIST OF BOOKS INDEXED

Ackerley, Chris, and Lawrence J. Clipper. *A Companion to "Under the Volcano."* Vancouver: University of British Columbia Press, 1984.

Adams, Stephen. *The Homosexual as Hero in Contemporary Fiction.* New York: Barnes & Noble, 1980.

Addison, James Clyde. *An Old-Spelling Critical Edition of Thomas Lodge's "A Margarite of America" (1596).* Salzburg: Institut für Anglistik und Amerikanistik, Universität Salzburg, 1980.

Adrian, Arthur A. *Dickens and the Parent-Child Relationship.* Athens: Ohio University Press, 1984.

Alexander, J. H., and David Hewitt, eds. *Scott and His Influence: The Papers of the Aberdeen Scott Conference, 1982.* Aberdeen: Association for Scottish Literary Studies, 1983.

Alkon, Paul K. *Defoe and Fictional Time.* Athens: University of Georgia Press, 1979.

Allen, Virginia M. *The Femme Fatale: Erotic Icon.* Troy, NY: Whitston, 1983.

Allott, Miriam, ed. *Essays on Shelley.* Totowa, NJ: Barnes & Noble, 1982.

Almeida, Hermione de. *Byron and Joyce through Homer: "Don Juan" and "Ulysses."* New York: Columbia University Press, 1981.

Altman, Janet Gurkin. *Epistolarity: Approaches to a Form.* Columbus: Ohio State University Press, 1982.

Amalric, Jean-Claude. *Bernard Shaw: Du réformateur victorien au prophète édouardien.* Paris: Didier, 1977.

Anand, Shahla. *Choice Ruminations on English Literature.* Washington, DC: University Press of America, 1983.

Anderson, James. *Sir Walter Scott and History: With Other Papers.* Edinburgh: Edina Press, 1981.

Apter, T. E. *Fantasy Literature: An Approach to Reality.* Bloomington: Indiana University Press, 1982.

Argyle, Gisela. *German Elements in the Fiction of George Eliot, Gissing, and Meredith.* Frankfurt: Peter Lang, 1979.

Aronson, Alex. *Music and the Novel: A Study in Twentieth-Century Fiction.* Totowa, NJ: Rowman and Littlefield, 1980.

Ashton, Rosemary. *George Eliot.* Oxford: Oxford University Press, 1983.

Aspects du sacré dans la littérature anglo-américaine. Reims: Centre de Recherches sur l'Imaginaire dans les Littératures de Langue Anglaise, 1979.

Atkins, Dorothy. *George Eliot and Spinoza.* Salzburg: Institut für Anglistik und Amerikanistik, Universität Salzburg, 1978.

Atkins, John. *The British Spy Novel: Styles in Treachery.* London: John Calder; New York: Riverrun, 1984.

Atkins, John. *J. B. Priestley: The Last of the Sages.* London: John Calder; New York: Riverrun, 1981.

Aubert, J., and M. Jolas, eds. *Joyce & Paris.* Lille: Publications de l'Université de Lille III, 1979.

Bassoff, Bruce. *Toward "Loving": The Poetics of the Novel and the Practice of Henry Green.* Columbia: University of South Carolina Press, 1975.

Batchelor, John. *The Edwardian Novelists.* London: Duckworth, 1982.

Batchelor, John. *H. G. Wells.* Cambridge: Cambridge University Press, 1985.

Bayer-Berenbaum, Linda. *The Gothic Imagination: Expansion in Gothic Literature and Art.* London: Associated University Presses, 1982.

Beauman, Nicola. *A Very Great Profession: The Woman's Novel, 1914–39.* London: Virago, 1983.

Becker, Alida, ed. *The Tolkien Scrapbook.* Philadelphia: Running, 1978.

Becker, George J. *D. H. Lawrence.* New York: Frederick Ungar, 1980.

Beckman, E. M. *The Verbal Empires of Simon Vestdijk and James Joyce.* Amsterdam: Rodopi, 1983.

Bedell, R. Meredith. *Stella Benson.* Boston: Twayne, 1983.

Beja, Morris, ed. *Critical Essays on Virginia Woolf.* Boston: G. K. Hall, 1985.

Bell, Ian A. *Defoe's Fiction.* Totowa, NJ: Barnes & Noble, 1985.

Bell, Michael. *The Sentiment of Reality: Truth of Feeling in the European Novel.* London: Allen & Unwin, 1983.

Bell, Michael, ed. *1900–1930.* New York: Holmes & Meier, 1980.

Bendau, Clifford P. *Colin Wilson: The Outsider and Beyond.* San Bernardino, CA: Borgo Press, 1979.

Ben-Ephraim, Gavriel. *The Moon's Dominion: Narrative Dichotomy and Female Dominance in Lawrence's Earlier Novels.* Rutherford, NJ: Fairleigh Dickinson University Press, 1981.

Benstock, Bernard. *James Joyce.* New York: Frederick Ungar, 1985.

Benstock, Bernard, ed. *The Seventh of Joyce.* Bloomington: Indiana University Press; Brighton: Harvester, 1982.

Benvenuto, Richard. *Emily Brontë.* Boston: Twayne, 1982.

Bergmann, Helena. *Between Obedience and Freedom: Woman's Role in the Mid-Nineteenth Century Industrial Novel.* Göteborg: Acta Universitatis Gothoburgensis, 1979.

Bergström, K. Gunnar. *An Odyssey to Freedom: Four Themes in Colin Wilson's Novels.* Uppsala: Acta Universitatis Upsaliensis, 1983.

Bernikow, Louise. *Among Women.* New York: Harmony Books, 1980.

Best, Nigel. *Dawn: A Study of the Present Age and "Finnegans Wake" through a Close Look at "FW" Page 594: One Page Sufficient for Our Time.* 2nd ed. New Plymouth, New Zealand: Dawn, 1979.

Bidwell, Bruce, and Linda Heffer. *The Joycean Way: A Topographic Guide to "Dubliners" & "A Portrait of the Artist as a Young Man."* Baltimore, MD: Johns Hopkins University Press, 1982.

Birdsall, Virginia Ogden. *Defoe's Perpetual Seekers: A Study of the Major Fiction.* Lewisburg, PA: Bucknell University Press, 1985.

Birmann, Marie-Claude. *"The Spire" de William Golding: La Flèche ou Le Désir Pétrifié.* St. Etienne: Centre Interdisciplinaire d'Etudes et de Recherches sur l'Expression Contemporaine, 1981.

Blake, N. F. *Non-Standard Language in English Literature*. London: André Deutsch, 1981.

Bleich, David. *Utopia: The Psychology of a Cultural Fantasy*. Ann Arbor, MI: UMI Research Press, 1984.

Bleiler, E. F., ed. *Science Fiction Writers: Critical Studies of the Major Authors from the Early Nineteenth Century to the Present Day*. New York: Scribner's, 1982.

Blodgett, Harriet. *Patterns of Reality: Elizabeth Bowen's Novels*. The Hague: Mouton, 1975.

Bloom, Harold, ed. *Samuel Beckett: Modern Critical Views*. New York: Chelsea House Publishers, 1985.

Boaden, Ann, ed. *The Masks of Comedy: Papers Delivered at the Humanities Festival, 1978—Augustana College*. Rock Island, IL: Augustana College Library, 1980.

Boardman, Michael M. *Defoe and the Uses of Narrative*. New Brunswick, NJ: Rutgers University Press, 1983.

Bode, Christoph. *Intellektualismus und Entfremdung: Das Bild des Intellektuellen in den frühen Romanen Aldous Huxleys*. Bonn: Bouvier, 1979.

Boitani, Piero, and Anna Torti, eds. *Medieval and Pseudo-Medieval Literature: The J. A. W. Bennett Memorial Lectures—Perugia, 1982–1983*. Tübingen: Gunter Narr; Cambridge: D. S. Brewer, 1984.

Bold, Alan. *Modern Scottish Literature*. London: Longman, 1983.

Bold, Alan, ed. *Muriel Spark: An Odd Capacity for Vision*. London: Vision; Totowa, NJ: Barnes & Noble, 1984.

Bold, Alan, ed. *Sir Walter Scott: The Long-Forgotten Melody*. London: Vision; Totowa, NJ: Barnes & Noble, 1983.

Bold, Alan, ed. *Smollett: Author of the First Distinction*. London: Vision; Totowa, NJ: Barnes & Noble, 1982.

Bolt, Sydney. *A Preface to James Joyce*. London: Longman, 1981.

Bolton, W. F. *The Language of 1984*. Knoxville: University of Tennessee Press, 1984.

Bonifas, Gilbert. *George Orwell: L'engagement*. Paris: Didier, 1984.

Bonney, William W. *Thorns & Arabesques: Contexts for Conrad's Fiction*. Baltimore, MD: Johns Hopkins University Press, 1980.

Boucé, Paul-Gabriel, ed. *Sexuality in Eighteenth-Century Britain*. Manchester: Manchester University Press; Totowa, NJ: Barnes & Noble, 1982.

Bowie, Malcolm, Alison Fairlie, and Alison Finch, eds. *Baudelaire, Mallarmé, Valéry: New Essays in Honour of Lloyd Austin*. Cambridge: Cambridge University Press, 1982.

Bowlby, Rachel. *Just Looking: Consumer Culture in Dreiser, Gissing and Zola*. New York: Methuen, 1985.

Boyum, Joy Gould. *Double Exposure: Fiction into Film*. New York: Universe Books, 1985.

Bradbury, Malcolm, and David Palmer, eds. *The Contemporary English Novel*. London: Edward Arnold, 1979.

Brandt, Helmut, and Nodar Kakabadse, eds. *Erzählte Welt: Studien zur Epik des 20. Jahrhunderts*. Berlin: Aufbau, 1978.

Braun, Thom. *Disraeli the Novelist*. London: Allen & Unwin, 1981.

Brebach, Raymond. *Joseph Conrad, Ford Madox Ford, and the Making of "Romance."* Ann Arbor, MI: UMI Research Press, 1985.

Brewer, Derek. *English Gothic Literature*. New York: Schocken Books, 1983.

Brigg, Peter. *J. G. Ballard*. Mercer Island, WA: Starmont House, 1985.

Brivic, Sheldon. *Joyce between Freud and Jung*. Port Washington, NY: Kennikat, 1980.

Brooke-Rose, Christine. *A Rhetoric of the Unreal: Studies in Narrative and Structure, Especially of the Fantastic*. Cambridge: Cambridge University Press, 1981.

Brooks, Chris. *Signs for the Times: Symbolic Realism in the Mid-Victorian Novel*. London: Allen & Unwin, 1984.

Brooks, Peter Newman, ed. *Reformation Principle and Practice: Essays in Honour of Arthur Geoffrey Dickens*. London: Scolar Press, 1980.

Broomfield, Olga R. R. *Arnold Bennett*. Boston: Twayne, 1984.

Brown, Carole, and Leo Knuth. *Bloomsday, The Eleventh Hour: The Quest for the Vacant Place*. Colchester: A Wake Newslitter Press, 1981.

Brown, David. *Walter Scott and the Historical Imagination*. London: Routledge & Kegan Paul, 1979.

Brown, James M. *Dickens: Novelist in the Market-Place*. London: Macmillan, 1982.

Brown, Julia Prewitt. *A Reader's Guide to the Nineteenth-Century English Novel*. New York: Macmillan, 1985.

Brown, Richard. *James Joyce and Sexuality*. Cambridge: Cambridge University Press, 1985.

Brownstein, Rachel M. *Becoming a Heroine: Reading About Women in Novels*. New York: Viking, 1982.

Bruffee, Kenneth A. *Elegiac Romance: Cultural Change and Loss of the Hero in Modern Fiction*. Ithaca, NY: Cornell University Press, 1983.

Bruns, Gerald L. *Inventions: Writing, Textuality, and Understanding in Literary History*. New Haven, CT: Yale University Press, 1982.

Brunsdale, Mitzi M. *The German Effect on D. H. Lawrence and His Works, 1885–1912*. Bern: Peter Lang, 1978.

Buhariwala, Shernavaz. *Arcades to a Dome: Humanism in Forster's Novels*. Bombay: Somaiya Publications, 1983.

Burgess, Anthony. *Flame Into Being: The Life and Work of D. H. Lawrence*. London: Heinemann, 1985.

Burke, John J., Jr., and Donald Kay, eds. *The Unknown Samuel Johnson*. Madison: University of Wisconsin Press, 1983.

Burns, Aidan. *Nature and Culture in D. H. Lawrence*. Totowa, NJ: Barnes & Noble, 1980.

Burns, Bryan. *The Novels of Thomas Love Peacock*. London: Croom Helm, 1985.

Burt, Forrest D. *W. Somerset Maugham*. Boston: Twayne, 1985.

Buschkühl, Matthias. *Die irische, schottische und römische Frage: Disraeli's Schlüsselroman "Lothair" (1870)*. St. Ottilien: EOS Verlag, 1980.

Bushman, Richard L., Neil Harris, David Rothman, Barbara Miller Solomon, and Stephan Thernstrom, eds. *Uprooted Americans: Essays to Honor Oscar Handlin*. Boston: Little, Brown, 1979.

Bushrui, Suheil Badi, and Bernard Benstock, eds. *James Joyce: An International Perspective—Centenary Essays in Honour of the Late Sir Desmond Cochrane*. Gerrards Cross, Bucks.: Colin Smythe; Totowa, NJ: Barnes & Noble, 1982.

Butler, Lance St. John. *Samuel Beckett and the Meaning of Being: A Study in Ontological Parable*. New York: St. Martin's, 1984.

Butler, Marilyn. *Peacock Displayed: A Satirist in His Context*. London: Routledge & Kegan Paul, 1979.

Büttner, Gottfried. *Samuel Beckett's Novel "Watt."* Trans. Joseph Dolan. Philadelphia: University of Pennsylvania Press, 1984. (*Samuel Becketts Roman "Watt": Eine Untersuchung des gnoseologischen Grundzuges*. Heidelberg: Carl Winter, 1981.)

Butturff, Douglas, and Edmund L. Epstein, eds. *Women's Language and Style*. Akron, OH: L & S Books, 1978.

Byrd, Max. *Tristram Shandy*. London: Allen & Unwin, 1985.

Cahalan, James M. *Great Hatred, Little Room: The Irish Historical Novel*. Syracuse, NY: Syracuse University Press, 1983.

Caie, Graham D., Michael Chesnutt, Lis Christensen, and Claus Faerch, eds. *Occasional Papers 1976–1977*. Copenhagen: University Press of Copenhagen, 1978.

Cain, William E., ed. *Philosophical Approaches to Literature: New Essays on Nineteenth- and Twentieth-Century Texts*. Lewisburg, PA: Bucknell University Press, 1984.

Calder, Jenni, ed. *Stevenson and Victorian Scotland*. Edinburgh: Edinburgh University Press, 1981.

Campbell, Ian, ed. *Nineteenth-Century Scottish Fiction: Critical Essays*. New York: Barnes & Noble, 1979.

Cantor, Paul A. *Creature and Creator: Myth-Making and English Romanticism*. Cambridge: Cambridge University Press, 1984.

Carlisle, Janice. *The Sense of an Audience: Dickens, Thackeray, and George Eliot at Mid-Century*. Athens: University of Georgia Press, 1981.

Carrabino, Victor, ed. *The Power of Myth in Literature and Film*. Tallahassee: University Presses of Florida, 1980.

Carter, Ronald, ed. *Language and Literature: An Introductory Reader in Stylistics*. London: Allen & Unwin, 1982.

Casagrande, Peter J. *Unity in Hardy's Novels: 'Repetitive Symmetries'*. Lawrence: Regents Press of Kansas, 1982.

Castillo, Debra A. *The Translated World: A Postmodern Tour of Libraries in Literature*. Tallahassee: Florida State University Press, 1984.

Castle, Terry. *Clarissa's Ciphers: Meaning & Disruption in Richardson's "Clarissa."* Ithaca, NY: Cornell University Press, 1982.

Coates, Paul. *The Realist Fantasy: Fiction and Reality since "Clarissa."* New York: St. Martin's, 1983.

Cohen, Keith. *Film and Fiction: The Dynamics of Exchange.* New Haven, CT: Yale University Press, 1979.

Colaiacomo, Paola, Giovanna Covi, Vita Fortunati, Giovanna Franci, and Bianca Tarozzi. *Come nello specchio: Saggi sulla figurazione del femminile.* Turin: La Rosa, 1981.

Coleman, William Emmet. *On the Discrimination of Gothicisms.* New York: Arno, 1980.

Collie, Michael. *George Borrow: Eccentric.* Cambridge: Cambridge University Press, 1982.

Conlon, John J. *Walter Pater and the French Tradition.* Lewisburg, PA: Bucknell University Press, 1982.

Connor, Steven. *Charles Dickens.* Oxford: Blackwell, 1985.

Conroy, Mark. *Modernism and Authority: Strategies of Legitimation in Flaubert and Conrad.* Baltimore, MD: Johns Hopkins University Press, 1985.

Cook, Cornelia. *Joyce Cary: Liberal Principles.* London: Vision; Totowa, NJ: Barnes & Noble, 1981.

Cook, Eleanor, Chaviva Hosek, Jay Macpherson, Patricia Parker, and Julian Patrick, eds. *Centre and Labyrinth: Essays in Honour of Northrop Frye.* Toronto: Toronto University Press, 1983.

Cope, Jackson I. *Joyce's Cities: Archaeologies of the Soul.* Baltimore, MD: Johns Hopkins University Press, 1981.

Cope, Jackson I., and Geoffrey Green, eds. *Novel vs. Fiction: The Contemporary Reformation.* Norman, OK: Pilgrim Books, 1981.

Cornu, Marie-Renée. *La Dynamique du "Quatuor d'Alexandrie" de Lawrence Durrell: Trois Etudes.* Montreal: Didier, 1979.

Cosslett, Tess. *The 'Scientific Movement' and Victorian Literature.* Brighton: Harvester; New York: St. Martin's, 1982.

823.912
W454c — Costa, Richard Hauer. *H. G. Wells.* Revised Edition. Boston: Twayne, 1985.

Coulson, John. *Religion and Imagination: 'In Aid of a Grammar of Assent'.* Oxford: Clarendon, 1981.

Coustillas, Pierre, Jean-Pierre Petit, and Jean Raimond. *Le roman anglais au XIXe siècle.* Paris: Presses Universitaires de France, 1978.

Cox, Don Richard. *Arthur Conan Doyle.* New York: Frederick Ungar, 1985.

Cox, Stephen D. *'The Stranger Within Thee': Concepts of the Self in Late-Eighteenth-Century Literature.* Pittsburgh, PA: University of Pittsburgh Press, 1980.

Coyle, William, ed. *Aspects of Fantasy: Selected Essays from the Second International Conference on the Fantastic in Literature and Film.* Westport, CT: Greenwood Press, 1986.

Crabbe, Katharyn F. *J. R. R. Tolkien.* New York: Frederick Ungar, 1981.

Craig, Patricia, and Mary Cadogan. *The Lady Investigates: Women Detectives and Spies in Fiction.* London: Victor Gollancz, 1981.

Crawford, Fred D. *H. M. Tomlinson.* Boston: Twayne, 1981.

Das, G. K., and John Beer, eds. *E. M. Forster: A Human Exploration—Centenary Essays*. New York: New York University Press, 1979.

Das, R. J. *Joseph Conrad: A Study in Existential Vision*. New Delhi: Associated Publishing House, 1980.

Datlof, Natalie, Edwin L. Dunbaugh, Frank S. Lambasa, Gabrielle Savet, William S. Shiver, Alex Szogyi, and Joseph G. Astman, eds. *George Sand Papers: Conference Proceedings, 1978*. New York: AMS Press, 1982.

Dave, Jagdish Chandra. *The Human Predicament in Hardy's Novels*. Atlantic Highlands, NJ: Humanities Press International, 1985.

David, Deirdre. *Fictions of Resolution in Three Victorian Novels: "North and South," "Our Mutual Friend," "Daniel Deronda."* New York: Columbia University Press, 1981.

Davidson, Cathy N., and E. M. Broner, eds. *The Lost Tradition: Mothers and Daughters in Literature*. New York: Frederick Ungar, 1980.

Davies, Stevie. *Emily Brontë: The Artist as a Free Woman*. Manchester: Carcanet, 1983.

Davis, Robert. *Gerald Griffin*. Boston: Twayne, 1980.

Davis, Robert Con, ed. *The Fictional Father: Lacanian Readings of the Text*. Amherst: University of Massachusetts Press, 1981.

Dawson, Carl. *Victorian Noon: English Literature in 1850*. Baltimore, MD: Johns Hopkins University Press, 1979.

Day, William Patrick. *In the Circles of Fear and Desire: A Study of Gothic Fantasy*. Chicago: University of Chicago Press, 1985.

Deakin, Motley F. *Rebecca West*. Boston: Twayne, 1980.

Dédéyan, Charles. *Dante dans le romantisme anglais*. Paris: Société d'Edition d'Enseignement Supérieur, 1983.

Denis, Yves. *G. K. Chesterton: Paradoxe et catholicisme*. Paris: Belles Lettres, [n.d.].

De Rose, Peter L. *Jane Austen and Samuel Johnson*. Washington, DC: University Press of America, 1980.

Dervin, Daniel. *A 'Strange Sapience': The Creative Imagination of D. H. Lawrence*. Amherst: University of Massachusetts Press, 1984.

DeSalvo, Louise A. *Virginia Woolf's First Voyage: A Novel in the Making*. Totowa, NJ: Rowman and Littlefield, 1980.

De Stasio, Clotilde. *Lo Scrittore e le due nazioni: Saggi sui vittoriani*. Bari: Adriatica, 1982.

DeVitis, A. A., and Albert E. Kalson. *J. B. Priestley*. Boston: Twayne, 1980.

DiBattista, Maria. *Virginia Woolf's Major Novels: The Fables of Anon*. New Haven, CT: Yale University Press, 1980.

DiBernard, Barbara. *Alchemy and "Finnegans Wake."* Albany: State University of New York Press, 1980.

Dillon, Bert. *A Malory Handbook*. Boston: G. K. Hall, 1978.

Di Pietro, John C. *Structures in Beckett's "Watt."* York, SC: French Literature Publications Co., 1981.

Dipple, Elizabeth. *Iris Murdoch: Work for the Spirit*. Chicago: University of Chicago Press, 1982.

Dircks, Richard J. *Henry Fielding*. Boston: Twayne, 1983.

Donaghy, Henry J. *Graham Greene: An Introduction to His Writings*. Amsterdam: Rodopi, 1983.

Doody,. Terrence. *Confession and Community in the Novel*. Baton Rouge: Louisiana State University Press, 1980.

Dowling, David. *Bloomsbury Aesthetics and the Novels of Forster and Woolf*. New York: St. Martin's, 1985.

Downie, J. A. *Jonathan Swift: Political Writer*. London: Routledge & Kegan Paul, 1984.

Doyle, Mary Ellen. *The Sympathetic Response: George Eliot's Fictional Rhetoric*. Rutherford, NJ: Fairleigh Dickinson University Press, 1981.

Drew, Philip. *The Meaning of Freedom*. Aberdeen: Aberdeen University Press, 1982.

Dubasinskij, I. A. *"Saga o Forsajtax" Dzona Golsuorsi*. Moscow: Vyssaja skola, 1979.

Duchet, Claude, B. Merigot, and A. P. Van Teslaar, eds. *Sociocritique*. Paris: Nathan, 1979.

Dunn, Richard J., ed. *Approaches to Teaching Dickens' "David Copperfield."* New York: Modern Language Association of America, 1984.

Durant, Jack M., and M. Thomas Hester, eds. *A Fair Day in the Affections: Literary Essays in Honor of Robert B. White, Jr.* Raleigh, NC: Winston, 1980.

Duthie, Enid L. *The Themes of Elizabeth Gaskell*. Totowa, NJ: Rowman and Littlefield, 1980.

Eagleton, Mary, and David Pierce. *Attitudes to Class in the English Novel: From Walter Scott to David Storey*. London: Thames and Hudson, 1979.

Eagleton, Terry. *The Rape of Clarissa: Writing, Sexuality and Class Struggle in Samuel Richardson*. Minneapolis: University of Minnesota Press, 1982.

Ebbatson, Roger. *The Evolutionary Self: Hardy, Forster, Lawrence*. Brighton: Harvester; Totowa, NJ: Barnes & Noble, 1982.

Ebbatson, Roger. *Lawrence and the Nature Tradition: A Theme in English Fiction, 1859–1914*. Brighton: Harvester; Atlantic Highlands, NJ: Humanities Press, 1980.

Echeruo, Michael J. C. *Joyce Cary and the Dimensions of Order*. New York: Barnes & Noble, 1979.

Eckley, Grace. *Children's Lore in "Finnegans Wake."* Syracuse, NY: Syracuse University Press, 1985.

Eco, Umberto, and Thomas A. Sebeok, eds. *The Sign of Three: Dupin, Holmes, Peirce*. Bloomington: Indiana University Press, 1983.

Edwards, Lee R. *Psyche as Hero: Female Heroism and Fictional Form*. Middletown, CT: Wesleyan University Press, 1984.

Edwards, Malcolm, and Robert Holdstock. *Realms of Fantasy*. Garden City, NY: Doubleday, 1983.

Ehrlich, Heyward, ed. *Light Rays: James Joyce and Modernism*. New York: New Horizon, 1984.

Elert, Kerstin. *Portraits of Women in Selected Novels by Virginia Woolf and E. M. Forster.* Umea: Acta Universitatis Umensis, 1979.

Elgin, Don D. *The Comedy of the Fantastic: Ecological Perspectives on the Fantasy Novel.* Westport, CT: Greenwood Press, 1985.

Elovaara, Raili. *The Problem of Identity in Samuel Beckett's Prose: An Approach from Philosophies of Existence.* Helsinki: Suomalainen Tiedeakatemia, 1976.

El-Shater, Safaa. *The Novels of Mary Shelley.* Salzburg: Institut für englische Sprache und Literatur, Universität Salzburg, 1977.

Emmerich, Janet. *Anthony Trollope: His Perception of Character and the Traumatic Experience.* Washington, DC: University Press of America, 1980.

Engel, Elliot, and Margaret F. King. *The Victorian Novel before Victoria: British Fiction during the Reign of William IV, 1830–1837.* New York: St. Martin's, 1984.

Erlebach, Peter, Wolfgang G. Müller, and Klaus Reuter, eds. *Geschichtlichkeit und Neuanfang im sprachlichen Kunstwerk: Studien zur englischen Philologie zu Ehren von Fritz W. Schulze.* Tübingen: Gunther Narr, 1981.

Ermarth, Elizabeth Deeds. *George Eliot.* Boston: Twayne, 1985.

Eruvbetine, Agwonorobo Enaeme. *Intellectualized Emotions and the Art of James Joyce.* Hicksville, NY: Exposition Press, 1980.

Essais sur le dialogue. Grenoble: Publications de l'Université des Langues & Lettres, 1980.

Esslin, Martin. *Mediations: Essays on Brecht, Beckett, and the Media.* Baton Rouge: Louisiana State University Press, 1980.

Etherington, Norman. *Rider Haggard.* Boston: Twayne, 1984.

Etudes anglo-américaines. Annales de la Faculté de Lettres et Sciences Humaines de Nice 27. Paris: Belles Lettres, 1976.

Etudes sur le XVIIIe siècle. Clermont-Ferrand: Association des Publications de la Faculté des Lettres, 1979.

Etudes sur "The French Lieutenant's Woman" de John Fowles. Caen: Centre National de Documentation Pédagogique, 1977.

Falk, Quentin. *Travels in Greeneland: The Cinema of Graham Greene.* London: Quartet Books, 1984.

Farrell, James T. *On Irish Themes.* Edited by Dennis Flynn. Philadelphia: University of Pennsylvania Press, 1982.

Farrell, John P. *Revolution as Tragedy: The Dilemma of the Moderate from Scott to Arnold.* Ithaca, NY: Cornell University Press, 1980.

Faulkner, Peter. *Against the Age: An Introduction to William Morris.* London: Allen & Unwin, 1980.

Faulkner, Peter. *Angus Wilson: Mimic and Moralist.* New York: Viking, 1980.

Fawkner, H. W. *The Timescapes of John Fowles.* Rutherford, NJ: Fairleigh Dickinson University Press, 1984.

Fréchet, Alec. *John Galsworthy: A Reassessment.* Translated by Denis Mahaffey. Totowa, NJ: Barnes & Noble, 1982.

Freedman, Ralph, ed. *Virginia Woolf: Revaluation and Continuity—A Collection of Essays.* Berkeley: University of California Press, 1980.

Freitag, Hans-Heinrich, and Peter Hühn, eds. *Literarische Ansichten der Wirklichkeit: Studien zur Wirklichkeitskonstitution in englischsprachiger Literatur—To Honour Johannes Kleinstück.* Frankfurt: Peter Lang, 1980.

Fricker, Robert. *The Unacknowledged Legislators: Ausgewählte Aufsätze zur englischen Literatur.* Edited by Werner Senn and Dimiter Daphinoff. Bern: Francke, 1979.

Fry, Carroll Lee. *Charlotte Smith, Popular Novelist.* New York: Arno, 1980.

Fryckstedt, Monica Correa. *Elizabeth Gaskell's "Mary Barton" and "Ruth": A Challenge to Christian England.* Uppsala: Acta Universitatis Upsaliensis, 1982.

Furber, Donald, and Anne Callahan. *Erotic Love in Literature: From Medieval Legend to Romantic Illusion.* Troy, NY: Whitston, 1982.

Fussell, Paul. *Abroad: British Literary Traveling between the Wars.* New York: Oxford University Press, 1980.

823.912
S274g

Gaillard, Dawson. *Dorothy L. Sayers.* New York: Frederick Ungar, 1981.

Gallagher, Catherine. *The Industrial Reformation of English Fiction: Social Discourse and Narrative Form, 1832–1867.* Chicago: University of Chicago Press, 1985.

Gallagher, S. F., ed. *Woman in Irish Legend, Life and Literature.* Gerrards Cross, Bucks.: Colin Smythe; Totowa, NJ: Barnes & Noble, 1983.

Gamerschlag, Kurt. *Die Korrektur der Waverley Novels: Textkritische Untersuchungen zu einer Autor-Korrector-Beziehung.* Bonn: Bouvier, 1979.

Gamerschlag, Kurt. *Sir Walter Scott und die Waverley Novels: Ein Forschungsbericht.* Darmstadt: Wissenschaftliche Buchgesellschaft, 1978.

Garber, Frederick. *The Autonomy of the Self from Richardson to Huysmans.* Princeton, NJ: Princeton University Press, 1982.

Gardner, Averil. *Angus Wilson.* Boston: Twayne, 1985.

Gardner, Philip. *Kingsley Amis.* Boston: Twayne, 1981.

Garrett, Peter K. *The Victorian Multiplot Novel: Studies in Dialogical Form.* New Haven, CT: Yale University Press, 1980.

Garvin, John. *James Joyce's Disunited Kingdom and the Irish Dimension.* Dublin: Gill and Macmillan; New York: Barnes & Noble, 1976.

Gaston, Georg M. A. *The Pursuit of Salvation: A Critical Guide to the Novels of Graham Greene.* Troy, NY: Whitston, 1984.

Geddes, Gary. *Conrad's Later Novels.* Montreal: McGill-Queen's University Press, 1980.

Genno, Charles N., and Heinz Wetzel, eds. *The First World War in German Narrative Prose: Essays in Honour of George Wallis Field.* Toronto: University of Toronto Press, 1980.

Le Genre du roman—les genres de romans. Paris: Presses Universitaires de France, 1980.

Le Genre pastoral en Europe du XVe au XVIIe siècle. Saint-Etienne: Publications de l'Université de Saint-Etienne, 1980.

George Orwell & "Nineteen Eighty-Four": The Man and the Book. Washington, DC: Library of Congress, 1985.

Ghinste, Josée van de. *Lawrence Durrell: "Le Quatuor Alexandrin" et le mythe de la création.* Paris: A.-G. Nizet, 1983.

Gibault, Henri. *John Galt: Romancier écossais.* Grenoble: Publications de l'Université des Langues et Lettres de Grenoble, 1979.

Gibson, Evan K. *C. S. Lewis: Spinner of Tales—A Guide to His Fiction.* Grand Rapids, MI: Christian University Press, 1980.

Gidal, Peter. *Understanding Beckett: A Study of Monologue and Gesture in the Works of Samuel Beckett.* New York: St. Martin's, 1986.

Giddings, Robert, ed. *The Changing World of Charles Dickens.* London: Vision; Totowa, NJ: Barnes & Noble, 1983.

Giddings, Robert, ed. *J. R. R. Tolkien: This Far Land.* London: Vision; Totowa, NJ: Barnes & Noble, 1983.

Giddings, Robert, and Elizabeth Holland. *J. R. R. Tolkien: The Shores of Middle-Earth.* Frederick, MD: University Publications of America, 1982.

Gifford, Don. *Joyce Annotated: Notes for "Dubliners" and "A Portrait of the Artist as a Young Man."* 2nd ed. Berkeley: University of California Press, 1982.

Gilbert, Sandra M., and Susan Gubar. *The Madwoman in the Attic: The Woman Writer and the Nineteenth-Century Literary Imagination.* New Haven, CT: Yale University Press, 1979.

Gilkes, Michael. *The West Indian Novel.* Boston: Twayne, 1981.

Gillie, Christopher. *A Preface to Forster.* New York: Longman, 1983.

Gillis, Christina Marsden. *The Paradox of Privacy: Epistolary Form in "Clarissa."* Gainesville: University Presses of Florida, 1984.

Gillon, Adam. *Joseph Conrad.* Boston: Twayne, 1982.

Gilmour, Robin. *The Idea of the Gentleman in the Victorian Novel.* London: Allen & Unwin, 1981.

Gilmour, Robin. *Thackeray: "Vanity Fair."* London: Edward Arnold, 1982.

Ginsberg, Elaine K., and Laura Moss Gottlieb, eds. *Virginia Woolf: Centennial Essays.* Troy, NY: Whitston, 1983.

Giordano, Frank R., Jr. *'I'd Have My Life Unbe': Hardy's Self-destructive Characters.* University: University of Alabama Press, 1984.

Glage, Liselotte, and Jörg Rublack. *Die gestörte Identität: Wahn und Wirklichkeit in James Hoggs "The Private Memoirs and Confessions of a Justified Sinner."* Heidelberg: Carl Winter, 1981.

Glover, Donald E. *C. S. Lewis: The Art of Enchantment.* Athens: Ohio University Press, 1981.

Gloversmith, Frank, ed. *Class, Culture and Social Change: A New View of the 1930s.* Brighton: Harvester; Atlantic Highlands, NJ: Humanities, 1980.

Gluck, Barbara Reich. *Beckett and Joyce: Friendship and Fiction.* Lewisburg, PA: Bucknell University Press, 1979.

Gooneratne, Yasmine. *Diverse Inheritance: A Personal Perspective on Commonwealth Literature*. Adelaide: Centre for Research in the New Literatures in English, 1980.

Gordon, John. *James Joyce's Metamorphoses*. Dublin: Gill and Macmillan; Totowa, NJ: Barnes & Noble, 1981.

Gordon, John. *Notes on Issy*. Colchester, Essex: A Wake Newslitter Press, 1982.

Gose, Elliott B., Jr. *The Transformation Process in Joyce's "Ulysses."* Toronto: University of Toronto Press, 1980.

Gottfried, Roy K. *The Art of Joyce's Syntax in "Ulysses."* Athens: University of Georgia Press, 1980.

Gould, Eric. *Mythical Intentions in Modern Literature*. Princeton, NJ: Princeton University Press, 1981.

Grace, Sherrill E. *The Voyage that Never Ends: Malcolm Lowry's Fiction*. Vancouver: University of British Columbia Press, 1982.

Grant, Allan. *A Preface to Dickens*. London: Longman, 1984.

Grant, Damian. *Tobias Smollett: A Study in Style*. Manchester: Manchester University Press; Totowa, NJ: Rowman and Littlefield, 1977.

Grassin, Jean-Marie, ed. *Mythes, images, représentations*. Paris: Didier, 1981.

Green, Brian, ed. *Generous Converse: English Essays in Memory of Edward Davis*. Cape Town: Oxford University Press, 1980.

Green, Martin. *The English Novel in the Twentieth Century: The Doom of Empire*. London: Routledge & Kegan Paul, 1984.

Green, Robert. *Ford Madox Ford: Prose and Politics*. Cambridge: Cambridge University Press, 1981.

Greenfield, Thelma N. *The Eye of Judgment: Reading the "New Arcadia."* Lewisburg, PA: Bucknell University Press, 1982.

Greenland, Colin. *The Entropy Exhibition: Michael Moorcock and the British 'New Wave' in Science Fiction*. London: Routledge & Kegan Paul, 1983.

Gregor, Ian, ed. *Reading the Victorian Novel: Detail into Form*. New York: Barnes & Noble, 1980.

Grenander, M. E., comp. *Proceedings of Asclepius at Syracuse: Thomas Szasz, Libertarian Humanist*. Albany: Institute for Humanistic Studies, State University of New York, 1980.

Griffin, Brian, and David Wingrove. *Apertures: A Study of the Writings of Brian W. Aldiss*. Westport, CT: Greenwood Press, 1984.

Groden, Michael. *"Ulysses" in Progress*. Princeton, NJ: Princeton University Press, 1977.

Grundy, Isobel, ed. *Samuel Johnson: New Critical Essays*. London: Vision; Totowa, NJ: Barnes & Noble, 1984.

Grünewald-Huber, Elisabeth. *Virginia Woolf: The Waves—Eine textorientierte psychoanalytische Interpretation*. Bern: Francke, 1979.

Grushow, Ira. *The Imaginary Reminiscences of Sir Max Beerbohm*. Athens: Ohio University Press, 1984.

Grylls, David. *Guardians and Angels: Parents and Children in Nineteenth-Century Literature*. London: Faber and Faber, 1978.

Guetti, James. *Word-Music: The Aesthetic Aspect of Narrative Fiction*. New Brunswick, NJ: Rutgers University Press, 1980.

Guiliano, Edward, ed. *Lewis Carroll: A Celebration*. New York: Potter, 1982.

Gurr, Andrew. *Writers in Exile: The Identity of Home in Modern Literature*. Brighton: Harvester; Atlantic Highlands, NJ: Humanities Press, 1981.

Gutierrez, Donald. *Lapsing Out: Embodiments of Death and Rebirth in the Last Writings of D. H. Lawrence*. Rutherford, NJ: Fairleigh Dickinson University Press, 1980.

Gysin, Fritz. *Model as Motif in "Tristram Shandy."* Bern: Francke, 1983.

Hadfield, Alice Mary. *Charles Williams: An Exploration of His Life and Work*. New York: Oxford University Press, 1983.

D'Haen, Theo. *Text to Reader: A Communicative Approach to Fowles, Barth, Cortázar and Boon*. Amsterdam: John Benjamins, 1983.

Hafner, Dieter. *"Tom Jones": Fieldings Roman und Osbornes Drehbuch—Untersuchungen zu einem Medienwechsel*. Bern: Francke, 1981.

Hagstrum, Jean H. *Sex and Sensibility: Ideal and Erotic Love from Milton to Mozart*. Chicago: University of Chicago Press, 1980.

Hague, Angela. *Iris Murdoch's Comic Vision*. London: Associated University Presses, 1983.

Haight, Gordon S., and Rosemary T. VanArsdel, eds. *George Eliot: A Centenary Tribute*. Totowa, NJ: Barnes & Noble, 1982.

Haley, Bruce. *The Healthy Body and Victorian Culture*. Cambridge: Harvard University Press, 1978.

Halio, Jay L., ed. *Critical Essays on Angus Wilson*. Boston: G. K. Hall, 1985.

Hall, Dennis. *Joyce Cary: A Reappraisal*. New York: St. Martin's, 1983.

Hall, Trevor H. *Dorothy L. Sayers: Nine Literary Studies*. Hamden, CT: Archon, 1980.

Haller, Robert S., ed. *Papers from the 1979 Mid-America Linguistics Conference, November 2–3, 1979, University of Nebraska-Lincoln*. Lincoln: Area Studies Committee in Linguistics, University of Nebraska, 1980.

Halper, Nathan. *Studies in Joyce*. Ann Arbor, MI: UMI Research Press, 1983.

Halperin, John. *The Life of Jane Austen*. Brighton: Harvester, 1984.

Halperin, John, ed. *Trollope Centenary Essays*. New York: St. Martin's, 1982.

Hammond, J. R. *A George Orwell Companion: A Guide to the Novels, Documentaries and Essays*. London: Macmillan, 1982.

Hammond, J. R. *An H. G. Wells Companion: A Guide to the Novels, Romances and Short Stories*. New York: Barnes & Noble, 1979.

Hammond, J. R. *A Robert Louis Stevenson Companion: A Guide to the Novels, Essays and Short Stories*. London: Macmillan, 1984.

Johansson, Stig, and Bjorn Tysdahl, eds. *Papers from the First Nordic Conference for English Studies, Oslo, 17–19 September 1980*. Oslo: Institute of English Studies, University of Oslo, 1981.

Johnson, Lee McKay. *The Metaphor of Painting: Essays on Baudelaire, Ruskin, Proust, and Pater*. Ann Arbor, MI: UMI Research Press, 1980.

Johnson, Mary Lynn, and Seraphia D. Leyda, eds. *Reconciliations: Studies in Honor of Richard Harter Fogle*. Salzburg: Institut für Anglistik und Amerikanistik, Universität Salzburg, 1983.

Johnson, Wendell Stacy. *Sons and Fathers: The Generation Link in Literature, 1780–1980*. New York: Peter Lang, 1985.

Johnson, Wendell Stacy, ed. *Charles Dickens: New Perspectives*. Englewood Cliffs, NJ: Prentice-Hall, 1982.

Johnston, Arnold. *Of Earth and Darkness: The Novels of William Golding*. Columbia: University of Missouri Press, 1980.

Johnstone, Richard. *The Will to Believe: Novelists of the Nineteen-thirties*. Oxford: Oxford University Press, 1982.

Jones, Michael P. *Conrad's Heroism: A Paradise Lost*. Ann Arbor, MI: UMI Research Press, 1985.

Jurgensen, Jean-Daniel. *Orwell ou la route de 1984*. Paris: Robert Laffont, 1983.

Kalpakgian, Mitchell. *The Marvellous in Fielding's Novels*. Washington, DC: University Press of America, 1981.

Kapur, Vijay. *Virginia Woolf's Vision of Life and Her Search for Significant Form: A Study in the Shaping Vision*. Meerut, India: Anu Prakashan, 1979.

Kavanagh, James H. *Emily Brontë*. Oxford: Blackwell, 1985.

Kavanagh, Peter. *Sacred Keeper: A Biography of Patrick Kavanagh*. The Curragh, Ireland: Goldsmith Press, 1979.

Kawin, Bruce F. *The Mind of the Novel: Reflexive Fiction and the Ineffable*. Princeton, NJ: Princeton University Press, 1982.

Keener, Frederick M. *The Chain of Becoming: The Philosophical Tale, the Novel, and a Neglected Realism of the Enlightenment—Swift, Montesquieu, Voltaire, Johnson, and Austen*. New York: Columbia University Press, 1983.

Kellman, Steven G. *The Self-Begetting Novel*. New York: Columbia University Press, 1980.

Kelly, Richard. *George Du Maurier*. Boston: Twayne, 1983.

Kelly, Richard. *Graham Greene*. New York: Frederick Ungar, 1984.

Kendrick, Walter M. *The Novel-Machine: The Theory and Fiction of Anthony Trollope*. Baltimore, MD: Johns Hopkins University Press, 1980.

Kenner, Hugh. *Joyce's Voices*. Berkeley: University of California Press, 1978.

Kenny, Virginia C. *The Country-House Ethos in English Literature 1688–1750: Themes of Personal Retreat and National Expansion*. Brighton: Harvester; New York: St. Martin's, 1984.

Kermode, Frank. *The Art of Telling: Essays on Fiction*. Cambridge: Harvard University Press, 1983.

823.912
J 73 w

Kosok, Heinz, ed. *Studies in Anglo-Irish Literature*. Bonn: Bouvier, 1982.

Kramer, Dale, ed. *Critical Approaches to the Fiction of Thomas Hardy*. London: Macmillan, 1979.

Krissdottir, Morine. *John Cowper Powys and the Magical Quest*. London: Macdonald & Jane's, 1980.

Kucich, John. *Excess and Restraint in the Novels of Charles Dickens*. Athens: University of Georgia Press, 1981.

Kulshrestha, J. P. *Graham Greene: The Novelist*. Delhi: Macmillan, 1977.

Kurismmootil, K. C. Joseph. *Heaven and Hell on Earth: An Appreciation of Five Novels of Graham Greene*. Chicago: Loyola University Press, 1982.

Kurrik, Maire Jaanus. *Literature and Negation*. New York: Columbia University Press, 1979.

Kush, Thomas. *Wyndham Lewis's Pictorial Integer*. Ann Arbor, MI: UMI Research Press, 1981.

La Bossière, Camille R. *Joseph Conrad and the Science of Unknowing*. Fredericton, NB: York Press, 1979.

Lamarca Margalef, Jordi. *Ciencia y literatura: El científico en la literatura inglesa de los siglos XIX y XX*. Barcelona: Ediciones de la Universidad de Barcelona, 1983.

Land, Stephen K. *Paradox and Polarity in the Fiction of Joseph Conrad*. New York: St. Martin's, 1984.

Landow, George P. *Images of Crisis: Literary Iconology, 1750 to the Present*. Boston: Routledge & Kegan Paul, 1982.

Landow, George P. *Victorian Types, Victorian Shadows: Biblical Typology in Victorian Literature, Art, and Thought*. Boston: Routledge & Kegan Paul, 1980.

Landow, George P., ed. *Approaches to Victorian Autobiography*. Athens: Ohio University Press, 1978.

Lane, Calvin W. *Evelyn Waugh*. Boston: Twayne, 1981.

Lansbury, Coral. *Elizabeth Gaskell*. Boston: Twayne, 1984.

Lansbury, Coral. *The Reasonable Man: Trollope's Legal Fiction*. Princeton, NJ: Princeton University Press, 1981.

Lascelles, Mary. *The Story-Teller Retrieves the Past: Historical Fiction and Fictitious History in the Art of Scott, Stevenson, Kipling, and Some Others*. Oxford: Clarendon, 1980.

Laurenson, Diana, ed. *The Sociology of Literature: Applied Studies*. Keele, England: University of Keele, 1978.

Lauritzen, Monica. *Jane Austen's "Emma" on Television: A Study of a BBC Classic Serial*. Gothenburg: Acta Universitatis Gothoburgensis, 1981.

Leclerq, Florence. *Elizabeth Taylor*. Boston: Twayne, 1985.

Lee, Hermione. *Elizabeth Bowen: An Estimation*. London: Vision; Totowa, NJ: Barnes & Noble, 1981.

Leech, Geoffrey N., and Michael H. Short. *Style in Fiction: A Linguistic Introduction to English Fictional Prose*. London: Longman, 1981.

Leinster-Mackay, D. P. *The Educational World of Daniel Defoe*. Victoria, BC: University of Victoria, 1981.

Lock, F. P. *The Politics of "Gulliver's Travels."* Oxford: Clarendon, 1980.

Lock, F. P. *Swift's Tory Politics.* Newark: University of Delaware Press, 1983.

Lombardo, Agostino, ed. *Studi inglesi: Raccoltà di saggi e ricerche.* Bari: Adriatica, 1978.

Longford, Elizabeth. *Eminent Victorian Women.* London: Weidenfeld and Nicolson, 1981.

Louis, Frances Deutsch. *Swift's Anatomy of Misunderstanding: A Study of Swift's Epistemological Imagination in "A Tale of a Tub" and "Gulliver's Travels."* Totowa, NJ: Barnes & Noble, 1981.

Loveday, Simon. *The Romances of John Fowles.* New York: St. Martin's, 1985.

Lusignan, Serge, and John S. North, eds. *Computing in the Humanities: Proceedings of the Third International Conference on Computing in the Humanities.* Waterloo, Canada: University of Waterloo Press, 1977.

MacAndrew, Elizabeth. *The Gothic Tradition in Fiction.* New York: Columbia University Press, 1979.

MacCabe, Colin. *James Joyce and the Revolution of the World.* New York: Barnes & Noble, 1979.

MacCabe, Colin, ed. *James Joyce: New Perspectives.* Brighton: Harvester; Bloomington: Indiana University Press, 1982.

McCarthy, John P. *Hilaire Belloc: Edwardian Radical.* Indianapolis: Liberty Press, 1978.

McCarthy, Patrick A. *Olaf Stapledon.* Boston: Twayne, 1982.

McCarthy, Patrick A. *The Riddles of "Finnegans Wake."* Rutherford, NJ: Fairleigh Dickinson University Press, 1980.

Macey, Samuel L. *Money and the Novel: Mercenary Motivation in Defoe and His Immediate Successors.* Victoria, BC: Sono Nis Press, 1983.

McClure, John A. *Kipling & Conrad: The Colonial Fiction.* Cambridge: Harvard University Press, 1981.

McCluskey, Kathleen. *Reverberations: Sound and Structure in the Novels of Virginia Woolf.* Ann Arbor, MI: UMI Research Press, 1986.

McConnell, Frank. *Storytelling and Mythmaking: Images from Film and Literature.* New York: Oxford University Press, 1979.

McCormack, W. J., and Alistair Stead, eds. *James Joyce and Modern Literature.* London: Routledge & Kegan Paul, 1982.

McCoy, Richard C. *Sir Philip Sidney: Rebellion in Arcadia.* New Brunswick, NJ: Rutgers University Press, 1979.

McCullen, Maurice L. *E. M. Delafield.* Boston: Twayne, 1985.

McDowell, Frederick P. W. *E. M. Forster.* Revised Edition. Boston: Twayne, 1982.

McEwan, Neil. *The Survival of the Novel: British Fiction in the Later Twentieth Century.* Totowa, NJ: Barnes & Noble, 1981.

McFate, Patricia. *The Writings of James Stephens: Variations on a Theme of Love.* New York: St. Martin's, 1979.

McGinn, Donald J. *Thomas Nashe.* Boston: Twayne, 1981.

Markel, Michael H. *Hilaire Belloc*. Boston: Twayne, 1982.

Marshall, Madeleine F., ed. *Science Fiction Miscellany: Approaches to the Study of Science Fiction*. Mayagüez: University of Puerto Rico, 1979.

Martin, Augustine. *James Stephens: A Critical Study*. Totowa, NJ: Rowman and Littlefield, 1977.

Martin, Graham. *"Great Expectations."* Milton Keynes, England: Open University Press, 1985.

Masih, I. K., ed. *An Indian Response to Samuel Beckett: For His Seventy Seventh Birthday*. Calcutta: P. Lal, 1982.

Mason, Philip. *The English Gentleman: The Rise and Fall of an Ideal*. New York: William Morrow, 1982.

Massa, Daniel, ed. *Individual and Community in Commonwealth Literature*. Msida: University of Malta Press, 1979.

Massie, Allan. *Muriel Spark*. Edinburgh: Ramsay Head Press, 1979.

Mathews, Richard. *Lightning from a Clear Sky: Tolkien, the Trilogy, and the Silmarillion*. San Bernardino, CA: Borgo Press, 1978.

May, Leland Chandler. *Parodies of the Gothic Novel*. New York: Arno Press, 1980.

Mayer, Hans. *Outsiders: A Study in Life and Letters*. Translated by Denis M. Sweet. Cambridge, MA: MIT Press, 1982.

Meier, Stefanie. *Animation and Mechanization in the Novels of Charles Dickens*. Bern: Francke, 1982.

Meisel, Perry. *The Absent Father: Virginia Woolf and Walter Pater*. New Haven, CT: Yale University Press, 1980.

Mellor, Anne K. *English Romantic Irony*. Cambridge: Harvard University Press, 1980.

Mengham, Rod. *The Idiom of the Time: The Writings of Henry Green*. Cambridge: Cambridge University Press, 1982.

Merrett, Robert James. *Daniel Defoe's Moral and Rhetorical Ideas*. Victoria, BC: University of Victoria, 1980.

Meyerowitz, Selma S. *Leonard Woolf*. Boston: Twayne, 1982.

Meyers, Jeffrey. *D. H. Lawrence and the Experience of Italy*. Philadelphia: University of Pennsylvania Press, 1982.

Meyers, Jeffrey, ed. *D. H. Lawrence and Tradition*. Amherst: University of Massachusetts Press, 1985.

Meyers, Jeffrey, ed. *Wyndham Lewis: A Revaluation—New Essays*. Montreal: McGill-Queen's University Press, 1980.

Meyers, Walter E. *Aliens and Linguists: Language Study and Science Fiction*. Athens: University of Georgia Press, 1980.

Mikhail, E. H., ed. *The Art of Brendan Behan*. New York: Barnes & Noble, 1979.

Milberg-Kaye, Ruth. *Thomas Hardy: Myths of Sexuality*. New York: John Jay Press, 1983.

Milbury-Steen, Sarah L. *European and African Stereotypes in Twentieth-Century Fiction*. New York: New York University Press, 1981.

Miller, Henry Knight. *Henry Fielding's "Tom Jones" and the Romance Tradition*. Victoria, BC: University of Victoria, 1976.

Niven, Alastair. *D. H. Lawrence: The Writer and His Work*. London: Longman, 1980.

Noel, Ruth S. *The Languages of Tolkien's Middle-Earth*. Boston: Houghton Mifflin, 1980.

Noel, Ruth S. *The Mythology of Middle-Earth*. Boston: Houghton Mifflin, 1977.

Nokes, David. *Jonathan Swift, A Hypocrite Reversed: A Critical Biography*. Oxford: Oxford University Press, 1985.

Nordic Rejoycings 1982: In Commemoration of the Centenary of the Birth of James Joyce. Stockholm: James Joyce Society of Sweden and Finland, 1982.

Norrman, Ralf. *Samuel Butler and the Meaning of Chiasmus*. New York: St. Martin's, 1986.

North, Michael. *Henry Green and the Writing of His Generation*. Charlottesville: University Press of Virginia, 1984.

Novak, Maximillian E. *Eighteenth-Century English Literature*. New York: Schocken Books, 1983.

Novak, Maximillian E. *Realism, Myth, and History in Defoe's Fiction*. Lincoln: University of Nebraska Press, 1983.

Odmark, John. *An Understanding of Jane Austen's Novels: Character, Value and Ironic Perspective*. Totowa, NJ: Barnes & Noble, 1981.

O'Hanlon, Redmond. *Joseph Conrad and Charles Darwin: The Influence of Scientific Thought on Conrad's Fiction*. Edinburgh: Salamander Press, 1984.

Omasreiter, Ria. *Travels through the British Isles: Die Funktion des Reiseberichts im 18. Jahrhundert*. Heidelberg: Carl Winter, 1982.

Ord, Priscilla A., ed. *Proceedings of the Sixth Annual Conference of the Children's Literature Association, University of Toronto, March, 1979*. Villanova, PA: Villanova University Press, 1980.

Orel, Harold. *The Literary Achievement of Rebecca West*. London: Macmillan, 1986.

O'Rourke, Brian. *The Conscience of the Race: Sex and Religion in Irish and French Novels, 1941–1973*. Dublin: Four Courts Press, 1980.

Overton, Bill. *The Unofficial Trollope*. Brighton: Harvester; Totowa, NJ: Barnes & Noble, 1982.

Pache, Walter. *Profit and Delight: Didaktik und Fiktion als Problem des Erzählens—Dargestellt am Beispiel des Romanwerks von Daniel Defoe*. Heidelberg: Carl Winter, 1980.

Page, Norman. *A Conrad Companion*. New York: St. Martin's, 1986.

Page, Norman. *E. M. Forster's Posthumous Fiction*. Victoria, BC: University of Victoria, 1977.

Page, Norman, ed. *Thomas Hardy: The Writer and his Background*. New York: St. Martin's, 1980.

Palmer, Jerry. *Thrillers: Genesis and Structure of a Popular Genre*. London: Edward Arnold, 1978.

Palusci, Oriana. *John R. R. Tolkien*. Florence: La Nuova Italia, 1982.

Panek, LeRoy L. *The Special Branch: The British Spy Novel, 1890–1980.* Bowling Green, OH: Bowling Green University Popular Press, 1981.

Panitz, Esther L. *The Alien in Their Midst: Images of Jews in English Literature.* London: Associated University Presses, 1981.

Paradis, James, and Thomas Postlewait, eds. *Victorian Science and Victorian Values: Literary Perspectives.* New York: New York Academy of Sciences, 1981.

Parkinson, Kathleen, and Martin Priestman, eds. *Peasants and Countrymen in Literature.* London: English Department, Roehampton Institute of Higher Education, 1982.

Parrinder, Patrick. *James Joyce.* Cambridge: Cambridge University Press, 1984.

Parrinder, Patrick. *Science Fiction: Its Criticism and Teaching.* London: Methuen, 1980.

Parrinder, Patrick, ed. *Science Fiction: A Critical Guide.* London: Longman, 1979.

Partlow, Robert B., Jr., and Harry T. Moore, eds. *D. H. Lawrence: The Man Who Lived.* Carbondale and Edwardsville: Southern Illinois University Press, 1980.

La Passion dans le monde anglo-américain aux XVIIe et XVIIIe siècles. Bordeaux: Société d'Etudes Anglo-Américaines des XVIIe et XVIIIe Siècles, Université de Bordeaux, 1979.

Patai, Daphne. *The Orwell Mystique: A Study in Male Ideology.* Amherst: University of Massachusetts Press, 1984.

Patey, Douglas Lane, and Timothy Keegan, eds. *Augustan Studies: Essays in Honor of Irvin Ehrenpreis.* Newark: University of Delaware Press, 1985.

Pattison, Robert. *The Child Figure in English Literature.* Athens: University of Georgia Press, 1978.

Paul, Ronald. *"Fire in Our Hearts": A Study of the Portrayal of Youth in a Selection of Post-War British Working-Class Fiction.* Gothenburg: Acta Universitatis Gothoburgensis, 1982.

Pawling, Christopher, ed. *Popular Fiction and Social Change.* New York: St. Martin's, 1984.

Peereboom, John James. *Fielding Practice: A Study of the Novels of Henry Fielding.* Amsterdam: Rodopi, 1984.

Perkins, Donald. *Charles Dickens: A New Perspective.* Edinburgh: Floris Books, 1982.

Perry, Ruth. *Women, Letters, and the Novel.* New York: AMS Press, 1980.

Peterson, Audrey. *Victorian Masters of Mystery: From Wilkie Collins to Conan Doyle.* New York: Frederick Ungar, 1984.

Peterson, Richard F. *Mary Lavin.* Boston: Twayne, 1978.

Peterson, Richard F., Alan M. Cohn, and Edmund L. Epstein, eds. *Work in Progress: Joyce Centenary Essays.* Carbondale and Edwardsville: Southern Illinois University Press, 1983.

Petit, Jean-Pierre. *L'oeuvre d'Emily Brontë: La vision et les thèmes.* Lyon: Edition L'Hermès, 1977.

Petty, Anne C. *One Ring to Bind Them All: Tolkien's Mythology.* University: University of Alabama Press, 1979.

Phillipps, K. C. *The Language of Thackeray.* London: André Deutsch, 1978.

Piazza, Paul. *Christopher Isherwood: Myth and Anti-Myth.* New York: Columbia University Press, 1978.

Pichanik, Valerie Kossew. *Harriet Martineau: The Woman and Her Work, 1802–76.* Ann Arbor: University of Michigan Press, 1980.

Pierce, Charles E., Jr. *The Religious Life of Samuel Johnson.* London: Athlone, 1983.

Piggott, Patrick. *The Innocent Diversion: A Study of Music in the Life and Writings of Jane Austen.* London: Douglas Cleverdon, 1979.

Pinion, F. B. *A George Eliot Companion: Literary Achievement and Modern Significance.* Totowa, NJ: Barnes & Noble, 1981.

Platzner, Robert Leonard. *The Metaphysical Novel in England: The Romantic Phase.* New York: Arno, 1980.

Polhemus, Robert M. *Comic Faith: The Great Tradition from Austen to Joyce.* Chicago: University of Chicago Press, 1980.

Poole, Roger. *The Unknown Virginia Woolf.* Cambridge: Cambridge University Press, 1978.

Poresky, Louise A. *The Elusive Self: Psyche and Spirit in Virginia Woolf's Novels.* Newark: University of Delaware Press, 1981.

Postlethwaite, Diana. *Making It Whole: A Victorian Circle and the Shape of Their World.* Columbus: Ohio State University Press, 1984.

Potter, Jonathan, Peter Stringer, and Margaret Wetherell. *Social Texts and Context: Literature and Social Psychology.* London: Routledge & Kegan Paul, 1984.

Le Pouvoir dans la littérature et la pensée anglaises. Aix-en-Provence: Centre Aixois de Recherches Anglaises, Université de Provence, 1981.

Powers, Katherine Richardson. *The Influence of William Godwin on the Novels of Mary Shelley.* New York: Arno, 1980.

Prasad, Keshava. *Graham Greene the Novelist.* New Delhi: Classical Publishing Co., 1982.

Prasad, Madhusudan. *D. H. Lawrence: A Study of His Novels.* Bara Bazar, Bareilly: Prakash Book Depot, 1980.

Pratt, Annis (with Barbara White, Andrea Loewenstein, and Mary Wyer). *Archetypal Patterns in Women's Fiction.* Bloomington: Indiana University Press, 1981.

Prickett, Stephen. *Victorian Fantasy.* Bloomington: Indiana University Press, 1979.

Probyn, Clive T., ed. *The Art of Jonathan Swift.* New York: Barnes & Noble, 1978.

Punter, David. *The Literature of Terror: A History of Gothic Fictions from 1765 to the Present Day.* London: Longman, 1980.

Purdy, Dwight H. *Joseph Conrad's Bible.* Norman: University of Oklahoma Press, 1984.

Purtill, Richard L. *J. R. R. Tolkien: Myth, Morality, and Religion.* San Francisco: Harper & Row, 1984.

Putzell-Korab, Sara M. *The Evolving Consciousness: An Hegelian Reading of the Novels of George Eliot.* Salzburg: Institut für Anglistik und Amerikanistik, Universität Salzburg, 1982.

Qualls, Barry V. *The Secular Pilgrims of Victorian Fiction: The Novel as Book of Life.* Cambridge: Cambridge University Press, 1982.

Quigly, Isabel. *The Heirs of Tom Brown: The English School Story.* London: Chatto & Windus, 1982.

Rabinovitz, Rubin. *The Development of Samuel Beckett's Fiction.* Urbana: University of Illinois Press, 1984.

Rabkin, Eric S. *Arthur C. Clarke.* West Linn, OR: Starmont House, 1979.

Rabkin, Eric S., Martin H. Greenberg, and Joseph D. Olander, eds. *The End of the World.* Carbondale and Edwardsville: Southern Illinois University Press, 1983.

Rabkin, Eric S., Martin H. Greenberg, and Joseph D. Olander, eds. *No Place Else: Explorations in Utopian and Dystopian Fiction.* Carbondale and Edwardsville: Southern Illinois University Press, 1983.

Rafroidi, Patrick, and Pierre Joannon, eds. *James Joyce Centenary Issue.* (*Etudes Irlandaises,* numéro spécial 1982.) Lille: Université de Lille III, 1982.

Rai, Gangeshwar. *Graham Greene: An Existential Approach.* New Delhi: Associated Publishing House, 1983.

Raleigh, John Henry. *The Chronicle of Leopold and Molly Bloom: "Ulysses" as Narrative.* Berkeley: University of California Press, 1977.

Rao, K. Bhaskara. *Paul Scott.* Boston: Twayne, 1980.

Radin, Grace. *Virginia Woolf's "The Years": The Evolution of a Novel.* Knoxville: University of Tennessee Press, 1981.

Rataboul, Louis J. *Le pasteur anglican dans le roman victorien: Aspects sociaux et religieux.* Paris: Didier, 1978.

Rawson, Claude, ed. *The Character of Swift's Satire: A Revised Focus.* Newark: University of Delaware Press, 1983.

Rawson, Claude, ed. (assisted by Jenny Mezciems). *English Satire and the Satiric Tradition.* Oxford: Blackwell, 1984.

Reddin, Chitra Pershad. *Forms of Evil in the Gothic Novel.* New York: Arno, 1980.

Reed, James. *Sir Walter Scott: Landscape and Locality.* London: Athlone, 1980.

Reed, John R. *The Natural History of H. G. Wells.* Athens: Ohio University Press, 1982.

Reed, Walter L. *An Exemplary History of the Novel: The Quixotic versus the Picaresque.* Chicago: University of Chicago Press, 1981.

Rees, Joan. *Exploring "Arcadia."* Birmingham: University of Birmingham, 1981.

Reilly, Patrick. *George Orwell: The Age's Adversary.* New York: St. Martin's, 1986.

Reilly, Patrick. *Jonathan Swift: The Brave Desponder.* Manchester: Manchester University Press, 1982.

Schakel, Peter J. *Reading with the Heart: The Way into Narnia.* Grand Rapids, MI: Eerdmans, 1979.

Schakel, Peter J. *Reason and Imagination in C. S. Lewis: A Study of "Till We Have Faces."* Grand Rapids, MI: Eerdmans, 1984.

Scheckner, Peter. *Class, Politics, and the Individual: A Study of the Major Works of D. H. Lawrence.* London: Associated University Presses, 1985.

Scheuermann, Mona. *Social Protest in the Eighteenth-Century English Novel.* Columbus: Ohio State University Press, 1985.

Schmidt, Dorey, and Jan Seale, eds. *Margaret Drabble: Golden Realms.* Edinburg, TX: School of Humanities, Pan American University, 1982.

Schmidt, Johann N., ed. *Of Private Vices and Publick Benefits: Beiträge zur englischen Literatur des frühen 18. Jahrhunderts.* Frankfurt: Peter Lang, 1979.

Schmuhl, Norbert. *Perspektivität und Aperspektivität in James Joyces "Ulysses."* Frankfurt: Peter Lang, 1976.

Schneider, Daniel J. *D. H. Lawrence: The Artist as Psychologist.* Lawrence: University Press of Kansas, 1984.

Schnitzler, Günter, Gerhard Neumann, and Jürgen Schröder, eds. *Bild und Gedanke: Festschrift für Gerhart Baumann zum 60. Geburtstag.* Munich: Fink, 1980.

Schofield, Mary Anne. *Eliza Haywood.* Boston: Twayne, 1985.

Schofield, Mary Anne. *Quiet Rebellion: The Fictional Heroines of Eliza Fowler Haywood.* Washington, DC: University Press of America, 1982.

Schofield, Mary Anne, and Cecilia Macheski, eds. *Fetter'd or Free? British Women Novelists, 1670–1815.* Athens: Ohio University Press, 1986.

Schöneich, Christoph. *Epos und Roman: James Joyces "Ulysses"—Beitrag zu einer historisierten Gattungspoetik.* Heidelberg: Carl Winter, 1981.

Schröder, Wolfgang. *Reflektierter Roman: Untersuchungen zu Samuel Becketts Romanwerk mit Berücksichtigung seiner implizierten Poetik, seiner Reflexionsstrukturen und seiner Beziehung zur romantischen Ironie.* Frankfurt: Peter Lang, 1981.

Schug, Charles. *The Romantic Genesis of the Modern Novel.* Pittsburgh, PA: University of Pittsburgh Press, 1979.

Schwarz, Daniel R. *Conrad: "Almayer's Folly" to "Under Western Eyes."* Ithaca, NY: Cornell University Press, 1980.

Schwarz, Daniel R. *Conrad: The Later Fiction.* London: Macmillan, 1982.

Schwarz, Daniel R. *Disraeli's Fiction.* New York: Barnes & Noble, 1979.

Schwarzbach, F. S. *Dickens and the City.* London: Athlone, 1979.

Scott, Bonnie Kime. *Joyce and Feminism.* Bloomington: Indiana University Press; Brighton: Harvester, 1984.

Scott, P. H. *John Galt.* Edinburgh: Scottish Academic Press, 1985.

Scott, P. J. M. *Anne Brontë: A New Critical Assessment.* London: Vision; Totowa, NJ: Barnes & Noble, 1983.

Scott, P. J. M. *E. M. Forster: Our Permanent Contemporary.* London: Vision; Totowa, NJ: Barnes & Noble, 1984.

Scott, P. J. M. *Reality and Comic Confidence in Charles Dickens*. New York: Harper & Row, 1979.

Sekine, Masaru, ed. *Irish Writers and Society at Large*. Gerrards Cross, Bucks.: Colin Smythe; Totowa, NJ: Barnes & Noble, 1985.

Selig, Robert L. *George Gissing*. Boston: Twayne, 1983.

Sell, Roger D. *The Reluctant Naturalism of "Amelia": An Essay on the Modern Reading of Fielding*. Abo: Abo Akademi, 1983.

Sellin, Bernard. *The Life and Works of David Lindsay*. Translated by Kenneth Gunnell. Cambridge: Cambridge University Press, 1981.

Senn, Fritz. *Joyce's Dislocutions: Essays on Reading as Translation*. Edited by John Paul Riquelme. Baltimore, MD: Johns Hopkins University Press, 1984.

Shahane, Vasant A., ed. *Approaches to E. M. Forster: A Centenary Volume*. New Delhi: Arnold-Heinemann, 1981.

Shaheen, Mohammad. *George Meredith: A Reappraisal of the Novels*. London: Macmillan; Totowa, NJ: Barnes & Noble, 1981.

Shalvi, Alice, ed. *"Daniel Deronda": A Centenary Symposium*. Jerusalem: Jerusalem Academic Press, 1976.

Shamsul Islam. *Chronicles of the Raj: A Study of Literary Reaction to the Imperial Idea towards the End of the Raj*. Totowa, NJ: Rowman and Littlefield, 1979.

Sharma, R. S. *"The Rainbow": A Study of Symbolic Mode in D. H. Lawrence's Primitivism*. Hyderabad: Trust, 1981.

Sharrock, Roger. *Saints, Sinners and Comedians: The Novels of Graham Greene*. Tunbridge Wells: Burns & Oates; Notre Dame, IN: University of Notre Dame Press, 1984.

Sheriff, John K. *The Good-Natured Man: The Evolution of a Moral Ideal, 1660–1800*. University: University of Alabama Press, 1982.

Shippey, T. A. *The Road to Middle-Earth*. London: Allen & Unwin, 1982.

Shoham, Shlomo Giora, and Francis Rosenstiel (assisted by Anita Tamari), eds. *And He Loved Big Brother: Man, State and Society in Question—Contributions to the [Council of Europe] George Orwell Colloquy, "1984: Myths and Realities."* London: Macmillan, 1985.

Showalter, Elaine. *A Literature of Their Own: British Women Novelists from Brontë to Lessing*. Princeton, NJ: Princeton University Press, 1977.

Shroff, Homai J. *The Eighteenth Century Novel: The Idea of the Gentleman*. Atlantic Highlands, NJ: Humanities Press, 1978.

Shrubsall, Dennis. *W. H. Hudson: Writer and Naturalist*. Tisbury, Wiltshire: Compton Press, 1978.

Shuttleworth, Sally. *George Eliot and Nineteenth-Century Science: The Make-Believe of a Beginning*. Cambridge: Cambridge University Press, 1984.

Sibley, Agnes. *Charles Williams*. Boston: Twayne, 1982.

Sidhu, C. D. *The Pattern of Tragicomedy in Bernard Shaw*. New Delhi: Bahri Publications, 1979.

Silver, Carole G., ed. *The Golden Chain: Essays on William Morris and Pre-Raphaelitism*. New York: William Morris Society, 1982.

Simon, Alfred. *Beckett.* Paris: Pierre Belfond, 1983.

Simon, Richard Keller. *The Labyrinth of the Comic: Theory and Practice from Fielding to Freud.* Tallahassee: Florida State University Press, 1985.

Simpson, David. *Fetishism and Imagination: Dickens, Melville, Conrad.* Baltimore, MD: Johns Hopkins University Press, 1982.

Simpson, Hilary. *D. H. Lawrence and Feminism.* DeKalb, IL: Northern Illinois University Press, 1982.

Simpson, K. G., ed. *Henry Fielding: Justice Observed.* London: Vision; Totowa, NJ: Barnes & Noble, 1985.

Sinha, S. K. *Thackeray: A Study in Technique.* Salzburg: Institut für Anglistik und Amerikanistik, Universität Salzburg, 1979.

Skulsky, Harold. *Metamorphosis: The Mind in Exile.* Cambridge: Harvard University Press, 1981.

Slusser, George E., and Eric S. Rabkin, eds. *Hard Science Fiction.* Carbondale and Edwardsville: Southern Illinois University Press, 1986.

Slusser, George E., George R. Guffey, and Mark Rose, eds. *Bridges to Science Fiction.* Carbondale and Edwardsville: Southern Illinois University Press, 1980.

Smith, Anne, ed. *The Art of Malcolm Lowry.* New York: Barnes & Noble, 1978.

Smith, Anne, ed. *George Eliot: Centenary Essays and an Unpublished Fragment.* London: Vision, 1980.

Smith, Anne, ed. *Lawrence and Women.* New York: Barnes & Noble, 1978.

Smith, Anne, ed. *The Novels of Thomas Hardy.* New York: Barnes & Noble, 1979.

Smith, Esther Marian Greenwell. *Mrs. Humphry Ward.* Boston: Twayne, 1980.

Smith, Grahame. *The Novel & Society: Defoe to George Eliot.* Totowa, NJ: Barnes & Noble, 1984.

Smith, John B. *Imagery and the Mind of Stephen Dedalus: A Computer-Assisted Study of Joyce's "A Portrait of the Artist as a Young Man."* Lewisburg, PA: Bucknell University Press, 1980.

Smith, Nathaniel B., and Joseph T. Snow, eds. *The Expansion and Transformations of Courtly Literature.* Athens: University of Georgia Press, 1980.

Smith, Nelson C. *James Hogg.* Boston: Twayne, 1980.

Smith, Peter. *Public and Private Value: Studies in the Nineteenth-Century Novel.* Cambridge: Cambridge University Press, 1984.

Smithers, David Waldron. *Dickens's Doctors.* Oxford: Pergamon, 1979.

Smitten, Jeffrey R., and Ann Daghistani, eds. *Spatial Form in Narrative.* Ithaca, NY: Cornell University Press, 1981.

Snipes, Katherine. *Robert Graves.* New York: Frederick Ungar, 1979.

Snitow, Ann Barr. *Ford Madox Ford and the Voice of Uncertainty.* Baton Rouge: Louisiana State University Press, 1984.

Snyder, Robert Lance, ed. *Thomas De Quincey: Bicentenary Studies.* Norman: University of Oklahoma Press, 1985.

Soldati, Joseph Arthur. *Configurations of Faust: Three Studies in the Gothic (1798–1820)*. New York: Arno, 1980.

Sörensen, Dolf. *James Joyce's Aesthetic Theory: Its Development and Application*. Amsterdam: Rodopi, 1977.

Soupel, Serge, and Roger A. Hambridge. *Literature and Science and Medicine: Papers Read at the Clark Library Summer Seminar 1981*. Los Angeles: William Andrews Clark Memorial Library, University of California, 1982.

Speck, W. A. *Society and Literature in England, 1700–60*. Dublin: Gill and Macmillan; Atlantic Highlands, NJ: Humanities Press, 1983.

Spiegel, Rotraut. *Doris Lessing: The Problem of Alienation and the Form of the Novel*. Frankfurt: Peter Lang, 1980.

Spilka, Mark. *Virginia Woolf's Quarrel with Grieving*. Lincoln: University of Nebraska Press, 1980.

Spisak, James W., ed. *Studies in Malory*. Kalamazoo: Medieval Institute, Western Michigan University, 1985.

Spivey, Ted R. *The Journey beyond Tragedy: A Study of Myth and Modern Fiction*. Orlando: University Presses of Florida, 1980.

Springer, Marlene. *Hardy's Use of Allusion*. Lawrence: University Press of Kansas, 1983.

Spurling, John. *Graham Greene*. London: Methuen, 1983.

Squier, Susan M. *Virginia Woolf and London: The Sexual Politics of the City*. Chapel Hill: University of North Carolina Press, 1985.

Squier, Susan Merrill, ed. *Women Writers and the City: Essays in Feminist Literary Criticism*. Knoxville: University of Tennessee Press, 1984.

Squires, Michael. *The Creation of "Lady Chatterley's Lover."* Baltimore, MD: Johns Hopkins University Press, 1983.

Stableford, Brian. *Scientific Romance in Britain, 1890–1950*. New York: St. Martin's, 1985.

Staley, Thomas F. *Jean Rhys: A Critical Study*. Austin: University of Texas Press, 1979.

Staley, Thomas F., ed. *Twentieth-Century Women Novelists*. Totowa, NJ: Barnes & Noble, 1982.

Stang, Sondra J., ed. *The Presence of Ford Madox Ford: A Memorial Volume of Essays, Poems, and Memoirs*. Philadelphia: University of Pennsylvania Press, 1981.

Stansky, Peter, ed. *On Nineteen Eighty-Four*. New York: W. H. Freeman, 1983.

Steiner, Wendy, ed. *The Sign in Music and Literature*. Austin: University of Texas Press, 1981.

Stern, J. P., ed. *The World of Franz Kafka*. New York: Holt, Rinehart and Winston, 1980.

Stewart, Grace. *A New Mythos: The Novel of the Artist as Heroine, 1877–1977*. St. Alban's, VT: Eden Press, 1979.

Stiller, Nikki. *Eve's Orphans: Mothers and Daughters in Medieval English Literature*. Westport, CT: Greenwood Press, 1980.

Torgovnick, Marianna. *The Visual Arts, Pictorialism, and the Novel: James, Lawrence, and Woolf.* Princeton, NJ: Princeton University Press, 1985.

Torrance, Robert M. *The Comic Hero.* Cambridge: Harvard University Press, 1978.

Tortosa, Francisco García, Manuel Almagro Jiménez, José Carnero González, and Paul Witkowsky, eds. *James Joyce: A New Language—Actas/Proceedings del Simposio Internacional en el Centenario de James Joyce.* Sevilla: Publicaciones de la Universidad de Sevilla, 1982.

Tracy, Ann Blaisdell. *Patterns of Fear in the Gothic Novel, 1790–1830.* New York: Arno, 1980.

Tredell, Nicolas. *The Novels of Colin Wilson.* London: Vision; Totowa, NJ: Barnes & Noble, 1982.

Tripodi, Vincenzo. *Studi su Laurence Sterne ed Ugo Foscolo.* Madrid: José Porrúa Turanzas, 1978.

Trombley, Stephen. *All that Summer She Was Mad: Virginia Woolf—Female Victim of Male Medicine.* New York: Continuum, 1982.

Tromly, Annette. *The Cover of the Mask: The Autobiographers in Charlotte Brontë's Fiction.* Victoria, BC: University of Victoria, 1982.

Tucker, Bernard. *Jonathan Swift.* Dublin: Gill and Macmillan, 1983.

Tucker, Lindsey. *Stephen and Bloom at Life's Feast: Alimentary Symbolism and the Creative Process in James Joyce's "Ulysses."* Columbus: Ohio State University Press, 1984.

Twitchell, James B. *The Living Dead: A Study of the Vampire in Romantic Literature.* Durham, NC: Duke University Press, 1981.

Urang, Sarah. *Kindled in the Flame: The Apocalyptic Scene in D. H. Lawrence.* Ann Arbor, MI: UMI Research Press, 1983.

Vaid, Sudesh. *The Divided Mind: Studies in Defoe and Richardson.* New Delhi: Associated Publishing House, 1979.

Van Caspel, Paul. *Bloomers on the Liffey: Eisegetical Readings of Joyce's "Ulysses."* Baltimore, MD: Johns Hopkins University Press, 1986.

Van Luchene, Stephen Robert. *Essays in Gothic Fiction: From Horace Walpole to Mary Shelley.* New York: Arno, 1980.

Vance, Norman. *The Sinews of the Spirit: The Ideal of Christian Manliness in Victorian Literature and Religious Thought.* Cambridge: Cambridge University Press, 1985.

Vannatta, Dennis. *H. E. Bates.* Boston: Twayne, 1983.

Vargish, Thomas. *The Providential Aesthetic in Victorian Fiction.* Charlottesville: University Press of Virginia, 1985.

Vasbinder, Samuel Holmes. *Scientific Attitudes in Mary Shelley's "Frankenstein."* Ann Arbor, MI: UMI Research Press, 1984.

Veitch, Douglas W. *Lawrence, Greene and Lowry: The Fictional Landscape of Mexico.* Waterloo, Canada: Wilfrid Laurier University Press, 1978.

Velicu, Adrian. *Unifying Strategies in Virginia Woolf's Experimental Fiction.* Uppsala: Acta Universitatis Upsaliensis, 1985.

Vesterman, William. *The Stylistic Life of Samuel Johnson.* New Brunswick, NJ: Rutgers University Press, 1977.

Williams, D. A., ed. *The Monster in the Mirror: Studies in Nineteenth-Century Realism*. Oxford: Oxford University Press for the University of Hull, 1978.

Williams, Ioan. *The Idea of the Novel in Europe, 1600–1800*. New York: New York University Press, 1979.

Williams, Merryn. *Women in the English Novel, 1800–1900*. New York: St. Martin's, 1984.

Williamson, Jack, ed. *Teaching Science Fiction: Education for Tomorrow*. Philadelphia: Owlswick Press, 1980.

Wilson, A. N. *Hilaire Belloc*. New York: Atheneum, 1984.

Wilson, A. N. *The Laird of Abbotsford: A View of Sir Walter Scott*. Oxford: Oxford University Press, 1980.

Wilson, Colin. *The Haunted Man: The Strange Genius of David Lindsay*. San Bernardino, CA: Borgo Press, 1979.

Wilt, Judith. *Ghosts of the Gothic: Austen, Eliot, & Lawrence*. Princeton, NJ: Princeton University Press, 1980.

Wilt, Judith. *Secret Leaves: The Novels of Walter Scott*. Chicago: University of Chicago Press, 1985.

Winner, Anthony. *Characters in the Twilight: Hardy, Zola, and Chekhov*. Charlottesville: University Press of Virginia, 1981.

Witemeyer, Hugh. *George Eliot and the Visual Arts*. New Haven, CT: Yale University Press, 1979.

Wohl, Anthony S., ed. *The Victorian Family: Structure and Stresses*. New York: St. Martin's, 1978.

Wolfe, Gary K. *The Known and the Unknown: The Iconography of Science Fiction*. Kent, OH: Kent State University Press, 1979.

Wolfe, Peter. *Jean Rhys*. Boston: Twayne, 1980.

Wolfe, Peter. *John Fowles, Magus and Moralist*. 2nd ed. Lewisburg, PA: Bucknell University Press, 1979.

Woodcock, Bruce. *Male Mythologies: John Fowles and Masculinity*. Brighton: Harvester; Totowa, NJ: Barnes & Noble, 1984.

Woodcock, George. *Orwell's Message: "1984" and the Present*. Madeira Park, B.C.: Harbour Publishing, 1984.

Woolf, David. *An Aspect of Fiction: Its Logical Structure and Interpretation*. Ravenna: Longo, 1980.

Worpole, Ken. *Dockers and Detectives: Popular Reading—Popular Writing*. London: Verso, 1983.

Worthen, John. *D. H. Lawrence and the Idea of the Novel*. Totowa, NJ: Rowman and Littlefield, 1979.

Wotton, George. *Thomas Hardy: Towards a Materialist Criticism*. Dublin: Gill and Macmillan; Totowa, NJ: Barnes & Noble, 1985.

Wright, Andrew. *Anthony Trollope: Dream and Art*. Chicago: University of Chicago Press, 1983.

Wright, David G. *Characters of Joyce*. Dublin: Gill and Macmillan; Totowa, NJ: Barnes & Noble, 1983.

Wright, Eugene P. *Thomas Deloney*. Boston: Twayne, 1981.

Yeazell, Ruth Bernard, ed. *Sex, Politics, and Science in the Nineteenth-Century Novel.* Baltimore, MD: Johns Hopkins University Press, 1986.

Yoke, Carl B., and Donald M. Hassler, eds. *Death and the Serpent: Immortality in Science Fiction and Fantasy.* Westport, CT: Greenwood Press, 1985.

Young, Robert, ed. *Untying the Text: A Post-Structuralist Reader.* Boston: Routledge & Kegan Paul, 1981.

Zatlin, Linda Gertner. *The Nineteenth-Century Anglo-Jewish Novel.* Boston: Twayne, 1981.

Zeman, Anthea. *Presumptuous Girls: Women and Their World in the Serious Woman's Novel.* London: Weidenfeld and Nicolson, 1977.